HUMAN RIGHTS IN THE DIGITAL DOMAIN

As digital technologies transform governance, communication, and public life, human rights frameworks must adapt to new challenges and opportunities. This book explores four fundamental questions: how digitalisation changes the application of human rights, how human rights law can respond to the challenges of digital technology, how freedom of expression applies online, and how vulnerable groups are affected by digitalisation. With contributions from leading scholars, the book combines legal analysis with insights from ethics, environmental education, and medical research. It examines critical topics such as AI regulation, platform accountability, privacy protections, and disinformation, offering an interdisciplinary and international perspective. By balancing different viewpoints, this book helps readers navigate the complexities of human rights in the digital age. It is an essential resource for anyone seeking to understand and shape the evolving landscape of digital rights and governance. This title is also available as open access on Cambridge Core.

Tiina Pajuste is Professor of International Law and Security Studies at Tallinn University and holds a PhD from Cambridge and an LLM from Helsinki. She is a member of the ESIL and COST networks, and she has contributed to major international projects shaping policy and practice in human rights and peace studies.

Human Rights in the Digital Domain

CORE QUESTIONS

Edited by

TIINA PAJUSTE

Tallinn University

CAMBRIDGE
UNIVERSITY PRESS

CAMBRIDGE
UNIVERSITY PRESS

Shaftesbury Road, Cambridge CB2 8EA, United Kingdom

One Liberty Plaza, 20th Floor, New York, NY 10006, USA

477 Williamstown Road, Port Melbourne, VIC 3207, Australia

314–321, 3rd Floor, Plot 3, Splendor Forum, Jasola District Centre, New Delhi – 110025, India

103 Penang Road, #05–06/07, Visioncrest Commercial, Singapore 238467

Cambridge University Press is part of Cambridge University Press & Assessment, a department of the University of Cambridge.

We share the University's mission to contribute to society through the pursuit of education, learning and research at the highest international levels of excellence.

www.cambridge.org
Information on this title: www.cambridge.org/9781009606240

DOI: 10.1017/9781009606295

When citing this work, please include a reference to the DOI 10.1017/9781009606295

First published 2026

A catalogue record for this publication is available from the British Library

Library of Congress Cataloging-in-Publication Data
NAMES: Pajuste, Tiina, editor.
TITLE: Human rights in the digital domain : core questions / edited by Tiina Pajuste, Tallin[n] University.
DESCRIPTION: Cambridge, United Kingdom ; New York, NY : Cambridge University Press, 2026. | Includes bibliographical references and index.
IDENTIFIERS: LCCN 2025015052 | ISBN 9781009606240 (hardback) | ISBN 9781009606295 (ebook)
SUBJECTS: LCSH: Human rights – Data processing. | Freedom of expression. | Freedom of information. | Information technology – Law and legislation. | Social media – Law and legislation. | Online social networks – Law and legislation. | Disinformation.
CLASSIFICATION: LCC K3240 .H85729 2026 | DDC 342.08/5–dc23/eng/20250401
LC record available at https://lccn.loc.gov/2025015052

ISBN 978-1-009-60624-0 Hardback
ISBN 978-1-009-60627-1 Paperback

Contents

Contributors

Barbora Baďurová – Independent researcher; previously Assistant Professor at Matej Bel University

Johanas Baltrimas – Associate Professor at Vilnius University, Faculty of Law

Wolfgang Benedek – Professor Emeritus at University of Graz, European Training and Research Centre for Human Rights and Democracy

Violeta Beširević – Professor at Union University Law School Belgrade

Raizza da Costa Lopes – PhD student in Environmental Education (Programa de Pós-Graduação em Educação Ambiental da Universidade Federal do Rio Grande, Brazil)

Vesna Crnić-Grotić – Professor at University of Rijeka, Faculty of Law

Philippe Jougleux – Associate Professor, European University Cyprus, Nikosia, School of Law

Artūrs Kučs – Associate Professor at University of Latvia, Riga, Faculty of Law

Eva Lievens – Associate Professor at Ghent University, Faculty of Law and Criminology, Law & Technology research group

Vygantė Milašiūtė – Associate Professor at Vilnius University, Faculty of Law

Tiina Pajuste – Professor at Tallinn University, School of Governance, Law and Society

Florent Pasquier – Associate Professor at Sorbonne University, Paris; President of Ciret (International Center for Transdisciplinary Research and Studies)

Samuel Lopes Pinheiro – PhD in Environmental Education (PPGEA FURG, Brazil)

Cristina Elena Popa Tache – Researcher at the Centre International de Recherches et Études Transdisciplinaires, Paris

Cathleen Powell – Until her death in 2025, Associate Professor at University of Cape Town, Faculty of Law

Oscar R. Puccinelli – Professor at Rosario National University, Law School

Cătălin-Silviu Săraru – Associate Professor at Bucharest University of Economic Studies, Faculty of Law

Birgit Schippers – Senior Lecturer at University of Strathclyde, Faculty of Humanities and Social Sciences, Law School

Sergio de Souza Salles – Associate Professor at Catholic University of Petropolis, Brazil

Saulius Stonkus – PhD candidate at Vilnius University, Faculty of Law

Mart Susi – Professor at Tallinn University, School of Governance, Law and Society

Paula Veiga – Associate Professor at University of Coimbra, Faculty of Law

Valerie Verdoodt – Postdoctoral Fellow at Ghent University, Faculty of Law and Criminology, Law & Technology research group

Jukka Viljanen – Professor at Tampere University, Faculty of Management and Business

Tomoe Watashiba – PhD student at Tallinn University, School of Governance, Law and Society

Skirgailė Žalimienė – Professor at Vilnius University, Faculty of Law

Acknowledgements

This volume is the result of four years of monthly Zoom meetings, lively discussions, and workshops in many inspiring locations. It would not have materialised without the active members of the Global Digital Human Rights Network (GDHRNet), many of whom are authors in this volume. Their expertise, research, and dedication have shaped this book, while non-author members have also played a crucial role by providing valuable feedback on chapters during workshops and discussions. The collective insights of the network have greatly informed the ideas and analyses presented here.

Special gratitude is owed to the COST Association (European Cooperation in Science and Technology), whose funding through COST Action CA19143 enabled the establishment of GDHRNet and made this collaborative work possible. COST support provided opportunities for research visits, conferences, and summer schools, which laid the ground for meaningful collaborations far beyond what we initially imagined. Additionally, COST funding covered the Open Access costs of this volume, ensuring that its findings and discussions are freely accessible to a global audience.

Sincere thanks are also due to Cambridge University Press for their guidance and support. The professionalism and dedication of the editorial team ensured a seamless and efficient publication process.

Table of Cases

EUROPEAN COURT OF HUMAN RIGHTS

EUROPEAN UNION COURTS

INTER-AMERICAN COURT OF HUMAN RIGHTS

DOMESTIC COURT DECISIONS

Canada

France

Germany

German Federal Court of Justice, II ZR 192/20, III ZR 179/20, 29 July 2021, 257

Ireland

Foley v. Sunday Newspapers Ltd [2005] IEHC 14, 85
Muwema v. Facebook Ireland Limited [2018] IECA 104, 85

US

Abrams v. United States, 250 US 616 (1919), 249, 323
Ashcroft v. Free Speech Coalition, 535 US 234 (2002), 248
Boos v. Barry, 485 US 312 (1988), 71
Brandenburg v. Ohio, 395 US 444 (1969), 71, 249
The Civil Rights Cases, 109 US 3 (1883), 69
Dipp-Paz v. Facebook, No. 18-CV-9037, WL 3205842 (SDNY 2019), 73
Edwards v. Aguillard, 482 US 578 (1987), 249
FAN v. Facebook, 18-CV-07041-LHK, 20 July 2019, 256
Federal Agency of News LLC v. Facebook, Inc., 395 F. Supp. 3d 1295 (ND Cal 2019), 73
Gonzalez v. Google LLC, 598 US 617 (2023), 73
Google LLC v. Oracle America, Inc., 593 US 1 (2021), 86
Kingsley Int'l Pictures Corp. v. Regents, 360 US 684 (1959), 71
Knight First Amendment Inst. at Columbia Univ. v. Trump, No. 1:17-cv-5205 (SDNY) No. 18-1691 (2d Cir.), 58
Kyllo v. US, 533 US 27 (2001), 291
Matal v. Tam, 582 US 218 (2017), 246
New York Times Co. v. Sullivan, 376 US 254 (1964), 220
Police Dept. v. Mosley, 408 US 92 (1972), 71
R.A.V. v. City of St. Paul, 505 US 377 (1992), 71
Reno v. ACLU, 521 US 844 (1997), 72
Shelley v. Kraemer, 334 US 1 (1948), 70
Simon & Schuster, Inc. v. Members of New York State Crime Victims Board, 502 US 105 (1991), 71
Twitter Inc. v. Taamneh, 598 US 471 (2023), 73
United States v. Alvarez, 567 US 709, 717–8 (2012), 252

1

Introduction

Tiina Pajuste

We are living in an era where the boundaries between the physical and digital worlds have blurred, as our interactions, communications, and expressions have increasingly migrated to the virtual realm. Digital technologies have transformed nearly every facet of human life, from how we communicate and work to how we learn, govern, and assert our rights. Our lives are now entwined with data, algorithms, and platforms, which shape our experiences and influence our choices (whether we are aware of this or not). This transformation has been rapid, pervasive, and, at times, deeply disruptive. While digital tools offer unprecedented opportunities for connection, innovation, and empowerment, they also challenge existing legal, ethical, and social frameworks, particularly in the realm of human rights. The United Nations (UN) Secretary-General has emphasised that '[t]echnologies provide new means to advocate, defend and exercise human rights, but they can also be used to suppress, limit and violate human rights'.[1]

Digital technologies can also magnify existing inequalities and create new vulnerabilities. The internet, artificial intelligence, and other digital tools are not neutral. They are shaped by the intentions of their creators, the dynamics of global markets, and the priorities of states and corporations. These technologies increasingly mediate fundamental rights such as privacy, freedom of expression, access to education, and equality. Yet our legal and ethical frameworks often lag behind, struggling to address the challenges posed by algorithmic bias, mass surveillance, online disinformation, and the commodification of personal data.

In order to competently traverse the vast landscape of the digital domain, we need to be aware of questions of ethics, privacy, security, and justice that arise in this context and have the potential to significantly impact the enjoyment of our human rights. Against this backdrop, this book explores the intersection of human rights and the digital environment, examining how to adapt our understanding,

[1] UN Secretary-General, 'Road map for digital cooperation: implementation of the recommendations of the High-level Panel on Digital Cooperation. Report of the Secretary-General', UN Doc. A/74/821, 29 May 2020, para. 38.

application, and governance of human rights in the digital age. The authors aim to provide a balanced view of human rights in the digital realm, addressing both the challenges to and opportunities for human rights protection stemming from the digital reality.

EXPERTISE FROM THE GLOBAL DIGITAL HUMAN RIGHTS NETWORK

This book was developed over the course of four years by scholars taking part in the European Cooperation in Science and Technology (COST) Action Global Digital Human Rights Network (GDHRNet).[2] GDHRNet investigates the theoretical and practical challenges to the protection of human rights posed by the online context and engages with the role of national governments and private online companies in addressing these challenges. The network explores whether international human rights law is sufficiently detailed to enable governments and private online companies to understand their respective obligations vis-à-vis the protection of human rights online. It also evaluates how national governments have responded to the task of providing a regulatory framework for online companies and how these companies have transposed the obligation to protect human rights and combat hate speech online into their community standards.

The network is composed of over 120 academics from diverse disciplines,[3] who examine the impact of digital technology on people (e.g., law, business and management, philosophy, information and communications technology, and health informatics). Each chapter and author benefited from interdisciplinary feedback and input from other members of the network during dedicated workshops and meetings. The network's cross-disciplinary engagement is reflected in the book's interdisciplinary approach. Human rights in the digital age cannot be understood through legal analysis alone; it requires insights from ethics, political science, sociology, and technology studies. While the book's primary focus is international (human rights) law, it also incorporates perspectives from other disciplines, such as ethics, environmental education, and medical research. This integrative approach enriches the analysis, offering readers a more comprehensive understanding of the challenges posed by digital technologies and actionable pathways for addressing them. By drawing on

[2] COST is a funding organisation for the creation of research networks, called COST Actions. These networks offer an open space for collaboration among scientists across Europe (and beyond) and thereby provide the impetus for research advancements and innovation (COST, 'About COST', www.cost.eu/about/about-cost/). Detailed information about COST Action CA19143 is available on the network website: Global Digital Human Rights Network, 'Objectives', https://gdhrnet.eu/overview/objectives/.

[3] The full list of participants is available at the COST website:www.cost.eu/actions/CA19143/#tabs+Name:Working%20Groups%20and%20Membership. Although the COST Action has ended, GDHRNet continues in the form of informal collaboration between people and institutions.

diverse expertise, the book underscores the need for interdisciplinary collaboration to navigate the intersection of human rights and digital transformation effectively.

FOCUS ON CORE QUESTIONS

Central to the coherence of the book's narrative is the innovative use of fundamental questions, each forming the cornerstones of the parts of the volume. These core questions serve as a scaffold for examining human rights in the digital domain, leading readers on a journey through diverse dimensions of the topic. This unique approach nurtures intellectual curiosity and encourages an active exploration of human rights in the context of the digital reality. Owing to the pervasive nature of digitalisation, not all aspects of human rights can be covered in one book. Therefore, the choice was made to focus on fundamental questions and provide different (non-exhaustive) perspectives on issues that are attached to each question.

The methodology for choosing the questions and the chapter focus areas was based on the following elements:

(a) *involving interdisciplinary expertise* – by involving experts from different backgrounds (leveraging the collective expertise of GDHRNet members in fields such as law, technology, sociology, ethics, and political science), the questions (and issues addressed in the chapters) would better capture the breadth of challenges posed by digital technologies.

(b) *having both practical and theoretical significance* – the questions should balance theoretical depth with practical relevance, addressing both foundational issues in human rights and actionable governance challenges. This balance ensures the questions are meaningful to academics, policymakers, and practitioners alike, bridging the gaps between theory and practice.

(c) *considering global and context-specific relevance* – the book should address universal human rights challenges while accounting for regional and contextual nuances. Digitalisation can sometimes impact regions differently, depending on socio-economic, legal, and technological contexts. Accordingly, the insights from the different focus areas should have broad applicability while recognising diverse experiences.

(d) *being collaborative and consensus-driven* – the questions should be selected and refined by network members collaboratively through iterative discussions, workshops, and consensus-building exercises.

(e) *including issues regarding vulnerability* – the process should include a focus on vulnerable populations, as their needs and experiences are often not addressed in policy documents and scholarship regarding human rights and digitalisation, even though they tend to be disproportionately affected by digitalisation. Addressing vulnerability ensures that structural inequalities and underrepresented perspectives are addressed.

The selection of the core questions was a collaborative process involving members of GDHRNet. The process began with scoping and brainstorming, where members identified both fundamental and pressing challenges in relation to human rights in the digital domain. These ideas were then organised into thematic categories such as governance, freedom of expression, right to privacy, inclusion, and regulatory adaptation. Next, through prioritisation exercises, members selected the most pressing and globally relevant issues. This was followed by an iterative refinement process, where draft questions were circulated for feedback to ensure clarity and relevance. Finally, the questions were validated against real-world cases to confirm their practical and theoretical significance. This rigorous process resulted in four core questions that address some of the most foundational and complex human rights challenges in the digital age, providing the foundation for the book's structure and discussions.

STRUCTURE OF THE BOOK

This volume is organised into four parts, each addressing a core question that reflects a distinct dimension of the human rights challenges in the digital age. The parts begin with an introduction that describes the relevance of the question and the focus areas of the chapters, provides an overview of the substance of the chapters and how the authors respond to the core question, and draws parallels between the different chapters and the themes addressed in them.

The first part focuses on how to adapt human rights to the digital world and responds to the question: *What difference does it make to move online?* The seven chapters in that part examine how the digital environment fundamentally changes the nature and scope of human rights. Moving online amplifies risks, such as disinformation and privacy violations, while also creating new rights dilemmas, such as the 'right to disconnect' or the governance of algorithmic decision-making. These challenges demand a re-evaluation of how rights are understood, protected, and enforced in a rapidly evolving digital landscape. The chapters explore these transformations through theoretical, legal, and practical lenses, offering insights into how courts, regulators, and individuals can adapt to these changes. This section is important because it lays the groundwork for understanding the broader themes addressed throughout the book. It underscores the importance of adapting human rights frameworks to ensure they remain effective and relevant in the digital age.

The second part addresses the question: *How should freedom of expression be applied in the digital environment?* The chapters in this part engage with one of the most complex areas of human rights in the digital age: freedom of expression. Digital platforms have transformed public discourse, enabling unprecedented access to information and empowered individuals to participate in global conversations. However, they have also amplified harmful phenomena such as disinformation, hate speech, and manipulation, posing serious risks to democratic values, social cohesion, and individual dignity. This section addresses the delicate balance between preserving the right to free speech and implementing safeguards to prevent harm in the digital space. Without clear guidance and accountability mechanisms, digital platforms risk becoming unregulated arenas where abuses of speech undermine trust, democratic integrity, and human rights. At the same time, over-regulation can stifle expression and innovation, creating a need for nuanced, rights-based approaches to this complex issue.

The third part focuses on the question: *How should human rights law respond to the challenges of digital technologies?* As digital technologies, such as artificial intelligence, drones, and surveillance systems become deeply embedded in governance, commerce, and daily life, they introduce new challenges to human rights. These technologies often outpace existing legal frameworks, raising urgent questions about how to protect privacy, ensure accountability, and promote equity in an increasingly digitised world. Addressing this question is particularly important because it helps understand the evolving relationship between human rights law and technological innovation at a time when the stakes for individual freedoms and societal well-being are higher than ever. Without proactive legal frameworks, the rapid advancement of these technologies risks deepening inequalities, eroding public trust, and enabling unchecked surveillance and exploitation. The four chapters in this section analyse both the theoretical and practical dimensions of these challenges and provide insights into how human rights law can adapt to balance the benefits of innovation with the protection of fundamental rights. They emphasise the need for global harmonisation to avoid fragmented governance, which can lead to inconsistencies and loopholes that undermine the protection of rights.

The fourth and final part aims to address the question: *What challenges do vulnerable groups face in the digital realm?* The chapters draw attention to the problem that vulnerable groups are often the ones most affected by the negative aspects of digitalisation. The authors highlight the unequal impact of digitalisation, focusing on vulnerable groups such as children, minority-language communities, precarious workers, and broadly those affected by the digital divide. They emphasise the intersectional nature of digital exclusion, advocating for inclusive policies and rights-based approaches that address the compounded vulnerabilities faced by marginalised populations. Including a section on vulnerable groups in a book about human rights in the digital realm is essential because digital technologies often amplify existing inequalities and create new forms of exclusion. Vulnerable groups face unique challenges in accessing and benefiting from digital tools and services. Highlighting their experiences ensures that human rights discussions go beyond general principles and address the specific barriers these groups encounter, such as affordability, digital literacy gaps, and online discrimination. This focus is critical for promoting inclusive digital policies that uphold the rights of all individuals.

CLARIFICATIONS REGARDING SCOPE

The primary focus of this book is on civil and political rights, as these rights are particularly challenged and redefined in the digital age. Issues such as privacy, freedom of expression, and the right to information are at the forefront of debates surrounding digital governance, platform regulation, and technological innovation. These rights are deeply intertwined with the mechanisms of democracy, individual autonomy, and accountability, making them central to understanding the impact of digital technologies on human rights frameworks.

However, the book does not neglect economic, social, and cultural rights. Several chapters address issues such as the right to education and the right to health, particularly in the context of vulnerable groups. For example, discussions of precarious labour in digital economies, internet addiction, and the digital divide highlight how economic, social and cultural rights are also deeply affected by technological advancements. This dual focus ensures that the book provides a well-rounded exploration of human rights challenges in the digital realm, acknowledging both the immediate political concerns and the broader social implications of digitalisation.

The book offers global perspectives, but places special emphasis on Europe. The prominent place of Europe in this book is not intended to suggest a Eurocentric perspective but rather to acknowledge Europe's role as a forerunner in digital governance. The General Data Protection Regulation (GDPR), for example, has shaped global debates on data protection, inspiring similar laws in jurisdictions as diverse as Brazil, South Africa, and California. Similarly, the Artificial Intelligence Act offers a proactive approach to regulating artificial intelligence that could serve as a blueprint for other regions. By analysing these frameworks, this book seeks to explore how rights-based digital governance strategies can be developed and adapted to other cultural, legal, and political contexts.

At the same time, the book takes a deliberately global approach, integrating perspectives from Africa, Asia, and the Americas to ensure that the discussion extends beyond European experiences. Chapters (co-)authored by scholars from Japan, South Africa, Brazil, and Argentina offer insights into how digital technologies intersect with human rights in different settings, addressing some of the unique challenges faced by the Global South and other under-represented contexts, and bridging regional experiences to highlight shared challenges and opportunities.

While the book acknowledges Europe's influence in shaping global digital policy, it does so within a broader effort to foster a more inclusive dialogue on digital human rights. The focus on Europe serves as a springboard for understanding how robust governance frameworks can emerge and evolve. However, the ultimate aim of this book is to provide a comprehensive and diverse exploration of digital rights that reflects the needs and perspectives of a global audience. In this way, Europe's place in the book is balanced by contributions that highlight the voices, experiences, and innovations of other regions, ensuring that the analyses resonate with a truly international readership.

The book sets out to provide a holistic perspective on the ways digital technologies reshape rights, responsibilities, and governance structures. It offers a panoramic view of the profound implications and challenges that accompany our move into the digital realm. The reader is led on a journey through a landscape that requires a delicate balance between freedom and responsibility. It is our hope that this broad examination of human rights in the digital domain will not only shed light on the complexities of our digital age but also inspire thoughtful discourse, further research, policy development, and advocacy, as well as to empower individuals, policymakers, and institutions to uphold and protect human rights in the digital era, ensuring a human-centric and ethically grounded technological landscape.

The digital transformation is still unfolding, and its full implications for human rights remain uncertain. However, what is clear is that the stakes are high. Without deliberate, inclusive, and rights-based approaches to governance, the digital environment risks deepening inequalities, eroding trust, and undermining democratic values. This book is not just an exploration of current challenges but a call to action – an invitation to rethink how we protect human rights in a rapidly changing world.

PART I

Adapting Human Rights to a Digital World

Introduction to Part I

What Difference Does It Make to Move Online?

Tiina Pajuste

As individuals, communities, and governments increasingly move online, longstanding legal frameworks face unprecedented challenges. The transition to the digital realm introduces new dimensions to established rights, amplifies existing vulnerabilities, and raises questions about whether current frameworks can adequately address the complexities of digitalisation. This first part of the book offers a comprehensive exploration of how the online context makes a profound difference in the application, governance, and enforcement of human rights. The seven chapters challenge readers to rethink traditional legal frameworks, adapt to the rapid pace of technological change, and embrace interdisciplinary solutions to ensure that human rights remain robust and relevant in the digital age. The chapters aim to answer a core question: *What difference does it make to move online?* The groundwork is then laid for understanding the digital transformation of rights and the need for innovative approaches to their protection. Through theoretical insights, case studies, and practical examples, the chapters collectively address key challenges related to governance, accountability, harm, and innovation in the digital sphere.

CHAPTER 2. IS THERE A NEED FOR NEW DIGITAL HUMAN RIGHTS IN AI GOVERNANCE?

Chapter 2 explores the evolving landscape of digital human rights. Wolfgang Benedek evaluates whether the emergence of digital technologies necessitates entirely new human rights (e.g., the right to digital self-determination) or whether existing rights can be extended to address new challenges (e.g., the right to privacy, freedom of expression). He focuses on artificial intelligence (AI) governance as a case study, examining regulatory initiatives by global, regional, and national actors. The discussion includes the role of the United Nations, the Council of Europe (CoE), and the European Union (EU) in addressing gaps in digital rights through frameworks such as the CoE Framework Convention on Artificial Intelligence and the EU Artificial Intelligence Act. The chapter also examines the interplay between state actors and private platforms in regulating AI and protecting digital rights. In response to the core question of the first part of the volume, the chapter notes the following: (a) human rights take on new dimensions in the digital context, requiring reinterpretation and the extension of traditional rights to address these challenges; (b) digital technologies introduce novel threats (e.g., disinformation, mass surveillance), which necessitate innovative legal responses; (c) moving online requires protection through binding international commitments, while non-binding soft law approaches are insufficient to enforce rights effectively; and (d) the borderless digital environment requires international co-ordination to avoid regulatory fragmentation.

CHAPTER 3. WHY AND HOW THE STATE SHOULD REGULATE THE INTERNET

Chapter 3 by Cathleen Powell examines the philosophical and practical foundations for state regulation of the internet, focusing on the relationship between individual rights and societal interests. It critiques the traditional view of rights as individualistic and argues for a more community-focused approach, emphasising that human rights should serve the common good. Powell argues that the digital realm introduces unique challenges – such as disinformation, manipulation, and hate speech – that require state intervention to preserve the integrity of public discourse and democratic values. Drawing on legal theory, particularly the ideas of Lon L. Fuller, she emphasises the importance of fostering trust, maintaining the rule of law, and balancing power between states, private actors, and users in internet governance. With regard to this part's core question (*What difference does it make to move online?*), the chapter identifies several transformative effects of moving online: (a) the digital realm magnifies the reach and impact of harmful content (e.g., disinformation and hate speech), making existing social and legal challenges more acute; (b) the internet's susceptibility to manipulation and false information erodes trust in public discourse and democratic institutions, making it harder for communities to reach shared understandings and maintain the rule of law; (c) online spaces, often privately owned, function as public forums, demanding state oversight to ensure that private governance aligns with public interests and fundamental rights; and (d) the state's regulatory power must be exercised in collaboration with non-state actors to prevent abuse and ensure responsiveness to public concerns. The chapter advocates a three-tiered model of internet governance involving self-regulation by platforms, oversight by independent regulatory bodies, and state intervention for serious threats such as hate speech or disinformation during elections.

CHAPTER 4. HOW TO TAME THE 'DIGITAL' SHREW: CONSTITUTIONAL RIGHTS GOING ONLINE

Chapter 4 examines the horizontal application of constitutional rights in the digital environment. It focuses on the accountability of social platforms, the limitations of current regulatory frameworks, and the growing role of private actors in regulating online spaces. Violeta Beširević analyses judicial practices in jurisdictions such as Germany, Canada, and the EU, and demonstrates how constitutional rights – traditionally enforceable only against the state – are being extended to regulate private actors, particularly social platforms, which now wield significant power over public discourse and individual freedoms. The chapter critiques the lack of adequate regulatory mechanisms for holding platforms accountable for human rights violations, emphasising their quasi-regulatory role in online governance. It advocates for a model of governance that enforces constitutional principles in the digital sphere, promoting accountability, transparency, and democratic legitimacy. The chapter responds to the core question by drawing attention to the following aspects: (a) the lines between public and private spaces have blurred (as private platforms such as Facebook and X function as public forums), so accordingly constitutional protections need to be extended to interactions governed by private actors; (b) as social platforms have quasi-regulatory roles, they should be recognised as duty bearers under constitutional rights; (c) the reach and permanence of digital actions amplify the potential harm caused by rights violations, necessitating stronger accountability mechanisms and legal protections; and (d) the online environment forces courts to reinterpret constitutional principles to address unique digital challenges (e.g., algorithmic decision-making and platform moderation).

CHAPTER 5. HOW DO WE DECIDE WHETHER MOVING ONLINE MAKES A DIFFERENCE?

Johanas Baltrimas continues the exploration of changes that occur in the digital environment in Chapter 5 by examining the legal reasoning behind determining whether the digital nature of an action or object requires different legal treatment to its offline equivalent. Through an analysis of court cases from different jurisdictions, he identifies two primary criteria that courts use to evaluate whether moving online makes a difference: (a) the purpose and function of the disputed object or action; and (b) the extent of harm caused by the disputed behaviour. Baltrimas highlights how courts compare digital cases with analogous offline situations to assess whether the online factor is legally relevant or whether traditional rules suffice. He provides a structured framework for evaluating the legal significance of moving online, addressing the following ways in which the digital realm impacts legal reasoning: (a) the online context often amplifies the extent of harm (e.g., the speed and scale of disinformation), which necessitates different legal responses; (b) moving online forces courts to reinterpret traditional laws and occasionally establish new rules when existing frameworks prove inadequate (e.g., the right to be forgotten); and (c) the difference made by moving online is not static – ongoing technological advancements continuously reshape the relevance of the online factor in legal disputes, requiring courts to remain adaptable.

CHAPTER 6. SOME REFLECTIONS ON THE NON-COHERENCE THEORY OF DIGITAL HUMAN RIGHTS

Chapter 6 by Mart Susi analyses the challenges of applying human rights frameworks to the digital realm through the lens of non-coherence theory. This theory posits that human rights in the digital domain differ fundamentally from their offline counterparts owing to shifts in meaning, scope, and application. Susi critically examines the assumption that offline human rights norms can be seamlessly transposed into the digital environment, highlighting the distortions and variances that arise in this process. He calls for a reimagining of human rights as adaptable, context-dependent principles that can address the unique dynamics of the digital age. In response to this part's core question – *What difference does it make to move online?* – the chapter demonstrates that moving online fundamentally alters the structure, interpretation, and implementation of human rights as follows: (a) the digital environment transforms the meaning and scope of established rights (e.g., privacy online often involves the desire not to be left alone); (b) moving online shifts human rights from being absolute to relative, as digital contexts require rights to be balanced against one another in ways that differ significantly from offline contexts; (c) the digital realm creates competing governance systems (e.g., private versus public regulation), leading to non-coherence between rights frameworks and fragmenting their application; and (d) the digital environment's fast-paced nature leaves little time for traditional legal processes (e.g., judicial balancing), compromising the effectiveness of rights protection.

CHAPTER 7. INTERNET ADDICTION AS A HUMAN RIGHTS ISSUE

After addressing broad conceptual and theoretical issues regarding human rights in the digital realm, Chapter 7 introduces a specific harm – internet addiction – that uniquely arises in the online environment. Vygantė Milašiūtė examines internet addiction through the lens of human rights, highlighting how the online environment amplifies the risks of addiction and introduces new legal and policy challenges. She explores the interplay between medical research and legal frameworks, analysing how internet addiction affects rights such as health, non-discrimination, and the rights of vulnerable groups such as children. The chapter also evaluates international and regional responses, including public health interventions, consumer protection laws, and the emerging concept of the 'right to disconnect'. With regard to the core question, the chapter provides a comprehensive analysis of how moving online changes the nature of addiction and introduces new challenges for human rights law: (a) the online environment's accessibility, anonymity, and engaging design features make addiction more prevalent and severe than in offline contexts, affecting vulnerable groups disproportionately; (b) digital tools blur the boundaries between leisure and harm, turning everyday internet use into a potential health risk that requires public health and regulatory interventions; (c) online platforms increasingly function as de facto regulators of user behaviour, raising questions about their responsibilities in mitigating addiction and the state's role in holding them accountable; and (d) the online context requires new approaches to existing rights (e.g., the right to health) and the creation of novel legal concepts such as the 'right to disconnect', which respond specifically to digital harms.

CHAPTER 8. JUST DON'T GET CAUGHT!

Chapter 8, the final chapter in the first part of the book, provides a different perspective, critically examining the limitations of legal regulations in governing the digital realm. Laws struggle to keep pace with technological advancements, leading to vague, inconsistent, or unenforceable rules in the digital space. Barbora Bad'urová explores the potential of digital ethics and education as complementary solutions. She highlights the challenges of regulating digital technologies, including the slow pace of legal development, the limitations of law enforcement, and the unique nature of the online environment, such as anonymity and global reach. Bad'urová emphasises the role of intrinsic motivation, individual responsibility, and moral education in addressing the ethical dilemmas posed by digital technologies. The chapter responds to the core question by noting the following: (a) the anonymity and lack of accountability online (making it difficult to detect and address violations effectively) amplifies the need for internal regulation and moral responsibility; (b) as digital activities transcend national borders and create regulatory challenges and inconsistencies, there is a need for universal ethical principles to address these gaps; and (c) as legal regulation lags behind technological advancements, it becomes essential to complement laws with flexible and forward-looking ethical education. The chapter argues for a multidimensional approach, combining legal regulation with the promotion of digital ethics and education, to effectively address the complexities of the digital realm.

SHARED THEMES AND INTERCONNECTIONS

The seven chapters collectively provide a nuanced exploration of how moving online transforms the nature, application, and governance of human rights. Each chapter addresses distinct facets of this transformation, but they converge around several overarching themes that highlight the fundamental differences introduced by the digital realm. Listed here are the key parallels across the chapters and their shared contributions to answering the question: *What difference does it make to move online?*

A. TRANSFORMATION OF RIGHTS

All chapters acknowledge that moving online reshapes the scope, interpretation, and enforcement of human rights, shifting their application from static, state-centred frameworks to dynamic, context-dependent interpretations:

- Chapter 2 on new digital rights emphasises that existing rights, such as privacy and freedom of expression, require reinterpretation in the context of AI and digital governance.
- Chapter 3 on state regulation of the internet shows how the internet amplifies risks such as disinformation and hate speech, necessitating reimagined frameworks to preserve public trust and democratic values.
- Chapter 4 on constitutional rights online explores how private platforms function as public forums, requiring constitutional rights to extend beyond state obligations to regulate platform behaviour.
- Chapter 5 on legal reasoning in digital contexts argues that courts must adapt their reasoning to address new harms and purposes unique to the online world, such as the permanence of digital information.
- Chapter 6 on non-coherence of digital rights argues that moving online disrupts the coherence of traditional human rights, leading to the relativisation of rights and the need for novel theoretical approaches.
- Chapter 7 on internet addiction discusses how digital environments amplify behavioural risks, such as addiction, which require integrating health and human rights approaches to governance.
- Chapter 8 on digital ethics and law critiques the limits of legal frameworks in addressing the unique challenges of the online space, emphasising the need for ethics and education.

B. AMPLIFICATION OF HARM AND VULNERABILITY

Each chapter highlights how the digital environment magnifies risks and harms that were less prominent offline:

- Chapter 2 shows how AI exacerbates risks such as bias, discrimination, and surveillance, amplifying existing inequalities.
- Chapter 3 illustrates how disinformation and manipulation online distort public discourse and erode trust at a scale unprecedented in offline contexts.
- Chapter 4 demonstrates that the privatisation of public spaces online amplifies the power of platforms to influence discourse, often to the detriment of individual freedoms.
- Chapter 5 notes that the reach and permanence of digital actions, such as online defamation or data breaches, heighten harm compared with their offline equivalents.

- Chapter 6 draws attention to the fact that the fast-paced and opaque nature of digital systems increases the likelihood of rights violations, complicating traditional legal safeguards.
- Chapter 7 shows how digital environments intensify the risk of addiction, particularly for vulnerable groups such as children, and require targeted public health interventions.
- Chapter 8 highlights how anonymity and the global reach of digital spaces amplify unethical behaviour, making it harder to enforce accountability.

C. SHIFTING DUTY BEARERS AND ACCOUNTABILITY

Most of the chapters discuss how moving online partly shifts responsibilities for rights protection from states to private actors, creating gaps in accountability:

- Chapter 2 notes the role of private AI developers in adhering to human rights standards, emphasising the need for public oversight.
- Chapter 3 advocates for shared responsibility between states, platforms, and independent regulators to address disinformation and other digital harms.
- Chapter 4 argues that constitutional rights must be horizontally applied to hold private platforms accountable for human rights violations.
- Chapter 6 points out the fragmented governance of digital rights, with overlapping responsibilities between states, platforms, and international bodies.
- Chapter 7 critiques platforms for failing to mitigate addictive design features, placing the burden on individuals and states to address the issue.
- Chapter 8 stresses the importance of ethical self-regulation alongside legal frameworks to address the accountability gaps created by anonymity and global reach.

D. FRAGMENTATION AND GLOBALISATION

Several of the chapters highlight the tension between the global nature of the internet and fragmented legal and regulatory frameworks, and advocate for harmonised regulatory frameworks based on international cooperation:

- Chapter 2 discusses the need for the harmonised international governance of AI to address cross-border rights violations.
- Chapter 3 emphasises the difficulty of regulating global platforms using national laws, advocating for international cooperation.
- Chapter 4 highlights how platform governance transcends national boundaries, necessitating transnational constitutional approaches.
- Chapter 5 illustrates how courts struggle to apply consistent reasoning when addressing global digital cases using local legal norms.
- Chapter 6 critiques the lack of coherence in global digital governance, arguing for more integrated frameworks.

E. THE NEED FOR COMPLEMENTARY APPROACHES

Several chapters also advocate for combining legal regulation with other mechanisms, such as ethics, education, and public awareness. Legal regulation alone cannot address the complexities of the digital realm, so complementary tools and cross-sectoral collaboration are essential:

- Chapter 2 stresses the need for enforceable legal obligations alongside ethical AI guidelines.
- Chapter 3 proposes a multi-tiered regulatory model combining self-regulation, independent oversight, and state intervention.
- Chapter 7 advocates for public health initiatives and digital literacy campaigns to mitigate addiction risks.
- Chapter 8 highlights the role of digital ethics and education in addressing gaps left by slow legal responses.

The seven chapters collectively argue that moving online fundamentally alters the nature of governance, accountability, and the protection of human rights. They draw attention to the amplified harms, shifting responsibilities, and global complexities of the digital environment, emphasising the need for innovative, multidisciplinary, and collaborative approaches to address the challenges posed by digital technologies.

2

Is There a Need for New Digital Human Rights in AI Governance?

Wolfgang Benedek

2.1 THE EMERGENCE OF (NEW) DIGITAL HUMAN RIGHTS

2.1.1 *Introduction*

Several recent initiatives have proposed new human rights for the digital sphere. This is in response to new challenges to human rights in an increasingly digitalised world. Recent developments to strengthen the governance of artificial intelligence (AI) have contributed to this debate. However, is there really a need for genuinely new digital human rights or would it suffice to adjust or extend existing rights by interpretation to deal with the new threats from cyberspace? As the proposals claim the emergence of new principles and rights, at which stage is the development of new digital human rights? How have European institutions reacted to the proposals and which regulatory efforts have they undertaken? If the new rights are proposed to be protected at the European level, what about the universal level of a global cyberspace, where there is a threat of increasing fragmentation?

Specific attention will be given to the regulation of AI from a human and fundamental rights perspective. In a dramatic move, a large number of renowned experts and scientists, among them developers of AI, have made a call in an open letter in March 2023 for a pause, a moratorium on the training of AI going beyond ChatGPT 4 in order to provide time to deal with the shortcomings in terms of reliability and some neglected aspects of the new technology. The letter also calls for quicker regulation by governments to provide a proper framework for the development and use of AI. This was complemented by concerns expressed by leading AI developers and even companies. The erratic Elon Musk has welcomed the suggested pause, and in view of the fact that ChatGPT cannot always distinguish between truth and falsehood, announced the development of a 'TruthGPT' as an alternative. Prompted by data protection concerns, Italy even temporarily prohibited the use of ChatGPT in order to obtain some assurances. The White House and the US Senate have called on the leaders of major companies to report on their activities. The Council of Europe (CoE) and the European Union (EU) have presented new regulatory approaches to AI, which will be analysed in a comparative way regarding their contribution to the protection of human and fundamental rights.

2.1.2 *Protection of Human Rights on the Internet*

The question of how to protect human rights online was first raised by civil society at the World Summit on the Information Society of the United Nations (UN), which took place in Geneva in 2003 and in Tunis in 2005. While the final documents of those conferences made only a few references to human rights,[1] the topic became a major concern in their follow-up in the form of the annual Internet Governance Forum (IGF).[2] For example, on the suggestion of the Association for Progressive Communications, which in 2006 produced an Internet Rights Charter, the Dynamic Coalition on Internet Rights and Principles established at the IGF in Rio in 2007 began elaborating the Charter of Human Rights and Principles for the Internet. The Charter was drafted in a broad process mainly by civil society and academia and presented as a draft version at the IGF in Vilnius in 2010, while the final version was presented at the IGF in Belgrade in 2011. The methodology was oriented towards the Universal Declaration of Human Rights in order to interpret it and other key UN human rights documents such as the International Covenants on Civil and Political as well as on Economic, Social and Cultural Rights, the UN Conventions on the Rights of the Child, and on the Rights of People with Disabilities for the Purposes of the Internet. The only new right identified was the right to access to the internet, which is formulated in Article 1 of the Charter.[3] The Charter contributed to the general debate on internet rights, which produced numerous proposals.[4]

The UN human rights bodies were thus far largely absent from the topic. Only in 2011 did the Special Rapporteur on the Promotion and Protection of the Right of Freedom of Opinion and Expression, Frank LaRue, produce a report with a focus on the internet.[5] In 2012, the UN Human Rights Council adopted its first resolution

1 See the outcome documents at ITU, World summit on the information society, Geneva 2003, www.itu.int/net/wsis/documents/doc_multi.asp?lang=en&id=1161|1160|2266|2267; see also W. Benedek, 'International organizations and digital human rights', in B. Wagner, M. C. Kettemann, and K. Veith (eds.), *Research Handbook on Human Rights and Digital Technology. Global Politics, Law and International Relations*, 2nd ed. (Cheltenham: Edward Elgar, 2024), pp. 311–26.

2 W. Benedek, 'Internet governance and human rights', in W. Benedek, V. Bauer, and M. C. Kettemann (eds.), *Internet Governance and the Information Society* (The Hague: Eleven, 2008), pp. 31–50, at 36 et seq.

3 See the Charter on the webpage of the Internet Rights and Principles Coalition, https://internetrightsandprinciples.org.

4 See A. Pettrachin, 'Towards a universal declaration on internet rights and freedoms?' (2018) 80 *International Communication Gazette* 4, 337–53, who analysed fifty-eight documents proclaiming internet-related human rights.

5 UNHRC, UN Special Rapporteur on the Promotion and Protection of the Right of Freedom of Opinion and Expression, Frank LaRue, 16 May 2011, UN Doc. A/HRC/17/27.

on human rights and the internet in which it used the famous formula that 'the same rights people have offline must also be protected online'.[6] This clarified that all human rights, in principle, are also applicable online, but does not exclude taking the particularities of the internet into account. Since that time, the UN has taken up issues related to the internet in several fora and recently prepared the Global Digital Compact that was agreed upon by its Summit for the Future of the Internet in September 2024. The compact deals with digital cooperation, including the application of human rights online.[7]

Already before the UN started to deal with the issue, the CoE engaged in the question of how to apply human rights, in particular the European Convention on Human Rights (ECHR) to the internet, and since has taken the lead among international organisations in the study and regulation of the new challenges to human rights brought by the internet.[8] Inspired by the Charter on Human Rights and Principles for the Internet, the CoE elaborated a guide on human rights for internet users, which contains a catalogue of the main digital human rights.[9] The European Court of Human Rights (ECtHR) has developed its case law on the issue, related mainly to access to the internet, freedom of expression,[10] and the right to privacy and data protection with regard to the new technologies.[11] The tech community has also shown awareness of the need to give adequate attention to human rights in regard to technological development by coining the concept of 'digital humanism'.[12]

2.1.3 *Proposals for New Digital Human Rights*

In recent years, several proposals for new digital human rights have been launched, such as the Charter of Digital Fundamental Rights of the EU, elaborated by a group

[6] UNHRC, 'Resolution on the promotion, protection and enjoyment of human rights on the internet', 16 July 2012, UN Doc. A/HRC/RES/20/8, para. 1. Since the resolution was renewed about every second year, see latest UNHRC Resolution 47/16 of 13 July 2021 with the same title, which repeats the principle in its para. 1.

[7] See UN Office of the Secretary-General's Envoy on Technology, www.un.org/techenvoy/global-digital-compact.

[8] Benedek, 'International organizations and digital human rights', 370 et seq.; see also W. Benedek and M. C. Kettemann, 'The Council of Europe and the information society', in R. Kicker (ed.), *The Council of Europe, Pioneer and Guarantor for Human Rights and Democracy* (Strasbourg: Council of Europe Publishing, 2010), p. 109 et seq.

[9] See the guide, Council of Europe, 'Guide to human rights for internet users', www.coe.int/en/web/freedom-expression/guide-to-human-rights-for-internet-users.

[10] See W. Benedek and M. C. Kettemann, *Freedom of Expression and the Internet*, 2nd ed. (Strasbourg: Council of Europe Publishing, 2020).

[11] See ECtHR, 'Factsheet – Access to internet and freedom to receive and impart information and ideas' (June 2024), www.echr.coe.int/documents/d/echr/FS_Access_Internet_ENG; and ECtHR, 'Factsheet – New technologies' (October 2024) www.echr.coe.int/documents/d/echr/FS_New_technologies_ENG.

[12] See the Vienna Manifesto on Digital Humanism, May 2019, https://caiml.org/dighum//dighum-manifesto/.

of mainly German experts and launched with the help of the Zeit Foundation in 2016 and updated in 2018.[13] The idea was to complement the EU Charter on Fundamental Rights drafted by a Convention in 2000, which became binding as part of the Treaty of Lisbon in 2009. The proposal contains, for example, the right that net neutrality must be provided in a non-discriminatory way (Article 11). Of particular interest are the rights related to automated systems and decisions; for example, that the criteria for automated decisions, such as in regard to digital profiling, must be transparent and be taken by natural or legal persons. Every person must have a right to the independent review of such decisions by a human being (Article 5). The rights should apply to the EU, state and non-state actors, including internet platforms.

Another initiative came in early 2021 from the author and lawyer Ferdinand von Schirach, who suggested six new fundamental rights to complement the EU Charter on Fundamental Rights, among them two new digital human rights: 'Everyone has the right to know that any algorithms imposed on them are transparent, verifiable and fair. Major decisions must be taken by a human being.' The other fundamental right proposed was the right to digital self-determination, according to which 'excessive profiling or the manipulation of people is forbidden'. This proposal was supported by the WeMoveEurope Foundation, which has collected more than 270,000 supporters.[14] While these definitions lack the necessary precision to be directly legally applicable, they may serve as principles or be concretised depending on the respective context. The proposal included the idea of organising a new Convention to discuss the enlargement of the EU Charter on Fundamental Rights on the basis of these rights. However, this proved not to be realistic. A right to informational self-determination with a focus on data protection is already part of German law.

The proposals are addressed in the first place to the bodies of the EU, such as the European Parliament, the European Commission, and the governments of European states. However, there has been no known direct response to the proposals, while the European Commission and Parliament have developed their own proposals in the field of digital human rights, to be presented later in this chapter.

2.1.4 *Methodology for 'Creating' New Digital Human Rights*

The various initiatives for the progressive development of digital human rights and principles raises the question of how such new rights are being created. There has been an abundance of declarations and recommendations by various institutions, and non-government and inter-governmental organisations, sometimes developed

[13] See the text at https://digitalcharta.eu/wp-content/uploads/DigitalCharter-English-2019-Final.pdf.

[14] See YouMove Europe, 'For new fundamental rights in Europe', https://you.wemove.eu/campaigns/for-new-fundamental-rights-in-europe.

with a multi-stakeholder approach.[15] With few exceptions, they are all of a soft law nature. Today, this is the norm in the progressive development of international legal obligations. If the authority of the proposed rules is high, they might be respected even without being legally binding. Therefore, the process of creation, whether by state initiatives or in a multi-stakeholder approach, whether by non-government initiatives or by regulatory bodies at the regional or universal level, makes a major difference. The regulation may not only come from public institutions but also from private platforms; for example, by way of self-regulation, which might follow recommendations from the public sphere, thus providing the horizontal protection of human rights – that is, of individuals against private companies. For example, in the case of the Human Rights Oversight Board of Facebook/Meta, individuals can launch appeals against company decisions that limit their freedom of expression.[16]

There is an obvious danger of an inflation of the use of the concept of 'rights', which requires appropriate standards for their recognition. Today, we are faced with many claims for new human rights in various fields, but whether they find their way to general recognition and finally into regulatory norm-setting is a process with many factors. Already in 1984, Alston proposed some criteria for quality control in the creation of new human rights, such as the social value added, non-repetition of existing rights, ability to achieve high international consensus, or being sufficiently precise to produce identifiable rights and obligations.[17] Rights might also be recognised only at national or regional levels, which raises the question whether human rights need universal standing to be recognised as human rights.[18] For example, the prohibition of the death penalty as a key human right in Europe applies only among the members of the CoE and a number of other states globally, and therefore is not a universal human right. However, this does not affect its human rights character. The Spanish government has drafted a Charter on Digital Rights, which contains a comprehensive set of rights for the digital environment, including the right to digital identity, to public participation by digital means, and the right of access to digital environments for older persons. In several cases, the details of the rights identified are to be specified by the law.[19]

[15] See Pettrachin, 'Towards a universal declaration', and J. Kulesza, 'Multistakeholderism – meaning and implications', in M. Susi (ed.), *Human Rights, Digital Society and the Law: A Research Companion* (London: Routledge, 2019), pp. 117–31; W. Benedek, 'Multi-stakeholderism in the development of international law', in U. Fastenrath et al. (eds.), *From Bilateralism to Community Interest: Essays in Honour of Judge Bruno Simma* (Oxford: Oxford University Press, 2011), pp. 201–10.

[16] See D. Wong and L. Floridi, 'Meta's oversight board: a review and critical assessment' (2023) 33 *Minds and Machines* 2, 261–84.

[17] P. Alston, 'Conjuring up new human rights: a proposal for quality control' (1984) 78 *American Journal of International Law* 3, 607–21.

[18] M. Susi, 'Novelty in new human rights: the decrease in universality and abstractness thesis', in A. von Arnauld, K. von der Decken, and M. Susi (eds.), *The Cambridge Handbook on New Human Rights: Recognition, Novelty, Rhetoric* (Cambridge: Cambridge University Press, 2020), pp. 21–33.

[19] See for the text of the Charter https://portal.mineco.gob.es/RecursosArticulo/mineco/ministerio/participacion_publica/audiencia/ficheros/Charter%20of%20Digital%20Rights.pdf.

Much depends on the protection needs identified by relevant actors. For example, while the focus in the past was on data protection, leading to various regulatory efforts such as the modernised Convention 108+ of the CoE or the General Data Protection Regulation (GDPR) of the EU, more recently the main concern has been with illicit content such as hate speech and disinformation on the internet, while today the protection of human rights in the development and use of AI takes centre stage. AI is also used for the Internet of Things. This produces non-personal data, which are not covered by the GDPR, but may still raise protection issues. Generally, the rights are to address protection needs, which in the digital environment can be structured into issues related to identity and access such as digital self-determination and protection from blocking and filtering as well as internet shutdowns, issues of protection against illicit digital content such as hate speech, disinformation, defamation, or online violence, and issues related to protection against technological threats such as surveillance, biometrical data use for facial recognition, and the use of AI to interfere with human rights or the harassment of bloggers or of digital human rights defenders.

Not all the digital rights proposed qualify as human rights. As an advocacy non-governmental organisation (NGO), European Digital Rights (EDRi) has established a network of NGOs from different countries to protect and promote digital rights.[20] In 2014, EDRi also produced a ten-point Charter on Digital Rights aimed mainly at members of the European Parliament preparing for (re-)election. In practice those rights were rather commitments in the form of principles covering a wide range of issues, such as the promotion of encryption or of free software.[21]

Various questions related to the emergence of new human rights have been studied in detail in a recent handbook on new human rights, which also looks at some examples from the digital world.[22] The development of new human rights is a process starting with the identification of new protection needs, as mentioned, their articulation in the form of rights, and finally their recognition and implementation. Mart Susi identifies several elements of inadequate protection on the basis of existing human rights as a reason for developing new human rights. For rights derived from other rights, he observes a decrease in abstractness.[23] This could also be said for rights derived from principles such as the right to informational self-determination, which goes back to a decision of the German Constitutional Court in 1983.[24] In most cases, an evolutionary interpretation as applied by the ECtHR will suffice. For example, the secrecy of correspondence by letter can be extended to personal

[20] See on its composition and activities, https://edri.org.

[21] See the EDRi Charter of Digital Rights, https://edri.org/wp-content/uploads/2014/06/EDRi_DigitalRightsCharter_web.pdf.

[22] A. von Arnauld, K. von der Decken, and M. Susi (eds.), *The Cambridge Handbook on New Human Rights: Recognition, Novelty, Rhetoric* (Cambridge: Cambridge University Press, 2020).

[23] Susi, 'Novelty in new human rights'.

[24] O. Puccinelli, 'The right to be forgotten 2.0', in von Arnauld, von der Decken, and Susi (eds.), *The Cambridge Handbook on New Human Rights*, pp. 300–10.

communication using the internet. But this also needed additional provisions on data protection, as in CoE Convention 108+, to address new privacy needs.[25]

In view of the particularities of the online domain, Susi developed the non-coherence theory of digital human rights, which claims a change of meaning and scope when human rights are transposed from the physical to the digital world. Accordingly, digital human rights are different by nature from the respective offline human rights.[26]

New human rights may be derived from parent rights ('implied rights') or be stand-alone rights. For example, the right to access to the internet has been derived by some from the freedom of expression and information, but others claim that because the relevance of meaningful access to the internet goes far beyond the freedom of expression it should be considered as a stand-alone right.[27] This is also supported by a report by the Office of the UN High Commissioner for Human Rights on Internet Shutdowns from a human rights perspective, which shows that many more rights are affected than just freedom of expression.[28] However, while the report refers to international commitments ensuring universal internet access, it does not speak of internet access as a human right, which shows that the right is not yet fully recognised as such at the UN level.[29]

Furthermore, the 'right to be forgotten' has been claimed to be a stand-alone right, while its formation is related to the right to privacy and data protection.[30] Based on a judgement of the European Court of Justice, it has been introduced as part of the GDPR rules of the EU.[31] In response, Google has received thousands of requests for the deletion of links to personal information. It was largely left to the private company how to deal with these. However, whether a new digital human right has really been created is also being questioned.[32] So far, it is legally codified only in Article 17 of the GDPR and a few national constitutions, and is thus not generally recognised. However, in *Biancardi v. Italy*, the ECtHR has upheld the right to be forgotten, without referring to it in that way, against the freedom of expression of a journalist. The delayed de-indexing of an article on criminal proceedings on the internet had been found damaging to the reputation of a person.[33]

25 See CoE, 'Privacy and data protection – explanatory memorandum', www.coe.int/en/web/freedom-expression/privacy-and-data-protection-explanatory-memo.

26 M. Susi, *The Non-Coherence Theory of Digital Human Rights* (Cambridge: Cambridge University Press, 2024).

27 See B. Cali, 'The right to meaningful access to the internet', in von Arnauld, von der Decken, and Susi (eds.), *The Cambridge Handbook on New Human Rights*, pp. 276–84.

28 OHCHR, 'Internet shutdowns: trends, causes, legal implications and impacts on a range of human rights', 13 May 2022, UN Doc. A/HRC/50/55.

29 Ibid., para. 2.

30 M. Susi, 'The right to be forgotten', in von Arnauld, von der Decken, and Susi (eds.), *The Cambridge Handbook on New Human Rights*, pp. 287–99, esp. 297.

31 T. Pajuste, 'The protection of personal data in the digital society: the role of the GDPR', in Susi (ed.), *Human Rights, Digital Society and the Law*, pp. 303–15.

32 Susi, 'The right to be forgotten', p. 287 et seq.

33 *Biancardi v. Italy*, Application no. 77419/16, Judgment of 25 November 2021.

Human rights can be individual and collective. Most experts will agree that a human right should be individually enforceable, otherwise we should better speak of principles. But there can also be a collective enforcement, as in the context of social rights. Some universally recognised human rights, such as the right to self-determination, and including the solidarity rights of peace, development, and the environment, can only be realised collectively. They are therefore sometimes called 'peoples' rights'. The African Charter on Human and Peoples' Rights contains several such rights. Therefore, it might be worth also distinguishing between individual and collective digital human rights. For example, some – such as the right to cybersecurity – are quite abstract and need concretisation to be applied to individuals. However, this is nothing unusual if we consider, for example, the right to water and sanitation or the right to a clean, healthy, and sustainable environment recognised respectively in 2010 and in 2022 by the General Assembly of the UN.[34] Most human or fundamental rights also need concretisation. This is why one function of the various human rights treaty bodies is to elaborate interpretations, mostly in the form of general comments, while the human rights courts can give binding interpretations in individual cases that may provide general directions.

2.2 GOVERNANCE OF AI AND HUMAN RIGHTS

2.2.1 *Introduction*

The impact of the development and application of AI (systems) on human and fundamental rights has become a priority concern for many actors, in particular since the company OpenAI backed by Microsoft has made ChatGPT 3 freely available.[35] The new technology opens new opportunities, but also new threats, such as the possibility of further facilitating the assessment of people according to their social behaviour (social scoring), as is already in use in China. While it produces astonishing results, which have generated heightened attention and expectations for its potential, there have also been warnings about its disruptive potential for democracy and society at large if used for disinformation. This culminated in the open letter of 22 March 2023 signed by key AI developers and thousands of concerned scientists asking for a six-month moratorium on the training of AI systems more powerful than ChatGPT 4. This is motivated by what the letter calls an out-of-control race, with AI labs 'developing and deploying ever more powerful digital

[34] See UNGA, 'The human right to water and sanitation', 28 July 2010, UN Doc. A/HRC/64/292; UNGA, 'The human right to a clean, healthy, and sustainable environment', 1 August 2022, UN Doc. A/RES/76/300.

[35] GPT stands for Generative Pretrained Transformer. First assessments of the new technology and its commercial successor GDP 4 show its strengths and weaknesses; see K. Rose, 'The brilliance and weirdness of ChatGPT', *New York Times*, 5 December 2022; C. Metz, 'OpenAI plans to up the ante in tech's A.I. race', *New York Times*, 14 March 2023.

minds that no one – not even their creators – can understand, predict and control'. One example given is the 'flooding of information channels with propaganda and untruth'. The uncontrolled race may lead to a 'loss of control of our civilization'. Consequently, it creates new challenges to democracy and human rights. Time should be taken to introduce much-needed regulation and to address planning and management needs, including the development of shared safety protocols for advanced AI design to be overseen by independent outside experts. AI developers should work with policymakers 'to dramatically accelerate the development of robust AI governance systems', including oversight of highly capable AI systems, auditing and certification systems, and liability for harm caused.[36]

The Human Rights Council of the UN also reacted by indicating the potential and risks of the emerging technologies and recommending certain measures to protect the human rights of individuals throughout the life cycle of AI systems. It also recommended strengthening the capacities of the Office of the High Commissioner for Human Rights (OHCHR) to advance human rights in the context of new and emerging technologies, and asked it to prepare a mapping report identifying challenges and gaps in this respect.[37] The report, presented in 2024, identified several gaps, including the provision of advice that should be provided by the OHCHR to Member States and all stakeholders to support them in integrating human rights from the design to the regulation of digital technologies.[38]

This development shows the limitations of the old approach that industry should lead on new technological developments and that regulation can come later in cases where economic considerations lead to the neglect of societal concerns. The corresponding approaches of self-regulation and declarations of ethical principles, while important, are insufficient in such circumstances where the largest tech giants match each other in regard to economic opportunities, while states only pursue their national interests. The Asilomar Principles on Beneficial AI already elaborated in 2017 with the purpose of ensuring the compatibility of the development of AI with human dignity, rights, and freedoms, were already concerned that AI systems remain under human control.[39] The Organisation for Economic Co-operation and Development (OECD) adopted a set of principles on AI in 2019,[40] while UNESCO adopted a consensus-based Recommendation on the Ethics of Artificial Intelligence in 2021.[41] OpenAI on its website expresses its commitment to ensure that artificial

36 See Future of Life Institute, 'Pause giant AI experiments: an open letter', 22 March 2023, https://futureoflife.org/open-letter/pause-giant-ai-experiments/.

37 See HRC, 'New and emerging digital technologies and human rights', 12 July 2023, UN Doc. A/HRC/RES/53/29.

38 OHCHR, 'Mapping report: new and emerging technologies', 24 June 2024, UN Doc. A/HRC/56/45.

39 The Asilomar Principles are part of another open letter; see Future of Life Institute, 'Asilomar AI Principles', 11 August 2017, https://futureoflife.org/open-letter/ai-principles/.

40 See the Recommendation of the OECD Council on Artificial Intelligence of 22 May 2019, https://legalinstruments.oecd.org/en/instruments/OECD-LEGAL-0449.

41 See the UNESCO Recommendation, https://unesdoc.unesco.org/ark:/48223/pf0000381137.

general intelligence benefits all humanity, and also commits to the principle of transparency.[42] However, the training of AI systems is presently taking place behind closed doors without state or societal control. The danger of serious harm created by these developments has led one of the AI pioneers at Google to resign from his position in order to be free to speak out.[43]

The call for the regulation of the development of AI and its application has accelerated ongoing efforts in Europe and beyond.[44] Besides the EU and the CoE, the US has responded with a non-binding AI Bill of Rights and a White House executive order. The AI Bill of Rights has a focus on addressing challenges to democracy and certain rights such as privacy and non-discrimination with a focus on serving the American people. It also foresees a right to opt out and of access to a human person to consider and remedy problems.[45] In reaction to the appeals for regulation, the heads of the main companies were called to the White House and the Senate, where even the chief executive of OpenAI called for regulation.[46] The issue is also on the agenda of the G7.

China has also adopted 'Interim Measures for the Management of Services of Generative AI', which are to complement existing laws on network security and data security. The regulation establishes the requirement that the contents should reflect the basic values of socialism, while the law should also prevent discrimination, hatred, violence, fakes, and other content that could interfere with the economic and social order.[47]

These different and partly competing approaches also carry some ideological baggage. American and European values or Chinese socialism create the danger of a further fragmentation of the internet. Accordingly, universal rules for global problems created by the use of generative AI would be necessary to counter the trend of fragmentation and polarisation. Digital constitutionalism aiming at a normative framework for the protection of human rights and the balancing of

42 See the Statement on Artificial General Intelligence, 24 February 2023, https://openai.com/blog/planning-for-agi-and-beyond.

43 See '"The Godfather of AI" leaves Google and warns of danger ahead', *New York Times*, 1 May 2023, www.nytimes.com/2023/05/01/technology/ai-google-chatbot-engineer-quits-hinton.html?te=1&nl=from-the-times&emc=edit_ufn_20230501.

44 W. Benedek, 'Digital human rights and artificial intelligence' (2023) 14 *Pravni Zapisi*, 2, 227–37.

45 See White House, 'Blueprint for an AI Bill of Rights – making automated systems work for the American people', www.whitehouse.gov/ostp/ai-bill-of-rights/; White House, 'Executive Order on the safe, secure and trustworthy development and use of artificial intelligence', 30 October 2023, www.whitehouse.gov/briefing-room/presidential-actions/2023/10/30/executive-order-on-the-safe-secure-and-trustworthy-development-and-use-of-artificial-intelligence/.

46 See 'Open AI's Sam Altmann urges regulation at Senate hearing', *New York Times*, 16 May 2023, www.nytimes.com/2023/05/16/technology/openai-altman-artificial-intelligence-regulation.html?te=1&nl=the-evening&emc=edit_ne_20230516.

47 See the Chinese 'Interim measures', www.pwccn.com/en/tmt/interim-measures-for-generative-ai-services-implemented-aug2023.pdf; M. Sheehan, 'China's AI regulations and how they get made', Carnegie Foundation, 10 July 2023, https://carnegieendowment.org/research/2023/07/chinas-ai-regulations-and-how-they-get-made?lang=en.

powers is one approach to addressing these concerns.[48] Strengthening international cooperation and closing digital divides are the main aims of the UN Global Digital Compact. It contains several principles and objectives for international cooperation and also aims at enhancing governance in the field of digital technologies for which purpose new institutional proposals have been made, such as the establishment of an International Scientific Panel on AI to conduct independent risk assessments and produce annual reports, a Global Dialogue on AI Governance, and a Global Fund for AI for Sustainable Development. In support of stakeholders, the Office of the High Commissioner for Human Rights in Geneva is to provide advice on ensuring human rights.[49]

As the non-binding recommendations and commitments to the self-regulation of AI were considered insufficient and some of the developers themselves were calling for a binding regulation, European regional organisations took the lead in elaborating new rules. Therefore, the efforts of the CoE and the EU will be studied here in greater detail using a comparative approach. Both of these started long before the hype around ChatGPT.

2.2.2 *The CoE on AI and Human Rights*

From a human rights perspective, major work on the regulation of AI has been undertaken by the CoE, which has traditionally taken the lead in the field of the internet and human rights. The methodology of the CoE aims to establish a committee by decision of the Committee of Ministers (CoM) for a particular topic to produce a report with a recommendation for adoption by the CoM. The committee is supported by the competent staff of the CoE and traditionally follows a multi-stakeholder approach as it brings together experts from Member States and civil society as well as academia, while the business community is also consulted. In the case of AI, the CoE has engaged in numerous activities since 2017 to study pertinent human rights issues and produce recommendations aimed towards guidance and regulation in this field.

In particular, the Parliamentary Assembly of the CoE adopted a recommendation in 2017 on technological convergence, AI, and human rights,[50] calling for the drafting of guidelines. In addition, the European Commissioner of Human Rights also came out in 2019 with a recommendation entitled 'Unboxing Artificial Intelligence: 10

[48] See G. De Gregorio and R. Radu, 'Digital constitutionalism in the new era of internet governance' (2022) 30 *International Journal of Law and Technology*, 1, 68–87.

[49] See the developments on the global digital compact at the website of the UN Envoy for technology, www.un.org/techenvoy/global-digital-compact.

[50] See European Parliament, Recommendation 2102 (2017), 'Technological convergence, artificial intelligence and human rights', 28 April 2017, http://assembly.coe.int/nw/xml/XRef/Xref-XML2HTML-en.asp?fileid=23726.

Steps to Protect Human Rights'.[51] It called for Human Rights Impact Assessments, information and transparency, independent oversight, non-discrimination, data protection, and remedies, to mention just the main steps. Also in 2019, the CoM established the Ad Hoc Committee on Artificial Intelligence (CAHAI), which was succeeded by the Committee on Artificial Intelligence (CAI) in 2021. Having adopted a declaration in 2019 on the manipulative capabilities of algorithmic processes,[52] one of the first recommendations by the CoM on the human rights impacts of algorithmic systems, with a set of guidelines attached, was adopted in 2020.[53] Based on a multi-stakeholder consultation, CAHAI with the help of three subgroups produced a comprehensive feasibility study on a legal framework for the development, design and application of AI.[54] It came to the conclusion that while there were several applicable instruments, a number of substantive and procedural legal gaps existed that could be best addressed by a new legal framework for which key elements were identified.[55]

In December 2021, after broad consultation, several studies, and conferences,[56] CAHAI adopted a report entitled 'Possible Elements of a Legal Framework for Artificial Intelligence, Based on CoE's Standards on Human Rights, Democracy and the Rule of Law',[57] which dealt with issues related to the development, design, and application of AI based on CoE's standards. For this purpose, the regulatory work of other international organisations such as UNESCO, the OECD, and the EU was taken into account.[58] It set out the main elements for a transversal convention creating a framework and possible additional legal or soft law instruments to apply generally or to specific sectors, and the public sector in particular. For example, a model for a human rights, democracy, and rule of law impact assessment on a soft law basis was proposed.[59] Mantelero, who has developed his own

[51] See CoE Commissioner for Human Rights, 'Unboxing artificial intelligence: 10 steps to protect human rights (2019), https://rm.coe.int/unboxing-artificial-intelligence-10-steps-to-protect-human-rights-reco/1680946e64.

[52] See CoE, 'Declaration by the Committee of Ministers on the manipulative capabilities of algorithmic processes', 13 February 2019, https://search.coe.int/cm/pages/result_details.aspx?objectid=0900001680 92dd4b.

[53] See CoE, Recommendation CM/Rec(2020)1 of the Committee of Ministers to member States on the human rights impacts of algorithmic systems', 8 April 2020, https://search.coe.int/cm/pages/result_details.aspx?objectid=09000016809e1154.

[54] See CAHAI, Feasibility study, 17 December 2020, https://rm.coe.int/cahai-2020-23-final-eng-feasibility-study-/1680a0c6da.

[55] See ibid., paras. 83–90 and paras. 95 et seq.

[56] See CoE, 'Artificial Intelligence, Council of Europe's work in progress', November 2024, www.coe.int/en/web/artificial-intelligence/work-in-progress.

[57] See CAHAI, 'Possible elements of a legal framework on artificial intelligence, based on the CoE's standards on human rights, democracy and the rule of law', 3 December 2021, https://rm.coe.int/cahai-2021-09rev-elements/1680a6d90d.

[58] See for UNESCO its Recommendation on the Ethics of Artificial Intelligence, 23 November 2021, https://unesdoc.unesco.org/ark:/48223/pf0000381137.

[59] See CAHAI, 'Possible elements of a legal framework on artificial intelligence', paras. 45 et seq.

Human Rights, Ethical and Social Impact Assessment, critically noted that the CoE approach might be too broad.[60]

Between 2022 and 2024, the CAI negotiated the text for a common legal instrument on AI. The drafts were provided by the secretariat and then discussed in the committee.[61] The Framework Convention on Artificial Intelligence, Human Rights, Democracy and the Rule of Law was designed as an open convention with a global vocation. There were fifty-seven states participating, among them some already established observer states of the CoE, including the USA, Canada, Mexico, and Japan, and also the EU. The Framework Convention was finally adopted by the CoM in May 2024 to be opened for signature in September 2024 at the meeting of ministers of justice in Vilnius. For it to enter into force, it needs only five ratifications. All states (including the EU) that have participated in its negotiation, as well as other states invited by the CoM of the CoE, can then become parties to the Convention.

The Framework Convention mainly contains principles for respecting existing human rights, but does not formulate new digital human rights. It also covers the obligations to protect the integrity of democratic processes and respect for the rule of law (Article 5).[62] The Convention contains relevant guidance for its parties such as the obligation to adopt and apply measures to protect human dignity and individual autonomy during the lifecycle of AI systems.[63] Its framework character implies that there might be additional instruments to address specific issues of AI governance. There are provisions on transparency and oversight, on accountability and responsibility, and on non-discrimination in the implementation of the Convention.[64] There is also a right to be informed when one is interacting with AI systems.[65] It also provides for a risk and impact management framework, which includes an obligation on parties to ensure that adverse impacts of AI systems on human rights, democracy, and the rule of law are adequately addressed.[66] There is no obligatory human rights, democracy, and rule of law impact assessment, but the CoE plans to elaborate a pertinent methodology. Regarding effective remedies, measures are to be foreseen that inform relevant bodies and where appropriate also affected persons about AI systems having the potential to significantly affect human rights, allowing them to contest decisions made or lodge a complaint to competent

60 A. Mantelero, *Beyond Data: Human Rights, Ethical and Social Impact Assessment in AI* (New York: Springer, 2022), p. 165.

61 See for the work of CAI and CoE, 'Artificial Intelligence. Committee on Artificial Intelligence', www.coe.int/en/web/artificial-intelligence/cai.

62 See on CAI, and the text of the Framework Convention, CoE, 'Artificial Intelligence. Committee on Artificial Intelligence', www.coe.int/en/web/artificial-intelligence/cai.

63 CoE Framework Convention on Artificial Intelligence and Human Rights, Democracy and the Rule of Law, CoE Treaty Series No. 225, Vilnius, 5 September 2024, Article 7.

64 Ibid., Articles 8, 9, and 17.

65 Ibid., Article 15, para. 2.

66 Ibid., Article 16.

authorities.[67] Measures to ensure that AI systems are not used to undermine the integrity of the democratic process and the rule of law are to be adopted.[68]

Parties should also establish effective oversight mechanisms. However, several general legal safeguards proposed in the elements for a convention by CAHAI, the predecessor of the CAI, such as the right to interaction with a human,[69] did not make it into the final version of the Convention, although they were partly taken up in the AIA.[70] With regard to the scope of the Convention, national security interests are excepted. The focus is on regulating public bodies. In view of resistance to including the private sector, the final version provides that parties will declare at the time of signature or ratification whether they will apply the principles and obligations also to private actors.[71] It seems that a watering down of the Convention was the cost of including the USA and other non-European states in the negotiations. States are free to use the legal tools they consider appropriate in implementing the Convention (Article 3). This would include the possibility of private self-regulation, which has been criticised by civil society, as it could undermine the binding character of the Convention. The general exception for national security has also been criticised.[72]

Like the Data Protection Convention (Convention 108+),[73] the Biomedicine (Oviedo) Convention and the Cybercrime (Budapest) Convention of the CoE, the Convention will also be open by invitation to non-European states. For this purpose, the interests of future parties from outside the European region, but also in the EU, which was finalising its Artificial Intelligence Act (AIA) in parallel, had to be taken into account in the negotiations.

The CoE therefore moved ahead with a legally binding approach, whereas the field of AI and human rights has so far been primarily the subject of soft law recommendations and guidelines. This approach also goes beyond the ethical dimension covered by UNESCO guidelines,[74] but aims at legally binding

67 Ibid., Article 14.

68 Ibid., Article 5.

69 See on the work of CAHAI, CoE, 'Artificial Intelligence. CAHAI – Ad hoc Committee on Artificial Intelligence', www.coe.int/en/web/artificial-intelligence/cahai.

70 See, e.g., Article 13 AIA on transparency and provision of information to deployers and in particular Article 14 on human oversight for high-risk AI systems and Article 50 – natural persons to be informed that they interact with certain AI systems or that content has been artificially created or manipulated (deep fakes).

71 See Article 3 of the CoE Framework Convention.

72 See the open letter by Algorithm Watch and numerous other NGOs of 5 March 2024 at: https://algorithmwatch.org/de/wp-content/uploads/2024/03/Open_letter_Council_of_Europe_AI_Convention.pdf.

73 Convention for the Protection of Individuals with regard to the Automatic Processing of Personal Data, Strasbourg, 28 January 1981, ETS 108, and its protocol of 2001, Additional Protocol to the Convention for the Protection of Individuals with regard to Automatic Processing of Personal Data regarding supervisory authorities and transborder data flows, Strasbourg, 8 November 2001, ETS 181.

74 See the UNESCO Recommendation on the Ethics of Artificial Intelligence, 23 November 2021, https://unesdoc.unesco.org/ark:/48223/pf0000381137.

obligations after soft law and self-regulation has been shown to be insufficient. There are obvious advantages and disadvantages to this approach. The advantage of a legally binding obligation and not just a soft law commitment is obvious if we look at the difficulties of having the multitude of recommendations and guidelines in the field respected in practice. The disadvantage is that a convention is negotiated mainly by states, which is also reflected in the composition of the CAI; this includes CoE member and observer states, and representatives of international organisations and private business, while selected members of civil society and academia can only participate if invited as observers. The outcome of the negotiation process needs to be ratified by national parliaments. As in the case of the Cybercrime Convention, only limited membership from non-European states can be expected. In order to achieve greater participation, standards had to be lowered. Therefore, whether the Convention can be expected to produce a valuable global response to the issues at stake is yet to be seen. It might remain a mainly European response to a global challenge, as the other open conventions of the CoE have. However, the effort to open up to the world needs to be recognised.

2.2.3 *The EU Act on Artificial Intelligence and Fundamental Rights*

The efforts of the EU in the field of regulating AI also aim to have an effect beyond the EU, as the EU, as in the case of the GDPR, aims at a 'Brussels effect'. In a broad process, the EU has worked on different aspects of AI including its definition and ethical principles, on which the Independent High-Level Group of Experts on AI has produced relevant proposals including guidelines on ethics.[75] In January 2022, the European Commission presented a European Declaration on Digital Rights and Principles for the Digital Decade, which also contains rights related to the use of AI jointly adopted with the European Parliament and the Council in December 2022.[76] It focuses on principles and claims that in the digital transformation of Europe people should be at the centre, but, however, avoids saying clearly whether people should have enforceable fundamental rights. The declaration was supposed to serve as a reference work for politics and business.[77] Under freedom of choice, the rather short declaration also contains principles on AI, such as ensuring transparency about the use of AI, avoiding discrimination, and ensuring that algorithms are not used to predetermine people's choices, which is reminiscent of some elements of

[75] See on ethics guidelines for trustworthy AI by the Independent High-Level Group of Experts of EU at European Commission, 'Shaping Europe's digital future. Ethics guidelines for trustworthy AI', 8 April 2019, https://digital-strategy.ec.europa.eu/en/library/ethics-guidelines-trustworthy-ai.

[76] See European Commission, 'Shaping Europe's digital future. European Declaration on Digital Rights and Principles', 15 December 2022, https://digital-strategy.ec.europa.eu/en/library/european-declaration-digital-rights-and-principles.

[77] Communication by the Commission, COM (2022) 27 final of 26 January 2022.

the rights proposed by the WeMoveEurope campaign. This paved the way for the EU AIA to regulate AI.

The proposed EU AIA,[78] of April 2021, was presented by the European Commission after wide public consultation with the involvement of all interested actors. The explanatory memorandum only saw advantages for fundamental rights,[79] and indeed compared with the present situation, improvements can be expected. Certain AI practices, such as the evaluation of the trustworthiness of a person leading to a social score, are to be prohibited. For AI, which interacts with humans and uses biometric data, certain transparency obligations should apply.[80] For non-high-risk AI, providers are encouraged to develop codes of conduct for which the AIA sets a framework.

The Artificial Intelligence Strategy of the EU of 2018 was mainly concerned with making the EU a world-class hub for AI.[81] While committed to a 'human-centric approach', it also includes rules for product safety and civil liability. The resolution adopted by the European Parliament in May 2022, on 'AI in a digital age',[82] focused on the competitive situation of the EU in the global context and addressed various sectors including AI and the future of democracy. It mentioned many challenges for the protection of fundamental rights, which were to be fully respected in the digital transition and the development of AI, and called for *ex ante* risk self-assessments, data protection impact assessments, and conformity assessments.[83] It was clear that the risk-oriented approach, for example, in the use of face recognition, surveillance, or transparency requirements, did affect significant fundamental rights issues internally and human rights concerns externally. In addition, the participation of AI users and their rights were considered to be key concerns. In reaction to the debate on ChatGPT, the European Parliament requested stricter rules for 'general purpose models' of AI, which are trained on broad data at scale and can be adapted to a wide range of distinct tasks. This includes generative AI such as ChatGPT, which can produce new content.

With regard to fundamental rights, the EU Agency on Fundamental Rights provided an overview in 2020 of the main issues related to AI.[84] There were

78 Proposal for a Regulation of the European Parliament and of the Council laying down harmonised rules on artificial intelligence (Artificial Intelligence Act) of 21 April 2021, COM (2021) 206 final, https://eur-lex.europa.eu/resource.html?uri=cellar:e0649735-a372-11eb-9585-01aa75ed71a1.0001.02/DOC_1&format=PDF; see also the Communication of the European Commission, 'Fostering a European approach to Artificial Intelligence', 21 April 2021, COM(2021) 205 final, https://eur-lex.europa.eu/resource.html?uri=cellar:01ff45fa-a375-11eb-9585-01aa75ed71a1.0001.02/DOC_1&format=PDF.

79 Draft AIA, ibid., 3.5.

80 Ibid., 5.2.4.

81 See the Communication of the Commission on Artificial Intelligence for Europe, 25 April 2018, Com. (2018) 237, https://digital-strategy.ec.europa.eu/en/library/communication-artificial-intelligence-europe.

82 See European Parliament resolution on AI in a Digital Age, 3 May 2022, www.europarl.europa.eu/doceo/document/TA-9-2022-0140_EN.html.

83 Ibid., para. 141.

84 European Union Agency for Fundamental Rights, *Getting the Future Right – Artificial Intelligence and Fundamental Rights* (Luxembourg: Publications Office of the EU, 2020) and its study on facial

suggestions for a more specific inclusion of fundamental rights concerns in the AIA.[85] A total of 115 European civil society organisations, including EDRi and Algorithm Watch, called for a number of amendments to the AIA to strengthen its impact on fundamental rights.[86] Besides a better mechanism to deal with new risks, the authors called for meaningful rights and redress for people impacted by AI systems, such as the right for the explanation of decisions taken, the right to a judicial remedy, and the requirement of accessibility to all AI systems. NGOs such as Algorithm Watch produced studies on how to protect worker rights when AI is used in the workplace or how to provide access to data for public interest research.[87]

After key committees of the European Parliament such as the Civil Liberties Committee had adopted a position on the AIA in which most of the concerns of civil society, such as the prohibition of predictive policing systems, emotion recognition, and real-time biometric identification in public spaces were taken into account, the EU Parliament adopted its position in June 2023.[88] The trilogue (an informal inter-institutional negotiation bringing together representatives of the European Parliament, the Council of the European Union, and the European Commission) ended with an agreement in December 2023 and further negotiations on the adoption of the revised draft by the European Parliament in March 2024. After a very tough negotiation process, the AIA was finally adopted on 21 May 2024.[89] The final text of the AIA was published in the EU Official Journal in July 2024 to enter into force the following month.[90]

The AIA provides for a risk-management system distinguishing between unacceptable risks, high risks, and lower risks in or from AI systems. With regard to high-risk AI systems, which are characterised by posing significant threats to health, safety, or fundamental rights,[91] before being placed on the market, providers should meet several requirements such as testing and mitigating foreseeable risks to health, safety, fundamental rights, the environment, rule of

recognition technology, FRA, 'Facial recognition technology: fundamental rights considerations in the context of law enforcement' (2020), https://fra.europa.eu/sites/default/files/fra_uploads/fra-2019-facial-recognition-technology-focus-paper-1_en.pdf.

[85] See, e.g., D. Onitsiu, 'How a human rights perspective could complement the EU's AI Act', LSE blog, 31 January 2022, https://blogs.lse.ac.uk/europpblog/2022/01/31/how-a-human-rights-perspective-could-complement-the-eus-ai-act/.

[86] See Civil Society statement, 'EU Artificial Intelligence Act for fundamental rights', 30 November 2021, https://algorithmwatch.org/en/eu-artificial-intelligence-act-for-fundamental-rights/.

[87] See AlgorithmWatch, 'Publications', https://algorithmwatch.org/en/publications/.

[88] European Parliament, 'AI Act: a step closer to the first rules on Artificial Intelligence', 11 May 2023, www.europarl.europa.eu/news/en/press-room/20230505IPR84904/ai-act-a-step-closer-to-the-first-rules-on-artificial-intelligence.

[89] For the legislative train schedule, see European Parliament, 'Legislative train schedule. Artificial Intelligence Act', www.europarl.europa.eu/legislative-train/theme-a-europe-fit-for-the-digital-age/file-regulation-on-artificial-intelligence#:~:text=The%20AI%20act%20was%20adopted,20%20days%20after%20its%20publication.

[90] See Regulation 2024/1689, 13 June 2024, OJ L of 12 July 2024.

[91] See ibid., Article 6, para. 3.

law, and democracy with the involvement of independent experts.[92] In Article 5, it defines several prohibited AI practices, such as manipulative techniques impairing the ability of persons to make an informed decision, social scoring and profiling, certain emotion recognition systems, and certain biometric identification systems, although there are numerous exceptions. Still, they create barriers against the violation of fundamental rights.

The AIA has binding force only in Member States of the EU, but there is the expectation that, similar to the GDPR, it will set a global standard for companies, and thus also have extra-territorial impact.[93] In this context, it is worth noting that the GDPR already sets some applicable standards of relevance for AI applications, such as the prohibition of automated decisions related to individuals except if they give their consent (Article 22), thus applying the principle of human intervention (human in the loop) regarding data controllers. The Digital Service Act of 2022, which came into force in 2024, regulates online platforms with provisions relating to liability for the deletion of illicit and fake content and to remedies. In line with the competences of the EU, the objectives of the AIA are not focused on fundamental rights issues, but more broadly on risks related to the use of AI and their impact on economic and commercial as well as consumer concerns. It deals with the use of a trustworthy AI in products and services, and thus also adopts a harmonising and conformity-oriented approach. Accordingly, its first objective is described as ensuring safety and conformity of AI systems with fundamental rights during the whole AI lifecycle. For this purpose, it distinguishes different risk categories. Unacceptable risks, such as social scoring or the use of biometric data in public spaces, are prohibited in general; high risks, such as profiling, predictive analysis, and so on, are subject to risk management via assessments and transparency obligations, such as the right to be informed on the use of AI or the right to human oversight. However, there are also large exceptions for law enforcement and the security sector is fully exempted. In addition, there are safety and liability rules as well as a right to effective remedies. Fewer obligations apply to limited-risk and lower or minimal-risk AI systems.

The AIA became applicable according to a phased approach in which the prohibition of AI of unacceptable risk started to apply six months after the entry into force of the AIA (i.e., February 2025), and the obligations of general purpose AI model providers or the appointment of authorities in competent member states started to apply after twelve months. Certain obligations related to high-risk systems listed in Annex III, such as AI systems in biometrics, will become enforceable only after twenty-four months and others only after thirty-six months. A clarification of

92 See L. Bertuzzi, 'AI Act: MEPs close in on rules for general purpose AI, foundation models', Euroactiv, 24 April 2023, www.euractiv.com/section/artificial-intelligence/news/ai-act-meps-close-in-on-rules-for-general-purpose-ai-foundation-models/.

93 See the report by A. Engler, 'The EU AI Act will have global impact, but a limited Brussels Effect', Brookings, 8 June 2022, www.brookings.edu/research/the-eu-ai-act-will-have-global-impact-but-a-limited-brussels-effect/.

the rules for the implementation will be provided by delegated acts and guidance from the Commission, as well as codes of practice by the EU AI Office, established in May 2024.[94] For example, only by early 2026 will the EU Commission guidelines on the classification of high-risk AI systems have to be issued. Consequently, owing to the complexities of the Act, its obligations will be phased in over several years, which raises the question of whether this might not come too late given the ongoing race for ever more powerful AI systems. However, in view of this fact, the European Commission has set up the AI Pact as a framework to assist companies to prepare for the AIA on a voluntary basis.[95]

2.2.4 *Possible Complementarity between the Two Regulatory Approaches*

While the CoE Convention on Artificial Intelligence, Human Rights, Democracy and the Rule of Law is fully focused on human rights and democracy standards, fundamental rights in the EU AIA only play a limited role, such as safeguarding against the undermining of existing standards as contained in the EU Charter on Fundamental Rights. While references to fundamental rights are included throughout the entire text of the AIA, they are limited to the rights contained in the Charter. This confirms the relevance of the EU Charter on Fundamental Rights for addressing AI. The EU, being represented in the drafting process of the AI convention of the CoE also contributed to its provisions from the EU background. In this way, possible differences were avoided. For example, the Convention provides that EU parties to the Convention shall in their mutual relations apply EU rules.[96]

Accordingly, while there is an alignment to be observed, the CoE Convention in terms of human and fundamental rights covers a much broader ground. For example, it also directly covers democracy, while the AIA is only of indirect relevance, although this has also been one of the important concerns in the EU process. In this regard, the two texts can also be seen as complementary. If, as can be expected, the EU becomes a party to the Convention, this complementarity will be particularly relevant. However, the EU might want to wait until a significant number of its member states have ratified the Convention. However, as the European Court of Justice has clarified in its opinion of 2021, issued on the request of the European Parliament on the accession of the EU to the Istanbul Convention, there is no need for a 'common accord' of all EU Member States before the Council decides to join the Convention.[97]

94 See preambular para. 179 of the AIA.

95 See European Commission, 'Shaping Europe's digital future. AI Pact', https://digital-strategy.ec.europa.eu/en/policies/ai-pact.

96 See Article 27, para. 2 of the CoE Convention.

97 European Court of Justice, Opinion 1/19 of the Court (Grand Chamber) of 6 October 2021.

One major issue highlighted by civil society is the use of invasive applications of AI, such as biometrics for mass surveillance or in the migration context.[98] The AIA sees the remote use of biometrics in publicly accessible places for law enforcement as a red line, but has exceptions for asylum and migration.[99]

One key problem is how to operationalise the right to digital self-determination in view of self-learning algorithms, which are black boxes even to their programmers. Accordingly, full transparency is technically not possible. Benefits and risks cannot always be fully determined in advance. To ensure that the persons affected remain in control has already shown to be difficult in the case of data protection rules. Therefore, the transparency obligation in Article 50 of the AIA contains the right to be informed if one is interacting with AI systems or if content is artificially created. The principle not to predetermine people's choices as in the draft EU Declaration on Digital Rights and Principles can hardly be applied in practice where decisions in penal systems or the migration context are often guided by algorithms proposing decisions based on a large number of cases. However, rules on consent, as in data protection, are missing in this context. This makes the principle that safeguards or remedies should be provided all the more important, but the EU principles lack precision in terms of whom those safeguards should be provided for, let alone how they should look. The CoE, in its preliminary reflections and drafts based on Article 13 of the ECHR on the right to effective remedy or safeguards was more precise,[100] while the EU Declaration does not even refer to Article 47 of its Charter on Fundamental Rights on the same right. However, the AIA contains certain mechanisms, such as a right to an appeal to be provided at the national level, but still needs progress on the issue of enforcement.

Regarding the regulation of AI by the CoE Framework Convention and the AIA, both regulation projects, having been finalised in parallel, did influence each other. For example, the definition of AI chosen for the AIA also appears in Article 2 of the Framework Convention. There was clearly an intention to ensure that where the two processes overlapped the negotiations should achieve complementary results. However, in cases of conflict for EU Member States, the AIA prevails, as the Framework Conventions allows them to give preference to their obligations under the AIA. The open letter calling for a moratorium has contributed to an acceleration of the legal regulations urgently needed to provide legal security and establish oversight institutions.

2.3 GENERAL CONCLUSIONS

The need for the protection of human rights in the regulation of the internet today is beyond doubt. The online dimension of human rights is receiving increasing

[98] See Access Now, 'The EU AIA: how to (truly) protect people on the move', 13 May 2022, https://edri.org/our-work/the-eu-ai-act-how-to-truly-protect-people-on-the-move/.

[99] EU Commission, Proposal for AIA, 5.5.2.

[100] See CAHAI, Feasibility study, paras. 91 and 113, and CAHAI, 'Possible elements of as legal framework on artificial intelligence', paras. 34 and 39 et seq.

attention, as are the emergence of digital human rights that may go beyond existing human and fundamental rights. Such rights may be claimed and recognised at different levels; for example, at the national, European, or universal level. Accordingly, their human rights nature does not depend on recognition at the universal level, although this might be the claim and ambition, in particular when new threats show a global nature. As the example of the right to access to the internet shows, it is widely but not as yet generally recognised as a new human right. In the case of the right to be forgotten, this new right has mainly been established in the EU. The human rights related to the use of AI are presently in the process of concretisation, starting from ethical principles and aiming at concrete obligations at least in some respects in the form of the Framework Convention adopted by the CoE or the AIA of the EU. The focus is on the progressive development and concretisation of general principles and rights, and not on the creation of new digital human rights, which, however, may also be the case in response to new challenges. For example, the AIA now contains the right to know whether one is interacting with an AI system. One could also identify a right to be protected against detrimental uses of AI leading to manipulation or biometric categorisation of natural persons by prohibitions or risk-management systems. In the process of identifying or designing digital human rights in line with a multi-stakeholder approach, civil and public actors may be involved. In the case of most new and emerging threats there is no need for new digital human rights, but existing rights can be extended by interpretation to cover the new challenges. Altogether, the emergence of (new) digital human rights is a highly dynamic part of the progressive development of international law in all its emanations, from soft law to hard law. The regulation of the development and application of AI has accelerated the process of meeting new threats on the basis of extended and new human and fundamental rights in order to close gaps identified in human rights protection in the digital environment.

3

Why and How the State Should Regulate the Internet

Cathleen Powell

3.1 INTRODUCTION

This volume explores the challenges posed to human rights by the digital environment. Grounded as they are in human rights law in general, and Western human rights law in particular, many of the contributions take the individual as their focal point. From this perspective, the broader society of which the individual forms a part is not excluded from the analysis, but it is overshadowed by the individual's interests. This focus can be found expressly in the preamble to the Charter of Fundamental Rights of the European Union (EU), which states that it 'places the individual at the heart of its activities'.[1]

By contrast, society, community, or the common good, is treated as a competing interest; a tension suggested most strongly in the limitations clauses of human rights instruments. These clauses focus on restricting the extent to which social or general interests can be allowed to limit an individual's rights. An example of such a clause is article 52 of the Charter of Fundamental Rights of the EU: 'Subject to the principle of proportionality, limitations may be made only if they are necessary and genuinely meet objectives of general interest recognised by the Union or the need to protect the rights and freedoms of others.'

The argument in this chapter is that the interests of society as a whole can and should play a more central role in the protection of human rights. In addition, I show that the heightened significance of societal interests has a particular implication for the digital environment.

My argument proceeds in three main parts. In Section 3.2, I explore the supposed tension between the individual and society, examining briefly how Western human

I am deeply grateful to the team of disinformation internet experts, lawyers and general thinkers who helped me tackle the intellectual, technical and practical challenges of this area. Thank you, especially, to Chris Newby, Navjothi Raju, Elisa Galgut, William Bird, Jesse Cann, Camaren Peter, Stewart Jones, Khomotso Moshikaro, Nurina Ally, and Tomoe Watashiba. And thank you to my doctoral committee at the University of Toronto (Jutta Brunnée, David Dyzenhaus, and Karen Knop), as I draw on my SJD thesis for much of my discussion of Lon L. Fuller.

[1] Charter of Fundamental Rights of the EU, OJ C 326, 26.10.2012, 391–407, preamble, para. 2.

rights law in particular tends to see these two entities as competing rather than interdependent units. I then set out some alternative approaches to the relationship between the individual and society, in particular, the natural law-based Common Good Constitutionalism and the interactional vision of the legal philosopher, Lon L. Fuller. I suggest that Fuller's view is particularly compelling in the context of internet regulation, as it emphasises the need for (genuine) social interaction as a prerequisite for individual agency.

In Section 3.3, I use Fuller's vision as the basis for a discussion of two seminal requirements of a healthy system of internet regulation: trust and the constraint of power. In Section 3.4, I flesh out how these requirements could best be realised to create an effective system to protect individual rights and society as a whole. Section 3.5 draws together the main points of my chapter.

I need to be clear at the outset that what I am aiming to do in this chapter is to explain why the state must regulate the internet at all; that is, to establish the baseline from which individual rights analyses could proceed. The harm that my suggested approach is aimed at countering is, broadly speaking, the use of (dis)information to manipulate users of the internet. The main examples of such harm are found in disinformation, manipulation of information, and hate speech. I set out an approach that, I submit, justifies the speedy removal of disinformation or even of accurate but misleading information from the internet, the reporting and banning of social media accounts and websites, and the creation of structures that monitor and respond to inaccurate or manipulative postings in both the short and the long term. Such forms of internet regulation are already known in parts of the globe, and some of the mechanisms I propose in my conclusion may appear familiar to the European readers of this volume.

However, it is important to set out some basic design elements of internet regulation and explore their foundation. This is for two reasons. The first is that the mechanisms need to be tailored to their specific social, political, and constitutional contexts. In states with authoritarian governments, weakened governments with less technological capacity, and societies in which the government is not trusted by the subjects of law, the main features of the European or Western system may need to be adjusted. For a successful adjustment, the purpose behind the mechanism needs to be properly understood. Having said this, my second reason for suggesting the design features that I set out in Section 3.4 is that *all* societies, even those with technologically advanced governments and a seemingly healthy rule of law, need ongoing engagement between internet users, internet providers, and government authorities to sustain healthy internet regulation, avoiding both the harm caused by individual users and that caused by the government suppression of information and ideas. Thus, even for societies that already implement the basic design that I am suggesting here, it is important to understand its rationale and its positive relationship with individual human rights.

3.2 DIFFERENT PERSPECTIVES ON THE RELATIONSHIP BETWEEN THE INDIVIDUAL AND SOCIETY

As mentioned earlier, limitation clauses in human rights instruments are often interpreted in a way that sees the individual and society as essentially in conflict. This emerges from the formulation of the clauses themselves – they make it clear that the individual and his or her rights come first – but also from the dominant role that the limitations enquiry tends to play in rights analysis. Consequently, the wording of the limitations clause might even be said to present the general interest as a necessary evil, and it certainly functions as a counterweight to the individual right. With some variation, all limitation clauses require a compelling case to be made that the limitation is necessary (not merely convenient) to achieve an important social good.

Second, the strong focus on the individual is reinforced by the tendency to shift most of the work of rights analysis to the limitations clause. Where rights are not phrased as absolute – where they are subject to limitations – the first step of rights analysis should be to determine the scope of the right in question, to see whether it has been limited or infringed. Only if the answer to the first test is 'yes' should courts and commentators consider whether the limitation/infringement is legally justifiable. However, as Michael Foran has noted, modern doctrine 'has a tendency to avoid difficult questions relating to the scope of rights, preferring instead to view virtually any interference with a claimed interest as an infringement that stands in need of legal justification'.[2] As the legal justification can only be found through the limitations clause, the court is constantly being required to weigh up the individual interest against the public interest. Such an approach assumes ongoing tension between the individual and society. It is important to note that the public interest is, in these cases, generally identified with the interests of the majority, the group purportedly represented by the legislature.[3] If this is how the public interest is to be understood, courts are repeatedly placed in the position of defending one person against a larger group. In Michael Foran's words: 'When the public is set up conceptually in tension with the individual, rights become the last great defence of the individual against an encroaching state demanding their sacrifice for the benefit of the rest of society'.[4]

How might such a stark dichotomy between individual and society be countered using legal theory? I examine two possible approaches briefly here. The first is based on natural law and the second on the philosophy of Lon L. Fuller.[5]

2 M. Foran, 'Rights, common good, and the separation of powers' (2023) 86 *The Modern Law Review* 3, 599–628, at 605, citing N. E. Simmonds, 'Constitutional rights, civility and artifice' (2019) 78 *The Cambridge Law Journal* 1, 175–99, at 175; J. Tasioulas, 'Saving human rights from human rights law' (2021) 52 *Vanderbilt Law Review* 5, 1167–1207.

3 Foran, 'Rights, common good, and the separation of powers', p. 605.

4 Ibid., p. 606.

5 L. L. Fuller, *The Morality of Law: Revised Edition* (New Haven: Yale University Press, 1969). See also J. Klabbers, 'Constitutionalism and the making of international law: Fuller's procedural natural law' (2008) 5 *No Foundations: An Interdisciplinary Journal of Law and Justice*, 84–112; D. Sturm, 'Lon

Common Good Constitutionalism sees the common good as 'the set of conditions necessary for each and every member of the community to flourish'.[6] The common good is therefore not limited to the interests of the majority, but refers to the good of all individuals within the community. From this perspective, there is no tension between the individual and the broader society, or the minority and the majority:

> It is a central tenet of the common good that there is no conflict between the good of the majority and the good of the minority, once both are properly understood. This is because the good of an individual cannot be separate from the good of the community: my life is better when my friends' lives are better. My membership within a civic community grounds the bonds of a civic friendship that connects all members of a polity. It is in our shared common interest that all members of our community be capable of leading flourishing lives and that they be treated with dignity and respect. To diminish the flourishing of others, to disrespect their dignity, in the name of the common good, is to fundamentally misunderstand what makes the common good common. It also fundamentally misunderstands what it means to pursue a good life, of which membership within a flourishing political community of equals is essential.[7]

A similar approach to the virtue and necessity of community is found in the African concept of *Ubuntu*, which, in its broadest meaning, recognises that humanity is attained through community.[8] This pre-colonial concept may lie at the root of the emphasis on peoples and community in African human rights instruments.[9] The African (Banjul) Charter expressly recognises the duties of individuals, and states these duties are owed to 'family and society, the State and other legally recognised communities and the international community'.[10] Furthermore, the Banjul Charter expressly mandates that '[t]he rights and freedoms of each individual shall be exercised with due regard to the rights of others, collective security, morality and common interest'.[11] Finally, this Charter is the only human rights instrument that recognises the rights of peoples and not just of individuals, thereby including the group within its focus.[12]

Common Good Constitutionalism makes particular demands of human rights analysis, in that the first stage of the analysis – determining the scope of the

Fuller's multidimensional natural law theory' (1965–6) 18 *Stanford Law Review* 3, 612–39. Fuller's procedural natural law is explored more fully later in this chapter.

6 Foran, 'Rights, common good, and the separation of powers', p. 628.

7 Ibid., p. 606. The citation within the text refers to John Finnis: J. Finnis, *Natural Law and Natural Rights* (Oxford: Oxford University Press, 1980), chapter 6.

8 T. W. Bennett, A. Munro, and P. J. Jacobs, *Ubuntu: An African Jurisprudence* (Cape Town: Juta, 2018), chapter 3.

9 OAU, African Charter on Human and Peoples' Rights ('Banjul Charter'), 27 June 1981, CAB/LEG/67/3 rev. 5, 21·ILM 58 (1982).

10 Ibid.

11 Ibid., Art. 27(2).

12 Ibid., Arts 19–24.

right – has to be taken seriously. The scope of the right must further be determined with reference to the common good. In this way, our very understanding of the right is informed by, and promotes, the values that allow members of the community to flourish.[13] The limitations analysis, with its conflict between the individual and society, will come into play less often.[14]

Since its introduction in 2020,[15] Common Good Constitutionalism has been strongly criticised as dangerous and authoritarian.[16] This chapter shows that a benign application of Common Good Constitutionalism is possible by drawing on Lon L. Fuller's legal philosophy to suggest both what the underlying values of the common good might be and to show that the understanding of that common good can, and should, be developed by the community to whose benefit it must be used, rather than by a disconnected authority.

Common Good Constitutionalism sits uneasily with liberalism to the extent that the latter excludes from a legal analysis questions 'relating to the flourishing of individuals or of what constitutes a good life',[17] adopting instead the neutrality principle.[18] Consequently, the nature of the good 'is either whatever a given individual says it is for them, or it is whatever a democratic institution determines it to be'.[19] Indeed, some liberal theorists hold that governments themselves must be neutral on 'what might be called questions of the good life … that political decisions must be, so far as is possible, independent of any particular conception of the good life or of what gives value to life'.[20] It would thus seem that the role we are prepared to afford to society, or public interest, in human rights analysis depends on whether we are prepared to accept the moral content that natural law locates within law itself.

13 Foran, 'Rights, common good, and the separation of powers', p. 605.

14 Ibid., p. 625.

15 Adrian Vermeule, who introduced the term to current legal discourse, expressly draws on the classical legal tradition when he uses the concept. See A. Vermeule, *Common Good Constitutionalism: Recovering the Classical Legal Tradition* (Cambridge: Polity Press, 2022); C. Casey and A. Vermeule, 'Myths of common good constitutionalism' (2022) 45 *Harvard Journal of Law and Public Policy* 1, 103–46.

16 See, e.g., G. Epps, 'Common-good constitutionalism: an idea as dangerous as they come', 3 April 2020, *The Atlantic*, www.theatlantic.com/ideas/archive/2020/04/common-good-constitutionalism-dangerous-idea/609385/; D. Dyzenhaus, 'Schmitten in the US', 4 April 2020, Verfassungsblog, https://verfassungsblog.de/schmitten-in-the-usa; M. D. Kelly, 'Challenging common good constitutionalism' (2024) 15 *Jurisprudence* 1, 418–40; L. C. McClain and J. E. Fleming, 'Toward a liberal common good constitutionalism for polarized times' (2023) 46 *Harvard Journal of Law and Public Policy*, 1123–48.

17 Ibid., pp. 1–2.

18 R. Dworkin, 'Liberalism', in S. Hampshire (ed.), *Public and Private Morality* (Cambridge: Cambridge University Press, 1978), pp. 113–43.

19 Foran, 'Rights, common good, and the separation of powers', p. 600.

20 Dworkin, 'Liberalism', p. 127. See also P. Neal, 'Liberalism & neutrality' (1985) 17 *Polity* 4, 664–84; R. J. Arneson, 'Liberal neutrality on the good: an autopsy' in S. Wall and G. Klosko (eds.), *Perfectionism and Neutrality: Essays in Liberal Theory* (Lanham, MD: Rowman & Littlefield Publishers, 2003), pp. 191–208.

Lon L. Fuller's approach could possibly be seen as a compromise between the two apparently opposing philosophies of liberalism and natural law. Fuller described his own philosophy as 'procedural natural law'.[21] The qualifier 'procedural' is important. Fuller remains neutral on (most) ethical issues within the content of law,[22] which would seem to exclude any discussion of the common good from legal enquiry. For Fuller, most substantive (what he would call 'external') moral questions fell outside the realm of law. Nonetheless, his vision of law is particularly useful for our analysis because of the minimum moral content, which he suggested is internal to law itself.[23] Second, the notions of the rule of law and equality before the law underpin the human rights documents consulted for this study.[24] If we adopt Fuller's understanding of the rule of law, then the human rights treaties themselves recognise a minimum level of common good that society needs to promote before it can meaningfully protect human rights.

What do we mean by the rule of law? Most legal philosophers agree on the basic requirements of the rule of law,[25] what Jeremy Waldron calls the 'laundry lists'.[26] These boil down to two basic ideas: first, that law must have a form that allows its subjects to understand what it demands of them and to ensure that their behaviour complies with it; second, that the law as laid down must be the law that is applied to them.[27] To fulfil the first requirement, law must be general, publicised,

[21] Fuller, *The Morality of Law*, pp. 96–7. See also Klabbers, 'Constitutionalism and the making of international law'; Sturm, 'Lon Fuller's multidimensional natural law theory'.

[22] K. Rundle 'The impossibility of an exterminatory legality: law and the Holocaust' (2009) 59 *University of Toronto Law Journal* 1, 65–125, citing the last chapter of the original edition of Fuller' s *Morality of Law* (L. L. Fuller, *The Morality of Law* (New Haven, Yale University Press, 1964)).

[23] Ibid., p. 69.

[24] The Charter of Fundamental Rights of the EU (OJ C 326, 26.10.2012, 391–407) expressly acknowledges the rule of law in its Preamble. A range of other human rights instruments require equality before the law and protection of the law in various formulations. See OAU, African Charter on Human and Peoples' Rights ("Banjul Charter"), 27 June 1981, CAB/LEG/67/3 rev. 5, 21 ILM 58 (1982), Art. 3; UN General Assembly, Universal Declaration of Human Rights, 10 December 1948, 217 A (III), in its Preamble, the International Convention on the Elimination of All Forms of Racial Discrimination, 21 December 1965, 660 UNTS 195, at 214, require equality before the law and the protection of the law; International Covenant on Civil and Political Rights, 16 December 1966, 999 UNTS 171, Arts 14 and 26; Convention on the Elimination of All Forms of Discrimination Against Women, 18 December 1979, 1249 UNTS 1249, Art. 15.

[25] C. Murphy, 'Lon Fuller and the moral value of the rule of law' (2005) 24 *Law and Philosophy* 3, 239–62, at 240.

[26] J. Waldron, 'Is the rule of law an essentially contested concept (in Florida)?' (2002) 21 *Law and Philosophy* 2, 137–64, at 154. The 'laundry list' is generally that there be (a) (general) rules, which are (b) publicised, (c) understandable, (d) not retroactive, and (e) internally consistent (that is, not contradictory). The rules must also be (f) relatively consistent over time; that is, they may not change so frequently that the legal subjects can no longer orient their conduct in compliance with the rules. In addition, (g) compliance must not be physically impossible; that is, the law cannot demand that legal subjects act beyond their powers. Finally, the (h) administration of law must reflect the rules as announced.

[27] Fuller, *The Morality of Law*, chapter 2.

understandable, consistent, and not impossible to comply with. To fulfil the second, it must be prospective, reasonably stable, and faithfully enforced.

Fuller's understanding of the concept of the rule of law differs from that of other scholars to the extent that he saw it as giving effect to a deeper, moral function, which was to protect and promote human agency:

> I have repeatedly observed that legal morality can be said to be neutral over a wide range of ethical issues. It cannot be neutral in its view of man himself. To embark on the enterprise of subjecting human conduct to the governance of rules involves of necessity a commitment to the view that man is, or can become, a responsible agent, capable of understanding and following rules, and answerable for his defaults. Every departure from the principles of law's inner morality is an affront to man's dignity as a responsible agent.[28]

Like liberalism, the agency-centred vision of the rule of law appears to take the individual as the quintessential and foundational element of law. Furthermore, Fuller's concept of agency maps closely onto the right to dignity and its associated notions of autonomy and freedom. However, law could protect agency in Fuller's conception only by coming into being and being sustained through community. Fuller used the term 'interaction' to describe the reciprocal process that shapes the content of the law, and this interaction required the engagement of the subjects of law with one another.[29] The interactional process, and not the fiat of government, creates and sustains law, because it is built on the shared understandings of the individuals who interact with one another. As Brunnée and Toope explain, the core moral quality of law, its capacity to allow its subjects to 'reason with law and make choices about their own lives',[30] generates fidelity 'to the rule of law itself and not merely to specific rules'.[31] As a result, while the ultimate purpose of law is to protect and build on human agency, its vehicle for doing so is a socially cohesive community through which the applicable norms can be created and applied.

Douglas Sturm made a similar point about Fuller's conception of freedom:

> It should be made clear that Fuller's understanding of freedom is not individualistic in character. More than once, Fuller has indicated his strong rejection of that theory of natural law whose substance consists in the proclamation of the 'natural, inalienable and sacred rights of man' precisely because of its individualistic bent. To posit the value or goal or goodness of freedom in Fuller's usage of that term is not to desire that each man attain a state of total and absolute independence. On

[28] Rundle, 'The impossibility of an exterminatory legality', citing the last chapter of the original edition of Fuller's *Morality of Law*.

[29] See Postema's discussion of the different aspects of interaction in G. Postema, 'Implicit law', in W. J. Witteveen and W. van der Burg (eds.), *Rediscovering Fuller: Essays on Implicit Law and Institutional Design* (Amsterdam: Amsterdam University Press, 1999), pp. 253–75, at 255.

[30] J. Brunée and S. Toope, *Legitimacy and Legality in International Law* (Cambridge: Cambridge University Press, 2010), pp. 29–30.

[31] Ibid., p. 53.

> the contrary, the choices one can make, the purposes one can pursue, without collaborative social effort and without appropriate forms of human intercourse are trivial, if any such totally independent choices are in fact possible. More definitively, the natural law of 'keeping alive the creative, choosing, and purposive side of man's nature' is *intrinsically* societal...[32]

Because community is a prerequisite for and guarantor of individual agency, it is inaccurate and misleading to treat the individual and the community as adversaries. To support human rights through regulating the internet, we should therefore encourage rules that strengthen the community and, in particular, ensure genuine engagement and communication.[33]

If human agency requires community and communication, then a healthy system to regulate the internet will promote trust between internet users and accurate information. This will require the active involvement of the state but, as I argue here, the state will need both the support and the constraint that is provided by non-state actors engaging with it. I explore each of these factors in more detail in the following sections.

3.3 SEMINAL FEATURES OF GOOD INTERNET REGULATION

3.3.1 *Trust*

For Fuller, communication had a pivotal moral function because he saw 'maintaining communication with our fellows' as the overriding aim of human aspiration.[34] Its further moral value lay in its role in creating law. In Fuller's theory, 'law is constructed through rhetorical activity producing increasingly influential mutual expectations or shared understandings of actors'.[35] Through interaction and rhetorical activity,[36] actors are also able to 'generate shared knowledge and shared understandings that become the background for subsequent interactions'.[37]

Communication must clearly be more than cheap talk to give rise to genuine interaction,[38] so we need to ask what *kind* of communication creates shared understandings and legal norms. Drawing on Habermas's notion of communicative

32 Sturm, 'Lon Fuller's multidimensional natural law theory', p. 616.

33 J. C. Barker, 'The politics of international law-making: constructing security in response to global terrorism' (2007) 3 *Journal of International Law and International Relations* 1, 5–24, at 24. For the form that this communication should take, see Brunée and Toope, *Legitimacy and Legality in International Law*, p. 31, and I. Johnstone, 'Legislation and adjudication in the Security Council: bringing down the deliberative deficit' (2008) 102 *American Journal of International Law* 2, 275–308, at 279.

34 Fuller, *The Morality of Law*, p. 185.

35 J. Brunée and S. Toope, 'International law and constructivism: elements of an interactional theory of international law' (2000) 39 *Columbia Journal of Transnational Law* 1, 19–74, at 65.

36 Brunée and Toope, *Legitimacy and Legality in International Law*, p. 31.

37 Ibid., p. 13.

38 Barker, 'The politics of international law-making', p. 27.

action, Cornelieu Bjola suggests that communication moves beyond 'instrumental bargaining on the basis of fixed preferences' to a more reasoned process, including 'a mode of interaction between actors based on the logic of arguing; that is, of convincing each other to change their causal or principled beliefs in order to reach a reasoned consensus'.[39] Similarly, Ian Johnstone points out that '[d]eliberation is not a communicative free-for-all, in which any argument is as good as any other; the felt need to offer reasons others can accept in principle sets the parameters of discourse'. Seen in this way, communication must be based on reason and principle.

Compare this standard with the kind of exchanges that result on the internet when users create and share disinformation or manipulate the processes of internet communication, either to amplify or suppress information or ideas, or to eviscerate the expertise and authority of qualified actors. The internet is particularly vulnerable to this form of abuse owing to the difficulty of verifying the identity of the persons behind the posts, or when a post is being artificially enhanced or suppressed by the manipulation of algorithms or the use of robots. Such abuse makes principled or reasoned discussion impossible, and every argument is indeed as good as the next because there is no way for the readers to ascertain which information or actors they can rely on. As a result, the posts that are more likely to be believed are those that align with the views that the reader already holds; a situation which reinforces existing divisions between groups in society rather than stimulating genuine interaction across boundaries of difference. This means that shared understandings cannot arise across a community as a whole. People misled by disinformation and manipulation will not have engaged in the process whereby shared understandings and norms are formed, they will not be able to make informed decisions themselves, and they will not trust the authorities who are attempting to make and implement informed decisions. Those governed by the law will not feel fidelity to it. As a result, disinformation and manipulation threaten the rule of law and also weaken government programmes set up to protect public health or welfare, or any other common good. It is therefore not surprising that the EU describes online disinformation practices as 'public harms', specifically harms to the integrity of electoral processes, and as 'threats to our way of life',[40] which undermine trust and confidence in democratic politics. One of the best examples was the disinformation around COVID-19, as reported by the EU,[41] and by monitoring bodies all over the globe.[42]

[39] C. Bjola, 'Legitimating the use of force in international politics: a communicative action perspective' (2005) 11 *European Journal of International Relations* 2, 266–303, cited by Barker, 'The politics of international law-making', p. 24.

[40] European Commission, 'Shaping Europe's digital future. The 2022 Code of Practice on disinformation', https://digital-strategy.ec.europa.eu/en/policies/code-practice-disinformation.

[41] EU, 'Fighting disinformation', https://commission.europa.eu/strategy-and-policy/coronavirus-response/fighting-disinformation_en.

[42] C. Cortés and L. F. Isaza, 'The new normal? Disinformation and content control on social media during Covid-19' (2021), CELE, Palermo University, www.palermo.edu/Archivos_content/2021/cele/papers/Disinformation-and-Content-Control.pdf.

The constitutive role of communication in the creation and maintenance of the legal and social order renders the integrity of internet communication particularly important. Expressed in terms of a rights analysis, the heightened social importance of reliable communication would suggest either that the scope of the individual's freedom of expression should be more narrowly defined, or that, if that freedom is found to have been limited by the regulation of the internet, society's interests should weigh more heavily in a proportionality analysis. In this regard, we can distinguish between the people who create or knowingly distribute false or misleading information and the people who unwittingly or negligently encourage or disseminate it. In the case of the former group, I would argue that the scope of freedom of expression does not extend to the right to knowingly misrepresent information or mislead. In the case of the latter group, the scope of freedom of expression can more plausibly be argued to include this group's behaviour; that is, to include the right to unknowingly disseminate false or misleading information. However, in this case, at the point where freedom of expression has been found to have been limited, society's interest in accurate and good faith communication should play a stronger role in justifying the limitation of that right.

The internet needs to be regulated because a lack of regulation leads to distrust and a breakdown of common values. But simply putting a regulator in charge of the internet with no way of ensuring that the regulator itself is trustworthy compounds the problem. In the area of COVID-19, for example, there were many examples of state actors spreading disinformation, either by denying the existence or spread of the disease or by suggesting cures with no medical efficacy.[43] Moreover, we have seen how control and censorship of the media (social and registered journalism) has been used to justify government abuses and war.[44] Ironically, the power to regulate cannot itself be left unregulated. It needs to be structured in an interactive manner, which ensures that the regulator is in dialogue with responsible stakeholders.

3.3.2 *(The Constraint of) Power*

States have a monopoly on legitimate violence within their territories, control over the executive arm of government, including its security apparatus, and the ability to pass new legislation. If states abuse this power, they pose a threat to democratic values and the common good. On the other hand, and despite the power they may enjoy over their subjects, states are simultaneously often weaker than powerful social media corporations, such as Meta and X. From both perspectives, states need

[43] UNHRC, 'Report of the Special Rapporteur on the Promotion and Protection of the Right to Freedom of Opinion and Expression – Disinformation and freedom of opinion and expression', 13 April 2021, UN Doc. A/HRC/47/25.

[44] M. Susi et al., *Governing Information Flows During War: A Comparative Study of Content Governance and Media Policy Responses After Russia's Attack on Ukraine* (Hamburg: Verlag Hans-Bredow-Institut, 2022).

to act in concert with non-state actors and broader society to be effective and compliant with the rule of law.

Fuller's theory explains why the state is both too weak and too strong to act alone. The state needs the buy-in of its subjects because law is formed out of the engagement of those subjects with each other and the government. Fuller claims that, in practice, interaction was part of all lawmaking, 'even … those [forms] apparently dominated by enacted law and formal law-making and law-applying institutions'.[45] This was both because there is a horizontal element in apparently vertical law-making procedures, such as adjudication or even the drafting of legislation,[46] and because the subjects of law are engaged in a vertical process of interaction with the lawgiver.[47] Non-state actors thus help the state to create the law.

Particularly in the context of internet regulation, there is a practical reason why the state needs the help of broader society. The state often cannot *enforce* the law; that is, it cannot effectively regulate the internet without the engagement of non-state actors. Particularly where the government is not fully trusted by its citizenry, and where that government does not have the expertise to quickly identify disinformation, manipulation of the internet, or hate speech, non-state actors need to assist and collaborate with the government if it is to respond effectively to such misuse. Collaboration of this kind actually empowers the state meaningfully to counter the dangers posed by the internet.

On the other hand, the engagement of non-state actors also prevents the imbalance of power between state and subject from threatening the rule of law. Interaction is necessarily a reciprocal process, even when there is a power imbalance between the parties to the interaction. As Cheng explains:

> To Fuller, no power relation is completely devoid of any measure of interaction between the power-holder and the subject of his power, especially over the course of time. This inevitable degree of reciprocity, in turn, imposes a constraint on the exercise of power by the power-holder, while allowing for the possibility of resistance and negotiation by those subject to the power.[48]

The state bears the primary moral duty of protecting the subjects of law against threats to their lives, health, and other resources.[49] It has the authority to exercise coercion, through regulation,[50] or even criminalisation,[51] when this proves necessary

45 Postema, 'Implicit law', p. 259.

46 D. E. Wueste, 'Fuller's Processual philosophy of law' (1986) 71 *Cornell Law Review* 6, 1205–30.

47 See Postema's discussion of the different aspects of interaction in Postema, 'Implicit law', pp. 259–65.

48 H. H. L. Cheng, 'Beyond forms, functions and limits: the interactionism of Lon L. Fuller and its implications for alternative dispute resolution' (2013) 26 *The Canadian Journal of Law and Jurisprudence* 2, 257–92, at 268.

49 R. A. Duff and S. E. Marshall, '"Abstract endangerment", two harm principles, and two routes to criminalisation' (2015) 3 *Bergen Journal of Criminal Law and Criminal Justice* 2, 131–61, at 148.

50 Ibid., p. 133, cites J. S. Mill, *On Liberty* (1859) in chapter 1, para. 9.

51 J. Feinberg, *Harm to Others* (New York: Oxford University Press, 1984), p. 26.

to fulfil its duty. But both criminalisation and regulation can be manipulated by the state to favour a particular party, such as the government in power, and silence the input of the other actors in the internet community. In the context of the internet, a reciprocal process of interaction needs to be built into the very design of the regulatory process to prevent the coercive power enjoyed by the state from threatening the rule of law.

3.4 A LAWFUL PROCESS OF REGULATION

In this concluding section, I suggest some basic design elements of a healthy system of internet regulation, one that permits and indeed requires of the state that it protect society against disinformation, manipulation, and hate speech, and yet constrains the power of the state in order to protect individual agency and the rule of law.

The outline of my suggested regulatory system must generally be broad, as the details of the particular mechanisms employed for regulation depend on a number of extraneous factors. These include whether and how states control the activities of transnational corporations within their own jurisdictions, the technological capacity the state and civil society can provide, and the traditional modes of civic engagement within any particular society. Nonetheless, I suggest there are common features that all well-regulated internet communities will share.

As set out in Section 3.3, we are aiming to ensure a community in which participants have a minimal level of trust in each other and the government, and in which power – both state and private – is sufficiently constrained. As argued in Section 3.2, the main tool to achieve these ends is ongoing engagement and responsiveness between the parties. This process, which we would call interaction under a Fullerian approach to the rule of law, ensures that the necessary shared understandings can arise; understandings that form the foundation of the legal system adopted by the participants. Particularly in the case of the internet, ongoing engagement will also help to monitor compliance with the norms that emerge from this foundation.

Ongoing and effective interaction is best achieved by a multi-tiered design. At the first level of such a framework, the internet and online service providers regulate themselves in dialogue with their users. At the second level, non-state actors monitor the use of the internet, engaging with both the service providers and the state. At the third level, the state plays an active role in internet regulation, co-ordinating between the first two tiers of non-state actors.

3.4.1 *Self-Regulation*

At the first level, service providers self-regulate. This term, 'self-regulation', is a slight misnomer, as I suggest that it be mandated by the state itself, and that penalties be attached to egregious failures by service providers to prevent serious harm through their users' traffic on the internet. However, the horizontal and internal nature of the regulation is important; the platform must itself publish and enforce a code of conduct based on international best practices, and encourage debate among users of its platform on what the code of conduct should look like.

Singapore provides an example of self-regulation that is promoted by the statutory authority,[52] the Infocomm Media Development Authority.[53] This government board encourages content providers to develop industry codes of practice in order to promote self-regulation and codes that complement existing internet content regulations.[54] The dialogue between users of the platform and the platform, and among the users themselves, provides the first step in developing shared understandings that recognise the harm that can be caused by internet traffic and build consensus on how to avoid the harm.

The role that the users of the internet can play is illustrated by the process followed in South Korea whenever the Korean Communications Standard Commission (KCSC) instructs an internet provider to remove content from its platform.[55] Upon receiving a request for deletion or rebuttal of the information, the provider of information and communications services must delete the information or take a temporary or any other necessary measure.[56] This content can be hidden, but not deleted, for thirty days, to allow either the platform or the user to challenge the decision. An example of such an engagement arose in 2015, when the entire platform of an adult cartoon service was blocked because part of its content had been considered obscene. The platform operator challenged this ruling on the basis that the site used an age authentication system and therefore complied with the law. The decision to block the site was met with public outcry, and subsequently the commission removed the blocking order.[57]

3.4.2 *Independent Regulatory Bodies*

The second tier of regulation needs to be provided by independent regulatory bodies. These bodies need to be structurally independent of the government and steered

[52] Infocomm Media Development Authority, 'Internet regulatory framework', www.imda.gov.sg/regulations-and-licensing-listing/content-standards-and-classification/standards-and-classification/internet.

[53] Infocomm Media Development Authority, 'Who we are', www.imda.gov.sg/About-IMDA/Who-We-Are.

[54] Infocomm Media Development Authority, 'Internet regulatory framework'.

[55] The operation of the KCSC is prescribed in chapter 5 of the Act on the Establishment and Operation of Korea Communications Commission (KCCA), last amended by Act No. 11711, 23 March 2013, www.law.go.kr/LSW/lsInfoP.do?lsiSeq=137296#0000.

[56] Article 44-2(2) of Act on Promotion of Information and Communications Network Utilization and Information Protection, https://elaw.klri.re.kr/eng_service/lawDownload.do?hseq=38422&type=PDF.

[57] Freedom House, 'South Korea: freedom on the Net 2021 country report', https://freedomhouse.org/country/south-korea/freedom-net/2021, citing Sung-won Yoon, 'Watchdog hit for excessive digital censorship', 30 March 2015, *Korean Times*, www.koreatimes.co.kr/www/news/tech/2015/04/133_176155.html.

by civil society. At the same time, these independent bodies must be designed and set up in such a way as to ensure that they genuinely do represent the public interest and operate in a transparent and accessible manner.

Recognition is growing that the involvement of civil society is crucial for healthy internet regulation. Civil society can fulfil two roles: developing the rules and policies by which the internet should be governed, and monitoring compliance with the normative system. A good example of the former can be found in the creation of the African Declaration on Internet Rights and Freedoms.[58] This declaration is a pan-African initiative aimed at 'promoting human rights standards and principles of openness in internet policy formulation and implementation' across the African continent.[59] The idea for the declaration emerged from the African Internet Governance Forum in Nairobi, Kenya, in 2013,[60] at which participants came from government, the private sector, civil society, and regional and international organisations.[61]

International bodies such as UNICEF can play a role in the constitution and functioning of internet regulation at the domestic level, and some of the domestic bodies fulfilling this function can be self-constituting, particularly those offering essential technical expertise.[62] However, non-state bodies require the backing of the government and need to remain in communication with it, for reasons explored further here.

I submit that these bodies need to be independent of the state because the government should not be identifying trends or disinformation itself, particularly in states with weak democracies. If an autocratic government exercises unilateral control over the internet, the rule of law is broken. Particularly egregious examples of this form of abuse have been seen when dictatorial governments in Africa have shut down the internet completely during protests or elections.[63] By contrast, if external bodies are doing the job of regulation, they can function as an interlocutor

58 African Declaration on Internet Rights and Freedoms, 'About the initiative', https://africaninternetrights.org/en/about.

59 Association for Progressive Communications, 'African Declaration on Internet Rights and Freedoms Coalition: promotion of freedom of expression a priority for Southern Africa', www.apc.org/en/news/african-declaration-internet-rights-and-freedoms-coalition-promotion-freedom-expression.

60 African Declaration on Internet Rights and Freedoms, 'About the initiative'.

61 In all, 195 participants attended from twenty-nine countries. See the African Internet Governance Forum – AfIGF 2013, 23 September 2013, 'Final draft report', www.intgovforum.org/en/filedepot_download/7508/1620.

62 An effective South African example of such a body is the Centre for Analytics and Behavioural Change. See The Centre for Analytics & Behavioural Change, https://cabc.org.za/. Real411, 'Report digital disinformation', www.real411.org/.

63 I. Gagliardone and A. Brhane, 'Ethiopia digital rights landscape report – digital rights in closing civic space: lessons from ten African countries' (2021), https://opendocs.ids.ac.uk/opendocs/bitstream/handle/20.500.12413/15964/Ethiopia_Report.pdf.; C. H. Powell and T. Schonwetter, 'Africa, the Internet and human rights', in M. Susi (ed.), *Human Rights, the Digital Society and Law: A Research Companion* (New York: Routledge Publishing, 2019), pp. 316–34.

with whom the government has to interact, and to whom it must justify its exercise of power. In this way, they help to ensure the necessary checks and balances in internet regulation.

Independence can be achieved only by the correct design of the regulatory body and of its connection with the state. First of all, the power to regulate must be given to an external body; that is, a body that is structurally separate from the state. But, second, the regulatory authority may not be subject to political interference. Singapore provides an example of a body without structural independence. Under the Protection from Online Falsehoods and Manipulation Act of Singapore, government ministers can order the publication of corrections and the retraction of content they assess to be false or against public interest.[64] The regulatory body is thus embedded within government itself. However, South Korea provides an example of an apparently independent regulatory body that is still subject to strong political interference. The KCSC is established through legislation and identifies itself as a private organisation; however, all nine members of the Commission are appointed by the president.[65] Consequently, a nominally independent 'private' organisation is factually 'under the direct control of the President'.[66]

In addition to politicised appointments, the KCSC has been criticised for its lack of transparency.[67] The norms that it applies when it suppresses internet communications are opaque, and it enjoys wide discretion in its decisions.[68] A similar criticism is levelled at the new power enjoyed by the Film and Publications Board in South Africa,[69] a board whose core members are also appointed directly by the relevant minister.[70]

The problematic role of the government in appointing incumbents to these regulatory bodies highlights another important design element of healthy internet regulation, namely, a transparent process for the selection of office holders. Such a selection process addresses two problems at once. First, it reduces the chance that the regulatory body will be beholden to the government and thus lack independence. But second, it also helps to ensure that such bodies do, in fact, represent the public interest. These independent bodies do not have a democratic mandate, which

64 Tech Against Terrorism, 'The Online Regulation series | Singapore – tech against terrorism', 5 October 2020, www.techagainstterrorism.org/2020/10/05/the-online-regulation-series-singapore/.

65 J. Lee, 'A private organization directly under the president? Structural contradiction of the Korea Communications Commission', www.mediatoday.co.kr/news/articleView.html?idxno=97350.

66 Ibid.

67 Freedom House, 'South Korea: freedom on the Net 2021 country report', https://freedomhouse.org/country/south-korea/freedom-net/2021, citing Sung-won Yoon, 'Watchdog hit for excessive digital censorship', 30 March 2015, *Korean Times*, www.koreatimes.co.kr/www/news/tech/2015/04/133_176155.html.

68 Ibid.

69 Bowmans, 'South Africa: Films and Publications Amendment Act comes into operation', https://bowmanslaw.com/insights/technology-media-and-telecommunications/south-africa-films-and-publications-amendment-act-comes-into-operation/.

70 South African Government 'Films and Publications Amendment Act, Act No. 11 of 2019', section 4.

means that some kind of public process is needed to ensure responsiveness and legitimacy for the authority that they exercise, particularly for those bodies that are formulating policy. The selection process should ideally consist of public interviews conducted by mixed panels representing both the legislature and experts in the field of internet regulation.[71] Such a process ensures the interaction from which shared understandings can be built by promoting trust in the incumbents of the regulatory bodies.

Legislation or regulation is then needed to confer on this body the power that resides, by default, in the state itself: the power to regulate the internet. These powers serve two functions. They are, on the one hand, a check on inadequate self-regulation by service providers, while on the other hand, they serve as both a check on and support for the government in its duty to prevent harm through internet usage. Particularly where the government faces challenges of technical capacity, there needs to be coordination between rapid information task teams, which are properly constituted, to respond effectively to immediate crises and provide watchdog analysis of future or emerging threats. In relation to disinformation, this needs to be a real-time response, so that inaccurate and damaging information can be removed immediately if needed.

However, immediate responses are not always necessary. Monitoring and response bodies can also be assigned to different target areas that need to be addressed, such as terrorism, incitement, hate speech, and xenophobia. Such bodies may react in a more long-term manner and even coordinate counter-campaigns against harmful internet initiatives.

Although these bodies need to be independent of the government, they need to be supported by the government to be effective, a point discussed further in the next section. They need to operate under clear rules and procedures, and remain responsive to the engagement of the public as well as the government. As seen in the example of the KCSC, public response to the rulings of this independent authority can help it to refine and clarify the norms that it is meant to be applying.

3.4.3 *The Role of the State*

The state is needed partly because deleting and retracting does not eliminate the activity behind the information shared online, such as terrorism, incitement, hate speech, and xenophobia. Engaging with this reality is beyond the capacity of the task team; this is when the involvement of the state is warranted. We have many recent examples of occasions when the state should have acted, but did not. The online trends and chatter leading up to the 6 January riots in the US in 2021 made the riots

[71] While these bodies themselves may be susceptible to political influence, the open nature of their interviews does at least provide some level of a check in the form of public responses to the interview process.

foreseeable. Similarly, the Centre for Analytics and Behavioural Change picked up the indicators of the approaching riots before they began in South Africa in June 2021.[72] The presence of the state, through the police, was needed, whether or not the police themselves were gathering the primary information.

The role of the state requires clear delineation because its involvement in internet governance must be a justifiable intervention addressing credible and serious threats to the peace and security of citizens and the state as a whole. It would intervene in two main contexts. The first is proactive suppression of a serious forthcoming danger, such as xenophobic attacks, riots, and insurrection. These threats call for a multi-departmental response that only the state has the capacity to execute. In these cases, the state's involvement should work based on the analysis, predictions, and recommendations made by independent task teams in the event that a pre-emptive response is required to maintain societal peace and security.

The second context in which the state has a role to play is in the prosecution of serious crimes committed online. These include hate speech in some jurisdictions and may also encompass the deliberate distribution of misinformation, especially during elections. And, of course, it includes all the offences that are also offences when committed offline. There is no reason why the normal law enforcement processes should be hindered because the crime is taking place in the digital space. Therefore, a component of the amendment to the internet regulation law in South Africa was that internet service providers were to inform the Film and Publication Board whether they had reported the presence of the prohibited content, as well as the particulars of the individual maintaining, hosting, distributing, or in any manner contributing to the content, to an official of the South African Police Service.[73]

3.5 CONCLUSION

In this chapter, I have attempted to pan out from an analysis of specific rights affected by internet regulation to then focus in on the basis for that regulation. I argue that this basis is the rule of law, and that the rule of law, properly understood, requires an approach to rights analysis that recognises and fosters the community in which the rights are exercised. Under such an approach, we interpret individual rights in such a way as to benefit all the members of the community, and we are prepared to limit individual rights if this is necessary to maintain genuine interaction between the subjects of law. In Fuller's view, this process of interaction creates the shared understandings from which a community develops a legal system, and nurtures

[72] The Centre for Analytics & Behavioural Change, '2021 June riots', https://cabc.org.za/search/2021 Juneriots/.

[73] *Business Tech*, 'South Africa's internet censorship laws are now in full effect – and legal notices are going out', 31 October 2022, https://businesstech.co.za/news/government/639087/south-africas-internet-censorship-laws-are-now-in-full-effect-and-legal-notices-are-going-out/.

and develops the particular norms that make communal life possible. It is thus a prerequisite for the very existence of the individual rights.

With the focus on maintaining interaction and responsiveness, I then suggest some basic design elements for internet regulation. The general model I propose is backed up by the coercive power of the state and allows for significant limitation of individual rights to prevent the manipulation of information. However, such limitations are themselves bounded by a structure in which the necessary actors remain in dialogue with one another and keep the state responsive to the views of internet users.

4

How to Tame the 'Digital' Shrew

Constitutional Rights Going Online

Violeta Beširević

'No man and no mind was ever emancipated
merely by being left alone.'

John Dewey, *The Public and Its Problems*

4.1 ON DANGERS AND SOLUTIONS

On 11 July 2017, the Knight First Amendment Institute at Colombia University filed a lawsuit against former President Trump and his aides for blocking several people from Trump's Twitter account following their criticism of his presidency and policies. The plaintiff asserted that the @realDonaldTrump account was a 'public forum' protected under the First Amendment, from which no one could be excluded based simply on their views.[1] The US Court of Appeals for the Second Circuit affirmed the district court's holding that such blocking violated the First Amendment.[2] This judicial finding confirms 'the key role that the Internet can play in mobilising the population to call for justice, equality, accountability [...] and better respect for human rights'.[3]

By way of contrast, assume now that Twitter has removed users' comments. The outcome would be different since Twitter, as a private actor, is not bound by constitutional obligations embodied in the First Amendment. Under such a scenario, First Amendment rights are illusory, as are sometimes privacy-related rights, whose online infringements can produce cascade results. Recently, a surveillance information technology company and social media made, what Danielle Citron calls

1 Knight First Amendment Institute at Columbia University, 'Knight Institute v. Trump: a lawsuit challenging President Trumps's blocking of critics on Twitter', https://knightcolumbia.org/cases/knight-institute-v-trump.

2 *Knight First Amendment Inst. at Columbia Univ. v. Trump*, No. 1:17-cv-5205 (SDNY) No. 18-1691 (2d Cir.).

3 Special Rapporteur on the Promotion and Protection of the Right to Freedom of Opinion and Expression, Frank La Rue, Human Rights Council, P2, U.N. Doc. A/HRC/17/27 (16 May 2011) www2.ohchr.org/english/bodies/hrcouncil/docs/17session/A.HRC.17.27_en.pdf.

'intimate privacy',[4] accessible to everyone possessing a computer or mobile phone. *MIT Technology Review* revealed how iRobot collected photos and videos from the homes of test users and employees and shared them with data annotation companies.[5] The investigation revealed that images of a minor and a tester on a toilet ended up on Facebook. It was a robot vacuum that took the pictures, not a person. Nevertheless, it would be too simple to blame iRobot for this infringement since humans were those who decided to steal and leak them.

But who is to blame? When during the 1990s the internet started the digital revolution, it was generally viewed that it should be free of regulation, that electronic commerce should be free, and that social platforms, that is, intermediaries, should not themselves be liable for content posted by third parties.[6] However, with the increasing influence of digital technology on everyday life, the concerns about human rights violations have also rapidly increased, making the issue of liability for the online infringement of human rights unavoidable. Modelling the liability of social platforms has become a pressing issue, along with emerging efforts to institutionalise the accountability of digital collective actors, which includes human–algorithmic association.[7] But to make social platforms liable, it is necessary to resolve the problem of the accountability of private actors for human rights violations traditionally immune to human rights challenges because social platforms are owned by private actors who also manufacture their contents, and coordinate and control them. To remedy the situation, different strategies are employed or offered.

First, the transnational nature of digital communication and unreadiness of states to step out of their traditional zone of control within their borders made room for social platforms to turn to self-regulation and develop what Gunther Teubner following David Sciulii calls 'societal constitutionalism'.[8] At the expense of democracy, by accumulating powers traditionally seen as public, the private actors have become responsive to values of fundamental rights through private actions. The Facebook Oversight Board's decision to uphold and partially revise Facebook's decision to suspend former US President Donald Trump's account indefinitely for the alleged influence of his posts on the violent attacks on Capitol Hill on 6 January 2021 clearly

4 See D. K. Citron, *The Fight for Privacy: Protecting Dignity, Identity, and Love in the Digital Age* (New York: W.W. Norton & Company, 2022).

5 E. Guo, 'A Roomba recorded a woman on the toilet. How did screenshots end up on Facebook?' (2022) *MIT Technology Review*, www.technologyreview.com/2022/12/19/1065306/roomba-irobot-robot-vacuums-artificial-intelligence-training-data-privacy/.

6 A. Savin, 'The EU Digital Service Act: toward a more responsible Internet' (2021) 24 *Journal of Internet Law* 7, 15–25.

7 See, e.g., A. Beckers and G. Teubner, 'Human-algorithm hybrids as (quasi-)organizations? On the accountability of digital collective actors' (2023) 50 *Journal of Law and Society* 1, 100–19.

8 G. Teubner, 'Societal constitutionalism: alternatives to state-centred constitutional theory?', in C. Joerges, I.-J. Sand, and G. Teubner (eds.), *Transnational Governance and Constitutionalism* (Oxford: Hart, 2004), pp. 3–28.

illustrates this trend.[9] What is more striking is that international law has encouraged such privatisation of public law, because it lacks legally binding instruments that would regulate the direct responsibility of non-state actors and profit-driven companies for human rights violations. Take, for example, the United Nations (UN) Guiding Principles on Business and Human Rights, whose greatest achievement suggests that corporate responsibility implies a negative obligation to respect human rights and a positive obligation to understand and mitigate the negative impacts on human rights with due diligence.[10] In the absence of state reactions, business actors, including social platforms, have become quasi-regulators.[11]

Second, despite the limits of international law and the fact that the European Convention for the Protection of Human Rights and Fundamental Freedoms generally obliges only states, the European Court of Human Rights has attempted to limit the power of social platforms, by ruling that, in principle, social platforms, in the role of content providers, are liable for third-party content.[12] Although this approach has been subject to substantial criticism because it might encourage social platforms to behave like censors to avoid liability or arbitrarily remove content, it is worth noting that the Court has made an effort to model a liability regime for human rights violations in the online context through its doctrine of positive obligations.[13]

Third, within the European Union (EU), a social platform's liability was initially perceived as non-existent, providing that in a specific case it 'has neither knowledge of nor control over the information which is transmitted or stored.'[14] In the opposite case, if it was established that the social platform possessed knowledge about the posted information and exercised control over it, the liability existed.[15] Today, the Court of Justice of the EU (CJEU) has become a significant regulator of the digital world, finding the balancing principle extremely helpful in disputes involving, on the one hand, the right of social platforms to conduct business, and on the other hand, the rights of individuals. Furthermore, the recently adopted Digital Service

[9] The Facebook Oversight Board, Case decision no. 2021-001-FB-FBR (2021).

[10] See the 2011 United Nations Guiding Principles on Business and Human Rights (UNGP).

[11] For more, see S. Deva and D. Bilchitz (eds.), *Human Rights Obligations of Business: Beyond the Corporate Responsibility to Respect* (Cambridge: Cambridge University Press, 2013).

[12] See *Delfi AS v. Estonia*, Application no. 64569/09, Judgment of 16 June 2015; *Magyar Tartalomszolgáltatók Egyesülete and Index.Hu Zrt v. Hungary* (*MTE v. Hungary*), Application no. 22947/13, Judgment of 2 February 2016.

[13] For more see M. Maroni, 'The liability of internet intermediaries and the European Court of Human Rights', in B. Petkova and T. Ojanen (eds.), *Fundamental Rights Protection Online: The Future Regulation of Intermediaries* (Cheltenham: Edward Elgar Publishing, 2020), pp. 255–79.

[14] Joined Cases C-236/08 to C-238/08, *Google France SARL and Google Inc. v. Louis Vuitton Malletier SA* (C-236/08), *Google France SARL v. Viaticum SA and Luteciel SARL* (C-237/08) *and Google France SARL v. Centre national de recherche en relations humaines (CNRRH) SARL and Others* (C-238/08) [2010] EU:C:2010:159, para. 113.

[15] Ibid., para. 114; see also Case C-291/13 *Sotiris Papasavvas v. O Fileleftheros Dimosia Etaireia Ltd and Others*, [2014] EU:C:2014:2209, para. 45.

Act, the Digital Market Act, and AI Regulation represent additional EU attempts to force platforms to act more responsibly.[16]

From a methodological perspective, although policymakers and judges have attempted to cope with the issue of intermediary liability for human rights violations within different fields, including data protection law, consumer law, privacy law, intellectual property law, and hate speech regulations,[17] on the theoretical level, the dominant way to frame this new phenomenon is to label it in constitutional terms. Starting from the fact that constitutionalism aims to limit government to protect individual rights, the emerging model of digital constitutionalism strives towards the same aim: to provide an understanding of how digital technology affects human rights, which are traditional tenants of constitutional law, and offer solutions for how to make private actors responsible for human rights infringements in the context of the digital world.[18]

On this account, some scholars have offered the recognition of the new rights as the exit strategy. In addition to already available rights, the right to explanation (in the context of data processing), the right to accessibility, and the right to obtain a translation from the language of technology into the language of human beings are perceived as means to regulate the relationship among three main participants of the information society – platforms, states, and individuals.[19] Others examined whether the horizontal application of constitutional rights in private law may be a possible response to the unlimited powers of social platforms.[20] Several years ago, the Council of Europe's Committee of Ministers acknowledged the significance of the horizontal effects strategy in regulating the responsibilities of online platforms

16 See, e.g., A. Savin, 'Digital sovereignty and its impact on EU policymaking', (2022) *CBS LAW Research Paper* 22–02.

17 S. Stalla-Bourdillon and R. Thorburn, 'The scandal of intermediary: acknowledging the both/and dispensation for regulating hybrid actors', in B. Petkova and T. Ojanen (eds.), *Fundamental Rights Protection Online: The Future Regulation of Intermediaries* (Cheltenham: Edward Elgar Publishing, 2020), pp. 141–74, at 145–6.

18 The literature on digital constitutionalism is growing. See, e.g., G. De Gregorio, *Digital Constitutionalism in Europe* (Cambridge: Cambridge University Press, 2022); G. De Gregorio, 'Digital constitutionalism across the Atlantic' (2022) 11 *Global Constitutionalism* 2, 297–324; E. Celeste, 'Digital constitutionalism: a new systematic theorization' (2019) 33 *International Review of Law, Computers & Technology* 1, 76–99; D. Redeker, L. Gill, and U. Gasser, 'Towards digital constitutionalism? Mapping attempts to craft an Internet Bill of Rights' (2018) 80 *International Communication Gazette* 4, 302–19. Despite the growing popularity, some argue that the digital constitutionalist approach may encounter specific problems owing to the technological embeddedness of governance mechanisms and the discrepancy between jurisdictional borders and digital processes of a transnational nature. See N. Palladino, 'The role of epistemic communities in the "constitutionalization" of Internet governance: the example of the European Commission High-Level Expert Group on Artificial Intelligence' (2021) 45 *Telecommunications Policy* 6, Article 102149, 1.

19 O. Pollicino, *Judicial Protection of Fundamental Rights on the Internet: A Road Towards Digital Constitutionalism?* (Oxford: Hart Publishing, 2021), pp. 204–6.

20 This approach has been debated in the works of G. De Gregorio and O. Pollicino. See De Gregorio, 'Digital constitutionalism across the Atlantic'; Pollicino, *Judicial Protection of Fundamental Rights on the Internet*.

and recommended to Member States to ensure the horizontal effects of constitutional rights in relations between private parties.[21]

Considering that human rights violations in the digital sphere are of a constitutional quality, this chapter identifies the horizontal application of constitutional rights as a possible response to human rights challenges raised by the actions of social platforms. The traditional view in constitutional law is that constitutional rights are shields only against the state. However, in this chapter, I will start from the premise that the focus should not be on the state's obligations but the individual's rights. Following Joseph Raz, who claims that 'rights precede obligations and therefore there is no closed list of obligations according to a certain law [but that] … changed circumstances can lead to the creation of new obligations according to an already existing law',[22] I will presuppose that constitutional rights correlate not only with different duties but also with different duty-bearers concerning the fulfilment of duties. In light of this conclusion, it is evident that digital technology has made social platforms a prominent duty-bearer toward constitutional rights. I intend to make progress on the issue of the liability of social platforms for individual rights violations by suggesting the horizontal application of constitutional rights as an available strategy to remedy individual rights infringements in the online environment. The issue of whether constitutional rights should be restructured to protect from all intrusions of the digital world (e.g., the digital code) and not only from the activities of social platforms is outside this discussion.[23]

This chapter is divided into five parts. After the introduction, in the second part, I will more closely explain the (non-)application of constitutional rights in offline private relations. In the third part, I will discuss different approaches to the emerging authority of constitutional rights online. The fourth part will advance understanding of how the horizontal application of constitutional rights in the online environment helps establish and maintain democratic control over digital technology. In the concluding part, I will summarize why an extension of constitutional rights in the digital sphere could be a driving strategy for protecting individual rights against the intrusive power of the algorithmic society.

4.2 RIGHTS TALK IN PRIVATE LAW

4.2.1 *The Meaning and Relevance of the Public/Private Law Distinction*

A distinction between private and public law provides a ground for the systematisation of law.[24] It first appeared in sixteenth-century legal treatises, which, largely

[21] Recommendation CM/Rec(2018)2 of the Committee of Ministers to Member States on the roles and responsibilities of internet intermediaries, adopted by the Committee of Ministers on 7 March 2018.

[22] J. Raz, *The Morality of Freedom* (Chicago: Clarendon Press, 1986), p. 171.

[23] On this account, see G. Teubner, 'Horizontal effects of constitutional rights in the Internet: a legal case on the digital constitution' (2017) 3 *The Italian Law Journal* 1, 193–205.

[24] H. Kelsen, *General Theory of Law and State*, trans. Andreas Wedberg (Cambridge, MA: Harvard University Press, 1945), p. 201.

ignoring the contrast in Roman law between *jus gentium* and *jus civile*, made a sharp distinction between *jus publicum* and *jus privatum*.[25] Ever since, what belonged to the first and what was covered by the second category, however, remained a subject of vivid discussion.

Broadly speaking, private law traditionally encompasses the law of contracts, tort, property, business associations, commercial transactions, and related fields governing relations between individuals.[26] The state here appears as a mere arbiter of the rights and duties that exist between private parties and is not the party with the interest.[27]

Figuring out the meaning of the term public law became more challenging. Thus, scholars have never had a complete control of the definition of public law. For example, public law was entirely omitted in Justinian's *civil law*, but Hale and Blackstone's *civil law* incorporated much of what the Romans would have called public law – including the rights and duties of the monarch, members of Parliament and other magistrates.[28] Issues of whether public law is an autonomous body founded on the autonomy of the political realm, whether it is isolated from morality, to which philosophy should we turn to specify its subject and tasks (e.g., to functionalist legal thought, legal positivism, Dworkinian legal interpretivism, or political theory), and which values are immanent within public law, have been subject to a modern passionate debate exemplified in the work of Loughlin, Craig, Harlow, and Cane.[29] At the highest level of abstraction, one may say that public law is inseparable from the government.[30] Following this argument, one can argue that constitutional law, criminal law, and administrative law are principal tenants of public law. Yet one should bear in mind that a lack of a clear definition of public law is also a result of still present differences among jurisdictions – despite emerging unifying trends, the tenants of public law are not the same in, for instance, France, the US, and England.[31]

The issue of whether public law is fundamentally different from private law slowly loses its attraction since, in contemporary times, it is often unclear whether

[25] See in H. J. Berman, *Law and Revolution, II: The Impact of the Protestant Reformations on the Western Legal Tradition* (Cambridge, MA, and London: Harvard University Press, 2003), pp. 156, 439, fn.1.

[26] Ibid., p. 439, fn.1; M. Rosenfeld, 'Rethinking the boundaries between public law and private law for the twenty-first century: an introduction' (2013) 11 *International Journal of Constitutional Law* 1, 125–8.

[27] Kelsen, *General Theory of Law and State*, p. 202.

[28] Berman, *Law and Revolution, II*, p. 298.

[29] See M. Loughlin, 'Theory and values in public law: an interpretation' (2005) *Public Law*, 48–66; P. Cane, 'Theory and values in public law', in P. Craig and R. Rawlings (eds.), *Law and Administration in Europe: Essays in Honour of Carol Harlow* (Oxford: Oxford University Press, 2003), pp. 3–21; P. Craig, 'Theory, "pure theory" and values in public law' (2005) *Public Law*, 440–7; C. Harlow and R. Rawlings, *Law and Administration*, 2nd ed. (London: Butterworths, 1997); C. Harlow, 'Public law and popular justice' (2002) 65 *Modern Law Review* 1, 1–18.

[30] Rosenfeld, 'Rethinking the boundaries', p. 125.

[31] V. Beširević, 'Introduction', in Violeta Beširević (ed.), *Public Law in Serbia: Twenty Years After* (London: European Public Law Organization and Esperia Publications Ltd, 2012), pp. 15–19, at 16.

the relevant institute, value, or principle derives from public or private law. This is why Kelsen's claim, that a distinction between private and public law is 'useless as a common foundation for a general systematization of law', is still valid.[32]

There is much more to be said on the distinction between public and private law, but what helps approach the issue of the impact of constitutional rights on private parties is Kelsen's view that traditionally, private law embraces norms governing relations between private parties, while public law embraces norms stipulating rights and duties between the state on the one hand, and private parties on the other.[33]

4.2.2 *The Riddle of Horizontality: From Natural Law to the Horizontal Enforcement of Constitutional Rights*

Individual rights were first theoretically articulated in natural law theory without any differentiation between duty bearers responsible for their violations and the state obligation to protect individual rights regardless of who a perpetrator was:

> The state of Nature has a law of Nature to govern it, which obliges everyone, and reason, which is that law, teaches all mankind who will but consult it, that being all equal and independent, no one ought to harm another in his life, health, liberty or possessions [...]. The great and chief end, therefore, of men uniting into commonwealths, and putting themselves under government, is the preservation of their property [...].[34]

Thus, John Locke never considered natural rights to create obligations only for states, nor did he think a state's duty to protect rights extended only to its intrusions. His vision found an expression in the first state documents stressing freedom and equality and acknowledging various duty holders vis-à-vis individual rights and a *total* state obligation to protect them from different intruders, not only from the state.[35]

While the idea of natural rights mostly proved short, the constitutionalisation of individual rights in different forms and through different generations continued to endure after its first occurrence in the US Bill of Rights. However, over time, the focus on the state's duties became the centre of constitutional protection as the state accumulated power and authority over its citizens.[36] As a result, constitutional rights, with fewer exceptions, extended only into the public law regime but not the regime

[32] Kelsen, *General Theory of Law and State*, p. 207.

[33] Ibid., pp. 201–2.

[34] J. Locke, *Two Treatises of Government* (Vermont: Everyman, 1997), pp. 107, 116–22, 159.

[35] Thus, The American Declaration of Independence proclaimed that '[...] All men are created equal, that they are endowed by their Creator with certain unalienable rights; that among these are life, liberty, and the pursuit of happiness... [T]o secure these rights, governments are instituted among men.' The French Declaration on the Rights of Man and the Citizen accented that 'The aim of all political association is the preservation of the natural and imprescriptible rights of man.'

[36] S. R. Ratner, 'Corporations and human rights: a theory of legal responsibility (2001) 111 *The Yale Law Journal* 3, 468–9.

of private governance. What followed on the theoretical level was the development of an animating idea that constitutional rights apply only vertically – in the relationship between a state and individuals – and not horizontally between private parties.

However, the fall of the Berlin Wall, the end of apartheid, and the return of many Latin American countries to democracy in the 1990s encouraged drafters of the new constitutions for post-communist, post-apartheid, and post-authoritarian societies, and constitutional law scholars, to rethink the nature and the purpose of the constitution, including the issue of its application in private law.[37] Furthermore, the phenomenon of globalisation, the increased activity of non-state actors in world conflicts, and the penetration of transnational corporations, non-government organisations, and digital platforms into the traditional public sector have imposed a critical theoretical question – who are the duty bearers to whom human rights (either constitutional or international) impose burdens and obligations?[38] Translated into this discussion, the starting position is that constitutional rights have become just as vulnerable to private actions as to the states, but unlike their constraint of the state in a Lockean sense, constitutional rights, in principle, do not constrain private actors.

Now, the academic discussion on whether constitutional rights should or should not produce effects in private law has brought to light three different positions regarding the applicability of constitutional rights in private law.

The first two positions are mutually exclusive. One, verticality, exposes the already elaborated traditional idea that constitutional rights protect only against the government and have no application in private law. Accordingly, they are judicially enforceable in public but not in private law. The main justification for insisting on verticality is the protection of individual autonomy in the private sphere, along with liberty or privacy, and the need for market efficiency.[39] A frequent argument is that autonomy in the private sphere should be isolated from any state action or control.[40] A constitution's mandate is to secure a limited government and not to regulate private relations, which should be based on free individual choice.

The other position rests on the opposite, horizontal, approach: although defined and determined in constitutional (i.e., public) law, constitutional rights are directly

37 S. Gardbaum, 'The structure and scope of constitutional rights', in R. Dixon and T. Ginsburg (eds.), *Research Handbook in Comparative Constitutional Law* (Cheltenham: Edward Elgar Publishing, 2011), pp. 387–403, at 393–4; See also W. Rivera-Perez, 'What the constitution got to do with it: expanding the scope of constitutional rights into the private sphere' (2012) 3 *Creighton International and Comparative Law Journal* 1, 189–214.

38 V. Beširević', '"Uhvati me ako možeš": o (ne)odgovornosti transnacionalnih korporacija zbog kršenja ljudskih prava' ['"Catch me if you can": reflections on legal (un)accountability of transnational corporations for human rights violations'] (2018) *Pravni zapisi* 1, 22–45.

39 Gardbaum, 'The structure and scope of constitutional rights', p. 392.

40 See, e.g., A. Sajó and R. Uitz, *The Constitution of Freedom: An Introduction to Legal Constitutionalism* (Oxford, Oxford University Press, 2017), pp. 399–401; J. Thomas, *Public Rights, Private Relations* (Oxford: Oxford University Press, 2015), pp. 34–5.

applicable in private law, meaning that constitutional rights protect not only against government but also against private parties. Apart from insisting on the vulnerability of human rights in relation to any actor, either state or private, some authors also assert that there is no reason to avoid the constitutional regulation of autonomy for the purpose of its protection, as autonomy is already regulated by non-constitutional law.[41] Others indicate the function of a constitution, arguing that as a *supreme law of the land* it should apply to all equally. For example, Mattias Kumm's *total constitution* claim derives from the premise that private law also involves political choices, and that political choices are subject to a constitutional rights review using proportionality analysis; this, in turn, suggests that decisions relating to private law should not be excluded from constitutional rights scrutiny.[42] Consequently, constitutional rights should be judicially enforceable in disputes between private parties.

The third position stands between the two extreme positions. It is grounded on an intermediate position, known as the indirect horizontal effect, and assumes that although constitutional rights apply directly only in public law against the government, they nevertheless indirectly apply, that is, produce effects, on private law.[43] While in the direct horizontal effect position, private actors are directly subjected to constitutional rights, in the indirect horizontal effects position, private laws are subjected to constitutional rights. Courts play a decisive role here as they must, in one way or another, take into account constitutional rights in deciding disputes between private parties.[44] What is indirect here is the fact that individuals are protected not directly by constitutional rights, but by the effects constitutional rights produce on private law.[45]

There is a further wrinkle here. Constitutional rights can produce either strong or weak indirect horizontal effects on private law. A *strong* indirect horizontal effect assumes that all private laws are subject to constitutional rights and may be challenged in private litigations, meaning that individuals are fully (yet indirectly through private law) protected by constitutional rights. Contrary to this, a *weak* indirect horizontal effect means that private law is not subjected to constitutional rights, but that courts can take constitutional values exemplified in applicable constitutional rights into account when interpreting or developing private laws in litigation between private parties.[46] What stands behind the *weak* indirect horizontal effect

[41] See E. Chemerinsky, 'Rethinking state action doctrine' (1985) 80 *Northwestern University Law Review*, 503–57.

[42] M. Kumm, 'Who is afraid of the total constitution? Constitutional rights as principles and the constitutionalization of private law' (2006) 7 *German Law Journal*, 4, 341–69.

[43] Gardbaum, 'The structure and scope of constitutional rights', p. 394; see also S. Gardbaum, 'The "horizontal effect" of constitutional rights' (2003) 102 *Michigan Law Review* 2, 387–459, at 436.

[44] Thomas, *Public Rights, Private Relations*, p. 28.

[45] Gardbaum, 'The structure and scope of constitutional rights', p. 394.

[46] G. Phillipson, 'The Human Rights Act, "horizontal effect" and the common law: a bang or a whimper?' (1999) 62 *The Modern Law Review* 6, 824–49, at 830.

is a claim that 'the actions of private individuals can produce similar or identical effects or harms to those of governmental'.[47]

4.2.3 *How Horizontality Works Offline*

The concept of the horizontal effects of constitutional rights is one of the basic coinages of modern constitutionalism. Although Ireland and South Africa are famously known for expanding constitutionalism in private law, horizontality is operational in some other jurisdictions, most notably in many Latin American countries, including Argentina, Bolivia, Chile, and Colombia,[48] and then in Malawi, Ghana,[49] and Slovenia.[50] As a rule, horizontality means different things in different jurisdictions.

The Irish Constitution itself contains an expressed commitment to direct horizontality: 'The State guarantees in its laws to respect, and, as far as practicable, by its laws to defend and vindicate the personal rights of the citizen.' Since 1965, the Irish courts have maintained that constitutional rights may have a direct horizontal effect and are not imposing obligations on the state alone.[51] The objections to the horizontal application of constitutional rights from liberal constitutional theory have played no role in judicial reasoning.[52]

South Africa has a specific approach to the horizontality issue.[53] Apart from verticality, its 1996 Constitution endorses the direct horizontal application of constitutional rights in private law 'taking into account the nature of the right and the nature of any duty imposed by the right'.[54] This is not the end of the story. The Constitution also authorises the indirect horizontal application of rights in disputes between private parties through the courts: 'When interpreting any legislation, and when developing the common law or customary law, every court, tribunal or forum must promote the spirit, purport and objects of the Bill of Rights.'[55]

An important footnote should be added here. Direct horizontality also works in France, but not as a constitutional matter. French legal culture does not recognise

47 Ibid.

48 Fourteen Latin American countries have adopted some form of direct horizontal effect: Argentina, Bolivia, Chile, Colombia, Costa Rica, Dominican Republic, Ecuador, Guatemala, Honduras, Paraguay, Pert, Puerto Rico, Uruguay, and Venezuela. See Rivera-Perez, 'What the constitution got to do with it', p. 198.

49 A. Nolan, 'Holding non-state actors to account for constitutional economic and social rights violations: experiences and lessons from South Africa and Ireland' (2014) 12 *International Journal of Constitutional Law* 1, 66–93.

50 P. Weingerl, 'The influence of fundamental rights in Slovene private law', in V. Trstenjak and P. Weingerl (eds.), *The Influence of Human Rights and Basic Rights in Private Law* (Cham, Heidelberg, New York: Springer, 2016), pp. 535–58, at 541–2.

51 See *Ryan v. The Attorney General*, [1965] I.R. 294; Thomas, *Public Rights, Private Relations*, p. 29.

52 Nolan, 'Holding non-state actors to account', pp. 69–71.

53 Ibid., pp. 76–86.

54 Section 8 (2) of the 1996 Constitution.

55 Ibid., Section 39 (2).

the horizontal effect of rights, and, in some way, it is incompatible with it because the state has never been perceived as a threat to rights but rather as the protector.[56] Nevertheless, rights do produce a direct effect in private law through the judicial application of the European Convention on Human Rights.[57]

In Germany and Canada, constitutional rights do not have a direct but an indirect horizontal effect. In the world of horizontality, Germany is best known for the application of the *Drittwirkung* doctrine, meaning third-party effect, which has produced a substantial horizontal effect in jurisprudence. The doctrine was born in the jurisprudence of the German Federal Constitutional Court. By specifying its premises in the famous *Lüth* case decided in 1958, the Court ended a decade-long passionate discussion among German scholars and courts about the scope of the then newly adopted Basic Law (1949).[58] The Federal Labour Court took a leading role in the discussion, asserting that the constitutional rights, protected in the Basic Law, were directly applicable to relations between the employer and employees.[59] Concerned with the fact that 'basic rights shall be binding for the legislative, executive and judicial powers', the Federal Constitutional Court did not accept the standing of the Federal Labour Court. Yet, more importantly, it did not fully reject the idea that fundamental rights could have produced effects on the relations between private parties. The Court adopted what is now called the indirect horizontal effect model, in which constitutional rights were understood as legal codifications of objective general values immanent to the whole legal order, including private law:

> This value system, which centres upon human dignity and the free unfolding of personality within the social community, must be looked upon as a fundamental constitutional decision affecting the entire legal system [...] It naturally influences private law as well; no rule of private law may conflict with it, and all such rules must be construed by its spirit.[60]

In short, although the *Drittwirkung* doctrine accepts that basic rights oblige only state organs, it nevertheless holds that: (a) all private law is directly subjected to constitutional rights and is invalid if it conflicts with constitutional rights, and (b) it is not on private actors to conform their actions with constitutional values, but rather,

[56] M. Troper, 'Who needs a third party effect doctrine? – The case of France', in A. Sajó and R. Uitz (eds.), *The Constitution in Private Relations: Expanding Constitutionalism* (Utrecht: Eleven International Publishing, 2005), pp. 115–28, at 119.

[57] For more see M. Hunter-Henin, 'Horizontal application of human rights in France: the triumph of the European Convention on Human Rights', in O. Dawn and J. Fedtke (eds.), *Human Rights and the Private Sphere – a Comparative Study* (Cavendish, London, and New York: Routledge, 2007), pp. 98–124.

[58] U. Preuß, 'The German *Drittwirkung* doctrine and its socio-political background', in A. Sajó and R. Uitz (eds.), *The Constitution in Private Relations: Expanding Constitutionalism* (Utrecht: Eleven International Publishing, 2005), pp. 23–32, at 23.

[59] Ibid.

[60] Bundesverfassungsgericht, Lüth, BVerfGE 7, 198–230.

it is on judges, bound by the basic rights under Article 3 of the Basic Law, to consider constitutional values when interpreting private laws.[61]

The German indirect horizontal effect model, with some variations, is also followed in Canada. Like Germany, Canada also supports verticality when it comes to the effects of the Charter of Fundamental Rights and Freedoms on legislation.[62] Yet the Supreme Court has distinguished between the constitutional rights and constitutional values embodied in the Charter, allowing constitutional values to influence the entire legal system, including private law, when 'private litigant disputes fall to be decided at common law'.[63] This means that the principal role of the rights embodied in the Charter is to protect citizens against the government, but the courts may 'apply and develop the principles of the common law in a manner consistent with the fundamental values enshrined in the Charter'.[64] Therefore, unlike in Germany, not all private law in Canada is directly subjected to constitutional review for its inconsistency with the Charter, but only common law, when the courts should check its consistency with Charter values (not rights). This solution directly derives from the separation of powers principle in the (British) common law tradition, under which the courts are allowed to develop common law in parallel with the Constitution.[65]

Compared with Germany and Canada, the US is an outlier in the world of horizontality, although it adheres to the same starting position – the constitutional rights – as they oblige only state actors. Influenced by the strong liberal tradition, in which individual autonomy is highly cherished in all law, not only that the constitutional text refers explicitly to the obligation of states when conferring rights (No state shall…), but also that the US Supreme Court has established the controversial 'state action doctrine', which, arguably, precludes the influence of constitutional rights in private law. Therefore, in the original case from 1903 – *The Civil Rights Cases* – in which the doctrine was born, the US Supreme Court held that since they apply only to government actions, the Thirteenth and Fourteenth Amendments are not an appropriate basis for Congress to pass laws protecting African-Americans from discrimination.[66] The Court emphasised that constitutional rights shielded by the Fourteenth Amendment were so designed that it had only negative effects – they imposed duties of restraint only on federal or state governments whose duty was

61 For more see Thomas, *Public Rights, Private Relations*, p. 32; Gardbaum, 'The "horizontal effect" of constitutional rights', pp. 404–6; D. Looschelders and M. Makowsky, 'The impact of human rights and basic rights in German private law', in V. Trstenjak and P. Weingerl (eds.), *The Influence of Human Rights and Basic Rights in Private Law* (Cham, Heidelberg, New York: Springer, 2016), pp. 295–317, at 299.

62 C. Saunders, 'Constitutional rights and the common law', in A. Sajó and R. Uitz (eds.), *The Constitution in Private Relations: Expanding Constitutionalism* (Utrecht: Eleven International Publishing, 2005), pp. 183–216, at 195–200.

63 *RWDSU v. Dolphin Delivery Ltd.* [1986] 2 SCR 573, para. 39.

64 Ibid.

65 Saunders, 'Constitutional rights and the common law', p. 200.

66 *The Civil Rights Cases*, 109 US 3 (1883).

to protect them only from actions taken by the state. However, the Court made an exception regarding the Thirteenth Amendment, arguing that 'Congress may probably pass laws directly enforcing its provisions, yet such legislative power extends only to the subject of slavery and its incidents [...].'[67]

The issue of who the state is for the state action doctrine has extended the reach of this doctrine to private parties providing that their conduct can be in different ways attributable to the state.[68] However, such situations are limited because the US Supreme Court has refused to find state action under many strands, apparently without clear criteria.[69] On the other hand, for those who are committed to debating the state action doctrine, a key concern is either which law is subject to constitutional scrutiny or whether courts, as state actors who enforce those laws, must be subject to constitutional rights scrutiny. Thus, focusing on the courts, the US Supreme Court itself ruled in *Shelley v. Kraemer* that it was unconstitutional for the courts to grant relief to enforce a racially restrictive covenant because this would constitute a state action under the Fourteenth Amendment.[70] Stephen Gardbaum even claims that the US adheres to the horizontal model when viewed through a comparative lens, as all law is fully and equally subject to constitutional rights scrutiny.[71] Nevertheless, the dominant position in the US is still that the Constitution limits the application of constitutional rights to public law. I hasten here to say that in cases involving constitutional rights infringements in a digital context the US Supreme Court has not shown any intention to change this position.

4.3 THE AUTHORITY OF CONSTITUTIONAL RIGHTS ONLINE: EMERGING TRENDS AND RESISTANCE

Having documented the horizontal effects of constitutional rights offline, I now turn to present similar efforts to validate the horizontal effects of constitutional rights online. This section takes the freedom of expression and the right to privacy as the focus of attention.

67 Ibid., 4. The Court also ruled that the denial of equal accommodations in inns, public conveyances, and places of public amusement, prohibited under the federal legislation under review, did not amount either to slavery or involuntary servitude, 'but at most, infringes rights which are protected from State aggression by the XIV Amendment'. Ibid.

68 Gardbaum, 'The "horizontal effect" of constitutional rights', 412–14; J. Miller, 'The influence of human rights and basic rights in private law in the United States', in V. Trstenjak and P. Weingerl (eds.), *The Influence of Human Rights and Basic Rights in Private Law* (Cham, Heidelberg, New York: Springer, 2016), pp. 473–86, at 481.

69 For the criticism, see Chemerinsky, 'Rethinking state action doctrine'; M. Kumm and V. Ferreres Comella, 'What is so special about constitutional rights in private litigation? A comparative analysis of the function of state action requirements and indirect horizontal effect', in A. Sajó and R. Uitz, *The Constitution of Freedom: An Introduction to Legal Constitutionalism* (Oxford: Oxford University Press, 2017), pp. 241–86; Gardbaum, 'The "horizontal effect" of constitutional rights', pp. 412–14.

70 *Shelley v. Kraemer*, 334 US 1 (1948). For comments, see Miller, 'The influence of human rights', p. 585.

71 Gardbaum, 'The structure and scope of constitutional rights', p. 396.

4.3.1 *Is the Internet a 'New Free Marketplace of Ideas' Immune to Constitutional Review?*

There are several reasons why freedom of speech deserves special status in constitutional democracies. First, freedom of speech essentially contributes to social progress and the moral and intellectual development of individuals.[72] Second, without citizens being free to express, deliberate, and accept different ideas, there is no democratic government.[73] Third, freedom of speech is indispensable for establishing the truth: in the famous words of Justice Oliver Wendell Holmes, truth should not be regulated, but determined in the 'marketplace of ideas'.[74]

Probably the world's best-known free speech clause is embodied in the US First Amendment. In case law, it is firmly established that the First Amendment does not permit the government to engage in a viewpoint-based regulation of speech without a compelling governmental interest, such as averting a clear and present danger of imminent violence.[75] Compared with the US, where the First Amendment provides almost an unlimited right to freedom of speech, the German Basic Law and the Canadian Charter, despite a presumption in favour of freedom of speech, offer mostly a qualified right, subject to limitations for different reasons. These different approaches have already been transplanted online. German and Canadian case law indicates that transplantation has followed the horizontality route. The American case shows that the US denied the horizontal applications of constitutional rights in the online context following its position in the offline world. Consider the following.

4.3.1.1 *The American Approach: Ignoring Horizontality from* LICRA *to* Gonzales *and* Taamneh

In 2000, the High Court in Paris famously ruled against Yahoo. The dispute began when two human rights organizations (La Ligue Internationale Contre Le Racisme Et l'Antisemitisme (LICRA) and L'Union Des Etudiants Juifs De France) sued Yahoo in France for allowing its users to offer Nazi-related items for sale on Yahoo .com, as the sale, exchange, or display of Nazi-related materials or Third Reich

[72] *Handyside v. UK*, Application no. 5493/72, Judgment of 7 December 1976, para. 49.

[73] For more, see V. Beširević, 'A short guide to militant democracy: some remarks on the Strasbourg jurisprudence', in W. Benedek et al. (eds.), *European Yearbook of Human Rights 2012* (Antwerp: Intersentia; Vienna: NW Verlag, 2012), pp. 243–58, at 248–52.

[74] See in *Abrams v. US*, 250 US 616, 630/631 (1919).

[75] See *R.A.V. v. City of St. Paul*, 505 US 377, 112 S.Ct 2538, 120 L.Ed.2d 305 (1992); *Simon & Schuster, Inc. v. Members of New York State Crime Victims Board*, 502 US 105, 112 S.Ct 501, 116 L.Ed.2d 476 (1991); *Boos v. Barry*, 485 US 312, 108 S.Ct 1157, 99 L.Ed.2d 333 (1988); *Police Dept. v. Mosley*, 408 US 92, 92 S.Ct 2286, 33 L.Ed.2d 212 (1972); *Brandenburg v. Ohio*, 395 US 444, 89 S.Ct 1827, 23 L.Ed.2d 430 (1969); *Kingsley Int'l Pictures Corp. v. Regents*, 360 US 684, 79 S.Ct 1362, 3 L.Ed.2d 1512 (1959).

memorabilia, represented a hate crime outlawed by the French Penal Code.[76] The French Court ruled that Yahoo's auction site violated the Penal Code and bluntly ordered Yahoo to preclude access to the auction site and other sites displaying Nazi-related material for French citizens and warn its users to refrain from accessing content prohibited by French law to avoid legal sanctions.[77]

In the US, however, the claim that everyone ought to have their rights protected against everyone, whether offline or online, is not appealing. The argument resurfaces in the *LICRA* case. Because the dispute also involved jurisdictional issues, the US District Court for the Northern District of California was asked by Yahoo to intervene and declare that the French Court's decision in LICRA was neither recognisable nor enforceable in the US.[78] The US Court specified that the lawsuit aimed to determine 'whether a United States court may enforce the French order without running afoul of the First Amendment'.[79] It issued a declaratory judgment and ruled, inter alia, that 'Yahoo has shown that the French order is valid under the laws of France, that it may be enforced with retroactive penalties, and that the ongoing possibility of its enforcement in the United States chills Yahoo's First Amendment rights.'[80] In the view of the US Court, the French Court's demand that Yahoo 'take all necessary measures to dissuade and render impossible any access via Yahoo.com to the Nazi artifact auction service and any other site' was too general and imprecise and amounted to censorship of protected speech.[81] The decision follows the US Supreme Court's finding that a law may violate the First Amendment if it is so 'overly broad' that it infringes protected and unprotected speech.

At this point, the basic considerations should be clear. In its landmark ruling on the online freedom of expression in *Reno v. ACLU*, the Supreme Court declared unconstitutional two provisions of the Communications Decency Act that criminalised 'obscene or indecent' speech transmitted to children and the delivery of 'patently offensive' information to children.[82] As a matter of fact, social platforms are exempted from liability for material posted by someone else on their sites, regardless of whether the posts violate the right to free speech. In such cases, Section 230 of the US Communications Decency Act exempts internet platforms from liability expressly providing that they would not be treated as 'publishers or speakers'.[83]

[76] Tribunal de Grande Instance de Paris, *Ligue contre le racisme et l'antisémitisme et Union des étudiants juifs de France c. Yahoo! Inc. et Société Yahoo! France*, RG 05308 (2000). See also in *Yahoo!, Inc., v. La Ligue Contre Le Racisme Et L'antisemitisme*, 169 F.Supp.2d 1181 (N.D.Cal.2001).

[77] Ibid., 1184–5.

[78] Ibid.

[79] Ibid., 1192.

[80] Ibid., 1194.

[81] Ibid., 1189.

[82] *RENO V. ACLU*, 521 US 844 (1997).

[83] Section 230 provides: 'No provider or user of an interactive computer service shall be treated as the publisher or speaker of any information provided by another information content provider.' 47 USC § 230(c) (2018).

Moreover, the established case law testifies that the state action doctrine does not apply to social platforms. The US federal courts have repeatedly rejected the notion that private corporations providing services via the internet are a public forum for the purposes of the First Amendment. Take, for example, the cases of *Dipp-Paz v. Facebook* and the *Federal Agency of News v. Facebook*.

In the *Dipp-Paz* case, the plaintiff asserted that Facebook violated his constitutional right to free speech by blocking his account.[84] However, the Court dismissed the claim finding that the plaintiff did not show that Facebook 'acted under the colour of a state "statute, ordinance, regulation, custom or usage"'.[85] The Court denied that Facebook is a public forum to which the First Amendment requirements applied, stressing that 'Facebook is a private corporation, and Plaintiff does not allege any facts suggesting that Facebook's actions are attributable to the state.'[86] The District Court for the Northern District of California followed the same reasoning in the *Federal Agency of News (FAN)* case, when Facebook blocked and removed the account of the Russian agency (FAN) allegedly involved in the US presidential elections in 2016.[87] The Court ruled that Facebook did not operate as a public forum and that its actions did not amount to state action under the public function test on the ground that Facebook was not a wilful participant in joint action with the government, nor did it conspire with the government to violate any constitutional rights.[88]

Some hope for a change was raised when recently the US Supreme Court was asked in *Google v. Gonzales* and *Twitter v. Taamneh* to shift the foundations of internet law by narrowing or revoking the protection that Section 230 secures for online platforms.[89] Both cases were initiated by the families of victims of ISIS terrorist attacks who alleged that Twitter and Google-owned YouTube helped the ISIS group carry out the attacks. Both opponents and proponents of Section 230 anxiously awaited the decisions. Eventually, the Supreme Court said nothing about Section 230 in either ruling. In *Twitter v. Taamneh*, it ruled exclusively on the grounds of the Justice Against Sponsors of Terrorism Act. After considering whether the defendant's conduct constituted aiding and abetting by knowingly providing substantial assistance, the Supreme Court found that the plaintiffs failed to establish their case. In the *Gonzales* case, the Court openly declined to address the application of Section 230 and, by unanimous vote, returned the case to the lower Court to rehear it in light of its decision in *Twitter v. Taamneh*, implying again that there was no need for Section 230 to be addressed.

84 *Dipp-Paz v. Facebook*, No. 18-CV-9037, WL 3205842 (SDNY 2019).

85 Ibid., 5.

86 Ibid.

87 *Federal Agency of News LLC v. Facebook, Inc.*, 395 F. Supp. 3d 1295 (ND Cal 2019).

88 Ibid., 1309–13.

89 See *Gonzalez v. Google LLC*, 598 US 617 (2023) and *Twitter Inc. v. Taamneh*, 598 US 471 (2023). The Court delivered decisions on 18 May 2023.

The Supreme Court's approach to these decisions could be read differently. Thus, one may claim that the Court purposely followed the judicial minimalism strategy to allow the voters and Congress to decide whether they want the internet to change. In constitutional cases of high complexity, which divide people on moral or other grounds, a minimalist path makes sense because democracy then urges the legislature to decide.[90] Any limitation of the freedom of speech, particularly in the context of new or changing circumstances, is such a case in the US. The narrow rulings could also suggest that nine justices appeared to postpone the ruling on Section 230 as 'other cases presenting different allegations and different records may lead to different conclusions', as Justice Jackson observed concurring in *Twitter v. Taamneh*. This may be so, particularly if one takes into account yet another possible reading. Strictly speaking, in *Gonzales* and *Taamneh*, the Supreme Court did not say online platforms were protected under Section 230, but rather it found no direct link between the terrorist attacks and online posts and videos. Notwithstanding which of these readings holds promise from a constitutional rights perspective, the Supreme Court's decision to avoid considering Section 230 alone represents a victory for online platforms, at least for the time being.

4.3.1.2 German and Canadian Approach: Horizontality Matters in Online Speech

Because social networks took over a significant portion of the public sphere, the constitutional dimension of their responsibility attracted profound attention among scholars in Germany. An initiative that called for intermediary responsibility under the same standards as the state was not taken seriously, but a discussion on the horizontal effects of the freedom of speech and the connected right of the platform to delete content gained significance.[91]

The approach insisting on the transplantation of the *Drittwirkung* doctrine in the digital sphere obtained judicial recognition. In its decision delivered in 2021, the German Federal Court of Justice, in a case involving hate speech online, took a more balanced approach than the French court in *LICRA* and solved the issue on the grounds of the indirect horizontal effect of constitutional rights.[92]

The Court was faced with two cases involving the Facebook decision to delete posts and partially block users' accounts with the explanation that hostile remarks about migrants amounted to hate speech. Unlike the French Court, which in *LICRA* paid no attention to the interests of Yahoo, the German Federal Court of

[90] C. Sunstein, *One Case at a Time: Judicial Minimalism on the Supreme Court* (Cambridge, MA: Harvard University Press, 1999), p. 5.

[91] T. Wischmeyer, 'What is illegal offline is also illegal online: the German Network Enforcement Act 2017', in B. Petkova and T. Ojanen (eds.), *Fundamental Rights Protection Online: The Future Regulation of Intermediaries* (Cheltenham: Edward Elgar Publishing, 2020), pp. 28–56, at 34.

[92] BGH, Urteil vom 29. Juli 2021 – III ZR 179/20.

Justice was more cautious. It balanced two constitutionally protected and conflicting rights: users' freedom of expression, protected under Article 5, and Facebook's occupational freedom, covered in Article 12 of the German Basic Law.[93] The Court found that, based on its right to occupational freedom, Facebook, in principle, was entitled to require users to respect specific communication standards and to block users' accounts responsible for possible breaches. At the same time, it emphasised that Facebook's right to occupational freedom is not unlimited. Facebook's terms of business, including standards for deleting posts or blocking users for a breach of standards, must, following Article 307 of the German Civil Code (the requirement for reasonable business terms), take into account the involved fundamental rights, as in this case, the freedom of expression.[94] Therefore, the Court ruled that Facebook's business terms related to deleting users' posts and blocking accounts in case of violation were invalid. Before blocking them or deleting the content that amounted to hate speech, Facebook should have consulted the affected users, informed them about the deletion, and made possible redress opportunities after the deletion.[95]

Eventually, the German Federal Court of Justice did not rule that Facebook, as a private company, had a constitutional obligation to respect freedom of expression. Rather, it used the *Drittwirkung* doctrine to order Facebook how to delete posts and block users' accounts for posting content with hate speech implications. The portion of the Court's decision requesting information obligations and complaint mechanisms mirrors the same solution embedded in the German Network Enforcement Act (NetzDG).[96] It also corresponds to the solutions proposed in the EU Digital Services Act, which requests online platforms to comply with obligations related to transparency, information obligations, and complaint mechanisms in relation to the removal of illegal content and the protection of users' fundamental rights online.[97]

Now, the situation in Canada is intriguing. The 2020 United States–Mexico–Canada Agreement limits the civil liability of online platforms for third-party content and does not treat them as content providers.[98] However, even since 2005, in the defamation context, the Canadian courts have ruled that online platforms could be liable for defamatory comments posted by third parties under certain

93 See press release, www.bundesgerichtshof.de/SharedDocs/Pressemitteilungen/DE/2021/2021149.html.

94 Ibid.

95 Ibid.

96 C. Etteldorf, '[DE] Federal Supreme Court finds Facebook terms of use ineffective in relation to hate speech', IRIS 2021-8:1/20, https://merlin.obs.coe.int/article/9273. For a discussion on NetzDG, see Wischmeyer, 'What is illegal offline is also illegal online', pp. 28–57.

97 Ibid. See also Regulation (EU) 2022/2065 of the European Parliament and of the Council of 19 October 2022 on a Single Market for Digital Services and amending Directive 2000/31/EC (Digital Services Act) (Text with EEA relevance).

98 See Trade Agreement at https://ustr.gov/trade-agreements/free-trade-agreements/united-states-mexico-canada-agreement/agreement-between. For comments, see, e.g., V. Krishnamurthy and J. Fjeld, 'CDA 230 goes North American? Examining the impacts of the USMCA's intermediary liability provisions in Canada and the United States', http://dx.doi.org/10.2139/ssrn.3645462.

circumstances.[99] Yet a breakthrough has been recently announced thanks to the availability of the horizontality doctrine. I will explain this in more detail by tracing the decision in the ongoing lawsuit in *Cool World Technologies Inc. v. Twitter Inc.*

Who governs online content in Canada is a major issue in this case initiated against Twitter for rejecting to promote posts relating to a Canadian documentary film.[100] The applicant (the publicity firm Cool World Technologies) alleged that Twitter wrongfully refused to sell advertising space on the Twitter social media platform, which ended in the violation of the applicant's freedom of speech.[101] The applicant relied on the influence of constitutional values related to the freedom of speech in Canadian contract law to support their claim. Because Twitter in Canada has such a political significance as to represent the 'town hall', the applicant asserted that the public policy of Canada, 'informed by Charter values related to freedom of expression, preclude Twitter from enforcing contract terms to exclude high value, non-harmful speech from its self-proclaimed town hall'.[102]

On the other hand, Twitter claimed that it had absolute and unfettered discretion to refuse any advertising posts and that all of Twitter's user accounts had no nature of the governing contract.[103] Besides, Twitter urged that the applicant was not entitled to allege the breach of Charter values, reminding that no right for one private party to sue another private party for breach of the Charter or breach of analogous Charter values existed.[104]

At the preliminary stage, the Court allowed the lawsuit to proceed, finding that the applicant could base their case on the effects that the constitutional guarantees of freedom of speech produce in contract law because of Twitter's central role in the public life of Canada.[105] Whether Twitter's unlimited power to control the content on its platforms in Canada will remain untouched by the end of the judicial proceedings remains to be seen. However, the indirect horizontality effect of constitutional values has opened the door for the judicial protection of freedom of speech on social platforms in Canada.

4.3.2 *Horizontality in Service of Privacy-Related Rights in Online Contexts*

Privacy-related rights are also frequently exposed to gross infringements in the digital environment. For the time being, all we know about the horizontal effect of

[99] See, e.g., *Carter v. B.C. Federation of Foster Parent Assn.*, 2005 BCCA 398 and *Pritchard v. Van Nes*, 2016 BCSC 686.
[100] See *Cool World Technologies Inc. v. Twitter Inc.*, 2022 ONSC 7156.
[101] Ibid., paras. 7, 10–13.
[102] Ibid., para. 13.
[103] Ibid., paras. 10–11.
[104] Ibid., para. 9.
[105] Ibid., para. 18.

privacy and privacy-related rights in the digital context mostly comes from the EU and the pioneering practice of the CJEU.

It has been quite a while since the constitutional nature of EU primary law and the constitutional value of rights in its legal order were emphasised.[106] The horizontal effects of certain equality-related rights were announced already in the Rome Treaty adopted in 1956. This came to the surface when the CJEU in 1976 ruled that Article 119 of the Rome Treaty, ensuring the principle of equal pay for male and female workers for work of equal value, obliged not only the Member States to whom the provision was directed but also private employers.[107]

In EU law, considerable attention has also been given to the horizontal effects of the EU Charter of Fundamental Rights. Although it has the same legal effect as the EU Treaties, the horizontal effect of its provisions has provoked much debate. The CJEU implicitly confirmed that, when applied within the scope of EU law, the Charter could create obligations for private parties if its provisions grant a legal right for an individual and not just a principle.[108] This finding seems reasonable, considering that the Charter has the status of EU primary law. The ultimate confirmation came in 2018 when, in four decisions, the CJEU established the direct horizontal effect of several Charter rights in disputes between private parties, specifically the right to non-discrimination, certain rights related to fair and just working conditions, and the right to an effective remedy and a fair trial.[109]

However, even before its 2018 revolutionary offline case law, the CJEU opened the door to the indirect horizontal application of fundamental rights online, in

[106] In 1986, the CJEU ruled that the Community treaties constituted the constitutional charter of the Community, based on the rule of law (see Case C-294/83, *Partiécologiste 'Les Verts' v. European Parliament* [1986] ECLI:EU:C:1986:166). Theoretically, several constitutional theories have explained the foundations of the EU's uncodified constitutional structure, including constitutional pluralism, constitutional synthesis, multilevel constitutionalism, and constitutional tolerance. For more about the constitutional nature of the EU and its primary law, see, e.g., J. Habermas, 'The crisis of the European Union in the light of a constitutionalization of international law' (2012) 23 *European Journal of International Law* 2, 335–48; V. Beširević, 'The constitution in the European Union: the state of affairs', in A. Dupeyrix and G. Raulet (eds.), *European Constitutionalism: Historical and Contemporary Perspectives* (Brussels: Peter Lang, 2014), pp. 15–35.

[107] Case C-43/75, *Defrenne v. Sabena* [1976] ECLI:EU:C:1976:56.

[108] See Case C-176/12, *Association de médiation sociale v. Union locale des syndicats CGT and Others* [2014] ECLI:EU:C:2014:2.

[109] See Case C-414/16, *Vera Egenberger v. Evangelisches Werk für Diakonie und Entwicklung e.V.* [2018] ECLI:EU:C:2018:257; Case C-68/17, *IR v. JQ* [2018] ECLI:EU:C:2018:696; Joined Cases C-569/16 and C-570/16, *Stadt Wuppertal and Volker Willmeroth als Inhaber der TWI Technische Wartung und Instandsetzung Volker Willmeroth e.K. v. Maria Elisabeth Bauer and Martina Broßonn* [2018] ECLI:EU:C:2018:871; Case C-684/16, *Max-Planck-Gesellschaft zur Förderung der Wissenschaften e.V. v. Tetsuji Shimizu* [2018] ECLI:EU:C:2018:874. For a discussion, see A. C. Ciacchi, 'The direct horizontal effect of EU fundamental rights: ECJ 17 April 2018, Case C-414/16, Vera Egenberger v Evangelisches Werk für Diakonie und Entwicklung e.V. and ECJ 11 September 2018, Case C-68/17, IR v JQ' (2019) 15 *European Constitutional Law Review* 2, 294–305.

particular, to privacy-related rights, embodied in Articles 7 and 8 of the Charter. In the *Google Spain* case, it articulated the right to be forgotten, relevant in the framework of the right to data protection and freedom of expression and information.[110] The case involved the interpretation of the Data Protection Directive in the dispute between Google and the Spanish data protection agency. It concerned the removal (delisting) of personal data available online. Among several questions addressed to the CJEU, important for this discussion is the question of whether, under the Directive, an individual who does not wish to make personal data available to internet users has the right to address a search engine directly and ask it to delist the personal information published on third parties' web pages.[111]

The CJEU resolved this question by famously concluding that if the activity of a search engine significantly affects the fundamental rights to privacy and the protection of personal data, the operator of the search engine 'must ensure [...] that the guarantees laid down by the directive may have full effect and that effective and complete protection of data subjects, in particular of their right to privacy [....]'.[112] Although the said Directive did not explicitly create the right for an individual to request the data processor to remove their personal data, the Court stressed that the Directive had to be interpreted as if it included such a right because of the effects the rights to privacy and the protection of private data, guaranteed in Articles 7 and 8 of the Charter, produced on the Directive.[113] Consequently, the CJEU concluded that, 'the data subject may, in the light of his fundamental rights under Articles 7 and 8 of the Charter, request that the information in question no longer be made available to the general public by its inclusion in such a list of results'.[114]

Although certifying that the Charter produced an indirect horizontal effect on EU secondary legislation, the CJEU nevertheless recognised that under the given circumstances, the legitimate general interest of the public in accessing information also existed. Balancing thus became necessary: 'A fair balance should be sought in particular between that interest [the legitimate interest of the public in accessing information] and the data subject's fundamental rights under Articles 7 and 8 of the Charter.'[115] The burden of the balance was put on the search engines, which, according to the CJEU, qualified as personal data controllers within the meaning

[110] Case C-131/12, *Google Spain SL and Google Inc. v Agencia Española de Protección de Datos (AEPD) and Mario Costeja González* [2014] ECLI:EU:C:2014:317, hereafter *Google Spain*. For the general comments of the case, see, e.g., F. Fabbrini and E. Celeste, 'The right to be forgotten in the digital age: the challenges of data protection beyond borders' (2020) 21 *German Law Journal* S1, 55–65.

[111] *Google Spain*, para. 20.

[112] Ibid., para. 38.

[113] Ibid., paras. 68–9.

[114] Ibid., para. 97. In subsequent rulings, the CJEU determined both the territorial and the material scope of the right to be forgotten. See Case C-507/17, *Google LLC v. CNIL* [2019] EU:C:2019:772 and Case C-136/17, *G.C. and others v. CNIL* [2019] EU:C:2019:773.

[115] *Google Spain*, para. 81.

of the Data Protection Directive and 'within its responsibilities, powers, and capabilities'.[116] According to this view, the CJEU acknowledged that these rights override, as a rule, the economic interest of the search engine operator and the general public's interest in having access to that information.[117]

Therefore, the ultimate outcome of the case carries the particular interest of the individual to have personal data delisted, the general interest of the public in accessing information, as well as the obligation of the search engine (e.g., Google), to balance the relevant rights when assessing users' requests to delist personal data from search results. The broader point here is that the *Google Spain* case exemplifies how consequential the indirect horizontal application of the Charter can be in practice, as the Court made both the Charter and the said Directive applicable in disputes between private parties.[118] Moreover, via its readiness to vest the Charter's privacy-related rights with horizontal effects, the CJEU reaffirmed another landmark decision on digital privacy in *Schrems I* – that the Data Protection Directive, since it regulates the processing of personal data and is liable to infringe fundamental freedoms, in particular, the right to respect private life, must always be interpreted in light of the Charter's rights.[119]

4.4 HOW THE HORIZONTALITY DOCTRINE HELPS PREVENT DIGITAL THREATS TO DEMOCRACY

The examples from German, Canadian, and the CJEU constitutional jurisprudence testify that the horizontal application of constitutional rights can accommodate both the concerns of those who object to any limitations to what is termed 'internet governance' and of those who insist on protecting rights online in the same manner as they are protected offline. Horizontality operating in the online world can also increase the democratic legitimacy of the online world. I will now turn my attention to this conclusion.

There is good reason to believe in the potential of the internet to upgrade democracy. Online communications and deliberations could help in developing an ideal, an internet-facilitated public sphere, with free discourse that could legitimise democratic government in Habermas's sense.[120] Illuminating such potentials, the UN Human Rights Council concluded that 'facilitating access to the internet for

[116] Ibid., para. 83.

[117] Ibid., para. 99.

[118] See more in De Gregorio, 'Digital constitutionalism across the Atlantic'; E. Frantziou, 'The horizontal effect of the Charter: towards an understanding of horizontality as a structural constitutional principle?' (2020) 22 *Cambridge Yearbook of European Legal Studies*, 208–32.

[119] Case C-362/14, *Maximillian Schrems v. Data Protection Commissioner* [2015] ECLI:EU:C:2015:650, para. 38. For more see Pollicino, *Judicial Protection of Fundamental Rights on the Internet*, pp. 132–41.

[120] J. Habermas, *The Structural Transformation of the Public Sphere: An Inquiry into a Category of Bourgeois Society* (Cambridge, MA: The MIT Press, 1991).

all individuals, with as little restriction to online content as possible, should be a priority for all States'.[121]

However, there is also good reason for concerns about digital threats to democracy, ranging from weakening election and referendum integrity (e.g., in the 2016 US elections and the Brexit referendum campaign) to disinformation or hate speech in the online public sphere and interference with opinion formation in social networks, especially when they produce extremism.[122] In the digital world, the allegations that democracy implies only the majority rule and that a democratic system should be highly responsive to popular will are more easily sold to the public than in the offline world. Consequently, social practices that form preferences may question the legitimacy of decision-making processes. In particular, as Stephen Holmes suggests, the individuals whose activities are left without constraints exercise more significant influence than those responsible for making decisions.[123] In the presence of the unconstrained majority, the garden-variety examples either from the offline or online worlds testify that individual rights are the first to suffer in these circumstances.

Now, what a democratic constitution tends to achieve is to minimise the tension between democracy and individual rights, as people are prone to overstate this tension.[124] Moreover, apart from the usual argument that human rights are undemocratic, some took comfort from the observation that individual rights could be reconciled with democracy only if perceived as serving majorities.[125] Yet, on this account, Cass Sunstein essentially denies that democracy is an antagonist to rights. On the contrary, a democratic constitution, he claims, protects rights and thus constrains 'what majorities can do to individuals or groups'.[126]

Following Sunstein, it is not hard to conclude that no other strategy to tame the power of the online platforms brings the online world closer to democracy than the radiating effect of constitutional rights on the internet. The explanation of why democratic control matters here is almost self-evident. On the one hand, in a functional constitutional democracy, human rights are subjected to effective protection, while sanctions for their violations are pre-conditioned by the government's democratic legitimacy, the rule of law, transparency requirements, and accountability under constitutional rules. On the other hand, the idea that the

[121] Special Rapporteur on the Promotion and Protection of the Right to Freedom of Opinion and Expression, Frank La Rue, Human Rights Council, P 2, U.N. Doc. A/HRC/17/27 (16 May 2011), www2.ohchr.org/english/bodies/hrcouncil/docs/17session/A.HRC.17.27_en.pdf.

[122] For more see M. L. Miller and C. Vaccari, 'Digital threats to democracy: comparative lessons and possible remedies' (2020) 25 *The International Journal of Press/Politics* 3, 333–56.

[123] S. Holmes, *Passions and Constraint: On the Theory of Liberal Democracy* (Chicago and London: The University of Chicago Press, 1995), p. 160.

[124] C. Sunstein, *Designing Democracy: What Constitutions Do* (Oxford: Oxford University Press, 2001), p. 7.

[125] See S. Moyn, 'On human rights and majority politics' (2019) 52 *Vanderbilt Law Review* 5, 1135–66.

[126] Sunstein, *Designing Democracy*, p. 7.

self-binding could be a strategy for the digital world was not comprehended initially. Those who maintained that some regulations were needed advocated the creation of a new system with no clear parallel in the offline world.[127] When internet governance emerged, it was established exclusively within the venue of private powers.

Thus, it turned out that those who make laws in the digital environment (a) order who can participate and who cannot in online communication, (b) design protocols and procedures in the case of digital rules' violations, and (c) are private entities, including online platforms and their self-regulating bodies. How they make choices related, for example, to freedom of speech, the protection of privacy, or the collection of personal data, even when they do it under formally observed human rights law, such as Facebook's Oversight Board, is left without democratic oversight. In other words, the power of the online platforms and their self-regulating bodies to design rules and control cyberspace compared with their accountability is underproportioned if not non-existent. The digital space's private order suffers from a democratic deficit, which, interpreted by Haggart and Keller, exists since 'private companies make the choices that set norms and directly influence the behavior of billions of users'.[128]

Adjusting the constitutional system to the horizontal effects of constitutional rights is a reactive strategy to what happens online, but it legitimises the rules affecting individual rights and delivers results grounded on the citizens' perceptions of what 'the correct outcome is' whenever rights should be balanced against general interests. In principle, when applied horizontally, the right to privacy or freedom of speech does not automatically prevail over the right of the online platform to conduct business but requires balancing, a process legitimised in the constitutional discourse whenever a court is asked to set aside a regulation of whatever kind, on the grounds of its non-compatibility with some constitutionally protected right.[129] On balance, it seems that under the horizontal model, no one loses; only democracy gains.

4.5 CONCLUSIONS

I have arrived at the end of a long trail of arguments offered to show why constitutional rights should be extended into the regime of internet governance, in particular to social platforms.

Social platforms have proven track records as to their capacity to pose harm to constitutional rights, which, according to the European Court of Human Rights, is

[127] D. R. Johnson and D. Post, 'Law and borders: the rise of law in cyberspace' (1996) 48 *Stanford Law Review* 5, 1367–402.

[128] B. Haggart and C. I. Keller, 'Democratic legitimacy in global platform governance' (2021) 45 *Telecommunications Policy* 6, Article 102152.

[129] Balancing is at the core of the proportionality doctrine that has origins in German and Canadian constitutional jurisprudence. For a discussion see, e.g., V. Jackson and M. Tushnet (eds.), *Proportionality: New Frontiers, New Challenges* (Cambridge: Cambridge University Press, 2017).

even greater than that posed by the press.[130] Although the view that constitutional rights protect all private persons but oblige only the state has been abandoned in some jurisdictions under the doctrine of the horizontal effects of constitutional rights, and although this doctrine is a ready-made vehicle to make social platforms responsible for the intrusions upon constitutional rights, the claim that everyone ought to have his or her rights protected against everyone is still disputable. To remind the reader, the division between public and private law still dominates in constitutional systems across the globe: it mirrors the position that individual rights impose obligations only on the state and not private actors. Therefore, rights do not regulate relations between private parties whose autonomy should remain free from the compulsory regime created by constitutions. However, knowing that the state is not the only bearer of political and economic power and that individual rights are also threatened by private actors, including those operating in the digital world, the rhetoric must be changed. This step does not require the recognition of new rights but the recognition of new duty holders in relation to existing rights, such as social platforms. The examples from Germany, Canada, and the EU, jurisdictions traditionally open to the horizontal enforcement of constitutional rights, illustrate its promising potential to remedy human rights abuses that happen online.

[130] *Editorial Board of Pravoye Delo and Shtekel v. Ukraine*, Application no. 33014/05, Judgment of 5 May 2011, para. 63.

5

How Do We Decide Whether Moving Online Makes a Difference?

Johanas Baltrimas

5.1 INTRODUCTION

One of the best ways to comprehend what difference it makes to move online is to compare cases that differ essentially on the basis of only one thing – one of them is online.

In some cases, moving online might make a difference to how the law works. Identifying those particular cases (as well as those where the digital factor does not make a difference) is a worthwhile theoretical task. However, there is another related question that carries a similar significance: How can courts decide whether in a particular case moving online should make a difference on how the law works? This chapter presents a study with the aim of exploring this question.

Getting acquainted with this process can provide greater clarity on this relatively new phenomenon and stimulate new theoretical insights. Having knowledge of criteria relevant for the discussed decisions has the potential of impacting legal practice by making judicial decisions more predictable and substantiated. Rich and comprehensive reasoning in legal documents is an attractive alternative to legal documents that provide scarce citations of laws and actual logical links, which lead to the conclusion of relying on the intuition of the lawyer.

5.2 BEFORE WE BEGIN

Legal theory proposes several ways to determine whether a new case requires a different treatment. In this context, the assessment would require to decide whether a new fact requires a departure. One of the most famous tests, which requires taking into account only the material facts, was devised by Arthur L. Goodhart for the application of precedents.[1] Julius Stone explained this method by directing to seek a reason that explains whether the later case provides grounds for the same outcome as the

[1] A. L. Goodhart, 'Determining the ratio decidendi of a case' (1930) 40 *Yale Law Review* 2, 161–83; A. L. Goodhart, 'The ratio decidendi of a case' (1959) 22 *Modern Law Review* 2, 117–30; T. Bustamante et al., *On the Philosophy of Precedent: Proceedings of the 24th World Congress of the International Association for Philosophy of Law and Social Philosophy, Beijing, 2009* (Stuttgart: Franz Steiner

precedent.[2] However, the more prevailing approach for precedents is the rule model that is sometimes described as the *ratio decidendi*, perceived as a legal rule that the judge used as necessary to justify the conclusion of the precedential judgment.[3] It is a widespread view that was aptly worded by Karl N. Llewellyn, that we have to keep in mind the reason for the rule (accordingly, apply it where the reason extends and rethink the rule where the reason becomes irrelevant or is found to be wrongful).[4] The concept of *purpose* is also discussed in the application of precedents. This can be used as the goal of a particular judicial precedent – the reasoning on which the precedent was based and the purpose of relevant legal categories, such as particular individual rights or obligations.[5] The purpose of judicial precedent can aid as a reason in the assessment of whether its *ratio decidendi* is applicable (according to the purpose that justifies it).[6] However, it can be hypothesised that evaluating the legal relevance of a factual difference is not chaotic beyond the limits of the aforementioned criteria, and a deeper examination reveals certain patterns, especially in the context of moving online.

A specific test to evaluate whether a digital factor affects the decision to apply a particular legal rule can be carried out only after there are general indications that the considered rule could be applicable. This chapter presents research on cases where a rule can be found, which was designed for legal relations in the non-digital space, and a new situation occurs, which differs in the sense that it takes place in a digital environment. However, before acknowledging that it is the only difference, a regular evaluation of the rule's applicability must first be conducted.

5.2.1 *Similar Aspects in Dissimilar Cases*

The discussed initial evaluation could be regarded as a typical process in everyday legal practice. However, it is worth remembering that these issues should not be confused with novel legal challenges posed by the cases of focus here. Otherwise, such confusion risks that the conventional tools of legal reasoning be neglected, where they are actually appropriate.

Verlag, 2012); I. McLeod, *Legal Method* (London: Palgrave Macmillan, 2007); J. L. Montrose, 'Ratio decidendi and the House of Lords' (1957) 20 *Modern Law Review* 2, 124–30.

2 J. Stone, *Precedent and Law: Dynamics of Common Law Growth* (Sydney: Butterworths, 1985), p. 123.

3 R. Cross and J. W. Harris, *Precedent in English Law* (Oxford: Clarendon Press, 2004), p. 72; W. M. Landes and R. A. Posner, 'Legal precedent: a theoretical and empirical analysis' (1976) 19 *Journal of Law and Economics* 2, 249–307, at 250; L. Alexander and E. Sherwin, 'Judges as rulemakers' (2004) 15 *University of San Diego Public Law and Legal Theory Research Paper Series*, 1–36; L. Alexander and E. Sherwin, *Demystifying Legal Reasoning* (Cambridge: Cambridge University Press, 2008).

4 K. N. Llewellyn, *Jurisprudence: Realism in Theory and Practice* (New Brunswick: Transaction Publishers, 2008), p. 117; K. N. Llewellyn, *The Bramble Bush: On Our Law and Its Study* (New York: Oceana Publications, 1991), p. 189.

5 G. Lamond, 'Do precedents create rules?' (2005) 11 *Legal Theory* 1, 1–26, at 7; J. Raz, *The Authority of Law. Essays on Law and Morality* (Oxford: Clarendon Press, 1979), p. 203.

6 J. F. Horty, *Rules and Reasons in the Theory of Precedent* (Cambridge: Cambridge University Press, 2011), p. 6.

On 19 April 2018, the Court of Appeal of Ireland delivered a judgment in *Muwema v. Facebook Ireland Limited* that is an important reminder in the context of the initial evaluation.[7] This case involved a legal problem regarding a required standard of proof to issue an order of disclosure. The order was requested against the operator of a social network – Facebook – to disclose the identity of its user. The respondent protested this request, arguing that the user in question would be exposed to arrest and ill-treatment at the hands of the authorities in Uganda whom he opposed. The court provided grounds for the solution of this issue in earlier precedents, which not only did not have the element of the digital space but was also established in rather different cases. The court mentioned *Foley v. Sunday Newspapers Ltd* (2005) regarding an injunction to prevent the publication by the defendant of an article that, if published, the plaintiff considered would place at real and serious risk his right to life and/or right to bodily integrity.[8] Another case was even more distant from the relevant circumstances and was decided in the context of the surrender of a person to Poland under a European arrest warrant. However, all these cases included the same sort of question of balancing one person's right to life and bodily integrity against other concepts guarded by law (e.g., another person's freedom of expression). The court relied on the aforementioned precedents and stated that 'there is no reason why the court should not require the same standard of proof in relation to an assertion by the plaintiff seeking a Norwich Pharmacal order where the court is required to carry out a balancing exercise between competing constitutional rights'. This common denominator can be formulated as follows – *where different cases involve the balancing of the same individual rights, this connection can be sufficient to make these cases comparable both in the digital and physical context.*

The most important takeaway from this example is that legal provisions might be relevant even if they do not contain a typically applicable legal rule. There are undoubtedly numerous examples, which confirm that in legal practice judicial precedents are not only used in cases where all material facts coincide but also where the cases are quite different. The Muwema case confirms that the explored class of cases cannot be held as an absolute exception of this tendency – going online does not cancel the ruling.

5.2.2 *Sometimes: Not Merely a Difference but a Wholly Different Affair*

Reasoning algorithms in the preparatory stage must consider a probable scenario where no applicable rule can be found in statutory law or judicial precedents. This type of crossroad leads to one of two paths: either courts (a) recognise there is no regulation, or somehow (b) justify the application of an old rule, which was not initially intended for such cases.

7 *Muwema v. Facebook Ireland Limited* [2018] IECA 104.
8 *Foley v. Sunday Newspapers Ltd* [2005] IEHC 14.

Naturally, courts can be inclined towards the second path, since the first can require the creation of new rules that is only in the power of parliaments, not the judiciary. However, the first path may not require this and can lead to an outcome that is strongly dependent on one of these principles – 'everything that is not forbidden is allowed' or 'everything that is not allowed is forbidden'. A particular outcome might vary according to the type of legal issue. If it is a matter of criminal liability, the defendant is acquitted. Similarly, a new type of commercial business cannot be treated as requiring a prior licence (and be seen as illegal) if it conceptually differs from the licensed form of commercial activities. However, in cases of a civil dispute between two private persons, different interests must be balanced – the court cannot refuse to resolve the dispute because there is no legal rule.

The last scenario applies usually in cases where courts might have to create a new rule. One case containing factual circumstances that do not have any analogical counterparts in the non-online environment is the *Google LLC v. Oracle America, Inc.* case.[9] It was resolved by the US Supreme Court judgment of 5 April 2021. This case concerned copyright infringement when a certain type of computer code was copied – the copied lines of code were part of a user interface for programmers to access prewritten computer code through the use of simple commands. As a result, this code is different from many other types of code. The copied lines are part of a tool called an Application Programming Interface. The court found applicable law in general provisions regarding copyright infringement, but it decided to distinguish the case from others regarding copying computer code – this unique type of code was treated differently. One of the reasons was that it was widely used by programmers and, given how much the programmers had invested in learning it, enforcement of copyright would limit the future creativity of new programs. Therefore, the enforcement would interfere with rather than further the copyright's basic creativity objectives – the 'copyright supplies the economic incentive to [both] create and disseminate ideas [...] and the reimplementation of a user interface allows creative new computer code to more easily enter the market'. This shows that the US Supreme Court took into consideration the social impact of the decision and objectives of the law, but, most importantly, this case demonstrates that even though judicial precedents could be found that, at first sight, appeared applicable, the Court decided to distinguish the case and, in a way, create a new rule.

5.3 PURPOSE AND FUNCTION OF THE DISPUTED OBJECT OR ACTIONS

Among the criteria used in the analysed cases, the purpose of the disputed object was used very frequently. One such example can be found in *Magyar Jeti Zrt v. Hungary*

9 *Google LLC v. Oracle America, Inc.*, 593 US 1 (2021).

of the European Court of Human Rights (ECtHR).[10] In this case, a violation of the European Convention on Human Rights (ECHR) was found after domestic authorities held an online news portal liable for posting a hyperlink leading to defamatory content. The courts established the objective liability of the news portal: although the practice of the domestic courts exempted the publishers from civil liability for the reproduction of statements made at press conferences, provided that they were reporting on a matter of public interest in an unbiased and objective manner, distinguished themselves from the source of the statement, and gave an opportunity to the person concerned to comment on the statement. However, the domestic courts decided that in this case of posting a hyperlink to defamatory information, the standard of objective liability applied, irrespective of the question of whether the author or publisher acted in good or bad faith and in compliance with their journalistic duties and obligations.

The ECtHR noted that:

> the very purpose of hyperlinks is, by directing to other pages and web resources, to allow Internet users to navigate to and from material in a network characterised by the availability of an immense amount of information. Hyperlinks contribute to the smooth operation of the Internet by making information accessible through linking it to each other. Hyperlinks, as a technique of reporting, are essentially different from traditional acts of publication in that, as a general rule, they merely direct users to content available elsewhere on the Internet. They do not present the linked statements to the audience or communicate its content, but only serve to call readers' attention to the existence of material on another website.[11]

Taking into account this and other reasons, the ECtHR decided that the domestic authorities violated the applicant's freedom of expression by applying the standard of objective liability, which was not used in similar non-digital circumstances.

In the C–264/14 case,[12] the European Court of Justice (ECJ) was faced with an issue regarding the taxation of transactions where traditional currency was exchanged for virtual currency – Bitcoin. The ECJ had to decide whether in this context virtual currency could be characterised as security and tangible property or fall into the same category as traditional currency. In this discussion, the purpose of virtual currency was also recognised as a relevant factor. The ECJ noted that:

> [t]ransactions involving non-traditional currencies, that is to say, currencies other than those that are legal tender in one or more countries, in so far as those currencies have been accepted by the parties to a transaction as an alternative to legal tender and have no purpose other than to be a means of payment, are financial transactions [...] the 'bitcoin' virtual currency has no other purpose than to be a means of payment and that it is accepted for that purpose by certain operators.

10 *Magyar Jeti Zrt v. Hungary*, Application no. 11257/2016, Judgment of 4 December 2018.
11 Ibid., paras. 73–4.
12 Case C-264/14, *Skatteverket v. David Hedqvist* [2015] ECLI:EU:C:2015:718.

This led the court to the conclusion that this virtual currency is neither a security conferring a property right, nor a security of a comparable nature.

Case No. C-360/13 of the same court concerned the legality of making digital cached copies of copyrighted material on the internet.[13] Among other things, the court considered the application of EU law, according to which an act of reproduction is exempted from the reproduction right on condition that it is temporary, it is transient or incidental, it is an integral and essential part of a technological process, its sole purpose is to enable a transmission in a network between third parties by an intermediary, or a lawful use of a work or other subject-matter to be made, and has no independent economic significance. Although, the purpose of a copy is a separate condition according to this rule, the court recognised the purpose of the disputed copies in consideration of other factors. The judgment states:

> As regards the other criterion mentioned in paragraph 39 above, an act of reproduction can be regarded as 'incidental' if it neither exists independently of, nor has a purpose independent of, the technological process of which it forms part [...] the *technological process in question wholly determines the purpose* for which those copies are created and used, although, as is apparent from paragraph 34 above, that process can function, albeit less efficiently, without such copies being made. Secondly, it is apparent from the documents before the Court that internet users employing the technological process at issue in the main proceedings cannot create the cached copies outside of that process [...] It follows that *the cached copies neither exist independently of, nor have a purpose independent of, the technological process* at issue in the main proceedings and must, for that reason, be regarded as 'incidental'. [emphasis added]

Another example is case No. C–390/18,[14] which revolved around the issue of applicable domestic law for a new sort of business provided by the Airbnb Ireland company. This issue was determined by answering the question: Can this new sort of economic activity be treated as the profession of a real estate agent? Doubts were substantiated, among other things, by the fact that apart from the service of connecting hosts and guests using an electronic platform, Airbnb Ireland offers hosts a certain number of other services, such as a format for setting out the content of their offer, with an option for a photography service, an optional tool for estimating the rental price with regard to market averages taken from that platform, and many other supplemental services. The ECJ took into account the purpose of those services – according to the court:

> ...it follows that an intermediation service such as the one provided by Airbnb Ireland cannot be regarded as forming an integral part of an overall service, the main component of which is the provision of accommodation. None of the other services [...] above, taken together or in isolation, call into question that finding.

[13] Case C-360/13, *Public Relations Consultants Association Ltd. v. Newspaper Licensing Agency Ltd and Others* [2014] ECLI:EU:C:2014:1195.

[14] Case C-390/18, *Airbnb Ireland UC* [2019] ECLI:EU:C:2019:1112.

On the contrary, *such services are ancillary in nature, given that, for the hosts, they do not constitute an end in themselves, but rather a means of benefiting from the intermediation service* provided by Airbnb Ireland or of offering accommodation services in the best conditions [emphasis added].

Case No. C–62/19 involved questions related to the legality of a smartphone application 'STAR TAXI – driver', which was used in the field of transportation services.[15] The dilemma in this case was of a similar kind to the one in the Airbnb Ireland case: Is the law for a traditional sort of business applicable to a new type of business? Accordingly, the similarity of this application to traditional taxi services had to be assessed. The ECJ emphasised the purpose of the disputed services from more than one perspective. First, it was noted that the direct contractors of the disputed Star Taxi App were legally authorised professional taxi drivers and the *purpose* of the contracts with drivers is:

> …to provide the drivers with an IT application, called *STAR TAXI – driver*, a smartphone on which the application has been installed, and a SIM card including a limited amount of data, in exchange for a monthly subscription fee […] Star Taxi App does not exercise any control over the quality of the vehicles or their drivers, or over the drivers' conduct.

The court recognised this as a material difference distinguishing this case from an earlier similar dispute regarding the intermediation of a taxi transportation service – in the precedent, the purpose of the intermediation service was to connect, by means of a smartphone application and for remuneration, non-professional drivers using their own vehicle with persons wishing to make urban journeys. In the precedent, the ECJ decided that the service was to be classified as a 'service in the field of transport', but the Star Taxi App was classified differently. Furthermore, the ECJ concluded that the disputed decision of the domestic authorities (which was restricting) related to:

> …intermediation services, the *purpose* of which is to put persons wishing to make urban journeys in touch, by means of a smartphone application and in exchange for remuneration, with authorised taxi drivers, it does no more, in broadening the scope of the term 'dispatching' […] so as to encompass that type of service, than to extend to that information society service a pre-existing requirement for prior authorisation applicable to the activities of taxi reservation centres [emphasis added].

5.4 ACTUAL HARM: DOES GOING ONLINE AFFECT THE EXTENT OF HARM/DAMAGES MADE BY THE DISPUTED ACT?

It is natural that a lawmaker chooses to forbid certain actions or inactions when they violate someone's individual rights, cause damage to values protected by law,

[15] Case C-62/19, *Star Taxi App SRL v. Unitatea Administrativ Teritorială Municipiul Bucureşti prin Primar General and others* [2020] ECLI:EU:C:2020:980.

or raises the risk of these occurrences. The line of lawfulness turns interference with someone's interests into an illegal violation of someone's individual rights. There are multiple examples of this criterion, such as violating property rights by damaging private property, violating the freedom of expression by imposing a fine for a published opinion, and so on. Illegal damage to values protected by law can sometimes have no interference with an individual's rights, but be in violation of what is often called public interest. Examples of the latter can be violations of environmental law, animal cruelty, tax evasion, and so on. But sometimes the law forbids actions that do none of these – the prohibition to drive under the influence of alcohol or without a seatbelt; to disregard safety requirements on building construction sites, and so on. Although this behaviour does not necessarily violate someone's individual rights or cause damage to values protected by law, it raises such risks; therefore this sort of legal regulation can be justifiable.

Although these considerations can usually be found in the process of lawmaking in parliaments, it is hard to find strong reasons to neglect them in the judicial interpretation of the law. Naturally, they are most relevant when the law is unclear and there are no precedents in similar cases or distinguishing the cases is considered. Disputes with a digital element are no exception.

In *Savva Terentyev v. Russia*,[16] the ECtHR found a violation of Article 10 of the ECHR because domestic authorities convicted the applicant and suspended the prison sentence for an offensive internet comment against police officers. Perhaps the most important reason the ECtHR relied on was the fact that the domestic courts did not evaluate the actual consequences of the comment, but merely relied on its text:

> …applicant posted his comment on an individual blog of his acquaintance, […] courts, however, do not appear to have ever attempted to assess whether Mr B.S.'s blog was generally highly visited, or to establish the actual number of users who had accessed that blog during the period when the applicant's comment remained available […] the applicant's comment had remained online for one month before the applicant, who found out the reasons for a criminal case against him, removed it […]. Although the access to the impugned statement had not been restricted, it drew seemingly very little public attention. Indeed, even a number of the applicant's acquaintances remained unaware of it, and, it appears it was only the criminal prosecution of the applicant for his online publication that prompted the interest of the public towards his comment […]. It is also important to note that, at the time of the events under examination, the applicant does not appear to have been a well-known blogger or a popular user of social media […], let alone a public or influential figure […], which fact could have attracted public attention to his comment and thus have enhanced the potential impact of the impugned statements. In such circumstances the Court considers that the potential of the applicant's comment

16 *Savva Terentyev v. Russia*, Application no. 10692/09, Judgment of 28 August 2018.

> to reach the public and thus to influence its opinion was very limited [...] although the wording of the impugned statements was, indeed, offensive, insulting and virulent [...], they cannot be seen as stirring up base emotions or embedded prejudices in an attempt to incite hatred or violence against the Russian police officers [...] The Court furthermore discerns no other elements, either in the domestic courts' decisions or in the Government's submission, which would enable it to conclude that the applicant's comment had the potential to provoke any violence with regard to the Russian police officers, and thus posed a clear and imminent danger which required the applicant's criminal prosecution and conviction.

Beizaras and Levickas v. Lithuania is another example of this sort of reasoning.[17] In this case, the ECtHR found a violation of the fourteenth article of the Convention because the domestic authorities refused to prosecute authors of serious homophobic comments on Facebook without an effective investigation beforehand. The applicants were two young men, one of whom had posted a photograph of the couple kissing on his Facebook page. This online post went viral and received hundreds of virulent homophobic comments (containing, for example, calls to 'castrate', 'kill', and 'burn' the applicants).

At the applicants' request, a non-government organisation upholding the rights of LGBTQ+ people (of which they were members) lodged a complaint with the prosecutor's office against thirty-one of these comments, asking the prosecution service to open an investigation for incitement to homophobic hatred and violence. The ECtHR agreed with the aforementioned NGO's position that 'the number of comments could constitute a circumstance determining the gravity of the crime or the extent of the culprit's criminal liability, but that it did not constitute an indispensable element of the crime under the above-mentioned provision of the Criminal Code'. The ECtHR continued to evaluate this by noting, while the comments were in the public sphere, what was the 'potential reach of comments on the Internet, as well as the danger they may cause, especially when published on popular Internet websites'; and that 'the photograph had "gone viral" online and received more than 800 comments'. It was mentioned that 'the potential impact of the medium concerned is an important factor'. Besides these circumstances, which can be found in the digital space, the judgment also includes a notion that 'the comments on the first applicant's Facebook page [...] affected the applicants' psychological well-being and dignity, thus falling within the sphere of their private life'. Although the ECtHR mentioned that 'the posting of even a single hateful comment, let alone a comment that such persons should be "killed," on the first applicant's Facebook page was sufficient to be taken seriously', the whole of the reasoning does not eliminate the real possibility that the court's final conclusion could have been different if the comments were not as serious and their reach was significantly lower.

[17] *Beizaras and Levickas v. Lithuania*, Application no. 41288/15, Judgment of 14 January 2020.

The judgment by the Grand Chamber of the ECtHR on 20 January 2020 in *Magyar Kétfarkú Kutya Párt v. Hungary* concerns a curious example of a new unique form of political campaigning enabled by internet technologies.[18] The ECtHR found that Hungarian authorities violated the freedom of expression of the applicant (the political party Magyar Kétfarkú Kutya Párt (MKKP)) by holding it liable for making available a mobile application allowing voters to share anonymous photographs of their ballot papers. The events occurred in a referendum related to the European Union's (EU's) migration relocation plan. The referendum was initiated by the Hungarian government, and the applicant, being an oppositional party, was campaigning against the referendum, encouraging voters to destroy their ballot papers. One of the ways the MKKP conducted the campaign was by making available a mobile application called 'Cast an invalid ballot', which enabled users to upload and share with other users, anonymously, photographs of their ballots or a photograph of the activity they were engaged in instead of voting. The ECtHR found that the domestic authorities imposed penalties for this act without a clearly prescribed law. The law, on which courts relied, established a principle of the exercise of rights in accordance with their purpose. The ECtHR stated that:

> having regard to the particular importance of the foreseeability of the law when it comes to restricting the freedom of expression of a political party in the context of an election or a referendum […], the Court takes the view that the considerable uncertainty about the potential effects of the impugned legal provisions applied by the domestic authorities exceeded what is acceptable under Article 10 § 2 of the Convention.

Here, the ECtHR decided on a matter that at first sight might seem to concern only the text of the statute – liability for an offence can be estimated as unprescribed by law when the statute does not expressly prohibit such behaviour. On the one hand, this can be said about the discussed case, but on the other hand, the law could also be regarded as abstract, and the ECtHR admits that in other cases some level of vagueness in the law can be tolerated, as long as it is clarified in the domestic judicial case law. With that in mind, the quote displays that the context where the freedom of expression was exercised involved political activities with the potential of significant societal impact. This impact might even concern the fundamental values of democratic order. In this case, an indirect equivalent of considered acts (the issuing of a mobile application) might have been some sort of physical display of analogical photographs, perhaps communicating them through less modern channels of communication. But in this case, the online factor was not decisive. The court followed a traditional path of legal reasoning, which coincidentally led to an unregulated field; therefore, there was a need for a new rule to be established

[18] *Magyar Kétfarkú Kutya Párt v. Hungary*, Application no. 201/17, Judgment of 20 January 2020.

according to judicial precedent, which was drafted with regard to the extent of damages from interference with the applicant's freedom of expression.

On 13 May 2014, the ECJ adopted a famous decision in *Google Spain SL, Google Inc. v. Agencia Española de Protección de Datos, Mario Costeja González* – case No. C-131/12,[19] regarding the right to be forgotten. This decision basically established that individuals have the right to request search engines, such as Google, to remove certain links from their search results if the information is outdated, irrelevant, or infringes their privacy rights. This decision includes the following statement: 'the effect of the interference with those rights of the data subject is heightened on account of the important role played by the internet and search engines in modern society, which render the information contained in such a list of results ubiquitous'.

What this precedent contrasts with in a non-digital environment is the legal status of the paper archives of newspapers. If the right to be forgotten rule was universal, there would be very little reason not to enforce it for public libraries and other archives. However, it was constructed and recognised only when the traditional paper archives attained a counterpart in a digital environment. This counterpart – internet search engines – differs mostly in terms of the ease of access to the requested data for a non-professional domestic user, which means that interference with a person's right to privacy in digital archives (i.e., search engines) is much greater than the same interference in non-digital archives, such as public libraries. This ECJ case is an example where the extent of harm/damages made by the disputed act in a digital environment had an enormous significance compared with other judicial cases.

5.5 AFTER WE FINISH

5.5.1 *Established Theory*

It is an understatement to say that some research has been conducted on legal reasoning or the impact of the internet: there is a plethora of academic publications tackling particular legal issues in the digital space. Among other things, they include artificial intelligence (AI) liability,[20] data protection and privacy,[21] copyright

[19] Case C-131/12, *Google Spain SL, Google Inc. v Agencia Española de Protección de Datos, Mario Costeja González* [2014] ECLI:EU:C:2014:317.

[20] E.g., G. Borges and C. Sorge (eds.), *Law and Technology in a Global Digital Society: Autonomous Systems, Big Data, IT Security and Legal Tech* (Cham: Springer Nature, 2022); G. Borges, 'Liability for AI systems under current and future law: an overview of the key changes envisioned by the Proposal of an EU Directive on Liability for AI' (2023) 24 *Computer Law Review International* 1, 1–8; P. H. Padovan, C. M. Martins, and C. Reed, 'Black is the new orange: how to determine AI liability' (2023) 31 *Artificial Intelligence and Law* 1, 136–67.

[21] E. K. Cortez (ed.), *Data Protection Around the World: Privacy Laws in Action* (The Hague: T.M.C. Asser Press, 2021); S. O'Leary, 'Balancing rights in a digital age' (2018) 59 *Irish Jurist*, 59–92; D. J. Solove, *Understanding Privacy* (Cambridge, MA: Harvard University Press, 2008).

law,[22] and others. However, very few address the issue of legal reasoning in this context. Naturally, a substantial number of findings on this topic are applicable to disputes in the field of modern internet technologies. It would be beyond the format of this publication to list all of the relevant insights on legal reasoning, but some of them are noteworthy because they focus on the matter of *refreshing* the law.

In legal disputes, the question 'what difference does going online make' (if at all) can be particularly hard to answer when judicial precedents can be found and they appear to come from similar cases. Often most of the material facts can be similar, except the online factor. Legal literature provides some insights into when precedents must be followed and when departed from.

Changes in the social, moral, and economic contexts are among the most widely mentioned reasons to overrule a judicial precedent.[23] Other, more detailed, justifications for a departure from precedents by overturning them include subsequent changes or developments in the law that undermine the rationale of the earlier decision; a need to bring a decision into agreement with experience and with facts newly ascertained; the precedent can be shown to have become a detriment to coherence and consistency in the law; a mistake exists in the precedent; the precedent is unworkable or badly reasoned; the departure can be justified by the possible significance of intervening events or the possible impact of settled expectations;[24] and where there are serious and objective reasons and where 'the new solution better reflects the *ratio legis*, changed circumstances or altered legal views'.[25] In summary, it can also be said that overruling a precedent, when deciding a case based on how it was resolved earlier is suitable for the former, but not the present situation, and in light of new circumstances, the same empirical results that were reached in the precedent case cannot be achieved in the present case using the same measures. Every time we consider a departure from a precedent, it is useful to evaluate the role of the judicial precedent's prerequisites in the particular case – how strong could the legal expectations have been, could the departure have been predicted, and so on.[26] Chris Reed is one of the few authors who have analysed in depth the issue of the legal significance of the internet (as a factor requiring different legal treatment).[27] In

[22] L. Bently et al., *Intellectual Property Law*, sixth edition (Oxford: Oxford University Press, 2022); P. Goldstein and B. Hugenholtz, *International Copyright: Principles, Law, and Practice* (Oxford: Oxford University Press, 2019).

[23] See, e.g., M. Jacob, *Precedents and Case-Based Reasoning in the European Court of Justice* (Cambridge: Cambridge University Press, 2014), p. 175; A. Ross, *On Law and Justice* (Clark, NJ: The Lawbook Exchange Ltd, 2004), p. 86.

[24] S. Brenner and H. J. Spaeth, *Stare Indecisis: The Alteration of Precedent on the Supreme Court, 1946–1992* (Cambridge: Cambridge University Press, 1995), p. 8.

[25] C. Baudenbacher and S. Planzer (eds.), *International Dispute Resolution. The Role of Precedent* (Stuttgart: German Law Publishers, 2010), p. 17.

[26] J. Baltrimas, 'Judicial precedent: authority and functioning', Summary of Doctoral Dissertation (2017), pp. 28–9.

[27] C. Reed, 'Online and offline equivalence: aspiration and achievement' (2010) 18 *International Journal of Law and Information Technology* 3, 248–73.

his paper 'Online and offline equivalence: aspiration and achievement', Reed lays down insightful observations on when the online factor is sufficient for a different legal treatment and proposes a methodology for the rules of behaviour regulation: (a) identifying the various interests that the rule needs to take into account; (b) analysing the ways in which the new rule is likely to affect those interests; and (c) evaluating the resultant balance of interests to decide if it is equivalent to the offline situation.[28] Although this test of interest-balancing is undoubtedly valuable for legal reasoning, the judicial judgments adopted after Reed's paper was published display a large set of supplemental modes or reasoning. In addition, the question of whether going online makes a difference is sometimes followed by the question of whether going online *still* makes a difference (or not). This issue is presented in the following section.

5.5.2 *Differences That Vanish*

Sometimes 'going online' makes a difference that is not permanent. Established precedents on the matter of a certain online phenomenon can become outdated if the underlying reasons for those precedents are no longer applicable because of technological developments. So, an important question to keep in mind is how judicial precedents on this matter function. It was already mentioned that with important changes precedents might become obsolete, which is partly illustrated by most of the cases presented in this chapter.

The presented cases show the significance of the purpose of the disputed object or actions and the significance of the actual extent of the harm from the act under consideration. But the theory on precedents in many of these cases provides an important notice – transferring to a digital environment is not the last step. *Going online often does make a difference but after we are there, developments of modern technologies can continue making changes.*

In the *Pihl v. Sweden* case,[29] the ECtHR found that an application regarding an alleged failure by domestic authorities to hold a service provider responsible for the content of third-party comments on a blog was inadmissible. The applicant included a complaint that, although a defamatory comment on the internet was removed and a new post was added on the blog by the association stating that the earlier post had been wrong and based on inaccurate information, according to the applicant, it was still possible to find the old post and the comment on the internet via search engines. The court responded to this by pointing out that 'the applicant is entitled to request that the search engines remove any such traces of the comment (see the ECJ judgment of 13 May 2014, *Google Spain* and *Google*, no. C-131/12, EU:C:2014:317)'. This offers room to speculate what would the ECtHR's view be if

[28] Ibid., p. 256.

[29] *Pihl v. Sweden* [ECHR], Application no. 74742/14, Judgment of 9 March 2017.

this case had taken place before the ECJ established the right to be forgotten. There cannot be a definitive answer, but if we strictly follow the rules of formal logic, this alternative hypothetical scenario should turn out differently (if there were no other decisive circumstances).

An even stronger example of the relevant developments is the case of *Ashcroft v. American Civil Liberties Union*, et al. 535 U.S. 564 (2002) presided over by the Supreme Court of the US. In this case the legality of the Child Online Protection Act (COPA) was reviewed. This act restricted publishing indecent material on the internet that can be harmful to children. One of the reasons mentioned in this case was a statement by the Court of Appeals that prior community standards jurisprudence 'has no applicability to the Internet and the Web' because 'Web publishers are currently without the ability to control the geographic scope of the recipients of their communications'. It was argued that 'COPA is "unconstitutionally overbroad" because it requires Web publishers to shield some material behind age verification screens that could be displayed openly in many communities across the Nation if Web speakers were able to limit access to their sites on a geographic basis'. The Court noted that 'given Internet speakers' inability to control the geographic location of their audience, expecting them to bear the burden of controlling the recipients of their speech, as we did in Hamling and Sable, may be entirely too much to ask, and would potentially suppress an inordinate amount of expression'. However, in today's world there are numerous cases where courts impose restrictions on the content on the internet that confine it to certain geographic locations. Contemporary technology is much more capable of controlling the geographic scope of the recipients, which makes the aforementioned US Supreme Court's reasoning in this *Ashcroft v. American Civil Liberties Union* case basically obsolete.

5.6 THE IMPLICATIONS

In legal practice, it is very common to follow a collection of universally recognised legal principles, such as the principle of proportionality, *nullum crimen sine lege*, *pacta sund servanda*, *in dubio pro reo*, *ignorantia legis neminem excusat*, and many others. In this, they are taken as a given, and it is rarely asked who (and when) created those principles. The usual first answer could be that they were crafted by ancient Roman legal scholars or (and) forged in judicial practice. Should it not be encouraged to keep raising the questions: Are we done with drafting legal principles? Are they all already discovered? Perhaps some of them already exist between the lines of judicial case law and the only step left is to give them the title of 'principles'.

If we do not require the sanction of the lawmaker to present the title 'principle', there is no other more reliable source for discovering legal principles than the tendencies in judicial case law. With proper respect to David Hume's guillotine, it cannot be denied that, when the statutory law is not amended, there is no better way to predict future judicial decisions than on the basis of past judicial decisions – to predict what will be done by recognising what is being done. Articulating those tendencies can help initiate a discussion about whether what the courts are doing should be amended. If we come to the conclusion that there is no such need, more extensive reasoning can better help reflect the reasoning process that took place in the judge's intuition or maybe even help her come up with a better solution overall. This consideration is reminiscent of a big-picture question concerning the goals of methods for legal reasoning overall: What are they? What should they be? If those goals include a more representative articulation of the judge's thought process and help to achieve a more just and beneficial judgment, then the search for principles that are yet to be given the title of 'principles' should be carried out.

In this chapter, two main tendencies of judicial practice were found – the relevance of the purpose or function of the disputed object or actions and the extent of harm. Judicial practice in the future has the tools to keep 'polishing' these and, perhaps, one day title them principles. The first has the potential to be worded as a principle that 'similar actions or objects in different contexts receive a similar legal treatment if their purpose and function does not differ'. The second – 'an act that is incompatible with the text of law but causes no harm or any risk of it will be treated as lawful'. The latter also might have the potential to be worded *a contrario* – 'an act which causes harm or the risk of it will be treated as unlawful, even if its incompatibility with the text of the law is vague'. Of course, these preliminary wordings are imperfect and legal professionals should be able to come up with significantly improved versions to describe the tendencies presented in this chapter.

5.7 CONCLUSIONS

The analysed cases illustrate that when faced with the task of resolving whether going online makes a difference, the courts, among other things, consider (a) the purpose and function of the disputed object or actions, and (b) the extent of harm/damages made by the disputed behaviour or act. These criteria might be helpful when analogical objects or actions can be found in a non-digital environment, which is already regulated by clearly established legal rules. The evaluation of similarities between cases according to these criteria focus on material facts and can be useful in concluding whether differences between similar cases in digital and non-digital environments are legally relevant or do not have more significance than the hair colour of the litigants.

The purpose and function of the disputed objects or actions can be relevant in comparison with the purpose and function of analogical objects or actions in a non-digital environment. If they are different, the 'online' case may receive a different legal treatment from its non-digital counterpart, and by contrast, when they are not different, they may receive the same legal treatment.

The extent of harm/damages made by the disputed act influences the conclusion about whether going online makes a difference in an intuitive way, which can be typical in all sorts of legal disputes – when there is no discernible harm, the behaviour can be treated as lawful. Correspondingly, when an act balances on the boundaries of legality according to the text of the law, it can be recognised as unlawful when this act causes considerable harm.

These findings also force us to propose a theoretical hypothesis: Can going online ever make a difference by itself? Perhaps a different legal treatment based solely on the difference of this circumstance is a rarity and can only be found when going online has other consequences (e.g., different levels of harm as a result of the illegal content being easier to access through the internet). However, since the presented study was not quantitative, further research would be necessary in order to confirm this statement.

The pure evaluation of whether going online makes a difference in itself is only part of the process arising from disputes in the context of technological innovations. There are important insinuations both before and after we begin the aforementioned evaluation. At the start, it is important to determine whether this test is appropriate at all. Afterwards, it must not be forgotten that developments of modern technologies can keep making differences perpetually. Accordingly, enforcers of the law and legal regulators must remain alert not to miss important developments, which might require them to supplement the system of the law based on new precedents.

6

Some Reflections on the Non-coherence Theory of Digital Human Rights

Mart Susi

6.1 INTRODUCTION

The non-coherence theory of digital human rights was introduced in a Cambridge University Press monograph in 2024,[1] and has thereafter been presented and discussed at various conferences and book launches. Academic discussion is at its inaugural stage. This chapter wishes to accomplish three goals. First, to summarise the main elements of the theory with some illustrative examples; second, discuss some points raised during oral discussions when the theory has been presented; and third, point to a major doubt about the relativity of human rights as opposed to universality, which seems to be logically concludable from the theory.

6.2 THE MAIN ELEMENTS OF NON-COHERENCE THEORY OF DIGITAL HUMAN RIGHTS

The non-coherence theory of digital human rights focuses partly upon the transposition of established human rights principles from the non-digital domain to the digital realm. The normative and practice landscapes of digital and non-digital human rights appear non-coherent; that is, the meaning and scope of well-established ideas, concepts, and the content of norms appear at variance to a certain degree. These are to some extent incompatible images. This observation raises significant ontological and epistemological concerns. The main concern – expressed in an abstract manner – is the mistaken assumption that 'A' means the same in both domains, whereas on closer inspection it appears that upon transposition the meaning of 'A' has undergone a transformation. 'A' stands here for any human right norm or principle that is encountered in both domains.

[1] M. Susi, *The Non-Coherence Theory of Digital Human Rights* (Cambridge: Cambridge University Press, 2024).

6.2.1 *The Scenarios of Normative Transformation*

The transfer of judicial ideas and norms by itself is a phenomenon that is detectable wherever and whenever there is a confrontation of two or more (more or less) established socio-judicial environments.[2] Various scenarios are possible. The first concerns a situation where a certain normative-ideological regulatory framework is carried to another socio-geographic environment, but is countered by an existing framework of normative ideas and practices. This scenario can be labelled the socio-geographic transposition of law and can be illustrated by the process of imposing 'colonial' supremacy upon territories of the indigenous or more established but different cultures. Saliha Belmessous has shown that colonisation of indigenous people in the Americas, Africa, Australia, and New Zealand was countered not only by force, but also by ideas and understandings of a law that should apply between people. She uses the expression of indigenous legal opposition to the European legislative framework and justifications.[3] From the perspective of legal scholarship, this opposition means contestation between ideas and procedures; that is, mechanisms for how the ideas are made to govern. Non-coherence theory has the assumption that there is no or only a minor contestation because contestation usually leads to the disappearance of one competing ideology. Yet such contestation may appear in time, when the normative power of the digital domain grows through self-normativity.

The second scenario concerns regime change, leading to the ideological transposition of law. Legal scholarship dominated by comparative methodology does not conclusively show the possibility of the full replacement of established legal ideologies and structures by an incompatible set of ideas, leading to an entirely different understanding of how the law should govern society.[4] The overthrow of the Russian tsarist regime by the Bolsheviks led to the enactment of socialist ideology, but the administrative and court systems were largely functionally retained. The French Revolution led perhaps, at least initially, to even broader chaos in terms of laws and procedures.[5] Regime change may go hand in hand with the adoption of legal

[2] See for discussion an overview of how legal systems around the world have been impacted by legal transfers: J. Gillespie and P. Nicholson, 'Taking the interpretation of legal transfers seriously: the challenge for law and development', in J. Gillespie and P. Nicholson (eds.), *Law and Development and the Global Discourses of Legal Transfers* (Cambridge: Cambridge University Press, 2012), pp. 1–26.

[3] S. Belmessous (ed.), *Native Claims: Indigenous Law against Empire, 1500–1920* (Oxford: Oxford University Press, 2012).

[4] Peter Reich has explored the impact of regime change upon legal change and has identified various outcomes. For example, he writes, regime change in the Second Empire in ancient Rome resulted in hybridization, in Canada regime change led to legal conundrums for decades, and in California gradual supplanting of the civil law system. See: P. L. Reich, 'Regime change and legal change – the legacy of Mexico's Second Empire' (2015) *Oxford University Comparative Law Forum* 1.

[5] R. G. Fuchs, *Contested Paternity: Constructing Families in Modern France* (Baltimore: Johns Hopkins University Press, 2008), pp. 34–41.

norms from a regime falling into the same ideological paradigm.[6] The common characteristic of regime change is the generic variance of the legal framework before and after the change, where the variance can always be characterised by degree. Such a scenario would not make sense in the initial stages after the appearance of the digital domain, for the simple reason that there was no regime to be changed. But this does not exclude the possibility that the regime may have appeared in time, either in disguise or openly, which is then subject to the aspiration of regime change from the offline domain. Yet the reverse is also possible, namely the aspiration of the digital domain to trigger the legal regime change of the offline domain.

The third scenario concerns a situation where people and institutions enter unknown territory with their own discursive history, ideas, and values, but for one reason or another note that their regulatory and ideological equipment does not fully work. We can term this scenario the transposition of law into a normative carte blanche. This position might take for granted that the digital domain could have been characterised – in the early years – as such an empty sheet open to the transposition of normative regulation; that is, there were no countering normative forces, and the offline regulatory and conceptual framework should have appeared welcome in the online context. A deeper examination questions this predisposition for the reason of the inadequacy of protection thesis, which I have developed elsewhere to explain the element of novelty in human rights development.[7] This thesis claims that the development of new human rights is explainable through the recognition of the incapability of established human rights to provide adequate protection for certain groups in comparison with others, or that the novel contemporary conditions challenge the capability of an established human right to provide sufficient protection of an important social value. The common element of both reasons leading to the articulation of new human rights according to the inadequacy of protection thesis is contestation. Application of this thesis to the internet is at the root of questions about whether it is possible to provide protection in the online domain that is comparable to the offline by using concepts entirely placed in and originating from offline, or whether offline remedies can be effectively applied online.

6.2.2 *Reflections on the Inadequacy of Protection Thesis*

The inadequacy of protection thesis when applied to the internet is offline-morphic and practice-dependent. Offline-morphic means the view from the offline domain, which is analogous to when an animal rights lawyer projects her understandings

6 P. Varul and H. Pisuke, 'Louisiana's Contribution to the Estonian Civil Code' (1999) 73 *Tulane Law Review* 4, 1027–34.

7 M. Susi, 'Novelty in new human rights: the decrease of universality and abstractness thesis', in A. von Arnaud, K. von der Decken, and M. Susi (eds.), *Cambridge Handbook on New Human Rights of the 21st Century: Recognition, Novelty, and Rhetoric* (Cambridge: Cambridge University Press, 2020), pp. 21–33, at 21–2.

onto other species and concludes that they exhibit behavioural patterns comparable to humans.[8]

The inadequacy of protection thesis offers a practical lens through which to examine non-coherence theory. This thesis posits a dichotomy between online and offline protection, where frameworks deemed adequate in the offline world may prove inadequate online. This offline-morphic perspective, analogous to projecting human understanding onto non-human contexts, highlights the subjective nature of assessing the adequacy of protection in the digital environment. The practice-dependent aspect of this thesis emphasises empirical observation. The presence of contestation – detailed arguments regarding the compatibility of offline human rights norms with online realities – indicates a non-coherent image. The theory distinguishes mere disagreement from actual contestation, requiring a critical mass of actors recognising the inadequacy of the protection. This contestation is manifested in various ways, including conflicting categorisations of legal transposition processes (e.g., the direct/indirect and receptive/unreceptive models). This contestation also reveals the evolving and dynamic nature of the non-coherent image of digital human rights, as the discrepancy between online and offline frameworks is not a static phenomenon but is subject to change over time.

6.2.3 *The Dual Nature Thesis*

Discussions about the non-coherence theory of digital human rights have raised the question of how to position this theory in the framework of existing approaches to legal transformations. What is the novel aspect of this theory – when the topic of transfers has been known as long as different cultures have collided – can and has been asked. My response is through the dual nature of the human rights thesis. It says that differently from legal transformation approaches where one domain has to yield to another, the digital and non-digital coexist in parallel, using similar human rights words, which carry a meaning in variation. The non-coherent image of human rights in the digital domain does not appear immediately and develops over time. It becomes evident once attempts to find in the digital domain an almost analogous image from the non-digital human rights system have proven illusory. The theory of non-coherence can explain this through the concept of the multi-stakeholderist veil thesis and the weakness of the sameness of rights doctrine.

6.2.4 *The Multi-stakeholderist Veil Thesis*

Multi-stakeholderism of internet governance, as formulated by Joanna Kulesza, is 'a distributed policymaking model based on the voluntary cooperation of key actors,

[8] M. C. Nussbaum, 'Animal rights: the need for a theoretical basis' (2001) 114 *Harvard Law Review* 5, 1506–52.

usually identified as: states, business, and civil society, operating "in their respective roles" through "rough consensus and running code"'.[9] For more than one party to connect, a genuine willingness from both sides is needed, otherwise the logical sequence of rhetorical functions comes to a standstill. In the digital human rights landscape it can be viewed as an attempt to incrementally transpose the offline human rights framework into the digital domain. Multi-stakeholderism as an end result in itself carries primarily non-regulatory aspirations, such as an advocacy tool for civil society or 'whitewashing' the aspirations of stakeholders who are more equal than others.[10]

This thesis is inspired by the various transposition scenarios described earlier. The rise of the internet in the late 1990s and early 2000s can be characterised by the expansion of technological horizons, overshadowing the absence of internet-specific regulation, thereby assuming that the law offline as we know it can be easily transposed to the digital. This was the period of transformation to carte blanche. The recognition of the unclear image led to the ideological transposition through the multi-stakeholderism scenario, where co-creation and dialogue were viewed as arriving at a clear image, while still relying on the conceptual and procedural building blocks from offline. In parallel, the online community construed its own understandings of human rights in the digital domain, either implicitly or explicitly intending to conceptually counter the offline framework. By the time the limitations of the multi-stakeholder approach became evident, the only scenario left was the rivalry between competing regulatory frameworks; that is, between the horizontal and vertical governance models. This condition of regulatory uncertainty and proliferation has an axiomatic effect on human rights in the digital domain, which can be viewed as an element of non-coherence. It has to suffice to say at this point that multishakeholderism as a holistic approach applied to reconcile the non-digital and digital domains has failed. Non-coherence has become a permanent condition of the coexistence of human rights in the digital and non-digital domains. Multi-stakeholderism is no longer needed.

6.2.5 *About the Sameness of Rights Approach*

With some imagination, it is possible to cite the claim of sameness from the Geneva Principles in 2003.[11] This result of an effort for which there are no *traveaux*

[9] See for the discussion about multi-stakeholderism: J. Kulesza, 'Multistakeholderism – meaning and implications', in M. Susi (ed.), *Human Rights, Digital Society and the Law: A Research Companion* (London: Routledge, 2019), pp. 117–31.

[10] A. Kovacs, 'Moving multistakeholderism forward: lessons from the NETmundial', *Internet Policy Review*, 12 May 2014, https://policyreview.info/articles/news/moving-multistakeholderism-forward-lessons-netmundial/281.

[11] World Summit on the Information Society, Geneva 2003 – Tunis 2005, Document WSIS-03/GEBEVA7DOC74-E, 12 December 2003, Declaration of Principles, Building the Information Society: a global challenge in the new millennium, https://digitallibrary.un.org/record/533621?v=pdf.

preparatoires, that lacks argumentation in support of its claims, and is thus representing a clear example of an instrument of faith. It reaffirms 'the universality, indivisibility, interdependence and interrelation of all human rights and fundamental freedoms [...]'.[12] One can say that such a statement is not a full acknowledgement of the idea of sameness, but it conveys the impression that human rights are not domain-dependent. Then it took almost ten years to reach an *expressis verbis* statement of the sameness in an international instrument. This is the United Nations (UN) Human Rights Council resolution from 29 June 2012, which '*[a]ffirms* that the same rights that people have offline must also be protected online, [...]'.[13] Sometimes the idea of the sameness does not appear as a direct statement, but is deductible from the context. Take for example the UN Human Rights Committee's General comment No. 34 to Article 19 of the UN General Declaration from 2011.[14] This comment acknowledges in paragraph 15 the substantial change in communication practices around the world owing to information and communication technologies. And yet implicitly it is based on accepting full transposition of human rights principles from offline to online.

It may be sufficient here to point to this idea's ubiquity on the basis of the commendable work of others. For example, Dror-Shpoliansky and Shany propose the normative equivalency paradigm, having shown how in a series of resolutions the Human Rights Committee and the General Assembly 'have reiterated the notion that human rights apply in the digital "online world" as they apply in the "offline world"'.[15] The normative equivalency, as they are asserting, contains a major flaw, which is about considering 'digital technology as a new tool or arena for exercising offline rights or governmental powers, as opposed to a conceptualization of digital space as giving rise to new human condition and governance domain'.[16] This view represents non-coherence between digital and non-digital domains in a narrow sense, not encompassing well-established rights from the offline domain, such as the right to privacy, and covers the so-called second generation rights.

I have raised two main objections against the doctrine of the sameness of rights. The first objection is from relativity and the second objection is from practicality. The objection from relativity is related to the basic or fundamental building blocks of human rights. There are certain ideas that are difficult to justify through explication, and even then, the element of belief in something remains relevant. For example, take the idea of the universality of human rights. Is this a premise that can

[12] Ibid., para. 3.

[13] UN Human Rights Council, 'The promotion, protection and enjoyment of human rights on the Internet', HRC 20th Session, UN Doc. A/HRC/20/L.13, 29 June 2012.

[14] Ibid., para. 1.

[15] D. Dror-Shpoliansky and Y. Shany, 'It's the end of the (offline) world as we know it: from human rights to digital human rights – a proposed typology' (2021) 32 *The European Journal of International Law* 4, 1249–82, at 1253.

[16] Ibid., 1265.

be verified through rational argumentation, or is this the result of discursive, political, and judicial practices? But its importance is evident from asking what would happen to the suggestion of the omnipotence of human rights if the idea was given up. The sameness idea carries similar connecting and rhetorical force. In today's human rights discourses, policies, judicial judgments, and civil society approaches, in other words, everywhere, any answer to the question of whether human rights offline and online are the same or not has far-reaching consequences. An affirmative answer means coherence of content and leads to the subsequent question of the breadth of non-coherence in enforcement instruments. However, if the negation of the sameness idea could claim validity as a general principle, then we can say that human rights online do not exist in a similar fashion as (we are accustomed to know them) in the offline domain. This leads us to say that the theory of non-coherence is one of relativity.

The objection in practicality terms is articulated by the advocacy group Article 19. This group translated the reaffirmation that 'the same rights that people have offline must also be protected online' in questions of practicality. It says that unless greater priority is placed on addressing violations and changes to law and practice, this statement of sameness is no more 'than words just written on paper'.[17] The non-coherence theory explains this image by suggesting that the sameness of rights remains at the highest level of generality, expressed in words only, and starts to evaporate once we enter the sphere of more detailed content and enforcement. There continue parallel roads with occasional crossings, to use a figurative expression.

6.2.6 *Double Nature of Privacy*

To give a robust example of the coexistence of the non-coherent concepts of rights, it can be shown that privacy offline exhibits different features to privacy online. The formulation of the right to privacy in the contemporary era is widely credited to Warren and Brandeis's formulation from 1890 as an interest 'to be let alone'.[18] Online privacy exhibits the opposite, namely, an interest not to be let alone. I have explained these opposites through fundamental differences of entry into non-digital and digital domains. We enter the non-digital domain involuntarily. This is the existentialist viewpoint, Jean-Paul Sartre's view that we are thrown into freedom, yet we do not choose to be free.[19] It can be said that the right to privacy in its original manifestation is part of the existentialist 'package', which we may or may not choose to

[17] ARTICLE 19 statement at the thirty-fifth session of the UN Human Rights Council on 14 June 2017, as part of the Item 3 General Debate, see www.article19.org/resources/article-19-at-the-unhrc-the-same-rights-that-people-have-offline-must-also-be-protected-online/.

[18] S. D. Warren and L. D. Brandeis, 'The right to privacy' (1890) 4 *Harvard Law Review* 5, 193–220.

[19] Sartre writes: 'Man is condemned to be free. Condemned, because he did not create himself, in other respect is free: because, once thrown into the world, he is responsible for everything he does.' See: J-P. Sartre, *Existentialism and Human Emotions* (New York: Philosophical Library Book, 1957), p. 15.

utilise. The entry into the digital domain is different and carries both voluntary and involuntary elements. Voluntary entry is the result of the conscious choice to use the digital domain for social communication, obtaining information, interacting with official government structures, or accessing vital services from private providers, such as financial or medical sectors. Involuntary entry happens despite one's position in regard to the digital domain and is connected to e-state and blockchain technologies, which are widely used to maintain official records of events and persons. A few more sentences are in order to express these differences in more detail.

Voluntary entry is related to the interest to exhibit oneself in the digital domain in the most suitable manner. It is not accompanied by the positive validity of one's image but is triggered by what one wishes to put forward and at the same time hide. Such a digital image has been termed the digital identity. Michalkiewicz-Kadziela and Milczarek have noted that 'human identity on the internet functions on completely different terms than outside it. The internet gives unlimited possibilities of creating subjective elements of one's own identity, but it also allows a change of objective elements'.[20] There are warnings from policy organisations that digital identity does not fit into the framework of human rights, and it entails a threat leading to totalitarianism.[21]

Involuntary entry into the digital domain is caused by the growing reliance on e-solutions by public and private authorities offering essential services. It is practically impossible to avoid that various digital surveillance mechanisms record us under Big Data, and that financial or medical institutions record our personal information. Here it is impossible to raise the interest of being left alone, and the only claim is related to requesting that the data be accurate through the newly emerged right to erasure.[22] Once someone enters involuntarily into the blockchain system, their interest to be let alone becomes meaningless. As put eloquently by Sullivan, this is because of 'considerable challenges in establishing not only that "I am who I say I am" but in establishing "I am not who the identity register says I am"'.[23]

At this point there is noticeable prima facie variance in the meanings of privacy offline and online. The variance is of such a degree that it should be more appropriate to refrain from the usage of the expression 'privacy' for the online environment. Non-coherence is centre stage here. Because the digital and non-digital domains

[20] E. Michalkiewcz-Kadziela and E. Milczarek, 'Legal boundaries of digital identity creation' (2022) 11 *Internet Policy Review* 1, 1–13, at 10.

[21] See, e.g., panel conclusions put forward by Geneva Internet platform digwatch in November 2018: S. Grottola, 'The future of digital identity and human rights', Geneva Internet platform digwatch, 13 November 2018, https://dig.watch/event/13th-internet-governance-forum/future-digital-identity-and-human-rights.

[22] E.g., under the GDPR article 17. It is worth mentioning here that the heading of this article 'right to erasure ("right to be forgotten")' is an example of how the various entitlements related to the reflection of offline privacy get mixed up.

[23] C. Sullivan, *Digital Identity: An Emergent Legal Concept. The Role and Legal Nature of Digital Identity in Commercial Transactions* (Adelaide: University of Adelaide Press, 2011), p. 140.

are interconnected and someone leads parallel lives in both domains, the right to privacy has meaning in the digital reality only so far as it enables the realisation of the interest to be let alone in the non-digital reality.

6.2.7 *Concerns Related to Time*

Among epistemological concerns the one related to time is of significance. In the non-digital domain, time can be regarded as a quality assurance for knowledge development, and as such is considered to have a positive effect upon human rights adjudication practice. This is because of the possibilities of reflection and discourse. However, the element of time becomes negativity in the digital domain because the time window for resolving online human rights conflicts appears immensely narrow. Liu articulates this aspect as follows: 'Instead of valuing enduring or permanent truths (the temporal version of "high" knowledge), the digital age is preoccupied with information of much shorter durations – time spans plunging down to the diurnal rhythm of blog posts, the microseconds of a data packet's TTL (time to live) [...]'.[24]

Elsewhere, I have shown that shortness of time weakens one of the basic instruments for offline rights conflict resolution – balancing.[25] Within any framework of judicial balancing, the courts have as much time as needed to claim a correct assessment of the concrete importance of conflicting rights and establish a proper balance. Conversely on the internet, the element of time is non-existent, as it would lead to the non-effective, retrospective recognition that rights were violated and proper balance was not achieved. Effective balancing online depends on swift decisions about whether certain information published overrides someone else's concern about an intrusion into his or her private domain or other rights. Here time is a different concern from the understanding that with the passage of time the balance of interests may reverse; for example, when processing personal data.[26] The shortness of time for reasoned decision-making can easily lead ultimately to the rejection of the rationality of online balancing.

A related doubt about whether balancing as we know it from the offline domain is at all possible in the digital domain is related to the matter of transparency. In online balancing via private entities, the transparency deficit of portals has been raised as a concern. This matter has been noticed for longer than a decade and there are calls to address it, but nothing has changed. For instance, the Council of Europe has stated that 'Internet service providers should put in place appropriate,

[24] A. Liu, 'Theses on the epistemology of the digital: advice for the Cambridge Centre for Digital Knowledge', 14 August 2014, https://liu.english.ucsb.edu/theses-on-the-epistemology-of-the-digital-page/.

[25] M. Susi, 'Internet balancing formula' (2019) 25 *European Law Journal*, Special Issue: Internet and Human Rights Law 2, 198–212.

[26] G. Sartor, 'The right to be forgotten: balancing interests in the flux of time' (2016) 24 *International Journal of Law and Information Technology* 1, 72–98.

clear, open and efficient procedures to respond within reasonable time limits to complaints from internet users alleging breaches of the principles included in the foregoing provisions […]'.[27] The UN calls upon 'all States to consider formulating, through transparent and inclusive processes with all stakeholders, and adopting national internet-related public policies that have the objective of universal access and enjoyment of human rights at their core'.[28] Similarly, La Rue encourages 'corporations to establish clear and unambiguous terms of service in line with international human rights norms and principles […]'.[29]

The transparency deficit leads to a phenomenon that can be termed the legitimacy deficit in relation to balancing conflicting rights online. There is a growing academic discourse on the topic. Enguerrand Marique and Yseult Marique search for the source of legitimacy when private platforms set rules, monitor compliance with their own rules, and finally, apply sanctions.[30] Noting the unilateral character of the 'contractual' horizontal relationship, they proceed to highlight that online portals give the 'take it or leave it' option without any possibility of negotiation, which in turn leaves the issue of the legitimacy of private content assessment undefined. It is suggested that new forms of legitimacy may develop based on public–private or hybrid interactions in setting and enforcing the regulatory order of the internet.[31] The legitimacy deficit is currently also apparent in a mathematical solution with practice-affecting aspiration, proposed by a multi-country scholarly community. For instance, a simplified model by Zufall, Kimura, and Peng uses the elements of privacy of information and nature of information, while the relevance of the intrusion is affected by time.[32] This solution isolates and polarises just one element from the conflicting rights to be balanced, because privacy of information is just one aspect of the level of intrusion into privacy, and nature of information is just one aspect allowing to determine the scope of the freedom of expression. The

[27] Council of Europe, Appendix to Recommendation CM/Rec(2016)1, para 6.1, see also CM/Rec(2018)2 / Recommendation of the Committee of Ministers to member States on the roles and responsibilities of internet intermediaries.

[28] UN Human Rights Council, 'The promotion, protection and enjoyment of human rights on the Internet', HRC 32nd Session, UN Doc A/HRC/32/L.20 (2016).

[29] F. La Rue, Report of the Special Rapporteur on the Promotion and Protection of the Right to Freedom of Opinion and Expression, HRC 17th session, UN Doc. A/HRC/17/27 (2011), para 48, see also Report of the Special Rapporteur on the promotion and protection of the right to freedom of opinion and expression, submitted to the United Nations General Assembly on 8 September 2015; the Summary has the following passage: 'In many situations, sources of information and whistle-blowers make access to information possible, for which they deserve the strongest protection in law and in practice.' See D. Kaye, Report of the Special Rapporteur on the promotion and protection of the right to freedom of opinion and expression, UN Doc. A/70/361 (2015), 2.

[30] E. Marique and Y. Marique, 'Sanctions on digital platforms: beyond the public-private divide' (2019) 8 *Cambridge University Law Journal* 2, 258–81.

[31] Ibid., p. 281.

[32] F. Zufall, R. Kimura, and L. Peng, 'A simple mathematical model for the legal concept of balancing of interests' ICAIL '21: Proceedings of the Eighteenth International Conference on Artificial Intelligence and Law, June 2021, 270–1.

matter of algorithmic simplicity was to be expected and possibly characterises some or many solutions in practical use today.

These brief observations convey the perception that balancing online stands at significant variance from balancing online owing to legitimacy and transparency deficits. This is a clear phenomenon of non-coherence.

6.2.8 *Some Additional Theses*

Space available for this chapter also permits me to give a brief introduction to some additional theses connected to the non-coherence theory.

While exploring the notion of digital dignity, I have formulated the relativisation of core values thesis, which is a logical consequence of the recognition that in the digital domain there are no absolute human rights – the space allocated to this chapter allows me only to make this as an assertion, which means that everything becomes relative. This is because the basic norm in which offline stands at the bottom of the structure of human rights norms and principles itself becomes relative. Online dignity does not possess the feature of absoluteness that we are accustomed to accepting offline – as the core value written into the preambles of various human rights instruments. Here in the digital domain the key notion of dignity will be measured against 'competing' rights and values. But it would no longer correspond to the place of dignity in the offline human rights realm. In this case, the weight of dignity in the offline and online domains becomes non-coherent. This lies in the simple recognition that while dignity is a constant offline, it is relative online.

A novel aspect of the transfer of human rights images and ideas can be described through the 'comfort in non-coherence thesis'. This refers to the simplistic perception that we prefer to operate in a realm that is at least to some extent familiar to us, as opposed to being confronted with a reality that is completely new, unfamiliar, and unpredictable. In such a reality, human rights ideas and concepts would not be meaningful, and the only reason for using human rights language would be to approach the new reality with tools that are familiar to us from the physical realm. The high level of variance in observations between non-digital and digital domains has become part of the mainstream in judicial discourse. For instance, Kettemann, Peukert, and Spiecker write in their 2022 edited volume on law in the digital space: 'The book reveals that the number of specifically digital and global phenomena, which raise unique regulatory questions, is increasing, and that the applicable digital law is characterised by private ordering, transnational standardisation, economisation but at the same time by persistent and possibly deepening legal fragmentation'.[33] Magarin lists structural concerns connected to limited free speech online in need of regulatory attention, among these being inequalities of access, power relationships

[33] M. Kettemann and A. Peukert, 'Conclusion', in M. Kettemann, A. Peukert, and I. Spiecker gen. Döhmann (eds.), *The Law of Global Digitality* (London: Routledge, 2022), pp. 250–5.

among governments, private speech intermediaries and internet users, and the ways in which the internet's architecture complicates effective regulation.[34] All these observations are about non-coherence between the two domains under review. The comfort thesis says that we prefer to live in an environment of double standards and fragmentation instead of an environment where one sphere is devoid of any normativity, be it rational or non-rational.

6.3 CONCLUDING REMARKS

6.3.1 *Conclusion by the Artificial Intelligence ChatGPT*

For the first time in my writing experience, I asked ChatGPT to write a short summary of my writing. I submitted the manuscript of the non-coherence theory of digital human rights, which is around 250 pages, and asked it to write a short one-page summary. The resulting text is as follows, which for the purposes of clarity is in quotation marks. The only curiosity of the text that follows – which I endorse for the purposes of knowledge sharing – is the choice of the only reference. Why ChatGPT chose Merleau-Ponty remains unknown.

'The theory's core premise is that the transposition of offline human rights law and practice to the online environment often results in a distorted, "non-coherent" image. This non-coherence stems from inherent discrepancies between the offline and online contexts, rendering the simple transferability of established norms problematic. The resulting lack of clarity regarding the application, realization, and enforcement of human rights online necessitates a re-evaluation of existing frameworks.

'The non-coherence theory emerges from the observation that established human rights principles, their implementation, related obligations, and remedies for violations, as understood in the "offline" world, lack clear analogues in the digital sphere. The central question becomes: Do offline human rights rules and principles maintain their integrity online, or do they undergo modifications, distortions, or even cease to apply altogether? This uncertainty, termed "non-coherence", arises when the transposition from the offline to the online context results in significant differences. While the terms "variance" and "distortion" are used interchangeably in this context, the critical distinction lies in the degree of difference. Minor variances may be acceptable, but substantial divergences indicate a distortion that may render the offline framework inapplicable or limit its scope in the digital context. This core concept challenges the assumption of the straightforward transposability of human rights from the offline to the online world. The theory anticipates potential objections, particularly regarding its theoretical underpinnings and the empirical evidence supporting its claims.

[34] G. P. Magarin, 'The internet and social media', in A. Stone and F. Schauer (eds.), *The Oxford Handbook of Freedom of Speech* (Oxford: Oxford University Press, 2021), pp. 350–70.

'These models differ fundamentally in their approach: vertical governance relies on the state's coercive power, while horizontal governance involves a partnership of diverse actors. Non-coherence theory is not concerned with the *content* of rights defined by these models but rather with the *processes* by which rights are established, enforced, and remedied. The simultaneous operation of these differing models illustrates the inherent unpredictability and inconsistency in the digital domain, undermining the notion of a unified and coherent human rights framework online. The coexistence and interaction between these models highlight the complex and often conflicting nature of online regulation.

'Non-coherence theory also explores the ontological and epistemological dimensions of digital human rights. Ontologically, the theory questions the very existence of human rights in the digital space, posing the fundamental question: Do human rights exist intrinsically for sentient beings entering the virtual realm or are they conferred by some external authority? The theory argues that even under ideal discursive conditions, the transposition of human rights concepts from the offline to the online domain leads to a loss of meaning and clarity, akin to Merleau-Ponty's concept of the subjective experience of colour.[35] The theory's focus is on how the offline image of human rights is reflected online, implying that even distorted reflections are meaningful for understanding the non-coherence. The inherent limitations of the practice-independent approach raise the question of the continued validity of applying non-positivist categories such as "human rights" to the digital domain, particularly given their possible transformation into merely "legal rights". This analysis requires an acknowledgement of the inherent subjectivity and context-dependence of human rights interpretations, and the theory's emphasis on how different frameworks interact within the digital environment highlights this further.

'Epistemologically, the theory examines how knowledge about human rights is created, articulated, and enforced in the digital sphere. The theory identifies a polarisation of views regarding the coherence of online and offline knowledge creation processes. It argues that even if the means of knowledge creation differ, this does not necessarily invalidate the claim of normative validity, highlighting the role of processes such as communicative rationality and the "wisdom of the crowd" in generating credible knowledge. However, the theory suggests a relativisation of truth in digital human rights. What is considered truthful in one domain may not be considered truthful in the other, highlighting the paradigm-dependent nature of truth claims and questioning the universal applicability of non-positivist concepts. The theory concludes that the non-coherence of digital human rights is not simply a hypothesis but an inherent feature of the digital environment,

[35] M. Merleau-Ponty, *The Visible and the Invisible*, edited by C. Lefort, translated by A. Lingis, Northwestern University Studies in Phenomenology and Existential Philosophy (Evanston, IL: Northwestern University Press, 1968), p. 130.

requiring a reconceptualisation of human rights frameworks in this space. Further research would need to elaborate on the specifics of how competing online and offline normative systems interact and the implications for the future of digital human rights.'

6.3.2 *Conclusion by the Author*

The central conclusion of non-coherence theory is relativity. It shows how the division into absolute and relative human rights evaporates in the digital domain, and the human rights landscape becomes uni-layered. Basic norms that stand at the base of the human rights architecture in the physical world – such as dignity – become relativised and subject to balancing with other principles of a lower degree of generality. Balancing that constrains and directs human rights adjudication in the physical world assumes a completely different nature owing to transparency and legitimacy deficits. Relativity deprives human rights of their universal power. Competing systems of human rights can claim equal legitimacy, which leads to the validation of conflicting contents of concrete human rights bearing similar labels.

Yet there can be some commonalities that are applicable in any domain where human rights can exist, independently from their concrete content. These commonalities would have universal nature, which restores at least partially the idea of universality into the human rights landscape. Building on the analogy with quantum mechanics, it can be asked whether certain human rights exist in a shared state. This would mean, for instance, whether the right to privacy exists in a shared state with the right to freedom of expression; or whether the right to reputation – leaving aside the issue of whether such a self-standing right can be justified – exists in a shared state with the right of access to information. If the premise of such a shared state is correct, then it would follow that change in the scope and meaning of one right (particle) in this shared state leads to a simultaneous change to the opposite in the other right (particle). To give a concrete example, if the scope of the right to privacy is broadening, then the scope of the right to freedom of expression has to narrow. Such correlation would then be assumed. To give an abstract example from the other side, when we can measure the broadening of the right to freedom of expression, say in an online portal, we know without additional measuring that the scope of the right to privacy is narrowing. For human rights, the matter is related to, first and foremost, the relative weight of rights against one another. A new thesis can be advanced. I would term this the equilibrium of relative rights thesis, which says that for those rights existing in a shared state, when the relative weight of one right increases, the relative weight of another right has to decrease by the respective amount. Validation of the universality of the equilibrium of relative rights thesis could partly restore universality to the human rights discourse.

7

Internet Addiction as a Human Rights Issue

Vygantė Milašiūtė

7.1 INTRODUCTION

This chapter examines internet addiction as a threat related to the use of the internet, which in a sense is not a new problem. Research shows that throughout history, there have been recurring waves of concern and fear over pathological media use. We have witnessed afflictions such as radio addiction, television (TV) addiction, internet addiction, and smartphone addiction. Concern about these afflictions especially addresses young people, who are presumed more reckless and irresponsible in their media use but also more vulnerable to its effects. Up to a third of US parents and half of teens believe they spend too much time online, and half of teens and more than one in four parents in the US describe themselves as addicted to their smartphone. In other words, even though clinical diagnoses are exceptionally rare, as a cultural phenomenon, internet addiction appears to be widespread. What is new is that the advent of information and communication technologies (ICTs) marked a shift from mass media to a 'personal communication society'. In particular, smartphones render us permanently online and connected.[1] This suggests that internet addiction may be more acute than any other technology-related media addiction and may raise new challenges for law and policymakers.

The phenomenon of internet addiction is global. Previously, abnormal internet-related behaviours mainly concerned Asian countries, but it is now established that internet addiction represents a global emerging public health issue, with relevant societal costs.[2] For example, one study showed that 31 per cent of undergraduate students in northern Tanzania were addicted to the internet. Internet addiction was

[1] M. M. Vanden Abeele and V. Mohr, 'Media addictions as Apparatgeist: what discourse on TV and smartphone addiction reveals about society' (2021) 27 *Convergence* 6, 1536–57.

[2] B. Dell'Osso and N. Fineberg, COST (European Cooperation for Science and Technology) Action CA16207, 'learning to deal with problematic usage of the internet', www.cost.eu/publication/learning-to-deal-with-problematic-usage-of-the-internet/, 48.

associated with using the internet at college, lengthy periods using the internet per day, and social networking.[3]

Although the problem of internet addiction is perceived as important, it has so far attracted limited attention from legal scholars. Law and policy responses to internet addiction have also been somewhat underdeveloped. Partly, this can be related to the lack of robust medical evidence of internet addiction as a diagnosis and a health issue that requires the attention of law and policymakers. There is, however, a rich and growing body of medical research into internet addiction issues.[4] This chapter will rely on medical research in order to identify concrete human rights issues that need to be addressed by law.

7.2 INTERPLAY OF MEDICAL AND LEGAL RESEARCH

From the medical perspective, issues of addiction to the internet or to content accessed via the internet are examined as an issue of problematic usage of the internet (PUI). This umbrella term used by mental health researchers encompasses all potentially problematic internet-related behaviours, including those relating to gaming, gambling, buying, pornography viewing, social networking, cyberbullying, and cyberchondria among others. PUI may have mental and physical health consequences.[5] A common element across all expressions of PUI is the excessive time spent online, which contributes to significant functional impairment with negative consequences for the daily life of the subjects involved and their relatives.[6] In medical terms, PUI covers conditions considered to be behavioural addictions and also a spectrum of conditions going beyond behavioural addictions and covering problematic, hazardous, and harmful usage.[7] In this chapter, we are interested in behavioural addictions and have therefore chosen the term 'internet addiction'.

In 1995, Ivan Goldberg coined the term 'Internet Addiction Disorder' and formulated a list of symptoms drawn from the characteristics of pathological gambling. The term remains widely used nowadays to indicate internet-related psychopathology. Around the same time (1995–9), Mark Griffiths proposed a conceptual distinction between addictions on the internet (those affecting individuals who simply use the internet as a medium to engage in a specific behaviour that could be conducted offline) versus addictions to the internet (where individuals are primarily addicted to content solely generated inside the World Wide Web).[8]

3 I. B. Mboya et al., 'Internet addiction and associated factors among medical and allied health sciences students in northern Tanzania: a cross-sectional study' (2020) 73 *BMC Psychology*, 8, Article 73.

4 Dell'Osso and Fineberg, 'Learning to deal with problematic usage of the internet'.

5 N. A. Fineberg et al., 'Manifesto for a European research network into problematic usage of the internet' (2018) 28 *European Neuropsychopharmacology* 11, 1232–46.

6 Dell'Osso and Fineberg, 'Learning to deal with problematic usage of the internet', p. 11.

7 H.-J. Rumpf, T. Effertz, and C. Montag, 'The cost burden of problematic internet usage' (2022) 44 *Current Opinion in Behavioral Sciences*, 101107.

8 Dell'Osso and Fineberg, 'Learning to deal with problematic usage of the internet', pp. 8–9.

Many studies have used the umbrella term 'Internet Addiction'. Other terms such as 'Smartphone Addiction' are used and have been criticised owing to the lack of specificity, as users of mobile devices rather show tendencies towards the problematic use of certain apps.[9]

For medical doctors, the term 'addiction to the internet' may be problematic as it is only specific behavioural patterns ('addictions'), such as 'internet gaming disorder', that have been officially recognised as requiring further study (i.e., having the potential to be recognised as a disorder) rather than addiction to the internet itself.[10]

From the legal perspective, there are more problematic aspects related to the usage of the internet in addition to those characterised by addiction. Cyberbullying, hate crime, the digital divide, and privacy threats are just some examples. This chapter, however, focuses solely on the aspect of addiction, viewing it primarily as a threat to health. Both aspects of addiction to the internet and addiction to specific content on the internet are covered. In human rights terms, this threat can affect the right to health, the right not to be discriminated against, and rights of specific vulnerable groups, such as the rights of the child. In certain contexts, this threat also affects consumer rights to the safety of products and services. Issues of internet addiction may also be relevant in the context of exercising other human rights, such as work or education-related human rights.

Robust mental health research data indicating that persons suffering from internet addiction actually suffer from a medical condition and need healthcare, could have implications for both how the law and policymakers should respond to the needs of such persons and how courts should take into account the characteristics of such individuals in applying the law to them.

Currently, however, there are limits to what psychiatry and neuroscience can prove. Individuals with indications of PUI do not necessarily meet the criteria for a psychiatric disorder. There is little evidence to suggest that they experience a high degree of behavioural dyscontrol and thus need to be exempted from certain requirements of the law. Where neuroscience suggests sexual internet addiction in an individual, it is not yet clear whether the diagnosis of a form of sexual disorder (e.g., paedophilia), regardless of the medium used, would be more appropriate than a PUI diagnosis. Although PUI has been the subject of growing research interest, this diagnosis has not been widely accepted among psychiatrists. PUI is not yet a valid diagnostic entity. Clear, operationalised criteria for PUI are still lacking. Given the lack of consensus regarding PUI, courts and forensic experts should examine claims of internet addiction critically. Specific attention should be paid to the issue

9 Rumpf, Effertz, and Montag, 'The cost burden of problematic internet usage'.

10 C. Megele and A. Longfield, *Safeguarding Children and Young People Online: A Guide for Practitioners* (Bristol: Bristol University Press, 2017), p. 98.

of whether the internet is the source of an individual's problems, or whether the root cause lies elsewhere.[11]

Domestic courts have so far been cautious to accept internet addiction arguments. In the US legal system, arguments based on the concept of internet addiction have been an issue in both civil and criminal litigation. In civil cases, individuals have brought lawsuits against video game developers owing to harm allegedly caused by their products (specifically, in-game 'loot boxes' – virtual items containing random rewards that can be purchased or earned). Notably, one complaint used emerging neuroscientific data to argue that adolescents are especially prone to addiction and risk-taking behaviour (such as gambling). Additionally, at least one plaintiff has contended that his internet addiction was a disability entitling him to protection under the Americans with Disabilities Act. In criminal cases, internet addiction arguments have been raised as a potential defence or mitigating factor to charges of sexual crimes, particularly those involving online child pornography or the sexual solicitation of minors. It was, however, only in one case that the concept of internet addiction has overcome a Daubert challenge (i.e., a hearing on the scientific validity and admissibility of expert testimony).[12]

Hence, this chapter looks into the issue of how medical research can inform legal research, and also how legal research into internet addiction should proceed in the absence of evidence from medical research.

7.3 TYPES OF INTERNET ADDICTION

Medical research provides sufficient evidence to identify the following subtypes of internet addiction: internet-related gaming disorder (excessive use of the internet for the purposes of playing online games that becomes associated with the development of loss of control of the gaming behaviour, prioritisation of gaming over other important everyday activities), internet-related gambling disorder (a pattern of persistent or recurrent gambling behaviour, which may be online or offline and which results in impaired control over gambling, increased priority given to gambling over other interests and activities, and the continuation or escalation of gambling despite the occurrence of negative consequences), internet-related buying or shopping disorder (extreme preoccupations with and craving for buying or shopping and irresistible urges to possess consumer goods), cyberchondria (an individual's excessive or repeated online search for medical information driven by a need to alleviate distress or anxiety regarding their health), cyberpornography addiction (excessively time-consuming, distressing, and difficult to resist use of the internet to view or interact with pornographic material), cyberbullying (the use of digital

[11] A. W. Blum and J. E. Grant, 'Legal aspects of problematic internet usage' (2022) 45 *Current Opinion in Behavioral Sciences*, 101142.

[12] Ibid.

technology to seek to harm, intimidate, or coerce other people online), and internet social media/forum addiction (excessive preoccupation with social media use as well as increased amounts of time using social media resulting in detrimental consequences on an individual's functioning and especially affecting the young). Limited scientific evidence exists to present excessive web surfing, mail checking, cyberhoarding and cyberstalking as specific internet addiction subtypes.[13] Other subtypes, such as binge-watching (watching multiple episodes of a TV programme in one sitting or in rapid succession), have been suggested by researchers,[14] but have not so far acquired universal acceptance.

Researchers have noted how one type of internet addiction can lead to another one, notably in situations of the problematic design of video games that contain elements such as loot boxes, because of which excessive online gaming can lead to excessive online gambling. The phenomenon of overlapping internet addictions is also noticeable in fantasy sports, where gaming often includes gambling and is accompanied by additional time spent online seeking relevant information or using internet forums for additional dialogues concerning the game.

Fantasy sports consist of selecting an online team of real-world players based on the rules of the particular fantasy sport. Participants are then awarded points based on the real-world statistics of those players. Gambling can play a major role in fantasy sports, especially in the form of Daily Fantasy Sports (DFS). DFS involves an accelerated version of fantasy sports where participants can bet on the performance of their players and win a proportion of their opponent's entry fees. DFS participants have been shown to have similar psychological and emotional characteristics to their traditional fantasy sports counterparts but have been associated with increased problem gambling behaviours. Gambling is common within traditional fantasy sports too, with one US study reporting 43.5 per cent of participants gambling on fantasy sports. Fantasy sports participants seek out online information to help them research and participate in fantasy sports, increasing their time spent online and the potential of developing an internet addiction. Participants using forums for additional discussions and information on fantasy sports are likely to be more avid users and may be more susceptible to developing an internet addiction owing to the increased amount of internet-based content consumed.[15]

More generally, researchers have found that internet addiction often co-occurs with other psychiatric disorders, such as anxiety disorders, mood disorders, obsessive-compulsive and related disorders, substance-related and addictive disorders,

[13] Dell'Osso and Fineberg, 'Learning to deal with problematic usage of the internet', pp. 10–17.

[14] K. T. Rahman and Z. U. Arif, 'Impact of binge-watching on Netflix during the Covid-19 pandemic' (2017) 2 *South Asian Journal of Marketing* 1, 97–112, at 98.

[15] D. Columb, M. D. Griffiths, and C. O'Gara, 'Fantasy football (soccer) playing and internet addiction among online fantasy football participants: a descriptive survey study' (2022) 20 *International Journal of Mental Health and Addiction* 2, 1200–11.

disruptive impulse-control and conduct disorders, personality disorders, and sleep/wake disorders. The relationship between internet addiction and other psychiatric disorders is mutual. People who suffer from internet addiction are at higher risk of developing anxiety, depression or other psychiatric conditions, and the occurrence of internet addiction in people with psychiatric problems is higher than in the general population.[16]

7.4 NEGATIVE CONSEQUENCES OF INTERNET ADDICTION

In regard to problems caused by excessive internet use, researchers have suggested that those problems can be divided into four areas, namely mental health problems, behavioural safety/accidents, physical health problems, and malfunctioning. In the case of mental health problems, depression, suicidal ideation, impulsiveness, attention deficit hyperactivity disorder (ADHD), smoking, and drinking are all increased in association with internet addiction. In the physical health area, eye disease, musculoskeletal disorders, sleep problems, and sudden death are reported to be related to excessive internet use. In the area of behavioural safety/accidents, increases in aggression and violence, accidents, cyberbullying, and risky sexual behaviours have been reported. In the area of malfunctioning problems, learning, intellectual abilities, and functioning in the family are all reported to suffer a decrease.[17] Problems, or threats, can also be divided into broader categories of individual and social threats.

Some examples of the findings on threats from specific studies into various aspects of internet addiction are presented here.

Studies of adolescents affected by internet addiction found increased rates of obesity to be linked with diminished physical activity or exercise, poor sleep quality, an irregular diet, eating snacks instead of regular meals, and inadequate or insufficient sleep. Importantly, obesity itself adversely affects self-esteem, further contributing to symptoms associated with anxiety and depression.[18]

As the internet is very often accessed via smartphones, findings related to the risk of smartphone addiction may also be relevant. Research shows that problematic smartphone use is moderately but robustly associated with both anxiety and depression. Problematic smartphone use can be viewed as an indicator of symptoms of anxiety and depression and a possible manifestation of these mental health problems in modern society. Furthermore, problematic smartphone use as a maladaptive coping behaviour may contribute by worsening these symptoms.[19]

[16] Dell'Osso and Fineberg, 'Learning to deal with problematic usage of the internet', p. 27.

[17] H. K. Lee and S. Chung, 'Conceptualization of internet addiction based on the public health perspective', in M. N. Potenza, K. A. Faust, and D. Faust (eds.), *The Oxford Handbook of Digital Technologies and Mental Health* (Oxford: Oxford University Press, 2020), pp. 87–96, at 89.

[18] Dell'Osso and Fineberg, 'Learning to deal with problematic usage of the internet', p. 29.

[19] C. Augner et al., 'The association between problematic smartphone use and symptoms of anxiety and depression – a meta-analysis' (2023) 45 *Journal of Public Health* 1, 193–201.

As the excessive use of social media is one subtype of internet addiction, research findings related to social media use risks are also relevant. The use of multiple social media platforms was found to be independently associated with symptoms of depression and anxiety, even when controlling for overall time spent in their use.[20]

In regard to social threats, it is noteworthy that one study conducted in Italy shows that adolescents who reported the problematic use of electronic media communication (mobile phone use and social media use) or internet addiction showed an increased risk of cyber-victimisation.[21]

In terms of the use of digital tools in the workplace, an exploratory qualitative study of professionals working in various industries in France showed that the majority of survey participants (93.4 per cent) either agreed or strongly agreed with the view that the digital tools were highly addictive. The findings of the study confirm that the use of digital tools at work is widespread. Heavy users of digital tools indicated that these tools provided a fertile ground for the development of professional exhaustion and burnout.[22]

More generally, addictive internet use can result in a goal conflict (i.e., a condition where two or more goals compete against each other and cause conflict in a person's mind) between entertainment and obligations, and negatively affect the social functioning of a person. In the case of binge-watching, for instance, the goal of getting enough sleep is offset by the goal of watching 'one more episode' before bedtime. The available evidence suggests that excessive binge-watching might lead to the impairment of daily functioning and disturbance in the quality of social life and sleep cycles.[23]

In addition to the problems described here, it needs to be kept in mind that problems caused by internet addiction have economic costs. The costs and burden from PUI not only accrue to the individuals suffering from the condition but also others, such as the individual's family or society as a whole, with regard to the impact on healthcare and other social security systems. Currently, the extent of such costs is unclear owing to the broad conditions related to digital technology use and insufficient data, but researchers are working on this issue and have proposed methodological requirements for an assessment of the cost burden of PUI, which includes but is not limited to internet addiction.[24]

20 H. Allam et al., 'Prevalence of problematic social media use among residents and teaching assistants in Ain Shams University Hospitals and faculty of medicine and its relationship to emotional distress' (2021) 114 (Supplement 1) *QJM: An International Journal of Medicine*, i216.

21 N. Marengo et al., 'Cyberbullying and electronic media communication problematic use in Piedmont. Data from HBSC study' (2020) 30 (Supplement 5) *European Journal of Public Health*, v869.

22 L. Pansu, 'Evaluation of "right to disconnect" legislation and its impact on employee's productivity' (2018) 5 *International Journal of Management and Applied Research* 3, 99–119.

23 Rahman and Arif, 'Impact of binge-watching on Netflix', p. 100.

24 Rumpf, Effertz and Montag, 'The cost burden of problematic internet usage'.

7.5 SPECIFIC FEATURES OF ADDICTION ONLINE

7.5.1 *Lack of Internet Specificity?*

One of the issues that arises in addressing the need for a law and policy response to the problem of internet addiction is whether there is a need for a specific response as the problem can be viewed as being part of a broader phenomenon of addiction to technologies or can be understood as being inaccurately named because it is not the medium of the internet but its problematic content (online gaming, gambling, pornography) that a person is addicted to that calls for law and policy measures regarding specific content, but not the internet in general.

Research suggests that internet addiction can be seen as one manifestation of the so-called technopanics where every new technology is met with fear about its pathological usage. As the internet is often accessed via smartphones, internet addiction analysis could benefit from smartphone addiction analysis. As smartphone addiction has similarities with TV addiction (similarities are most visible when TV and smartphone addiction are discussed as medical conditions),[25] the problem of internet addiction can be usefully compared to TV addiction. As excessive use of a mobile phone (irrespective of whether internet features are used) has similarities with excessive use of the internet (specifically, the paradox of technology facilitating communication but leading to an erosion in social well-being),[26] mobile phone addiction analysis could inform the analysis of the problem of internet addiction. In practical terms, the law and policy response to other technological addictions can have an indirect effect on internet addiction, which would suggest the need for a general rather than specific approach to internet addiction. The same would be true when addressing specific problematic content. As online gambling has similarities to gambling generally or as online pornography viewing is similar to viewing pornography using other media, addressing gambling addiction and pornography addiction would also tackle online gambling addiction and online pornography viewing addiction.

Research also shows, however, that certain features of the internet create favourable conditions for developing an addiction.

7.5.2 *Features of the Internet Which Contribute to Addiction*

The internet as a medium has features that reinforce problematic behaviour potentially leading to addiction. For example, features of internet-related gaming include the ease of accessing a game via portable or handheld devices, the possibility of

[25] Vanden Abeele and Mohr, 'Media addictions as Apparatgeist', pp. 1536–57.

[26] M. Seo, J.-H. Kim, and P. David, 'Always connected or always distracted? ADHD symptoms and social assurance explain problematic use of mobile phone and multicommunicating' (2015) 20 *Journal of Computer-Mediated Communication* 6, 667–81.

engaging in competitions with other gamers, the perception of oneself in a manner that is more rewarding and less impacted by real-world issues, and the specific genres, designs, and content of the games that are played, including the possibility of financial rewards or achieving winning status. In online gambling, new types of gambling (in addition to the traditional games such as poker, casino games, and sports betting) are available online, and online gambling is more accessible than gambling in the real world. Online shopping can be considered more addictive than shopping in the real world because e-commerce provides a range of potential addictive features, such as immediate product availability, anonymity, easy access, and affordability.[27] Pornography viewing has expanded substantially in the era of the internet, likely because of specific aspects of the internet (relating to anonymity, affordability, and availability).[28]

7.5.3 *Increased Vulnerability Online*

Everybody using the internet is subject to increased vulnerability. Two aspects are particularly important. First, every user of the internet is vulnerable to internet platforms, especially large ones, because of the power the platforms often have in defining, interpreting, and applying the rules governing online matters. Second, everybody is exposed to the possibility of technological vulnerabilities owing to the large amounts of personal data available online, lack of clarity regarding the algorithms used by platforms, possibilities of targeting individuals based on their profile, and so on. These two features make everybody vulnerable and in need of protection against the platforms interested in gaining attention for their products and designing their products accordingly, without necessarily warning the users of the danger of excessive use or addiction.

At the same time, some groups of internet users are particularly vulnerable (such as children) and require special protection, which suggests that the law and policy response should combine measures aimed at the general protection of all internet users and specific protection of particular vulnerable groups.

7.5.4 *Specific Vulnerable Groups*

Only a minority of internet users develop addiction, but belonging to certain groups increases the likelihood of developing such an addiction.

European studies show that relevant proportions of the population suffer from internet addiction, particularly in young age groups. Internet addiction is associated with the male gender, younger age, mental health problems, and unfavourable

[27] Dell'Osso and Fineberg, 'Learning to deal with problematic usage of the internet', pp. 12–14.

[28] Lee and Chung, 'Conceptualization of internet addiction', pp. 477–9.

social conditions.[29] Research confirms the importance of gender, age, mental health issues, personality, and neuroscientific traits, as well as social factors as risk factors for developing an internet addiction.

In terms of gender, even though the male gender is a bigger risk factor (as shown, for example, in a study concerning the relationship between internet addiction and obesity),[30] in some cases (such as explored in a study on cyber-victimisation and internet addiction where thirteen-year-old girls reported the highest proportions of both cyber-victimisation and electronic media communication problematic use),[31] females are more vulnerable.

Severe forms of internet addiction are more likely in people of a young age.[32] However, older persons are not immune to internet addiction, but the risk factors for older and younger people are different. Internet addiction for older individuals is strongly associated with obsessive-compulsive disorder and generalised anxiety disorder, whereas internet addiction in the young is strongest among those with ADHD and social anxiety disorder.[33]

In terms of mental health problems, research has confirmed that the occurrence of internet addiction in people with psychiatric problems is higher than in the general population. All substance use, early alcohol use, and smoking strongly indicate a high risk of developing internet addiction. Abuse of multiple substances is even more strongly associated with internet addiction. There is a high rate of internet addiction in people suffering from ADHD. Obsessive-compulsive personality traits such as rigidity, perfectionism, being dependent on others, and harm avoidance are common in problematic internet users, suggesting that an obsessive temperament may also predispose an individual to the development of an internet addiction.[34]

More generally, personality traits can be important. Research findings have shown that depression seems to be the strongest risk factor for internet addiction and the trait of optimism has a protective effect. In addition, the personality factor of extraversion was found to be associated negatively with internet addiction.[35]

Research suggests that neuroscientific traits can be important too. Recent studies suggest a neurobiological component for internet addiction. Anatomical and

29 H.-J. Rumpf, 'General population-based studies of problematic internet use: data from Europe', in M. N. Potenza, K. A. Faust, and D. Faust (eds.), *The Oxford Handbook of Digital Technologies and Mental Health* (Oxford: Oxford University Press, 2020), pp. 57–64.

30 A. K. Tsitsika et al., 'Association between problematic internet use, socio-demographic variables and obesity among European adolescents' (2016) 26 *European Journal of Public Health* 4, 617–22.

31 Marengo et al., 'Cyberbullying and electronic media communication'.

32 Dell'Osso and Fineberg, 'Learning to deal with problematic usage of the internet', p. 5.

33 Ibid., 28.

34 Ibid., 27–8.

35 J. Benka, O. Orosova, and L. Hricova, 'Risk and protective factors of problematic internet use in the context of prevention: Jozef Benka' (2016) 26 (Supplement 1) *European Journal of Public Health*, 367–8.

functional changes, genetic polymorphisms, and impairment of neurotransmitter systems have been found in brains of individuals with an internet addiction.[36]

Social factors, such as family life and parent–child relationships play a strong role in the development of persistent behaviours (e.g., gaming to escape parental conflict).[37] Maternal depression is related to children's internet addiction; in particular, mothers at graduate level or above, male children, and a child's normal or better academic performance show the strongest relationship with child internet addiction.[38]

Furthermore, we should not overlook the legal requirement to be connected and the prevailing culture of connectivity as risks that may contribute to the development of internet addiction.

This outline of risk factors enables us to identify vulnerable groups characterised by one or more such factors. Law and policymakers should adopt evidence-based measures targeted at most vulnerable groups, primarily children, especially where other risk factors co-occur.

7.5.5 *Specific Challenges: Conflicting Findings regarding the Harms and Benefits of Internet Usage*

One specific challenge in trying to prevent and fight internet addiction is related to conflicting findings regarding the overall assessment of the harms and benefits of internet usage. The internet paradox – that the technology provides conditions for better communication but using it leads to worsening social interactions – is well known. Some researchers have suggested that online social interaction and ICT use are likely to undermine social bonds as well as decrease social capital at both individual and societal levels, arguing that the more time one spends online, the less one can spend socialising with others. On the other hand, others have found that digital media use is associated with an increase in interpersonal communication and community participation, and in turn may provide both bridging and bonding of social capital.[39] The internet provides an important source of information and a precious channel for communication. More generally, it is considered to be a medium where human rights are exercised. Therefore, notwithstanding the risks associated with the excessive use of the internet, limiting access to the internet is frowned upon, as it limits opportunities to exercise human rights.

36 R. Pezoa-Jares and I. Espinoza-Luna, '629 – neurobiological findings associated with internet addiction: a literature review' (2013) 28 (Supplement 1) *European Psychiatry*, 1.

37 D. L. King and P. H. Delfabbro, 'The natural history of problematic internet use and gaming: recent findings, challenges, and future directions', in M. N. Potenza, K. A. Faust, and D. Faust (eds.), *The Oxford Handbook of Digital Technologies and Mental Health* (Oxford: Oxford University Press, 2020), pp. 65–74.

38 D. W. Choi et al., 'The association between parental depression and adolescent's internet addiction in South Korea' (2018) 17 *Annals of General Psychiatry*, Article 15.

39 E. Hargittai and Y. P. Hsieh, 'Digital inequality', in W. H. Dutton (ed.), *The Oxford Handbook of Internet Studies* (Oxford: Oxford University Press, 2013), pp. 129–50.

The possibility of different viewpoints on the harms and benefits of the internet practically results in a difference of attitudes of various government agencies based on their functions and relative interest in public health and economic value.[40] This makes it difficult to promote a consistent approach regarding, for example, limiting supply of online products containing addictive features and limiting screen time in the process of education, among others.

Another challenge related to the use of online media is the lack of knowledge on how to safely use the internet. Knowledge gaps in the domain of digital media use may be more severe than gaps in uses of traditional media, given that meaningful internet use requires new skill sets, such as refined search strategies and critical approaches to evaluating content credibility that are less associated with using traditional media.[41] Recognising the addictive design of online products, applying protective strategies, and knowing where to turn for professional help when everything else fails are the skills that need to be taught to diminish the threat of internet addiction.

7.6 LAW AND POLICY RESPONSES AND SOLUTIONS

Law and policy responses and solutions in different legal systems vary and are not necessarily very elaborate or comprehensive. Four approaches are presented by way of example here.

7.6.1 *Public Health Policies: Comprehensive Approach*

Given the predominance of health aspects in addressing PUI, one could expect health policy responses to internet addiction. At present, there have been limited public health interventions with regard to many forms of PUI, with the partial exception of online gambling disorder and gaming disorder. Public health approaches have been attempted in countries particularly affected by online gaming disorder, including South Korea, China, Japan, and Germany. Broadly in line with existing approaches to substance use disorders, these interventions have largely focused on (a) limiting supply, (b) reducing demand, and (c) reducing harms.[42]

Researchers note that the substance use disorders approach is suitable because internet addiction has similar clinical characteristics to, for example, an alcohol use disorder.

The public health model of alcoholism, which is composed of three risk factors (including host, agent, and the environment) can also be applied to excessive (or addictive) internet use. This differs from the medical model, which explains a

[40] Lee and Chung, 'Conceptualization of internet addiction', pp. 94–5.

[41] Hargittai and Hsieh, 'Digital inequality', pp. 129–50.

[42] D. J. Stein and A. Hartford, 'Health-policy approaches for problematic internet use: lessons from substance use disorders' (2022) 45 *Current Opinion in Behavioral Sciences*, 101151.

disease mainly based on individual vulnerability. Under the public health model, public health policy interventions are necessary to reduce all the relevant internet addiction risk factors.

Furthermore, people using the internet can be grouped as regular users, users at the initial stage of the addiction process, and an addicted group experiencing clear addiction symptoms with various impairments in a wide range of areas. Similar to substance addiction, internet addiction should also be understood as a problem on a continuum. Therefore, public health policy interventions need to be adjusted to the severity of the internet addiction. Such a model has already been applied to alcohol and gambling.

Preventative education in combination with the public health promotion campaigns proposed in gambling addiction can be proposed as a primary intervention targeting the general population. Secondary interventions would implement screening and intensive prevention programmes using screening tools. Educating individuals who are most likely to encounter others with internet addiction problems and help them cope with their addiction is another form of secondary intervention. Tertiary interventions involve constructing an infrastructure to employ evidence-based treatment programmes, fostering addiction experts, and constructing a community-based aftercare system for relapse prevention.

The Korean public health policy response to internet addiction has largely followed the public health model described here, as it addresses various risk factors and is adjusted to different levels of the severity of internet use.

In response to the internet addiction problem, Korea established the Third Internet Addiction Prevention & Resolution Comprehensive Plan in 2016, led by the Ministry of Science, ICT, and Future Planning in cooperation with the Ministry of Culture, Sports, and Tourism (governing game contents), and the Department of Education, the Ministry of Gender Equality and Family, and the Ministry of Health and Welfare (governing youth protection services). Measures applied include education and group counselling at schools aimed at prevention, screening students and providing counselling for those identified as at risk, and psychiatric treatment for excessive gamers. Help is provided inter alia via Internet Addiction Response Centres in sixteen metropolitan cities, internet addiction counsellors in the forty-five Education District Offices, Excessive Gaming Healing Centres, the Rescue School (a short-term residential treatment programme), community-based Addiction Management Centres, and social service institutions. One of the institutional challenges is to ensure better collaboration and avoid overlap of activities conducted by different agencies. Owing to conflicting perspectives in regard to the public health risks and economic value of the digital media industry, there are different attitudes to internet addiction-related problems even in government agencies.[43]

43 Lee and Chung, 'Conceptualization of internet addiction', pp. 87–96.

The European Union (EU) also considers taking a comprehensive public health policy approach to address the problem of internet addiction. Public health policy options offered by researchers for consideration to the European Parliament (EP) include health promotion, strengthening health services available for internet users that engage in harmful use, and the creation of units to address the harmful use of the internet within various EU Commission Directorates-General and Member State ministries. Information campaigns can create awareness and help users to develop skills that prevent harm. Public recognition of internet addiction as a disorder is believed to encourage people to seek help. Strengthening health services means providing support for health professionals so that they are able to recognise cases of harmful internet use and offer clinical services. If internet addiction were to be recognised as a mental disorder, this would (a) enhance psychological and pharmacological treatment options ('digital detox') available to individuals affected by this condition, (b) facilitate reimbursement by insurance companies, and (c) increase the screening that could be undertaken for children with preliminary symptoms of internet addiction.[44]

7.6.2 *Consumer Protection: Product Safety Standards*

Loot boxes have been identified as an example of a problematic element of computer game design, which is akin to gambling and can potentially lead to addiction to gambling online. Some game designs resemble addictive designs of conditioning known, for example, from slot machines.

Loot boxes are subject to general national legislation on contracts and consumer protection. In addition, several national authorities have investigated the conditions under which loot boxes may qualify as gambling. With the exception of Belgium, the Netherlands, and Slovakia, no EU country has come to the conclusion that loot boxes fulfil their national gambling criteria. As a result, only those countries have so far taken or are considering taking regulatory steps to ban loot boxes. In those countries that have already banned them, this has led to the withdrawal of the loot box feature from games in these markets. In other countries, less invasive action has been taken including awareness raising and developing guidelines for parents and players.

As gambling belongs to the sphere of national competence, it has been suggested that the EU could approach the issue of loot boxes and problematic game design more generally from the consumer protection perspective.[45]

Qualifying loot boxes as gambling may not work also in those cases where loot boxes are just one element of chance in an otherwise skill-based game, which was the

[44] G. Quaglio and S. Millar, 'Potentially negative effects of internet use' (2020), European Parliamentary Research Service, www.europarl.europa.eu/RegData/etudes/IDAN/2020/641540/EPRS_IDA(2020)641540_EN.pdf.

[45] A. Cerulli-Harms et al., 'Loot boxes in online games and their effect on consumers, in particular young consumers' (2020), European Parliament Research Service, www.europarl.europa.eu/RegData/etudes/STUD/2020/652727/IPOL_STU(2020)652727_EN.pdf.

verdict reached by the Dutch Administrative Jurisdiction Division in overturning a fine for developers of the FIFA game,[46] who had previously been fined €10 million over a failure to obtain a gambling licence to operate 'Ultimate Team' packs, which gave in-game players who pay for the packs access to an unspecified group of players they could add to their squad or onwards trade.[47]

The practice of marking the products as fit for a certain age based on inter alia its loot box feature is in line with the consumer protection rationale. Germany introduced such marking as of 2023.[48]

In 2023, the EP adopted a resolution on consumer protection in online video games in line with a European single market approach.[49] The resolution calls for gamers to be better protected from addiction and other manipulative practices and stresses that children's games must take into account their age, rights, and vulnerabilities. At the same time, it notes the enormous potential for growth and innovation in the video game sector and its need of support.[50] The resolution contains specific proposals on how to enhance consumer protection in this field. It notes that aggressive commercial practices used in the manipulative design of some games are already prohibited under EU law (para. 15). It calls on the Commission to assess whether the current consumer law framework is sufficient to address all the consumer law issues raised by loot boxes and in-game purchases and, if not, to present the necessary legislative proposals. 'These proposals should assess whether an obligation to disable in-game payments and loot box mechanisms by default or a ban on paid loot boxes should be proposed to protect minors, avoid the fragmentation of the single market and ensure that consumers benefit from the same level of protection, no matter their place of residence' (para. 27). It suggests an *ex-ante* child impact assessment might be required from providers of online video games (para. 28). The resolution also calls on the Commission and the Member States' consumer protection authorities to ensure that consumer law is fully respected and enforced (para. 48).

7.6.3 *Vulnerable Groups Approach: Rights of the Child*

Taking a consumer protection perspective and protecting children from the harm of loot boxes and other problematic video game design features is one example of

[46] T. Phillips, 'EA's €10m Dutch FIFA loot box fine overturned' (2020), www.eurogamer.net/eas-10m-dutch-fifa-loot-box-fine-has-been-overturned.

[47] G. Van Mansfeld, 'Consumer law arguments raised against gaming "loot boxes"' (2022), www.pinsentmasons.com/out-law/news/consumer-law-arguments-gaming-loot-boxes.

[48] D. O'Boyle, 'Germany to add loot boxes to video game age-rating criteria' (2022), https://igamingbusiness.com/esports/video-gaming/germany-to-add-loot-boxes-to-video-game-age-rating-criteria/.

[49] EP resolution of 18 January 2023 on consumer protection in online video games: a European single market approach (2022/2014(INI)).

[50] European Parliament, 'Protecting gamers and encouraging grow in the video games sector', 18 January 2023, www.europarl.europa.eu/news/en/press-room/20230113IPR66646/protecting-gamers-and-encouraging-growth-in-the-video-games-sector.

the vulnerable group protection approach. Other examples of activities aimed at protecting children from internet addiction abound.

At the global level, the World Health Organization has been defining standards of healthy sedentary screen time for children of various age groups. Under its recent guidelines, for children under one year screen time is not recommended. For one-year-olds, sedentary screen time (such as watching TV or videos, playing computer games) is not recommended. For those aged two years, sedentary screen time should be no more than one hour; less is better.[51] On the other hand, medical research also suggests that with twenty-four-hour connectivity and when digital and social media technologies are an integral part of the experiences and identities of children and young people, it is the quality and nature of engagement rather than its quantity that determine inappropriate use of digital media or the internet.[52]

The need for an approach that enables the reaping of the benefits of internet use while avoiding the risks of its overuse has been highlighted by international human rights bodies both at the global and regional level.

The United Nations (UN) Committee on the Rights of the Child (CRC) in its General Comment on children's rights in relation to the digital environment recognises that the digital environment affords new opportunities for the realisation of children's rights,[53] but also poses a risk of their violation or abuse (para. 3). It recognises health risks related to the use of digital tools but does not specifically identify the problem of internet addiction as a health issue. It does, however, admit the importance of a healthy balance of digital and non-digital activities and sufficient rest (para. 98), which resembles the rationale of public health policy interventions aimed at limiting screen time for those suffering from internet addiction. The CRC also recognises the need to address other risks that are related to internet addiction. Notably, the CRC admits that measures may be needed to prevent unhealthy engagement in digital games or social media, such as regulating against digital designs that undermine children's development and rights (para. 96). Furthermore, the General Comment mentions the increasing importance of children gaining an understanding of the digital environment, including its infrastructure, business practices, and persuasive strategies (para. 105). These two provisions remind us of the internet addiction research into the problematic design of video games, such as loot boxes, as a result of which online gaming can lead to online gambling and develop into an addiction.

The Council of Europe, in its guidelines to respect, protect and fulfil the rights of the child in the digital environment,[54] recognises that access to and use of the digital

[51] World Health Organization, 'To grow up healthy, children need to sit less and play more', 24 April 2019, www.who.int/news/item/24-04-2019-to-grow-up-healthy-children-need-to-sit-less-and-play-more.

[52] Megele and Longfield, *Safeguarding Children and Young People Online*, p. 116.

[53] UN Committee on the Rights of the Child (CRC), 'General comment No. 25 (2021) on children's rights in relation to the digital environment' (2 March 2021) CRC/C/GC/25.

[54] CoE, 'Guidelines to respect, protect and fulfil the rights of the child in the digital environment', Recommendation CM/Rec(2018)7 of the Committee of Ministers.

environment is important for the realisation of children's rights and fundamental freedoms. Where children do not have access to the digital environment or where this access is limited owing to poor connectivity, their ability to fully exercise their human rights may be affected (para. 10). The Guidelines recognise some health risks related to the use of the internet – excessive use, sleep deprivation, and physical harm (para. 51) – but do not specifically identify internet addiction as a health risk. They do, however, recognise the importance of safety by design as a guiding principle for product and service features and functionalities addressed to or used by children (para. 54), and, despite the strong protection of the right of access to the internet, recognise the legitimacy of and encourage the development of parental controls installed in various products as a measure to mitigate risks for children in the digital environment (para. 54). The Guidelines also specifically recognise the problem of premature exposure to the internet (para. 55). States are expected to require the use of effective systems of age verification to ensure children are protected from products, services, and content in the digital environment that are legally restricted with reference to specific ages (para. 56) and to take measures to ensure that children are protected from commercial exploitation in the digital environment, including exposure to age-inappropriate forms of advertising and marketing (para. 57).

7.6.4 *Right to Disconnect and Its Insufficiency*

There is growing attention to 'disconnection' as a solution to digital technology overuse. Disconnection is a new area of focus for both tech and health and wellness industries, which develop and sell a wide range of digital well-being interventions, ranging from digital detox programmes to screen time monitoring apps to products that create physical barriers to use. These interventions are intended to help individuals achieve a 'healthier' relationship to their technology, and therefore stand in opposition to conceptualisations of 'unhealthy' overuse.[55] Disconnection also features as a research question in new media studies.[56] Researchers have acknowledged the existence of the so-called digital divide of disconnection as certain individuals and social groups lack the privilege to disconnect.[57] Importantly, the right to disconnect has also become an object of law and policymaking.

According to Eurofound (the EU Agency for the Improvement of Living and Working Conditions), the right to disconnect refers to a worker's right to be able to disengage from work and refrain from engaging in work-related electronic communications, such as emails or other messages, during non-work hours.[58] This

[55] Vanden Abeele and Mohr, 'Media addictions as Apparatgeist', pp. 1536–57.

[56] S. Lomborg and B. Ytre-Arne, 'Advancing digital disconnection research: introduction to the special issue' (2021) 27 *Convergence* 6, 1529–35.

[57] Vanden Abeele and Mohr, 'Media addictions as Apparatgeist'.

[58] European Observatory of Working Life, 'Right to disconnect' (2021), www.eurofound.europa.eu/observatories/eurwork/industrial-relations-dictionary/right-to-disconnect.

applies in the context of work and refers to one aspect of safe and healthy working conditions.

In January 2017, France passed a new employment law allowing workers in organisations with more than fifty employees to negotiate the conditions of a 'right to disconnect' from work after working hours. Article 55 under Chapter II 'Adapting the Labour Law to the Digital Age' of the Labour Code was introduced, aiming to protect workers against the problems associated with the increasing use of digital technology in the workplace.[59] Scholars do not necessarily see this law as a solution to the problem of being required to be connected. Some consider that with the passing of this law, it would seem that the employee can no longer invoke this 'right' under the traditional conditions of waged labour, where it would be on a par with one's unpaid or free time. Instead of protecting the employee, the law runs the risk of turning *all* our available hours into the time of (unwaged) labour, thus feeding into the very problematic it tries to oppose, a problematic that characterises our current 'culture of connectivity'.[60]

Notwithstanding the lack of clear evidence that legislation on the right to disconnect effectively contributes to solving the problem of the requirement to be connected, some other EU Member States have also adopted or debated the need to adopt similar legislation. According to a 2021 Eurofound report, to date, Belgium, France, Italy, and Spain have legislation that includes the right to disconnect and in five other EU Member States (Finland, Germany, Lithuania, Slovenia, Sweden) policy debate on the right to disconnect was in progress.[61] In various EU Member States, the right to disconnect was also an object of company-level initiatives. In Germany, Volkswagen was reportedly the first company to implement a company-wide freeze on out-of-hours emails in 2012.[62] Moreover, the German Labour Ministry itself has also adopted policies regarding after-hours communication, in order to encourage other employers to follow suit. The ministry has banned any communication with staff outside working hours, except in emergencies, and implemented rules that do not allow managers to take disciplinary action against employees who switch off their mobile devices or fail to respond to communication after working hours.[63]

The EP adopted a resolution in 2021 on the right to disconnect,[64] inter alia calling on the Commission to prepare a directive 'that enables those who work

[59] Eurofound, *Right to Disconnect: Exploring Company Practices* (Luxembourg: Publications Office of the European Union, 2021), p. 18.

[60] P. Hesselberth, 'Discourses on disconnectivity and the right to disconnect' (2018) 20 *New Media & Society* 5, 1994–2010.

[61] Eurofound, *Right to Disconnect.*

[62] European Observatory of Working Life, 'Right to disconnect'.

[63] K. Müller, 'The right to disconnect' (2020) European Parliamentary Research Service, p. 4.

[64] European Parliament resolution of 21 January 2021 with recommendations to the Commission on the right to disconnect, OJ C 456, 10.11.2021, pp. 161–76.

digitally to disconnect outside their working hours'. This directive 'should also establish minimum requirements for remote working and clarify working conditions, hours and rest periods'. Members of the EP believe that 'workers' right to disconnect is vital to protecting their physical and mental health and well-being and to protecting them from psychological risks', requesting the Commission to submit a proposal for an act on the right to disconnect. In its EU strategic framework on health and safety at work, the Commission explains that it will 'ensure appropriate follow-up'. The Commission admits that working remotely full time, which increased during the pandemic together with other remote-working trends, such as permanent connectivity, a lack of social interaction, and the increased use of ICT, has given an additional rise to psychosocial and ergonomic risks.[65] Importantly, the EP resolution among risks posed by excessive use of technological devices mentions (in recital E) techno-addiction (along with isolation, sleep deprivation, emotional exhaustion, anxiety and burnout), which implies that the right to disconnect might also be instrumental for addressing concerns related specifically to internet addiction.

The right to disconnect is also included in the Declaration on Digital Rights and Principles for the Digital Decade signed on 15 December 2022 by the presidents of the EU Commission, the EP, and the Council.[66] The preamble (para. 4) mentions that the EP called for a strengthened protection of 'workers' rights and a right to disconnect'. The main body of the declaration (para. 6) contains a commitment to 'ensuring that everyone is able to disconnect and benefit from safeguards for work–life balance in a digital environment'.

Academic debate on the right to disconnect in the EU focuses on a possible need to redefine the rest period under the Working Time Directive to ensure that a person is entitled to be not only outside the workplace but also beyond the employer's reach, to urge Member States to consider introducing the right to disconnect into their domestic law,[67] or to do nothing as the issue can already be resolved using existing EU legislation or settled case law.[68] The EU has the necessary competence to pass legal acts on the right to disconnect. Even if there is no enacted or proposed EU regulation that directly addresses the right to disconnect, Articles 153 and 154 TFEU could be the basis for the adoption of directives setting out minimum requirements,

65 Communication from the Commission to the European Parliament, the Council, the European Economic and Social Committee and the Committee of the Regions, 'EU strategic framework on health and safety at work 2021–2027, Occupational safety and health in a changing world of work', COM(2021) 323 final.

66 European Commission, 'Digital rights and principles: Presidents of the Commission, the European Parliament and the Council sign European Declaration', 15 December 2022, https://ec.europa.eu/commission/presscorner/detail/en/ip_22_7683.

67 L. Mitrus, 'Potential implications of the Matzak judgment (quality of rest time, right to disconnect)' (2019) 10 *European Labour Law Journal* 4, 386–97.

68 M. Glowacka, 'A little less autonomy? The future of working time flexibility and its limits' (2021) 12 *European Labour Law Journal* 2, 113–33.

as well as supporting and complementing the activities of the Member States in the area of working conditions.[69]

Domestic legal standards related to the right to disconnect were also adopted or debated beyond Europe. On 2 December 2021, the Ontario government in Canada introduced the 'Right to Disconnect' policy in the Employment Standards Act of 2000. Employers that employ twenty-five or more employees are required to have a written policy on disconnecting from work in place for all employees. The Employment Standards Act of 2000 defines 'disconnecting from work' as 'not engaging in work-related communications, including emails, telephone calls, video calls or the sending or reviewing of other messages, so as to be free from the performance of work'. This is not an exhaustive list, meaning that other forms of work-related communications can also fall under this definition. The goal of the right to disconnect law is to allow employees to disconnect from work and enjoy downtime. Ideally, the ability to disconnect from work will protect an employee's mental well-being and avoid burnout.[70] The Working for Workers Act was proposed by the provincial government in 2021 in response to concerns around burnout, particularly during the pandemic, when working from home meant lines between work and home blurred even further.[71]

Although the right to disconnect may be seen as contributing to the prevention of internet addiction, it is of limited value for this purpose.

First, for those addicted to the internet, merely having a right to disconnect would not suffice to change their addictive behaviour patterns. In an exploratory qualitative study of professionals working in various industries in France, some participants indicated setting barriers to protect themselves from the negative side of being always hyperconnected. However, they felt it was not easy to overcome a technology addiction as it required willpower and wisdom to regain control of the technology. As not everyone manages to regulate it by themselves, some interviewees pinned their hope on the law as a way to help protect workers from the overuse of digital tools. Although almost every survey participant declared being in favour of the 'right to disconnect' legislation, they were not sure how the law could make them more productive. The study also revealed the importance of educative actions. Awareness campaigns and training sessions advising on how to use digital tools more productively and reminding workers of the benefits of disconnecting could help significantly.[72]

69 Müller, 'The right to disconnect'.

70 Monkhouse Law, 'Right to disconnect Ontario – the law in Ontario 2022', 13 September 2022, www.monkhouselaw.com/right-to-disconnect-ontario/.

71 S. Ho, 'Ontario's 'right to disconnect' law: who qualifies and what are the loopholes?', 7 June 2022, www.ctvnews.ca/business/ontario-s-right-to-disconnect-law-who-qualifies-and-what-are-the-loopholes-1.5936773.

72 L. Pansu, 'Evaluation of 'right to disconnect' legislation and its impact on employee's productivity' (2018) 5 *International Journal of Management and Applied Research* 3, 99–119.

Second, research shows that being connected when required to do so (notably, for the purpose of studying) is less likely to result in an internet addiction than being connected during leisure time. Research carried out in Lithuania shows that for schoolchildren of all ages it is the length of screentime as well as internet activities specifically aimed at amusement that increase the risk of PUI.[73] In north Tanzania, undergraduate students using the internet at the college were less likely to be addicted to the internet compared with those using it both at a hostel or home and college.[74] Therefore, the right to disconnect, if its application was limited to the work context, would not be of use in those situations where internet addiction manifests itself when digital tools are used in other contexts.

This suggests that to combat the overuse of digital tools, more proactive methods, such as raising awareness of the dangers and the safe use of the internet, are necessary, and even being required to disconnect could be considered.

Arguably, the requirement to disconnect has already become a cultural requisite and a lifestyle component for some. Media researchers note the prevalence of the self-responsibility narrative, which now takes the form of the 'responsibility to disconnect' as a precondition to keeping up with digital society. This expectation of self-discipline also comes with a heavy moral component: Societal assumptions about what is healthy or good feed into a moral superiority for those who can dutifully disconnect and shame for those who cannot. By framing 'failure to disconnect' as a problem of willpower, feelings of shame and guilt are legitimised and even capitalised on as mechanisms that could be used to effect change. In doing so, disconnection is implicitly framed as an act of self-improvement.[75] In the legal context, the requirement to disconnect has been attempted for schools in some countries where a ban on the use of cell phones was introduced, notably in France, the province of Ontario in Canada, and the state of Victoria in Australia.

Research shows that for most children across Europe, smartphones are now the preferred means of going online. This often means that they have 'anywhere, anytime' connectivity, with the majority of children reporting using their smartphones daily or almost all the time.[76] One study has shown that the restrictions on the use of smartphones can have a positive impact on academic performance. Restricting mobile phone use can also be a low-cost policy to reduce educational inequalities.[77]

[73] R. Jusienė et al., 'Ilgalaikis ekranų poveikis vaikų fizinei ir psichikos sveikatai: mokslinio projekto ataskaita' (Valstybinis visuomenės sveikatos stiprinimo fondas, 2022) ['Long-term effects of screen exposure on children's physical and mental health: scientific project report' (State Public Health Strengthening Fund)], https://lt.mediavaikai.lt/copy-of-results, p. 39.

[74] Mboya et al., 'Internet addiction and associated factors among medical and allied health sciences students in northern Tanzania', p. 8.

[75] Vanden Abeele and Mohr, 'Media addictions as Apparatgeist'.

[76] D. Smahel et al., 'EU Kids Online 2020: Survey results from 19 countries' (2020), DOI: 10.21953/lse.47fdeqj01ofo, p. 6.

[77] L.-P. Beland and R. Murphy, 'Ill communication: technology, distraction & student performance' (2015), https://cep.lse.ac.uk/pubs/download/dp1350.pdf.

In France, the ban was introduced at the level of national legislation. Under the Code of Education as amended in 2018, schoolchildren are not allowed to use mobile phones or any other electronic communication at schools and during all school activities even if they are held outside school. Exceptions are allowed for teaching purposes and for children with special needs. The phone can be confiscated for a certain period if the rule is not followed.[78] At the time of the ban, the French Education Minister mentioned the problem of screen addiction as a phenomenon of bad mobile phone use and talked about the role of the state in protecting children by means of education.[79] In the state of Victoria in Australia, the ban on the use of mobile phones at schools was introduced in 2020,[80] as a policy of the Minister of Education,[81] aimed at improving student performance and managing risks related to the use of technology, without specifically identifying the problem of addiction but mentioning that the use of mobile phones requires more and more of the user's time. In Canada, the ban was introduced in the province of Ontario in 2019,[82] but not in Quebec after a debate leaving the decision for the management of individual schools.[83] Similarly, in the UK and the US it is up to individual schools to set their own rules. In the UK, parents seem to support the idea of such a ban. In the US, the situation is different. Owing to the spate of school shootings, parents tend to want the reverse – the opportunity to contact their children to remain open. Reportedly, this was one of the reasons why a school cell phone ban in New York was overturned in 2015.[84] Such variety of approaches shows that the problematic use of the internet among schoolchildren and the value of being temporarily disconnected is recognised, the bans on the use of the internet are not necessarily recognised as a necessary approach and even when such bans are introduced they apply only in certain situations, for certain people and not without exceptions. Finally, the role of education and educators in creating a culture of better managed use of the internet is acknowledged, which suggests that responsibility to disconnect or disconnection as a lifestyle can be taught.

78 République française, Code de l'éducation, Article L511-5, www.legifrance.gouv.fr/codes/article_lc/LEGIARTI000037286581.

79 R. Smith, 'France bans smartphones from schools', CNN, 31 July 2018, https://edition.cnn.com/2018/07/31/europe/france-smartphones-school-ban-intl/index.html.

80 Government of Victoria, Australia, 'Mobile phones in schools', www.vic.gov.au/mobile-phones-schools.

81 Government of Victoria, Australia, 'Mobile phones – student use, a ministerial policy formally issued by the Minister for Education under section 5.2.1(2)(b) of the Education and Training Reform Act 2006 (Vic)', last updated in 2022, www2.education.vic.gov.au/pal/students-using-mobile-phones/policy.

82 The Canadian Press, 'Cellphone ban in Ontario classrooms comes into effect today', *CTV News*, 4 November 2019, https://toronto.ctvnews.ca/cellphone-ban-in-ontario-classrooms-comes-into-effect-today-1.4668824.

83 S. Parent, 'Québec rejette l'interdiction des cellulaires à l'école comme en Ontario', 14 March 2019, www.rcinet.ca/fr/2019/03/14/quebec-rejette-linterdiction-des-cellulaires-a-lecole-comme-en-ontario/.

84 A. Ledsom, 'The mobile phone ban in French schools, one year on. Would it work elsewhere?', 30 August 2019, www.forbes.com/sites/alexledsom/2019/08/30/the-mobile-phone-ban-in-french-schools-one-year-on-would-it-work-elsewhere/.

7.7 HOW INTERNATIONAL HUMAN RIGHTS LAW CAN HELP

International and European human rights law provide the necessary preconditions for protecting a person against the human rights harms caused by internet addiction, but those preconditions have not been spelled out in the context of concrete cases. Nevertheless, international human rights law is slowly growing as soft law instruments on internet addiction-related matters are adopted.

7.7.1 *Existing Norms at the Global Level*

International human rights law already contains norms relevant for preventing and addressing internet addiction. The best interests of the child, which is one of the underlying principles of the UN system of the protection of the rights of the child, encompasses interests related to the safe usage of the internet. The fact that the UN Committee on the Rights of the Child has already addressed the issue of rights in the digital realm is important as it provides a basis for further interpretations of what it takes to ensure that children do not develop unhealthy habits when using the internet.

The right of everyone to the enjoyment of the highest attainable standard of physical and mental health provided for in Article 12 of the International Covenant on Economic, Social and Cultural Rights is a basis for interpretations requiring states to take measures to prevent internet addiction and to provide medical services for those affected. As demonstrated in this chapter, efforts by the state should be directed at the development of a comprehensive public health model aimed inter alia at the problem of internet addiction. The challenge in this respect is that under a surviving dichotomic civil and political versus socio-economic rights system, the right to health enjoys relatively weak protection as its implementation is dependent on the available resources of the state. One way to diminish this weakness is to rely either on the core of the right to health, which under the concept of core obligations needs to be guaranteed in any circumstances,[85] or on the non-discrimination element of the right to health, which is required irrespective of existing limitations as to available resources.[86]

Protection from discrimination in the context of internet addiction is possible on various grounds. On the ground of young age and on the ground of sex it can be claimed that children and, depending on the context, boys or girls require special protection against internet addiction compared with the general population. On the ground of disability, claiming that internet addiction because of resulting obstacles amounts to a disability (an approach inspired by Canadian experience: the Ontario Human Rights Commission takes an expansive and flexible approach to defining

85 UN Committee on Economic, Social and Cultural Rights (CESCR), 'General Comment No. 3: The Nature of States Parties' Obligations (Art. 2, Para. 1 of the Covenant)' (14 December 1990) E/1991/23, para. 10.

86 Ibid., para. 1.

mental health disabilities and addictions that are protected by the Ontario Human Rights Code; it considers that the Code protects people with mental health disabilities and addictions from discrimination and harassment on the grounds of disability),[87] it could be argued that it is under the UN Convention of the Rights of Persons of Disabilities that states should take measures to provide the required services for those afflicted by internet addiction.

7.7.2 *Avenues to be Explored Based on Regional Experience*

Regional human rights law often acts as a laboratory in which new definitions and interpretations of human rights are developed and tested. In regard to internet addiction, the Council of Europe approach towards the protection of children in the digital realm is an example of how this process of identifying existing threats and developing the required standards gradually progresses (even though at present internet addiction has not yet been clearly identified by the Council of Europe as a human rights issue).

EU law has tools that enable it to expand into new areas faster than would be possible under international (global or regional) human rights law. The EU fundamental rights catalogue – the Charter of Fundamental Rights – is not limited to any specific type of human rights and, notably, contains provisions on health (as an element of working conditions and in Article 35 on healthcare) and consumer protection (Article 38). Even though official explanations of the Charter state that both Article 35 and Article 38 contain principles rather than rights,[88] Charter provisions have the potential to be transformed from vaguely described principles to specifically defined rights. This potential derives from the fact that the EU can concretise its commitments by way of adopting, within the scope of its competencies, secondary legal acts. Moreover, the EU's fundamental rights can be a trump card in a political discussion on the need to adopt further legal acts on a certain issue. If the Charter applies in a certain type of legal relationship, this indicates that a fundamental right is at issue, and in this manner raises the importance of the question at issue.

When we specifically consider internet addiction, the EU approach of addressing problematic video game design via the consumer rights perspective is novel and instructive, as consumer rights protection is included in the catalogue of human (fundamental) rights only in the EU Charter of Fundamental Rights but not in international human rights law documents. Similarly, the right to disconnect, which first became a subject matter of certain domestic laws, entered the rights debate first in the EU where, even though it is not a right contained in the Charter, it was included in the declaration on digital rights, where it will serve as an indicator

[87] Ontario Human Rights Commission, 'Policy on preventing discrimination based on mental health disabilities and addictions' (2014), www3.ohrc.on.ca/en/policy-preventing-discrimination-based-mental-health-disabilities-and-addictions Chapter 4.

[88] Explanations relating to the Charter of Fundamental Rights, OJ C 303, 14.12.2007, pp. 17–35.

for EU institutions that the protection of this right will have to be further developed. As international human rights law follows a similar path of putting ideas into soft law and then gradually transforming these into hard law, it is advisable to consider including the ideas tested in the EU in texts of non-binding resolutions of relevant international institutions (such as the UN Human Rights Council and UN human rights treaty bodies documents) to spark further debate on the required action at the global level. Reflecting on the experience of regional human rights law systems, such as the Council of Europe, should also continue to be an inspiration in developing the global system for the protection of human rights and, in particular, addressing the problem of internet addiction.

7.8 CONCLUSION

This chapter has shown that a multidisciplinary approach is useful for the purpose of identifying human rights issues related to the phenomenon of internet addiction and, ultimately, for improving human rights law. Mental health research, in particular, can provide lawyers with evidence necessary to assess the severity of internet addiction-related threats, to identify the most vulnerable groups and the required legal response. Understanding that children are the most vulnerable group but that other age groups are not immune to internet addiction is one example where medical research findings can lead to legal research on which human rights instruments can provide protection for persons of different ages afflicted by internet addiction. Importantly, mental health research also shows that moving online makes certain addictions more likely, which proves that internet addiction is a novel type of addiction that requires a novel human rights law response.

Within the discipline of law, the interaction of various legal systems is necessary to transplant best practices from one legal system to another. Whether or not 'the right to be disconnected' will continue its journey from domestic legal systems to international human rights law via its most recent appearance in EU law, remains to be seen, but the fact that there are domestic practices related to disconnecting seems to invite further dialogue of legal systems.

Finally, as we see the limits of available medical evidence to validate diagnoses of internet addiction and realise that the law may remain uninformed by medical research for some time to come, human rights law and its interpretation can be influenced by cultural factors. Where the connectivity (or 'always on') culture is perceived as increasing the risk of burnout, and disconnection for a short time is seen as an escape, further research into the right to disconnect as a human rights issue seems to be required. Disconnection as a lifestyle can possibly alleviate the severity of internet addiction problems, but whether it is states or internet platforms that can act as better influencers promoting such practices and what is the minimum required from states in this case by international human rights law (e.g., can the state leave it to the platforms to promote healthy internet use?) is a question for further research.

8

Just Don't Get Caught!

Barbora Bad'urová

8.1 INTRODUCTION

We can observe various forms of harm, wrongdoing and crime in the digital environment, violating traditional or newly modified digital human rights.[1] 'Globalisation, digitalisation and smart technologies have escalated the propensity and severity of cybercrime.'[2] A serious increase in cybercrime and cyberattacks has been reported,[3] and estimations for the year 2020 predicted that cybercrime would cost the global economy around US$1 trillion, which is a 50 per cent increase in comparison with 2018.[4] However, the financial impact is not the only problem resulting from the unregulated possibilities in the digital world. For instance, as stated in 2018, around 45 per cent of adult internet users in the UK had experienced some form of online harm;[5] potential harm is affecting not just adults but also children,[6] and not just private individuals but also larger entities such as companies, organisations, and so on. The harm can also be psychological, social, ethical, and medical.

1 Department for Digital Culture, Media and Sport, 'Online harms feasibility study' (2021), https://assets.publishing.service.gov.uk/media/639b0511e90e072180b2a7c6/DCMS_Online_Harm_Feasibility_study_v2.pdf.

2 F. Cremer et al., 'Cyber risk and cybersecurity: a systematic review of data availability' (2022) 47 *The Geneva Papers on Risk and Insurance – Issues and Practice*, 698–736, at 698.

3 E. Decker, 'Full count? Crime rate swings, cybercrime misses and why we don't really know the score' (2018) 5 *Journal of National Security, Law and Policy*, 583–604.

4 Cremer et al., 'Cyber risk and cybersecurity', p. 698.

5 Kantar Media, 'Internet users' experience of harm online: summary of survey research' (2018), www.ofcom.org.uk/siteassets/resources/documents/research-and-data/online-research/online-harms/2018/internet-harm-research-2018-report.pdf?v=323453, 66.

6 J. Holdoš (ed.), 'EU kids online Slovensko – správy z výskumu' (2022), https://euko.ku.sk/wp-content/uploads/2022/04/EU-Kids-Online-Slovensko-spravy-z-vyskumu_ed_J_Holdos.pdf; V. Gill, L. Monk, and L. Day, 'Qualitative research project to investigate the impact of online harms on children' (2022), https://assets.publishing.service.gov.uk/government/uploads/system/uploads/attachment_data/file/1167838/Online_Harms_Study_Final_report_updated_51222_updated_290623.pdf; N. Hudson et al., 'Content and activity that is harmful to children within scope of the Online Safety Bill: a rapid evidence assessment', 27 May 2022, https://assets.publishing.service.gov.uk/government/uploads/system/uploads/attachment_data/file/1123421/Content_and_Activity_that_is_Harmful_to_Children_within_Scope_of_the_Online_Safety_Bill__REA__accessible_.pdf.

Many experts, leaders, stakeholders, even laypeople claim that legal restrictions are what would help. At first glance, legal regulations have several advantages:

- they provide clear guidelines for everyone,
- they set national/international standards,
- the legal system is based on institutions,
- having an authoritative institution facilitates reporting violations of rights.

The legal system clearly has the advantage that rules when well written are transparent and clear to everyone, and provide a set of standards and guidelines about what is prohibited and permitted in the digital realm.[7] The legal rules provide national and international standards of conduct, which can be helpful to orientate agents, citizens, and other legal persons. Rules can be guaranteed by institutions, which represent the distribution of power between the legislature, executive, and judiciary. As pointed out by many social contract theorists (e.g., John Locke),[8] it is reasonable to transfer certain duties; for example, judging and punishing wrongdoers, to an entity that is above individuals and thus independent and acts in a just and commensurate manner. The violation of rights can then be claimed to the authority, and the authority provides protection for individuals. For instance, internet fraud, such as stealing an identity, can be reported to the police, and they can then act accordingly to execute the law.

8.2 PROBLEMS ASSOCIATED WITH THE LEGAL REGULATION OF THE DIGITAL REALM

However, there is also the other side of the coin that legal restrictions are not an ideal and flawless solution. The problems associated with legal rules include, for instance:

- the development of legal regulations is too slow,[9]
- legal standards are not yet developed because the cause of human rights violations in the online realm is not yet adequately understood,[10]

7 Of course, it depends also on the legal system: some systems are more focused on precedents and also consider the constitution as a living tree.

8 J. Locke, *Two Treatises of Government* (Cambridge: Cambridge University Press, 1967), p. 525.

9 See, e.g., L. B. Moses, 'Adapting the law to technological change: a comparison of common law and legislation' (2003) 26 *UNSW Law Journal* 2, 394–417; S. Greenstein, 'Preserving the rule of law in the era of artificial intelligence' (2022) 30 *Artificial Intelligence and Law*, 291–323, at 396.

10 T. Pajuste (ed.), 'Specific threats to human rights protection from the digital reality: international responses and recommendations to core threats from the digitalised world' (2022), https://graphite.page/gdhrnet-threats-to-human-rights-protection/, p. 9; A. Strowel and W. Vergote, 'Digital platforms: to regulate or not to regulate? Message to regulators: fix the economics first, then focus on the right regulation' (2016), https://ec.europa.eu/information_society/newsroom/image/document/2016-7/uclouvain_et_universit_saint_louis_14044.pdf.

- the field and the legal context is country specific,[11]
- there can be vagueness, limited scope, and conflicting interpretations of the law,[12]
- law enforcement can be problematic,[13]
- some crimes go unreported.[14]

The problem of the regulation of digital issues stems from the rapid exponential growth of what is possible with digital technology and the comparatively slow development of legal restrictions. 'As technological developments take place faster than regulation can catch up, the guidelines and rules that have been adopted have not provided solutions to many of the issues, including the human rights implications of digital activities.'[15]

A related problem is that the restriction of certain areas focusing on, for instance, the regulation of digital human rights is not yet fully understood, and thus the regulation is not yet developed in some areas at all. As an example, we could mention that 'a threat of cancel culture and social engineering in the context of elections where the harm of manipulated voting is obvious but how exactly the prohibited acts should be defined or how they could be prevented is an open question. Similarly, a question to what extent the risk of addiction to the Internet could provide entitlements to health care services.'[16]

A more general problem of the law and legal restrictions is that situations are often country specific, and it is difficult to find common ground for legal norms in the international global context. Countries have citizens and inhabitants with various beliefs and they represent the plurality of diverse cultures. Other problems related to legal rules stem from how they are written and presented, and this is related to uncertainty, limited scope, or divergent interpretations of law. Another interesting aspect of law, the legal system, and the state distribution of power is law enforcement. The problem is thus not only whether the legal rules are well made, timely, and targeting relevant issues, but also whether the violation of the law is treated in a relevant manner and the criminals punished.

[11] See, e.g., Y. Shany, 'Digital rights and the outer limits of international human rights law' (2023) 24 *German Law Journal* 3, 461–72, at 464; J. Kleijssen and P. Perri, 'Cybercrime, evidence and territoriality: issues and options' (2017) 47 *Netherlands Yearbook of International Law*, 147–73, at 155.

[12] Pajuste (ed.), 'Specific threats to human rights protection', p. 9; M. Greenberg, 'Legal interpretation' (2021), *Stanford Encyclopedia of Philosophy*, https://plato.stanford.edu/entries/legal-interpretation/.

[13] A. Ivanov, D. Gorelik, and K. Prokofiev, 'Law enforcement in the context of digitalization: problems and prospects for improving efficiency' (2020) 171 *Advances in Economics, Business and Management Research, volume*, Proceedings of the 1st International Scientific Conference 'Legal Regulation of the Digital Economy and Digital Relations: Problems and Prospects of Development' (LARDER 2020); V. Ceccato, 'Special issue: crime and control in the digital era' (2019) 20 *Criminal Justice Review* 10, 1–6, at 3.

[14] US Department of Justice, 'Report of the Attorney General's cyber digital task force' (2018), www.justice.gov/archives/ag/page/file/1076696/dl.

[15] Pajuste, 'Specific threats to human rights protection', p. 4.

[16] Ibid., p. 9.

Similarly, the detection of a violation of the law needs to be well monitored in order to catch the criminal. If the system fails, for instance, if the victim does not report a bully because the victims are not aware of their rights or are afraid to do so, the legal regulation does not fully help diminish the problem. In the digital world, the problem of unreported violations and harms can be quite fruitful owing to its potential for anonymity. According to the US Federal Bureau of Investigation (FBI), approximately only one in seven cybercrimes were reported in 2017.[17]

This prompts a question: How can we achieve better regulation of the digital realm?

It seems there are multiple possible solutions, and they can be summed up as follows within the framework of a better legal system:

- better regulation, better laws, and law enforcement,
- developing better legal standards,
- better law enforcement,
- stricter regulation and control.

There are many emerging developments in the national and international context of aiming to better regulate the digital environment.[18] However, as ideal as it may seem at first sight, these approaches also have their Achilles heels, including:

- not all societies and citizens are developed enough to be able to follow the law and manage proper law enforcement,[19]
- the motivation for action is mostly – not to get caught.

It is obvious that some societies are suffering with greater problems of law enforcement. For instance, this is related to the high level of corruption that affects the impartiality, justness, and fairness in the decision-making of responsible agents.[20]

[17] FBI, 'Internet crime: IC3 a virtual complaint desk for online fraud' (2017), www.fbi.gov/news/stories/ic3-virtual-complaint-desk-for-online-fraud.

[18] See, e.g., M. L. Chiarella, 'Digital Markets Act (DMA) and Digital Services Act (DSA): New rules for the EU digital environment' (2023) 9 *Athens Journal of Law* 1, 33–58; European Commission, Proposal for a regulation of the European Parliament and of the Council laying down harmonised rules on artificial intelligence (Artificial Intelligence Act) and amending certain union legislative acts (2021), https://eur-lex.europa.eu/legal-content/EN/TXT/?uri=celex%3A52021PC0206; Council of the EU, Press Release, 'DSA: Council gives final approval to the protection of users' rights online' (2022), www.consilium.europa.eu/en/press/press-releases/2022/10/04/dsa-council-gives-final-approval-to-the-protection-of-users-rights-online/.

[19] This can be illustrated by the differences in the trust that citizens have in the police in different countries, see, e.g., D. Schaap and P. Scheeper, 'Comparing citizens' trust in the police across European countries: an assessment of cross-country measurement equivalence' (2014) 24 *International Criminal Justice Review* 1, 82–98; R. I. Mawby, 'Comparing police systems across the world', in G. Bruinsma and D. Weisburd (eds.), *Encyclopedia of Criminology and Criminal Justice* (New York, NY: Springer, 2014), pp. 478–88.

[20] See, e.g., Transparency International, 'Corruption Perceptions Index' (2022), www.transparency.org/en/cpi/2022.

8.3 THE PROBLEM OF SURVEILLANCE

One option would be to say, all right, we can still make it work and focus on the following:

- monitoring agents,
- even stricter regulations – cameras, tracking devices everywhere, use of facial recognition,[21]
- provide better control and data about who is doing what, so that the responsible institutions can protect citizens and other stakeholders.

There is quite a fruitful debate currently regarding surveillance systems, for instance in China, but also other countries. As pointed out by Peter Königs, non-democratic states nowadays and in recent history 'known for their extensive surveillance systems include the GDR, the People's Republic of China, the Soviet Union, and North Korea. In the past few decades, however, established liberal democracies have been increasingly ready to monitor their citizens on a massive scale. One notorious surveillance program run by an alliance of democracies was uncovered by Edward Snowden.'[22] The proponents of surveillance present arguments regarding greater safety and crime prevention, and the resulting benefits for everyone involved. Unfortunately, such Big Brother concepts are not ideal.[23] 'Government surveillance and the erosion of privacy it is associated with are being discussed as a cause of distrust and feelings of vulnerability, as a potential source of discrimination and unjust domination, and as a threat to democracy and the integrity of the public sphere, to name but a few concerns.'[24] Therefore, as mentioned earlier, reducing harms in the digital realm by increasing surveillance also has its downsides, which stem from:

- the right to privacy,[25]
- possible abuses of information, data, systems.[26]

The concept of the protection of privacy is central in relation to human rights, and relates to the threat of the abuse of information, its manipulation, use in an

[21] See, e.g., A. M. Jansen et al., 'The influence of the presentation of camera surveillance on cheating and pro-social behavior' (2018) 9 *Frontiers in Psychology*, Article 1937; T. Golda et al., 'Perception of risks and usefulness of smart video surveillance systems' (2022) 12 *Applied Sciences* 20, Article 10435; C. Ziller and M. Helbling, 'Public support for state surveillance' (2021) 60 *European Journal of Political Research* 4, 994–1006.

[22] P. Königs, 'Government surveillance, privacy, and legitimacy' (2022) 35 *Philosophy & Technology*, 1, Article 8.

[23] For educational aspects regarding surveillance see workshop proposal related to the Erasmus+ project PLATO'S EU, that I got a chance to test at the University of Skovde, Sweden and Frederick University, Cyprus.

[24] Königs, 'Government surveillance, privacy, and legitimacy', section 1.

[25] See, e.g., S. Quach et al., 'Digital technologies: tensions in privacy and data' (2022) 50 *Journal of the Academy of Marketing Science* 6, 1299–323.

[26] See, e.g., Königs, 'Government surveillance, privacy, and legitimacy'.

inappropriate context, even stealing an identity. For instance, the idea of transparency is helping not to conflate the protection of privacy by masking other inappropriate actions, such as cheating, stealing, and other forms of wrongdoing.

8.4 MOTIVATIONS

Another aspect of this problem relates to what motivates a person or agent in the digital world. The motivation not to get caught.

If the agents are mostly motivated to not do certain things (e.g., cheat online) by the idea of not getting caught, they may try to find ways to avoid punishment. The problem is in the system but also in human character. For instance, the ancient philosopher Aristotle already sketched the problem of the human character in relation to the state.[27]

Even with controlling devices and greater surveillance, there is a danger that the people who work with them can manipulate the data or evidence, and can be bribed to do so. So there is the question of who controls those who are in power and those who should control others. Of course, there again the solution of the division of power emerges, but as we can observe even that can be abused if individuals with an unsuitable character end up in these roles.

When we consider the legal restrictions, we may ask: What is the motivation to act legally?

It seems that the motivation is, as already sketched out, not to get caught. We can, of course, speculate and consider that in the end it is not important to act based on certain motives, but the consequences are what matters. Even if we act in compliance with the law and out of a fear of punishment, we can still act well and the consequences can be good. Nevertheless, it seems this is not always optimal either, as there is still room to act in ways that are not so beneficial for society if we expect no one can catch us.

Therefore, we may go further and ask: What if no one can see us?

The digital world offers us several potential threats that are often not so prevalent offline, related to anonymity, the idea of 'no identity', or creating a 'new' identity.[28] It seems to be easier to remain anonymous using a fake identity online than offline. Of course, even in the pre-digital era, we could send anonymous (paper) letters, or wear masks, or modulate our voice; however, nowadays the possibilities in the online world are more numerous and can have a much greater impact. It is possible to identify an IP address or other digital traces; however, at the same time there are ways to avoid being spotted.

[27] Aristotle, *The Nicomachean Ethics* (London: Penguin Books, 2004).

[28] See, e.g., A. Lareki et al., 'Fake digital identity and cyberbullying' (2022) 45 *Media, Culture & Society* 2, 338–53.

8.5 INDIVIDUAL REGULATION

There are various forms of regulation online, but they are also related to different motivations. Since the idea of regulation presented here is not flawless, we should consider other options. Therefore, there emerges the issue of individual regulation.

Our motivation should be more than just to not get caught and could also include:

- individual responsibility,
- internal/intrinsic regulation/ motivation.

By individual responsibility, we mean the responsible behaviour of an individual, considering the consequences of his or her actions and being aware and able to be held accountable for them. The responsible person is aware of his or her own actions and makes qualified judgements and decisions. He or she does not rely only on external forms of authority, telling him or her what to do and what not, but also on rational understanding of the situation.

The idea of internal or intrinsic regulation and motivation exists in contrast with external, extrinsic regulation and motivation. An example of external, extrinsic regulation is a police officer standing at an intersection regulating the traffic, where it affects motivation, and people act in the requested manner in the given situation in order to not incur a fine or end up in jail.

On the other hand, the idea of intrinsic or internal regulation is about regulation not from outside but rather from inside. Therefore, to put it simply, there is no policeman on the street but our internal policeman or conscience tells us we should not exceed the speed limit. The reason is, for instance, because it will very likely endanger other passengers, pedestrians, or even ourselves, and it is not good to take such a risk without sufficient justification.

To imagine a situation in the digital realm, we can think of examples such as an authority checking the identity of a user by validating their credentials (e.g., password, biometric data, phone number) as a form of external regulation preventing users accessing another person's account. The motivation for not trying to access someone else's account is the fear of punishment. On the other hand, internal regulation in this situation is when the user is aware that it is not right to hack into another person's account and steal his or her identity or finances.

However, we may ask whether there is a necessary connection between internal regulation and internal motivation, or external regulation and external motivation. Of course, it seems it is not so straightforward, since it is possible to have, for instance, external regulation and at the same time internal motivation to act in compliance with the law.

At the same time, we also need to be aware that internal or intrinsic motivation and the related regulations also have some limits; for instance, they:

- need time and effort to develop,
- rely on people's conscience.

There are also problems with regulations set and adopted by private companies; they can set their own standards and create diverse responses, as there are many (often mostly financial) interests. Then such rules are often referred to as 'ethics washing'; that is, they pretend the company is regulated to the benefit of society but in fact the benefit is only aimed at a narrow group of people. Despite the fact that this area is an interesting topic, in this chapter I will focus on the ethical regulation of individuals.

There have been quite fruitful discussions about the nature of intrinsic and extrinsic motivation.[29] The debate is not just at the conceptual level but also explores the emerging problem of how to deal with this in practice. The obvious question, therefore, is how we can implement internal regulation.

One plausible answer is that agents internalise existing rules and act according to them.[30] This seems quite a good idea at first sight. Citizens, agents become informed and educated about the legal norms in relation to the digital environment and understand the importance of them for themselves and others, and also understand that violating them will be punished, and they will internalise such rules and act accordingly.

Regarding the regulation and compliance motivation, there are many interesting ideas.[31] However, unfortunately, there are also some problems with this approach, as mentioned at the beginning of the chapter, such as the fact that:

- legal norms regarding the digital realm are evolving slowly,
- the legal system is evolving, but the legal norms are not always right,
- people can manipulate the rules,
- there is a problem with freedom and autonomy,
- internalising the rules may not be effective or efficient.

29 See, e.g., F. Gomez and M. Artigot i Golobardes, 'Intrinsic and extrinsic motivations to comply with legal rules: comment on B. Deffains and D. Demougin, "Class Actions, Compliance, and Moral Cost"', in S. Grundmann, F. Möslein, and K. Riesenhuber (eds.), *Contract Governance: Dimensions in Law and Interdisciplinary Research* (Oxford: Oxford Academic, online edn., 2015), pp. 241–8; L. S. Morris et al., 'On what motivates us: a detailed review of intrinsic v. extrinsic motivation' (2022) 52 *Psychological Medicine* 10, 1801–16; R. Ryan and E. L. Deci, 'Intrinsic and extrinsic motivations: classic definitions and new directions' (2000) 25 *Contemporary Educational Psychology* 1, 54–67; R. Bénabou and J. Tirole, 'Intrinsic and extrinsic motivation' (2003) 70 *Review of Economic Studies* 3, 489–520; A. Van den Broeck et al,. 'Beyond intrinsic and extrinsic motivation: a meta-analysis on self-determination theory's multidimensional conceptualization of work motivation' (2021) 11 *Organizational Psychology Review* 3, 240–73; A. Turner, 'How does intrinsic and extrinsic motivation drive performance culture in organizations?' (2017) 4 *Cogent Education* 1, Article 1337543.

30 See, e.g., S. Larcom et al., 'Follow the leader? Testing for the internalization of law' (2019) 48 *The Journal of Legal Studies* 1, 217–44; J. Benka et al., 'Internalization of rules and risk-behavior among early adolescents and relevance for public health' (2019), 29 *European Journal of Public Health*, Issue Supplement 4, 367–8; M. Kim, 'Legalization and norm internalization: an empirical study of international human rights commitments eliciting public support for compliance' (2019) 7 *Journal of Law and International Affairs* 2, 337–81.

31 See, e.g., P. J. May, 'Regulation and compliance motivations: examining different approaches' (2005) 65 *Public Administration Review* 1, 31–44; P. J. May, 'Compliance motivations: affirmative and negative bases' (2004) 38 *Law & Society Review* 1, 41–68.

Therefore, even this approach is problematic and is not a flawless solution.

It seems that we need something more. One idea is to use various nudges to motivate people to act in a desirable way; however, this can also be understood as manipulation and can be abused by the authorities or certain people.[32]

8.6 DIGITAL ETHICS AND EDUCATION

It seems that we need something else. And that could be ethics and moral norms.[33] What more do they add to legal regulation? They are often oriented towards internal regulation, and therefore can help even in situations when agents are in a setting where no one can see them, when there is no surveillance, and it can even help them deal with situations when there are no existing legal rules regulating their actions.

Therefore, when mentioning digital ethics as a solution, the question of whether it should fully replace legal regulation of the digital realm can emerge.[34] Of course not – both have their pros and cons, and therefore their mutual enrichment could be beneficial. They should be understood as complementing each other – internal should complement external regulation.

Similarly, we could mention Lawrence Kohlberg and his theory of moral development here, where he speaks about associating the lower stages with external regulation and the higher stages with the internal regulation of moral actions.[35] For instance, the pre-conventional level is oriented towards avoiding punishment and focused on obtaining praise, while the other stages are more oriented towards compliance with rules, the law for the benefit of society, and the highest stages are related to greater moral competence in moral judgements. How can we put ideas about digital ethics into practice?

There seem to be quite a rich debate regarding digital ethics regulating agents online, and many companies show they have a code of conduct dealing with such issues or that ethics committees exist; however, there is a risk of using this merely as

[32] L. Congiu and I. Moscati, 'A review of nudges: definitions, justifications, effectiveness' (2022) 36 *Journal of Economic Surveys* 1, 188–213.

[33] 'Ethics is generally understood to be the study of "living well as a human being". This is the topic of works such as Aristotle's Nicomachean Ethics, in which the aim of human beings is to exemplify human excellence of character.' – J. Driver, 'Moral theory' (2022), *Stanford Encyclopedia of Philosophy*, https://plato.stanford.edu/entries/moral-theory/. However, it is often understood more broadly as a discipline of practical philosophy dealing with right and wrong conduct.

[34] Digital ethics can be understood as a branch of practical or applied ethics, which deals with ethical issues related to digital technologies. As in other areas of practical ethics it is highly interdisciplinary and overlaps with or includes other areas of investigation as well as other areas of practical ethics (e.g., ethics of technology, ethics of AI, environmental ethics, ethics of law). Digital ethics is sometimes falsely interpreted as dealing only with etiquette online, so called netiquette. However, ethics is not possible to conflate with etiquette. Both deal with questions regarding right conduct but ethics deals more with the idea of harm, which is not that important in etiquette.

[35] L. Kohlberg, *The Philosophy of Moral Development* (New York, NY: Harper and Row, 1981).

marketing to wash their hands so consumers do not question their actions.[36] At the same time, as mentioned earlier, although I think well-made self-regulation of companies can supplement the overall regulation of digital issues, here I will focus more on the regulation of individuals. So how can we make digital ethics work?

There is room for digital ethics education to help to implement the ideas of digital ethics. It should focus on:

- the development of internal regulation,
- critical thinking and moral judgement,
- a deeper understanding of ethical dilemmas in the digital realm.

There are various approaches to digital education and digital ethics education,[37] and various challenges emerge related to the following:

- targeting individuals on different levels – children, adults,[38]
- the means of teaching,
- dealing with disagreements,
- having qualified teachers,
- having good teaching materials.

It seems reasonable to focus not just on children but also on adult education in the area of digital ethics. There are several approaches to teaching ethics,[39] but I propose that ethics education be oriented towards the development of critical thinking and not merely training about ethics – indoctrination or rules without any critical examination and reflection. Reflection and critical analysis has the advantage of being flexible in seeking the best solution to moral dilemmas. Digital ethics

36 In relation to AI digital ethics see, e.g., B. Wagner, 'Ethics as an escape from regulation. From "ethics-washing" to ethics-shopping?', in E. Bayamlioğlu, I. Baraliuc, and L. Janssens (eds.), *Being Profiled: Cogitas Ergo Sum. 10 Years of Profiling the European Citizen* (Amsterdam: Amsterdam University Press, 2018), pp. 84–8.

37 See, e.g., B. O'Brien, 'Digital ethics in higher education' (2020) *Educause Review*, https://er.educause.edu/articles/2020/5/digital-ethics-in-higher-education-2020; E. Zvereva, 'Digital ethics in higher education: modernizing moral values for effective communication in cyberspace' (2023) 13 *Online Journal of Communication and Media Technologies* 2, e202319; E. Wulandari and W. Triyanto, 'Digital citizenship education: shaping digital ethics in society 5.0' (2021) 9 *Universal Journal of Educational Research* 5, 948–56; D. Olcott, Jr et al., 'Ethics and education in the digital age: global perspectives and strategies for local transformation in Catalonia' (2015) 12 *RUSC* 2 Special Issue.

38 See, e.g., K. Moore, 'The three-part harmony of adult learning, critical thinking, and decision-making' (2010) 39 *Journal of Adult Education* 1, 1–10; H. Boxler, 'Quest for the grail? Searching for critical thinking in adult education' (2002) *Adult Education Research Conference*, Conference Proceedings; D. R. Garrison, 'Critical thinking and adult education: a conceptual model for developing critical thinking in adult learners' (1991) 10 *International Journal of Lifelong Education* 4, 287–303; H. Tinmaz et al., 'A systematic review on digital literacy' (2022) 9 *Smart Learning Environments*, Article 21; T. Ott and M. Tiozza, 'Digital media ethics: benefits and challenges in school education' (2022) 14 *International Journal of Mobile and Blended Learning* 2, 1–8.

39 See, e.g., the forthcoming book that I am editing with J. Irwin – *Ethical Education Across European Systems – Concepts, Practices, Dilemmas* (Lausanne: Peter Lang Publishing, 2025).

education should be oriented towards critical thinking, where the focus is not primarily on what to think but rather on method or how to think.[40] It is also about focusing on understanding why. The potential for disagreements about what is right and what is wrong also needs to be taken into account; however, this approach should also help us learn how to communicate clearly, effectively, logically, and how to evaluate arguments.

However, what if the critical thinking collides with legal norms? It seems that in open societies it can even be desirable to have citizens who are able to critically evaluate the existing legal system and norms.[41]

Of course, the problem may be in finding qualified teachers and having good teaching materials and manuals. The lack in these areas is addressed for instance by various initiatives and projects: digital education is often oriented towards the technical or psychological aspects of using digital technologies, which is important since based on empirical findings in Slovakia, for example, 20 per cent of children do not know that they can block a contact on social media and 40 per cent do not know that they can report a case when someone is bullying them online.[42] At the same time, it is also important to address digital ethics with regard to what is right and what is wrong and why, and what we should do in a given situation. The problem of digital ethics education has been addressed by various projects, for instance, Erasmus+ PLATO'S EU, where the team has developed teaching materials and manuals for teachers as well as organizing workshops for students in order to promote philosophical methods of thinking as a tool for dealing with issues online.[43]

8.7 CONCLUSION

This chapter has explored the problem of digital regulation, and the idea of digital ethics and education has been proposed as a complementary solution.[44] The main idea presented is that we need to focus not just on external regulation and the

[40] See, e.g., L. M. Murawski, 'Critical thinking in the classroom … and beyond' (2014) 10 *Journal of Learning in Higher Education* 1, 25–30; K. Larsson, 'Understanding and teaching critical thinking – a new approach' (2017) 84 *International Journal of Educational Research*, 32–42; O. L. U. Enciso et al., 'Critical thinking and its importance in education: some reflections' (2017) 19 *Rastros Rostros* 34, 78–88; Y. E. L. Zuluaga et al., 'A study of critical thinking in higher education students' (2020) 16 *Revista Latinoamericana de Estudios Educativos* (Colombia) 2, 256–79; L. Campo et al., 'Methodologies for fostering critical thinking skills from university students' points of view' (2023) 13 *Education Sciences* 2, Article 132; J. Huang and G. Sang, 'Conceptualising critical thinking and its research in teacher education: a systematic review' (2022) 29 *Teachers and Teaching* 6, 638–60.

[41] See, e.g., B. Sheehy et al., 'Shifting from soft to hard law: motivating compliance when enacting mandatory corporate social responsibility' (2023) 24 *European Business Organization Law Review* 4, 693–719; A. S. Rosenberg, 'Motivational law' (2008) 56 *Cleveland State Law Review* 1, 111–36.

[42] Holdoš, 'EU kids online Slovensko', pp. 120, 137.

[43] Plato's EU website, https://platos-eu.org.

[44] As presented also in earlier material on the topic under GDHR – Pajuste, 'Specific threats to human rights protection', pp. 20–2.

motivation to act in compliance with legal norms out of fear of being caught and punished, but also on the development of an internal moral compass in our citizens. Various advantages and disadvantages to the different approaches to regulation have been presented.

Legal norms are not considered in contrast with digital ethical regulation but as complementary. As mentioned in an earlier publication of the COST Global Digital Human Rights Network project: 'there is the inherently multidimensional nature of compliance with human rights in the digital realm, which requires a multidimensional response, including in the context of awareness raising and training. Law should be complemented by ethics and the training on cyber ethics should be provided along with training on digital human rights law.'[45]

Internal regulation and intrinsic autonomous motivation seem to be an important area for further development towards the regulation of the digital realm. The topic of internal regulation is very fruitful, and has been investigated by philosophers and ethicists since ancient times also in terms of people flourishing and realising their full human potential.

45 Pajuste, 'Specific threats to human rights protection', pp. 9–10.

PART II

Freedom of Expression in the Digital Domain

Introduction to Part II

How Should Freedom of Expression Be Applied in the Digital Environment?

Tiina Pajuste

The second part of this book focuses on freedom of expression. Freedom of expression is a cornerstone of human rights and democratic governance, 'providing the vehicle for the exchange and development of opinions'.[1] The internet (social media platforms in particular) has transformed how people communicate and exchange ideas, democratised access to information, and decentralised public discourse. At the same time, it has created a broad range of new threats, such as disinformation, platform monopolies, online hate speech, regulatory tensions, and the potential to undermine democratic principles.[2] This part looks at some of these challenges while aiming to answer the following core question: *How should freedom of expression be applied in the digital environment?* Examining this question is essential to ensure that this right continues to foster democratic participation and safeguard individual autonomy.

This part includes four chapters on different issues connected to the freedom of expression online – positive state obligations, new media doctrines, disinformation, and the potential digital imperialism of the EU. The combination of these topics tries to demonstrate the complexities of freedom of expression and provide a basis for understanding how freedom of expression can continue to be protected, balanced with other rights, and adapted to the realities of the digital age. This is achieved by examining the obligations of different actors, global regulatory tensions, and the challenges to democratic principles.

1 UN Human Rights Committee, 'General Comment No. 34. Article 19: Freedoms of opinion and expression', 12 September 2011, UN Doc. CCPR/C/GC/34, para. 2.

2 The UN Special Rapporteur on freedom of opinion and expression has reported on many such issues (e.g., gendered disinformation, media freedom and safety of journalists in the digital age, online hate speech, online content regulation, surveillance and human rights): UN, 'Special Rapporteur on freedom of opinion and expression. Annual thematic reports', www.ohchr.org/en/special-procedures/sr-freedom-of-opinion-and-expression/annual-thematic-reports).

CHAPTER 9. FREEDOM OF EXPRESSION AND POSITIVE OBLIGATIONS OF THE STATE IN SOCIAL MEDIA

Chapter 9 opens the discussion with Artūrs Kučs' exploration of the evolving role of states in safeguarding freedom of expression within the digital environment, particularly on social media platforms. States have both negative obligations (to avoid undue interference) and positive obligations (to actively protect and ensure the right to freedom of expression). The latter include creating a favourable environment for public debate, protecting speakers from harm, and ensuring media pluralism. These obligations extend to relations between private parties, including users and internet intermediaries. The chapter responds to the core question of this part of the volume by noting the following aspects that should be central to applying freedom of expression online: (a) balancing it with protections against harmful content; (b) maintaining ultimate responsibility for safeguarding freedom of expression with states (not outsourcing decisions on limits of that freedom to private entities); (c) ensuring judicial oversight over content moderation; and (d) providing adequate legal regulation with effective remedies.

CHAPTER 10. THE DEVELOPMENT OF NEW MEDIA DOCTRINES ON FREEDOM OF EXPRESSION: HOW TO DEFEND DEMOCRATIC SOCIETY AND THE RULE OF LAW

Chapter 10 examines the evolution of freedom of expression doctrines in the context of digital media. Jukka Viljanen and Tomoe Watashiba look at how the European Court of Human Rights has adapted traditional doctrines to address challenges in the new media environment. Social media has expanded the concept of 'public watchdogs' beyond traditional media to include non-governmental organisations, bloggers, and activists, which may amplify the risk of disinformation and online hate and require a rethinking of liability issues. The authors explore how freedom of expression can balance individual rights, societal interests, and the regulation of disinformation and hate speech in the digital age. In relation to the core question, the chapter draws attention to the following aspects: (a) limitations on freedom of expression need to be guided by principles such as proportionality and the prohibition of the abuse of rights; (b) freedom of expression in digital spaces requires balancing individual rights with broader societal needs; (c) traditional doctrines (such as ensuring pluralism and protecting public watchdogs) must evolve to include the unique dynamics of digital media; (d) clear rules should be set for social media platforms without enabling censorship; and (e) pre-emptive measures, such as promoting media literacy and safeguarding public debate, must be adopted to protect democracy in the face of disinformation and authoritarian threats.

CHAPTER 11. DISINFODEMIC THREATS. REAL, FALSE, AND FAKE NEWS: A CONTRIBUTION TO FIGHT DISINFORMATION WITHOUT AFFECTING THE FREEDOM OF EXPRESSION

Chapter 11 delves even deeper into the issue of disinformation. Oscar Puccinelli shows how the rapid dissemination of false, manipulated, and misleading information poses a threat to human rights, democracy, and public trust. Disinformation erodes public trust, affects electoral integrity, threatens public health, and harms individuals' rights to information and privacy. The chapter outlines the historical roots of disinformation, the technological factors that enable it, and the responses by public and private actors to mitigate its harmful effects. Puccinelli emphasises the need for cooperation among governments, civil society, and technology companies to develop rights-based responses to disinformation. He stresses the importance of international frameworks, such as the United Nations declarations, to guide balanced approaches. In response to the core question of this part – *How should freedom of expression be applied in the digital environment?* – the chapter asserts the following: (a) efforts to regulate false information must avoid overreach and comply with the principles of legality, necessity, and proportionality; (b) measures must address the harms caused by disinformation (e.g., hate speech, incitement to violence, threats to public health); (c) digital platforms need to have greater transparency in their operations; and (d) media literacy programmes need to be promoted to empower individuals to critically evaluate information, reduce the impact of disinformation, and to use their freedom of expression without spreading disinformation.

CHAPTER 12. ONLINE FREEDOM OF EXPRESSION: A NEW EU IMPERIALISM?

In Chapter 12, the final chapter of this part, Philippe Jougleux examines the evolving role of the European Union (EU) in regulating online freedom of expression and the global implications of these efforts. The author frames EU interventions, such as the General Data Protection Regulation (GDPR) and the Digital Services Act (DSA), as examples of digital imperialism, whereby the EU's legal frameworks impose European values and legal standards on other jurisdictions (and create potential for global legal conflicts). The chapter explores key topics such as copyright law, content moderation, hate speech, and the right to be forgotten, while contrasting the EU's approach with the US's philosophy of free speech. The EU's rights-based approach to balancing free expression with societal harm contrasts sharply with the US emphasis on the marketplace of ideas and minimal restrictions. In response to the core question, the chapter focuses on the following aspects: (a) freedom of expression must be balanced against other societal interests, such as privacy, hate speech mitigation, and copyright protection; (b) there is a need for international consensus on freedom of expression in digital spaces (and subsequent joint regulation); (c) it is important to recognise the central role of online platforms in public debate and, accordingly, regulating them to ensure accountability while safeguarding freedom of expression; and (d) a balanced approach that reconciles regional legal traditions with the global nature of the internet should be adopted.

SHARED THEMES AND INTERCONNECTIONS

Although these four chapters explore diverse aspects of freedom of expression in the digital environment, they converge on the challenges of balancing this fundamental right with other human rights, societal needs, regulatory obligations, and technological realities. In the following, parallels are drawn through shared themes and how each chapter addresses the core question of this part: *How should freedom of expression be applied in the digital environment?*

A. BALANCING FREEDOM OF EXPRESSION WITH REGULATION

All four chapters highlight the tension between protecting freedom of expression and regulating harmful content or behaviour. They advocate for a balance between preventing harm (e.g., through disinformation and hate speech) and avoiding overly restrictive or arbitrary regulations that hinder democratic debate.

- Chapter 9 on the positive obligations of states in social media stresses the need for states to protect freedom of expression while setting clear rules for content moderation, ensuring private platforms do not overstep in censoring speech.
- Chapter 10 on new media doctrines on freedom of expression emphasises proportionality and context in applying freedom of expression doctrines, noting that digital platforms must balance rights with responsibilities, particularly in kerbing disinformation and hate speech.
- Chapter 11 on the threat of the disinfodemic discusses how combating disinformation requires targeted measures, but warns against overreach that stifles legitimate expression.
- Chapter 12 on EU imperialism critiques the EU's regulatory frameworks (e.g., DSA, GDPR) for imposing global standards, which can over-regulate platforms and risk excessive censorship.

B. THE ROLE OF STATES AND PLATFORMS

Each of the chapters engages with the issue of the division of responsibility between states and platforms in safeguarding freedom of expression. The authors maintain that states should assume primary responsibility for protecting freedom of expression and setting clear regulatory frameworks while ensuring that platforms are transparent and accountable in their content moderation practices.

- Chapter 9 focuses on the positive obligations of states to provide judicial oversight and emphasises the need to prevent private platforms from being the ones setting the boundaries of freedom of expression.
- Chapter 10 advocates for state-level interventions to ensure platforms uphold free expression without succumbing to profit-driven biases.
- Chapter 11 is critical of the delegation of the regulation of disinformation to platforms and calls for stronger state oversight to protect users from arbitrary content removal.
- Chapter 12 warns that EU regulations often delegate too much power to platforms, enabling them to act as gatekeepers of public discourse and risking private censorship.

C. TRANSPARENCY AND ACCOUNTABILITY

The importance of transparency in platform decision-making and accountability in content moderation processes is a recurring theme in the chapters of this part. Transparent, rights-based approaches to content moderation are essential for safeguarding freedom of expression in the digital age.

- Chapter 9 supports judicial oversight and user access to remedies as safeguards against opaque moderation practices by platforms.
- Chapter 10 argues that platforms must adopt transparent practices to foster public trust and accountability while addressing systemic risks such as hate speech.
- Chapter 11 advocates for platforms to disclose their moderation criteria and establish mechanisms for users to contest content removal decisions.
- Chapter 12 critiques the lack of transparency in algorithmic content moderation and calls for mechanisms to address issues such as shadow banning and disproportionate content filtering.

All four chapters also point out the need for international cooperation and international standards, which are necessary for freedom of expression to exist consistently across the global digital landscape, and to avoid fragmentation.

The chapters in this part collectively emphasise the intricate balance required to uphold freedom of expression in the digital age. By addressing the evolving obligations of states, the role of platforms, and the challenges posed by disinformation and regulatory disparities, these contributions provide insights into how this fundamental right can be preserved and adapted to the digital environment. Together, they emphasise the importance of safeguarding democratic principles, fostering accountability, and promoting international collaboration to ensure that freedom of expression remains a cornerstone of human rights in the face of rapid technological and societal changes.

9

Freedom of Expression and Positive Obligations of the State in Social Media

Artūrs Kučs

9.1 INTRODUCTION

The European Court of Human Rights (ECtHR) has long established that freedom of expression is crucial to the existence of a democratic society. A free society is impossible without a free exchange of information and opinions. Freedom of expression also entails both the imparting as well as receiving of information. The internet has given unprecedented power for new platforms to realise this right.

Information society services and especially intermediary services, including social media platforms, have become an important part of our daily lives. At the same time, the digital transformation and increased use of those services has also resulted in new risks and challenges, both for individual users and for society as a whole.[1]

The ECtHR and other bodies in numerous cases have pointed to a positive obligation for the state to protect the right to freedom of expression. At the same time, such an obligation has so far not been expressly attributed to the online environment by the ECtHR, while some other human rights protection bodies and institutions have pointed towards it only indirectly.

Therefore, the aim of this chapter is to analyse the positive obligations of states to protect freedom of expression in the online environment, especially on social media platforms. To achieve this aim, the first part of the chapter will set the background by analysing the general positive obligations of the state in the context of freedom of expression as found by various international bodies, most notably the ECtHR. The second part of the chapter will look at how the current regulation of social media and internet intermediaries impacts freedom of expression. Consequently, the third part will evaluate the requirements of the state in terms of its positive obligations and current regulation in the context of freedom of expression.

[1] European Commission, 'Proposal for a Regulation of the European Parliament and of the Council on a Single Market for Digital Services (Digital Services Act) and amending Directive 2000/31/EC', COM (2020) 825 final, recital 1.

It must be noted that this chapter is not intended as a general overview of the definition and characteristics of positive obligations under human rights law or as exhaustive research on the rules governing the liability of social media platforms and internet intermediaries. It is rather a merging of both of these topics, drawing attention to problematic situations and indicating their possible solutions.

9.2 FREEDOM OF EXPRESSION AND POSITIVE OBLIGATIONS OF THE STATE

Almost all human rights protection documents recognise the positive obligation of the state to ensure the protection of the rights enshrined in each particular document. For example, Article 1 of the European Convention on Human Rights (ECHR) provides that the Member States have a duty to secure for everyone within their jurisdiction the rights and freedoms defined therein. In addition, Article 13 of the ECHR guarantees the availability, at the national level, of a remedy to enforce the substance of ECHR rights and freedoms in whatever form they might happen to be secured in the domestic legal order. This requires the provision of a domestic remedy to deal with the substance of a complaint under the ECHR and to grant appropriate relief.[2] Therefore, states have a positive obligation to investigate allegations of a human rights infringement. The procedures followed must enable the competent body to decide on the merits of the complaint of the violation of the Convention and to sanction any violation found but also to guarantee the execution of decisions taken.[3]

Similarly, under Article 2 (3) of the International Covenant on Civil and Political Rights (ICCPR), state parties must ensure that persons whose rights under the Covenant have been violated have an effective remedy.[4] The Charter of Fundamental Rights of the European Union (CFREU) contains a rule that is comparable to the previously mentioned Article in the ICCPR and the ECHR. Namely Article 51 of the CFREU requires EU institutions and the Member States to 'respect the rights, observe the principles and promote the application thereof'. At the same time, it must be noted that obligations contained in the CFREU have some limitations. The same article prescribes that this obligation is applicable only as far as EU law is being implemented and does not extend the field of the application of EU law.

It is the ECtHR that can be thought of as the most prominent advocate of imposing positive obligations on the state to protect particular human rights. In addition, it holds that although the essential object of many provisions of the ECHR is to

[2] *Kaya v. Turkey*, Application no. 22729/93, Judgment of 19 February 1998, para. 106.

[3] *Smith and Grady v. UK*, Application nos. 33985/96 and 33986/96, Judgment of 27 September 1999, VI 72.

[4] UNHRC, 'Report of the Special Rapporteur on the promotion and protection of the right to freedom of opinion and expression', 11 May 2016, UN Doc. A/HRC/32/38, para. 68.

protect the individual against arbitrary interference by public authorities, there may in addition be positive obligations inherent in an effective respect of the rights concerned. The Court has emphasised that the effective exercise of certain freedoms does not depend merely on the state's duty not to interfere, but may require positive measures of protection.[5] Although the ECtHR has not provided a general definition of the concept of positive obligation, from its case law it can be deduced that the prime characteristic of positive obligations is that they require in practice national authorities to take the necessary measures to safeguard a right.[6]

The positive obligations of the state can be divided into several groups. First, there are substantive positive obligations and procedural positive obligations. Second, there are positive obligations of a vertical kind or those that protect the individual from the state and positive obligations of a horizontal kind or those that protect individuals against other individuals. Third, there are positive obligations that relate to the legal and administrative frameworks and those that encompass more practical measures that states need to take.[7]

These positive obligations can be found in relation to almost every human right laid down in the Convention, including freedom of expression. As the ECtHR has put it: 'Genuine, effective exercise of this freedom does not depend merely on the State's duty not to interfere, but may require positive measures of protection, even in the sphere of relations between individuals.'[8] This is because of the key importance of freedom of expression as one of the preconditions for a functioning democracy; therefore, states must ensure that private individuals can effectively exercise the right of communication between themselves.[9]

In deciding whether a positive obligation relating to the freedom of expression exists, the ECtHR has emphasised that there must be regard for the kind of rights of expression at stake, their capability to contribute to public debate, the nature and scope of restrictions on expression rights, the ability of alternative venues for expression, and the weight of the countervailing rights of others or the public.[10] It should

5 Council of Europe/ECtHR, 'Research report. Positive obligations on member States under Article 10 to protect journalists and prevent impunity', December 2011, www.echr.coe.int/documents/research_report_article_10_eng.pdf, 4.

6 J.-F. Akandji-Kombe, *Positive Obligations under the European Convention on Human Rights: A Guide to the Implementation of the European Convention on Human Rights* (Strasbourg: Council of Europe, 2007), p. 7.

7 L. Lavrysen, 'Blog seminar on positive obligations (3): positive obligations to protect fundamental rights – any role to be played by the European Court of Justice?', 10 October 2016, https://strasbourgobservers.com/2016/10/10/blog-seminar-on-positive-obligations-3-positive-obligations-to-protect-fundamental-rights-any-role-to-be-played-by-the-european-court-of-justice/, 7; ibid.

8 *Özgür Gündem v. Turkey*, Application no. 23144/93, Judgment of 16 March 2000, ECHR 2000-III 1, para. 43.

9 D. Bychawska-Siniarska, *Protection the Right to Freedom of Expression under the Convention on Human Rights: A Handbook for Legal Practitioners*' (Strasbourg: Council of Europe, 2017), p. 91.

10 *Appleby and Others v. the United Kingdom*, Application no. 44306/98, Judgment of 6 May 2003, ECHR 2003-VI 185, paras. 42–3, 47–9.

be noted, however, that the Court itself looks at these criteria cumulatively in each particular case, attributing more or less weight to any one or set of these criteria, depending on the circumstances.

The ECtHR has emphasised several positive obligations of the state in the context of freedom of expression. For example, the state has to protect the right to freedom of expression by ensuring a reasonable opportunity to exercise the right of reply and an opportunity to contest a newspaper's refusal in suing for a right to reply in the courts.[11] It has also recognised a rather broad obligation to create a favourable environment for participation in public debate for all persons concerned, enabling them to express their opinions and ideas without fear.[12] Moreover, the state has a positive obligation to protect speakers, especially journalists,[13] from physical attacks from other individuals in connection with the exercise of its freedom of expression.[14] Recognising that there can be no democracy without pluralism,[15] in the context of access to the broadcast market, the ECtHR has emphasised that states must put in place an appropriate legislative and administrative framework to guarantee effective pluralism.[16]

Other human rights protection bodies have also recognised that states not only have a duty to refrain from limiting the right to freedom of expression, but also have a positive obligation to protect and guarantee it. Although not explicitly recognising the concept of positive obligations under Article 11 of the CFREU, the Court of Justice of the EU has argued that it must be possible for national courts to check that interference of the information rights of internet users is justified.[17]

Furthermore, the United Nations (UN) Special Rapporteur on the promotion and protection of the right to freedom of opinion and expression in his report has emphasised that governments must adopt and implement laws and policies that protect private development and the provision of technical measures, products, and services that advance freedom of expression.[18]

Therefore, it can be argued that freedom of expression not only prohibits unjustified interferences from states, but may also require an active participation on behalf of them. At the same time, the positive obligations of the state should not be

[11] *Melnychuk v. Ukraine*, Application no. 17707/02, 19 October 2004, ECHR 2005-IX 397.

[12] *Dink v. Turkey* Application No. 2668/07, Judgment of 14 September 2010.

[13] *Khadija Ismayilova v. Azerbaijan*, Application nos. 65286/13 and 57270/14, Judgment of 10 April 2019, paras. 158–66.

[14] *Özgür Gündem v. Turkey*, Application no. 23144/93, Judgment of 16 March 2000, ECHR 2000-III 1, paras. 44–6.

[15] H. Tomlinson, 'Positive obligations under the European Convention on Human Rights', 21 July 2012, https://adminlaw.org.uk/wp-content/uploads/SC-2012-by-Tomlinson-QC.docx.

[16] *Manole and Others v. Moldova*, Application no. 13936/02, Judgment of 17 September 2009, ECHR 2009-IV 213, para. 98; *Informationsverein Lentia and Others v. Austria* (1993) Application nos. 13914/88, 15041/89, 15717/89, 15779/89, 17207/90, Judgment of 24 November 1993, Series A no 276, para. 39.

[17] Case C-314/12, *UPC Telekabel Wien*, [2014] ECR 166, paras. 56–7.

[18] UNHRC, 'Report of the Special Rapporteur on the promotion and protection of the right to freedom of opinion and expression', 11 May 2016, UN Doc. A/HRC/32/38, para. 86.

understood too broadly. They have been recognised as applicable to a limited number of situations touching upon the very essence of the freedom of expression. In addition, they are more often than not formulated in a manner that provides states with a rather wide margin of appreciation.

In the second part of this chapter, I will analyse whether the existing rules on regulating social media platforms and internet intermediaries in general ensure the positive obligations of the state in protecting and ensuring freedom of expression in the online environment.

9.3 REGULATION OF SOCIAL MEDIA PLATFORMS AND INTERNET INTERMEDIARIES: A THREAT TO FREEDOM OF EXPRESSION?

There are several types of actors participating in the flow of information in the online environment. First, there are internet users – natural persons – who access information stored online. Sometimes these also share information, thereby in essence becoming content producers, which are the second category of online actors. Possibly the most complex of the three is the third category – the internet intermediaries, including social media platforms. They differ from content producers as those individuals or organisations who are responsible for producing information in the first place and posting it online.[19] Internet intermediaries give access to, host, transmit, and index content originated by third parties or provide internet-based services to third parties.[20] The means by which they do this is almost without exception technical, meaning that the intermediaries are generally not aware of the content of the information they process and provide accessibility to. Such a role is unprecedented in the offline environment. Exactly because of this complexity, the regulation of internet intermediaries, including social media platforms, and their impact on freedom of expression is one of the focal points of this chapter.

The general and so far traditional rules of liability for internet intermediaries in the EU are set out in the E-Commerce Directive and recently in the Digital Services Act (DSA). The Directive exempts intermediaries from liability for the content they manage if they fulfil certain conditions. First, the service providers hosting illegal content need to remove it or disable access to it as fast as possible once they are aware of the illegal nature of the content. Second, only services that play a neutral, merely technical and passive role towards the hosted content are covered by the liability exemption.[21] For the Directive to become effective, it was transposed by the

[19] Article 19, *Internet Intermediaries: Dilemma of Liability* (London: Article 19, 2013), p. 6.

[20] K. Perset, 'The economic and social role of internet intermediaries', OECD Digital Economy Papers No. 171, April 2010, www.oecd.org/internet/ieconomy/44949023.pdf, 6.

[21] Directive 2000/31/EC of the European Parliament and of the Council of 8 June 2000 on certain legal aspects of information society services, in particular electronic commerce, in the Internal Market OJ L 178 17.7.2000, arts. 12–14.

EU Member States into their national laws. Therefore, the E-Commerce Directive laid the groundwork for a notice-and-take-down procedure but did not provide any additional guidelines with regard to its implementation. Instead, the Directive left the subject matter to the discretion of the Member States.[22]

Certain Member States have developed more detailed, formal notice-and-take-down procedures. Possibly the most known of these is the German Network Enforcement Act, which was adopted in 2017. Among other rules, it orders big social networks to remove or block access to content that is manifestly unlawful within twenty-four hours of receiving a complaint about it.[23] Administrative penalties of up to €5 million can be applied in cases where the social network fails to comply with the rules set out in the Network Enforcement Act.

The majority of the Member States opted for a verbatim transposition of the Directive, resulting in a lack of any firm safeguards for the content removal procedures in most EU countries.[24] For example, the Latvian Law on Information Society Services in Article 10 provides rules for the liability of an intermediary service provider. Nevertheless, like the E-Commerce Directive, it does not specify what amounts to actual knowledge or immediate action of the service provider.

Recognising these issues and the need to harmonise intermediary liability rules throughout the EU, the Commission of the EU has proposed new rules for digital platforms.[25] The Regulation of the European Parliament and of the Council on a Single Market For Digital Services (DSA) amending the E-Commerce Directive, as stated by the Commission, strives to maintain the core principles of the E-Commerce Directive and at the same time provide more protection for fundamental rights in the online environment, as well as online anonymity wherever technically possible.[26] Although the proposed regulation clarifies some aspects that were previously unclear under the guidance of the E-Commerce Directive, the general rules on intermediary liability have been maintained.[27] For instance, the DSA maintains the exemption of online platforms from liability provided the social media platform was not actively involved in the transmission or took action to delete the illegal information upon obtaining knowledge. However, one noticeable distinction in regard

22 Ibid., recital 46.

23 Act to Improve Enforcement of the Law in Social Networks 2017 (Netzwerkdurchsetzungsgesetz), s 3 (2).

24 A. Kuczerawy, 'The power of positive thinking: intermediary liability and the effective enjoyment of the right to freedom of expression' (2017) 8 *Journal of Intellectual Property, Information Technology and Electronic Commerce Law* 3, 226–37.

25 European Commission, 'Europe fit for the Digital Age: Commission proposes new rules for digital platforms', 15 December 2020, https://ec.europa.eu/commission/presscorner/detail/en/ip_20_2347.

26 European Commission, 'Explanatory memorandum. Proposal for a Regulation of the European Parliament and of the Council on a single market for digital services (Digital Services Act) and amending Directive 2000/31/EC' COM (2020) 825 final', https://eur-lex.europa.eu/legal-content/en/TXT/?qid=1608117147218&uri=COM%3A2020%3A825%3AFIN.

27 Directive 2000/31/EC of the European Parliament and of the Council of 8 June 2000 on certain legal aspects of information society services, in particular electronic commerce, in the Internal Market OJ L 178 17.7.2000, Art 14; Ibid., Art. 5.

to liability rules is the fact that the DSA further develops the due diligence obligations applicable to social media platforms and includes new rules related to illegal content, content moderation, and algorithm oversight. While such due diligence obligations are dependent on the role, size, and impact of social media platforms, the fines for non-compliance are high and can reach a maximum of 6 per cent of a company's annual worldwide turnover.[28]

Other pieces of EU legislation also impose an obligation on intermediaries deciding on which content should and which should not be available online. For example, the Audiovisual Media Services Directive promotes co-regulation and self-regulation.[29] It also imposes duties on video sharing platforms to eliminate such harmful content from their platforms as incitement to violence and hatred.[30] Under the General Data Protection Regulation, internet search engines are required to balance freedom of expression and privacy rights in applying the right to be forgotten.[31] The Code of Conduct on Countering Illegal Hate Speech Online announced by the Commission in May 2016 incentivises information technology companies to tackle hate speech online on their own initiative.[32] Therefore, for now, and it seems also for the foreseeable future, the balancing of various interests at stake is delegated to internet intermediaries.

Therefore, essentially it is the internet intermediaries, not the judiciary of states, that must take decisions on balancing freedom of expression, privacy, and other rights online. Although such a mechanism comes with some bonuses, such as speedy procedures and reduction of workload for the courts, there are several issues that arise from it, most visibly the threats to the freedom of expression of users of social media platforms and access to information removed by intermediaries by the public at large. Furthermore, after social media platforms imposed indefinite suspensions of former US President Trump, one can add prior censorship concerns. The one issue that is closely related to the positive obligations of the state to ensure protection mechanisms for freedom of expression is that in general this type of intermediary liability regime puts private intermediaries in the position of having to make decisions

[28] Regulation (EU) 2022/2065 of the European Parliament and of the Council of 19 October 2022 on a Single Market for Digital Services (Digital Services Act) and amending Directive 2000/31/EC.

[29] Directive (EU) 2018/1808 of the European Parliament and of the Council of 14 November 2018 amending Directive 2010/13/EU on the coordination of certain provisions laid down by law, regulation or administrative action in Member States concerning the provision of audiovisual media services (Audiovisual Media Services Directive) in view of changing market realities [2018] OJ L303/69, recital 14.

[30] Ibid., Art. 28b.

[31] Regulation (EU) 2016/679 of the European Parliament and of the Council of 27 April 2016 on the protection of natural persons with regard to the processing of personal data and on the free movement of such data, and repealing Directive 95/46/EC (General Data Protection Regulation) [2016] OJ L119/1, Art. 17 (3).

[32] European Commission, 'Code of Conduct on countering illegal hate speech online', 30 June 2016, https://ec.europa.eu/info/policies/justice-and-fundamental-rights/combatting-discrimination/racism-and-xenophobia/eu-code-conduct-countering-illegal-hate-speech-online_en.

about the lawfulness or unlawfulness of the content and create incentives for private censorship.[33] Several international organisations,[34] and other stakeholders,[35] have pointed to the fact that intermediaries should not be expected to conduct a quasi-adjudicatory exercise that weighs the rights of their users. They have argued that the fact that intermediaries have the technical means to prevent access to content does not mean that they are the best placed to evaluate the legality of the content in question, and whether measures affecting fundamental rights should be applied by an independent court rather than by private bodies.[36] Intermediaries are commercial entities whose fear of potential liability, or lack of resources to fully address requests for removal of information, may motivate an overzealous response to individual requests that information be delisted.[37] As private actors, intermediaries are not necessarily going to consider the value of freedom of expression when making decisions about content created by third parties for which they might be held liable.[38]

Another criticism of entrusting the balancing of fundamental rights to internet intermediaries is that by enlisting internet intermediaries as watchdogs, governments delegate online enforcement to algorithmic tools with limited or no accountability. Due process and fundamental guarantees are mauled by technological enforcement, curbing fair uses of content online and silencing speech according to the mainstream ethical discourse.[39] In addition, until the obligations contained in the DSA are implemented, the algorithms in most cases are known to the intermediary alone or are even considered to be a commercial secret. Such a lack of transparency in the intermediaries' decision-making processes can obscure discriminatory practices or political pressure affecting the companies' decisions. Consequently, transferring regulation and adjudication of rights to freedom on the internet to private actors does jeopardise fundamental rights in general – such as freedom of information, freedom of expression, and freedom of business – by limiting access to

33 IACHR, 'Freedom of expression and the internet', Special Rapporteur for Freedom of Expression, Catalina Botero Marino, 31 December 2013, OEA/Ser.L/V/II. CIDH/RELE/INF. 11/13, www.oas.org/en/iachr/expression/docs/reports/2014_04_08_internet_eng%20_web.pdf, para. 105.

34 S. Banerji et al., 'The "right to be forgotten" and blocking orders under the American convention: emerging issues in intermediary liability and human rights', September 2017, www-cdn.law.stanford.edu/wp-content/uploads/2017/09/The-_Right-to-Be-Forgotten_-and-Blocking-Orders-under-the-American-Convention-Emerging-Issues-in-Intermediary-Liability-and-Human-Rights_Sep17-.pdf, 47; UNHRC, 'Report of the Special Rapporteur on the promotion and protection of the right to freedom of opinion and expression', 11 May 2016, UN Doc. A/HRC/32/38, para. 44.

35 Article 19, *Internet Intermediaries*, p. 2.

36 Ibid., p. 14.

37 D. Keller, 'Europe's right to be forgotten in Latin America', 1 February 2017, http://cyberlaw.stanford.edu/publications/europes-right-be-forgotten-latin-america-0, para. 17.

38 IACHR, 'Freedom of expression and the internet', para. 99; P. Bernal, 'Self-regulation of internet intermediaries: public duty versus private responsibility', 2017, www.semanticscholar.org/paper/Self-regulation-of-internet-intermediaries%3A-public-Bernal/2204f0f30ae84b46f0994dcbd6ec9fc5666abfd6, 14.

39 G. Frosio, 'Why keep a dog and bark yourself? From intermediary liability to responsibility' (2018) 26 *Oxford International Journal of Law and Information Technology* 1, 1–33, at 14.

information, causing chilling effects, or curbing due process.[40] More particularly and closer to the topic of this chapter, it also influences the capacity of the states to carry out their positive obligations.

In the first part of this chapter, it was concluded that states must create a favourable environment for participation in public debate, protect speakers, and put in place an appropriate legislative and administrative framework to guarantee effective pluralism. We must remember that the ECtHR has recognised the state as an object of these duties, and human rights law does not, as a general matter, directly govern the activities or responsibilities of private business.[41] Yet, as emphasised earlier, the EU rules on intermediary liability follow different logics.

Since internet intermediaries through advertising or the payment of subscription fees benefit from disseminating third-party content online, it seems only fair that they should bear responsibility for preventing access to illegal or harmful material.[42] At the same time, while seeking the most effective enforcement mechanism, the regulation introduced by EU law and transposed into national law, shifts the balancing duty from the state to private companies – social media platforms. That means that not the states, but online platforms are the ones creating the environment for participation in public debate. Until recently, the limited potential to review decisions, often made using algorithms, is inevitably linked with limited possibilities to ensure the protection of speakers. It also involves very few options for influencing pluralism in the online environment, which is becoming the principal source of information and communication in many countries.

Therefore, although the intermediary liability regime itself does not interfere with the freedom of expression, it creates a situation of horizontal interference resulting from a failure of the legislature to effectively protect the right to freedom of expression – a form of 'State interference by proxy'.[43] The measures introduced by the DSA, which focus on ensuring more transparency and better protection of citizens' fundamental rights online, including the obligation to provide information to users and establish a complaint and redress mechanism, is a huge step in the right direction. However, these steps should not be considered a substitute for the positive obligations of the state arising from the human rights standards set by the ECtHR and other international bodies.

9.4 SAFEGUARDS FOR FREEDOM OF EXPRESSION

As just concluded, states have an obligation to effectively protect human rights from interference by other private individuals. Although not specifically mentioning the

40 Ibid., p. 33.

41 UNHRC, 'Report of the Special Rapporteur on the promotion and protection of the right to freedom of opinion and expression', 11 May 2016, UN Doc. A/HRC/32/38, para. 9.

42 Article 19, *Internet Intermediaries*, p. 14.

43 Kuczerawy, 'The power of positive thinking', p. 30.

positive obligations of the state, the ECtHR has already argued that the state should protect freedom of expression online, not only by avoiding any limitations to it, but also by creating an appropriate legal framework. In *Ahmet Yıldırım v. Turkey*, one of the most important cases dealing with the accessibility of information online,[44] it indicated that Article 10 of the ECHR requires a law to provide safeguards that are intended to protect against the over-removal of information from the internet.[45]

In addition, according to the UN Guiding Principles on Business and Human Rights, which requires businesses to avoid causing or contributing to adverse impacts on human rights, the duty to protect and to provide access to an effective remedy for violations of human rights is essentially incumbent on states.[46] Therefore, even though the document emphasises the duties of private stakeholders, it still underlines the role of the state in the protection of human rights.

Arguments supporting the positive obligations of the state in the context of freedom of expression and intermediary liability can also be found in legal doctrine. These arguments are based upon the idea that as many powerful social media platforms have become central to communication and information exchange, the legal framework in which they exist must be compatible with human rights standards.[47] Therefore, the content removal mechanisms should have a sufficient basis in law. To meet this requirement, the legislature should introduce specific legal provisions to clarify removal procedures. Legislation providing for content removal procedures should meet the requirement of 'quality'. This means that rules should be clear and sufficiently precise for those subject to them to foresee the consequences and adjust their behaviour accordingly.[48]

The positive obligations of states to protect freedom of expression are perhaps of even more relevance if such interferences are accepted, or even encouraged by the states,[49] as is the case in the rules dealing with intermediary liability. The current intermediary liability regime, the most notable documents of which are the E-Commerce Directive and the DSA, includes (especially in the latter) some safeguards that could ensure the protection of the right to freedom of expression.[50] But its application across Europe is yet to be seen and it does not relieve the state as an

[44] Council of Europe/ECtHR, 'Internet: case-law of the European Court of Human Rights', June 2015, www.echr.coe.int/Documents/Research_report_internet_ENG.pdf, 44.

[45] *Ahmet Yildrim v. Turkey*, Application no. 3111/10, Judgment of 18 December 2012, 2012-VI 465, para. 68.

[46] UNHRC, 'Report of the Special Representative of the Secretary General on the issue of human rights and transnational corporations and other business enterprises. Guiding Principles on Business and Human Rights: Implementing the United Nations "Protect, Respect and Remedy" Framework', 21 March 2011, UN Doc. A/HRC/17/31.

[47] E. Shattock, 'Is it time for Europe to reassess internet intermediary liability in light of coronavirus misinformation?', 20 April 2020, https://europeanlawblog.eu/2020/04/20/is-it-time-for-europe-to-reassess-internet-intermediary-liability-in-light-of-coronavirus-misinformation/.

[48] Kuczerawy, 'The power of positive thinking', 33.

[49] Ibid., 8.

[50] Ibid., 38.

ultimate actor to ensure fundamental rights also online. As stated earlier, the doctrine of the positive obligations of states in the context of freedom of expression may provide for the further legal protection of the users of social media platforms, their right to express themselves, and their right to have access to information.

9.5 EFFECTIVE REMEDIES AND PROCEDURAL SAFEGUARDS

When freedom of expression is violated, appropriate remedies to this situation may include access to information about the violation and grievance mechanisms.[51] In order for these safeguards for freedom of expression to be effective, the states should ensure that the principles of due process and access to independent and accountable redress mechanisms are respected in the application of them.[52]

First of all, users should be provided with the right to learn about the removal of the information they have published online.[53] Otherwise, they practically cannot protect their right to freedom of expression.[54]

Although there is a chance that such a practice could backfire and once removed information could resurface again through different channels, a notification to webmasters and content providers should be issued by internet intermediaries whenever they restrict access to information created by these actors. Such an approach is supported, for example, by the UN Special Rapporteur on the promotion and protection of freedom of opinion and expression.[55] It is also prevalent in the doctrine applied by the courts in cases concerning intellectual property rights in the US and Brazil.[56] The notification should, as far as possible, include the reasoning of

[51] UNHRC, 'Report of the Special Rapporteur on the promotion and protection of the right to freedom of opinion and expression', 11 May 2016, UN Doc. A/HRC/32/38, para. 74.

[52] Council of Europe, 'Recommendation CM/Rec(2012)3 of the Committee of Ministers to member states on the protection of human rights with regard to search engines', 4 April 2021, www.coe.int/en/web/freedom-expression/committee-of-ministers-adopted-texts/-/asset_publisher/aDXmrolovvsU/content/recommendation-cm-rec-2012-3-of-the-committee-of-ministers-to-member-states-on-the-protection-of-human-rights-with-regard-to-search-engines-adopted-by, para 15.

[53] Kuczerawy, 'The power of positive thinking', 35.

[54] F. Louis et al., 'Statement according to Art. 23 of the Statute of the Court of Justice and Art. 96 of the rules of procedure of the Court of Justice of the Reporters Committee for Freedom of the Press in Case C-507/17', 29 November 2017, www.rcfp.org/sites/default/files/2017-11-29%20-%20Statement%20CJEU%20in%20Googe%20v.%20CNIL%20(RCFP%20et%20al.)%20-%20as%20filed.pdf, 4; J. Riordan, *The Liability of Internet Intermediaries* (Oxford: Oxford University Press, 2016), p. 344; S. Banerji et al., 'The right to be forgotten', 34.

[55] UNHRC, 'Report of the Special Rapporteur on the promotion and protection of the right to freedom of opinion and expression', 11 May 2016, UN Doc. A/HRC/32/38.

[56] For more on doctrine, see Kuczerawy, 'The power of positive thinking'. Regarding the US, see D. Erods, 'Communicating responsibilities: the Spanish DPA targets Google's notification practices when delisting personal information', 21 March 2017, https://inforrm.org/2017/03/21/communicating-responsibilities-the-spanish-dpa-targets-googles-notification-practices-when-delisting-personal-information-david-erdos/; and regarding Brazil, D. Rousseff et al., 'Establishes the principles, guarantees, rights and obligations for the use of Internet in Brazil', 23 April 2014, www.publicknowledge.org/assets/uploads/documents/APPROVED-MARCO-CIVIL-MAY-2014.pdf.

the decision that, if necessary, can be later challenged. Even more, in accordance with the Manila Principles of intermediary liability, before such a removal becomes permanent, the intermediary should weigh the arguments of the author of the information in question.[57] The DSA apparently ensures this remedy by introducing the concept of 'notice and action' and obliging social media platforms to inform users of the removal of their information. Consequently, this rectifies the existing lacuna in the EU legal framework. However, the DSA only applies as far as to intermediaries who offer their services in the EU single market.

Second, users who are notified by the service provider that their content has been flagged as unlawful should have the option of challenging the block or filtering of their content and to seek clarifications and remedies.[58] The possibility to appeal could come in various forms – using procedures provided by the intermediary or by a competent judicial authority.[59]

The DSA notes that first and foremost the internet intermediaries themselves should have a review procedure in place. Such an idea is nothing new and some intermediaries have worked on this already. In 2018, Facebook already announced that it will create an independent oversight body to adjudicate appeals on content moderation issues.[60] The Board reviews a select number of highly emblematic cases and determines if decisions were made in accordance with Facebook's stated values and policies.[61] Individual users can bring appeals to the Board, and Facebook as a company is able to refer cases for expedited review if they could have urgent real-world consequences.[62] Most notably the Oversight Board accepted a case referral from Facebook to examine their decision to indefinitely suspend former US President Donald Trump's access to post content on Facebook and Instagram. Facebook has also requested policy recommendations from the Board on suspensions when the user is a political leader.[63]

57 The Manila principles on intermediary liability, 2015, www.eff.org/files/2015/10/31/manila_principles_1.0.pdf, principle 5.

58 Council of Europe, 'Recommendation CM/Rec(2008)6 of the Committee of Ministers of the Council of Europe to member states on measures to promote the respect for freedom of expression and information with regard to internet filters', 26 March 2008, www.coe.int/en/web/freedom-expression/committee-of-ministers-adopted-texts/-/asset_publisher/aDXmrolovvsU/content/recommendation-cm-rec-2008-6-of-the-committee-of-ministers-to-member-states-on-measures-to-promote-the-respect-for-freedom-of-expression-and-informati?inheritRedirect=false, para. 47.

59 Report of the Special Rapporteur on the promotion and protection of the right to freedom of opinion and expression, 16 May 2011, A/HRC/17/27, para. 47.

60 C. Newton, 'Facebook will create an independent oversight group to review content moderation appeals', 15 November 2018, www.theverge.com/2018/11/15/18097219/facebook-independent-oversight-supreme-court-content-moderation.

61 Oversight Board, 'The purpose of the board', www.oversightboard.com.

62 Newton, 'Facebook will create an independent oversight group to review content moderation appeals'.

63 Oversight Board, 'Oversight Board accepts case on former US President Trump's indefinite suspension from Facebook and Instagram', www.oversightboard.com/news/236821561313092-oversight-board-accepts-case-on-former-us-president-trump-s-indefinite-suspension-from-facebook-and-instagram/.

At the same time, the opportunities to contest the decisions of online platforms should complement, yet leave unaffected in all respects, the possibility to seek judicial redress.[64] There should always exist the option of judicial redress to ensure effective legal protection of the right to freedom of expression.[65] Indeed, the safeguards would become redundant if there were no option to receive a judicial overview of the decisions made by internet intermediaries. The liability placed upon private companies to remove third-party content without judicial oversight would not be compatible with international human rights law and freedom of expression specifically.[66]

Although internet intermediaries are technically the best placed to evaluate applications for content removal and act upon them, such a mechanism might not be completely compatible with the requirements of legality and quality of law. While the practice of implementing the transparency rules provided by the DSA on online platforms is unclear, so far the internal decision-making procedures of the intermediaries are not always very transparent. Therefore, removal orders issued by independent and impartial bodies provide a much greater degree of legal certainty.[67]

Third, the independence of internal complaint and redress mechanisms and the readiness of social media platforms to follow the decisions of oversight boards depend also on the goodwill of the platforms. The change in ownership in 2022 of one of the biggest social media platforms, Twitter, illustrates how rapidly the existing policies of the social media platform can change and how fragile reliance only on internal redress mechanisms created by the platform can be. A court or similar authority would operate with greater safeguards for independence, autonomy, and impartiality,[68] and would have greater capacity to evaluate the rights at stake and offer the necessary assurances to the user.[69] Such authorities as public bodies (not private) would also be better placed to make the determination of whether a particular content is illegal, which requires careful balancing of competing interests and consideration of defences.[70]

The positive obligation of states to protect freedom of expression entails the creation of a system that would allow individuals and other content creators to protect their freedom of expression also in case it is exercised through social media

64 European Commission, 'Proposal for a Regulation of the European Parliament and of the Council on a Single Market for Digital Services (Digital Services Act) and amending Directive 2000/31/EC', COM (2020) 825 final, recital 44.

65 Kuczerawy, 'The power of positive thinking', 36.

66 OHCHR, Special Rapporteur on the promotion and protection of the right to freedom of opinion and expression 'Comment on Social Networks bill (Netzdurchführungsgesetz)', 1 June 2017, www.ohchr.org/Documents/Issues/Opinion/Legislation/OL-DEU-1-2017.pdf, 4.

67 Article 19, *Internet Intermediaries*, p. 2.

68 Report of the Special Rapporteur on the promotion and protection of the right to freedom of opinion and expression, 16 May 2011, A/HRC/17/27.

69 IACHR, 'Freedom of expression and the internet', para. 106.

70 UNHRC, 'Report of the Special Rapporteur on the promotion and protection of the right to freedom of opinion and expression', 11 May 2016, UN Doc. A/HRC/32/38, para. 42.

platforms and internet intermediaries. These intermediaries should abide by the rules of freedom of expression themselves, but at the end of the day, the state cannot rely on these private players to protect speech online. The DSA envisages a new enforcement mechanism, which will complement the internal complaint and redress tools established by social media platforms. This mechanism will consist of the Commission and independent national authorities to supervise how online intermediaries, including social media platforms, adapt their systems to new requirements. To safeguard the freedom of expression, the independence of these bodies and the possibility of challenging their decisions in the courts are of crucial importance. The criticism so far has been correctly expressed that the oversight of very large platforms is subject to the European Commission, which is not an independent regulator but the executive arm of the EU.[71]

9.6 RULES ON BALANCING

At this point, it is clear that monitoring and restricting access to information online would be impossible without the involvement of internet intermediaries. They act as gatekeepers with direct access to the keys needed to close the gates to malicious or otherwise illegal information. The keys available to states are much more robust and take longer to activate. This means that to ensure effective protection of human rights online, the states have to cooperate with internet intermediaries. Therefore, besides the creation of a mechanism for protecting freedom of expression online, states have to set clear rules for internet intermediaries to follow in deciding which information remains accessible and which should be removed. The importance of clear rules at the national level is especially relevant, since only some illegal content is defined at the EU level, while some content might be found illegal and subject to removal only in certain states.

Internet users should always be able to understand why certain information has been removed.[72] The changes introduced by the DSA apparently ensure that social media platforms notify users of the reasons for removing their content and the option to contest such decisions.

The states should ensure that removal of information or blocking access should be undertaken in the observance of the principle of freedom of expression.[73]

[71] Article 19, 'At a glance: does the EU Digital Services Act protect freedom of expression?' (2021), www.article19.org/resources/does-the-digital-services-act-protect-freedom-of-expression/.

[72] Council of Europe, 'Recommendation CM/Rec(2008)6 of the Committee of Ministers of the Council of Europe to member states on measures to promote the respect for freedom of expression and information with regard to Internet filters', 26 March 2008, www.coe.int/en/web/freedom-expression/committee-of-ministers-adopted-texts/-/asset_publisher/aDXmrolovvsU/content/recommendation-cm-rec-2008-6-of-the-committee-of-ministers-to-member-states-on-measures-to-promote-the-respect-for-freedom-of-expression-and-informati?inheritRedirect=false.

[73] European Commission, 'Proposal for a Regulation of the European Parliament and of the Council on a Single Market for Digital Services (Digital Services Act) and amending Directive 2000/31/EC', COM (2020) 825 final, recital 22.

In mediating the public interest and individual rights online, a delicate regulatory balance is required.[74] Therefore, the state should provide guidance for intermediaries on how to achieve this.[75] The DSA could play a role in establishing standards and best practices in this area as it tries to balance measures imposed on platforms to remove harmful information against the restrictions to freedom of expression. Yet the application of the DSA both at the EU and national level is yet to be seen.

9.7 CONCLUSIONS

Social media platforms and internet intermediaries in general are becoming, and in many societies already are, the dominant actors in providing an environment for freedom of expression and communication. Yet the legal regulation of platforms has not always followed technological developments and changes in society so as to ensure respect for freedom of expression and other fundamental rights. The idea during the emergence of the online environment that it should be left free and unregulated to ensure the marketplace of ideas was gradually changed with increasing regulation from the states in order to protect other fundamental rights, for instance human dignity, and ensure non-discrimination. The signs of this shifting attitude of states and international bodies was evidenced by the judgement of the ECtHR in the case of *Delfi v Estonia*,[76] which for the first time imposed the liability on a news platform for not removing derogatory comments created by its users in a timely manner. The Court came to such a decision despite the fact that the platform acted quickly after the notice was received. This judgment was followed by laws restricting freedom of expression and imposing more obligations on social medial platforms in a number of European countries,[77] and even debates in the US about changes to section 230 of the Communications Act of 1934, which grants websites legal immunity for much of the content posted by their users.[78]

While such moves by states are understandable in order to protect other fundamental rights and currently provide measures against the spread of misinformation

[74] E. Shattock, 'Is it time for Europe to reassess internet intermediary liability in light of coronavirus misinformation?', 20 April 2020, https://europeanlawblog.eu/2020/04/20/is-it-time-for-europe-to-reassess-internet-intermediary-liability-in-light-of-coronavirus-misinformation/.

[75] Article 19, 'Germany: the Act to improve enforcement of the law in social networks', August 2017, www.article19.org/wp-content/uploads/2017/09/170901-Legal-Analysis-German-NetzDG-Act.pdf, 2.

[76] *Delfi v. Estonia*, Application no. 64569/09, Judgment of 16 June 2015, ECHR 2015-II 319.

[77] Act to Improve Enforcement of the Law in Social Networks 2017 (Netzwerkdurchsetzungsgesetz); Law on Countering Online Hatred 2020 (Projet de loi Avia) (FR); Law No. 5651 on Regulating Internet Publications and Combating Crimes Committed by Means of Such Publications (Internet Ortaminda Yapilan Yayinlarin Düzenlenmesi Ve Bu Yayinlar Yoluyla İşlenen Suçlarla Mücadele Edilmesi Hakkinda Kanunda Değişiklik Yapilmasina Dair Kanun) (2020) (TUR).

[78] Communications Act of 1934, s 230 (c) (1): 'No provider or user of an interactive computer service shall be treated as the publisher or speaker of any information provided by another information content provider'.

and harmful content in the online environment, the safeguards for freedom of expression seems to have been forgotten in this process. Online intermediaries, which have implemented different technical tools to block and to remove information in response to demands by states, are actually now in charge of setting the boundaries of freedom of expression – a role that should be performed by states. The role of freedom of expression in democracies is essential, and states should not shirk their obligations in ensuring freedom of expression and deciding about its limits by outsourcing this function to private corporations. Social media platforms and internet intermediaries in general have neither democratic legitimacy nor do they in many cases share the goal of protecting this fundamental right, and the process of limiting expressions is in most cases accompanied by a lack of clear rules, transparency, and access to remedies. We must remember that the right to freedom of expression entails not only the negative obligations of the state, but also positive ones. The doctrine of these positive duties is still developing and awaits clarification, especially in the context of information published online. However, it can be argued that it can already be applied in order to improve the safeguards for freedom of expression for users of social media platforms, and discourage the platforms from the over-removal of content to avoid liability. The DSA is certainly a step forward; however, its scope is limited and its application is yet to be seen.

Last but not least, the majority of existing legal standards focus on the development of content moderation rules, which would balance freedom of expression and the removal of illegal content by social media platforms. Still, another and similarly important threat to freedom of expression in the online environment is the fact that the vast majority of public discourse takes place on a very small number of platforms, which hold excessive power over information flow.[79] As stated earlier, the ECtHR has emphasised that states must put in place an appropriate legislative and administrative framework to guarantee effective pluralism in the media ecosystem.[80] Therefore, states are obliged to decentralise the channels of public discourse and develop rules that favour the development of new social media platforms.

[79] Article 19, 'At a glance'.

[80] *Manole and Others v. Moldova*, Application no. 13936/02, Judgment of 17 September 2009, ECHR 2009-IV 213; *Informationsverein Lentia and Others v. Austria* (1993) Application nos. 13914/88, 15041/89, 15717/89, 15779/89, 17207/90, Judgment of 24 November 1993, Series A no. 276.

10

The Development of New Media Doctrines on Freedom of Expression

How to Defend Democratic Society and the Rule of Law

Jukka Viljanen and Tomoe Watashiba

10.1 INTRODUCTION

Democracy and freedom of expression are intertwined in the European Court of Human Rights (hereinafter, 'the ECtHR' or 'the Court') case law. Article 10 (Freedom of Expression) of the European Convention on Human Rights (hereinafter, 'the ECHR' or 'the Convention') introduces obligations on Member States to protect the right to freedom of expression. The scope of the right is broad, and as such, it clarifies that any limitation on the freedom of expression must be prescribed by law, pursue a legitimate aim, and be necessary in a democratic society (e.g., protecting the reputation or rights of others). In addition, Articles 17 (Prohibition of abuse of rights) and 18 (Limitation on use of restrictions on rights) of the ECHR are also relevant in assessing the scope and legitimacy of restrictions against the freedom of expression. In protecting the right to the freedom of expression and robust public debate, which are the foundations and pre-conditions for a democratic society, strong safeguards have been developed by the ECtHR in its case law interpreting the Convention.

Within this case law, the defence of democracy as a legitimate aim of limiting the freedom of expression is a relatively unnoticed part of European case law. More often, the discussion has been on the abuse of rights provision, which is closely related to extreme political movements that try to promote undemocratic ideologies. In this connection, the Court has reiterated that the general purpose of Article 17 is to prevent individuals or groups with totalitarian aims from exploiting the principles enunciated in the Convention in their own interests.[1]

There has been consensus on certain fundamental doctrines related to freedom of expression and defending democracy. However, these are more designed

[1] *Paksas v. Lithuania*, Application no. 34932/04, Judgment of 6 January 2011, paras. 87–8 refer to established continuum in the field of Article 17. Mentioning, e.g., denying Nazi war crimes against the Jewish community, the use of freedom of expression for Islamophobic and anti-Semitic purposes respectively.

for a traditional media environment that does not reflect the prevailing internet-based system of expression in our current society. In the contemporary system, the defence of democracy is a more complex and multifaceted phenomenon than just guaranteeing the protection of democracy from extreme movements and the most serious hate speech. That is, pre-emptive measures have become a key part of the tools for defending democracy. This means that there need to be strong foundations for securing public debate, including a diverse and pluralist media environment that would enable safeguards against disinformation and other attacks on the democratic system. In contemporary society, the concept of the media as a public watchdog has also evolved into more of a diverse network of watchdogs, consisting of different actors, from the media to non-governmental organisations (NGOs) and even academics.

In addition, there is a fear of abuses of the defence of democracy argument. Sanctions and other restrictive measures could be used to silence critical voices and democratic opposition. This development in applying ulterior purposes is inevitable when looking at how Article 18 of the Convention has emerged in the Court's case law. There is more evidence of using different sanctions for ulterior motives, especially against those in opposition.

Against this background, this chapter tries to systematise current interpretative doctrines that the ECtHR applies in cases related to defending democracy and the rule of law under Article 10. In addition, it looks at the approach to contextualism taken by the Facebook's Oversight Board. The idea is to analyse these doctrines in light of present-day conditions and to evaluate how the doctrines are adaptable to the new media environment. In so doing, this chapter first focuses on the question of how European history and the historico-political context have been taken into account and what the key principles have been in assessing the width of the margin of appreciation in relation to the right to freedom of expression in the Court's interpretation in particular regard to defending democracy. Section 2 will then further outline established doctrines of defending democracy in the Court's case law. Section 3 of the chapter delves more into how the emergence of internet-based media and enhanced access to a space of social debate has further complicated the case law, where the focus has shifted more to encompassing freedom of expression online for upholding democracy as a system rather than merely restricting extremists or hate speech. The section also considers the threats of disproportionately restrictive measures on public debate, which might undermine democracy and fall under Article 18. The section also looks into the positive obligations and how a regulatory framework requiring pluralism would be essential as a pre-emptive measure against threats to democracy. The final section provides a concluding observation on how the ECtHR has dealt with the defence of democracy argumentation in relation to freedom of expression and the evolving nature of such established doctrines in the face of the current media environment and democratic society.

10.2 HISTORICAL CONTEXT AND STABILITY OF DEMOCRACY ARGUMENTATION

According to the Court's case law, the defence of democracy argumentation must be interpreted in light of European history. Consequently, the argumentation of protecting democracy is founded on the history of the twentieth century and especially on how fragile democracy can be in times of transition and where certain resurfacing ideologies pose a threat to democracy, referring to the ideologies and even symbols of authoritarian regimes, whether under Nazism or Communism.

Context is part of the defending democracy doctrines, and the Court emphasises a careful examination of context,[2] particularly when symbols with multiple meanings are used for the expression of political views.[3] Therefore, the Court does not exclude that certain symbols are not always 'equally permissible in all places and [at] all times', stating that 'the display of a contextually ambiguous symbol at the specific site [of mass murders] may in certain circumstances express identification with the perpetrators of those crimes' and that a ban on demonstrations when held on a specific day of remembrance may 'represent a pressing social need' and thus 'necessitate an interference with the right to freedom of expression'.[4]

In the case of *Vogt v. Germany*, history was essential for assessing whether the restriction on the freedom of expression in the name of defending democracy was in accordance with the Convention. The Court analysed whether a legitimate aim existed to restrict the rights of civil servants when the political loyalty requirement was applied to a teacher in a public school who was a member of a communist party and was dismissed on account of her political activities. The political loyalty requirement requires that state employees are loyal in actively upholding a free democratic constitutional system. The Court noted that the notion of the civil service being 'the guarantor of the Constitution and democracy has special importance in Germany because of that country's experience under the Weimar Republic, which, when the Federal Republic was founded after the nightmare of Nazism, led to its constitution being based on the principle of a "democracy capable of defending itself" (wehrhafte Demokratie)'.[5]

The same idea of historical experiences and using democratic processes to promote totalitarian movements was also mentioned in the *Refah Partisi* case (2003).[6] The communist authoritarian past was relevant in the *Ždanoka v. Latvia*

[2] *Öllinger v. Austria*, Application no. 76900/01, Judgment of 29 June 2006, para. 47.
[3] *Faber v. Hungary*, Application no. 40721/08, Judgment of 24 July 2012, para. 36.
[4] Ibid., para. 58.
[5] *Vogt v. Germany*, Application no. 17851/91, Judgment of 26 September 1995, para. 51.
[6] *Refah Partisi (the Welfare Party) and Others v. Turkey*, Application nos. 41340/98, 41342/98, 41343/98, and 41344/98, Judgment of 13 July 2003, para. 99, 'it is not at all improbable that totalitarian movements, organised in the form of political parties, might do away with democracy, after prospering under the democratic regime, there being examples of this in modern European history'.

case, where the Court established and consolidated the current criteria for the 'self-defence' of democracy. The *Ždanoka* judgment includes an extended doctrinal summary under the title *Democracy and its protection in the Convention system*, where it acknowledges that 'democracy constitutes a fundamental element of "European public order"' and the Preamble of the Convention makes a connection between the realisation and the maintenance of human rights and fundamental freedoms with 'effective political democracy'.[7] It also refers to the common heritage of political traditions, ideals, freedom, and the rule of law of European countries enshrined within the Convention, where, in fact, on many occasions, the Court has reiterated that the Convention exists 'to maintain and promote the ideals and values of a democratic society'.[8] According to the *Ždanoka* judgment, democracy is the only political model contemplated by the Convention and, accordingly, the only one compatible with it.[9]

In the *Ždanoka* case, the Court referred to the principle that:

> in order to guarantee the stability and effectiveness of a democratic system, the State may be required to take specific measures to protect itself. Thus, in the above-cited *Vogt* judgement, with regard to the requirement of political loyalty imposed on civil servants, the Court acknowledged the legitimacy of the concept of a 'democracy capable of defending itself' (paras. 51 and 59).[10]

The Court applies very careful reference to the historico-political background, which makes the same measure acceptable in one country and yet incompatible in another with different historico-political contexts.[11] Regarding a state with a less established democratic tradition or institutions, or those with a totalitarian past, therefore, the Court considers that the margin of appreciation is different, noting in such a state, national authorities would be better placed to 'assess the difficulties faced in establishing and safeguarding the democratic order'.[12] Under the Court's scrutiny, the Latvian context was different because the Court acknowledged that there might be a threat against the new democratic order and a 'resurgence of ideas which, if allowed to gain ground, might appear capable of restoring the former regime'.[13]

One of the key arguments in this contextual approach was that in the field of election-related rights, there was a wide margin of appreciation, but also in the Latvian context, the Court affirmed that the Parliament should keep statutory restrictions under constant review.[14] The Court also referred to European integration

7 *Ždanoka v. Latvia*, Application no. 58278/00, Judgment of 16 March 2006, para. 98.
8 Ibid.
9 Ibid.
10 Ibid., para. 100.
11 Ibid., para. 133.
12 Ibid., para. 134.
13 Ibid., para. 133.
14 Ibid., para. 135.

as one of the key elements to be taken into account as a contributing factor for Latvia's stability. Therefore, the election context impacts the proportionality test and gives more discretion to national authorities.

In this section, we have looked at the Court's deliberation so far based on European history and historico-political contextuality in its judgments in relation to defending democracy and protecting the freedom of expression of individuals, especially when political views are expressed. We can say that the foundational correlation between democracy and the Convention has been clearly demarcated in its interpretations, and democratic society is a central concept in the ECHR. Moreover, the ECtHR has applied the democracy argumentation since the start of its work, particularly when talking about the general principles of interpretation, as the Court founded its argumentation in the *Soering* case that as '[t]he general spirit of the Convention, [is] an instrument designed to maintain and promote the ideals and values of a democratic society'.[15]

Furthermore, 'an effective political democracy' is mentioned in the Preamble and 'democratic society' appears in six of the Articles (6, 8, 9, 10, 11, and 2 of Protocol 4) of the ECHR. The emphasis on the value of protecting the democratic system is deeply rooted in European history and human rights atrocities, and the reason to draft the Convention and establish its supervisory system in the spirit of the Universal Declaration of Human Rights was to ensure that such events would never be repeated in Europe.

10.3 ESTABLISHED DOCTRINES ON DEFENDING DEMOCRACY IN THE ECTHR CASE LAW AND HECKLER'S VETO

Now that we have looked at the approach that the Court has taken in regard to the defence of democracy and the freedom of expression in its case law, in this section, we will highlight some of the established doctrines and principles related to defending democracy.

The key doctrinal element in defending democracy is the Prohibition of the Abuse of Rights, enshrined in Article 17 of the Convention. Against the background of the provision is the idea that a state, group, or person does not have a right to activities aimed at the destruction of the rights and freedoms of others. For example, the Court has, in the case of *Refah Partisi et al. v. Turkey*, reiterated that 'no one should be authorised to rely on the Convention's provisions in order to weaken or destroy the ideals and values of a democratic society'.[16] In the case of *Ždanoka v. Latvia*, furthermore, by referring to the consideration during the drafting of the Convention,

[15] *Soering v. the United Kindgdom*, Application no. 14038/88, Judgment of 7 July 1989, para. 87.

[16] *Refah Partisi (the Welfare Party) and Others v. Turkey*, Application nos. 41340/98, 41342/98, 41343/98, and 41344/98, Judgment of 13 July 2003.

the Court acknowledged that certain rights could not be used in order to 'destroy' certain other rights set forth by the Convention, stating:

> It was precisely this concern which led the authors of the Convention to introduce Article 17, which provides: 'Nothing in this Convention may be interpreted as implying for any State, group or person any right to engage in any activity or perform any act aimed at the destruction of any of the rights and freedoms set forth herein or at their limitation to a greater extent than is provided for in the Convention'.[17]

The Court has also set forth the principles for assessing the breadth of the margin of appreciation afforded to national authorities in its freedom of expression case law. Freedom of expression is closely related to democracy. According to the Court, freedom of expression constitutes one of the essential foundations of a democratic society, and the basic conditions for its progress and each individual's self-fulfilment.[18] As such, the Court states, 'in a democratic system, the actions or omissions of the government must be subject to the close scrutiny not only of the legislative and judicial authorities but also of public opinion'.[19] This means that authorities should tolerate even harder criticisms from the public, yet the key principle is set that 'where such remarks incite violence against an individual or a public official or a sector of the population, the State authorities enjoy a wider margin of appreciation when examining the need for interference with freedom of expression'.[20] As stated in the joint dissenting opinion in *Sürek and Özdemir v. Turkey*, judges have expressed that even though freedom of expression constitutes one of the foundations of democratic society, speech inciting violence undermines democracy.[21]

As such, the Court has accepted that states can limit rights guaranteed under the Convention in order to defend democracy.[22] Furthermore, these measures can also be implemented in a pre-emptive manner. That is, states cannot be required to wait for authoritarian forces 'to take steps that might prejudice civil peace and the country's democratic regime' before intervening.[23] The Court referred to the possibility of preventing attempts against democratic regimes even before they occur. It approached the situation with the purpose of deference to national courts and other authorities. Therefore, the national courts, after detailed scrutiny of European

[17] *Ždanoka v. Latvia*, Application no. 58278/00, Judgment of 16 March 2006, para. 99.

[18] *Guja v. Moldova*, Application no. 14277/04, Judgment of 12 February 2008, para. 69.

[19] *Sürek and Özdemir v. Turkey*, Application nos. 23927/94 and 24277/94, Judgment of 8 July 1999, para. 60.

[20] Ibid.

[21] Joint dissenting opinion of Wildhaber, Kūris, Strážnická, Baka, and Traja in *Sürek and Özdemir v. Turkey*, Application nos. 23927/94 and 24277/94, Judgment of 8 July 1999, 'Violence as a means of political expression being the antithesis of democracy, irrespective of the ends to which it is directed, incitement to it will tend to undermine democracy.'

[22] See, e.g., *Refah Partisi (the Welfare Party) and Others v. Turkey*, Application nos. 41340/98, 41342/98, 41343/98, and 41344/98, Judgment of 13 July 2003, paras. 86 and 99.

[23] Ibid., para. 102.

supervision, can take restrictive measures to protect democracy. However, there are different contexts to be taken into account in the discourse of defending democracy; that is, how much the line should be stretched to tolerate minority opinions.

In contemplating this question, let us examine the *Vajnai v. Hungary* case, where the Court deliberated over disproportionate restrictions in the name of defending democracy and was concerned that free speech and opinion would be subjected to *a heckler's veto*, which would negate freedom of expression.[24] The heckler's veto is invoked in situations where hecklers or demonstrators silence a speaker without the intervention of the law. The heckler's veto is thought to happen when the government considers restrictions on a speech with the anticipated or actual reactions of the opponents of the speech.[25]

In this case, Attila Vajnai was convicted of using a symbol of an international workers' movement, which was considered a totalitarian symbol and prohibited in Hungary. The Court recognised the systematic terror of communist rule in several countries and regarded that 'it remains a serious scar in the mind and heart of Europe'.[26] It is understandable that these symbols can cause uneasiness or seem disrespectful. Such sentiments cannot limit the freedom of expression. However, the Court went on to consider that this was about feelings rather than rational fears. The Court reviewed the proportionality of restrictions against Vajnai and considered that such a restriction based on satisfying 'the dictates of public feeling – real or imaginary – cannot be meeting the pressing social need requirement in a democratic society'.[27]

The disproportionate conviction obviously reflects the legislative framework that did not previously provide any further qualification for wearing certain symbols. The authorities did not have to weigh wearing the symbol and other interests in order to find a fair balance. In their report to the Committee of Ministers, they referred to the new formulation of legislation, which does not base criminal conviction on the mere display of a symbol, but also includes an additional formulation, stating 'in a manner that is capable of disturbing public peace, in particular that violates the human dignity of victims of totalitarian systems or the due reverence for the dead'.[28] The national legislation now determines more precisely the condition under which wearing such a symbol is prohibited and leads to a conviction.

So far, the established doctrine reflects an era where democracy was organised by political parties. However, a contemporary democratic system has a more complex

24 *Vajnai v. Hungary*, Application no. 33629/06, Judgment of 8 July 2008, para. 57.

25 Heckler's veto is considered to be unconstitutional in the US Supreme Court case law. See *Terminiello v. Chicago*, 337 US 1 (1949). The Court held that the First Amendment protects the right to make comments that are so controversial that they may stir a crowd into anger. The Court set a high bar for public comments to be considered so disruptive to public order that it can be limited.

26 *Vajnai v. Hungary*, Application no. 33629/06, Judgment of 8 July 2008.

27 Ibid.

28 See DH-DD(2019)1220 24/10/2019, 1362nd meeting (December 2019) (DH) – Action report (15/10/2019) – Communication from Hungary concerning the *VAJNAI group of cases v. Hungary* (Application No. 33629/06).

structure with different layers. In addition to the model of a representative democratic system, there is also a direct democracy element, with NGOs having a major impact on the public debate on specific questions of interest.

10.4 DISTINGUISHING BETWEEN TRADITIONAL AND INTERNET-BASED MEDIA AND FREEDOM OF EXPRESSION

In terms of assessing the balance of journalistic freedom and the legitimate restriction of the freedom of expression by a state in the context of traditional media, the Court identified four key elements to be considered in the hate speech case of *Jersild v. Denmark* in 1994. Those were (a) the manner in which the feature was prepared, (b) its contents, (c) the context in which it was broadcast, and (d) the purpose of the programme.[29] In this case, the applicant, a journalist, made a documentary containing extracts from a television interview he had conducted with three members of a group of young people calling themselves the Greenjackets, who had made abusive and derogatory remarks about immigrants and ethnic groups in Denmark. The applicant was convicted of aiding and abetting the dissemination of racist remarks, and he alleged a breach of his right to freedom of expression.

While the national courts laid emphasis on issues different from those of the Court, considering that the applicant had intended to include the racist remarks and edited the feature in that way, the Court took a different view and considered that the objective purpose of the feature was not the propagation of racist views and ideas. The Court drew a distinction between the members of the Greenjackets, who had made openly racist remarks, and the applicant, who had sought to expose, analyse, and explain this particular group of youths and to deal with 'specific aspects of a matter that already then was of great public concern'.[30] It was opined that the documentary as a whole was not aimed at propagating racist views and ideas but at informing the public about a social issue. Accordingly, the Court held that there had been a violation of Article 10 of the Convention.

What was interesting in the different approaches taken by the national courts and the European Court was the consideration of the scope of the assessment. That is, the Court considered that there were editorial decisions, especially related to the news value of the items that were broadcast by the media. According to the Court, there was no reason to question the editorial staff's own appreciation of the news or information value of the impugned item, and emphasis was also placed on the fact that it was part of a serious news programme.[31]

Now, how has the established case law since the *Jersild* case reflected the situation in social media and the responsibility of social media giants such as Twitter/X

[29] *Jersild v. Denmark*, Application no. 15890/89, Judgment of 23 September 1994, para. 31.
[30] Ibid., para. 33.
[31] Ibid., paras. 33–4.

and Facebook? How can we apply the four factors mentioned in the *Jersild* case to internet-based media? First of all, the 'context in which something is broadcast' is one of the trickiest parts of transforming the broadcast context to social media because one of the key features of social media has been its ability to provide everyone with access to the social discussion in a more or less public sphere. It should not matter whether a person is mostly providing his or her own personal comments or whether a person is representing his or her institutional position. But are there, or should there be, different requirements for those with a more formal media status?

For some time, the internet's role in the media environment and public debate has been acknowledged in the Court's case law. Internet-based media has become one of the key focal points in the Court's interpretation of freedom of expression in recent years, as seen in the case of *Delfi v. Estonia*. In this case, the Court reminded us of the important role played by the internet in enhancing the public's access to news and facilitating the dissemination of information,[32] and later the Court elaborated further, noting that the function of bloggers and popular users of social media may also be assimilated to that of public watchdogs,[33] insofar as the protection afforded by Article 10 is concerned. An essential factor in the Court's argumentation was the interrelationship between the functioning of the political system and the role of the press and NGOs.[34]

The Court has also articulated a need for a legislative framework applicable to the imparting of information received from the internet. For example, in the Ukrainian case of the *Editorial Board of Pravoye Delo and Shtekel*, the Court considered that the absence of a sufficient legal framework could have negative consequences for the freedom of expression. It found that the lack of legislation at the domestic level allowing journalists to use information obtained from the internet without fear of sanctions for such use seriously hinders the exercise of the vital function of the press as a public watchdog.[35]

Online media outlets are also often now applicants before the Court. One recent interesting judgment was in the case of *OOO Memo v. Russia*, where an executive body of the state instigated the defamation case. The Court made a new interpretative approach and considered that executive bodies do not have the same rights as legal entities. In previous cases, the question was more about proportionality, and in the *OOO Memo* case, the Court chose a different line of interpretation. That is, the argumentation comes from the need for the close scrutiny of public power in order to prevent the abuse of power and corruption of public office in a democratic system. The Court saw that if executive bodies could file civil defamation cases, it

32 *Delfi v. Estonia*, Application no. 64569/09, Judgment of 16 June 2015, para. 133.

33 *Magyar Helsinki Bizottság v. Hungary*, Application no. 18030/11, Judgment of 8 November 2016, para. 168.

34 Ibid., para. 167.

35 *Editorial Board of Pravoye Delo and Shtekel v. Ukraine*, Application no. 33014/05, Judgment of 5 May 2011, para. 64.

would place an excessive and disproportionate burden on the media, creating an inevitable chilling effect. The conclusion was that restricting the freedom of expression on the basis of the defamation inflicted on the executive body did not have a legitimate aim.[36]

In another case, *Cicad v. Switzerland*, the Court considered it proportionate that, through a court order, the applicant was to remove an article from a website and publish the main findings on its website.[37] In the Hungarian case of *Magyar Tartalomszolgáltatók Egyesülete* and Index.hu *Zrt*, other special features of the internet were considered necessary to be taken into account when deciding whether certain measures are proportionate or not, including expressions in the comment area. According to the Court, 'comments, albeit belonging to a low register of style, are common in communication on many internet portals – a consideration that reduces the impact that can be attributed to those expressions'.[38]

Another aspect that is typical of the contemporary media environment is that there are actors who deliberately aim to use different forms of disinformation as a way of destabilising democratic systems and societies through abusing the freedom of expression. The flood of disinformation and other hybrid tactics used in the new media environment can be described as, according to some scholars, information disorder and information pollution.[39] According to the Council of Europe report, the forms of disinformation are (a) false context, (b) imposter content, (c) manipulated content, and (d) fabricated content. In these distributions of disinformation, the role of different types of new media has become an essential factor to be taken into account.[40] Often, this means that social media platforms, for example, are taking a key role in the dissemination process and spreading distrust in the democratic system. The Joint Declaration from the United Nations (UN) and the Organization for Security and Co-operation in Europe (OSCE), African Union, and Organization of American States rapporteurs have emphasised the positive duties of states especially in promoting a free, independent, and diverse media environment.[41]

As we have previously seen, the defence of democracy doctrine has been developed in the context of protecting the democratic system from those with totalitarian beliefs and a totalitarian history, especially in relation to electoral candidates or the loyalty requirements set for civil servants, but also in relation to pre-emptively

36 *OOO Memo v. Russia*, Application no. 2840/10, Judgment of 16 June 2022, paras. 44–5, 48.

37 *Cicad v. Switzerland*, Application no. 7211/06, Judgment of 7 June 2016, paras. 62–3.

38 *Magyar Tartalomszolgáltatók Egyesülete and Index.hu Zrt v. Hungary*, Application no. 22947/13, Judgment of 2 February 2016, para. 77.

39 C. Wardle and H. Derakhshan, 'Information disorder: toward an interdisciplinary framework for research and policy making', Council of Europe Report DGI (2017) 09, 27 September 2017, https://rm.coe.int/information-disorder-report-version-august-2018/16808c9c77.

40 Ibid.

41 OSCE – The Representative on Freedom of the Media, 'Joint Declarations of the representatives of intergovernmental bodies to protect free media and expression', 2013, www.osce.org/files/f/documents/5/5/99558.pdf.

dissolving political parties with objectives that are contrary to, and thus weakening or destructive to, the democratic system.

In the course of this development, the question of anti-democratic forces and their imminent threat to democracy has led to accepting pre-emptive measures against such forces, even accepting the dissolution of political parties. Some scholars have warned about the risks of abuse and unclear limits of defending democracy. This was raised, especially in the context of peace-time limitations.[42] Of course, given the current situation, this criticism has to be reviewed in light of Russia's war against Ukraine. The threat of using disinformation to overthrow democratic governments, and even more generally to destabilise democratic processes that might have been previously seen as highly unlikely, is now very concrete in countries neighbouring Russia, and even elsewhere where Russian influence and hybrid tactics can cause imminent danger to the democratic system.

In a new media environment, which needs to be distinguished from earlier interpretative lines of print and audiovisual media, one of the significant issues involves anonymity. It has become an important part of social media that people are allowed to express views while maintaining their anonymity. Its value in social media posts and different digital platforms has been widely accepted. The idea behind anonymity is that it provides the opportunity to avoid reprisals or unwanted attention and thus promotes the free flow of opinions, ideas, and information, as was mentioned in one of the key cases in this context, that of *Standard Verlagsgesellschaft mbH v. Austria (no. 3)*.

> In the instant case, the lack of any balancing between the opposing interests [(see paragraph 94 above)] overlooks the function of anonymity as a means of avoiding reprisals or unwanted attention and thus the role of anonymity in promoting the free flow of opinions, ideas and information, in particular if political speech is concerned which is not hate speech or otherwise clearly unlawful. In view of the fact that no visible weight was given to these aspects, the Court cannot agree with the Government's submission that the Supreme Court struck a fair balance between opposing interests in respect of the question of fundamental rights.[43]

This is, however, one extension that also caused criticism within the Court. Judge Eicke saw that the Court's line of argument could cause problems for victims of abusive speech, stating that:

> the extension of Article 10 in this context will not be capable of being limited to service providers under the E-Commerce Directive who are also media companies but will ultimately have to be applied to any 'bloggers and popular users of

[42] J. A. Sweeney, 'Freedom of religion and democratic transition', in A. Buyse and M. Hamilton (eds.), *Transitional Jurisprudence and the ECHR, Justice, Politics and Rights* (Cambridge: Cambridge University Press, 2011), pp. 103–30, at 122–3.

[43] *Standard Verlagsgesellschaft mbH v. Austria (no. 3)*, Application no. 39378/15, Judgment of 7 December 2021, para. 95.

the social media', with the consequent (negative) impact on the ability of victims of abusive posts to seek access to court for the purposes of protecting themselves and their reputation.[44]

Another interesting case is that of *Ecodefence and 60 others v. Russia*, where one of the most elaborate attempts by a state to create a legal regime placed a significant chilling effect on different NGOs and their choice to seek or accept any amount of foreign funding, especially in respect of politically sensitive or domestically unpopular topics. The case concerned the Foreign Agent Act and its concept of political activities carried out by so-called foreign agents, which could also include any views expressed in interviews or even social media posts by those 'foreign agents'.[45]

There is a more rigorous approach to online media hatred that also emphasises the role of governments in criminalising hate speech. This has especially been seen in recent cases against minority groups. Hate speech related to a person's sexual orientation is a key factor in the case of *Oganezova v. Armenia*, where an inadequate response was considered a violation of Article 3 of the Convention together with Article 14.[46]

10.4.1 *From Article 17 to Article 18: From Restricting Extremists to Using Defending Democracy as an Excuse to Control Opposition*

In the Court's case law, Article 17 (prohibition of the abuse of rights) has allowed measures, especially restrictions and sanctions against those extreme groups denying the rights of others, particularly when comments amounted to hate speech and countered the values and ideologies enshrined in the Convention.[47] This was the provision used in the cases reviewing convictions of neo-Nazi groups in Germany. It was later used in cases involving those denying the Holocaust and atrocities committed during the Second World War,[48] and also against those who clearly did not accept the same democratic values that were part of European heritage.

44 Ibid., Partly dissenting opinion of Judge Eicke, para. 16.

45 *Ecodefefence and 60 others v. Russia*, Applications nos. 9988/13 and 60 others, Judgment of 14 June 2022.

46 *Oganezova v. Armenia*, Application no. 72961/12, Judgment of 17 May 2022, para. 120.

47 See *Erbankan v. Turkey* where the Court stated:

> [T]olerance and respect for the equal dignity of all human beings constitute the foundations of a democratic, pluralistic society. That being so, as a matter of principle it may be considered necessary in certain democratic societies to sanction or even prevent all forms of expression which spread, incite, promote or justify hatred based on intolerance …, provided that any 'formalities', 'conditions', 'restrictions' or 'penalties' imposed are proportionate to the legitimate aim pursued (*Erbakan v. Turkey*, Application no. 59405/00, Judgment of 6 July 2006, para. 56).

48 E.g., see *Garaudy v. France*, Application no. 65831/01, Decision of 24 June 2003; *M'Bala M'Bala v. France*, Application no. 25239/13, Decision of 20 October 2015; and *Pastörs v. Germany*, Application no. 55225/14, Judgment of 3 October 2019.

One of the interesting questions to be discussed relates to the future role of Article 17. Some scholars have argued that focusing hate speech cases on Article 17 can lead to a chilling effect and consider that it is better to use an argumentation based on Article 10 instead when reviewing hate speech.[49] Cannie and Voorhof consider that the current situation has led to inconsistent argumentation when some cases are considered under Article 17 and some under Article 10.

The Court itself acknowledged that there should be a high threshold in applying Article 17 in the *Perincek v. Switzerland* case, as follows:

> However, Article 17 is, as recently confirmed by the Court, only applicable on an exceptional basis and in extreme cases (see *Paksas v. Lithuania* [GC], no. 34932/04, § 87 *in fine*, 6 January 2011). Its effect is to negate the exercise of the Convention right that the applicant seeks to vindicate in the proceedings before the Court. In cases concerning Article 10 of the Convention, it should only be resorted to if it is immediately clear that the impugned statements sought to deflect this Article from its real purpose by employing the right to freedom of expression for ends clearly contrary to the values of the Convention (see, as recent examples, *Hizb ut-Tahrir and Others v. Germany* (dec.), no. 31098/08, §§ 73–74 and 78, 12 June 2012, and *Kasymakhunov and Saybatalov v. Russia*, nos. 26261/05 and 26377/06, §§ 106–13, 14 March 2013).[50]

This high threshold has been applied to new media cases such as *Lilliendal v. Iceland*, where the comments of the applicants were considered under Article 10 of the Convention, and the Court saw no reason to substitute the views of a national court. The Court's approach after *Perincek* seems to focus primarily on the review under Article 10 of the Convention rather than giving too much weight to the abuse clause consideration. However, the abuse clause can be seen as an interpretative aid for the balancing test in Article 10 of the Convention.

The abuse of rights discourse in Article 17 is founded on the idea that the state does not act in bad faith, and state authorities would not abuse their powers for their own ulterior purposes. And for those authorities that operate in bad faith, there is Article 18 (Limitation on the use of restrictions on rights). The new era, which requires the application of Article 18, refers inherently to the use of different kinds of sanctions by a state (or a dominant party) to cause fear among those in opposition, for example, by using various public interest reasonings as an excuse for controlling and restricting the activities of opposition parties. These bad faith acts suppress political pluralism; for example, sanctioning political opponents by referring to public safety, which is a worrying trend, as states are ready to use courts and authorities for ulterior purposes, especially those that suit those in power and against their political adversaries.

[49] See H. Cannie and D. Voorhof, 'The abuse clause and the freedom of expression in the European Convention on Human Rights – an added value for democracy and human rights protection' (2011) 29 *Netherlands Quarterly of Human Rights* 1, 54–83.

[50] *Perincek v. Switzerland*, Application no. 27510/08, Judgment of 15 October 2015, para. 114.

In terms of its application, there is a high threshold to apply Article 18, since the Court has also acknowledged that the restrictions, coming from governments, can also serve to pursue a plurality of purposes simultaneously.[51]

Using restrictions for political purposes against opposition has been a relevant issue in many European countries in recent years. In the *Navalnyy v. Russia* case (GC), the Court applied Article 18, saying that there was an ulterior purpose for the restrictions, 'namely to suppress that political pluralism, which forms part of "effective political democracy" governed by "the rule of law", both being concepts to which the Preamble to the Convention refers'.[52] The Court continues by saying, '[A]s the Court has pointed out, notably in the context of Articles 10 and 11, pluralism, tolerance and broadmindedness are hallmarks of a democratic society'.[53]

10.4.2 *Changing Responsibilities and Obligations in the Field of Freedom of Expression*

One of the most interesting questions concerning defending democracy relates to the distribution of responsibility. To what extent can we transport the key rules of liability from traditional media to internet-based media, and what factors distinguish media platforms with editorial procedures compared with social media platforms? This leads to questions on the responsibilities of individuals and of those providing the platforms for unlawful expression. From the outset, the responsibilities differ from traditional media, in which clear rules place the onus on the publisher, who is ultimately responsible for every publication.

In internet-based media in the instance of speech that could cause instability and threaten the democratic system, no similar editorial structures exist to pre-emptively prevent any such speech from being published. The question is more about the obligation to remove material that would be unlawful and incite hatred and violence afterwards. Emphasis is also placed on social media rules, such as the Facebook community standards, which are monitored.[54] Facebook community standards emphasise social media as an environment not based on intimidation and exclusion. Facebook's hate speech policy is founded on anti-discrimination. The prohibited hate speech includes attacks against people on the basis of their 'protected characteristics' – race, sexual orientation, sex, gender identity, disability, or serious disease – but it also includes people's immigration status. The attacks can be violent

[51] *Merabishvili v. Georgia*, Application no. 72508/13, Judgment of 28 November 2017, para. 292. 'The question in such situations is whether the prescribed purpose invariably expunges the ulterior one, whether the mere presence of an ulterior purpose contravenes Article 18, or whether there is some intermediary answer.'

[52] *Navalnyy v. Russia*, Application nos. 29580/12 and 4 others, Judgment of 15 November 2018, para. 175.

[53] Ibid.

[54] Meta, 'Facebook community standards on hate speech', https://transparency.fb.com/policies/community-standards/hate-speech/.

speech, dehumanising speech, or mocking of concepts, events, or victims of hate crimes. Some exceptions are made when the content is satirical.

A number of detailed examples provided by the Facebook community standards are quite astounding. It is also interesting to note that the recent decision by Facebook's Oversight Board (hereinafter, 'Board' or 'Oversight Board') refers to a strong contextual approach. The Board has taken decisions where it has already dealt with several questions of contextual interpretation. The Board recently overturned a decision to remove a post (2022-008-FB-UA) comparing the Russian army in Ukraine to Nazis and quoting a poem that calls for the killing of fascists. The basis of the Board's review was the six-part threshold test mentioned in the Rabat Plan of Action.[55] The test includes (a) context, (b) speaker, (c) intent, (d) content and form, (e) extent of speech act, and (f) likelihood, including imminence.

The ECtHR doctrine on Facebook and social media responsibilities is under development. The Grand Chamber reviewed Facebook-related issues in the case of *Sanchez v. France* (15.5.2023). The case was referred to the Grand Chamber after the judgement of that Chamber found no violation of Article 10 of the Convention. The Grand Chamber came to the same conclusion that there was no violation of Article 10 of the Convention, but elaborated the reasoning and developed the necessity test. The Grand Chamber's argumentation is based on an assessment *in concreto* of the specific circumstances of the case.

The Grand Chamber presented an argumentation based on an assessment *in concreto* of the specific circumstances of the case and the margin of appreciation. The applicant was convicted because he did not delete unlawful comments (incitement to violence against Muslims) on the 'wall' of his Facebook account. The Grand Chamber found that the decisions of the domestic courts were based on relevant and sufficient reasoning.[56] The *Sanchez* case is interesting because it analysed the standards applied by national authorities and whether they were in conformity with the principles embodied in Article 10. The proportionality of the impugned penalty followed the test set out in the Chamber judgement: (a) the context of the comments, (b) the steps taken by the applicant to remove the comments once posted, (c) the possibility of holding the authors liable instead of the applicant, and lastly, (d) the consequences of the domestic proceedings for the applicant.[57] The elaborate argumentation relates to the context and developments in the function of the internet. The Grand Chamber considered that because the internet has become one of the principal means for individuals to express their opinion, any interference should be examined particularly carefully in order to avoid a chilling effect, carrying a risk

55 OHCHR, 'The Rabat Plan of Action on the prohibition of advocacy of national, racial or religious hatred that constitutes incitement to discrimination, hostility or violence', 5 October 2012, UN Doc. A/HRC/22/17/Add.4, www.ohchr.org/sites/default/files/Documents/Issues/Opinion/SeminarRabat/Rabat_draft_outcome.pdf.

56 *Sanchez v. France* [GC], Application no. 45581/15, Judgment of 15 May 2023, para. 209.

57 Ibid., paras. 167–8.

of self-censorship. At the same time, there are other dangers related to the dissemination of hate speech. The Court applies the concepts of defamatory speech and other types of clearly unlawful speech, including hate speech and speech inciting violence.[58]

In the electoral context, there is broad freedom of expression, but 'in the case of a racist or xenophobic discourse, such a context contributes to stirring up hatred and intolerance, as the positions of the candidates will inevitably harden and slogans or catchphrases become more prominent than reasoned arguments'. The entire argumentation relates to the concern that reasonable argumentation has suffered and 'the impact of racist and xenophobic discourse is then likely to become greater and more harmful'.[59] The argumentation is based on the premise that the role of politicians is to avoid comments that foster intolerance. They should be careful to defend democracy and its principles, their ultimate aim being to govern.[60] The context of an election makes racist and xenophobic discourse more harmful.[61] The Court developed its review under the premise of the shared liability of all actors involved. Therefore, it is not only the responsibility of the producer. Nevertheless, to exempt producers from all liability might facilitate or encourage abuse and misuse, including hate speech and calls to violence, but also manipulation, lies, and disinformation.[62]

There are also other contributions to the discussion of context. The UN Special Rapporteur Frank La Rue focused his report on this question and highlighted the perspective that context should be taken into account while analysing hate speech.[63] His basic argumentation was that 'what is deeply offensive in one community may not be so in another'. La Rue pointed out that the various factors worthy of consideration could relate to tensions between different racial and religious communities, discrimination against the targeted group, the tone and content of the speech, the person inciting hatred, and the means of disseminating the expression of hate. La Rue also considered the difference of weight for publications to small and restricted groups versus publications on a mainstream website.

The applicant's own behaviour is also relevant in assessing the proportionality of sanctions. The Court suggested in particular that a politician experienced in communication must be aware of the greater risk of excessive and immoderate remarks that might appear and necessarily become visible to a wider audience. The Court refers to the deliberate choice of the applicant in making his 'wall' public and also to his being a professional in matters of online communication strategy.[64] The Court's

58 Ibid., paras. 162 and 184.
59 Ibid., paras. 153 and 176.
60 Ibid., para. 150.
61 Ibid., para. 176.
62 Ibid., para. 185.
63 F. La Rue, 'Report of the Special Rapporteur on the Promotion and Protection of the Right to Freedom of Opinion and Expression', 2011, A/HRC/17/27/Add.1.
64 Ibid., para. 193.

scrutiny is closely related to facts and whether the applicant was reasonably expected to review the content of the comments and if necessary delete them. In the case of the applicant, excessive traffic that might prevent the applicant from effectively monitoring the situation did not exist.[65]

This is one of the most controversial parts of the Chamber's interpretation. To what extent is a person responsible for something published on their Facebook 'wall', which cannot be compared to professional websites or a journalistic website? If the liability is extended to the owner of the Facebook 'wall', what kind of monitoring is adequate, and would this kind of sanction lead to self-censorship?

The problem is also related to the question of demonstrating the intent of incitement to hatred. For example, the European Commission against Racism and Intolerance (ECRI) has reminded us that it is often difficult to establish intent because the speech might not articulate intent clearly. The speech might be unambiguous, and the intent to incite racial hatred might be inferred from the strength of the language of the speech or other relevant circumstances. The ECRI mentions in connection with this the former behaviour of the speaker.[66]

One of the ongoing topics is how community standards impact countries with weak national human rights protection. The Oversight Board has been particularly concerned about 'Facebook removing content on matters in the public interest in countries where national legal and institutional protections for human rights, in particular freedom of expression, are weak'.[67] This is reiterated especially in the Russian and Turkish context and the problems with freedom of expression in these countries. In the Pro-Navalnyy protest case (2021-004-FB-UA), the Board considered that Facebook should have considered the situation in Russia.[68] The Board stated: 'Facebook should have considered the environment for freedom of expression in Russia generally, and specifically government campaigns of disinformation against opponents and their supporters.'[69] The Board explains its approach in the Pro-Navalnyy protest case, balancing values used in the community standard: 'The decision to remove this content failed to balance Facebook's values of "Dignity" and "Safety" against "Voice". Political speech is central to the value of "Voice" and should only be limited where there are clear "Safety" or "Dignity" concerns.'[70] The Board especially considered 'Voice' as especially important in a country such as Russia, where freedom of expression is routinely suppressed.

65 Ibid., para. 200.

66 ECRI, 'General Policy Recommendation No. 15 on comparing hate speech', adopted on 8 December 2015, https://rm.coe.int/ecri-general-policy-recommendation-no-15-on-combating-hate-speech/16808b5b01, 18.

67 The Oversight Board, 'Öcalan's isolation', www.oversightboard.com/decision/ig-i9dp23ib/.

68 The Oversight Board, 'Pro-Navalny protests in Russia', www.oversightboard.com/decision/FB-6YHRXHZR.

69 Ibid., para. 8.3. III.

70 Ibid., Key findings.

The Oversight Board also overturned a Turkish case where the applicant's Instagram post was originally removed.[71] The post was encouraging people to discuss the solitary confinement of Abdullah Öcalan, a founding member of the Kurdistan Workers' Party (PKK). The user did not advocate violence in their post and did not express support for Öcalan's ideology or the PKK. Instead, he or she sought to highlight human rights concerns about Öcalan's prolonged solitary confinement, which had also been raised by international bodies. As the post was unlikely to result in harm, its removal was not necessary or proportionate under international human rights standards.[72]

One of the interesting continuums that also sheds light on the limits of argumentation over protecting democratic states relates to case law under Article 11 and cases where political parties have been faced with a dissolution. The objective of these dissolutions has often been related to a threat to democracy that these parties cause with their political activities. One recent key case was *DTP v. Turkey*, where the Turkish court approved the dissolution of the Party for a Democratic Society (DTP), supporting a peaceful resolution to the Kurdish problem.[73] In this case, the Court did not accept the government's argumentation that the political party's goals were themselves against democracy. The DTP fully supported a peaceful solution to the Kurdish question and recognised Kurdish identity in Turkey. The Court assessed whether the DTP project was against the democratic system. The political system must, if functioning properly, allow parties to introduce views that are contrary to the prevailing guidelines.[74] According to the Court, the DTP political project did not seek to undermine the democratic system, but emphasised the fact that it refused to use violence.[75]

10.4.3 *The Role of Public Watchdogs and the Promotion of a Free, Independent, and Diverse Media Environment in the Court's Case Law*

Noting that freedom of expression is acknowledged as one of the foundations of a democratic society, this naturally means that the interpretation of freedom of expression should also reflect the changing nature and characteristics of the prevailing democratic society. In this respect, it is imperative to note that, looking at past decades, freedom of expression has been understood mostly from the perspective of traditional media, that is, print and audiovisual media, which is different from the more diverse current media environment.

71 The Oversight Board, 'Öcalan's isolation', www.oversightboard.com/decision/ig-i9dp23ib/.

72 Ibid.

73 See *Party for a Democratic Society (DTP) and Others v. Turkey*, Application nos 3870/10, 3870/10, 3878/10, 15616/10, 21919/10, 39118/10 and 37272/10, Judgment of 12 January 2016.

74 Ibid., para. 78.

75 Ibid., para. 81.

Democracy has always been closely related to public debate and the maintenance of transparency within the system, but the views of those engaging in public debate in the past have not been as diverse as they could have been. As such, we can say that the traditional understanding of those whose speech should be protected is also in transition. As a consequence, how to balance the pluralism and diverse views expressed in the media and at the same time uphold the independence of the media have become essential questions to consider.

In a democratic system, the media has an important role as a public watchdog. It has a right to impart news and ideas and disseminate information on difficult and controversial issues. In order to have public debate on important social issues, the Convention allows reporting on issues that might include expressions not protected by the Convention. In the balancing process between freedom of expression and restrictions based on protecting democracy and the rights of others, context is a key factor and has an obvious impact on the limits of free speech.

The role of the media as a public watchdog has often been mentioned in the Court's case law since the *Barthold* case,[76] and has applied pressure to both print and broadcast news. It has been used in the context of public debate and in arguing how important it is in a democratic society not to hamper public debate with disproportionate sanctions. In the famous *Jersild* case, the role of news reporting and interviews was emphasised as one of the most important means whereby the press is able to play a vital role as public watchdog.[77] Later, the protection of sources was considered to be vital to the role of the press as a public watchdog, and in *Goodwin v. the UK* the Court also acknowledged the chilling effect that the disclosure of sources would cause.[78]

These cases in the 1980s and 1990s reflect the traditional media environment and the media's role in the democratic system. However, the watchdog concept has evolved in recent years to include a larger group of actors, which is better suited to the new media environment. In a number of cases, the Court has discussed the different kinds of roles public watchdogs could perform in a democratic society, especially the impact of restrictions on public debate in the case of censorship in the name of personality rights.[79] In particular, the case of *Magyar Helsinki Bizottság v. Hungary* (2016) specified what kinds of actors would qualify as public watchdogs in the context of freedom of expression. The Court based its interpretation on the key task in a democratic society, which is to facilitate and foster the public's right to receive and impart information and ideas.[80]

[76] *Barthold v. Germany*, Application no. 8734/79, Judgment of 25 March 1985, para. 58.

[77] See *Jersild v. Denmark*, Application no. 15890/89, Judgment of 23 September 1994, para. 35.

[78] See *Goodwin v. the United Kingdom*, Application no. 17488/90, Judgment of 27 March 1996, para. 39.

[79] See *Társaság a Szabadságjogokért v. Hungary*, Application no. 37374/05, Judgment of 14 April 2009, para. 37.

[80] *Magyar Helsinki Bizottság v. Hungary*, Application no. 18030/11, Judgment of 8 November 2016, para. 165.

The Court mentioned in the *Magyar Helsinki* case the creation of platforms for public debate. The Court used an analogy between the press and NGOs, drawing attention to matters of public interest. The Court used the characterisation of the social watchdog as warranting similar protection. In this line of consideration, the role of civil society was recognised as making an 'important contribution to discussion of public affairs'.[81] The Court also recognised the roles of scholars. According to the Court, a high level of protection also extends to academic researchers and authors of literature on matters of public concern.[82]

More recently, the Court has extended its approach to the media environment. The key concepts in the *NIT SRL v. Moldova* case are media pluralism and independent media. The *NIT SRL* case introduces key concepts relevant in creating a media environment that in itself provides the pre-emptive self-defence of democracy. In *NIT SRL*, the Court considered the key principles of pluralism in the media, stating that it is ultimately part of the positive obligation to guarantee that diverse political programmes are proposed and debated. The Court mentioned that these also mean programmes that question the current system, provided that they do not harm democracy. It is not only sufficient to provide a plurality of channels, but it is also necessary to provide effective access to such channels and guarantee the diversity of programmes reflecting, as far as possible, the variety of opinions in society.[83] The Court considers it dangerous that some corporations have a dominant position and can exercise pressure on broadcasters and eventually curtail their editorial freedom, undermining freedom of expression.[84] It is important to note that external and internal pluralism should not be considered in isolation, as external pluralism normally refers to multiple channels, and internal pluralism allows the content of the channel to be diverse.

The Court referred to the multifaceted character and sheer complexity of issues concerning media pluralism. There are a variety of means to be deployed by the state to regulate effective pluralism. Therefore, there is a wide margin of appreciation for authorities regarding the choice of means to ensure media pluralism.[85]

This wider discretion relates to the choice of means, but the Court also referred to a long tradition of case law, acknowledging that the margin is narrow when it comes to editorial freedom of the press and choosing what appropriate journalistic methods to use. The *NIT SRL* case gives a detailed analysis of Moldova's regulatory system and background, going into how the regulatory framework was operated and which kind of oversight was provided. It was noticed that legislation existed behind the regulatory framework that was drafted in order to provide proportionality. The legislation was made with careful consideration and genuine effort to strike a fair

81 Ibid., para. 166.

82 Ibid.

83 See *NIT S.R.L v. Moldova*, Application no. 28470/12, Judgment of 5 April 2022, para. 185.

84 Ibid., para. 186.

85 Ibid., para. 193.

balance between competing interests. That this fair balance was achieved at parliamentary level is paramount. According to the Court, the regulative framework was also supervised, and the state operated well within its margin of appreciation.

In addition to journalistic sources (*Goodwin v. the UK*) becoming more important than ever, it is also a question of protecting whistleblowers under the scope of Article 10 and defending democracy. There is a strong continuum that has emphasised the importance of imparting information and reporting on illegal conduct and wrongdoings.[86] The same has also been confirmed by the UN Special Rapporteur, who referred to an expanded view on the concept of journalism expressed by the Human Rights Committee, that the practice of journalism is carried out by 'professional full-time reporters and analysts, as well as bloggers and others who engage in forms of self-publication in print, on the Internet or elsewhere (Human Rights Committee, general comment No. 34, para. 44)'.[87]

Spreading an increasing amount of disinformation leads to disturbing impacts on trust and confidence in a democratic system. Distributing disinformation seeks to control media and public opinion. There are often ulterior motives behind disinformation.[88] These reasons are often part of political tactics, and their purpose can be misleading in the discussion. It is also often part of a state's hybrid tactics to destabilise other states during elections and other democratic processes by using disinformation and other forms of influence.

While previous case law has approached defending democracy from the perspective of traditional forms of activities related to election rights, new restrictions under the Court's scrutiny often reveal a widespread aim of preventing opposition forces from participating in public debate rather than using old-fashioned media channels. Recent cases also reflect that the Court has become active in requiring positive obligations to protect those who are victims of hate speech, especially towards minorities. When you cannot control the media as previously, the measures seem severe, and the rights protected under the Convention are questioned comprehensively.

The role of media companies has become instrumental, especially in recognition of media pluralism in a healthy democracy. In addition to national media outlets, social media giants can influence the distribution of disinformation. What is the responsibility of those giving a platform to hate speech and disinformation? What is

[86] *Guja v. Moldova*, Application no. 14277/04, Judgment of 12 February 2008.

[87] D. Kaye, 'Promotion and protection of the right to the freedom of opinion and expression', 8 September, 2015, UN Doc. A/70/361, 8-9. See also HRC, 'General Comment No. 34, Article 19: Freedoms of opinion and expression', 12 September 2011, UN Doc. CCPR/C/GC/34.

[88] Ulterior motives are often mentioned in the case-law. Especially this is connected to attacking against opposition parties and their leadership. It is related to the discussion of the misuse of power, see, e.g., *Merabishvili v. Georgia* [GC], Application no. 72508/13, Judgment of 28 November 2017, with reference to comparative material, 'There is misuse of power when an authority uses its power for a purpose other than the one for which it was conferred.' The Court also refers to situations where there are real and ulterior purposes at the same time, and the review concerns whether an ulterior purpose was predominant or not.

the role of Article 17 that so far has been related to a rather small number of extremist opinions? Could it be used by those who are distributing disinformation? What is the role of extraterritorial jurisdiction doctrine in new media? These are some of the essential questions to be answered in order to deal with those abusing their freedom of expression for hate speech and disinformation.

10.5 CONCLUDING OBSERVATIONS

So far, the development of the defending democracy doctrine has been considered to involve only very narrow extreme political movements pursuing totalitarian ideologies. The relevance of the historico-political context, and especially the history of events in Europe, have made it necessary for the Court to establish a doctrine based on the 'self-defence' of democracy. The Court has repeatedly reminded us of the scars related to Nazism and Communism. It has also reminded us about specific threats related to religious extremism. The historico-political context in different countries, especially the stability of the democratic system, constitutes one of the relevant issues to be assessed in the process of achieving a fair balance. On the one hand, this has allowed different standards in countries that have close historical connections to human rights atrocities in the past; for example, those who are denying historical events such as the Holocaust are considered under Article 17, thus examining their conduct as an abuse of rights. On the other hand, historical context is relevant in states with a short democratic history and, in some cases, forces with support for old authoritarian regimes.

But the contextual discussion is also currently bringing another side of contextualism. The proportionality test should also take into account the prevailing level of protection of the freedom of expression in the country. This is apparent in the recent cases before Facebook's Oversight Board, considering that weak protection should also have an impact on applying community standards and considering whether removing posts is proportionate. Obviously, the Board has acknowledged that in countries such as Russia and Turkey, there should be a higher threshold for removing Facebook posts.

The European Court's doctrines on the breadth of the margin of appreciation can provide a clear sign that regulating a complex and multifaceted issue requires a wider margin. Still, when authorities enter into the questions at the core of journalistic activities, such as the choice of journalistic methods, the margin is obviously narrow.

Democracy should be founded on pluralistic media, which, as one of the public watchdogs, ensures critical public debate on issues of public interest. When the authorities start making decisions on what is an acceptable issue to be discussed and what is not, this will ultimately lead to restrictions that jeopardise the core of freedom of expression. The Court states that it is not for the authorities or the Court 'to review the press's own appreciation of the news or information value of an item or to substitute their views for those of the press on what methods of objective and balanced reporting should be adopted by journalists'.[89]

When regulating audiovisual media, it has been necessary to take into account practical issues related to limited frequencies. Case law has continued to adopt, little by little, new elements related to a contemporary democratic system, in which democracy is something beyond elections and more about a comprehensive democratic system. On a global level, we are already seeing increasing repressions of freedom of expression and media integrity under the guise of fighting disinformation and protecting infrastructure against cyber-attacks.[90] This kind of trend can also be detrimental to European countries.

Threats in the new media environment are, to a certain extent, similar to traditional print or audiovisual media. The Court founded its case law on the idea of the chilling effect that different sanctions can have on the media. It was important that the media and journalists were able to impart information to the public without censorship. The media's access to information was key to performing as a public watchdog over those in power. With the democratic system becoming more complex, including multiple other actors in addition to the media, who are directly imparting information, it is necessary to talk of public watchdogs in the plural, including those who challenge the government and corporations, whether they be individual activists or networks of activists.

However, an even more significant development in the case law is related to understanding that the defence of democracy is related to understanding how modern democracy works and especially how one of the foundations of democratic society, freedom of expression, has transformed in the new media environment. There is ultimately a fear that restrictions become rules and protection comes as an exception. The Oversight Board has revealed many fundamental failings in respect to social media giants such as Facebook and Instagram removing posts, leading to a quest for transparency and specified rules on removing posts because the policy currently applied is in danger of silencing social debate.

Freedom of expression has changed substantially in the sense that governments are acting in bad faith against opposition parties. From Article 17 and extreme groups, it is now Article 18 that is not just an infrequent curiosity of the Convention but trending in cases such as *Navalnyy*. At the same time, more restrictions towards NGOs are being discussed, as in the case of *Ecodefence and 60 others v. Russia*. The linking issue in these cases is that the aim is to have a chilling effect and control the social debate.

[89] *Jersild v. Denmark*, Application no. 15890/89, Judgment of 23 September 1994, para. 31.

[90] See International IDEA, 'Global state of democracy report 2022: forging social contracts in a time of discontent' (2022), www.idea.int/democracytracker/sites/default/files/2022-11/the-global-state-of-democracy-2022.pdf, 21. The IDEA report mentions, e.g., Bangladesh's Digital Security Act, Vietnam's Cybersecurity Law, Kyrgyzstan's False Information Bill, and Singapore's Protection from Online Falsehoods and Manipulation Act.

There is a lack of clear interpretative guidance, especially concerning social media posts and applying traditional freedom of expression doctrines to them. It is not simply a case of proceeding with the *Jersild* doctrine, when at that time the situation was much clearer as to 'informing the public about a social issue'. In the new media environment, there is a strong need to develop criteria for freedom of expression and how best to apply these in different contexts. The Court has already decided several cases since *Delfi v. Estonia*. Despite the idea of source neutrality, a different context must be taken into account when modifying doctrines to be relevant to cases where the role of digital media has become central.

11

Disinfodemic Threats. Real, False, and Fake News

A Contribution to Fight Disinformation without Affecting the Freedom of Expression

Oscar R. Puccinelli

11.1 INTRODUCTION

The dissemination of false, incomplete, erroneous, distorted, or intrusive information is a phenomenon as old as humanity, but since the development of information and communication technologies (ICTs), it has re-emerged with a vigour never seen before. The causes and effects have varied considerably to the point of becoming a very dangerous threat not only to human rights but also to the stability of the democratic system.

As the United Nations (UN) Special Rapporteur on the promotion and protection of the right to freedom of opinion and expression, Irene Khan, explains:

> More than 2,000 years ago, Octavian spun a vicious disinformation campaign to destroy his rival Mark Anthony and eventually become the first Roman emperor Augustus Caesar. Since those ancient times, information has been fabricated and manipulated to win wars, advance political ambitions, avenge grievances, hurt the vulnerable and make financial profit.
>
> What is new is that digital technology has enabled pathways for false or manipulated information to be created, disseminated and amplified by various actors for political, ideological or commercial motives at a scale, speed and reach never known before. Interacting with political, social and economic grievances in the real world, disinformation online can have serious consequences for democracy and human rights.[1]

Among the many examples of the use of false information with the purpose of manipulating the population (or certain sectors of it), the alleged impact *fake news* (selectively or widely disseminated through social media) could have on recent elections is usually cited. More concretely, the 2016 referendum in the UK on whether

[1] Report of the Special Rapporteur on the promotion and protection of the right to freedom of opinion and expression, Irene Khan, 'Disinformation and freedom of opinion and expression', UN doc. A/HRC/47/25, 13 April 2021, 2.

or not it should continue to be part of the European Union (EU), so-called Brexit, the presidential election in the same year held in the US where Donald Trump was elected, the resulting Facebook/Cambridge Analytica scandal, and the Italian elections in 2018. Even though there is no consensus that the impact of fake news on these processes has been significant, the tight results obtained suggested that it was decisive.[2]

The use of fake news for political and electoral purposes was not the only preoccupying reality. Soon other uses appeared and turned the phenomenon of disinformation into a much more worrying matter, as can be recognised in the context of the COVID-19 pandemic, during which a large amount of false information circulated – even without the objective of manipulating the population – with mournful results.

In this regard, Khan held:

> In recent years, in a number of countries, State-led disinformation campaigns have sought to influence elections and other political processes, control the narrative of public debates or curb protests against and criticisms of Governments. In the context of the COVID-19 pandemic, there have been various instances of State actors disseminating unverified claims about the origins of the virus responsible for COVID-19, denying the spread of the disease or providing false information on infection rates, fatality figures and health-care advice. Such disinformation has been detrimental to efforts to control the pandemic, endangering the rights to health and life, as well as people's trust in public information and State institutions.[3]

These misconducts by high-ranking public officials, deputies, and even presidents were also verified in many cases in Latin America.[4] This worrying reality has been favoured particularly by the appearance, within the framework of Web 2.0, of

[2] On Trump's election, see Y. Benkler, R. Faris, and H. Roberts, *Network Propaganda: Manipulation, Disinformation, and Radicalization in American Politics* (Oxford: Oxford University Press, 2018), and about the Italian elections and their impact on the populist vote in Trentino and Tirol del Sur during the 2018 general elections, see M. Cantarella, N. Fraccaroli, and R. Volpe, 'Does fake news affect voting behavior?', Dipartimento di Economia Marco Biagi, Università Degli Studi di Modena e Reggio Emilia, Working Paper Series No. 146, June 2019, http://155.185.68.2/wpdemb/0146.pdf.

[3] Report of the Special Rapporteur on the promotion and protection of the right to freedom of opinion and expression, Irene Khan, 'Disinformation and freedom of opinion and expression', UN doc. A/HRC/47/25, 13 April 2021.

[4] Among various examples, two Argentine national deputies recommended the use of chlorine dioxide to combat the virus despite the contra-indications published by the World Health Organization; a Ministry of Brazil published a video stating that the use of masks was not effective to combat the virus and even that it was harmful to health, and the former President Jair Bolsonaro maintained that hydroxychloroquine, azithromycin, ivermectin, anitta, zinc, and Vitamin D were successful in treating COVID-19, this despite the lack of scientific evidence in this regard and disregarding the existence of side effects. The president of Guatemala, Alejandro Giammattei, did the same; he assured at an international event that ivermectin is a substitute for the vaccine against COVID-19. In the same sense, in Chile, the Mayor of Santiago falsely argued that there is no scientific evidence to show that public transport is a source of COVID-19 contagion (Center for Studies on Freedom of Expression and Access to Information, 'Are public officials' lies unsustainable or do they have far reaching effects? A study on the obligations of the government and its officials to prevent the proliferation of disinformation', August 2021, www.palermo.edu/Archivos_content/2021/cele/papers/Disinformation-and-public-officials.pdf).

social media (websites and computer programs that allow people to communicate and share information on the internet using a computer or a mobile phone), where the use of social networks and of *deepfakes* emerged as the preferred and most effective way of communicating fake news to people likely to believe them.[5] But the phenomenon of fake news is not only due to the technological factor but to other epistemological, economic, affective, and political factors.

As Melo points out when considering those factors:

> rumors and falsehoods spread in two different ways: social cascades and group polarization [...]. A cascade is born when a group of influential people say or do something and others follow in their footsteps. Group polarization occurs when people with intellectual affinities come together, and thus end up defending a more extremist version than the one they held before they began to communicate with each other [...].
>
> Cascades are generated because all people tend to depend on others: if most of the people we know believe a rumor, we are also inclined to believe it. In the absence of our own information, we accept the opinions of others [...]. In the economy, rumors can give rise to speculative bubbles... in public health they can generate anti-vaccination movements [...]. Rumors and falsehoods are often responsible for sowing panic [...]. [F]ear spreads quickly from one person to another, and if rumors provoke strong emotions, such as fear or indignation, it is much easier for them to spread.
>
> How to manage the risk that cascades and polarisations lead to people believing false rumours? The most intuitive answer is related to freedom of expression: people should be offered objective information and the necessary corrections from those who know the truth, but this does not always work [...]. Many people trust the market of ideas as a way to guarantee the truth.[6]

In this context, owing to the importance of public and private interests at stake, neither states and the international community nor the mass media and other social media actors (websites and applications that enable users to create and share content or to participate in social networking) have remained static, and have gradually come to face the need to set limits on freedom of expression in order to prevent or even to reduce the pernicious effects or spread of false information. As Warren and Brandeis pointed out, when new inventions converged at the end of the nineteenth century (the telegraph, the telephone, photography, and the rotary press) and competition between newspapers became more acute (causing the appearance of 'yellow journalism' or 'infotainment', as it is called today):

> That individual shall have full protection in person and in property is a principle as old as the common law; but it has been found necessary from time to time to

[5] According to the Collins dictionary, a deepfake is 'a way of adding a digital image or video over another image or video, so that it appears to be part of the original [...] an image or video that has been changed in this way' – Collins, 'Definition of 'deepfake', www.collinsdictionary.com/dictionary/english/deepfake#:~:text=uncountable%20noun,a%20real%20threat%20to%20democracy.

[6] V. E. Melo, *Fake News* (Buenos Aires: La Ley, 2022), pp. 6–8.

> define anew the exact nature and extent of such protection. Political, social, and economic changes entail the recognition of new rights, and the common Law, in its eternal youth, grows to meet the demands of society.[7]

In the most relevant declarations and constitutions of the late nineteenth century, freedom of expression has been recognised as a preferred freedom, and as a consequence of this, even false or erroneous speech has been protected. However, following the ideas of Warren and Brandeis,[8] this freedom to inform – originally conceived almost absolutely – began to be subject to restrictions. Mechanisms such as the right of reply or the right to be forgotten in its pre-internet version (conceived not as a right to de-index content but as a right to be compensated for the consequences of publishing old information without current relevance that unjustifiably harms a person) are two clear examples. More recently, the new factual configurations claim new responses from governments, the international community, and the private sector, especially from information society services, who have a special responsibility when providing them. This need was seen much more clearly in the last decade, when false information was disseminated as knowingly false to alter electoral processes or influence in the context of the war between Russia and Ukraine and even in the COVID-19 pandemic scenario. As was clearly stated:

> COVID-19 became the perfect storm for platforms. The increasing pressure they had been facing to remove problematic content became a public health issue. Disinformation surrounding the pandemic spread like the virus – at the hands of political leaders and influencers – community social media guidelines were insufficient and inconsistent, and those responsible for enforcing them had to confine themselves to their homes. Amid the confusion, platforms quickly began announcing new rules and measures to deal with misinformation. Regarding community rules, the actions reported during the pandemic have focused more on the rules on the content of the publications, than on rules about inauthentic activities.[9]

The main problem in adopting those concrete and multiple measures in the more recent and complex context to combat disinformation in general and fake news in particular, is how to evaluate the veracity of information and which kinds of measures, adopted both from public and private sectors, could be compatible with democracy and human rights.

The purpose of this chapter is precisely to analyse in general terms the phenomenon of disinformation in the new technological context (which added to its already wide field of action of traditional media the vaster field of the internet and social

7 S. Warren and L. Brandeis, 'The right to privacy' (1890), 4 *Harvard Law Review* 5, 193–220, at 193.

8 Ibid.

9 C. Cortés and L. F. Isaza, 'The new normal? Disinformation and content control on social media during COVID-19', CELE, Palermo University, April 2021, www.palermo.edu/Archivos_content/2021/cele/papers/Disinformation-and-Content-Control.pdf, 11.

networks), and more particularly of fake news, which has become even more popular in recent years as a weapon to achieve political or economic gains, leading to the 'disinfodemic' and to interesting and relevant conflicts between freedom of expression and various individual and collective rights (e.g., access to information, privacy, data protection).

There are, of course, other serious issues that have been generated and will continue to be generated by the new information technologies that are closely linked to the problem of false news, which we will not discuss here for reasons of space, but which must at least be mentioned: dangerous speech (including hate speech, which can be combated by the same tools that we will describe here); the effects on the rights of a specific person caused by the permanence on the internet of negative information that is true and that, although it was lawfully published at the time, has lost relevance owing to the passage of time (which finds a partial remedy in the right to be forgotten), and the appearance of cancel or call out culture, which condemns those who are deemed to have acted or spoken in an unacceptable manner aimed to ostracise, boycott, or shun (situations for which the right to be forgotten is clearly insufficient and requires other forms of mitigation).[10]

[10] Cancelling, calling out, calling in, and boycotting are all distinct actions. Calling in is speaking to an individual privately about their perceived harmful or problematic actions or opinions. Calling out is criticising an individual or organisation publicly, usually on social media. This kind of action can be a useful tactic when calling in fails, or when the problematic individual or company is too powerful or distant from someone to be called in (e.g., a celebrity). Calling out is seen by some activists as an effective way to create change and reduce harm while allowing an offending individual to learn, grow, and change. Boycotting is withholding financial support from a company in order to force change within that company's policies or practices. Once demands have been met, support is resumed. Cancelling is a collective attempt to ruin the reputation and livelihood of an individual or organisation in response to a problematic or harmful action or opinion. All these different actions share a commonality: their overarching goal is to reduce perceived harm to an individual or class, thereby creating social change. In other words, these four different terms draw attention to actions or opinions that may be hurting people in order to ultimately phase those behaviours or opinions out of the culture. Cancel culture is taking away support for an individual, their career, popularity, and/or fame because of something they've said or done that's considered unacceptable. To be cancelled is effectively to be boycotted, with the intent that the person will be ostracised and no longer benefit financially, personally, or professionally from their elevated position; in short, culturally blocked from having a prominent public platform or career. The cancel culture affects more public figures than politicians and public officials (ideological positions and partisan alignments play a huge role here) and obviously non-public persons. Most of the time, people are cancelled because he or she is a public figure with influence over a huge audience and what has been done or said is alleged to have caused harm to a particular person, group of people, or community. Some see participating in cancel culture as the most effective way to hold public figures to account, especially if no other lawful way appears to be working. By bringing the grievance public, it forces the accused's employers and others to confront the situation and distance themselves from the perpetrator. In other words, it rebalances the power gap between those with huge audiences and the people or communities who could be negatively affected. However, others believe cancel culture is more of a 'mob mentality' that's gone out of control. (E. Bunch, 'The cancel-culture glossary for cancelling, boycotting, calling out, and calling in', 23 July 2020, www.wellandgood.com/cancel-culture-examples/#:~:text=Canceling%2C%20calling%20out%2C%20calling%20in,demographic%2C%20thereby%20creating%20social%20change).

11.2 REAL AND FALSE NEWS: INFORMATION, DISINFORMATION, MISINFORMATION, MALINFORMATION, PROPAGANDA, FAKE, AND FABRICATED NEWS

According to the Cambridge dictionary, information means 'facts about a situation, person, event, etc.' (UK), 'news, facts or acknowledge' (USA) and in business lexicon 'facts or details about a person, company, product, etc.'.[11]

In the same dictionary, disinformation is 'false information spread in order to deceive people';[12] misinformation is 'wrong information, or the fact that people are misinformed';[13] fake news is 'false stories that appear to be news, spread on the Internet or using other media, usually created to influence political views or as a joke';[14] and propaganda is defined as 'information, ideas, opinions, or images, often only giving one part of an argument, that are broadcast, published, or in some other way spread with the intention of influencing people's opinions'.[15]

Malinformation and real, false, and fabricated news are not defined in the dictionary. Beyond its association with the concept of news, the meaning of 'information' is not exempt from debate because some authors think that 'information encapsulates truth, and hence that false information fails to qualify as information at all', and explain that the distinction between 'information as true, and misinformation and disinformation as false, collapses due to the possibility of true misinformation and true disinformation'.[16]

In short, the defined terms are few and, furthermore, these definitions do not have unanimous agreement in the academic field, so we will address them here in order to draw on such other sources.

11.2.1 *Disinformation, Misinformation, Malinformation*

Within the wide range of modalities that disinformation encompasses, for academic purposes, it is worth distinguishing between the next information disorders:

(a) Disinformation (false information shared intentionally to cause harm, for example, fabricated or deliberately manipulated content; intentionally created conspiracy theories or rumours),

[11] Cambridge dictionary, 'information', https://dictionary.cambridge.org/dictionary/english/information.
[12] Cambridge dictionary, 'disinformation', https://dictionary.cambridge.org/dictionary/english/disinformation.
[13] Cambridge dictionary, 'misinformation', https://dictionary.cambridge.org/dictionary/english/misinformation.
[14] Cambridge dictionary, 'fake news', https://dictionary.cambridge.org/dictionary/english/fake-news.
[15] Cambridge dictionary, 'propaganda', https://dictionary.cambridge.org/dictionary/english/propaganda.
[16] K. Santos-D'Amorim and M. K. Fernandes de Oliveira Miranda, 'Misinformation, disinformation, and malinformation: clarifying the definitions and examples in disinfodemic times' (2021) 26 *Revista eletrônica de biblioteconomia e ciência da informação* e76900, 7, www.redalyc.org/journal/147/14768130011/movil/.

(b) Misinformation (false information shared with no intention of causing harm, caused, for example, by unintentional mistakes such as inaccurate photo captions, dates, statistics, translations, or when satire is taken seriously), and
(c) Malinformation ('genuine information shared with the intention to cause harm'[17]; for example, the publication of private information for personal or corporate interest, such as revenge porn).

About the use of the term 'disinformation', in a recent report, Khan explains:

> There is no universally accepted definition of disinformation. While the lack of agreement makes a global response challenging, the lack of consensus underlines the complex, intrinsically political and contested nature of the concept [...]. Part of the problem lies in the impossibility of drawing clear lines between fact and falsehood and between the absence and presence of intent to cause harm [...].
>
> The European Commission has described disinformation as verifiably false or misleading information that, cumulatively, is created, presented and disseminated for economic gain or to intentionally deceive the public and that may cause public harm [...] The Broadband Commission for Sustainable Development, on the other hand, has approached disinformation as false or misleading content with potential consequences, irrespective of the underlying intention or behaviours producing and circulating messages. National laws and regulations dealing with disinformation cover a varied combination of false or misleading information, the intention to cause harm or not and the nature of the harm caused or intended. Disinformation is often described in broad, ill-defined terms not in line with international legal standards [...].
>
> Academics have developed a taxonomy of an information disorder in which 'disinformation' is described as false information that is knowingly shared with the intention to cause harm, 'misinformation' as the unintentional dissemination of false information and 'malinformation' as genuine information shared with the intention to cause harm [...]. By setting out a holistic and interconnected picture of the problem, the information disorder framework encourages a multidimensional, varied and contextualized approach to disinformation [...].
>
> Some academics have framed the phenomenon of disinformation as 'viral deception' consisting of three vectors: manipulative actors, deceptive behaviour and harmful content. (Camille François, 'Actors, behaviors, content: a disinformation ABC' (Transatlantic Working Group, September 2019). The focus is on online behaviour rather than on the veracity of content. Some large social media platforms, including Facebook, refer to these vectors to inform their policies on responding to coordinated inauthentic behaviour [...].
>
> Ultimately, the lack of clarity and agreement on what constitutes disinformation, including the frequent and interchangeable use of the term misinformation, reduces the effectiveness of responses. (Submission from the United Nations

[17] C. Wardle and H. Derakhshan, *Information Disorder: Toward an Interdisciplinary Framework for Research and Policymaking* (Strasbourg: Council of Europe, 2017), p. 5.

> Educational, Scientific and Cultural Organization. A/HRC/47/25 4) It also leads to approaches that endanger the right to freedom of opinion and expression. It is vital to clarify the concepts of disinformation and misinformation within the framework of international human rights law [...].
>
> For the purposes of the present report, disinformation is understood as false information that is disseminated intentionally to cause serious social harm and misinformation as the dissemination of false information unknowingly. The terms are not used interchangeably [...].[18]

11.2.2 *Real and False News: Fake or Fabricated News*

Even at the risk of oversimplification, false news, by exclusion, can be understood as information about something that has happened recently that is totally or partially not true. Obviously, to fully understand the scope of this definition – that obviously presents an information disorder – we must first determine what is meant by real news.

11.2.2.1 Real News

The definition of 'real news' has its complexity and can vary based on geographical and personal factors; it involves many other difficulties because:

(a) the notion of truth depends on the subjective interpretation of reality,
(b) to decide whether something is 'real' or not, it needs a grounding of truth (e.g., the 'collective consensus'), and
(c) most definitions take into account the editorial decision-making process followed to determine the credibility and accuracy of the information, considering that the journalistic labour is governed by the principles of verification, independence, and the obligation to report the truth (this is so because false news typically imitates real information in its shape, but not in organisational process or intent).

Real news is created through journalism, and includes 'hard news' – serious important news that is considered to be of interest to many people, either in a particular area or country, or in the world;[19] 'breaking news' – information that is received and broadcast about an event that has just happened or just begun;[20] and 'soft news' – news that is a mixture of information and entertainment, often relating to people's private lives.[21]

[18] Report of the Special Rapporteur on the promotion and protection of the right to freedom of opinion and expression, Irene Khan, 'Disinformation and freedom of opinion and expression', UN Doc. A/HRC/47/25, 13 April 2021, 3.

[19] Cambridge dictionary, 'hard news', https://dictionary.cambridge.org/dictionary/english/hard-news.

[20] Cambridge dictionary, 'breaking news', https://dictionary.cambridge.org/dictionary/english/breaking-news.

[21] Cambridge dictionary, 'soft news', https://dictionary.cambridge.org/dictionary/english/soft-news.

In order to distinguish real news from not real, Molina et al. indicate that real news has the following specific differential features:

I. Message and linguistic:
   (a) factuality: fact-checked, impartial reporting, uses last names to cite,
   (b) evidence: statistical data, research-based,
   (c) message quality: journalistic style, edited and proof read,
   (d) lexical and syntactic: frequent use of 'today', past tense,
   (e) topical interest: conflict, human interest, prominence.
II. Sources and intentions:
   (a) Sources of the content: verified sources, quotes and/or attributions, heterogeneity of sources,
   (b) pedigree: originated from a well-known site/organisation, written by actual news staff,
   (c) independence: organisation associated with the journalist.
III. Structural:
   (a) URL: reputable ending, URL has normal registration,
   (b) About Us section: will have a clear About Us section, authors and editors can be verified, contact Us section, e-mails are from the professional organisation.
IV. Network:
   (a) Metadata: Metadata indicators of authenticity.[22]

Complementing this idea, Verma et al. point out that any fake news detection system used to decide whether an article is fake or not should exploit not only the textual features of tweets (e.g., writing style and emotions) but also the characteristics of users (e.g., follower count and verified profile) who propagate fake news, and in this direction, various computational techniques, including long short-term memory, hierarchical attention networks, and natural language process, are utilised to design the fake news detection system with improved accuracy.[23]

11.2.2.2 False Information: False News

Section 11.2.2.1 established that false news should be understood as information that, for different reasons, does not conform to the truth and for that reason constitutes an information disorder that can lead to disinformation, misinformation, or malinformation – even though it is clear that people who create or disseminate the flawed content are not always aware of this and even do not intend to harm.

[22] M. D. Molina, S. S. Sundar, T. Le, and D. Lee. '"Fake news" is not simply false information: a concept explication and taxonomy of online content' (2021) 65 *American Behavioral Scientist* 2, 180–212.

[23] V. Verma et al., 'Fake news detection on Twitter', in S. Tiwari et al. (eds.), *Advances in Data and Information Sciences: Proceedings of ICDIS 2022* (New York: Springer, 2022), pp. 141–9.

According to Verma, Rohilla, Sharma, and Gupta, the false information that, with a greater or lesser degree of fraudulence, circulates on social media, exhibits various modalities and can be classified according to its contents and to the intentionality of the action, as follows:

(a) satire or parody (one that, although it does not seek to cause damage, has misleading potential),
(b) false connections (titles, images, and quotes are not faithful to the content),
(c) misleading content (information is distorted to create a different reality),
(d) false context (genuine information located in a factual or temporal context different from the real one),
(e) imposter content (the identity of genuine sources is impersonated),
(f) manipulated content (information or images manipulated to deceive), and
(g) fabricated content (totally false content, designed to deceive and cause damage).[24]

A recent paper by D'Amorim and Fernandes de Oliveira Miranda includes the next mis-, dis-, mal- information disorders:

(a) Fake news (information that is completely fabricated for the purpose of either making money or advancing a particular political or social agenda, typically by discrediting others, such as exposed fabrications, hoaxes, and news satire).
(b) Hoaxes (another type of deliberate fabrication or falsification in the mainstream or social media, such as rumours, fake graphics or tables, false attribution of authorship, and dramatic images).
(c) News satire or parody (usually found in humorous news websites based on irony, often in a mainstream format).
(d) Fake reviews (especially used in e-commerce platforms to influence the purchasing of products and services).
(e) Bias (belief bias, confirmation bias, and anchoring).
(f) Propaganda (commonly used as a dangerous persuasive political tool to shape a large-scale opinion, influencing people through Pavlov's theory of conditioned response that pairs a stimulus with a conditioned response).
(g) Retracted papers (e.g., about 500 papers were backed by the false discovery of the 'Piltdown man' a supposed hominid fossil forged about 100 years ago that was supposed to reveal facts about the evolution of man, but was a fraud that took about forty years to be detected).
(h) Conspiracy theories popularised on internet forums and social media (e.g., the COVID-19 anti-vaccine and flat-earthers movements, undermining efforts to end a pandemic and challenging even already consolidated scientific discoveries).

[24] AECOC Innovation hub, 'Facebook lucha contra las "fake news"' (Facebook fights against fake news), www.aecoc.es/innovation-hub-noticias/facebook-lucha-contra-las-fake-news/.

(i) The incorrect use of maps, charts, and graphics (misleading representations with the attempt to support arguments).
(j) Phishing as a malinformation mechanism that misuses personal and/or confidential information. Identity theft, attempts to tarnish a reputation, profile cloning, denying access to email, and financial loss are, for example, results of phishing.
(k) Filter bubbles (algorithm-based, can amplify and at the same time isolate viewpoints and narratives, spreading misinformation by creating a personal ecosystem of information)
(l) Echo chambers (selective exposure of information or messages to users that have a more emotional relationship with information, favouring the circulation of information that reinforces their pre-existing views, maximising ideological polarisation and reinforcing different types of intolerance).
(m) Political use of sensitive information (exaggerations or purposely inflating or deflating numbers to make a point).
(n) Misuse of personal/confidential information (e.g., the Facebook/Cambridge Analytica scandal, an unprecedented data breach involved the harvesting of private information from over 50 million Facebook profiles).[25]

11.2.2.3 Fake News and Propaganda

The broad dissemination of false information is commonly known as *false* or *fake* news, but these terms do not have the same meaning around the globe. Even though some authors consider them as synonymous, as said, others view false news as a genre that includes fake news, a concept that was more precisely coined, first to refer to false expressions emanating from high-profile public officials and later to include the expressions of the press and the criticisms disseminated through social networks.

The power of fake news lies in the ability to offer information in accordance with existing convictions of like-minded people, and for this reason the cosmos of social media in general and social networks in particular is a fertile field for its gestation since the business model of this applications leads to the generation of content and information that can be seen as credible and attractive. In this sense:

> what makes fabricated news unique is the information environment we currently live in, where social media are key to dissemination of information and we no longer receive information solely from traditional gatekeepers. Nowadays, it is not necessary to be a journalist and work for a publication to create and disseminate content online. Laypersons write, curate, and disseminate information via online media. Studies show that they may even be preferred over traditional professional sources. This is particularly troublesome given that individuals find information

[25] D'Amorim and Fernandes de Oliveira Miranda, 'Misinformation, disinformation, and malinformation'.

> that agrees with prior beliefs as more credible and reliable, creating an environment that exacerbates misinformation because credible information appears alongside personal opinions.[26]

We stated before that the fabrication and dissemination of false news for political reasons is an ancient phenomenon, but this phenomenon unexpectedly re-emerged with great vigour in the last decade, and clear evidence of this is that the Oxford dictionary selected 'post-truth' as the word of the year in 2016 and the Collins dictionary did the same with the term 'fake news' in 2017.

As recently stated:

> the concept known as 'disinformation' during the World Wars and as 'freak journalism' or 'yellow journalism' during the Spanish war, can be traced back to 1896 (Campbell, 2001; Crain, 2017). Yellow journalism was also known for publishing content with no evidence and therefore factually incorrect, often for business purposes (Samuel, 2016). In Yarros' (1922) critique of yellow journalism is characterized as 'brazen and vicious "faking," and reckless disregard of decency, proportion and taste for the sake of increased profits.' As if history were repeating itself, the phenomenon regained attention during the 2016 U.S. Presidential elections.[27]

The very recent resurgence of fake news has brought new uses and a conceptual constraint (most exclude the publication of false stories used as a joke from this term). As Wardle points out, the term has been recently used by politicians (e.g., the former president of the US, Donald Trump), 'as a weapon to attack a free and independent press'.[28] In accordance with this, Barclay restrictedly defines fake news as 'information that is completely fabricated for the purpose of either making money or advancing a particular political or social agenda, typically by discrediting others'.[29]

As Botero Marino points out, if we understand fake news as the publication or massive dissemination of false information of public interest, knowing its falsehood and with the intention of deceiving or confusing the public or a fraction of it, the concept is based on three elements: a material element (the massive dissemination of false information), a cognitive element (the effective knowledge of the falsity of the information that is manufactured and/or divulged), and a volitional element (the intention to deceive or confuse the public or a fraction of it). The volitional element is particularly useful in order to distinguish fake news from satire. Satire can consist of the publication of false information, knowing that it is false, without – or with – the intention of misleading or confusing the public. Satire, in accordance

26 Molina et al., '"Fake news" is not simply false information'.

27 Ibid.

28 C. Wardle, 'How you can help transform the internet into a place of trust', TED talk, 2019, www.youtube.com/watch?v=3iD4HwJ-67Q&t=89s.

29 D. A. Barclay, 'Confronting the wicked problem of fake news: a role for education?' Cicero Foundation Great Debate Paper, n.18/03, May 2018, www.cicerofoundation.org/lectures/Donald_Barclay_Confronting_Fake_News.pdf, 6.

with the jurisprudence of the European Court of Human Rights (*Vereinigung Bildender Künstler v. Austria*),[30] enjoys special and reinforced protection from the right to freedom of expression.[31]

As a consequence of this new and restricted concept, it is more obvious that the dissemination of fake news is a core component of propaganda, as both constitute forms of distorting reality in order to influence the opinions and actions of a given audience and obtain beneficial results.[32]

Molina et al. refer to the different possible contents included in the concept of fake news:[33]

(a) false news/hoaxes,[34]
(b) commentary, opinion and feature writing,[35]
(c) misreporting,[36]
(d) polarised and sensationalist content,[37]
(e) satirical news,[38]
(f) persuasive information,[39] and
(g) citizen journalism.[40]

[30] *Vereinigung Bildender Künstler v. Austria*, Application no. 68354/01, Judgment of 25 January 2007, para. 33.

[31] C. Botero Marino, 'La regulación estatal de las llamadas "noticias falsas" desde la perspectiva del derecho a la libertad de expresión', in OAS, Office of the Special Rapporteur for Freedom of Expression, 'Libertad de expresión: A 30 años de la Opinión Consultiva sobre la colegiación obligatoria de periodistas' (Freedom of expression: 30 years after the Advisory Opinion on the compulsory registration of journalists) (2017), www.oas.org/es/cidh/expresion/docs/publicaciones/OC5_ESP.PDF, 69.

[32] Benkler, Faris, and Roberts, propose the following definitions: (a) 'Propaganda' and 'disinformation': manipulating and misleading people intentionally to achieve political ends; (b) 'Network propaganda': the ways in which the architecture of a media ecosystem makes it more or less susceptible to disseminating these kinds of manipulations and lies, (c) 'Misinformation': publishing wrong information without meaning to be wrong or having a political purpose in communicating false information (Benkler, Faris, and Roberts, *Network Propaganda*, p. 24).

[33] Molina et al., '"Fake news" is not simply false information'.

[34] Information that is intentionally false, and are often malicious stories propagating conspiracy theories. Although this type of content shares characteristics with polarised and sensationalist content, where information can be characterised as highly emotional and highly partisan, it differs in important features.

[35] Commentary and other similar editorial pieces are different from real news in that the journalist does not abide by principles of opinion-free reporting typically seen in hard news stories.

[36] Misinformation, or unintentional false reporting from professional news media organisations.

[37] This content is not completely false but is characterised by its 'goodness-of-fit with a particular ideology'. A common strategy utilised by polarised content is the use of highly emotional and inflammatory content. These assertions typically lack evidence and are based on appeals to emotion and pre-existing attitudes.

[38] An intentionally false story meant to be perceived as unrealistic, which uses journalistic style as a parody of the style, to mock issues and individuals in the news, or to disseminate a prank.

[39] Persuasive information is decomposed in native advertisement (defined as promotional material of persuasive intent, often masked as a news article), and promotional (political or non-political) content.

[40] Citizen journalism includes two categories: blogs and websites from citizens, civil societies, and organisations with content originally created by such users, on one side, and on the other, subsites of

In addition, they conclude that identifying fabricated information online before it becomes viral is imperative for maintaining an informed citizenry able to make decisions required in a healthy democracy, so that using machine learning and including several types of indicators could provide a solution for the identification of fabricated information, despite its overlapping boundaries with other types of information.[41] With this in mind, they propose an original taxonomy of online content, as a precursor to identifying signature features of fabricated news, including a table in which seven indicators (fact checked, emotionally charged, source verification, registration inconsistency, site pedigree, narrative writing, and humour) converted into yes/no questions (for a decision-tree algorithm) are provided to distinguish between fake news and other types of content, precisely in order to develop algorithms for fabricated news detection, and not to impinge on users' right to express their opinions, or journalists' endeavours, but to stop the dissemination of false information.[42]

11.2.2.4 Ten Keys Suggested by the Private Sector and Academia to Detect and Stop the Spread of Fake News

In a recent study where it was detected that 86 per cent of Spaniards have difficulty distinguishing between real and false information, the researchers provided the following ten tips for detecting when information is false:

(a) *Be wary of headlines.* Fake news often has eye-catching headlines in all caps with exclamation marks and often shocking and unheard of information.
(b) *Always examine the URL.* A fake web address or one that copies a real one can indicate fake news. Check the characters of the URL well because there are always small details.
(c) *Investigate the source of the news,* particularly before sharing or disseminating it. Some social networks such as Facebook (until 2025) or Google have enabled the Fact Checking button so that users can certify the veracity of the information.
(d) *Pay attention to the format.* Many fake news sites have misspellings or weird layouts.
(e) *Take a close look at the photos and do an image search.* Fake news often contains manipulated images or videos, even based on authentic photos taken out of context.

professional journalism sites providing a forum for citizen reporting (e.g., CNN's iReport). Features to distinguish this content from other online information include message aspects such as not adhering to journalistic style of reporting and verification. Additionally, its contents are more emotionally driven and subjectively reported. Last, there are essential structural components. For instance, the URL and 'about us' section are giveaways of the site being a blog, personal site, or a site specifically meant for citizen reporting.

41 Molina et al., '"Fake news" is not simply false information'.

42 Ibid.

(f) *Check the dates.* Fake news can have a nonsensical timeline or include altered dates.
(g) *Check the facts and the author's sources to confirm that they are accurate.* If the identity of supposed experts is not mentioned, it is possible that the news is false.
(h) *Check other news.* If no other news source is reporting the same story, it may be false.
(i) *Consider that the story may be a joke,* especially when the source of the news is known for its parodies. If the details and the tone suggest that it has been written in a humorous way, it is not fake news.
(j) *Be critical.* Some stories are false on purpose and for hidden or malicious purposes.[43]

11.2.3 *The Four Top-Level Disinformation Responses*

The crisis generated by the disinfodemic phenomenon has led both public and private sectors (particularly the international community, states, digital service providers, and non-governmental organisations) to adopt measures to mitigate it.

In particular, state responses seek to punish administratively or criminally the authors or broadcasters, following the recommendations of the UN Special Rapporteur for Freedom of Opinion and Expression, who recently reported that the responses by states to the growing phenomenon of disinformation refer fundamentally to internet closures and different kinds of regulations: criminal laws on defamation, consumer protection, financial fraud, social media, and social networks, and recommends that, '[i]n consonance with their obligation to respect human rights, States should not make, sponsor, encourage or disseminate claims that they know or should reasonably know to be false [...]'.[44]

In the case of private stakeholders, they mainly responded by adopting self-regulation (rushed by the pressure of governments on large internet platforms, perceived as 'facilitators' of the phenomenon) deployed via:

(a) social media (in the USA, the *Washington Post*'s FactChecker; in France, *Libération*'s Desintox and *Le Monde*'s Les Décodeurs; in the UK, the Channel 4 News' Fact Check and *The Guardian*'s Reality Check Blog, among others),
(b) social networks (e.g., various tools used by Facebook to facilitate detection and reporting: a search initiative, a news literacy campaign, and a monitoring of the work done in News Feed),

[43] 'Study on the impact of fake news in Spain', carried out by market research company 'Simple Lógica' and the investigation group in psychology of testimony of the Complutense University of Madrid, www.amic.media/media/files/file_352_3350.pdf.

[44] Report of the Special Rapporteur on the promotion and protection of the right to freedom of opinion and expression, Irene Khan, 'Disinformation and freedom of opinion and expression', UN Doc. A/HRC/47/25, 13 April 2021.

(c) other internet service providers (e.g., Google's Fast Check and some browser's extensions, such as Pinocchio alerts, FiB Stop Living a Lie, This is Fake, B.S. Detector, and Fake News Alert), and
(d) non-governmental organisations (e.g., Fast Check CL in Chile, Newtral in Spain, FactCheckEU.org in Europe, FactCheck.org and Potitifact.com in the USA, Africa Check, in Africa, Chequeado.com in Argentina and AltNews in India; they check the quality of high social impact content and warn about any possible falsehood). In this direction, the Pointer Institute for Media Studies has been developing, with several civil and media organisations from around the world, the International Fact-Checking Network, and recently approved a code of principles on fact checking.

We will focus *infra* on these efforts, following the 'four top-level disinformation responses' classified by the Broadband Commission in the recent report on Freedom of Expression and Addressing Disinformation on the Internet.[45]

11.2.3.1 Identification Responses

These kinds of responses involve the monitoring and analysis of information channels in order to detect the presence of disinformation through two kinds of activities (called subtypes in the report):

(a) Monitoring and fact-checking: carried out by internet communications companies, academia, and news, civil society, and independent fact-checking organisations and their partnerships.[46]
(b) Investigative responses, aimed at determining whether a given message or content is totally or partially false and to provide insights into disinformation campaigns, including the originating actors, degree of spread, and affected communities.[47]

11.2.3.2 Law and Policy Responses Aimed at Producers and Distributors

These kinds of responses are addressed to alter the environment that governs and shapes the behaviour of producers and distributors of disinformation, specifically:

45 UNESCO, ITU, and Broadband Commission for Sustainable Development, *Balancing Act: Countering Digital Disinformation while respecting Freedom of Expression* (Geneva: ITU, 2020), https://unesdoc.unesco.org/ark:/48223/pf0000379015.

46 D. Teyssou, J. Posetti, and S. Gregory, 'Monitoring and fact-checking responses', in UNESCO, ITU, and Broadband Commission for Sustainable Development, *Balancing Act: Countering Digital Disinformation while Respecting Freedom of Expression* (Geneva: ITU, 2020), https://unesdoc.unesco.org/ark:/48223/pf0000379015, pp. 66–86.

47 D. Teyssou, J. Posetti, and S. Gregory, 'Investigative responses', in UNESCO, ITU, and Broadband Commission for Sustainable Development, *Balancing Act: Countering Digital Disinformation while Respecting Freedom of Expression* (Geneva: ITU, 2020), https://unesdoc.unesco.org/ark:/48223/pf0000379015, pp. 87–95.

(a) Legislative, pre-legislative, and policy responses, encompassing regulatory intervention.[48]
(b) National and international counter-disinformation campaigns, tending to focus on the construction of counter-narratives.[49]
(c) Specific responses aimed at combating election-related disinformation and designed to detect, track, and counter disinformation that is spread during elections, owing to its impact on democratic processes and citizen rights. This involves a combination of monitoring and fact-checking, legal, curatorial, technical, and other responses, which will be cross-referenced as appropriate.[50]

11.2.3.3 Responses within the Processes of Production and Distribution

These include:

(a) Curatorial responses, primarily editorial and content policy and 'community standards.'[51]
(b) Technical and algorithmic responses implemented by social media platforms, video-sharing platforms and search engines, but can also be third-party tools (e.g., browser plug-ins) or experimental methods from academic research using algorithms and/or artificial intelligence to detect and limit the spread of disinformation, or provide context or additional information on individual items and posts.[52]
(c) De-monetisation responses, designed to stop profit and thus discourage the creation of clickbait, counterfeit news sites, and other kinds of for-profit disinformation.[53]

[48] T. Meyer et al., 'Legislative, pre-legislative and policy responses', in UNESCO, ITU, and Broadband Commission for Sustainable Development, *Balancing Act: Countering Digital Disinformation while Respecting Freedom of Expression* (Geneva: ITU, 2020), https://unesdoc.unesco.org/ark:/48223/pf0000379015, pp. 97–112.

[49] T. Meyer, C. Hanot, and J. Posetti, 'National and international counter-disinformation campaigns', in UNESCO, ITU, and Broadband Commission for Sustainable Development, *Balancing Act: Countering Digital Disinformation while Respecting Freedom of Expression* (Geneva: ITU, 2020), https://unesdoc.unesco.org/ark:/48223/pf0000379015, pp. 113–22.

[50] D. Teyssou, J. Posetti, and K. Bontcheva, 'Electoral-specific responses', in UNESCO, ITU, and Broadband Commission for Sustainable Development, *Balancing Act: Countering Digital Disinformation while Respecting Freedom of Expression* (Geneva: ITU, 2020), https://unesdoc.unesco.org/ark:/48223/pf0000379015, pp. 123–39.

[51] T. Meyer, C. Hanot, and J. Posetti, 'Curatorial responses', in UNESCO, ITU, and Broadband Commission for Sustainable Development, *Balancing Act: Countering Digital Disinformation while Respecting Freedom of Expression* (Geneva: ITU, 2020), https://unesdoc.unesco.org/ark:/48223/pf0000379015, pp. 141–68.

[52] S. Gregory et al., 'Technical/algorithmic responses', in UNESCO, ITU, and Broadband Commission for Sustainable Development, *Balancing Act: Countering Digital Disinformation while Respecting Freedom of Expression* (Geneva: ITU, 2020), https://unesdoc.unesco.org/ark:/48223/pf0000379015, pp. 169–89.

[53] K. Bontcheva, 'Demonetisation and advertising-linked responses', in UNESCO, ITU, and Broadband Commission for Sustainable Development, *Balancing Act: Countering Digital Disinformation while*

11.2.3.4 Responses Supporting the Target Audiences (Victims) of Disinformation Campaigns

These responses include guidelines, recommendations, resolutions, media and data literacy, content credibility labelling initiatives, and other tools to influence curation in terms of the prominence and amplification of certain content. They are sub-classified in the report into:

(a) Ethical and normative responses carried out on international, regional and local levels involving the public condemnation of acts of disinformation or recommendations and resolutions aimed at thwarting these acts and sensitising the public to these issues.[54]
(b) Educational responses aimed at promoting media and information literacy, critical thinking, and verification in the context of online information consumption, as well as journalist training.[55]
(c) Empowerment and credibility labelling efforts around building content verification tools and web content indicators, in order to empower citizens and journalists to avoid falling prey to online disinformation.[56]

11.2.4 *International and Inter-American Human Rights System Responses*

The worrying current reality of the fake news phenomenon has led the international community to propose the adoption of measures and effective tools to combat fake news, but making clear both the scope of freedom of expression and the limits that measures aimed at combating disinformation must respect.

In this direction the UN Special Rapporteur for Freedom of Opinion and Expression, the Representative for Freedom of the Media of the Organization for Security and Cooperation in Europe (OSCE), the Organization of American States (OAS) Special Rapporteur for Freedom of Expression, and the Special Rapporteur on Freedom of Expression and Access to Information of the African Commission

Respecting Freedom of Expression (Geneva: ITU, 2020), https://unesdoc.unesco.org/ark:/48223/pf0000379015, pp. 190–201.

54 J. Posetti, 'Normative and ethical responses', in UNESCO, ITU, and Broadband Commission for Sustainable Development, *Balancing Act: Countering Digital Disinformation while Respecting Freedom of Expression* (Geneva: ITU, 2020), https://unesdoc.unesco.org/ark:/48223/pf0000379015, pp. 203–17.

55 K. Bontcheva, J. Posetti, and D. Teyssou, 'Educational responses', in UNESCO, ITU, and Broadband Commission for Sustainable Development, *Balancing Act: Countering Digital Disinformation while Respecting Freedom of Expression* (Geneva: ITU, 2020), https://unesdoc.unesco.org/ark:/48223/pf0000379015, pp. 218–230.

56 D. Maynard, D. Teyssou, and S. Gregory, 'Empowerment & credibility labelling responses', in UNESCO, ITU, and Broadband Commission for Sustainable Development, *Balancing Act: Countering Digital Disinformation while Respecting Freedom of Expression* (Geneva: ITU, 2020), https://unesdoc.unesco.org/ark:/48223/pf0000379015, pp. 231–47.

on Human and Peoples' Rights adopted several documents that, with greater or lesser specificity, refer to fake news and disinformation issues: in 2017, the Joint Declaration on Freedom of Expression and Fake News, Disinformation and Propaganda; in 2018, the Joint Declaration on Media Independence and Diversity in the Digital Age; in 2019, the Twentieth Anniversary of the Joint Declaration: Challenges to Freedom of Expression in the Next Decade; in 2020, the Joint Declaration on Freedom of Expression and Elections in the Digital Age; in 2021, the Joint Declaration on Politicians and Public Officials and Freedom of Expression, and in 2022 the Joint Declaration on Freedom of Expression and Gender Justice.[57] Also in 2022, and clearly facing the consequences of fake news during the Russia and Ukraine war, the UN Special Rapporteur for Freedom of Opinion and Expression also published a report on Disinformation and Freedom of Opinion and Expression during Armed Conflicts.[58]

11.2.4.1 The 'Standards on Disinformation and Propaganda' Settled in the Joint Declaration on Freedom of Expression and Fake News, Disinformation and Propaganda

This document states that general prohibitions on the dissemination of information based on vague and ambiguous ideas, including 'false news' or 'non-objective information', are incompatible with international standards for restrictions on freedom of expression; criminal defamation laws and civil liability are only legal if defendants cannot prove the truth and do not have other defences, such as fair comment.[59]

It also states that state actors should not make, sponsor, encourage, or further disseminate statements that they know or reasonably should know to be false (disinformation) or which demonstrate a reckless disregard for verifiable information (propaganda), and should take care to ensure that they disseminate reliable and trustworthy information, including about matters of public interest, such as the economy, public health, security, and the environment.

The principles settled in that document are as follows:

(a) States may only impose restrictions on the right to freedom of expression in accordance with the test for such restrictions under international law, namely that they be provided for by law, serve one of the legitimate interests recognised under international law, and be necessary and proportionate to protect that interest.

[57] OAS, 'Joint declarations', www.oas.org/en/iachr/expression/basic_documents/declarations.asp.

[58] Report of the Special Rapporteur on the promotion and protection of the right to freedom of opinion and expression, 'Disinformation and freedom of opinion and expression during armed conflicts', UN Doc. A/77/288, 12 August 2022.

[59] OAS, 'Joint declaration on freedom of expression and fake news, disinformation and propaganda' (2017), www.oas.org/en/iachr/expression/showarticle.asp?artID=1056&lID=1.

(b) Restrictions on freedom of expression may also be imposed, as long as they are consistent with the requirements noted in paragraph 1(a), to prohibit advocacy of hatred on protected grounds that constitutes incitement to violence, discrimination, or hostility (Article 20(2), International Covenant on Civil and Political Rights).
(c) Intermediaries should never be liable for any third-party content relating to those services unless they specifically intervene in that content or refuse to obey an order adopted in accordance with due process guarantees by an independent, impartial, authoritative oversight body (such as a court) to remove it and they have the technical capacity to do that.
(d) Consideration should be given to protecting individuals against liability for merely redistributing or promoting, through intermediaries, content of which they are not the author and which they have not modified.
(e) State mandated blocking of entire websites, IP addresses, ports, or network protocols is an extreme measure that can only be justified where it is provided by law and is necessary to protect a human right or other legitimate public interest, including in the sense that it is proportionate, there are no less intrusive alternative measures that would protect the interest, and it respects minimum due process guarantees.
(f) Content filtering systems that are imposed by a government and are not end-user controlled are not justifiable as a restriction on freedom of expression.

11.2.4.2 The Joint Declaration on Media Independence and Diversity in the Digital Age

This document states that restrictions on what may be disseminated through the media must be ruled by law, serve one of the legitimate interests recognised under international law, and be necessary and proportionate to protect that interest.[60] It rejects the use of vague notions, such as 'information security' and 'cultural security', as a basis for restricting freedom of expression.

It also states that media outlets and online platforms should enhance their professionalism and social responsibility, including potentially by adopting codes of conduct and fact-checking systems, and putting in place self-regulatory systems or participating in existing systems, to enforce them.

11.2.4.3 The Twentieth Anniversary Joint Declaration: Challenges to Freedom of Expression in the Next Decade

This document, considering private control as a threat to freedom of expression, states that there is an urgent need to adopt measures that address the ways in which

[60] OAS, 'Joint declaration on media independence and diversity in the digital age' (2018), www.oas.org/en/iachr/expression/showarticle.asp?artID=1100&lID=1.

the advertising-dependent business models of some digital technology companies create an environment that can also be used for viral dissemination of inter alia deception, disinformation, and hateful expression.[61] It also urges human rights sensitive solutions to the challenges caused by disinformation, including the growing possibility of deep fakes, in publicly accountable and targeted ways, using approaches that meet the international law standards of legality, legitimacy of objective, and necessity and proportionality.

11.2.4.4 The Joint Declaration on Freedom of Expression and Elections in the Digital Age

This document states that Member States should ensure that any restrictions on freedom of expression that apply during election periods comply with the international law three-part test requirements of legality, legitimacy of aim, and necessity, which implies the following:[62]

(a) There should be no prior censorship of the media, including through means such as the administrative blocking of media websites or internet shutdowns.
(b) Any limits on the right to disseminate electoral statements should conform to international standards, including that public figures should be required to tolerate a higher degree of criticism and scrutiny than ordinary citizens.
(c) There should be no general or ambiguous laws on disinformation, such as prohibitions on spreading falsehoods or non-objective information. It also states that the media, both legacy and digital, should be exempted from liability during election periods for disseminating statements made directly by parties or candidates unless the statements have specifically been held to be unlawful by an independent and impartial court or regulatory body, or the statements constitute incitement to violence and the media outlet had a genuine opportunity to prevent their dissemination.

About restrictions during elections, it recommends Member States to consider supporting positive measures to address online disinformation, such as the promotion of independent fact-checking mechanisms and public education campaigns, while avoiding adopting rules criminalising disinformation. It also states that online intermediaries should not be held liable for dis-, mis-, and malinformation that has been disseminated over their platforms unless they specifically intervene in that content or fail to implement a legally binding order to remove that content.

[61] OAS, 'Twentieth anniversary joint declaration: challenges to freedom of expression in the next decade' (2019), www.oas.org/en/iachr/expression/showarticle.asp?artID=1146&lID=1.

[62] OAS, 'Joint declaration on freedom of expression and elections in the digital age' (2020), www.oas.org/en/iachr/expression/showarticle.asp?artID=1174&lID=1.

It also states that digital media and online intermediaries should make a reasonable effort to address dis-, mis-, and malinformation and election related spam, including through independent fact-checking and other measures, such as advertisement archives, appropriate content moderation, and public alerts.

11.2.4.5 The Joint Declaration on Politicians and Public Officials and Freedom of Expression

This document recommends Member States to repeal or refrain from adopting general prohibitions on the dissemination of inaccurate information, such as false news or fake news laws, and also to respect the following standards in relation to disinformation and false news:[63]

(a) adopt policies that provide for disciplinary measures to be imposed on public officials who, when acting or perceived to be acting in an official capacity, make, sponsor, encourage, or further disseminate statements that they know or should reasonably know to be false;
(b) ensure that public authorities make every effort to disseminate accurate and reliable information, including about their activities and matters of public interest.

It also states that, given the harm done by hate speech, including the ability of its targets to exercise their right to freedom of expression and to participate in political activities, Member States should:

(a) prohibit by law any advocacy of hatred that constitutes incitement to discrimination, hostility, or violence, in accordance with international law;
(b) undertake a range of activities – including education and counter-messaging – to combat intolerance and promote social inclusion and intercultural understanding.

In this regard, several international organisations have begun to focus their attention on public servants' obligations to make truthful statements, highlighting those made by public officials and candidates for elected positions.

Knowingly or recklessly disregarding a falsehood about the truth finding is the basis of the doctrine of 'actual malice' enshrined by the US Supreme Court in the case *New York Times v. Sullivan* for the freedom of expression and the press.[64] This criterion has been taken up by the Inter-American human rights system, where due diligence is required for – and not only for – journalistic activity,[65]

[63] OAS, 'Joint declaration on politicians and public officials and freedom of expression' (2021), www.oas.org/en/iachr/expression/showarticle.asp?artID=1214&lID=1.
[64] *New York Times Co. v. Sullivan*, 376 US 254 (1964).
[65] In the same way, the Joint Declaration on Freedom of Expression and Fake News, Disinformation and Propaganda states: 5.

since officials must affirm true facts, and before making a judgement they must act with verification criteria superior to that of any person, and failure to do so in certain circumstances can generate consequences ranging from criminal to relevant ethical. Therefore, within the framework of Article 13 of the American Convention on Human Rights, the establishment of specific responsibilities and obligations to tell the truth or not lie, intentionally or negligently, for certain persons owing to their functions does not necessarily constitute an illegitimate restriction on the right to freedom of expression, and therefore false expression knowing its falsehood – standard of real malice – excludes the protection that a priori false expression enjoys.

In this direction, in the jurisprudence of the Inter-American Court, officials are charged – owing to their function and the position in society – with the duty to verify the facts (higher than in the case of an ordinary person) and to satisfy both the publicity of government acts and the access to public information.

As stated by the Inter-American Court in two resounding cases ruled against Venezuela,[66] the exercise of freedom of expression is not the same for a mere private subject as it is for public officials, since in a democratic society it is not just legitimate; rather, it is sometimes the duty of state authorities to rule on matters of public interest. However, in doing so they are subject to certain limitations insofar as they must reasonably, although not necessarily exhaustively, verify the facts on which they base their opinions, and they should do so with even greater diligence than that employed by individuals, by reason of its high investiture, the wide scope, and eventual effects that its expression may have on certain sectors of the population, and to prevent citizens and other interested persons from receiving a manipulated version of certain events.

The Court adds that the limitations on the duty to express oneself are clearly based on the damage that false expressions can cause and given that public officials perform the role of guarantor of the fundamental rights of the people, their statements cannot ignore them or constitute forms of direct or indirect interference or harmful pressure on the rights of those who seek to contribute to public deliberation through the expression and dissemination of their thoughts.

Journalists and Media Outlets a. The media and journalists should, as appropriate, support effective systems of self-regulation whether at the level of specific media sectors (such as press complaints bodies) or at the level of individual media outlets (ombudsmen or public editors) which include standards on striving for accuracy in the news, including by offering a right of correction and/or reply to address inaccurate statements in the media. b. Media outlets should consider including critical coverage of disinformation and propaganda as part of their news services in line with their watchdog role in society, particularly during elections and regarding debates on matters of public interest.

66 I/A Court HR, *Ríos et al. V. Venezuela*, 'Preliminary objections, merits, reparations and costs, judgment of 28 January 2009', Series C No. 194, www.corteidh.or.cr/docs/canes/articulos/seriec_194_esp.pdf and *Perozo et al. v. Venezuela*, 'Preliminary objections, merits, reparations and costs, judgment of 28 January 2009', Series C No. 195, www.corteidh.or.cr/docs/cases/articulos/seriec_195_esp.pdf.

This duty of special care is particularly accentuated in situations of greater social conflict, disturbances of public order, or social or political polarisation, precisely because of the set of risks that may be implied for certain people or groups at any given time.[67]

More recently, in the context of the COVID-19 pandemic, the Inter-American Court adopted a resolution in which it refers to the obligations of Member States, recommending they:

> Observe special care in the pronouncements and statements of public officials with high responsibilities regarding the evolution of the pandemic. In the current circumstances, it is a duty for state authorities to inform the population, and when pronouncing in this regard, they must act diligently and have a reasonable scientific basis. Also, they must remember that they are exposed to greater scrutiny and public criticism, even in special periods. Governments and Internet companies must deal with and transparently combat the disinformation that circulates regarding the pandemic.[68]

In projection of these premises, provisions of a criminal and administrative nature in Latin America can be found in internal laws, such as codes and laws of ethics for public functions and even health regulations, from which the obligations of public officials to tell the truth arise.

Consequently, in criminal matters, in the protection of public faith, mendacious actions by public officials are punished for their crimes in the ideological falsification of public instruments,[69] and in the field of administrative law damage to trust in the administered in the face of acts of power ('legitimate confidence'), and when this is violated, the administrative act is nullified.[70] Among the codes and laws of ethics in the public function, honesty and integrity stand out as express demands in the work

[67] Ibid.

[68] IACHR, Resolution 1/2020, Pandemic and Human Rights in the Americas, 10 April 2020, www.oas.org/es/cidh/decisiones/pdf/Resolucion-1-20-es.pdf, para. 34.

[69] Article 286 of the Colombian Penal Code punishes whoever 'consigns a falsehood or totally or partially reveals the truth'. Protecting the public faith: the Argentine Penal Code contemplates the crime of ideological falsification of a public instrument in its article 293 to 'whoever inserts or causes to insert in a public instrument false statements, concerning a fact that the document must prove, so that it may result in damage'. Brazil: article 299 of the Penal Code. Chile: article 193. Costa Rica: article 360. Guatemala: article 322. Mexico: article 243 of the Penal Code, and article 63 of the General Law of Administrative Responsibilities of 2016 that creates the crime of contempt of anyone who answers requests with false information, does not respond, or deliberately delays. Panama: article 366 of the Penal Code. Paraguay articles 246 and 250 of the Penal Code. Peru: article 428 of the Penal Code. Dominican Republic: article 145 to 147 of the Penal Code.

[70] Argentina: law 19,549 of administrative procedure, articles 7 and 14. Colombia Article 88 of the Code of Administrative Procedure and Administrative Litigation on the presumption of legality and veracity. Costa Rica: Article 132 General Law of Public Administration. Peru: article 51 of the Law of General Administrative Procedure. Dominican Republic: Articles 9 and 10 of Law 107 of 2013 describe the presumption of validity of administrative acts in Article 9. 10 and 14.

of public officials.[71] These rules have also been incorporated into both regional and global soft law norms.[72]

There are also specific regulations aimed at health officials, especially regarding the obligation not to produce false or misleading messages, which mainly refer to advertising pharmaceuticals and public health issues.[73]

Legal obligations are also established for candidates for elected public office, particularly in the prevention of 'dirty' campaigns (those in which offences are used, information is invented, and slanders intrude on the private life of a candidate), which have been denounced recently in Latin America,[74] and have given rise to regulation, especially in electoral laws and political parties.[75]

[71] Argentina: article 23 of the Framework Law for the Regulation of National Public Employment (No. 25,164) and article 2 of the Law of Ethics in the Exercise of Public Function. Uruguay: Article 13 of Law No. 19,823. Chile: Law 20,880 on Probity in the Civil Service and Prevention of Conflicts of Interest regulates the principle of probity. Colombia regulates 'honesty' in the Integrity Code of the Colombian Public Service. Mexico: article 12 of the Code of Ethics of Public Servants of the Federal Government and article 7 of the General Law of Administrative Responsibilities of July 18, 2016. Panama: article 8.4. of the Code of Conduct for Public Servants of the Comptroller General. Peru; In its articles 6.2 and 6.5 of Law 27,815, it requires probity and truthfulness.

[72] Thus, in the Ibero-American Charter of Ethics and Integrity in the Public Function, approved in July 2018 by the XVIII Ibero-American Conference of Ministers of Public Administration and State Reform, it is expressly indicated in the Preamble that the Charter seeks to promote a system of solid integrity that strengthens what they understood to be the common practice in the Ibero-American administrations: the honest behavior of public servants. One of the objectives detailed in the document is 'Promote the integrity of those responsible and public servants' (https://clad.org/wp-content/uploads/2020/10/1-Carta-Iberoamericana-de-%C3%89tica-e-Integridad-en-la-Function%C3%B3n-P%C3%BAblica-2018-CLAD.pdf). For its part, the UN Office on Drugs and Crime under its Education for Justice initiative in line with its Global Program for the Implementation of the Doha Declaration prepared the document 'Public Integrity and Ethics': 'The integrity of the public sector – or public integrity – refers to the use of powers and resources entrusted to the public sector effectively, honestly and for public purposes.' Additional related ethical standards that the public sector is expected to uphold include transparency, accountability, efficiency, and competence. UN staff members, for example, must 'maintain the highest standards of efficiency, competence and integrity', and integrity is defined in the United Nations Staff Regulations and Rules, which includes, but is not limited to: 'Probity, impartiality, fairness, honesty and truthfulness in all matters that affect their work and status' (Staff Regulations of the United Nations, UN Doc. ST/SGB/2023/1, 1 January 2023, Regulation 1.2 (b)).

[73] Argentina: resolution 20/2005 of the Ministry of Health and Environment and Provision 4980/2005 of the ANMAT. Colombia, Consumer Statute Law 1480 of 2011. Costa Rica: Article 113 of Law No. 7472 on the Promotion of Competition and Effective Defense of the Consumer and its respective regulations. Guatemala: Articles 15 to 17 of the Advertising Ethics Code, clearly self-regulated by the private sector. Panama, Articles 161 and 171 of Executive Decree 189 of 1999 for advertising broadcast on radio and television. Peru: articles 3 and 4 of Law No. 27808 Law of Transparency and Access to Public Information and Title V (Penalty Regime) and article 121 of Law No. 26842, General Health Law. Dominican Republic: Resolution 016-2014 and Technical Regulations of the Ministry of Public Health.

[74] There were complaints about manoeuvres of this type in the presidential elections in Mexico (2000 and 2006), Colombia (2014), and the Dominican Republic (2015), and in the referendum to modify the Bolivian Constitution regarding presidential re-election (2016), where it was appealed to unsubstantiated allegations of illegal campaign finance; corruption in the concession of public works or questions of the private life of the candidates.

[75] Mexico: article 247.2 of the General Law of Electoral Institutions and Procedures; Argentina: article 140 of the National Electoral Code; Honduras: arts. 146 and 148 of the Electoral and Political

In this sense, the Broadband Commission for Sustainable Development, co-founded by UNESCO and the International Telecommunication Union (ITU), recommends in a recent report that:

> Political parties and other political actors could: 1) Speak out about the dangers of political actors as sources and amplifiers of disinformation and work to improve the quality of the information ecosystem and increase trust in democratic institutions. 2) Refrain from using disinformation tactics in political campaigning, including the use of covert tools of public opinion manipulation and 'dark propaganda' public relations firms.[76]

In any case, when weighing the rights involved and when giving concrete solutions, it appears advisable to consider what Sunstein has said:

> In life and in politics, truth matters. In the end, it might matter more than anything else. It is a precondition for trust and hence for cooperation. But what, exactly, can governments do to restrict the dissemination of falsehoods in systems committed to freedom of speech? In brief: Much less than some of them want, but much more than some of them are now doing. I have argued in favor of a general principle: False statements are constitutionally protected unless the government can show that they threaten to cause serious harm that cannot be avoided through a more speech-protective route. I have also suggested that when lies are involved, the government may impose regulation on the basis of a weaker demonstration of harm than is ordinarily required for unintentional falsehoods. Reasonable people can disagree about how to apply these ideas in concrete cases. In general, however, this general principle, and the accompanying suggestion, give a great deal of constitutional protection to falsehoods and even lies.
>
> […] public officials have considerable power to regulate deepfakes and doctored videos. They are also entitled to act to protect public health and safety, certainly in the context of lies, and if falsehoods create sufficiently serious risks, to control such falsehoods as well. In all of these contexts, some of the most promising tools do not involve censorship or punishment; they involve more speech-protective approaches, such as labels and warnings.[77]

11.2.4.6 The Joint Declaration on Freedom of Expression and Gender Justice

This document promotes the adoption of 'education programs, social policies, cultural practices, and laws and policies that prohibit discrimination and sexual and

Organizations Law, in addition to an extraordinary agreement of 2018 of the National Electoral Chamber by which a 'Register of social media accounts and official websites of candidates, political groups and highest authorities is created'; Brazil: Article 9 of Resolution 23.610 / 2019 of the Superior Electoral Court and article 323 of the Electoral Code; Peru: Article 42 of Law No. 28094 – Law of Political Organizations.

[76] UNESCO, ITU, and Broadband Commission for Sustainable Development, *Balancing Act: Countering Digital Disinformation while Respecting Freedom of Expression* (Geneva: ITU, 2020), https://unesdoc.unesco.org/ark:/48223/pf0000379015, p. 263.

[77] C. Sunstein, *Liars: Falsehoods and Free Speech in an Age of Deception* (Oxford: Oxford University Press, 2021), pp. 131, 133.

gender-based violence and to promote equality and inclusion', considering specifically that 'online gender-based violence, gendered hate speech and disinformation, which cause serious psychological harm and can lead to physical violence, are proliferating with the aim of intimidating and silencing women, including female politicians, journalists and human rights defenders'.[78]

11.2.4.7 The UN Special Rapporteur for Freedom of Opinion and Expression Report on Disinformation and Freedom of Opinion and Expression during Armed Conflicts

In this report, Khan examines the challenges that information manipulation poses to freedom of opinion and expression during armed conflict. She notes that the information environment in the digital age has become a dangerous theatre of war in which state and non-state actors, enabled by digital technology and social media, weaponise information to sow confusion, feed hate, incite violence, and prolong conflict.[79]

Emphasising the vital importance of the right to information as a 'survival right' on which people's lives, health, and safety depend, she recommends that human rights standards be reinforced alongside international humanitarian law during armed conflicts; urges states to reaffirm their commitment to upholding freedom of opinion and expression and ensuring that action to counter disinformation, propaganda, and incitement is well grounded in human rights; she recommends that social media companies align their policies and practices with human rights standards and apply them consistently across the world, and concludes by reiterating the need to build social resilience against disinformation and promote multistakeholder approaches that engage civil society as well as states, companies, and international organisations.

11.2.4.8 The European Commission Communication on 'Tackling Online Disinformation: A European Approach' and the Report on the Implementation of This Communication

In March 2015, the European Council invited the High Representative to develop an action plan to address Russia's ongoing disinformation campaigns, which resulted in the creation of the East Stratcom Task Force, effective as planned since September 2015.

In a June 2017 resolution, the European Parliament called upon the Commission 'to analyse in depth the current situation and legal framework with regard to fake

[78] OAS, 'Joint declaration on freedom of expression and gender justice' (2022), www.oas.org/en/iachr/expression/showarticle.asp?artID=1233&lID=1.

[79] Report of the Special Rapporteur on the promotion and protection of the right to freedom of opinion and expression, 'Disinformation and freedom of opinion and expression during armed conflicts', UN Doc. A/77/288, 12 August 2022.

news and to verify the possibility of legislative intervention to limit the dissemination and spreading of fake content'.[80]

In March 2018, the European Council stated: 'social networks and digital platforms need to guarantee transparent practices and full protection of citizens' privacy and personal data',[81] and subsequently the European Commission adopted the Communication 'Tackling online disinformation: a European Approach',[82] focused on combating the effects of online disinformation through: (a) a more transparent, trustworthy, and accountable online ecosystem, (b) secure and resilient election processes, (c) fostering education and media literacy, (d) support for quality journalism as an essential element of a democratic society, and (e) countering internal and external disinformation threats through strategic communication.

Later in the same year, the European Commission adopted a Report on the implementation of that Communication,[83] which delineates the challenges online disinformation present to our democracies and outlines five clusters of actions for private and public stakeholders that respond to these challenges.

The four measures that the Communication on tackling online disinformation suggested are analysed here.

11.2.4.8.1 A MORE TRANSPARENT, TRUSTWORTHY, AND ACCOUNTABLE ONLINE ECOSYSTEM. The first set of actions involves four objectives: (a) online platforms to act swiftly and effectively to protect users from disinformation, (b) strengthening fact checking, collective knowledge, and monitoring capacity on disinformation, (c) fostering online accountability, and (d) harnessing new technologies.

11.2.4.8.1.1 Online Platforms to Act Swiftly and Effectively to Protect Users from Disinformation. This objective, achieved through:

(a) the adoption of a code of practice to be used by online platforms and the advertising industry in order to increase transparency,
(b) the creation of an independent European network of fact-checkers to establish common working methods, exchange best practices, and achieve the broadest possible coverage across the EU,

80 European Parliament resolution of 15 June 2017 on online platforms and the digital single market (2016/2276(INI)), EU Doc. P8_TA(2017)0272, para. 36.
81 European Council, Conclusions of European Council meeting 22 Match 2018, EU doc. EUCO 1/18, 23 March 2018, para. 7.
82 Communication from the Commission to the European Parliament, the Council, the European Economic and Social Committee and the Committee of the Regions, 'Tackling online disinformation: a European approach', EU Doc. COM/2018/236 final. Document 52018DC0236, https://eur-lex.europa.eu/legal-content/EN/TXT/?uri=CELEX%3A52018DC0236.
83 Report from the Commission to the European Parliament, the Council, the European Economic and Social Committee and the Committee of the Regions on the implementation of the Communication 'Tackling online disinformation: a European approach', EU Doc. COM/2018/794 final.

(c) the promotion of voluntary online identification systems for the traceability and identification of suppliers of information, and
(d) the use of the EU research and innovation programme (Horizon 2020) to mobilise new technologies, such as artificial intelligence, block chain, and cognitive algorithms.

The commitments are organised under five fields, monitored by the Commission in the implementation of a self-regulatory Code of Practice on Disinformation drafted in 2018 in a Multistakeholder Forum on Disinformation:

(a) *Scrutiny of ad placements* (deploy policies and processes to disrupt advertising and monetisation incentives for relevant behaviours).
(b) *Political advertising and issue-based advertising* (all advertisements should be clearly distinguishable from editorial content; enable public disclosure of political advertising; devise approaches to publicly disclose 'issue-based advertising').
(c) *Integrity of services* (put in place clear policies regarding identity and the misuse of automated bots on their services; put in place policies on what constitutes impermissible use of automated systems).
(d) *Empowering consumers* (invest in products, technologies, and programmes to help people make informed decisions when they encounter online news that may be false; invest in technological means to prioritise relevant, authentic and authoritative information where appropriate in searches, feeds, or other automatically ranked distribution channels; invest in features and tools that make it easier for people to find diverse perspectives about topics of public interest; partner with civil society, governments, educational institutions, and other stakeholders to support efforts aimed at improving critical thinking and digital media literacy; encourage market uptake of tools that help consumers understand why they are seeing particular advertisements).
(e) *Empowering the research community* (support good faith independent efforts to track disinformation and understand its impact; not prohibit or discourage good faith research into disinformation and political advertising on platforms; encourage research into disinformation and political advertising).[84]

11.2.4.8.1.2 Strengthening Fact Checking, Collective Knowledge, and Monitoring Capacity on Disinformation. The Commission committed, as a first step, to supporting the creation of an independent European network of fact-checkers.

As a second step, it committed to launching a secure European online platform on disinformation, offering analytical tools and cross-border data collection, including Union-wide open data and online platforms usage data to support detection and analysis of disinformation sources and dissemination patterns.

[84] Ibid., section 2.1.1.

The Commission organised a series of technical workshops with representatives of the fact-checking community in 2018. It selected relevant projects under the research and innovation programme Horizon 2020. Furthermore, in cooperation with the European Parliament, it organised a fact-checking conference in view of the European elections.

These actions have contributed to: (a) mapping and networking independent fact-checking organisations in the Member States, (b) ascertaining which tools and services are essential and facilitating the improvement of fact-checking activities and their impact (e.g., access to EUROSTAT data, translation tools, automated stream of fact-checks produced by the relevant fact-checking organisations), (c) identifying professional and ethical standards for independent fact-checking, and (d) providing tools and infrastructural support to fact-checking organisations.

To prepare the second step, the Commission proposed the creation of a new digital service infrastructure under the Connecting Europe Facility work programme 2019 for the establishment of a European Platform on Disinformation. In this direction, in June 2020, the Commission launched the European Digital Media Observatory (EDMO), but some civil society actors fear that the inclusion of a former Facebook executive and several organisations sponsored by Google could impact EDMO's missions, especially those that involve monitoring how online platforms follow the EU's code of practice on disinformation, which was signed in 2018 by the online platforms Facebook, Google, and Twitter, Mozilla, by advertisers and parts of the advertising industry (who presented their roadmaps to implementation), and then by Microsoft in 2019 and by TikTok in 2020. The strengthened Code of Practice in 2021 will evolve towards a co-regulatory instrument as outlined in the Digital Services Act (DSA).[85]

11.2.4.8.1.3 ***Fostering Online Accountability.*** With a view to increasing trust and accountability online, the Commission committed to promoting the use of voluntary online systems allowing the identification of suppliers of information based on trustworthy electronic identification and authentication means.[86]

11.2.4.8.1.4 ***Harnessing New Technologies.*** The Commission committed to making full use of the Horizon 2020 framework programme to mobilise new technologies and explore the possibility of additional support for tools that combat disinformation, accelerating time-to-market for high-impact innovation activities, and encouraging the partnering of researchers and businesses.

Furthermore, in the proposal for the Horizon Europe programme, the Commission has proposed dedicating efforts to: (a) safeguard democratic and economic stability through the development of new tools to combat online disinformation, (b) better

[85] Ibid., section 2.1.2.
[86] Ibid., section 2.1.3.

understand the role of journalistic standards and user-generated content in a hyper-connected society, and (c) support next generation internet applications and services including immersive and trustworthy media, social media, and social networking.[87]

11.2.4.8.2 SECURE AND RESILIENT ELECTION PROCESSES. The second set of actions addresses manipulative and disinformation tactics employed during electoral periods, in order to enable secure and resilient election processes, for which the Communication proposed to initiate continuous dialogue to support Member States in the management of risks to the democratic electoral process from cyber-attacks and disinformation.[88]

11.2.4.8.3 FOSTERING EDUCATION AND MEDIA LITERACY. The third set of actions focuses on fostering education and media literacy. The life-long development of critical and digital competences is crucial to reinforce the resilience of our societies to disinformation. The Communication proposed new actions to this end, including: (a) supporting the provision of educational materials by independent fact-checkers and civil society organisations to schools and educators, (b) organising a European Week of Media Literacy, (c) exploring the possibility of adding media literacy to the criteria used by the Organisation for Economic Co-operation and Development in its comparative reports on international student assessment, and (d) further encouraging the implementation of ongoing initiatives on digital skills, education, and traineeship.[89]

11.2.4.8.4 SUPPORT FOR QUALITY JOURNALISM AS AN ESSENTIAL ELEMENT OF A DEMOCRATIC SOCIETY. The fourth set of actions aims to support quality journalism as an essential element of a democratic society. Quality news media and journalism can uncover and dilute disinformation, providing citizens with high-quality and diverse information. The Communication proposed to enhance the transparency and predictability of state aid rules for the media sector by making available an online repository of decisions. The Communication also proposed to launch a call in 2018 for the production and dissemination of quality news content on EU affairs through data-driven news media and to explore increased funding opportunities to support initiatives promoting media freedom and pluralism, and the modernisation of news rooms.[90]

11.2.4.8.5 COUNTERING INTERNAL AND EXTERNAL DISINFORMATION THREATS THROUGH STRATEGIC COMMUNICATION. In line with the April communication, the European Commission worked to ensure the internal coordination of its

[87] Ibid., section 2.1.4.
[88] Ibid., section 2.2.
[89] Ibid., section 2.3.
[90] Ibid., section 2.4.

communication activities aiming at tackling disinformation. In this context, it created an internal Network against Disinformation, the primary purpose of which is to enable its services to better detect harmful narratives, support a culture of fact-checking, provide fast responses, and strengthen more effective positive messaging.

The Commission reinforced cooperation with the European Parliament and East Strategic Communication Task Force through a tripartite forum that aimed to operationalise the institutions' respective efforts in countering disinformation ahead of the 2019 European elections. In May 2021, the Commission presented a Guidance to strengthen the Code of Practice on Disinformation, which aims to address gaps and shortcomings and create a more transparent, safe, and trustworthy online environment and lays out the cornerstones for a robust monitoring framework for its implementation. It also aims at evolving the existing Code of Practice towards a co-regulatory instrument foreseen under the DSA, offering an early opportunity to design appropriate measures to address systemic risks related to disinformation stemming from the functioning and use made of the platforms' services in view of the anticipated DSA risk assessment and mitigation framework.[91]

More recently, the assembly, grouping the signatories of the Code and new signatories willing to subscribe to and take on commitments under the 2021 Code, met on 8 July 2021 to start the process that will strengthen the Code of Practice on Disinformation. Members of the Assembly have approved a vade mecum on the organisation and functioning of the process to shape and draft the strengthened Code of Practice on Disinformation.[92]

11.2.5 *Rules Emerging Both from International Regulations and Recommendations regarding Freedom of Expression and Other Individual and Collective Rights Involved in the Creation and Dissemination of False Information*

A proactive and efficient intervention to combat the disinfodemic phenomenon, respectful of conflicting rights and in particular the freedom of information, needs to first determine what kind of information requires an intervention without unduly affecting freedom of expression, and second, which obligations and responsibilities both public and private sectors have.

Now, little has been done to distinguish when disinformation requires some kind of intervention and to determine what kind of measures must be taken in accordance with the specific obligations that each sector has and even the different responsibilities of those who disseminate it, particularly when it is information

91 Ibid., section 2.5.

92 European Commission, 'Shaping Europe's digital future. The 2022 Code of Practice on Disinformation', https://digital-strategy.ec.europa.eu/en/policies/code-practice-disinformation.

issued by public officials and candidates for elected positions, on whom, depending on each legal system, ethical and legal obligations weigh that are even more intense when the dissemination of these manifestations can cause serious damage.

Referring to the emerging rules of the inter-American human rights system and based on what we have stated previously, Botero Marino indicates that there are two important standards applicable to any state effort aimed at prohibiting or regulating fake news:

(a) the simple objective falsehood of the expression cannot be the object of prohibition or state sanction, and
(b) it is only justified to restrict freedom of expression in order to protect the rights of third parties or public order understood from a narrowly defined democratic perspective.

She adds that to attend precisely to the protection of the rights of third parties and of democratic public order without undue restrictions, a test must be carried out that involves various relevant factors to define whether to act on false expressions – and to what extent – and eventually on those who generate and distribute them.[93]

Complementing this perspective, Sunstein affirms that what should be considered includes: (a) the intentionality of the declarant (if he/she is knowingly lying, if he/she is negligent, if he/she doubts and is not interested in corroborating the veracity, if he/she believes that what he says is true); (b) the damage that its expression can cause in terms of its magnitude (serious, moderate, slight, non-existent); (c) the probability of it taking place (certain, probable, improbable, impossible); and (d) the moment in which it will occur (immediate, near future, not near future, distant future).[94]

To measure the probability of damage, it is also relevant to consider the social position of the speaker, since it clearly affects his or her credibility (a minister of health referring to treatments against COVID-19 is not the same as what can be sustained by any person lacking the support of specific studies). And of course, in order to measure the personal consequences on the speaker, it will be necessary to assess whether specific legal obligations weigh on the speaker to tell the truth or to take any special care before issuing the statement, either because of his or her function or because of having contractually submitted to certain obligations (e.g., the acceptance of uses and conditions of a social network, which establishes guidelines on how to express oneself and the consequences that can lead to the administrator of the network restricting or deleting an account, as happened recently

93 C. Botero Marino, 'La regulación estatal de las llamadas "noticias falsas" desde la perspectiva del derecho a la libertad de expresión', in OAS, Office of the Special Rapporteur for Freedom of Expression, 'Libertad de expresión: A 30 años de la Opinión Consultiva sobre la colegiación obligatoria de periodistas' (Freedom of expression: 30 years after the Advisory Opinion on the compulsory registration of journalists) (2017), www.oas.org/es/cidh/expresion/docs/publicaciones/OC5_ESP.PDF, 65–83.

94 Sunstein, *Liars*, pp. 131, 133.

with the Facebook sanction of former president Donald Trump, whose account was suspended when he was in office and for two years because the expressions dumped on the network incited the assault on the Capitol).

Based on the combination of these parameters, it is clear that actions by both the states and the private sector must be based on a correct weighing of the conflicting interests at stake and, based on this, decide whether and to what extent it is feasible to intervene. In this direction, mathematical formulas similar to the one Susi proposes for the application of the right to be forgotten online (RTBF 2.0), should help.[95]

Facing the crisis generated by disinformation has provoked either state responses that seek to punish administratively or criminally their authors or broadcasters and private responses, based on self-regulations deployed both by social networks (e.g., various tools used by Facebook to facilitate detection and report, such as ranking and flagging; a search initiative, a news literacy campaign, and a monitoring of the work done in News Feed) and other internet service providers (e.g., Google's Fast Check), including non-governmental organisations that check the quality of content that may have a high social impact and warn about its possible falsehood (e.g., at a global level, the Fact Checking Network).

Botero Marino warns that the use of algorithms as a means to combating the spread of fake news is only compatible with freedom of expression, as stated by the special rapporteurs for freedom of expression in their 2017 Joint Declaration, if it: (a) is based on transparent and objectively justifiable criteria, (b) fully guarantees the right to due process of the interested parties, and (c) includes the participation of citizen initiatives dedicated to fact-checking based on transparent codes of ethics.

She also remembers that prohibiting or regulating fake news at the state level is not only not the least restrictive remedy for freedom of expression to combat this particular type of speech, but it is also structurally incompatible with the very functioning of democracy, since in it, the best remedy for lies is free democratic debate. And about fact-checking, she says that, although it is a growing trend, there are still very few organisations that are dedicated to it. For this reason, only for some news is its corresponding fact-check available on the network. There is also the problem that, even with the fact-checking of news, it is not always easy to find it on the World Wide Web. For this reason, different organisations dedicated to fact-checking have designed practical guides so that (in theory) anyone can independently verify any news, such as those of FactChecker.org, AfricaCheck, FullFact, and Les Décodeurs. Even PolitiFact.com offers a blacklist of web portals dedicated to spreading deliberately false information. The common idea behind

95 The Internet Balancing Formula is a mathematical instrument to increase the rational and transparent aspects of balancing conflicting human rights online. It is based on the relative weight and intensity of conflicting rights. The numerical value of these rights is arrived at by applying mathematical scales to various input elements. This formula is easy to use and could be applied globally by private online stakeholders (M. Susi, 'The internet balancing formula' (2019) 25 *European Law Journal* 2, 198–212.).

these guides is, to use the expression of the Supreme Court of the US, that 'each person is his own guardian of the truth'.[96]

11.2.6 *Actions Adopted by the Media and Civil Society Organisations to Detect and Report Fake News*

As mentioned earlier, both the media and civil society organisations have got to work to help detect and consequently combat fake news. Among various initiatives, the creation of websites, extensions for browsers, and applications dedicated to such a combat stand out. In order to provide a few samples, it is worth mentioning the following initiatives:

(a) Maldito Bulo (Damn Hoax): website, more profiles on Twitter, Facebook, and Instagram where false news and hoaxes are reported. Internet users can help by tagging posts with #MalditoBulo.
(b) El Tragabulos (The Gobbler): section of the Verne supplement of the newspaper *El País* aimed at denying hoaxes and identifying false news and information that has become viral through the internet and social networks.
(c) WikiTribune: promoted by one of the co-founders of Wikipedia, it is a collaborative editing project that offers journalistic information verified by experts before publication.
(d) The Trust Project Mirror: various important media outlets (among them, the newspapers *El Mundo* and *El País*) are responsible for alerting the major search engines that the information being disseminated is false.
(e) Canales de Vost Spain (Vost Spain channels): Vost Spain is the platform for emergency volunteers, and it becomes essential for events and emergency notifications.
(f) Salud sin Bulos (Health without hoaxes): this initiative is thanks to the Association of Researchers in eHealth and offers reliable and responsible information on such sensitive issues as health alerts, medicines, and news that affects the health field.
(g) Fake News Detector: extension for Firefox and Chrome browsers that facilitates marking and detecting fake news and reporting it on social network profiles.
(h) Oficina de Seguridad del Internauta (Internet Security Office): warnings and denials of hoaxes are constantly posted on the website, in addition to reporting threats and cybersecurity advice.
(i) Facterbot: provides the user with a bot that periodically sends information about fake news through Facebook Messenger.

[96] Botero Marino, 'La regulación estatal de las llamadas "noticias falsas" desde la perspectiva del derecho a la libertad de expresión', 81–2.

11.2.7 *Actions Adopted by Social Media Platforms: Three Examples*

The first approach by social media companies facing the aforementioned electoral crises of the last decade was very moderate, but the persistence of information disorders, exacerbated by the appearance of COVID-19, provoked important changes and led them to be proactive in fighting against the pernicious effects of fake news. Before the pandemic, platforms had been taking a rather passive role in the face of content causing disinformation by focusing their intervention on the authenticity of the accounts and the visibility of the publications. The leaders of these companies reasonably argued that they should avoid becoming judges of the public debate and also explained that from a commercial and political perspective, arbitrating content was already a costly and time-consuming task, and trying to evaluate the veracity of information would end up confronting social media platforms with political parties, governments, and civil society. In short, in the pre-pandemic world, social media approached disinformation delicately, with a minimal and exceptional intervention in content.

But the COVID-19 emergency constituted the perfect storm and forced the change, and the platforms began to focus on identifying inauthentic actions and judging the content through moderation processes that rely heavily on human analysis through people trained to make complex decisions on a massive scale, without sufficient context, and under a lot of emotional pressure.

The human intervention was inevitable because although algorithms can detect suspicious behaviour, spam, and certain types of content – especially regarding videos and photos – they do not know how to solve dilemmas inherent to the context of an expression, much less decide on the veracity of information. This mode of damage control has been characterised by inconsistent rules and processes with slow transparency progresses.[97]

In this direction, as has been stated in recent studies, these kinds of stakeholders adopted four types of responses:

(a) *Awareness actions*: political actions by the platforms, including partnerships with other actors, the promotion of educational campaigns, digital and media literacy, and so on. These are actions that seek to build a positive ecosystem regarding disinformation, to empower actors and strategies that are expected to combat the phenomenon. By definition, they do not involve changes to the platforms' codes or policies.

(b) *Changes to the code of the platforms*: including changes to the algorithms for recommendations, visibility, and scope of content.

[97] C. Cortés and L. F. Isaza, 'The new normal? Disinformation and content control on social media during COVID-19', CELE, Palermo University, April 2021, www.palermo.edu/Archivos_content/2021/cele/papers/Disinformation-and-Content-Control.pdf.

(c) *Policy changes and moderation actions*: including actions that implement internal policies or external mandates for the removal of content reported as illegal or contrary to community guidelines.
(d) *Transparency and public relations actions*: revealing information about the operation of the platform, generated by the platforms and by independent researchers, and abstract or wishful statements from platforms on how to deal with the challenge of disinformation.[98]

We will now discuss the evolution of the measures adopted, respecting the public interest exception contained in their community rules, by three of the most important social networks: Facebook, Twitter, and YouTube, especially following the two previously mentioned studies.[99]

11.2.7.1 Facebook: Meta

Before the pandemic, the publication of fake news through this platform did not violate its community rules. Therefore, pressured by the facts, governments, civil society organisations, and public opinion, it began to take action against fake news through specific policies, but weighing the public interest at stake with the risk of harm, taking into account international human rights standards and considering in each case several factors, such as the particularities of each country (i.e., if it recognises the freedom of the press, if an election is in progress, or if the country is at war), the content of what was said (i.e., posts that can lead to violence and harm), and if it relates to governance or politics. However, the use of the public interest exception highlighted some inconsistencies.[100]

In the case of publications related to politicians, Mark Zuckerberg alluded to the newsworthiness exception when he stated:

> A handful of times a year, we leave up content that would otherwise violate our policies if the public interest value outweighs the risk of harm. Often, seeing speech

[98] R. Álvarez Ugarte and A. Del Campo, 'Fake news on the Internet: actions and reactions of three platforms', CELE, Palermo University, February 2021, www.palermo.edu/Archivos_content/2021/cele/papers/Fake-news-on-the-Internet-2021.pdf.

[99] Ibid. and Cortés and Isaza, 'The new normal'.

[100] In September 2020, Facebook deleted for violation of its policy against incitement to violence a picture of a candidate (who was later elected) to the United States Congress for the state of Georgia where she posed with a rifle along with three photographs of Democratic politicians. That month, Facebook deleted a post by a Louisiana congressman promising the use of deadly force against protesters. In contrast, the platform kept online a message from President Trump in which he argued, almost threateningly, that 'when the looting starts, the shooting starts' also in the context of a public demonstration. COVID-19 has also shed light on inconsistencies in the use of policies: a video by Jair Bolsonaro in which he spoke in favor of the use of hydroxychloroquine in the treatment of the virus was removed from Facebook in March 2020, but a Trump post with the same message was kept up. However, another message in which Trump compares COVID-19 to the flu was removed from Facebook.

> from politicians is in the public interest, and in the same way that news outlets will report what a politician says, we think people should generally be able to see it for themselves on our platforms.[101]

In any case, he admitted that Facebook would begin to label the content it leaves online, in the application of the exception, and that it would allow people to share it in order to condemn it.

Until 2025 Facebook had the following approach. Generally, it did not remove content, but rather reduced its distribution relying on advanced third-party verification (concrete fact-checking by civil society organisations), alerting the person who saw it or who was going to share it, penalising by reducing its visibility in the news section, and taking restricting actions over the accounts that created or shared it repeatedly. Once a piece of content was flagged, it activated proactive detection methods for possible duplicates.

The company also:

(a) bans the spreading of content that shows, confesses, or encourages acts of physical harm to human beings, false calls to emergency services, or participation in high-risk viral challenges in the community rules, more precisely in the section 'coordinating harm and publicizing crime',
(b) as reported in blog posts, deleted disinformation about health that may contribute to imminent physical harm, and
(c) focuses significant efforts on identifying 'information or influence operations', such as coordinated actions that use automated and human accounts to amplify content, intimidate other users, and capture conversations and trends.[102]

Since January 2020, when COVID-19 was not yet a global pandemic, the company announced that it was controlling disinformation in labelling, filtering, and content removal and would disable the option to search for virus-related augmented reality effects on Instagram; excluded content or organic accounts related to COVID-19 from the recommendations; and alerted people who had interacted with content (with 'likes', reactions, or comments) that had been discredited, including recommendations for reliable information, practices that were extended to Instagram.

The company adopted various measures concerning paid advertising: the content to be advertised was previously presented by the contracting parties and approved or not by the platform (in the second case if there were possible violations to the community rules), so there is no content removal but unauthorised content.

[101] BBC, 'Facebook to tag "harmful" posts as boycott widens', 27 June 2020, www.bbc.com/news/business-53196487.

[102] Meta, 'Community standards', https://transparency.meta.com/en-gb/policies/community-standards/?source=https%3A%2F%2Fwww.facebook.com%2Fcommunitystandards%2F.

In this direction, before the declaration of the pandemic, the platform banned ads that sought to create panic or denote urgency regarding supplies and products linked to COVID-19 and that guaranteed the cure or prevention of the virus, and in March 2020 banned sales of COVID-19 masks, hand sanitisers, disinfecting wipes, and test kits, but from August allowed the promotion of non-medical masks (subject to compliance with certain requirements), hand sanitisers, and disinfecting wipes.

With the approval of COVID-19 vaccines, they began to remove false claims (such as the ones that affirmed that the vaccines are a cure for the virus) and conspiracy theories about them that could cause harm in accordance with the opinion of public health experts and authorities. It also banned advertised content where vaccination kits were sold or accelerated access to the vaccine was promoted, when the vaccines were near to being available. And similar actions were taken regarding advertised content that may affect the availability of biosafety items, even if the advertisements are not misinformative.

11.2.7.2 Twitter [X]

Twitter traditionally sustained that it should not become an arbiter of the truth owing to its nature as an open platform. However, before 2020, Twitter changed the community policies and confronted misinformation by focusing more on the activity of actors (accounts), rather than on the content, concentrating its efforts on avoiding automated use of the platform for manipulation purposes. The company began to include some prohibitions related to disinformation in the context of electoral processes, prohibiting the posting of misleading information about how to participate, voter suppression, and intimidating content, and false or misleading information about political affiliations. Then, the platform introduced the possibility for users to report tweets that violate this Election Integrity policy (later renamed Civic Integrity policy, facing the 2020 US census and presidential election campaign).

Twitter turned from being the platform that intervened the least in user content to the most active, but applying the public interest test, considering that a piece of content is of public interest to be weighed against the possible risk and severity of damage 'if it constitutes a direct contribution to the understanding or debate of a matter that concerns the whole public'. In this regard, the community rules consider that the exception is:

(a) more likely to apply in some cases (e.g., hate speech or harassment, or when the tweet includes a call to action), and
(b) less likely to apply (e.g., in cases of terrorism, violence, or electoral integrity, when the tweet is directed at government officials or when it provides important context for ongoing geopolitical events).

No exceptions are made for multimedia content related to child sexual exploitation, non-consensual nudity, and violent sexual assault on victims.[103]

In October 2019, Twitter addressed the use of the exception for world leaders in order to ensure people's right to know about their leaders and demand accountability. When using the exception, a filter can be put in place.[104]

In March 2020, the platform warned that it would expand its definition of harm to include content that goes directly against the instructions of authorised sources in global and local public health.[105] Then, it prohibited tweets that deny the recommendations of the authorities with the intention that people act against them, encourage breaking social distancing, recommend ineffective treatments (even if they are not harmful or if they are shared humorously), recommend harmful treatments, deny scientific data on the transmission of the disease, make statements that incite action, cause panic, discomfort, or disorder on a large scale, include false or misleading information about the diagnosis or make claims that specific groups or nationalities are not susceptible or are more susceptible to the virus. In this direction, the platform acted on tweets from presidents Bolsonaro and Trump and even temporarily suspended the account of Trump's lawyer, Rudy Giuliani, for similar reasons.[106]

The exceptions only apply to tweets from elected and government officials, and candidates for political office. If a tweet covered by this exception is kept online, Twitter adds a warning or filter that provides context about the breach of the rules (before someone can view the content, an interstitial warning appears). This also makes the tweet not recommended by the Twitter algorithm and limits the ability of users to interact with what is posted. Twitter applied the exception to a tweet by Donald Trump for violation of its rules on disinformation and COVID-19.[107] However, the implementation of these measures was not consistent and has interpretative issues.[108]

[103] X, 'The X rules', https://help.x.com/en/rules-and-policies/x-rules.

[104] J. C. Wong, 'Twitter lays out rules for world leaders amid pressure to rein in Trump', 16 October 2019, www.theguardian.com/us-news/2019/oct/15/twitter-explains-how-it-handles-world-leaders-amid-pressure-to-rein-in-trump.

[105] A. Hern, 'Twitter to remove harmful fake news about coronavirus', 19 March 2020, *The Guardian*, www.theguardian.com/world/2020/mar/19/twitter-to-remove-harmful-fake-news-about-coronavirus.

[106] T. Porter, 'Twitter deleted a tweet by Rudy Giuliani for spreading coronavirus misinformation', 29 March 2020, *Business Insider*, www.businessinsider.com/coronavirus-twitter-deletes-giuliani-tweet-for-spreading-misinformation-2020-3.

[107] G. Kolata and R. C. Rabin, '"Don't be afraid of Covid", Trump says, undermining public health messages', 5 October 2020, *New York Times*, www.nytimes.com/2020/10/05/health/trump-covid-public-health.html.

[108] While a couple of tweets from the then president of the US, Donald Trump, did not warrant any response from Twitter – a decision that would be explained by reasons of public interest – the platform did act on a tweet from the former president of Brazil, Jair Bolsonaro, and even temporarily suspended the account of Trump's lawyer, Rudy Giuliani, for similar reasons. Thread published by President Trump on 21 March 2020, where he promotes unproven medical treatments against COVID-19. This tweet promoting the use of hydroxychloroquine, published on March 27, 2020, was deleted by Twitter

In May 2020, Twitter updated its approach related to COVID-19 information and explained that it will act on content based on misleading information, controversial statements, and unverified claims, but will remove content only in cases of misleading information with a propensity for severe harm, and for all other cases will use labels (phrases below the tweet, accompanied by an exclamation mark, referring to reliable information) and filters or notices (hiding the questioned tweet to notify the user that the content differs from the guidance of public health experts).[109]

Regarding ads, since April 2020, Twitter has banned sensationalist or panic-inducing content and advertisements with inflated prices. Likewise, it prohibited the sale of masks and sanitisers and did not allow mention of vaccines, treatments, or test kits, except for information published by media outlets that the platform exempts under its policy of political advertisements (afterwards, in August 2020, these bans were limited to medical masks).

Since the acquisition of the company by Elon Musk, freedom of expression has been strengthened in the policies of use, as expressed by its new owner, when he stated in a tweet published in November 2022: 'New Twitter policy is freedom of speech, but not freedom of reach. Negative/hate tweets will be max deboosted & demonetised, so no ads or other revenue to Twitter. You won't find the tweet unless you specifically seek it out, which is no different from rest of Internet.'[110]

11.2.7.3 YouTube

YouTube's general strategy against disinformation rests on three principles:

(a) the preservation of content on the platform unless it violates its community guidelines,
(b) the possibility of monetising publications is a privilege, and
(c) the videos must meet exacting standards for the platform to recommend them.[111]

The Community Guidelines do not properly regulate the public interest exception, but the platform's chief executive officer has argued that they could keep content posted by politicians that violates its rules because it is important for people to know what they think. Other exceptions are granted to certain kinds of speech with

and earned Giuliani the temporary suspension of his account. In November 2020, the vice-president of the company argued, in a hearing before the US Congress, that Donald Trump would not have these protections when his term ends, which is questionable.

109 Y. Roth and N. Pickles, 'Updating our approach to misleading information', 11 May 2020, X blog, https://blog.x.com/en_us/topics/product/2020/updating-our-approach-to-misleading-information.

110 E. Musk's post on Twitter, 18 November 2022, https://twitter.com/elonmusk/status/159367333982621286 4?s=48&t=7Bs_I1KvLcG_xO5uZgOZTQ.

111 YouTube, 'Community guidelines', www.youtube.com/howyoutubeworks/policies/community-guidelines/.

educational, documentary, scientific or artistic content, but are not applicable in cases of harmful or dangerous content, violent or graphic content, incitement to hatred or violence, publications that promote, recommend, or assert that the use of harmful substances or treatments may have health benefits, and that manipulate or modify content that seeks to deceive the user and may involve serious risk of blatant harm.[112]

Trying to ensure authentic behaviour, YouTube prohibits publications that deceptively seek to redirect users to other sites or artificially increase engagement metrics (views, comments, 'likes'), as well as creating playlists with misleading titles or descriptions that make users believe that they will watch different videos than those in the list. Furthermore, only quality videos can be monetised, but in each intervention with the published content, YouTube always analyses the context to understand the intent of a video.[113]

The eruption of the COVID-19 pandemic led to the creation of a new 'policy on medical misinformation related to Covid-19', and owing to its 'serious risk of flagrant harm' it removed content that discloses erroneous medical information that contradicts the guidelines of the World Health Organization or local health authorities regarding the treatment, prevention, diagnosis, or transmission of the virus. With the first violation, the user receives a warning, and after a strike is added, three strikes results in permanent removal of the channel.[114]

11.3 BRIEF CONCLUSIONS

As initially stated, fake news is not a new phenomenon, but in the heat of the unthinkable technological changes that have taken place in recent decades (especially in the last two), they have become a huge problem for societies in general and particularly in the functioning of democracies, constituting an enormous challenge both for the international community and for governments, companies, and civil society.

The regulation of fake news became essential for various political reasons and owing to public health, both events that emerged with great force in the last half of the past decade, but regulation is still incomplete and in some cases confusing.

What is not in doubt, beyond the conflicts when dealing with freedom of expression, is the need for the regulation that has existed up to now, whether international, national, or from the private sector, to deepen, with clear and homogeneous guidelines across the globe, good practices, and intelligent initiatives, and in this, international cooperation becomes essential.

The task is not easy, but it is not impossible to carry out either. Let us keep working on it.

112 Ibid.

113 Ibid.

114 YouTube, 'Policy on medical misinformation related to Covid-19', https://support.google.com/youtube/answer/13813322?hl=et&ref_topic=9282436&visit_id=638734359219561926-1572933843&rd=1.

12

Online Freedom of Expression

A New EU Imperialism?

Philippe Jougleux

12.1 INTRODUCTION

The term 'European imperialism' in reference to the European Union (EU) legislator's actions emerged in the context of internet law concerning data protection.[1] Europeans have recognised the futility of creating one of the world's most robust data subject protection systems without ensuring its effectiveness beyond their borders. Consequently, the EU legislator introduced various mechanisms explicitly aimed at ensuring the global applicability of the EU General Data Protection Regulation (GDPR). These mechanisms include controlling the transnational flow of data and extending the GDPR's reach to any online platform actively seeking to collect personal data from European citizens. As a side effect, European data protection regulations not only impacted the digital lives of millions of Europeans but also indirectly influenced the legal frameworks of numerous countries seeking to maintain e-commerce ties with the EU, primarily the US,[2] notwithstanding the role of China as a third pillar in this game of internet governance,[3] an analysis of its role and influence would exceed the limits of this research.

Such an evolution was inevitable because, by its very nature, the internet has global reach. Regulating the internet on a regional basis is feasible but will invariably have worldwide implications. Similarly, freedom of expression and its boundaries constitutes another global struggle involving various actors. The American perspective on freedom of expression holds sway on the internet by default, considering that all five 'GAFAM' (Google, Amazon, Facebook – now Meta, Apple, Microsoft) companies are headquartered in California. Indeed, the fight for digital

[1] C. Mannion, 'Data imperialism: the GDPR's disastrous impact on Africa's e-commerce markets' (2020) 53 *Vanderbilt Journal of Transnational Law* 2, 685–711.

[2] M. Klar, 'Binding effects of the European General Data Protection Regulation (GDPR) on US companies' (2020) 11 *Hastings Science & Technology Law Journal* 2, 101–54.

[3] J. T. Pigatto, M. W. Datysgeld, and L. G. P. D. Silva, 'Internet governance is what global stakeholders make of it: a tripolar approach' (2021) 64 *Revista Brasileira de Política Internacional* 2, e011.

sovereignty is, first of all, a fight of states against companies.[4] The EU legislator is then faced with an impossible dilemma – since a regional response in a globalised environment is doomed to fail, should it grant its legislation global reach, falling into a sort of digital imperialism and provoking economic conflict with its partners (mainly, the US), or should it restrict itself to regional scope?

This chapter will first examine the various interventions made by the EU legislator in the field of internet law that have directly affected freedom of expression worldwide (Section 12.2). This examination is crucial not only because it establishes substantial elements of the law regarding legitimate restrictions on freedom of expression, but also because it expressly focuses on the responsibilities of online service providers. Subsequently, it will demonstrate how this perspective clashes with the American philosophy on freedom of expression (Section 12.3). In light of the imminent prospect of a fragmented and divided internet, there is a pressing need to rethink online freedom of expression on an international scale and to seek consensus (Section 12.4).

12.2 THE BIRTH OF AN EU INTERNET LAW AND ITS IMPACT ON ONLINE FREEDOM OF EXPRESSION

In this section, some examples of recent interventions from the EU legislator or developments from the European courts that have an impact on freedom of expression will be described, with emphasis on their explicit or implicit, and regional or global, reach. More specifically, the following topics will be analysed as legitimate interferences with freedom of expression from the European perspective: the rise of filters in online copyright law (Section 2.1), the question of the reach of injunctions in the context of the protection of reputation (Section 2.2), the innovations inserted by the Digital Service Act (Section 2.3), the measures taken at European level to fight the propagation of hate speech in digital environments (Section 2.4), the right to be forgotten (Section 2.5), and pictures of sexual content (Section 2.6).

12.2.1 *Copyright Law*

The enforcement of copyright law online is likely one of the most characteristic areas where a united position gradually diverged into substantial differences between US and EU perspectives. It cannot be denied that the EU's original stance on this issue, as expressed through the E-Commerce Directive (Directive 2000/31), which implemented a safe harbour protecting online intermediaries from liability, was heavily influenced by the American Digital Millennium Copyright Act, signed in 1998. It is worth noting that the regulation establishes the principle of prohibiting

[4] L. Floridi, 'The fight for digital sovereignty: what it is, and why it matters, especially for the EU' (2020) 33 *Philosophy & Technology* 3, 369–78.

general internet monitoring, which remains in force today. However, as discussed later, efforts to create mechanisms of a priori control of the content have multiplied.

However, Europe's position shifted, primarily through judicial activism, particularly in its strict interpretation of the safe harbour under 'passive role' theory.[5] The focus on a strict notice and takedown procedure inherently carries the danger of a 'broad censorial attitude',[6] with adverse effects on freedom of expression.[7]

Furthermore, *Telekabel* jurisprudence paved the way for a new mode of the online enforcement of copyright law at the expense of freedom of expression.[8] In this case, the European Court of Justice (ECJ) admitted that an injunction against an internet service provider requesting the intermediary to implement filtering measures to block access to a website infringing copyright does not violate freedom of expression. This stance can be seen as a form of censorship, as it blocks user access to online information. However, the Court takes care to add two fundamental safeguards: the injunction should be effective, and it should never have the effect of blocking access to legal content.

One of the most significant and widely discussed interventions of the EU legislator regarding freedom of expression for copyright protection is Article 17 of Directive 2019/790. The purpose of Article 17 is to compel major internet service providers (modelled after Alphabet's YouTube platform) to install filters that automatically block the uploading of copyright-infringing content. However, after extensive discussions and political negotiations, the term 'filter' itself does not appear in the final text of the Article. Article 17(4) only states that online service providers must make their best efforts to block this content; otherwise, they cannot rely on the old safe harbour mechanism.

Similar to the *Telekabel* case, it is evident how this regulation directly impacts freedom of expression. As a form of censorship, providers are required to block any attempts by users to communicate. This issue was immediately brought to the attention of the ECJ, which issued its ruling in the *EU Commission vs. Poland* case. The Court considered that Article 17(4) should indeed be interpreted as a restriction on freedom of expression. Still, it justified this restriction by citing the legitimate interest of protecting the rights holders. The Court outlined multiple safeguards: a system of internal and swift complaint mechanisms against abuse, limiting the filter to identified and protected works of intellectual property, restricting the filter's algorithm to obvious situations of plagiarism, and protecting fundamental rights through exceptions such as short citations and parody.

5 Case C-324/09, *L'Oréal SA and Others v. eBay International AG and Others* [2011], ECLI:EU:C:2011:474.

6 G. Sartor, 'Providers liability: from the eCommerce Directive to the future' (2017), Directorate General for Internal Policies, European Parliament, IP/A/IMCO/2017-07, 13.

7 A. Kuczerawy, 'Intermediary liability & freedom of expression: recent developments in the EU notice & action initiative' (2015) 31 *Computer Law and Security Review* 1, 46–56.

8 Case C-314/12, *UPC Telekabel Wien GmbH v. Constantin Film Verleih GmbH and Wega Filmproduktionsgesellschaft mbH* [2014], ECLI:EU:C:2014:192.

12.2.2 *Protection of Reputation*

The ECJ's landmark case, *Eva Glawischnig-Piesczek v. Facebook*,[9] initially arose as a classic defamation and right of publicity case. Someone on the social media platform Facebook posted a photograph of a famous politician along with personal insults. Importantly, the victim in this case not only requested the removal of the illegal content from the platform but also asked Meta to take adequate measures to ensure that the same or similar content would not be posted again in the future. Once again, the question of prior control of content through filtering, or preventive censorship, arose. The Court had to evaluate the legality of such an injunction.

The judges accepted that such an injunction may be legal, provided that it is not interpreted as imposing on the host provider an obligation to generally monitor the information it stores or to actively seek facts or circumstances indicating illegal activity. In other words, the provider would only have an obligation to make reasonable efforts to block the same content.

This case is particularly important in the context of this chapter as it explicitly addresses the issue of the global or regional reach of EU internet law. Regarding the question of the worldwide or regional impact of such an injunction, the ECJ concluded that the E-Commerce Directive does not impose any limitation, including a territorial one, on the scope of measures that Member States are entitled to adopt in accordance with the directive.[10] Therefore, there is no reason to limit the territorial impact of such an injunction.

12.2.3 *The Digital Service Act (DSA)*

The substantial impact of the DSA is well documented,[11] as research already pointed out before the regulation was adopted.[12] The regulation substantially built on the acquis of the E-Commerce Directive, preferring a system of self-moderation to state-censorship. Under this system, the primary responsibility for notifying and reporting content that allegedly violates the terms and conditions of the service lies with the users of the online service. The platform, in turn, has a duty to respond and intervene as necessary.

9 Case C-18/18, *Eva Glawischnig-Piesczek v. Facebook Ireland Limited* [2019], ECLI:EU:C:2019:821.

10 Ibid., para. 49.

11 Regulation (EU) 2022/2065 of the European Parliament and of the Council of 19 October 2022 on a Single Market for Digital Services and amending Directive 2000/31/EC (Digital Services Act), OJ L 277, 27.10.2022.

12 V. Golunova and J. M. Regules, 'The Digital Services Act and freedom of expression: triumph or failure?' (2021), www.hiig.de/en/the-digital-services-act-and-freedom-of-expression-triumph-or-failure/; J. Barata, 'The Digital Services Act and its impact on the right to freedom of expression: special focus on risk mitigation obligations (2021)', Platforma por la Libertad de Infoacion, https://libertadinformacion.cc/wp-content/uploads/2021/06/DSA-AND-ITS-IMPACT-ON-FREEDOM-OF-EXPRESSION-JOAN-BARATA-PDLI.pdf, 12.

At the forefront of this attention is once again the adoption of content-filtering technology. For very large online platforms (VLOPs) and search engines, defined by a set of strict economic conditions, the DSA takes a significant step away from the classic safe harbour approach and imposes a duty to mitigate the risks of illegal content proliferation.

Article 34 introduces a risk assessment, designed to tailor the VLOP's obligations to the specific dangers associated with their platforms. Article 35 builds upon this risk assessment by requiring VLOPs to implement 'reasonable, proportionate, and effective mitigation measures' to address these risks.

Officially, the DSA is presented as an act aimed at protecting digital sovereignty. However, the global reach of such a transformative regulation is evident and not hidden. For example, the EU Commission's website states that one of the DSA's two goals is 'to establish a level playing field to foster innovation, growth, and competitiveness, both in the European Single Market and globally'.[13] Consequently, it has already been observed that this practical function of the DSA as the global regulator of the internet 'will likely provoke a clash in free expression standards between the U.S. and the EU'.[14]

12.2.4 *Online Hate Speech*

There is a strong international legal background concerning the prevention of hate speech proliferation online. The most fundamental milestone at the international level is the first Additional Protocol to the Convention of Europe, commonly known as the Budapest Convention, on cybercrime.[15] Nevertheless, hate speech does constitute one of the most sensitive issues between the US and EU from the perspective of the delimitation of the boundaries of freedom of expression. It should be noted that the US, while participating in the drafting of the text, chose not to sign the first Additional Protocol covering the criminalisation of acts of a racist and xenophobic nature committed through computer systems.[16] In parallel, in the EU, the EU legislator decided to integrate this criminalisation of public incitement to violence or hatred into EU law. Council Framework Decision 2008/913 states:[17] 'Each Member State shall take the measures necessary to ensure that the following intentional conduct is punishable: (a) publicly inciting to violence or hatred directed

[13] European Commission, 'The Digital Services Act package', https://digital-strategy.ec.europa.eu/en/policies/digital-services-act-package.

[14] I. Tourkochoriti, 'The Digital Services Act and the EU as the global regulator of the Internet' (2023) 24 *Chicago Journal of International Law* 1, 129–47.

[15] Convention on Cybercrime, Budapest, 23 November 2001, ETS No. 185.

[16] Additional Protocol to the Convention on Cybercrime, concerning the criminalisation of acts of a racist and xenophobic nature committed through computer system, Strasbourg, 28 January 2003, ETS No. 189.

[17] Council Framework Decision 2008/913/JHA of 28 November 2008 on combating certain forms and expressions of racism and xenophobia by means of criminal law, OJ L 328, 6.12.2008, 55–8.

against a group of persons or a member of such a group defined by reference to race, colour, religion, descent, or national or ethnic origin'.[18]

In contrast, in the US, hate speech is protected by the First Amendment. For example, in a case related to a trademark allegedly using a racial slur, the Supreme Court determined that the registration office was not entitled to refuse its registration. The Court held that 'Speech that demeans on the basis of race, ethnicity, gender, religion, age, disability, or any other similar ground is hateful; but the proudest boast of our free speech jurisprudence is that we protect the freedom to express the thought that we hate'.[19]

The EU legal framework is not limited to the criminalisation of hate speech. Through soft law, specifically the EU Code of Conduct against online hate speech, the EU legislator aimed to engage major internet actors in the fight against hate speech. Furthermore, with the support of new powers provided by the DSA, the Commission may enforce this code of conduct and monitor its application. The DSA specifically mentions 'illegal hate speech' as one area where the mitigation duty of VLOPs must differ from general moderation policies, particularly in terms of speed and effectiveness (Article 35(1)(c) of the DSA refers to expeditious removal or disabling access to hate speech, and adds that dedicated resources for content moderation must be adopted). These efforts aim to compel internet service providers to structurally modify their services and integrate hate speech moderation in their design.

12.2.5 *The Right to Be Forgotten in the* Google Spain *Jurisprudence*

The circumstances and findings of the landmark *Google Spain* decision are well known.[20] The ECJ determined that freedom of expression, specifically the right to be informed, should yield to the data subject's right to 'oblivion', and in certain circumstances, the data subject is entitled to request that a search engine remove online content that reveals their personal data.

It should be immediately noted that this limitation on freedom of expression is not absolute. First, the right pertains not to the existence of the content itself online but only to it being referenced by search engines. Second, in light of the principle of proportionality, it must be demonstrated that there is an effective legitimate interest justifying the request for de-referencing and that, conversely, the information is not of sufficient public interest for the right to be informed to prevail.[21]

Therefore, the right to be forgotten is aptly named, as time itself is not the sole factor in assessing the various legitimate interests. For instance, the accuracy of the

[18] Ibid., Article 1(1).

[19] *Matal v. Tam*, 582 US 218 (2017).

[20] Case C-131/12, *Google Spain and Google* (GC) [2014], ECLI:EU:C:2014:317.

[21] C. M. Wulff, 'The right to be forgotten in post-Google Spain case law: an example of legal interpretivism in action?' (2020) 26 *Comparative Law Review* 1, 255–79.

information plays a more crucial role. In cases involving fake news, for example, search engines may be compelled to comply with de-referencing requests, as evidenced in the case of *Google (Déréférencement d'un contenu prétendument inexact)*.[22] Nevertheless, the passage of time remains significant, assuming that the public interest in current information decreases over time.

Once again, the practical importance of this right raises questions about its reach. Should the right influence the behaviour of search engines worldwide, or should it only have regional applicability? This issue was addressed in the *Google v. CNIL* case,[23] where, this time, the theory of global reach was rejected by the Court. Specifically, the ECJ concluded that an:

> operator is not required to carry out that dereferencing on all versions of its search engine but on the versions of that search engine corresponding to all the Member States, using, where necessary, measures which, while meeting the legal requirements, effectively prevent or, at the very least, seriously discourage an internet user conducting a search from one of the Member States on the basis of a data subject's name from gaining access, via the list of results displayed following that search, to the links which are the subject of that request.

12.2.6 *The Fight against Child Pornography*

It might have been expected that a consensus would be reached on combating the highly sensitive issue of child pornography. Indeed, under the framework of the Budapest Convention on cybercrime, both the US and the EU agree on repressing this form of communication. However, an issue has been left to the appreciation of the convention's signatories, illustrating the extent of the conceptual divergences between Americans and Europeans regarding the topic of freedom of expression.

Indeed, in EU Directive 2011/93/EU on combating the sexual abuse and sexual exploitation of children and child pornography,[24] child pornography is defined in four alternative ways, aligning with the definition provided by the Budapest Convention on cybercrime. More interestingly, the fourth alternative definition considers as child pornography 'realistic images of a child engaged in sexually explicit conduct or realistic images of the sexual organs of a child, for primarily sexual purposes'. This means that even in the absence of real abuse, the mere drawing or computer-imaging of a situation of child abuse is considered child pornography. This definition therefore encompasses various modern techniques such as deepfakes

[22] Case C-460/20, *Google (Déréférencement d'un contenu prétendument inexact)* [2022], ECLI:EU:C:2022:962.

[23] Case C-507/17, *Google v. CNIL* [2019], ECLI:EU:C:2019:772.

[24] Directive 2011/93/EU of the European Parliament and of the Council of 13 December 2011 on combating the sexual abuse and sexual exploitation of children and child pornography, and replacing Council Framework Decision 2004/68/JHA, OJ L 335, 17.12.2011, 1–14.

(replacing a face in a video with another),[25] or AI-generated pictures and videos.[26] By contrast, in the US, the case of *Ashcroft v. Free Speech Coalition* limits the range of the definition of child pornography to real content only,[27] considering that in the case of imaginary content (even realistic) freedom of speech should prevail. This stance is generally considered incompatible with the Budapest Convention, which acknowledges virtual child pornography and calls for its criminalisation.[28] However, on the aftermath of the decision in *Ashcroft*, the American Congress added what could be seen as a very restrictive interpretation of the Convention, amending the law and limiting the ban to any visual depiction 'that is, or is indistinguishable from, that of a minor engaging in sexually explicit conduct'.[29]

Moreover, the EU has engaged in discussions on a more active implication of online platforms in fighting child pornography. More specifically, the EU Commission has proposed a new regulation in 2022 to Prevent and Combat Child Sexual Abuse (CSA).[30] The text has created controversy and the opposition of the EU Parliament and the Council, as it aims to impose advanced moderation and detection duties to online service providers. The complimentary impact assessment produced by the European Parliament's Committee on Civil Liberties, Justice and Home Affairs was, in particular, extremely critical of the proposal.[31] It details how the new legislation would infringe the prohibition of general monitoring and the prohibition of general data retention principles that are enshrined in EU law and developed in the ECJ's case law. While a detailed analysis of this proposal and of the subsequent criticism would exceed the limits of this present research, it should be mentioned that the CSA regulation, if adopted, would have substantial consequences worldwide, as it would force online service providers to rethink how and when encrypted end-to-end communication services are provided to users.

12.3 FREEDOM OF EXPRESSION VERSUS FREEDOM OF SPEECH: THE FALSE TWINS

This section conducts a comparative analysis of the concept of freedom of expression in the EU and the US. As previously discussed, the US serves as the de facto

25 M. H. Maras and A. Alexandrou, 'Determining authenticity of video evidence in the age of artificial intelligence and in the wake of Deepfake videos' (2019) 23 *The International Journal of Evidence and Proof* 3, 255–62.

26 C. Ratner, 'When "sweetie" is not so sweet: artificial intelligence and its implications for child pornography' (2021) 59 *Family Court Review* 2, 386–401.

27 *Ashcroft v. Free Speech Coalition*, 535 US 234 (2002).

28 Budapest Convention, Article 9(2)(c).

29 PROTECT Act, 18 USC § 2252(B)(b).

30 Proposal for a Regulation of the European Parliament and of the Council laying down rules to prevent and combat child sexual abuse, COM/2022/209 final.

31 Op 't Hoog et al., *Proposal for A Regulation Laying Down the Rules to Prevent and Combat Child Sexual Abuse: Complementary Impact Assessment* (Brussels: European Union, 2023).

model for information technology (IT) companies regarding freedom of expression, operating under the belief that this notion possesses a consensual and universally accepted definition in all modern democracies. First, the conceptual differences between European freedom of expression and the American freedom of speech will be explored (Section 3.1), and then the practical example of the recent policies adopted by X (formerly Twitter) will be used as a case study to illustrate these divergences (Section 3.2).

12.3.1 *Freedom of Expression versus Freedom of Speech*

While there is consensus that freedom of expression is one of the fundamental pillars of democracy, this unanimity conceals a significant divergence of viewpoints regarding its definition.

In the US, freedom of speech is defined with reference to the famous theory of the marketplace of ideas. In a dissenting opinion in the landmark case of *Abrams v. United States*,[32] Justice Oliver Wendell Holmes argued that the First Amendment protects the right to dissent in response to the government's viewpoints and objectives. The theory of the marketplace of ideas posits that truth and by extension the common good will naturally emerge from the free exchange of ideas. In other words, all ideas should be freely expressed because they all contribute to the formation of a well-informed public opinion. In 1969, the US Supreme Court's decision in *Brandenburg v. Ohio* solidified this theory as the dominant public policy in US free speech law,[33] explaining that the government cannot penalise inflammatory speech unless that speech is 'directed at inciting or producing imminent lawless action and is likely to incite or produce such action'.

Nevertheless, multiple authors have warned against an overly literal interpretation of the theory of the marketplace of ideas. It has been pointed out that the classical interpretation depends on impossible assumptions for its coherence,[34] and Gordon in 1997 demonstrated that the theory, taken absolutely, would only create a situation where the views of the most powerful and/or the most numerous prevail.[35] In consequence, the theory of the marketplace of ideas has evolved over time. For instance, in the landmark *Edwards v. Aguillard* (1987) case, the US Supreme Court considered that a law stating that if one theory is exposed at school, the other theory must also be presented (referring to the principle of natural evolution, as opposed to the dogma of creationism), is unconstitutional.[36]

32 *Abrams v. United States*, 250 US 616 (1919).

33 *Brandenburg v. Ohio*, 395 US 444 (1969).

34 C. E. Baker, 'Scope of the First Amendment freedom of speech' (1977) 25 *UCLA Law Review* 964. See also S. Ingber, 'The marketplace of ideas: a legitimizing myth' (1984) 1 *Duke Law Journal* 1, 1–91.

35 J. Gordon, 'John Stuart Mill and the "marketplace of ideas"' (1997) 23 *Social Theory and Practice* 2, 235–49.

36 *Edwards v. Aguillard*, 482 US 578 (1987).

In Europe, on the contrary, the indelible scars of the Holocaust have led to the adoption of a rather different stance on freedom of expression. In this context, a free marketplace of ideas is considered a utopia. Under the prism, implicitly, of the theory of memes,[37] society is seen as an ecosystem where some ideas act as viruses, contaminating people's minds and jeopardising democracy. Therefore, freedom of expression, as enshrined in Article 10 of the Convention on Human Rights and Article 11 of the Charter of Fundamental Rights, is not perceived as absolute, as illustrated in the famous 'little red schoolbook' case.[38] While restrictions on freedom of expression are accepted, they must pass a three-part test, as recast in cases such as *Mouvement Raëlien Suisse v. Switzerland*,[39] and *Animal Defenders International v. the United Kingdom*;[40] the limitation must be provided by law, pursue a legitimate aim, and be necessary in a democratic society. This last condition has been further explained by case law, with emphasis on the notion of the 'pressing need of society'. In other words, for a restriction to freedom of expression to be legitimate in the European perspective, it is not enough for the restriction to serve a public interest. The restriction must be unavoidable in a democratic society. All the restrictions analysed above (copyright law, child pornography, protection of reputation, data protection, hate speech) have been subjected to the three-part test.

It is commonly accepted that the American philosophy of freedom of speech is much broader than the European one, but it is essential to temper this notion, as in some respects, the American concept is more restrictive than the European one. First, the American human rights framework has primarily been constructed as a defence mechanism against state intrusion, under the 'state action doctrine',[41] resulting in the impossibility of horizontal application. Meanwhile, in European traditions, some forms of horizontal application are permitted.[42] Second, American freedom of speech is largely conceived from an individualistic standpoint, whereas the European perspective could be described as multidimensional, encompassing not only the freedom to express ideas but also the protection of pluralism,[43] and the right to be informed.[44]

In conclusion, the American and European approaches to freedom of expression converge in terms of their core, which is the right to provoke. However, the

37 R. Brodie, *Virus of the Mind: The New Science of the Meme* (Carlsbad: Hay House, Inc, 2009).

38 *Handyside v. UK*, Application no. 5493/72, Judgment of 7 December 1976.

39 *Mouvement raëlien suisse v. Switzerland* [GC], Application no. 16354/06, Judgment of 13 July 2012.

40 *Animal Defenders International v. the United Kingdom* [GC], Application no. 48876/08, Judgment of 22 April 2013.

41 W. R. Huhn, 'The state action doctrine and the principle of democratic choice' (2005) 34 *Hofstra Law Review* 4, 1379–460.

42 E. Frantziou, 'The horizontal effect of the Charter of Fundamental Rights of the EU: rediscovering the reasons for horizontality' (2015) 21 *European Law Journal* 5, 657–79.

43 *Centro Europa 7 S.R.L. and Di Stefano v. Italy*, Application no. 38433/09, Judgment of 7 June 2012.

44 *Association BURESTOP 55 et autres c. France*, Application no. 56176/18 et al., Judgment of 1 July 2021.

various social functions of freedom, its role in society, and, most importantly, its limits are subjects of significant divergence between the birthplace of the internet and the EU.

12.3.2 *Case Study: The Situation of X (formerly Twitter)*

The recent policy changes of X (formerly Twitter) following its acquisition by Elon Musk should be used as a case study to illustrate the potential conflicts that can arise from this divergence. Indeed, the new president of the famous social media platform, who is a self-declared free speech absolutist,[45] has chosen to implement an orthodox American freedom of speech's perspective on X's functioning and moderation policies.

Consequently, the company lost around half of its workforce in 2022 (among them a substantial percentage were employees who focused on ethics and moderation) and then started to reinstall contentious accounts that had been suspended. Unsurprisingly, the platform almost immediately saw a rise in hate speech in its content.[46]

However, according to Twitter's advertising audience data from July 2022, the social network currently has 30.6 million users in Western Europe, and 27.2 million in Northern Europe.[47] Therefore, it is not surprising that, when Elon Musk tweeted 'the bird is freed' (after acquiring the company), the Internal Market Commissioner Thierry Breton replied '[i]n Europe, the bird will fly by our rules'.[48] Furthermore, in 2023, the European Commission Vice President focused on X in a press statement, highlighting the misfunctioning moderation system of the platform.[49]

Indeed, data shows that X is having the 'largest ratio of mis/disinformation posts' among platforms that submitted reports to the EU. In the context of information wars and while the existence of 'fake news factories' have been demonstrated,[50] the reactions of the EU and the US diverge again, as they are based on their definition of freedom of expression. The EU pushes for stricter control of posted content; for

45 A. Hassan, 'Is the bird free? The implication of Elon Musk's Twitter takeover', 7 November 2022, https://papers.ssrn.com/sol3/papers.cfm?abstract_id=4488697.

46 B. Benton et al., 'Hate speech spikes on Twitter after Elon Musk acquires the platform', 1 November 2022, School of Communication and Media, Montclair State University, www.montclair.edu/school-of-communication-and-media/wp-content/uploads/sites/20/2022/11/Montclair-State-SCM-Study-Increases-in-Twitter-Hate-Speech-After-Elon-Musks-Acquisition.pdf.

47 A. Turner, 'How many users does X (formerly Twitter) have?' (2024), www.bankmycell.com/blog/how-many-users-does-twitter-have.

48 W. Preussen, 'EU Commissioner to Elon Musk: Twitter will play by our rules', 28 October 2022, Politico.eu, www.politico.eu/article/eu-commissioner-to-musk-twitter-will-play-by-our-rules/.

49 Press statement of Vice-President Jourova on the meeting with the Code of Practice on Disinformation Signatories, 26 September 2023, SPEECH/23/464.

50 A. Renda, *The Legal Framework to Address 'Fake News': Possible Policy Actions at the EU Level* (Brussels: European Parliament, 2018).

instance, by putting forward the model of the 'trust flagger' in the DSA, organisms charged with the mission to accompany and guide the moderation teams of the online platforms.

By contrast, in the US, the case *United States v. Alvarez*,[51] where the Supreme Court ruled that the crime of falsely claiming military honour is unconstitutional, clearly stated that even disinformation is by presumption protected by free speech. Only under strict scrutiny may a content-based restriction of freedom of speech be accepted by exception in the US.[52]

12.4 THE NEED FOR A SOLUTION THROUGH INTERNATIONAL CONSENSUS

This section examines the consequences of EU interventions into online freedom of expression in the context of divergences with the US on the scope of this human right. The primary concern is the potential risk of a fragmented digital landscape (Section 4.1), which would undermine the internet's purpose and philosophical basis. Given the significant economic implications of this situation, the World Trade Organization (WTO) is proposed as an adequate forum of discussion for potential attempts at solutions (Section 4.2). Nonetheless, any attempt at solving the divergences on the boundaries and limitations of the human right must involve a reformulation of the concept itself. Online freedom of expression is effective only when its enforcement fully embraces the concept of the digital public space (Section 4.3).

12.4.1 *The Danger of a Fragmented Internet*

Based on the observations in Section 12.2, it can be concluded that the EU legislator, in conjunction with jurisprudence, does not hold an absolute position on the question of whether EU internet law should have regional or global reach. While the *CNIL* decision accepted that the right to be forgotten could only have regional reach, the *Eva Glawischnig* case, on the contrary, applied global reach. The situation is even more complicated concerning the mitigation duty stemming from the DSA and the Article 17 filter, where no indication exists regarding the reach of the legal framework. Generally speaking, any legislation that would allow for regional reach alone would be structurally flawed, as users could easily circumvent such regulations by using a virtual private network (VPN). Nevertheless, the National Security Agency revelations in the past have potentially damaged trust on internet governance in Europe, and ever since there has existed a deep current

[51] *United States v. Alvarez*, 567 US 709, 717–8 (2012).

[52] A. Park and K. H. Youm, 'Fake news from a legal perspective: the United States and South Korea compared' (2019) 25 *Southwestern Journal of International Law* 1, 100–19.

towards global reach in EU regulation of the internet, leading to a fragmentation of the internet.[53]

Furthermore, online law enforcement is also a matter of the protection of democratic values for EU institutions. Characteristically, in the 2023 European Declaration on Digital Rights and Principles for the Digital Decade,[54] the EU institutions declared with force that 'the digital transformation should not entail the regression of rights. What is illegal offline, is illegal online.'[55] Nonetheless, the global character of the digital environment pushes the boundaries of private international law. For instance, the GDPR explicitly considers it applies from the moment that EU data subjects are specifically targeted by the processing, even if neither the data controller nor the processing is in the EU. In any case, it has to be accepted that in any matter that concerns criminal law (such as hate speech), the EU is also entitled to defend the enforcement of its legal framework in the digital environment.

From a practical standpoint, it is doubtful that major companies would invest substantial resources in compliance with legislation that applies regionally or risk non-compliance with various European obligations, only to find out that European courts view them as obliged to comply because European citizens are indirectly affected by their activities. This phenomenon can be observed in the functioning over time of some of the most popular generated language artificial intelligence models, such as ChatGPT. Various white papers show that the company has taken a precautionary approach regarding mitigation of the risks of generating 'illicit content', including safeguarding anti-racist and anti-hate speech content.[56]

As a consequence, American proponents of the internet face three options: comply with the EU legislator's expectations worldwide, ignore them and limit their market, potentially losing one of the largest digital markets in the world, or offer differentiated services depending on the user's location. The third option may seem appealing at first: IT companies would not lose any market or antagonise any legislator. The simplest solution would be to distinguish the service based on user internet protocol (IP) address, or even implement geo-blocking. For instance, some American newspapers automatically block access to viewers with European IP address, fearing the adoption of the GDPR.[57] However, this 'soft division' of the internet provides more legal uncertainties. Indeed, as the use of VPNs constantly

[53] J. Liebenau and S. Elaluf-Calderwood, 'Challenges to European internet business models: governing a fragmented internet' (2014), http://eprints.lse.ac.uk/63880/1/Challenges%20to%20European%20Internet%20.pdf.

[54] European Declaration on Digital Rights and Principles for the Digital Decade 2023/C 23/01, PUB/2023/89, OJ C 23, 23.1.2023, 1–7.

[55] Ibid., Recital 3.

[56] Open AI, 'GPT-4V(ision) System Card' (2023), https://cdn.openai.com/papers/GPTV_System_Card.pdf.

[57] N. Thurman et al., 'Forbidden fruit or soured grapes? Long-term effects of the temporary unavailability and rationing of US news websites on their consumption from the European Union' (2022) 84 *International Communication Gazette* 7–8, 698–720.

increases in the population, the general awareness of the 'geo-unblocking' capabilities of such networks also expands,[58] to the extent that in a foreseeable future any geo-blocking attempt will be deemed inefficient on the prism of the principle of proportionality.

Alternatively, there is a risk of a 'hard division' or fragmentation of the internet. China for instance, following its own agenda of absolute national control of communications, has developed native alternative internet technologies that could splinter the global internet's shared and ubiquitous architecture.[59]

It has been argued that the territorialisation of cyberspace does not necessarily entail risking the fragmentation of the internet.[60] However, the arguments proposed are unconvincing because it is challenging to ignore how, in a globalised context, efforts to protect digital sovereignty can be seen as a form of digital imperialism.

A high-stakes game is currently unfolding – while Europe would not benefit from the GAFAMs leaving the internal market, the companies also have no incentive to abandon it. In this context, Meta's behaviour, first threatening to leave the market after the US-EU Safe Harbor and Privacy Shield agreements were struck down by the ECJ,[61] and then launching its Twitter-like social network Threads in the EU, should be seen as diplomatic attempts to push back against the EU legislator's imperialist view of the digital landscape.

12.4.2 *The Need for an International Structure of Conciliation*

Several international organisations have shown interest in resolving the challenge of enforcing laws in the digital realm without infringing upon online freedom of expression. The Council of Europe, in particular, has a long history of issuing guidelines on this topic.[62] In general, the question of global internet governance

58 E. Khan et al., 'Stranger VPNs: investigating the geo-unblocking capabilities of commercial VPN providers', in A. Brunstrom, M. Flores, and M. Fiore (eds.), *Passive and Active Measurement. PAM 2023* (Cham: Springer, 2023), pp. 46–68.

59 S. Hoffmann, D. Lazanski, and E. Taylor, 'Standardising the splinternet: how China's technical standards could fragment the internet' (2020) 5 *Journal of Cyber Policy* 2, 239–64.

60 D. Lambach, 'The territorialization of cyberspace' (2020) 22 *International Studies Review* 3, 482–506.

61 C. Kwan, 'Meta's threat to leave Europe hints at waning big tech influence', 13 February 2022, ZDNET, www.zdnet.com/article/metas-threat-to-leave-europe-hints-at-big-tech-influence-waning/.

62 Recommendation CM/Rec(2022)13 of the Committee of Ministers to Member States on the impacts of digital technologies on freedom of expression, Recommendation CM/Rec(2021)8 on the protection of individuals with regard to automatic processing of personal data in the context of profiling, Recommendation CM/Rec(2020)1 on the human rights impacts of algorithmic systems, Recommendation CM/Rec(2018)2 on the roles and responsibilities of internet intermediaries, Recommendation CM/Rec(2016)5 on Internet freedom, Recommendation CM/Rec(2016)1 on protecting and promoting the right to freedom of expression and the right to private life with regard to network neutrality, Recommendation CM/Rec(2015)6 on the free, transboundary flow of information on the Internet, Recommendation CM/Rec(2014)6 on a Guide to human rights for Internet users,

has been discussed as long as the internet has existed. It could be proposed that the United Nations is a natural choice for this debate, especially through its action via the Internet Governance Forum (IGF),[63] which embraces the 'multistakeholder model' (with all its flaws).[64] However, the actions of the IGF and the limitations of its mandate suggest that it may not be an effective platform for discussing the boundaries of online freedom of expression.

In this context, while the choice of the WTO may seem unusual at first considering it is primarily an economic organisation, there are arguments in favour of this option. First, the interstate Dispute Settlement Understanding is a highly efficient mechanism, and it is believed that enforcement through the WTO has been easier than through other international instruments.[65] Second, the divergent definitions of online freedom of expression impose significant economic costs on IT companies, which can be viewed as an economic factor. It has thus been argued that the WTO has a role to play in limiting China's online censorship policies.[66] Third, while differences in perspectives on freedom of expression are deeply rooted in constitutional systems, the WTO is seemingly independent of specific legal traditions. While the search for a synthesis between EU and US approaches to online freedom of expression involves complex reasoning and considerable effort, the use of a comparative approach privileged by the organisation would provide some insights on the issue. Finally, the human rights approach is not foreign to the WTO, and how the WTO is involved in resolving disputes related to freedom of expression has already been analysed,[67] using the concept of 'public morals' as a legitimate limitation to freedom of expression.[68]

12.4.3 *Through the Protection of Digital Public Spaces*

Finding a structure capable of resolving international disputes over online freedom of expression is not enough; it should also be recognised that the existing definitions, both American and European, are insufficient to fully protect online freedom of

Recommendation CM/Rec(2013)1 on gender equality and media, Recommendation CM/Rec(2012)4 on the protection of human rights with regard to social networking services, Recommendation CM/Rec(2012)3 on the protection of human rights with regard to search engines, Recommendation CM/Rec(2011)7 on a new notion of media, and Recommendation CM/Rec(2007)16 on measures to promote the public service value of the Internet.

63 S. Antonova, 'Internet and the emerging global community of rights: the human-rights debate at the internet governance forum' (2013) 4 *Journal of International Law* 1, 84–98.

64 L. DeNardis and M. Raymond, 'Thinking clearly about multistakeholder internet governance' (2013), https://papers.ssrn.com/sol3/papers.cfm?abstract_id=2354377.

65 M. H. Randall, 'Human rights within a multilayered constitution: the example of freedom of expression and the WTO' (2012) 16 *Max Planck Yearbook of United Nations Law* 1, 183–280, 252.

66 M. Ting, 'The role of the WTO in limiting China's censorship policies' (2011) 41 *Hong Kong Law Journal*, 285–310.

67 Randall, 'Human rights within a multilayered constitution'.

68 See for instance the case WTO, China – Publications, WT/DS363/AB/R, 19 January 2010.

expression. In other words, online freedom of expression requires not only a structure but also substantial legal adjustments. One of the fundamental aspects of the protection of online freedom of expression today is its heavy reliance on free access to social media platforms. However, these platforms are owned by private companies, which raises new challenges for the freedom of expression. Some authors then refer to the 'platformisation of the public sphere'.[69] Digital public spaces are governed by algorithms of presentation and management of the information flow. The huge potential of these algorithms in influencing public opinion has been demonstrated. The 2023 Declaration on Digital Rights and Principles expressly mentions this issue, stating that:

> Online platforms, particularly very large online platforms, should support free democratic debate online. Given the role of their services in shaping public opinion and discourse, very large online platforms should mitigate the risks stemming from the functioning and use of their services, including in relation to misinformation and disinformation campaigns, and protect freedom of expression.[70]

Furthermore, it is also argued that the digitalisation of the public space entails 'antagonistic and networked-individualistic flows of populist communication',[71] and effectively, the bubble effect of social media is nowadays well documented.[72]

One of these issues is the need for the horizontal application of freedom of expression. Here, 'horizontal effect' refers to the ability of end users to initiate private litigation against an online platform for violating their human rights, specifically by filing a complaint when their freedom of expression has been infringed owing to abusive moderation. In the US, no margin of appreciation is recognised for the horizontal effect of freedom of expression. For example, in the *District Court in California FAN v. Facebook* case,[73] it was ruled that private internet service providers such as Facebook are entitled to shut down users' accounts, as social media does not operate as a public forum.

By contrast, the EU tradition allows for greater application regarding the horizontal effect of freedom of expression (see for instance the *Viking Line* judgement,[74] where the ECJ adopted the German theory of the indirect horizontal effect of human rights). Furthermore, the landmark *Egenberger* and *Bauer* cases directly acknowledge a direct horizontal effect to some provisions of the Charter (the principle of

69 N. Smyrnaios and O. Baisnée, 'Critically understanding the platformization of the public sphere' (2023) 38 *European Journal of Communication* 5, 435–45.

70 European Declaration on Digital Rights and Principles for the Digital Decade, section 15.

71 S. Sevignani, 'Digital transformations and the ideological formation of the public sphere: hegemonic, populist, or popular communication?' (2022) 39 *Theory, Culture and Society* 4, 91–109.

72 D. Spohr, 'Fake news and ideological polarization: filter bubbles and selective exposure on social media' (2017) 34 *Business Information Review* 3, 150–60.

73 District Court in California, *FAN v. Facebook*, 18-CV-07041-LHK, 20 July 2019.

74 Case C-438/05, *International Transport Workers' Federation and Finnish Seamen's Union v. Viking Line ABP and OÜ Viking Line Eesti* [2007], ECLI:EU:C:2007:772.

non-discrimination and effective judicial protection).[75] These two cases have substantial importance for EU constitutional law,[76] and this reasoning could be seen as opening the door for further recognition of the horizontal effect. However, it is uncertain, in the absence of relevant secondary EU legislation, whether the reasoning employed in these two cases can be used by extension for freedom of expression.

Therefore, in the US without any doubt, and in the EU most probably, the enforcement of online freedom of expression against private actors, even those managing very large social platforms and acting as de facto gatekeepers of public spaces, remains uncertain. This has very practical consequences: How is it possible to prohibit a platform from banning an account or imposing a 'shadow ban' on a communication (through algorithmic moderation to restrict the range of a publication), thus manipulating opinion and enforcing private censorship, without having any control? Shadow banning, as a conscious form of moderation, might be a myth.[77] Nonetheless, the automatic consequence of algorithmic information presentation is that certain content, based on predefined criteria, may experience reduced visibility. In the EU, the DSA constitutes a first step towards regulation of this practice.[78]

Consequently, the protection of online freedom of expression currently relies on an indirect and imperfect legal framework, which combines contract law with consumer protection. For example, in Germany, in the *Facebook Terms of Service* Case,[79] it was determined that Facebook's terms of service on deleting user posts and blocking accounts for violations of its Community Standards were invalid. Similarly, in France, in the '*nombril du monde*' case,[80] the court found that by moderating the posting of a painting without explanations, Facebook had violated the general duty of good faith in the execution of the contract, as mandated by the Civil Code.

This situation is far from satisfactory. The philosophy and methodology of contract law cannot be seen as an ideal method to guarantee freedom of expression. It is time for a re-evaluation of online freedom of expression that takes into consideration the practical reality of some social media platforms as digital public spaces. As a result, no obstacles should be placed against the enforcement of freedom of expression in these digital public spaces.

75 *Egenberger*: Case C-414/16, *Vera Egenberger v.Evangelisches Werk für Diakonie und Entwicklung eV* [2018], ECLI:EU:C:2018:257; *Bauer*: Joint Cases C-569/16 and C-570/16, *Stadt Wuppertal v Maria Elisabeth Bauer and Volker Willmeroth v Martina Broßonn* [2018], ECLI:EU:C:2018:871.

76 A. Colombi Ciacchi, 'The direct horizontal effect of EU fundamental rights: ECJ 17 April 2018, Case C-414/16, Vera Egenberger v Evangelisches Werk für Diakonie und Entwicklung e.V. and ECJ 11 September 2018, Case C-68/17, IR v JQ' (2019) 15 *European Constitutional Law Review* 2, 294–305.

77 L. Savolainen, 'The shadow banning controversy: perceived governance and algorithmic folklore' (2022) 44 *Media, Culture & Society* 6, 1091–109.

78 P. Leerssen, 'An end to shadow banning? Transparency rights in the Digital Services Act between content moderation and curation' (2023) 48 *Computer Law & Security Review*, 105790.

79 German Federal Court of Justice, II ZR 192/20, III ZR 179/20, 29 July 2021.

80 Civil Court Paris, *Frédéric X / Facebook*, 15/03/2018, n° 12/12401.

12.5 CONCLUSION

The term 'imperialism' typically carries a historical and negative connotation. However, in the context of this chapter, it does not imply a deliberate intent of hegemony on the part of European institutions. Rather, it is an automatic consequence of safeguarding digital sovereignty in a globalised environment. This sheds light on fundamental conceptual differences regarding the interpretation of freedom of expression. Nevertheless, these differences give rise to political struggles with economic implications, highlighting the need for a solution to bridge these divides.

It must be accepted, then, that the EU institutions indeed endorse a certain amount of 'digital imperialism'. While the thorny issue of the governance of a globalised network is as old as the internet itself, the quest for the digital sovereignty of the EU is a novel concept that encompasses a will to promote the defence of European values online more actively.[81]

The argument here is that while this policy is justified from a democratic perspective, it may result in increasing confrontations that could hinder internet growth and potentially lead to network fragmentation. Instead, this chapter suggests that international negotiations with trusted partners, based on shared core elements of the concept of freedom of expression, should be prioritised. Such a solution could find support within the framework of the WTO, necessitating a re-evaluation of online freedom of expression. One of the main potential dangers of this clash between the US and the EU on the legitimate boundaries of freedom of expression may not be the potential fragmentation of the internet, but the occultation of a debate on the need to re-evaluate this human right in a way that enhances its scope in digital public spaces.

[81] J. Pohle and T. Thiel, 'Digital sovereignty' (2020) 9 *Internet Policy Review* 4, 1–19.

PART III

Challenges Posed by Digital Technologies

Introduction to Part III

How Should Human Rights Law Respond to the Challenges of Digital Technologies?

Tiina Pajuste

Technological development has transformed the way societies function, creating unprecedented opportunities while giving rise to complex human rights issues. Digital technologies, from artificial intelligence and algorithmic decision-making to data collection and surveillance systems, have altered systems of governance and individual autonomy. While these technologies have the potential to enhance human rights – by improving access to information, supporting equality, and fostering innovation – they also risk undermining them through privacy violations, discrimination, and erosion of accountability. As the United Nations Secretary-General has emphasised, we need to 'ensure that new technologies are anchored in the values of [...] the Universal Declaration of Human Rights'.[1] Accordingly, this part of the volume examines how human rights law should adapt to the ever-evolving situation. Each chapter addresses the core question: *How should human rights law respond to the challenges of digital technologies?* By delving into specific issues such as online disinformation, privacy violations, public health surveillance, and the intersection of digitisation with foreign investment, the chapters collectively explore the tensions between innovation and human rights protection, offering insights into how legal frameworks can adapt to contemporary technological realities.

These topics reflect key challenges where digital technologies intersect with human rights. Microtargeted disinformation threatens democratic participation and free expression, requiring legal responses to preserve public trust. The case study of COVID-19 apps highlights the balance between public health and privacy, offering lessons for future crises. The rise of drones necessitates safeguards to prevent privacy violations and misuse. Finally, the interplay between foreign investment and digitisation shows how human rights can shape global economic and regulatory strategies. Together, these chapters illustrate the need for a legal framework that protects human rights while fostering responsible innovation.

[1] UN Secretary-General, 'Strategy on new technologies' (2018), www.un.org/en/newtechnologies/.

CHAPTER 13. THE PARADOX OF DIGITALISATION IN THE CASE OF THE COVID-19 APPS: WHAT LESSONS CAN WE LEARN FROM THIS STRANGE EXPERIENCE?

Chapter 13 examines the role of digital technologies, particularly contact-tracing apps, during the COVID-19 pandemic and draws lessons from this experience that should be taken into consideration when crisis situations occur. Paula Veiga expresses how these technologies were developed and implemented as public health tools and digs into the reasons for their widespread failure in Western countries, despite their technical feasibility. She provides insight into how digitalisation impacts public trust, governance, and human rights. Digital technologies have reshaped societal norms, created new types of data-centric goods, and introduced novel legal challenges, such as redefining rights and the role of public authorities. The chapter shows how the pandemic highlighted tensions between public health measures, privacy, and the rule of law. The exceptional circumstances required balancing individual freedoms with collective security. In relation to the core question of this part of the volume, the chapter refers to the following ways in which human rights law should adapt to address digital technologies: (a) in balancing human rights with other considerations (such as public health) during crises, the temporary measures taken need to be proportionate; (b) legal frameworks should include mechanisms to build and maintain public trust (e.g., transparency in data use, clear communication); (c) the focus should be on inclusivity, ensuring that digital technologies do not deepen existing inequalities; and (d) new human rights (e.g., the right to digital education, the right to neutrality on the internet) should be recognised and formally included in international human rights frameworks.

CHAPTER 14. AERIAL SURVEILLANCE IN THE DIGITAL AGE: DRONE-RELATED PRIVACY CONCERNS AND THE PROTECTION OF OTHER HUMAN RIGHTS

In Chapter 14, Skirgailė Žalimienė and Saulius Stonkus explore the challenges and opportunities presented by drone technology, focusing on the human rights implications of its widespread adoption. The chapter examines how drones, as platforms integrating advanced technologies (e.g., cameras, the Global Positioning System, artificial intelligence), enable extensive surveillance capabilities that pose significant risks to privacy and other human rights. It also addresses the regulatory landscape, particularly within the European Union (EU), and notes how current regulations often lag behind technological advancements, with unclear or inadequate provisions for drone registration, data minimisation, and cybersecurity. The chapter offers recommendations for striking a balance between enabling innovation and safeguarding fundamental rights. In response to this part's core question – *How should human rights law respond to the challenges of digital technologies?* – the chapter notes the following: (a) human rights law should anticipate technological developments and establish forward-looking regulatory frameworks; (b) legal frameworks should require the integration of privacy-enhancing measures (e.g., automatic anonymisation) within technologies; (c) the principle of proportionality should be used as a guiding method, when the need arises to balance different human rights; and (d) a co-ordinated global approach is critical for ensuring consistency in legal standards.

CHAPTER 15. ONLINE DISINFORMATION, MICROTARGETING, AND FREEDOM OF EXPRESSION: MOVING BEYOND HUMAN RIGHTS LAW?

Chapter 15 studies the rise of microtargeted online disinformation (MOD) and its implications for human rights, democracy, and regulatory frameworks. Birgit Schippers looks at how microtargeting – a practice that uses data analytics to deliver tailored messages to specific audiences – amplifies the spread of disinformation, distorts public discourse, and impacts democratic processes. The chapter highlights the challenges posed by MOD to freedom of expression and privacy while evaluating the adequacy of current legal frameworks, particularly within the EU. It demonstrates how human rights law, particularly Article 10 of the European Convention on Human Rights, limits state interference with speech, making it difficult to regulate disinformation. Schippers answers this part's core question by suggesting that (a) human rights law alone may not sufficiently address MOD (and other human rights issues in the digital environment), so complementary approaches (e.g., media literacy initiatives) are needed; (b) regulatory measures must balance the need to counter disinformation with protecting free speech to avoid disproportionate restrictions; and (c) international cooperation is necessary to address cross-border human rights challenges such as disinformation, harmonise regulatory standards, and counteract the influence of global tech platforms.

CHAPTER 16. DIGITAL BOOM: CURRENT ISSUES FROM INTERNATIONAL INVESTMENT TO HUMAN RIGHTS

Chapter 16 explores the relationship between international investments, digital technologies, and human rights. Cristina Elena Popa Tache, Cătălin-Silviu Săraru, and Sergio de Souza Salles demonstrate how digitalisation has transformed international investment practices and created new legal challenges, particularly regarding data protection, privacy, and equitable access to technology. The authors propose a human rights-centred approach to regulating digital investments, focusing on balancing innovation, investment protection, and fundamental rights.

In relation to the core question of this part of the volume, they note the following: (a) digitalisation amplifies the need for legal frameworks that protect human rights while fostering technological innovation and international investment; (b) legal systems should anticipate technological advancements by adopting forward-looking frameworks that address potential human rights implications before they arise; (c) effective governance should reconcile state sovereignty, international investment interests, and the protection of human rights, ensuring legal systems can respond to evolving digital challenges; and (d) a multi-stakeholder approach should be adopted (involving states, businesses, and international organisations) to harmonise global standards.

SHARED THEMES AND INTERCONNECTIONS

The four chapters illustrate some of the ways in which human rights law can respond to the challenges posed by digital technologies, offering insights into areas ranging from health and surveillance to microtargeting and international investment. In the following, their common themes and approaches are summarised to highlight how they converge in addressing the question of this part: *How should human rights law respond to the challenges of digital technologies?*

A. BALANCING HUMAN RIGHTS WITH TECHNOLOGICAL INNOVATION

Each chapter emphasises the need to strike a balance between safeguarding human rights and enabling technological development. The authors share the view that human rights law must evolve to navigate the tension between regulating technology to prevent harm and fostering innovation that supports societal progress:

- Chapter 13 on COVID-19 apps explores how public health technologies must balance privacy with the right to health, highlighting the need for proportionality in emergencies.
- Chapter 14 on drone surveillance argues that regulations must balance privacy with public safety and innovation in drone use.
- Chapter 15 on microtargeted online disinformation emphasises that countering disinformation requires balancing freedom of expression with protections for privacy and democracy.
- Chapter 16 on digital investments emphasises the necessity to reconcile the drive for international digital investments with the need to protect rights such as equitable access and privacy

B. PROPORTIONALITY AS A GUIDING PRINCIPLE

All chapters recognise the importance of proportionality as a key legal principle and tool to be utilised in applying human rights law in the digital environment. Proportionality is seen as having the potential to ensure that regulatory responses to digital technologies are targeted, avoiding unnecessary or overly restrictive measures that may infringe on fundamental rights:

- Chapter 13 discusses proportionality in using emergency measures to ensure they are temporary and necessary without becoming tools for long-term surveillance.
- Chapter 14 advocates for proportionality in drone regulations to prevent overreach while addressing privacy concerns.
- Chapter 15 highlights proportionality in regulating disinformation to avoid a chilling effect on free expression.
- Chapter 16 states that proportional regulations are essential for balancing investment growth and human rights.

C. TRUST, TRANSPARENCY, AND ACCOUNTABILITY

The chapters highlight trust and transparency as critical components of effective digital governance. They note that trust in digital governance can be fostered through transparency, vigorous accountability mechanisms, and public engagement.

- Chapter 13 stresses the importance of public trust in ensuring the success of health technologies, facilitated by transparency in data usage.
- Chapter 14 emphasises accountability mechanisms to prevent the misuse of surveillance technologies.
- Chapter 15 highlights the need for transparent content moderation and data usage practices to counter the effects of microtargeting.
- Chapter 16 argues for transparent and inclusive governance in digital investments to prevent exploitation and exclusion.

Like the chapters in Part II, all four chapters in this part of the volume also call for international cooperation and harmonised legal standards. The global nature of digital technologies necessitates co-ordinated international responses to protect human rights effectively while promoting innovation and economic growth.

The chapters collectively emphasise that human rights law and its implementation must evolve to address the challenges posed by digital technologies. This involves balancing regulation with innovation, expanding the scope of human rights frameworks (or their interpretation), fostering transparency and trust, and adopting a globally harmonised, multi-stakeholder approach. Together, these insights (and others contained in the chapters) outline a strategy for ensuring that human rights are protected in the face of rapid digital transformation.

13

The Paradox of Digitalisation in the Case of the COVID-19 Apps: What Lessons Can We Learn from This Strange Experience?

Paula Veiga

13.1 INTRODUCTION

The rise of the internet and digitalisation have profoundly changed social relations and spread their influence in the juridical field. There is nothing new about this realisation. But the failure of COVID-19 apps during the pandemic in the Western world indicates that the trend of social adherence to digitalisation is neither automatic nor without restraint.

The mainstream analysis of contact-tracing apps is commonly closely related to data protection standards and digital surveillance technologies in order to obtain important gains: to prevent mass surveillance, and to protect human rights and the rule of law.[1] I reiterate 'closely related' because this second millennium has brought dramatic progress towards the recognition and enforcement of human rights, which is a positive development.

In this chapter, another perspective is sought – a broader one, perhaps even more comprehensive – based on the perplexity from our recent experience of contact-tracing apps, which embodies, as already said, a non-adherence to digital platforms in this particular case, unlike other areas (online shopping contracting, networks…).[2] These mentioned areas also pose several juridical problems, namely one of the real threat of the 'private' profiling of citizens and exploiting their vulnerabilities for commercial purposes. Therefore, one cannot assess the contact-tracing app experience in light of this element only. The scenario may be more complex than that.

Perhaps a broader analysis of this experience can answer how human rights law should develop in the face of the challenges of digital technologies.

[1] The literature is extensive. See, e.g., L. Bradford, M. Aboy, and K. Liddell, 'COVID-19 contact tracing apps: a stress test for privacy, the GDPR, and data protection regimes' (2020) 7 *Journal of Law and the Biosciences* 1, 1–34.

[2] The literature on digitalisation is starting to be extensive. Some recent thoughts can be seen in C. Kaufmann, 'Responsible business in a digital world – what's international law got to do with it?' (2021) 81 *Heidelberg Journal of International Law* 3, 781–815; J. F. MacLennan, 'Facing the digital future: public service broadcasters and state aid law in the European Union' (2017) 2 *Cambridge Yearbook of European Legal Studies*, 159–202.

In the first two decades of the twenty-first century, the rule of law scenario and its paradigms changed through digitalisation, the exceptionalism of the pandemic, and the need for the protection of human rights worldwide.[3] That is the background to the contact-tracing app experience, and we must take a deeper and more serious look at this apparently transitory phenomenon.

13.2 THE IMPACT OF DIGITALISATION: SOME HIGHLIGHTS FROM THE PUBLIC LAW PERSPECTIVE

Digitalisation is a hyper-complex phenomenon that uses new resources and new formats, and creates new problems in the juridical realm. The internet is not just an information platform, nor an ordinary channel of communication; it is the new centre of social communications. Almost all areas of our lives are reflected in cyberspace: economy, politics, trade, education, family, financial transactions, but also criminal activities, terrorism, and so on. This means that the issue is not only technological or economic, but also legal. The technological process has changed cultural norms and social behaviour, which also changes legal behaviour.

Among the juridical problems, there is one that deserves to be specifically mentioned: digitalisation has created a new good, very different from the classical physical goods we were used to – that is, data. In the twenty-first century, data will be the most valuable asset, especially personal data, and, as far as we can see, policy will struggle to control the flow of data. Data demands a different approach to regulating juridical relations, as it is not intended for exclusive use as the classical physical goods were. As we immediately intuited, this will be reflected in legal concepts as it is warrantable that classical notions, such as 'ownership', can be modified to form new or alternative concepts. It is now clear that digitalisation will always be accompanied by the collection, storage, and processing of large amounts of data, so-called big data, that will differ in terms of shape, size, and speed. Before the digital age, data essentially meant information about a certain content, collected by identifiable people. This has changed with digitalisation. Data is now a *container* for information. As the historian Yuval Noah Harari says, in a rather pessimistic view, there is a

[3] About these changes in the juridical paradigm, caused by digitalisation, see S. Koloß, 'Facebook and the rule of law' (2020) 80 *Heidelberg Journal of International Law* 2, 509–31; D. Harvey, *Collisions in the Digital Paradigm: Law and Rule-making in the Internet Age* (Oxford: Hart Publishing, 2017); M. Belov, *Rule of Law at the Beginning of the Twenty-first Century* (The Hague: Eleven International Publishing, 2018); about general changes in the twenty-first century, see A. v. Bogdandy, 'Globalization and Europe: how to square democracy, globalization and international law' (2004) 15 *European Journal of International Law* 5, 885–906. A notion of an international approach to rule of law can be seen in E. Katselli, 'The rule of law and the role of human rights in contemporary international law', in R. Dickinson et al. (eds.), *The Rule of Law and the Role of Human Rights in Contemporary International Law* (Cambridge: Cambridge University Press, 2012), pp. 131–52. My recent thoughts about the issue can be found in P. Veiga, *Direito Constitucional e Direito Internacional no Contexto do Constitucionalismo Global: Um Roteiro Pedagógico* (Lisbon: Petrony, 2020).

new universal narrative that replaces religious authority and the humanist ideology with the authority of the algorithm and big data.[4]

Another aspect that deserves special attention in light of public law is connected to more recent activities in the digital world. While in the early years of this century, discussions focused on the opportunities and risks of the internet, namely the protection of privacy and data; we are now facing a new type of activity, and therefore new challenges – those associated with the globalisation of communication infrastructures and markets, artificial intelligence (AI), big data, and its consequences for the collective interest (e.g., health services, political elections). Considering this, some of the most important problems caused by digitalisation in public law concern the information and technology revolution and its connections with the humanist traditions in which constitutions are based. How is it possible to enhance the legitimacy of the new information order, the impact of digitalisation on democracy and will-formation processes, the impact of digitalisation on the courts and administrations, namely the limits of digital justice, and the impact of the digital revolution on data protection, privacy, and human rights.

At the constitutional level, since the constitutional state and constitutions were built around the principle of human dignity, it is inevitable that the domain of the machine and the emergence of AI, with its new paradigms (acceleration, instantaneous action, and connectivity), will bring changes to several pillars of constitutionalism, namely the pillar of rights, the institutional pillar, and the pillar of legitimacy.

In this field, the most immediate concerns of digitalisation are related to: (a) the protection of rights, (b) the birth of new rights (e.g., the right to be forgotten, the right to social access to the internet), (c) the new understanding of competences, since the internet goes beyond the jurisdiction of state or region (legal orders, both national and international, are based on the Westphalian concept of sovereignty and state-centred power), and (d) public discourse and the formation of political will.

This means a change in the constitutional system, especially because the internet increases the ability of citizens to exercise their fundamental rights, but also increases the risk of threats to fundamental rights, and, related to the public sphere, the internet emphasises the special role of private actors. To express this succinctly, digitalisation can be a tool for both protecting and violating human rights, with direct implications for the cyber- and physical security of individuals.

Besides the pillar of rights, States must of course reorganise their classical functions that were based on territoriality. Some authors argue that there is a trend to territorialise cyberspace (aka 'sovereignty fever'). I feel it is too soon to reach that conclusion. As already stated, space and territory have been important as bases for the law for several centuries (in fact, territory is even a political construction in the legal field). All these have changed with the internet and digitalisation.

4 Y. N. Harari, *21 Lessons for the 21st Century* (New York, NY: Vintage Publishing, 2019).

The (new) public sphere is public–private, fragmentary, immediate, and egocentric.[5] This makes it difficult to distinguish between individual information and press information, and therefore the exact new notion of public opinion. Still considering the pillar of rights, the existing rights have gained a new dimension in the context of applying new technologies, and this necessitates a reinterpretation. We can also see the emergence of *new* digital rights.

Overlooking the rights themselves, and considering both the categories of fundamental rights and human rights, digitalisation implies, above all, a redefinition of privacy and other (personal) rights related to free will, as well as all rights connected with communication through the media (namely, freedom of expression and freedom of press and media). In addition to the framework of rights already broadly affirmed, there is the legal consecration (at constitutional and international levels) of new rights (digital rights), such as the right to access the internet irrespective of economic condition, the right to digital education, the right to neutrality on the internet, the right of access online data, innovations, creations, and knowledge generated by public funds, and the right to be forgotten.

There is (as yet) no international Bill of Digital Rights, which, in order to be approved, should be under the auspices of the United Nations. But in international law new configurations of human rights arise, especially the rights to freedom of expression and privacy. In this context, we can recall the UNESCO Recommendation concerning the promotion and the use of multilingualism and universal access to cyberspace (2003), that states the need for the coexistence of public and private, as well as civil society at the local, national, regional, and international levels, and the principle of universal access to the internet as a service of public interest.[6] The World Summits on the information society (Geneva, 2003; Tunis, 2005) should also not be forgotten.

In the European law context, and considering the Europeanisation of the protection of fundamental rights through technology, it is worth mentioning Directive 2009/136/EC of the European Parliament and the Council,[7] a process that was initiated with the first Directive on the protection of personal data.[8] We should also

5 About the classical public sphere, see J. Habermas, *The Structural Transformation of the Public Sphere: An Inquiry into a Category of Bourgeois Society* (Cambridge: Polity Press, 1989).

6 UNESCO, Recommendation concerning the Promotion and Use of Multilingualism and Universal Access to Cyberspace, 15 October 2003, www.unesco.org/en/legal-affairs/recommendation-concerning-promotion-and-use-multilingualism-and-universal-access-cyberspace.

7 Directive 2009/136/EC of the European Parliament and of the Council of 25 November 2009 amending Directive 2002/22/EC on universal service and users' rights relating to electronic communications networks and services, Directive 2002/58/EC concerning the processing of personal data and the protection of privacy in the electronic communications sector, and Regulation (EC) No 2006/2004 on cooperation between national authorities responsible for the enforcement of consumer protection laws (Text with EEA relevance), OJ L 337, 18.12.2009, 11–36.

8 Directive 95/46/EC of the European Parliament and of the Council of 24 October 1995 on the protection of individuals with regard to the processing of personal data and on the free movement of such data, OJ L 281, 23.11.1995, 31–50.

remember Regulation 2015/2120, which establishes measures dealing with access to the open internet and amends Directive 2002/22/EC on universal service, as well as Regulation 531/2012 on roaming on public mobile communications networks in the European Union (EU),[9] and, finally, the well-known Regulation on Data Protection (Regulation 2016/679), which repealed the aforementioned Directive 95/46/EC.[10]

13.2.1 *The Specific Case of Digitalisation among Health Norms*

One of the areas crucial to digitalisation is that of public services, in which health services are usually included.[11] This implies the development of a digital citizenship, a citizenship that will entail a new way of understanding relations between administrations and citizens where recognition of rights are concerned, namely the confidence for citizens about electronic ways of working (e.g., privacy and security issues). Of course, the EU is trying to develop a common vision of how e-government services will develop, and subsequently is committed to its implementation.

Alternatively, digitalisation is favouring the development of a new 'health market', namely through the reorganisation of therapy and business models offered by digital platforms, such as tablets with computer chips, implants with sensors, fingerprints, fitness trackers, and medical apps. The use of digital technologies concerning health poses special technical as well as philosophical and juridical problems, as this involves dealing with well-recognised sensitive data.[12] But doctors, pharmacists, and companies have banded together to develop applications that promise to redefine the way medicine is practised. There will likely be a need for new models, such as patient-oriented care and a more efficient system (perhaps an interconnected and smart-healthcare system capable of solving complicated situations in the healthcare sector using digital tools). Insurance companies will require special attention, as they will be responsible for handling sensitive data.

The main framework is already enacted by the General Data Protection Regulation (GDPR) (generally, processing data can be carried out without the consent of the individual). This health issue is also well known from the pandemic, as all over the world, and especially in Europe, the Council of Europe Member States moved forward in an attempt to make use of digital technology to slow down the

[9] Regulation (EU) 2015/2120 of the European Parliament and of the Council of 25 November 2015 laying down measures concerning open internet access and amending Directive 2002/22/EC on universal service and users' rights relating to electronic communications networks and services and Regulation (EU) No 531/2012 on roaming on public mobile communications networks within the Union (Text with EEA relevance), OJ L 310, 26.11.2015, 1–18.

[10] General Data Protection Regulation (GDPR), OJ L 119, 04.05.2016; cor. OJ L 127, 23.5.2018.

[11] An analysis can be found in V. L. Raposo, 'The doctor just poked you: os novos desafios da e-health' (2014) 57 *Boletim das Ciências Económicas* 3, 2903–33.

[12] See, for all, how GDPR deals with health data.

spread of the virus.[13] The COVID-19 apps could, therefore, if they had been successful in Europe, have served as an experiment for the digitalisation of healthcare. This was not, in general terms, the case (one exception, at least in the first period of the pandemic, was the Italian Immuni). One should never forget that smart management of healthcare ('telemedicine') includes treatments connected to the use of medical apps, through which independent owners collect data, including healthcare data on the person concerned, which can be used for different purposes.

13.3 COVID-19: DIGITALISATION METHODS AND JURIDICAL CONCERNS

13.3.1 *The Most Fundamental Constitutional Problems Posed by COVID-19*

A constitutional and pluralist view of public law sees citizens and communities as subjects of legitimacy, and in this context the ability of the law to achieve political inclusion. That is why constitutionalism focuses above all on the impact of governance arrangements on human rights.

On 11 March 2020, the World Health Organization (WHO) recognised the spread of the disease as a pandemic and soon states and their governments needed to take specific measures. Apart from disrupting international supply chains, adding popularity to anti-migrant policies, and weakening globalisation, the administration of the crisis led to restrictions on several human rights (e.g., quarantine, travel, isolation) and forced states to resort to the use of public coercion and protective measures, including business closures and social distancing.[14]

At the constitutional level, the pandemic implies a return to two classical and constitutionally protected juridical concepts that were required to be balanced: freedom and security.[15] The complex agreement between these two concepts – freedom and collective interest – explains why COVID-19 primarily posed three constitutional issues among occidental constitutional states: (a) the place of parliaments in epidemic (emergency) circumstances and the operationalisation of the 'law of the crisis' that signifies, as a rule, a rebalancing of the various powers, determining the centrality of the executive power, in general, and the government, in particular (a

[13] In this context, see P. Donaldson, 'Covid-19 vaccines. A global common good' (2020) 1 *The Lancet Healthy Longevity* 1, e6–e8.

[14] The implications of COVID-19 in the human rights field are well listed in E. Gilmore, 'La lucha contra COVID-19 es una batalla por los derechos humanos', 17 April 2020, EU External Action, https://bit.ly/2FXqdhT.

[15] The balance needed is particularly evident in F. Piovesan and M. Morales Antoniazzi, 'Covid-19 e a necessidade de uma abordagem holística e integral da proteção dos direitos humanos', 25 April 2020, Blog Constitucional; *M. Morales Antoniazzi and S. Steininger*, 'How to protect human rights in times of Corona? Lessons from the inter-American human rights system', 1 May 2020, EJIL:Talk!, www.ejiltalk.org/how-to-protect-human-rights-in-times-of-corona-lessons-from-the-inter-american-human-rights-system/.

stronger executive); (b) the adequacy of the legal basis of the measures adopted; and (c) the proportionality of the measures materially adopted.

In terms of the justice systems, it is worth noting that there was almost an automatic response from states considering the suspension of the judicial service and the procedural deadlines that represents an impact on the universality of access to process and effective judicial protection. There were also several influences on the functioning of democracy, such as the postponement of elections, restriction of the rights of freedom, and the right to assembly.

All rights are susceptible to being restricted under certain conditions. In light of the European Convention on Human Rights, those restrictions shall not affect the legality principle, must have a legitimate aim, and must respect the proportionality principle. This instrument even has its own Article (Article 15) that rules the derogation of the Convention in times of emergency, under certain limits.[16]

13.3.2 *Apps during the Pandemic: Their Possible Significance and Role*

The COVID-19 pandemic made us face many problems and also contradictions.[17] One was its 'cosmopolitanism' – COVID-19 spread all over the world – on the one hand, and the national response to it on the other. Indeed, despite the fact that there is nowadays undeniably more international coordination than during previous pandemics (namely through the WHO), the fight against the virus continued to take place within the national framework, which reinforced the notion of sovereignty that was otherwise dissolving through the globalisation and digitalisation processes. At least in Europe, borders regained a new meaning with COVID-19.

When COVID-19 initially spread, proposals for monitoring the epidemic through technology soon emerged all across the world, but in Europe in particular, both organised by the EU and by each national state. In general, the European proposals were

[16] Article 15 (*Derogation in time of emergency*) of the European Convention on Human Rights:

1. In time of war or other public emergency threatening the life of the nation any High Contracting Party may take measures derogating from its obligations under this Convention to the extent strictly required by the exigencies of the situation, provided that such measures are not inconsistent with its other obligations under international law.
2. No derogation from Article 2, except in respect of deaths resulting from lawful acts of war, or from Articles 3, 4 (paragraph 1) and 7 shall be made under this provision.
3. Any High Contracting Party availing itself of this right of derogation shall keep the Secretary General of the Council of Europe fully informed of the measures which it has taken and the reasons therefor. It shall also inform the Secretary General of the Council of Europe when such measures have ceased to operate and the provisions of the Convention are again being fully executed.

[17] I have had the opportunity to reflect on some of them in P. Veiga, 'Uma lição da pandemia: renúncia à globalização ou limites a essa renúncia? Ressignificação do Estado', in A. S. Pinto Oliveira and P. Jerónimo (eds.), *Liber Amicorum Benedita Mac Crorie*, vol. II (Braga: UMinho Editora, 2022), vol. II, pp. 381–90.

concerned with defending the rule of law and two particular human rights – data security and privacy. The key features were the aggregation of data (and subsequent anonymisation), the purpose, principle, and voluntariness.[18] The apps, according to European parameters, were designed to the highest standards of data privacy and data security. Their aim was not to track individuals and not to hold personal information. But even in the EU, where there is sophisticated regional integration, the response to the pandemic was far from uniform and efficient.

Of course, an app does not replace the human side of constraining the disease, but it is generally accepted that it can help. Like a piece in a puzzle, it is a tool to facilitate the resolution of the problem. These systems would enable people who had tested positive for COVID-19 to share information about their recent contacts, so that those individuals could be contacted and given appropriate public health advice to help limit the spread of the virus.

The official response, both from the European Data Protection Committee (EDPC) and the Council of Europe were issued in April 2020. The EDPC enacted Guidelines No. 4/2020 on the use of location data and contact-tracing tools in the context of COVID-19, on 21 April, with the Council issuing a document on 7 April. The European Commission also highlighted that contact tracing was just an instrument within the public health strategy, while clearing the advantages in creating a single app for mobile devices at the European level. However, the responses were fragmented and uncoordinated. Examples of national responses include the Italian Immuni, the German Corona Warn, the Irish COVID Tracker, and the Portuguese StayAway Covid.

In light of the rule of law and the right to privacy, there are five basic ideas to be kept in mind: (a) the pandemic was an exceptional scenario and called for exceptional measures; (b) the proportionality principle has a different meaning in normal times and times of exception; (c) privacy is intrinsic to the idea of the Rule of Law; (d) the Right to Privacy is a fundamental right and a human right (protected in Europe by Article 8 of the European Convention on Human Rights); and (e) Protection of Data and Privacy are two different rights, but both are protected in the European context.

This immediately means a juridical framework to treat personal data, informed consent, and the responsibility of treating data – all statutes in the GDPR.

The contact-tracing apps can be integrated into individual measures in the pandemic to avoid infection, alongside testing and vaccination – this implies responsibility, in addition to liberty.

[18] Initiatives from the European Data Protection Board and from the Council of Europe, both from April 2020. European Data Protection Board, 'Guidelines 04/2020 on the use of location data and contact tracing tools in the context of the Covid-19 outbreak', 21 April 2020, www.edpb.europa.eu/our-work-tools/our-documents/guidelines/guidelines-042020-use-location-data-and-contact-tracing_en and European Council, Council of the European Union, 'Covid-19', www.consilium.europa.eu/en/topics/covid-19/.

Traditional contact tracing is performed by teams of trackers who have to rebuild all the interactions a positive person had. This process consumes both time and resources. The time needed to identify contacts is a critical issue. The stress on responsibility is very important in the case of this tool, with statements that included the idea of a shared responsibility between communities and governments. The implicit value of the app was, therefore, beyond its technology; it instilled a sense of responsibility for the citizens to be part of the solution in addressing the spread of the COVID-19 virus. But it seems that beyond privacy concerns, other issues were at stake, namely efficacy, lack of transparent communication, and sacrifice of privacy when the sacrifice was not worthwhile (disbelief in the usefulness of the app).

All in all, while testing and vaccination were a relative success, contact-tracing apps were a complete failure in Western states. The main tool to combat the pandemic was, of course, vaccines, authorised from December 2020, as voluntary and free for all citizens.

It is also worth remembering that the success of the contact-tracing apps depended on the willingness of the citizens to permanently install and use them; in other words, voluntariness. But, once again, vaccines were also voluntary. That is why the question remains: why did citizens refuse to subscribe to this tool when it comes to the protection of public health, if they normally download applications for other (minor) purposes, which also have juridical consequences? What justifies this dual use of technology in the light of the law?

We must keep in mind that technology should guard patient privacy, but equity and collective benefit are also issues of concern.

13.3.3 *An Effort to Find a Justification ...*

The COVID-19 period was trying, but its consequences were far-reaching. A major proof of this is given by the UN Security Council Resolution 2532 (2020), a symbolic mark, which characterised COVID-19 as a threat to peace and international security, demanding, therefore, for the first time in history, a humanitarian pause in world conflicts.[19]

The pandemic caused the mobilisation of a state of emergency in most countries and in Portugal, in particular, within the framework of the 1976 Constitution for the first time since its entry into force (even though emergency powers have been in the Constitution from the outset). In the Portuguese case, the first patient was diagnosed on 2 March 2020 and the first death occurred fourteen days later.[20]

19 UN Security Council resolution 2532 (2020) [on cessation of hostilities in the context of the coronavirus disease (Covid-19) pandemic], 1 July 2020, S/RES/2532 (2020).

20 State of emergency is ruled especially in articles 19 and 138 of 1976 Portuguese Constitution (the text is available in English at www.parlamento.pt/sites/EN/Parliament/Documents/Constitution7th.pdf). The regime is explained in English by C. Santos Botelho, 'Covid-19 and stress on fundamental rights

States were faced with the legal projection of the effects of a pandemic in terms of fundamental rights, a crisis framed by a normative framework that is easily blurred. The admixture of these components gives rise to several questions. Among them are the distinction between situations of normality and situations of exception, the central role played by the executive in the context of the response to the crisis, and the subordination of exceptional measures to the rule of law.

Alternatively, we should never forget that digitalisation and, with it, mass surveillance, are omnipresent in society. Measures of surveillance (all at the heart of the digitalisation process) and privacy infringements are not always of the same degree and must be highlighted in categories, identifying the severity of possible human rights infringements. Let us hierarchise those according to three possible degrees: highly intrusive responses, intrusive responses, and mildly intrusive responses.

That said, it is necessary that one asks why contact-tracing apps were so inefficient during an era of digital applications, especially keeping in mind that the guiding principles of all action in times of a pandemic are freedom and responsibility, as already noted. In other words, in this balance between freedom and responsibility, it is worth asking why the contact-tracing apps were perceived as such a serious interference in informational self-determination. The first idea that one can imagine is the fear of being segregated or marginalised in communities once it became known that a citizen tested positive. But the scenario can be more complex than that.

First, because if it is true that the Western legal system is not built to impose restrictions on personal freedom when there is no culpability or direct benefit, it is also worth remembering that in an emergency situation rights are under stress.[21] Second, the COVID-19 pandemic led to restrictions in a range of areas. Common examples are the right to freedom of movement and assembly, the right to a fair trial, the right to education, and the right to private and family life.

I believe that the first important lesson to learn from this strange experience is the urgent need to regulate the health market properly, based on the ideas that digitalisation demands de-territorialisation, de-centralisation, and de-nationalisation. In technological terms, the system worked. However, the new wave of techno-optimism was in doubt. The problem was that technology was not enough. I believe the main threats felt by citizens were: (a) the use of the data produced by such tools for disease modelling and epidemic dashboards; (b) the information on health decisions through technology-driven disease testing; and (c) the use of technology to counter health-related discrimination.

in Portugal: an *intermezzo* between the state of exception and constitutional normality' (2020) *Revista Catalana de Dret Public (Catalan Journal of Public Law)*, special issue.

21 The stress on human rights in a pandemic crisis is demonstrated by an unprecedented number of states derogating from the International Covenant on Civil and Political Rights and from regional human rights conventions during COVID-19: S. Molloy, 'Covid-19 and derogations before the European Court of Human Rights', 10 April 2020, Verfassungsblog, https://verfassungsblog.de/covid-19-and-derogations-before-the-european-court-of-human-rights/.

In addition, there are always contextual issues. Social, political, economic, and psychological factors can affect citizens when adopting and/or using technology. We can imagine how attitudes towards the pandemic and the general attitude of the people before and during the pandemic can change (from negative – dissatisfaction, unhappiness, compliance, etc., to positive – satisfaction, appreciation, etc.).

In the Portuguese example (the one I know best), people were not sufficiently encouraged to start using the app. This involves two simple steps – the first is how to install the app and the second is instructions on how to operate the app using a smartphone. However, we must not forget that Portugal has many citizens without digital skills (especially the elderly who may not be conversant with new technologies), and the developers of the app did not consider them.

There was not enough public awareness about the app, and information and knowledge on usage was limited. The main efforts came from the government. However, the media did not promote the use of the app, either in the press or on radio stations, unlike what happened in other countries (e.g., Germany, with the Corona-Warn-App).[22] Specialists at the time reported that we would need at least 60 per cent of the population to download and actively use the contact-tracing app in order for it to be useful.

Let us go beyond the surface and utilise this experience to reflect on digitalisation and its implications in the juridical area. The digital transformation in the legal world can generate two paths: (a) the need for the right to 'give in' to new technologies, reducing the level of legal protection for those rights negatively affected by technologies; and (b) the call to update and reconceptualise the existing legal framework to accommodate new technological developments.

The real and critical challenge for public law and human rights protection in the digital age is finding and maintaining the appropriate balance between the advantages and disadvantages that the application of technology brings; that is, how to ensure that technological development moves within a framework that provides the well-being of human society.

13.4 THE LESSONS LEARNED

In contemporary democracies, trust in public and political institutions has collapsed in the last decade of the twentieth century and the beginning of the twenty-first century.[23] This is probably one substantial explanation for the non-adherence to the COVID-19 app in the Western states (first lesson). Added to that, the COVID-19 crisis highlighted the issue of trust in democracies, as governments had to both

[22] See C. Brause, 'Mit dieser Warn-App will die Regierung das Leben wieder normaler machen', 1 April 2020, *Welt*, www.welt.de/wirtschaft/article206935981/Coronavirus-Mit-dieser-Warn-App-will-die-Regierung-das-Leben-wieder-normaler-machen.html.

[23] G. Abiri and J. Buchheim, 'Beyond true and false: fake news and the digital epistemic divide' (2022) 29 *Michigan Technology Law Review*, 59–109.

undertake (unprecedented) restrictive measures to manage the spread of COVID-19 and to rely on the citizens' willingness to adhere to these measures.

Cyberspace is a global network, primarily for private entities and institutions, and that includes public institutions – which poses a fundamental question about the role of the state in this new world of goods and services.

A constitutional approach means a policy that deals with digital technologies from a perspective also aimed to protect fundamental rights and democratic values, which includes framing the debate within the information society; this is increasingly subject to the power of public and private actors implementing automated decision-making technologies. As a first consequence, far from simply applying existing law in cyberspace, there is an urgent need for online laws, such as the GDPR (second lesson). Especially in the healthcare field, we should amplify the call for building and strengthening stable global healthcare data and technology governance frameworks to assist digital surveillance suitable for overall healthcare systems. An appropriate institutionalisation of a rights-based framework would enhance trust, as well as longer-term geographical equity and comprehensive health and care. With the COVID-19 app experience, we have learned that technology as embellishment does not work at all.

In that field, the Council of the EU has considerable experience, as it played a crucial role in consolidating the constitutional dimension of the right to privacy and data protection in Europe, through the Data Protection Directive. So it is desirable that the institution focus on strengthening governance of digital healthcare systems, with at its heart the concept that healthcare is a public good (rather than health data as a public good).

The notion of the rule of law is also at stake. Indeed, the crisis of the rule of law is the crisis of trust. To exemplify that, just remember two recent European situations: the non-enforcement of refugee laws in Europe and high-level corruption in public entities. These two quite different examples prove that rules are also not being obeyed in Europe, which generates a problem of trust.

Trust, in light of the rule of law, is not trust in persons but trust in institutions (e.g., courts) and systems (e.g., the EU). This problem of trust has been reinforced by several measures in some states during the pandemic, as proven by people attending street events, criticisms of political leaders, and divided institutions.

The main problem of trusting institutions is related to the classical notion of the rule of law (the formal rule of law concept). One knows that there is an intrinsic ambiguity across legal traditions in this concept (there are differences between the English idea of 'the rule of law', the German *Rechtsstaat*, the French *l'Etat de droit*, the Italian *Stato di diritto*, etc.), but they all mean a relationship between state, constitution, governing, and law. In other words, this traditional concept is clearly related to notions of the separation of powers, general and public rules for all, and consistent and transparent regulation.

This system of checks and balances, along with the principle of the separation of powers, represents the common core of constitutionalism. The ideal of limited government, intrinsic to any form of constitutionalism, requires the adoption of a system of reciprocal control among different branches or decision-making centres of the state, and rejects the unwarranted concentration of power in the general constitutional design (third lesson).

This is the core of public law, even with digitalisation in progress. That is why we should identify a new notion of public authority, which includes acts, institutions, and relations of states, supranational institutions, and international bodies, and apply it in these normative dimensions of public law, both offline and online. Indeed, all public institutions must act according to the standards of democratic public law, no matter if they are acting offline or online.

A healthy suspicion of power provides democracy its vitality, but, and let us stress this point, democracy depends on trust. Besides, liberty in democracy is not only individual liberty, but also collective liberty.

We should try to continue and widely reflect on this lack of trust. Modern societies are creating particularised trust based on race, ethnicity, lifestyle, moral identity, or religion. I am not sure if this scenario is helping the real standards of trust. What is clear is that public policy has to cope with diversity, but trust can withstand the pressure that diversity poses. One thing is certain: in the end, a failure of trust is a failure for democracy.

Public entities must assure trust in justice (perception of the judiciary), maintain awareness of any (dis)satisfaction with public services, pay attention to corruption, and its perception, and govern with transparency and accountability. There is no need to stress that good governance practices influence citizens' attitudes and behaviours towards the government (fourth lesson).

In Europe, the problem of trust is a problem both for political institutions and the courts, not only in European institutions, but also in national institutions. This means a long path to develop a collaborative way forward, where trust is seen as a value by institutions.

Besides, ensuring anonymity is not enough. The technology used in the social context must be considered; for example, when providing additional support to citizens that have experienced discrimination because they contracted the COVID-19 virus. Furthermore, the use of a smartphone application to trace those individuals that an infected person has been in contact with in order to prevent the spread of COVID-19 is not such a novel situation.

From a broader perspective, there are benefits in enabling voluntarism, solidarity, and public modes of association, even in political relations (fifth lesson). The simple fact that national decision-making has shifted from domestic policies to policies that result from participation in a global or transnational decision-making process alters the dynamics of all decision-making. This will mean limiting coercive organisation in favour of voluntary association, enabling broader participation. Not all, but certain kinds of rights – in particular, rights of association, speech, and political participation – must shift from problem-solving mode and from a coercive manner to include participatory relations (according to the all affected principle). This principle says, roughly, that all those who are affected by a decision should have a right to participate in making it. The explanation is simple: it is only when strangers are no longer treated as bearers of malign intent that the possibilities of extensive trust can develop.

It is clear that globalisation and the proliferation of communicative platforms is taking people away from 'vertical' interactions in which representative politics is typical, toward more distributed, flatter, or 'horizontal' modes of sociality, working, and organising, which poses special problems for democracy itself, as this leaves us in a 'post-representative' political moment, which means that the advent of online communication has had both good and bad effects on the practice of democracy.

It is also pointless to recall the normative concept developed by Jürgen Habermas – the public sphere. For Habermas, modernity was formed from the development of a division between state and society.[24] The public sphere became politicised and was transformed into a political public sphere and this concept – the political public sphere – is the most difficult and controversial issue in terms of the constitutional power posed by digitalisation. It suffers a profound alteration in the Habermasian sense; that is, as a sphere of communication. Habermas explains this situation as one where individuals can discuss critical issues and gain knowledge of public issues. In this way, political public opinion is formed – a public and shared space in which decisions are made through dialogue.

Indeed, communication, an essential element for the formation of will within a community, is now guided by a new paradigm. I even question if digital communication is still 'only' a way of exercising freedom of expression.

This new paradigm is more accelerated, more instantaneous, and more connected. The public sphere, as already stated, became fragmentary, immediate, egocentric, and public–private. Besides, it includes a great divergence of publics, the political, the cultural, and so on. Knowledge is generated and disseminated in a decentralised manner and the reconstruction of meaning is carried out by acceptance and reproduction without any control. The protagonists are unknown. They are no longer ministers of religious cults, artists, or intellectuals. But will it be the will of leaders (political, business, etc.) or instead the will of the media? Or even none of these? Within the political will, new methodologies merge (informal information, fact-checking), where fact and opinion become mixed.

To sum up, all these changes represent a considerable challenge for the logic of constitutionalism in terms of legitimacy. This is why I can ask what the concrete manifestations are today of living in democratic spaces mediated by technology. In the spaces of discourse, which ones can be characterised as spaces of civic interaction and as spaces of political intervention? The control of access to resources

[24] F. Dallmayr, 'The discourse of modernity: Hegel and Habermas' (1987) 84 *The Journal of Philosophy* 11, 682–92.

and communications platforms indeed has considerable power to (re)configure discourses, and the answers to these questions are crucial. We should not forget the unequal distribution of the potential associated with such technologies, and the specific state of the virtual public sphere also distorts intercultural dialogue. In other words, virtual social networks can limit and distort the dialogue between cultures because of the virtual public sphere they create. That is one of the reasons I am in favour of encouraging the public financing of online communications so that they are not co-opted by commercial interests. Cultivating a will towards civic participation in society, keeping non-profits involved so that access remains affordable, is essential to democracy and the protection of fundamental rights. A virtual self-government by 'cyberians' is highly problematic, since the real world, through the state, is the only institutional structure that seems able to fulfil the important and irreplaceable task of promoting social and political integration that forms the collective identity (the formula that contains in itself the ideas of common interest and community). In this sense, there are several discussions, namely about 'echo chambers', specific platforms created by political parties, parliamentary decisions via AI, possible uses of AI for the realisation of social rights, and so on.

It is clear that the new regulations have to address one basic distinction: the exercise of democracy through the internet and the exercise of democracy on the internet. In the former, cyber-attacks, namely from authoritarian governments and non-state actors, pose a clear and increasing threat to democracies across the world, especially through their interference in free and fair elections (we must keep in mind that there is state influence on the internet by some states and international legal protection from that interference), and the manipulation of information sources for political discourse and decision-making. In the latter scenario, besides considering the rule of law, a new premise for democracy itself arises as technology becomes an integral part of a truly democratic global society. Indeed, in this new scenario, democracy itself and its realisation involves monitoring strategies that deal with the asymmetry of information and imbalance of power. Of course, an appropriate approach in confronting and criticising government power, a logical and rational critique of political, economic, social, and cultural issues, bilateral dialogue, and free audience (all) with government officials can help.

Good governance theory advocates the responsible, accountable, and transparent management of human, financial, economic, and natural resources for the sustainable and equitable development of all institutions. First of all, this requires the government to be accountable for its actions by implying transparency and access to information for its citizens. Governments also need to be responsive to people's needs by exhibiting responsiveness and safeguarding human rights, in order to achieve public trust. On the other hand, public authorities must use common-sense at the core of their speeches, embedded in an overall togetherness narrative. This will lead to mutual agreement, pragmatic rationality, and cooperative compliance from citizens. Building a common public culture is essential for trust in public affairs. Otherwise, we experience the division of society into parallel societies with little to no intergroup trust and the risk of mutual suspicion.

With the digitalisation of the public environment, it is not only the state and public authorities that can be a threat to our rights, but also private entities. That was the idea in the birth of fundamental rights in the eighteenth century. Today, the threat can come from both sides, but that is a completely different question and it is not addressed in this chapter.

This is, I believe, the core provided by the legal frameworks of public and private law. They follow different rationales. Private law allows actors to act solely in pursuit of their self-interest, whereas public law requires a higher standard, often referred to as the pursuit of a common interest. The public character of an act or behaviour thus derives from its relation to that common interest. It depends on the social sphere from which it originates. If the activity is part of the sphere where self-interest is a sufficient justification, the act is private; if it belongs to the sphere where common interests are predominant, it is public.

In times of crisis, such as the COVID-19 pandemic, citizen trust in the system is one of the central features ensuring citizen compliance and the functioning of a democratic society, which includes the role of democracy and how citizens assess its performance. That evaluation also comes from the published discourse. We cannot forget that it was that public discourse that associated the use of apps with surveillance, questioning whether these measures are 'typically' European.

13.5 CONCLUSION

It is time to conclude. From all that has been written, it is clear that I believe that trust, regulation, redefining the rule of law, and the role of the state are crucial factors in overcoming the general perception of the loss of rights. That perception has developed since the beginning of digitalisation and was particularly clear during the experience of contact tracking to control COVID-19. That is why I believe this represents a new set of challenges in the art of the law. It is important to keep in mind that we have online and offline rights, national and international orders, and states that will not give up their roles, and, last but not least, citizens who have claims relating to privacy and also protection and security.

14

Aerial Surveillance in the Digital Age

Drone-Related Privacy Concerns and the Protection of Other Human Rights

Skirgailė Žalimienė and Saulius Stonkus

14.1 INTRODUCTION

Innovation and digitalisation are perceived as an enabler of growth and a catalyst for the development of modern aviation in Europe.[1] In the view of the European Commission 'drones are a technology that is already bringing about radical changes, by creating opportunities for new services and applications, as well as new challenges'.[2] As it stated in the title of the Communication from the European Commission to the European Parliament and the Council, opening the aviation market to the civil use of drone technology marks '[a] new era for aviation'.[3] A similar view of drone technologies is shared by other countries.[4]

[1] For example, see European Commission, 'An aviation strategy for Europe', COM(2015) 598 final.

[2] The term 'drone' is often used to describe virtually any device that is able to fly without a pilot on board. A more technical term is unmanned aerial vehicle (UAV), which in conjunction with the equipment necessary to control it forms an unmanned aircraft system (UAS). The latter can be divided into remotely piloted aircraft systems (RPAS) or drones, which are piloted by remote pilots (humans), and autonomous aircraft, which do not require any human input during flight at all (with some exceptions, e.g., in accordance with Article 3 § 31 of Regulation (EU) 2018/1139 (commonly referred to as the 'Basic Regulation'), even when operating an autonomous aircraft, the remote pilot is still responsible for monitoring its course and remaining able to intervene and change the course at any time, whereas according to International Civil Aviation Organization (ICAO) terminology as autonomous aircraft are regarded as only those unmanned aircraft that do not allow pilot intervention in the management of the flight. Although the integration of fully autonomous aircraft into airspace is not expected to happen in the near future, the possibility for a remote pilot to intervene in a UAV flight and take over control is an important issue to discuss, as it is highly relevant when dealing with the liability for damage caused by autonomous aircraft (see International Civil Aviation Organization, *Unmanned Aircraft Systems* (2011), Cir 328, AN/190, ix, 3).

[3] See European Commission, 'A new era for aviation – opening the aviation market to the civil use of remotely piloted aircraft systems in a safe and sustainable manner', COM(2014) 207 final.

[4] For example, the President of the US in his 2021 executive order acknowledged the 'great potential' of drones (White House, 'Executive Order on Promoting Competition in the American Economy', 9 July 2021, www.whitehouse.gov/briefing-room/presidential-actions/2021/07/09/executive-order-on-promoting-competition-in-the-american-economy/) and the UK Regulatory Horizons Council pointed out in a 2021 exploratory study that 'drone technology, powered by advances in robotics,

Indeed, the commercial drone industry has flourished in recent years, and the technology, which a few decades ago was exclusively a part of modern military equipment, became available to the general public. The number of drone operations in Europe alone has already come close to manned aviation.[5] Drones are widely used by various state authorities, as well as commercial entities and private persons for purposes as diverse as policing, search and rescue, environment monitoring, film-making, mapping, agriculture, and entertainment.

Drones are undoubtedly very useful and represent tremendous opportunities. With evolving drone technologies various new business models emerge, such as parcel delivery by air, aerial photography, air taxis, and drone journalism. Drones offer new services and applications going far beyond traditional aviation and allow us to perform existing services in a more affordable and environmentally friendly way by increasing the efficiency of different activities. In addition, drones are hard to replace, especially in difficult situations; for example, when restoring communications or carrying out search and rescue missions after natural disasters. Even the pandemic caused by the COVID-19, when physical contact was restricted, became an opportunity to demonstrate the extremely wide range of possible drone applications and promote their use in everyday life, seeking a more positive public attitude towards the application of drone technology.[6] In principle, the capabilities of drones are almost limitless, making them applicable in any field.

However, among other reasons, to meet safety requirements, modern drones as a rule are equipped with high-end technologies, which can capture, store, and upload online or to other devices huge amounts of data, including private data. Drones can range in size from being big enough to carry a human to as small as a hummingbird, and very quiet, making them extremely hard to notice. In

battery power and artificial intelligence, is "on the cusp" of delivering new breakthrough capabilities' (Regulatory Horizons Council, 'The regulation of drones: an exploratory study' (2021), https://assets.publishing.service.gov.uk/government/uploads/system/uploads/attachment_data/file/1029834/rhc-drones-report.pdf).

5 See ICAO, 'European Regional Aviation Safety Plan 2020–2022' (2020), www.icao.int/EURNAT/EUR%20and%20NAT%20Documents/EUR%20Documents/EUR%20RASP/Archive/EUR%20RASP%202020-2022_EN.pdf, 23.

6 For example, in Lithuania, drones were used to monitor public places for possible violations of quarantine restrictions and to warn residents if such violations were observed (see Vilnius city website, 'Vilniuje karantino priežiūrai į dangų pakelti dronai' (2020), https://vilnius.lt/lt/2020/03/30/vilniuje-karantino-prieziurai-i-dangu-pakelti-dronai/); one man in Cyprus used a drone to take his dog for a walk while he was in lockdown because of COVID-19 (see L. Eadicicco, 'A man used a drone to take his dog for a walk while he was in lockdown because of the coronavirus' (2020), www.businessinsider.com/video-dog-being-walked-by-drone-cyprus-coronavirus-lockdown-2020-3?r=US&IR=T); in China and India drones were used to spray public areas with disinfectant – and such utilisation of drones was also considered in the UK (see Z. Kleinman, 'Coronavirus: should the UK use drones to disinfect public spaces?' (2020), www.bbc.com/news/health-52109824); even UNICEF prepared guidelines for how drones can be used to combat COVID-19 (see UNICEF, 'How drones can be used to combat COVID-19' (2020) www.unicef.org/supply/media/5286/file/%20Rapid-guidance-how-can-drones-help-in-COVID-19-response.pdf).

addition, drones are piloted remotely or, in some cases, using advanced artificial intelligence (AI) technology that is able to develop flight patterns with the only human input specifying the destination,[7] which makes it very hard to trace the actual drone users.[8] Therefore, with the use of drones private data can not only be easily accessed and collected in areas where people reasonably expect privacy, but it can also be achieved anonymously. Hence, along with all the new possibilities and benefits, the massive deployment of drones in public life also bring serious privacy issues, as drones like any other technology can be misused. According to Zuboff, in the absence of countervailing restrictions and sanctions, every digital application that *can* be used for surveillance and control *will* be used for surveillance and control, irrespective of its original intention.[9] Therefore, emerging drone technology requires an appropriate legal response, as it is impossible to disinvent the technology – drones are here to stay.

Privacy is a constitutional value recognised in the vast majority of countries. According to Privacy International, one of the world's major watchdogs on surveillance and privacy, over 130 countries in every region of the world have constitutional statements regarding the protection of privacy.[10] The right to privacy is also enshrined in major international and regional human rights documents (conventions, declarations, charters, etc).[11] Although legal scholars often acknowledge that drones pose a serious threat to privacy, in making such a conclusion they simply presume the potential dangers, usually limiting themselves to a few examples, but

7 Such autonomous drones are already available on the market (see the Skydio Autonomy website at www.skydio.com/skydio-autonomy).

8 Owing to the issue of identifying the actual pilot of a drone, a new type of profession – drone detectives (forensics) – has evolved in recent years (e.g., see P. Marks, 'How police catch drone-flying criminals' (2017), www.bbc.com/future/article/20170731-how-cops-catch-drone-flying-criminals).

9 S. Zuboff, *In the Age of the Smart Machine: The Future of Work and Power* (New York: Basic Books, 1988); S. Zuboff, 'The surveillance paradigm: be the friction – our response to the new Lords of the Ring' (2013), *Frankfurter Allgemeine Zeitung*, www.faz.net/aktuell/feuilleton/the-surveillance-paradigm-be-the-friction-our-response-to-the-new-lords-of-the-ring-12241996.html.

10 For more information see Privacy International, 'What is privacy?', 23 October 2017, https://privacyinternational.org/explainer/56/what-privacy.

11 For example, Article 5 of the American Declaration of the Rights and Duties of Man, Bogotá, 2 May 1948, 1 Annals of the OAS. 130 (1949); Article 12 of the United Nations Declaration of Human Rights, GA Res. 217A (III), UN Doc. A/810, at 71 (1948); Article 8 of the European Convention on Human Rights, Rome, 4 November 1950, Council of Europe, European Treaty Series No. 5; Article 17 of the International Covenant on Civil and Political Rights, New York, 16 December 1966; Article 11 of the American Convention on Human Rights, San Jose, 22 November 1969, 1144 UNTS 123; Article 16 of the Convention on the Rights of the Child, New York, 20 November 1989, 1577 UNTS 3; Article 10 of the African Charter on the Rights and Welfare of the Child, Addis Ababa, 11 July 1990, 29 ILM 1458; Article 14 of the International Convention on the Protection of the Rights of All Migrant Workers and Members of Their Families, New York, 18 December 1990, 2220 UNTS 3; Article 7 of the Charter of Fundamental Rights of the European Union, Nice, 7 December 2000, Official Journal of the European Union (OJ), 2000/C 364/01; Articles 16 and 21 of the Arab Charter on Human Rights, Tunis, 22 May 2004, 12 ILM 307); Article 21 of the Association of Southeast Asian Nations Human Rights Declaration, Phnom Penh, 18 November 2012, 52 ILM 1010, etc.

do not discuss in more detail the privacy violations that the use of drone technology can cause.

A deep understanding of drone related threats to privacy, the diverse ways that drone technology can affect privacy, the way it can interfere with other human rights, the various restrictions to drone use that may be implicated, and the need to mitigate these tensions by maintaining the right balance together form the cornerstone to ensuring the successful integration of drones in modern society. Therefore, the aim of Section 14.2 is to present a broader discussion of the major privacy concerns arising from the mass introduction of drones into everyday life,[12] provide a more detailed description of the relevant threats, as well as to highlight possible clashes between privacy and other human rights invoked by the use of drone technology, emphasising the need to strike a fair balance between these conflicting values. In Section 14.3, the current regulatory developments on drone technologies in relation to identified human rights concerns are analysed, focusing primarily on the European context and seeking to determine the main shortcomings that must be rectified in order to effectively manage the threats associated with the use of drones.

14.2 DRONES AND THEIR USE: MAJOR PRIVACY CONCERNS AND OTHER HUMAN RIGHTS ISSUES

Article 7 of the Charter of Fundamental Rights of the European Union (the Charter) holds that everyone has the right to respect for his or her private and family life, home, and communications. While Article 8 of the Charter enshrines protection of personal data, stating in its first paragraph that everyone has the right to the protection of personal data concerning him or her. The Court of Justice of the European Union (CJEU) when applying Articles 7 and 8 of the Charter has noted on numerous occasions that Article 7 of the Charter, regarding the right to respect for private and family life, contains rights corresponding to those guaranteed in Article 8(1) of the Convention for the Protection of Human Rights and Fundamental Freedoms (ECHR), and that the protection of personal data is of fundamental importance to a person's enjoyment of his or her right to respect for private and family life, as guaranteed by Article 8 of the ECHR. In accordance with Article 52(3) of the Charter, Article 7 of the Charter is thus to be given the same meaning and the same scope as Article 8(1) ECHR, as interpreted by the case law of the European Court of Human Rights (ECtHR).[13] The same is true for other rights protected by the Charter which correspond to rights guaranteed by the ECHR. Therefore, the CJEU

[12] For the purposes of this chapter, the right to privacy is regarded as including the right to protection of personal data (except if stated otherwise).

[13] See, for instance, Case C-345/17, *Sergejs Buivids v Datu valsts inspekcija* [2019], ECLI:EU:C:2019:122, para. 65; Case C-460/20, *TU, RE v Google LLC* [2022], ECLI:EU:C:2022:962, para. 59.

often relies on the jurisprudence of the ECtHR when interpreting the meaning and the scope of the rights recognised by the Charter. Nevertheless, this provision does not prevent EU law providing more extensive protection.

The ECtHR has emphasised in its case law that the concept of private life extends to aspects relating to personal identity, such as pictures of a person.[14] A person's image constitutes one of the chief attributes of his or her personality, as it reveals the person's unique characteristics and distinguishes the person from his or her peers. The right to the protection of one's image is thus one of the essential components of personal development.[15] It primarily presupposes the individual's right to control the use of that image, including the right to refuse its publication, which is also relevant for publications online.[16] And namely in the light of drone technology, the most evident threat to privacy is when using a drone equipped with a camera, which usually comes as a standard element of drone equipment and is able to capture images (photographs and videos).

The right to one's image is recognised virtually worldwide as a part of the right to private life or regarded as a separate right with a special provision in national laws to protect it; nevertheless, it is closely related to the right to respect for private life.[17] Therefore, the unlawful surveillance of a person and recording, collecting, processing, or using that data may lead to the violation of his or her right to privacy. As evident from the jurisprudence of the ECtHR, everyone, including people known to the public, has a legitimate expectation that his or her private life will be protected.[18] However, a person's reasonable expectation of privacy is a significant though not necessarily conclusive factor, since there are occasions when people knowingly or intentionally involve themselves in activities that are or may be recorded or reported

14 See *Schüssel v. Austria* (dec.), Application no. 42409/98, Decision of 21 February 2002; *Von Hannover v. Germany*, Application no. 59320/00, Judgment of 24 June 2004, para. 50; *von Hannover v. Germany (no. 2)* [GC], Applications nos. 40660/08 and 60641/08, Judgment of 7 February 2012, para. 95.

15 See *López Ribalda and Others v. Spain* [GC], Applications nos. 1874/13 and 8567/13, Judgment of 17 October 2019, paras. 87–91 and the references cited therein.

16 See *Reklos and Davourlis v. Greece*, Application no. 1234/05, Judgment of 15 January 2009, para. 40; *von Hannover v. Germany (no. 2)* [GC], Applications nos. 40660/08 and 60641/08, Judgment of 7 February 2012, para. 96.

17 For example, see S. R. Barnett, 'The right to one's own image: publicity and privacy rights in the United States and Spain' (1999) 47 *The American Journal of Comparative Law* 4, 555–81; E. H. Reiter, 'Personality and patrimony: comparative perspectives on the right to one's image' (2002) 76 *Tulane Law Review* 3, 673–726; H. Trouille, 'Private life and public image: privacy legislation in France' (2000) 49 *International and Comparative Law Quarterly* 1, 199–208.

18 See *von Hannover v. Germany (no. 2)* [GC], Applications nos. 40660/08 and 60641/08, Judgment of 7 February 2012, para. 97; *Sciacca v. Italy*, Application no. 50774/99, Judgment of 11 January 2005, para. 29; *Reklos and Davourlis v. Greece*, Application no. 1234/05, Judgment of 15 January 2009, para. 40; *Von Hannover v. Germany*, Application no. 59320/00, Judgment of 24 June 2004, para. 51; *Leempoel & S.A. ED. Ciné Revue v. Belgium*, Application no. 64772/01, Judgment of 9 November 2006, para. 78; *Standard Verlags GmbH v. Austria (no. 2)*, Application no. 21277/05, Judgment of 4 June 2009, para. 48; *Hachette Filipacchi Associés (ICI PARIS) v. France*, Application no. 12268/03, Judgment of 23 July 2009, para. 53.

in a public manner.[19] Therefore, there are a number of elements relevant to the consideration of whether a person's private life is concerned by measures effected outside a person's home or private premises.[20] As a result, according to the ECtHR, it is relevant if the surveillance exceeded an extent of exposure possible to a passer-by or to security observation and beyond a degree surpassing that which the individual could possibly have foreseen.[21]

In this sense the use of drones in the light of the right to privacy is quite problematic. Drones can be very small and quiet, and so hard to detect, and the ever-decreasing size of various drone components constantly leads to less detectable devices. Owing to these features, people may often not be aware of being surveilled; among other issues, it creates opportunities for more frequent voyeuristic attacks. Drones can also be very light and easy to carry, they can take off quickly and almost from anywhere, usually there is no need for lengthy preparation and/or special take-off and landing sites. In addition, they are relatively cheap. These are definitely the advantages of drones in comparison with conventional aircraft, as they make aerial surveillance, which was previously quite expensive and usually available only to state authorities, easily accessible to everyone. However, this poses a serious challenge to ensuring adequate protection of the right to privacy because it may lead to systematic mass surveillance, which can in turn cause serious negative psychological consequences in society by making people feel less free and force a sort of self-censorship by restricting their behaviour.

Private life, in the ECtHR's view, includes a person's physical and psychological integrity; the guarantee afforded by Article 8 of the ECHR is primarily intended to ensure the development, without outside interference, of the personality of each individual in his relations with other human beings.[22] There is therefore a zone of interaction with others, even in public contexts, which may fall within the scope of private life.[23] The ECtHR, for example, has found video surveillance of public places where the visual data are recorded, stored, and disclosed to the public as falling under Article 8 of the ECHR.[24] According to the ECtHR, although monitoring the

[19] See *Bărbulescu v. Romania* [GC], Application no. 61496/08, Judgment of 5 September 2017, para. 73; *Köpke v. Germany* (dec.), Application no. 420/07, Decision of 5 October 2010.

[20] See *P. G. and J. H. v. the United Kingdom*, Application no. 44787/98, Judgment of 25 September 2001, para. 57.

[21] See, for instance, *Peck v. United Kingdom*, Application no. 44647/98, Judgment of 28 January 2003, para. 62.

[22] See *Von Hannover v. Germany*, Application no. 59320/00, Judgment of 24 June 2004, para. 50; also, mutatis mutandis, *Niemietz v. Germany*, Application no. 13710/88, Judgment of 16 December 1992, para. 29; *Botta v. Italy*, Application no. 21439/93, Judgment of 24 February 1998, para. 32.

[23] See, mutatis mutandis, *P. G. and J. H. v. the United Kingdom*, Application no. 44787/98, Judgment of 25 September 2001, para. 56; *Peck v. United Kingdom*, Application no. 44647/98, Judgment of 28 January 2003, para. 57.

[24] In particular, the disclosure to the media for the broadcast use of video footage of an applicant whose suicide attempt was caught on surveillance television cameras was found to be a serious interference with the applicant's private life, notwithstanding that he was in a public place at the time (see *Peck*

actions of an individual in a public place using photographic equipment that does not record the visual data does not, as such, give rise to an interference with the individual's private life,[25] the recording of the data and the systematic or permanent nature of the record may give rise to such considerations, regardless of whether the surveillance is covert or overt.[26] Therefore, the ECtHR has concluded that the compilation of data by security services on particular individuals, even without the use of covert surveillance methods, constitutes an interference with the applicants' private lives.[27] This comes in line with 'mosaic theory', developed in light of the Fourth Amendment to the US Constitution.[28] According to this theory, a certain amount of data as an aggregated whole can implicate reasonable expectations of privacy even though the separate constituent parts of such data do not.[29] Hence, it is evident that private life is a broad term 'not susceptible to exhaustive definition'.[30]

Threats posed by drones equipped only with sound recorders and no ability to capture video or images should also not be neglected, as they can secretly listen to and record private conversations. Moreover, modern technologies make it possible to perform a sort of human profiling based on timbre and other voice characteristics and/or identify a particular person (i.e., a speaker) using voice recognition technology.[31] Accordingly, voice recordings, as well as images in the case of facial recognition, can be further processed into biometric data using advanced technologies, which makes it possible to relate real people with their profiles in the digital domain. Such unforeseen use of photographs, videos, and sound recordings can constitute an interference with the right to private life.[32] In the ECtHR's view, the rapid development of increasingly sophisticated techniques allowing, among

v. United Kingdom, Application no. 44647/98, Judgment of 28 January 2003, paras. 57–63, 87). For example, video surveillance in a supermarket by an employer (see *López Ribalda and Others v. Spain* [GC], Applications nos. 1874/13 and 8567/13, Judgment of 17 October 2019, para. 93) and in a university amphitheatre (see *Antović and Mirković v. Montenegro*, Application no. 70838/13, Judgment of 28 November 2017) also fall within the scope of Article 8 of the ECHR.

[25] See, for instance, *Herbecq and the association 'Ligue des droits de l'homme' v. Belgium*, Applications no. 32200/96 and 32201/96, Decision of 14 January 1998.

[26] See *P. G. and J. H. v. the United Kingdom*, Application no. 44787/98, Judgment of 25 September 2001, para. 57; *Peck v. United Kingdom*, Application no. 44647/98, Judgment of 28 January 2003, para. 59.

[27] See, for instance, *Rotaru v. Romania* [GC], Application no. 28341/95, Judgment of 4 May 2000, paras. 43–4; *Amann v. Switzerland* [GC], Application no. 27798/95, Judgment of 16 February 2000, paras. 65–7.

[28] See, e.g., O. S. Kerr, 'The mosaic theory of the Fourth Amendment' (2012) 111 *Michigan Law Review* 3, 311–54; D. C. Gray and K. D. Citron, 'A shattered looking glass: the pitfalls and potential of the mosaic theory of Fourth Amendment privacy' (2013) 14 *North Carolina Journal of Law & Technology* 2, 381–429.

[29] See Kerr, 'The mosaic theory of the Fourth Amendment', 311–54.

[30] See, for instance, *P. G. and J. H. v. the United Kingdom*, Application no. 44787/98, Judgment of 25 September 2001, para. 56; *Peck v. United Kingdom*, Application no. 44647/98, Judgment of 28 January 2003, para. 57.

[31] See, e.g., R. Singh, *Profiling Humans from their Voice* (Singapore: Springer, 2019).

[32] See, for instance *Peck v. United Kingdom*, Application no. 44647/98, Judgment of 28 January 2003.

other things, facial recognition and facial mapping techniques to be applied to individuals' photographs without a doubt amounts to interference with his or her right to private life within the meaning of Article 8 § 1 of the ECHR, which makes the taking of their photographs and the storage and possible dissemination of the resulting data problematic.[33] Therefore, recording and storing voices may also in itself constitute an interference with the right to private life. As the ECtHR has ruled in the case *P. G. and J. H. v. the United Kingdom* (§ 59–60), the recordings taken for use as voice samples cannot be regarded as falling outside the scope of the protection afforded by Article 8 of the ECHR.

The risk of interference with the right to privacy may arise not only when photographing and/or filming individuals but also their private property.[34] Even when such images (e.g., of an enclosed courtyard) are not related to an identified or identifiable natural person, it may still infringe one's privacy, as the right to respect for private life also includes the inviolability of the home. While drones can easily overcome fences of any size and construction or even fly inside buildings,[35] where persons reasonably expect to maintain their privacy, the inviolability of the home gains even more significance.[36] In addition to this, cameras used in

[33] See *Gaughran v. the United Kingdom*, Application no. 45245/15, Judgment of 13 February 2020, para. 70.

[34] E.g., Article 29 of the Data Protection Working Party in Opinion 01/2015 on Privacy and Data Protection Issues relating to the Utilisation of Drones (01673/15/EN, WP 231), adopted on 16 June 2015, has concluded that the processing of images (including images of houses, vehicles, driving licence plates, etc.) related to an identified or identifiable natural person carried out by the data processing equipment on-board a drone may have an impact on privacy and data protection, and therefore trigger the application of data protection legislation.

[35] E.g., an indoor security camera drone was recently introduced to the market (see J. Siminoff, 'Introducing Ring always home cam: an innovative new approach to always being home' (2020), https://blog.ring.com/products-innovation/introducing-ring-always-home-cam-an-innovative-new-approach-to-always-being-home/).

[36] Even legal entities (corporations) can rely on the right to privacy, although, e.g., CJEU has excluded legal persons from data protection (see Joined cases C-92/09 and C-93/09, *Volker und Markus Schecke GbR and Hartmut Eifert v. Land Hessen* [2010] ECR I-11063, paras. 52, 53 and 87). In this regard, the ECtHR has emphasised in the case *Bernh Larsen Holding AS and others v. Norway,* that the word 'home', appearing in the English text of Article 8 of the ECHR (the word '*domicile*' in the French text has a broader connotation) covers residential premises and may extend also to certain professional or business premises. It includes not only the registered office of a company owned and run by a private individual, but also that of a legal person and its branches and other business premises. Accordingly, in certain cases concerning complaints under Article 8 of the ECHR related to the search of business premises and the search and seizure of electronic data, the ECtHR found an interference with 'the right to respect for home' and 'correspondence'. Nevertheless, according to the jurisprudence of ECtHR, in such cases the Contracting States retain their entitlement to 'interfere' to the extent permitted by paragraph 2 of Article 8 of the ECHR, and that entitlement might well be more far-reaching where professional or business activities or premises were involved than would otherwise be the case (see *Bernh Larsen Holding AS and others v. Norway*, Application no. 24117/08, Judgment of 14 March 2013, paras. 104–5 and the references cited therein). The corporate right to privacy is acknowledged in US legal doctrine as well, yet this topic is still controversial (see, e.g., E. Pollman, 'A corporate right to privacy' (2014) 99 *Minnesota Law Review* 1, 27–88; also K. Robinson, 'Corporate rights and individual

modern drones have advanced optical and digital zoom capabilities, which make it possible to capture high resolution images from a long distance.[37] Combined with advanced infra-red, radar, laser, holographic, computer, and other technologies and theoretical scientific knowledge, drones equipped with high zoom cameras enable to form a detailed spatial (3D) projection from captured data, revealing in detail the geometric, physical, and other properties of objects and their interrelationships.[38] Furthermore, this feature (high zoom capability) is also an issue in relation to privacy concerns as far as it helps to maintain the secrecy of surveillance by facilitating a large distance from the subject of interest, in addition to the anonymity of the drone pilot owing to remote control. In turn, the individual not being aware of ongoing surveillance is one of the most significant challenges to privacy in relation to drones, when either way the actual transgressor (pilot) may remain anonymous.

Drones can capture and store a great variety of data – beside sound recordings and standard images (photos or videos), drones can also capture thermal images, geo-location and geo-spatial data, which poses no less threat to privacy than the former. For example, thermal image technology makes it possible to see through walls, obtaining an image of people and objects inside buildings without even entering.[39] In this respect, for example, the Supreme Court of the United States in the case *Kyllo v. US* (2001) has ruled that the use of such technology to capture the internal thermal image of a person's home constitutes a search within the meaning of the Fourth Amendment to the United States Constitution.[40] It may also be concluded from ECtHR jurisprudence that sophisticated surveillance methods with enhanced video monitoring capabilities, such as thermal imaging, infra-red, or night vision, will likely interfere with Article 8 of the ECHR, as they surpass the ordinary surveillance measures available to the general public and thus exceed reasonable expectations of privacy in certain circumstances (making individuals exposed in an unforeseen way).[41]

Most basic modern drones also have Global Positioning System (GPS) functionality, accelerometers, inclinometers, and other sensors necessary for safe drone operation and the functioning of such features as 'return home', 'follow me', and

interests: the corporate right to privacy as a bulwark against warrantless government surveillance' (2015) 36 *Cardozo Law Review* 6, 2283–320).

37 E.g., one of the largest drone manufacturers DJI offers drones with the integrated aerial zoom camera Zenmuse Z30, which has a 30x optical zoom and 6x digital zoom with a total magnification up to 180x (see DJI website at www.dji.com/lt/zenmuse-z30/info).

38 See B. Jiang, J. Yang, and H. Song, 'Protecting privacy from aerial photography: state of the art, opportunities, and challenges' (2020) *IEEE Conference on Computer Communications Workshops*, 799–804.

39 See J. Celso, 'Droning on about the Fourth Amendment: adopting a reasonable Fourth Amendment jurisprudence to prevent unreasonable searches by unmanned aircraft systems' (2014) 43 *University of Baltimore Law Review* 3, 461–94.

40 *Kyllo v. US*, 533 US 27 (2001).

41 See, for instance, *Peck v. United Kingdom*, Application no. 44647/98, Judgment of 28 January 2003, para. 62.

so on.[42] Meanwhile recording the GPS data makes it possible to track a person's movement and can interfere with the right to private life, especially in conjunction with other captured data (e.g., images).[43] In fact, GPS coordinates are often automatically assigned to images (photos and videos) taken by drones as metadata, making it possible to identify the specific location they were captured. This is a clear example of how new data (in a qualitative sense) can be created by combining various pieces of data, especially with the use of AI-driven data mining and data harvesting techniques, which make it possible to unearth new interesting and unexpected patterns and relationships between existing, at first sight completely unrelated, data by discovering the missing details of the information and linking such data in a logical way, creating a detailed picture of the subject under study. As Gray and Citron have noticed, 'technological advances have made it possible for public and private actors to watch us and to know us in ways that once seemed like science fiction'.[44] In this regard, the aforementioned mosaic theory becomes significant. The CJEU also shares this view and emphasises that various data, taken as a whole, may allow very precise conclusions to be drawn concerning the private lives of the persons whose data has been retained, such as their everyday life habits, permanent or temporary places of residence, daily or other movements, activities, their social relationships, and the social environments they frequent.[45]

With advanced computer programs and AI technology, besides providing such functions as face recognition or identification of vehicle licence plate numbers or autonomously tracking the target, drones can also perform many other tasks; for example, intercept or block mobile communications,[46] recognise and scan radio-frequency identification (RFID) tags (i.e., information stored in them), which form the basis of various identification methods (identity cards, pass cards, etc.),[47] and much more. However,

42 The 'follow me' function can also enable a drone to autonomously track a specified 'target' (person of interest), without any input from the pilot.

43 See, for instance, *Uzun v. Germany*, Application no. 35623/05, Judgment of 2 September 2010, paras. 49–53.

44 See Gray and Citron, 'A shattered looking glass', 386–7.

45 See, for instance, Joined Cases C-293/12 and C-594/12, *Digital Rights Ireland Ltd v Minister for Communications, Marine and Natural Resources and Others and Kärntner Landesregierung and Others*, ECLI:EU:C:2014:238, para. 27.

46 Tapping and other forms of the interception of communications represent a serious interference with private life and correspondence (see, for instance *Dragojević v. Croatia*, Application no. 68955/11, Judgment of 15 January 2015).

47 RFID is a form of wireless communication that incorporates the use of electromagnetic or electrostatic coupling in the radio frequency portion of the electromagnetic spectrum to uniquely identify an object, animal, or person; it is often used in passports, for access control (e.g., key cards), tap-and-go credit card payments, and tracking various assets. RFID systems are becoming increasingly used to support internet of things deployments. Combining the technology with smart sensors and/or GPS technology enables sensor data including temperature, movement, and location to be wirelessly transmitted (see S. Amsler and S. Shea, 'RFID (radio frequency identification)', www.techtarget.com/iotagenda/definition/RFID-radio-frequency-identification). At the same time, RFID technology can be used to transmit information about the drone and its pilot (e.g., registration number, pilot's

drones can be hacked and intercepted themselves, making it not only possible to use them for the unlawful collection of private data by taking over their control, but also to retrieve the data already stored in the drone's internal memory. Therefore, despite the fact that personal data may sometimes be gathered by drones lawfully, it is necessary to subsequently ensure adequate protection of such data. However, the cybersecurity of drones is questionable,[48] especially if even state-of-the-art military drones can be hacked.[49] This low level of cybersecurity poses a threat to drone technology itself, as it can erode public confidence in such technology, and drones, which are now rapidly gaining popularity among modern society, may no longer look so attractive.[50]

By using a well-established wireless (mobile) network, drones are able to transmit captured data directly to other devices (including other drones), upload the data online, or simply broadcast publicly over the internet, including through popular social networks and other platforms. Similarly, drones connected to a mobile network can download data from various databases and combine it with real time surveillance data. Notwithstanding, storing and processing personal data relating to the private life of an individual also falls within the right to privacy.[51] This raises another issue regarding the cross-border exchange of data,[52] while at the same time ensuring adequate protection of personal data.[53]

location) to devices on the ground; e.g., passers-by, smartphones. This is an example of how a technology that is seen as posing threat to privacy can also be employed to help protect it.

48 Several studies have showed the vulnerability of drone cybersecurity. E.g., see R. Altawy and A. M. Youssef, 'Security, privacy, and safety aspects of civilian drones: a survey' (2016) 1 *ACM Transactions on Cyber-Physical Systems* 2, 1–25; B. Siddappaji and K. B. Akhilesh, 'Role of cyber security in drone technology', in K. B. Akhilesh and D. P. F. Möller (eds.), *Smart Technologies* (Singapore: Springer, 2020), pp. 169–78.

49 E.g., see L. Mungin, 'Iran claims released footage is from downed U.S. drone' (2013), CNN World, https://edition.cnn.com/2013/02/07/world/meast/iran-drone-video/.

50 Public acceptance of UAV technology is recognised as key to the growth of drone services. E.g., see Riga declaration on remotely piloted aircraft (drones) 'Framing the future of aviation', Riga, 6 March 2015, https://eu2015.lv/images/news/2016_03_06_RPAS_Riga_Declaration.pdf; also European Parliament resolution of 29 October 2015 on safe use of RPAS, commonly known as UAVs, in the field of civil aviation (2014/2243(INI)), OJ J C 355.

51 See, for instance, *Amann v. Switzerland* [GC], Application no. 27798/95, Judgment of 16 February 2000, paras. 65; *Copland v. United Kingdom*, Application no. 62617/00, Judgment of 3 April 2007, para. 43.

52 In recent decades, information, including personal data, has been rapidly exchanged in both private and public sectors, and personal data is being transferred beyond national territories (see S. Žaltauskaitė-Žalimienė et al., *Europos Sąjungos Pagrindinių teisių chartijos taikymas supra- ir nacionaliniu lygmenimis* (Vilnius: Vilnius University Press, 2019), p. 237). Such growing cross-border movement of personal data owing to the ongoing economic and social integration in the world caused by globalisation will inevitably pose greater threats to privacy in the future, as national regulations in this area differ in many respects and the practice has already shown the shortcomings of existing protection mechanisms (see, for instance, Case C-362/14, *Maximillian Schrems v. Data Protection Commissioner*, ECLI:EU:C:2015:650; Case C-311/18, *Data Protection Commissioner v. Facebook Ireland Limited and Maximillian Schrems*, ECLI:EU:C:2020:559).

53 E.g., despite various legislative attempts, there is still legal uncertainty in relation to data exchange between the EU and US, which led to announcements by Meta, the parent company of Facebook

The ability of drones to communicate (interact) with each other makes it possible to form an interoperable drone *swarm*, making it possible to monitor multiple targets at the same time and/or maintain continuous long-term aerial surveillance using different drones in shifts. This kind of communication, as part of the Internet of Things, has led to the emergence of the terms Internet of Drones or Internet of Drone Things.[54] As the President of the European Commission, Ursula von der Leyen, has stressed in her political guidelines for 2019–24, the Internet of Things (thus, also the Internet of Drones) is connecting the world in new ways, as physical devices and sensors are now linking up with each other so that huge and increasing amounts of data are being collected; although data and AI are ingredients for innovation, in order to release that potential it is crucial to balance the flow and wide use of data while preserving high privacy standards, as well as ensuring safety and security.[55] This is a serious issue because combining drones with huge databases and aggregation software controlled by private entities may lead to significant shifts in the distribution of power in society, creating powerful private entities that can tend to abuse the available data. The AI technology used to manage such data can also lead to discrimination by misinterpreting individual behaviour and creating prejudices.

Technological development in recent decades has been notably moving towards higher levels of automation in various areas, including air transport.[56] Automation plays an ever-increasing role in aviation, where many processes are in fact already entrusted to technologies capable, for example, of keeping an aircraft on course, identifying conflicting traffic, proving resolution advisories to avoid potential mid-air collisions, plotting and executing optimal descent profiles, and in some cases even controlling aircraft take-off or landing, with the pilot becoming a simple observer of these high-end systems.[57] Accordingly, aviation is increasingly focusing on the application of AI technology in the air transport sector,[58] including, for

and Instagram, that it may be forced to shut down its two popular social media platforms in Europe as a result of the strict EU data protection regulation (see S. Shead, 'Meta says it may shut down Facebook and Instagram in Europe over data-sharing dispute', 7 February 2022, CNBC, www.cnbc.com/2022/02/07/meta-threatens-to-shut-down-facebook-and-instagram-in-europe.html).

54 See, e.g., Z. Lv, 'The security of Internet of drones' (2019) 148 *Computer Communications*, 208–14; A. Nayyar, B.-L. Nguyen, and N. G. Nguyen, 'The Internet of drone things (IoDT): future envision of smart drones', in A. Luhach et al. (eds.), *First International Conference on Sustainable Technologies for Computational Intelligence. Advances in Intelligent Systems and Computing* (Singapore: Springer, 2020), pp. 563–80; R. Krishnamurthi, A. Nayyar, and A.E. Hassanien (eds.), *Development and Future of Internet of Drones (IoD): Insights, Trends and Road Ahead* (Cham: Springer International Publishing, 2021).

55 See U. von der Leyen, *Political Guidelines for the Next European Commission 2019–2024* (Luxembourg: Publications Office of the European Union, 2019), p. 13.

56 As one of the laws formulated by Zuboff states, in *In the Age of the Smart Machine*, everything that can be automated will be automated.

57 See ICAO, *Unmanned Aircraft Systems* (2011), Cir 328, AN/190, at 5.

58 The progress of the whole aviation sector is based on AI technology (see European Organisation for the Safety of Air Navigation, *The FLY AI Report – Demystifying and Accelerating AI in Aviation / ATM* (2020)).

example, the use of passenger face recognition technology at airports to speed up the boarding process,[59] or the automation of air traffic control to increase aviation safety, inter alia by safely integrating drones into the non-segregated airspace.[60] As already mentioned, AI technology is widely used in drones themselves, with drones being regarded as high-risk AI systems.[61] This aspect of the digital transformation reflects the fourth industrial revolution, which is 'characterized by a fusion of technologies that is blurring the lines between the physical, digital, and biological spheres' and will change society in unpredictable ways.[62] In this regard the European Commission predicts that the use of drones is likely to grow significantly, as automation enables them to fly further, and declares that 'European rules promote the sustainable growth of drone operations, paving the way for a digital future.'[63]

Unmanned aerial vehicles are exceptional in the sense that they are able to integrate many different modern technologies into a single whole, acting like a platform (base) that additionally gives wings to these technologies. Drones are essentially flying robots capable of capturing and processing extremely large amounts of various types of data, and this process can be more or less automated, which makes them perfect surveillance tools. Despite the fact that the majority of the technologies used in drones (e.g., cameras, sound recorders, GPS sensors) are not so new, and that therefore they are quite well known (including the threats they pose to privacy), drone technology (specifically, their ability to fly and the remote control option) brings these to the next level of danger, making private data, which is so valuable and often regarded as the new currency, more vulnerable than ever.[64] Just as the emergence of instantaneous photographs in the gutter press was once seen as a game changer, requiring us to re-estimate the protection of the right to privacy

59 E.g., such technology is already implemented in practice at Narita International Airport in Tokyo (see K. Ishihara et al., 'Introducing Face Express, a new boarding procedure using face recognition (One ID at Narita Airport)' (2021) 16 *NEC Technical Journal* 1, 49–53.

60 E.g., the U-space initiative in Europe, aimed at ensuring safe and secure management and integration of drones in airspace, is largely based on AI and machine learning (see SESAR, 'Smart ATM: U-space and urban air mobility', www.sesarju.eu/U-space). It is estimated that over time U-space services will evolve as the level of automation of drones increases and advanced forms of interaction with the environment are enabled (including manned and unmanned aircraft) (see SESAR, *U-space Blueprint* (Luxembourg; Publications Office of the European Union, 2017)).

61 See draft report of the European Parliament Committee on Legal Affairs with recommendations to the Commission on a Civil liability regime for AI, 2020/2014(INL), 27 April 2020, 24. Also see B. C. Stahl, *Artificial Intelligence for a Better Future. An Ecosystem Perspective on the Ethics of AI and Emerging Digital Technologies* (Cham: Springer, 2021), p. 63.

62 K. Schwab, *The Fourth Industrial Revolution* (Geneva: World Economic Forum, 2016).

63 See European Commission, 'Aviation safety', https://transport.ec.europa.eu/transport-modes/air/aviation-safety-policy-europe_en.

64 See G. Clayton, 'Safeguarding the world's new currency' (2002) 36 *Information Management Journal* 3, 18–24; C. Gates and P. Matthews, 'Data is the new currency' (2014) *Proceedings of the 2014 New Security Paradigms Workshop*, 105–16.

in order to meet the demands of society,[65] today drones invoke the same necessity owing to the increased scope of aerial surveillance they afford.[66]

Along with the mass introduction of drones in everyday life, sophisticated surveillance techniques emerge.[67] Traditionally, the state was seen as the source of such surveillance concerns,[68] but increased usage of modern technologies in public life (including the commercial drone industry) has created what Zuboff calls 'surveillance capitalism', which stems from the exploitation and control of human nature as private entities control most of the data.[69] The immense deployment of drones in public life may lead to the so-called chilling effect on the fundamental right to privacy, creating a Panopticon environment, where individuals feel less free and may resort to self-preservation (self-censorship) by restricting their behaviour to avoid being watched even when no drones are in operation.[70] This requires an appropriate legal response, especially in light of increasing public concerns regarding bulk interception.

However, some data is captured and processed by drones for safety and security reasons – modern drones inevitably must capture, store, and process some specific data in order to ensure their safe and secure integration into the non-segregated airspace and our everyday life. For example, it would be hard (if not impossible) to safely use a long-distance drone without a camera, gyroscope, GPS, and other modern sensors, especially when performing BVLOS flights.[71] Such sensors are also necessary for the proper functioning of Detect and Avoid technology, which can automatically avoid obstacles (including humans); therefore, requiring the drone to constantly monitor the surrounding environment and process that data in real time. GPS data is also crucial for the proper operation of the return home function, which can safely return a drone to its take-off or other pre-arranged location; for example, in case of the loss of the remote control or when the drone battery is

65 See S. D. Warren and L. D. Brandeis, 'The right to privacy' (1890) 4 *Harvard Law Review* 5, 193–220.

66 It has to be noted that all of the aforementioned features of modern drones are just the tip of the iceberg. Owing to the extremely rapid progress in technological development and the wide range of possible uses of drones, it is difficult to foresee all the challenges that may arise to privacy from the use of drones. Therefore, this chapter does not aim to provide an exhaustive list of these challenges, essentially limiting them to the main threats that best illustrate the issues in the area in question.

67 Now drones are widely used by state authorities, commercial entities, and private persons for various purposes, examples being mapping, agriculture, environment monitoring, filmmaking, policing, search and rescue, and entertainment.

68 See D. Lyon, *Surveillance Society: Monitoring Everyday Life* (Buckingham: Open University Press, 2001).

69 S. Zuboff, *The Age of Surveillance Capitalism: The Fight for a Human Future at the New Frontier of Power* (New York: Public Affairs, 2019).

70 See, e.g., R. Clarke, 'The regulation of civilian drones' impacts on behavioural privacy' (2014) 30 *Computer Law and Security Review* 3, 286–305; R. L. Finn, D. Wright, and M. Friedewald, 'Seven types of privacy', in D. Gutwirth et al. (eds.), *European Data Protection: Coming of Age* (Dordrecht: Springer, 2013), pp. 3–32; P. McBride, 'Beyond Orwell: the application of unmanned aircraft systems in domestic surveillance operations' (2009) 74 *Journal of Air Law and Commerce* 3, 627–62.

71 Beyond Visual Line of Sight.

running low. This is also necessary for the geo-fencing technology used in restricted areas for security reasons (e.g., above nuclear plants, military bases, government buildings, airports).[72] Therefore, aviation safety and security implications must also be taken into account when analysing the privacy concerns raised by the use of drones because the collection, processing, storage, and use of certain (private) data may inevitably be necessary.

Moreover, although increasing drone usage primarily raises privacy concerns, at the same time, drone technology creates new opportunities for diverse applications and services. Therefore, the restrictions imposed on their use in order to protect the right to privacy may interfere with other human rights, necessitating a fair balance to be struck between these conflicting values.

As already stated, evolving drone technologies have led to the emergence of new business models, such as parcel delivery by air and aerial photography. Accordingly, drones are now widely used in various professions, including estate agents, photographers, cinematographers, advertisers, and others. In this regard, Articles 15 and 16 of the Charter enshrine that everyone has the right to engage in work and to pursue a freely chosen or accepted occupation, and the freedom to conduct a business in accordance with the law is recognised. Freedom to choose an occupation and the right to engage in work is also recognised by other international human rights documents.[73] Therefore, any restrictions on drone usage that affect professions dependent on this technology may be regarded as interfering with the freedom to choose an occupation, the right to engage in work, and the freedom to conduct a business.

Such restrictions may also interfere with the right to property, as protected by Article 17 of the Charter, Article 1 of Protocol No. 1 of the ECHR, among others. This is not only the case in the meaning of the use and peaceful enjoyment of drones themselves as physical possessions, but also in a broader sense. For example, the ECtHR has concluded in its case law that the economic interests connected with running a business include 'possessions' for the purposes of Article 1 of Protocol No. 1 of the ECHR, and maintenance of the licence can be regarded as one of the principal conditions for carrying on a business; thus its withdrawal could constitute interference with the right to the 'peaceful enjoyment of [one's] possessions'.[74] This

[72] Accordingly, Regulation (EU) 2018/1139, whose principal objective is to establish and maintain a high uniform level of civil aviation safety in the EU (Article 1), states that in order to ensure safety for people on the ground and other airspace users during the operation of unmanned aircraft, unmanned aircraft must be safely controllable and manoeuvrable, as necessary under all anticipated operating conditions including following the failure of one or, if appropriate, more systems, and must be operated only if it is in airworthy condition and where the equipment and the other components and services necessary for the intended operation are available and serviceable (see Annex IX to Regulation (EU) 2018/1139, establishing the essential requirements for unmanned aircraft).

[73] See, e.g., Article 23(1) of the Universal Declaration of Human Rights.

[74] See, for instance, *Traktörer Aktiebolag v. Sweden*, Application no. 10873/84, Judgment of 7 July 1989, para. 53; *Capital Bank AD v. Bulgaria*, Application no. 49429/99, Judgment of 24 November 2005, para. 130.

means that any legal regulation that may restrict the use of drones for business purposes in favour of the protection of the right to privacy, as a general (public) interest, must be reasonably proportionate to the aim sought. In other words, a fair balance must be struck between these conflicting values, and the requisite balance will not be found if the person or persons concerned have to bear an individual and excessive burden.

One profession that immediately took advantage of the emergence of drone technology is journalism, which is also closely related to the freedom of expression and the right to information.[75] Article 11 of the Charter, Article 10 of the ECHR, and other human rights instruments protect the right to receive information without interference by a public authority regardless of frontiers.[76] In light of this right, drone journalism becomes highly important, as drones allow reporters to access information in difficult and dangerous situations while maintaining a safe distance, such as in violent demonstrations, flooded areas, and the sites of other environmental disasters, where they could not otherwise be present or their presence would be of a very limited scope. Such an opportunity, besides helping to gather information, could also help promote human rights protection by documenting possible human rights violations (e.g., in war zones, during riots). Therefore, policies regarding the use of drones can be linked to the World Press Freedom Index and can be seen as a test of the freedom of expression, with top-ranked countries being the least restrictive about the use of drones and authoritarian countries completely prohibiting the journalistic use of this technology.[77]

Drone technology, as an instrument for remote observation, may also be relevant in the sense of the integration of persons with disabilities. Article 26 of the Charter states that the EU recognises and respects the right of persons with disabilities to benefit from measures designed to ensure their independence, social and occupational integration, and participation in the life of the community. Article 27 § 1 of the Universal Declaration of Human Rights also recognises, that everyone has the right freely to participate in the cultural life of the community and to share in scientific advancement and its benefits. Meanwhile, drones equipped with cameras, microphones, and speakers in some cases may be regarded as one way (if not the only way) for people with movement disabilities to engage in public life (at least remotely) and interact with others.

However, the intrusive nature of drone surveillance discussed in Section 14.1 could also affect the freedom of movement of others protected by Article 45 of the Charter, Article 2 of Protocol No. 4 of the ECHR, Article 13 of the Universal

[75] E.g., see P. Chamberlain, *Drones and Journalism – How the Media is Making Use of Unmanned Aerial Vehicles* (London: Routledge, 2016).

[76] E.g., see Article 19 of the Universal Declaration of Human Rights.

[77] E.g., see E. Lauk et al., 'Drone journalism: the newest global test of press freedom', in U. Carlsson (ed.), *Freedom of Expression and Media in Transition: Studies and Reflections in the Digital Age* (Gothenburg: Nordicom, 2016), pp. 117–25.

Declaration of Human Rights, among others. In this regard it must be noted that constant surveillance caused by such digital interaction, could damage freedom of movement in the sense that it may lead to a chilling effect, when individuals feel less free and resort to a form of self-preservation (self-censorship) by restricting their behaviour and feeling forced to avoid such drone-filled public places.

Another important issue is the right to life:[78] as already mentioned, drones inevitably must capture, store and process certain data owing to aviation safety and security considerations (see Section 14.1). The main aim of such aviation safety and security-based measures is not only to protect people in the air (e.g., crews and passengers of manned aircraft, against a collision with a drone), but also people on the ground (e.g., passers-by who may be injured by flying drones), as well as their property, which could be damaged or destroyed. A slightly more distant implication in this regard is related to drone usage during natural disasters and other difficult situations, when drone technology can be crucial in restoring communications and carrying out search and rescue missions, thereby saving lives.[79]

14.3 DEVELOPMENTS OF DRONE REGULATIONS: MAINTAINING THE BALANCE BETWEEN CONFLICTING HUMAN RIGHTS FROM A EUROPEAN PERSPECTIVE

In recent years, the vast development of drone technology has led to the important evolution of legal regulation worldwide. However, standards set by individual countries could lead to a significant weakening of the protection of the right to privacy, given the possible diversity of views in relation to it. Hence, it is worth looking into EU drone regulation in more detail, as the EU is characterised by its integrative nature and declares the expressed aim of becoming a world leader in international aviation, a global model for the development of next-generation aviation technologies in full respect of fundamental human rights.[80] It is clear from the jurisprudence of the ECtHR that when it comes to balancing competing values in relation to the use of modern technologies (e.g., in this case, drones), any state claiming a pioneer role in the development of new technologies bears special responsibility for striking the right balance in this regard.[81] Accordingly, with drones

[78] Enshrined, e.g., in Article 2 of the Charter, Article 2 of the ECHR, Article 3 of the Universal Declaration of Human Rights.

[79] E.g., see the white paper by Alliance for Telecommunications Industry Solutions (ATIS) on the use of UAVs for restoring communications in emergency situations, ATIS-I-000071, December 2018; also see J. N. McRae et al., 'Utilizing drones to restore and maintain radio communication during search and rescue operations' (2021) 32 *Wilderness and Environmental Medicine* 1, 41–6.

[80] See European Commission, 'An aviation strategy for Europe', COM(2015) 598 final.

[81] See, for instance, *S. and Marper v. the United Kingdom* [GC], Applications nos. 30562/04 and 30566/04, Judgment of 4 December 2008, para. 112.

considered to be the future of aviation,[82] there have been important developments in EU regulation in recent years.

In particular, the new Regulation (EU) 2018/1139 on common rules in the field of civil aviation was adopted (commonly referred to as the Basic Regulation), thereby also establishing an EU Aviation Safety Agency. It brought all aircraft, regardless of their operating mass, into EU competence. In other words, since the adoption of the Basic Regulation, all drones fell within the scope of EU regulation.[83] This comes in line with the opinion of the European Commission, expressed earlier in its Communication to the European Parliament and the Council COM(2014)207 'A new era for aviation', that rules allowing civil drone operations while guaranteeing at the same time the required high levels of privacy must be established at the European level, because such harmonised rules are seen as a necessary precondition for public (societal) acceptance of this disruptive technology.

Acknowledging public acceptance as key to the growth of drone services was also the standpoint of the European aviation community (which the European Parliament later agreed with and fully supported as one of the essential principles for future drone technology development),[84] which pointed out in the 2015 Riga declaration that in order to achieve this public acceptance the respect of citizens' fundamental rights, such as the right to privacy and the protection of personal data, must be guaranteed. The aviation community confirmed the importance of joint European action and stressed the necessity for European regulators to ensure that all conditions are met for the safe and sustainable emergence of innovative drone services, but at the same time highlighted that regulations must help the industry to thrive and adequately deal with citizens' concerns. This point of view reflects the importance of striking a fair balance between different competing values.

Following the adoption of the Basic Regulation, which provided a mandate to the European Commission to adopt legislation in relation to the operation of unmanned aircraft, as well as requirements for their production and certification, the Commission delegated Regulation (EU) 2019/945 on unmanned aircraft systems and on third-country operators of unmanned aircraft systems and the Commission implementing Regulation (EU) 2019/947 on the rules and procedures for the operation of unmanned aircraft were adopted and came into force, with the latter applied since 2021. In general, the Basic Regulation together with the aforementioned two regulations of the European Commission, brought in important changes regarding drone operations, especially in relation to the right to privacy. For example, the obligation was introduced to register drones and their users and to

82 See European Commission, 'A new era for aviation – opening the aviation market to the civil use of remotely piloted aircraft systems in a safe and sustainable manner', COM(2014) 207 final.

83 Until then all activities with aircraft lighter than 150 kg were under the regulatory competence of the EU Member States.

84 See European Parliament resolution of 29 October 2015 on the safe use of RPAS, commonly known as UAVs, in the field of civil aviation (2014/2243(INI)), OJ J C 355.

install direct remote identification systems in unmanned aircraft, it also established that courses and exams for remote pilots should include subjects on the right to privacy and data protection, with examination certificates valid only for a limited period of time (currently five years), which means that remote pilots will have to periodically renew their knowledge on this matter.

As pointed out in recital 28 of the Basic Regulation,

> The rules regarding unmanned aircraft should contribute to achieving compliance with relevant rights guaranteed under Union law, and in particular the right to respect for private and family life, set out in Article 7 of the Charter of Fundamental Rights of the European Union, and with the right to the protection of personal data, set out in Article 8 of that Charter and in Article 16 of the TFEU [Treaty on Functioning of European Union], and regulated by Regulation (EU) 2016/679 of the European Parliament and of the Council [General Data Protection Regulation (GDPR)].

Therefore, it is enshrined in Annex IX to the Regulation (EU) 2018/1139, that unmanned aircraft and operations with unmanned aircraft must comply with relevant rights guaranteed under Union law. But at the same time, it follows that 'unmanned aircraft […] operations should be subject to rules that are proportionate to the risk of the particular operation or type of operation'.[85] The European legislator therefore seems to be sharing the view of the aviation community, by taking the risk-based approach towards drone regulation in the search for a fair balance between conflicting legal values. However, at first sight it does not seem to be completely successful, to the detriment of the right to privacy and data protection, although the EU promotes high standards when it comes to the protection of these fundamental rights.

The analysis of the EU drone regulations concerned shows that there are a lot of exceptions from such important mechanisms as the registration of drones and their users or the direct remote identification of unmanned aircraft, which hardly seems to be well founded and makes it quite difficult to ensure the effectiveness of these measures while protecting the right to privacy and ensuring personal data protection. For example, the Basic Regulation states that operators of unmanned aircraft shall be registered in accordance with the acts adopted by the Commission when they operate unmanned aircraft, the operation of which presents risks to privacy or protection of personal data, and such unmanned aircraft shall be individually marked and identified.[86] Therefore, it seems that the obligations related to registration should apply whenever a drone with any sensor that allows the capture of private or personal data is used or is going to be used. Yet Regulation (EU) 2019/947 adds some ambiguity regarding registration, because according to it such registration is

85 See recital 26 of the Regulation (EU) 2018/1139.

86 See Annex IX 4.2–4.3.

mandatory only when operating a drone equipped with a sensor able to capture exclusively *personal* data, which covers only information related to an identified or identifiable natural person (data subject),[87] leaving aside the data, which strictly does not fall within the scope of the definition of personal data, despite the fact that collection of such data could infringe the right to privacy. Moreover, the obligation to register is not applied when using drones that are considered to be toys within the meaning of Directive 2009/48/EC, although the latter also can be fitted with cameras, microphones, and various other sensors capable of capturing and storing both private and personal data. Therefore, as the remote pilot of an unmanned aerial vehicle (UAV) and the pilot of a manned aircraft ultimately have the same responsibility for following the legal regulations when operating their aircraft,[88] the obligation to register is highly important when dealing with their anonymity issue, as it can ease traceability in the case of their possible liability for failing to comply with those rules. This was also the standpoint of the European Parliament, noting that all drones in line with a risk-based approach should be equipped with an ID chip and registered to ensure traceability, accountability, and the proper implementation of civil liability rules.[89]

The same goes for a direct remote identification system,[90] which, despite the European Parliament's expressed view that the question of identifying drones, of whatever size, is crucial,[91] does not apply to drones categorised as C0 class (i.e.,

[87] Article 4 of the GDPR.

[88] See ICAO, *Unmanned Aircraft Systems* (2011), Cir 328, AN/190, p. 5.

[89] See European Parliament resolution of 29 October 2015 on safe use of RPAS, commonly known as UAVs, in the field of civil aviation (2014/2243(INI)), OJ J C 355.

[90] As stated in Delegated regulation (EU) 2019/945, 'direct remote identification' means a system that ensures the local broadcast of information about a UA in operation, including the marking of the UA, so that this information can be obtained without physical access to the UA. Remote identification system must:

(a) allow the upload of the UAS operator registration number in accordance with Article 14 of Implementing Regulation (EU) 2019/947 and exclusively follow the process provided by the registration system;
(b) ensure, in real time during the whole duration of the flight, the direct periodic broadcast from the UA using an open and documented transmission protocol, of the following data, in a way that they can be received directly by existing mobile devices within broadcasting range: (i) the UAS operator registration number; (ii) the unique physical serial number of the UA compliant with standard ANSI/CTA-2063; (iii) the geographical position of the UA and its height above the surface or take-off point; (iv) the route course measured clockwise from true north and ground speed of the UA; and (v) the geographical position of the remote pilot or, if not available, the take-off point; and
(c) ensure that the user cannot modify the data mentioned under paragraph (b) points ii, iii, iv and v.

A similar technical solution was introduced by the US Federal aviation administration in December 2020 (see Department of Transportation, Federal Aviation Administration, 'Remote identification of unmanned aircraft' (2020), www.faa.gov/sites/faa.gov/files/2021-08/RemoteID_Final_Rule.pdf).

[91] See European Parliament resolution of 29 October 2015 on safe use of RPAS, commonly known as UAVs, in the field of civil aviation (2014/2243(INI)), OJ J C 355.

drones with an operating mass less than 250 g) or C4 class (i.e., drones already made available on the market) within the meaning of delegated Regulation (EU) 2019/945,[92] although this system is essential for effectively dealing with the issue of drone users' anonymity and ensuring their traceability; that is, remote ID is crucial for individuals to be able to take measures to protect their privacy from aerial surveillance by such drones. It is hard to understand the grounds for this exception because it does not seem that such an obligation could be regarded as unsuitable, unnecessary, or disproportionate, even when talking about the drones already made available on the market, as direct remote identification according to the same Regulation (EU) 2019/945 can be provided as a separate add-on, which can be retrofitted on drones by their users themselves.[93] This is especially the case when in 2017 one of the world's leading drone manufacturers had released a white paper outlining a concept in which each drone could transmit its location as well as a registration number or similar identification code using inexpensive radio equipment that is already on board many drones today and that could be adopted by all manufacturers.[94]

Furthermore, the delegated Regulation (EU) 2019/945 sets out the requirements for a geo-awareness system, which should alert remote pilots when a potential breach of airspace limitations is detected so that they can take effective immediate action to prevent that breach; for example, in areas where drone use is restricted owing to privacy concerns. But this system is not mandatory, not to talk about a geo-fencing system, which is completely omitted from the EU drone regulations, although it could automatically prevent drones from entering or launching in restricted (no-fly) zones and help to ensure privacy in these areas.[95] However, some drone manufacturers tend

92 See Annex of Delegated regulation (EU) 2019/945.

93 Part 6 of the Annex of Delegated regulation (EU) 2019/945, which sets out the requirements for a direct remote identification as a separate add-on, and requires for it to be placed on the market with the clear instructions on how to install the module on the unmanned aircraft.

94 See A DJI Technology Whitepaper, '"What's in a name?" A call for a balanced remote identification approach', 22 March 2017, www.dropbox.com/s/v4lkyr2kdp8ukvx/DJI%20Remote%20Identification%20Whitepaper%203-22-17.pdf?dl=0). In order to help solve this issue and increase pilot accountability some drone manufacturers also include a specific permissions clause in their software licence agreement permitting access to pilot location data and some identifying information about them (e.g., see Dedrone, www.aerialarmor.com/blog/how-to-track-a-drone-operator-trace-drone-pilots-with-aerial-armor).

95 There is a counterview among scholars that aerial surveillance by drone is not solely a privacy issue and should be regulated through property law, more specifically, landowners' airspace rights. Rule emphasises in his article 'Airspace in an age of drones' that 'the growing affordability of drones is jeopardizing the ability for low-altitude airspace to serve in its long-held role as a privacy buffer', because 'camera-equipped drone flights can enable drone operators to cheaply gaze onto private land areas that would otherwise be visible only from airplanes or helicopters at much higher altitudes'. Accordingly, he argues in favour of increasing the scope of landowners' airspace rights and states that in order 'to preserve a level of privacy […] comparable to what landowners enjoyed prior to the drone era, laws clarifying landowner airspace rights should define these rights as extending all the way up to the navigable airspace line of 500 feet above-ground in most locations': T. A. Rule, 'Airspace in an age of drones' (2015) 95 *Boston University Law Review* 1, 155–208. Following this idea, Blank, Kirrane, and Spiekermann proposed the software framework, which could enable drone operators to determine whether a selected drone flight path intersects with a restricted area, by considering privacy

to install geo-fencing systems in their drones voluntarily, which shows that business awareness extends far beyond that of the legislators.[96] What is more, alarming drone cybersecurity issues are not covered by the EU regulations either.[97]

Of course, the EU legislator acknowledges the need to further develop requirements regarding the registration of drones and their pilots, as well as geo-awareness and remote identification systems, as these are seen as the foundations of the U-space system, which is being developed to safely integrate drones into the airspace.[98] However, this step-by-step approach, based on the current state of drone technology development, considering the fast pace of technological progress in comparison to the evolution of legal regulation, risks lagging far behind the technology and does not correspond to the standpoint of the European Parliament expressed in a 2015 resolution on the safe use of remotely piloted aircraft systems (RPAS) in the field of civil aviation that the global regulatory framework for drones should be part of a long-term perspective, taking into account possible future developments.[99]

From the global perspective, it is quite clear that a similar approach to drone regulation is being taken by legislators worldwide; for example, in the US,[100] Canada,[101] and Australia,[102] where specific requirements for drone registration, pilot licensing, built-in remote identification systems, operations above gatherings of people, minimum distance from airports, other people and property, geo-fencing and/or geo-awareness systems, among others, are being established. Some of these are

preferences that can be configured by citizens themselves: P. Blank, S. Kirrane, and S. Spiekermann, 'Privacy-aware restricted areas for unmanned aerial systems' (2018) 16 *IEEE Security and Privacy* 2, 70–9. Unfortunately, the latter proposal, because of the plausible segregation of airspace, would jeopardise aviation safety, as it would become more difficult to plan and execute safe flight routes, especially bearing in mind the constantly increasing number of drone operations. And as already mentioned, advanced optical and digital zoom capabilities of modern cameras used in drones enable the capture of high resolution images from a large distance. Therefore, acknowledging landowner airspace rights up to the specific line above the ground would also be of little use when ensuring the protection of the right to privacy, although it could serve as a safeguard (though very limited) for drones with low-definition cameras.

96 E.g., see DJI, 'DJI GO app now includes a GEO geofencing system' (2016), www.dji.com/newsroom/news/dji-go-app-now-includes-geo-geofencing-system.

97 Although it may be concluded from Article 2.1.7 of Annex IX to Regulation (EU) 2018/1139 that the EU legislator seeks to solve this issue by imposing an obligation for organisations involved in the design of unmanned aircraft to take precautions so as to minimise the hazards arising from conditions, both internal and external, to the unmanned aircraft and their systems, that experience has shown to have a safety impact, which includes protection against interference by electronic means.

98 See, e.g., recital 26 of Implementing regulation (EU) 2019/947.

99 European Parliament resolution of 29 October 2015 on the safe use of RPAS, commonly known as UAVs, in the field of civil aviation (2014/2243(INI), OJ C 355.

100 For more information see US Department of Transportation, Federal Aviation Administration, 'Drones', www.faa.gov/uas/.

101 For more information see Government of Canada, 'Drone safety', https://tc.canada.ca/en/aviation/drone-safety.

102 For more information see Australian Government, Civil Aviation Safety Authority, 'Drone rules', www.casa.gov.au/knowyourdrone/drone-rules.

already being implemented; others are still in progress (in a transitional period).[103] Meanwhile, in other European (non-EU) countries, such as the UK,[104] Norway,[105] and Iceland,[106] drone regulation is based on common EU drone rules or the latter are de facto applied. The aforementioned countries also share a risk-based approach – like the EU, other countries tend to differentiate drone regulations based on the type of operation (i.e., different flight purposes: recreational, commercial), drone size and weight, other drone characteristics (e.g., with or without camera), level of pilot competence, and so on. This regulatory approach in a sense materialises the vision of the European Parliament that a 'harmonised and proportionate European and global regulatory framework needs to be developed on a risk-assessed basis, which avoids disproportionate regulations for businesses that would deter investment and innovation in the [drone] industry, whilst adequately protecting citizens'.[107]

Although such an approach at first glance may seem beneficial for industry, it is not the case in the context of drone technologies. When the legislator avoids taking more decisive steps in order to develop a clear and well-defined provision, this creates a sort of 'chicken and egg' problem, whereby regulators are reluctant to develop standards until the industry comes forward with technologies for authorisation; however, the industry is reluctant to invest in developing the necessary technologies without certainty surrounding how they will be regulated. Such a deadlock is dangerous from the human rights perspective and suggests a failure on the part of the legislator to balance conflicting values, and nor does it help the industry to thrive. As the ECtHR has ruled on several occasions, it is essential to have clear and detailed rules on the subject, especially as the technology available for use is continually becoming more sophisticated, and there must be adequate and effective safeguards against abuses.[108] Such rules must form part of a legislative framework affording sufficient legal certainty, so that all parties can foresee the consequences for themselves.[109]

[103] E.g., in the US all drone pilots required to register their UAV will have to operate their aircraft in accordance with the rule on remote identification (ID); that is, equipped with a remote ID system, which provides ID and location information that can be received by other parties during flight, beginning 16 September 2023. Accordingly, drone manufacturers have until 16 September 2022 to produce drones with built-in standard remote ID, and the FAA encourages the early production of remote ID broadcast modules for retrofitting (see US Department of Transportation, Federal Aviation Administration, 'Remote identification of drones', www.faa.gov/uas/getting_started/remote_id/, and US Department of Transportation, Federal Aviation Administration, 'Remote ID for industry and standards bodies', www.faa.gov/uas/getting_started/remote_id/industry/).

[104] For more information see UK Civil Aviation Authority, 'Drones: information about all aspects of remotely piloted aviation and drones', www.caa.co.uk/consumers/remotely-piloted-aircraft/.

[105] For more information see CAA Norway, 'Drones', https://luftfartstilsynet.no/en/drones/.

[106] For more information see Icelandic Transport Authority website: www.icetra.is/aviation/drones/.

[107] See European Parliament resolution of 29 October 2015 on the safe use of RPAS, commonly known as UAVs, in the field of civil aviation (2014/2243(INI)), OJ J C 355.

[108] See, for instance, *Kruslin v. France*, Application no. 11801/85, Judgment of 24 April 1990, paras. 33–5.

[109] See, for instance, *Valenzuela Contreras v. Spain*, Application no. 27671/95, Judgment of 30 July 1998, paras. 59–61.

This brings to mind the control dilemma elaborated by Collingridge, following which, influencing technological developments is easy when their implications are not yet manifest, but once we know these implications, they are difficult to change. In other words, when a technology is still at an early stage of development, it is possible to influence the direction of its development, but we do not yet know how it will affect society. On the other hand, when the technology has become societally embedded, we can recognise the implications, but by then it is very difficult to influence its development. Nevertheless, legislators should not put human rights at risk, but should refrain from a step-by-step approach based on the current state of technological progress, as such an approach tends to lag behind the development of technologies. Shifting from a reactive to proactive legislation and establishing a sufficiently clear and balanced legal framework could help foster further technological development, while at the same time ensuring adequate protection of human rights. As the deployment of drones may inevitably raise tensions between the right to privacy and other human rights, a holistic approach must be taken when regulating the use of drones, focusing not merely on the protection of the right to privacy, but paying more attention to other fundamental freedoms and human rights, and seeking a well-balanced legal framework.[110]

In this regard, Article 52 § 1 of the Charter establishes that any limitation on the exercise of the rights and freedoms recognised by this Charter are subject to the principle of proportionality. This principle is also considered the most important tool for interpreting the ECHR and is widely applied by the ECtHR.[111] Therefore, in continental (Romano-Germanic) legal systems, the proportionality principle prevails as a balancing method. Despite the very concept of balancing being perceived slightly differently in non-continental legal systems,[112] the substantial objective remains the same – to strike a fair balance between conflicting legal values. Legislators worldwide should rely more on the principle of proportionality (or other legal balancing methods) when regulating the usage of drone technology in order to reconcile conflicting human rights. As technological development in this field is inevitable and drone usage in modern society seems to keep growing rapidly, further discussion of these issues is of great importance.

110 The European Parliament in resolution 2014/2243(INI) has also stressed that the use of drones must respect not only the fundamental right to privacy and data protection, but also the freedom of movement and freedom of expression, and that the potential risks connected to these rights, regarding both surveillance of individuals and groups and the monitoring of public spaces (including borders), need to be addressed.

111 See E. Leonaitė, 'Proporcingumo principas Europos Žmogaus Teisių Teismo Jurisprudencijoje', PhD thesis, Vilnius University (2013), 45.

112 E.g., in the US, when the balancing test is applied, often the burden of a restriction of a right is weighed against the importance of the general interest. Meantime, in the UK, such criteria as legality, *ultra vires* doctrine, or Wednesbury's unreasonableness (or irrationality) test are usually applied. Furthermore, various other methods for balancing different values are distinguished in legal literature (e.g., see D. A. De Vries, 'Balancing fundamental rights with economic freedoms according to the European Court of Justice' (2013) 9 *Utrecht Law Review* 1, 169–92, at 171–2).

14.4 CONCLUSIONS

This study has revealed that the use of drone technology can interfere with the right to privacy in diverse ways. Although many of the discussed dangers that the use of drones pose to the right to privacy are not new relatively speaking, the frequency and severity of privacy violations may increase significantly owing to the capabilities of drones. In this regard drones pose a dual threat: (a) as a technology that inexpensively 'gives wings' to other technologies (e.g., cameras, sound recorders, GPS, infrared and other sensors, etc.), thus allowing their use in a completely new environment (i.e., in the air) and opening up new surveillance possibilities, and (b) as a platform (base) that integrates various technologies into one whole, including the incorporation of AI technology, thus creating qualitatively new surveillance instruments.

However, various restrictions imposed on the use of drones in favour of privacy protection could undermine other human rights that are equally important; for example, the right to engage in work and the freedom to conduct a business, the right to property, freedom of expression, and the right to information, or even the right to life. This requires a holistic approach from legislators in order to strike a fair balance between these conflicting values. It is important, when regulating the usage of drone technology, to rely more on the proportionality principle (or other legal balancing methods) in order to reconcile conflicting human rights.

The legal response to the threats posed by the use of drones tends to lag behind the development of these technologies, and various poorly grounded and extensive exceptions are being established. Illustrated by the example of the EU, the study reveals that further joint action must be taken to develop legal requirements regarding the registration of drones and their users, as well as geo-awareness and remote identification systems, while also establishing common rules related to drone cybersecurity, geo-fencing, and others. More attention should be paid to by-design and by-default measures (e.g., minimisation of the data gathered by drones, automatic anonymisation or removal of unnecessary data, etc.), possible obligations for online service providers (e.g., remote signal blocking, restrictions for data sharing, etc.) and AI related issues in drone systems.

The legislators should foster the development of standards using a long-term perspective. In order to be effective, the legislation has to shift from reactive to proactive, and establish a more future-orientated legal framework taking into account possible future developments, rather than a step-by-step approach based on the current state of technological progress. The industry, regulators, and the public must come together to seek a harmonised global regulatory framework and to guarantee legal certainty while balancing competing values. As drone usage in modern society keeps growing, it is of great importance to tackle these challenges in a timely manner and ensure that all the conditions are met for the safe and sustainable emergence of innovative drone services, enabling the industry to thrive and at the same time adequately deal with human rights concerns.

15

Online Disinformation, Microtargeting, and Freedom of Expression

Moving beyond Human Rights Law?

Birgit Schippers

15.1 INTRODUCTION

Concerns over the harmful impact of online disinformation on the integrity of electoral processes, on democratic political cultures and values, and on human rights arose globally in 2016, when the UK held its referendum to leave the European Union (EU), and Donald Trump was first elected as president of the US.[1] Almost ten years later, following the experiences of the COVID-19 pandemic, wars in Ukraine and in Gaza, and the return of Trump to the US presidency, these concerns have not receded.[2] Worries over disinformation, colloquially referred to as 'fake news',[3] centre on its global reach and ease of access, but also on the thorny challenge of regulating online communication, and with it the power of platforms and search engines that facilitate the dissemination of inaccurate and misleading content. This chapter argues that the disinformation problematic is compounded by the proliferation of fake news via the practice of microtargeting, a term that describes the surgical spread of political and other messages to homogeneous social groups, drawing on the analysis of people's personal data.[4] The chapter contends that the spread of microtargeted disinformation is of concern to human rights and democracy, as it distorts and fragments the information ecosystem, with harmful consequences for the right to freedom of expression and for democratic discourse.

I wish to thank Tiina Pajuste and Oscar Raúl Puccinelli for their generous and thoughtful comments on an earlier version of this chapter.

1 See, e.g., BBC World, 'Fake news in 2016: what it is, what it wasn't, how to help', 30 December 2016, www.bbc.co.uk/news/world-38168792.

2 See, e.g., D. M. West, 'How disinformation defined the 2024 election narrative', 7 November 2024, Brookings Institution, www.brookings.edu/articles/how-disinformation-defined-the-2024-election-narrative/. See also M. Susi et al. (eds.), *Governing Information Flows During War: A Comparative Study of Content Governance and Media Policy Responses After Russia's Attack against Ukraine* (Hamburg: Verlag Hans-Bredow-Institut 2022), graphite.page/gdhrnet-wp4/.

3 In 2017, 'fake news' was voted word of the year by the dictionary publisher Collins. See BBC News, 'What is 2017's word of the year?', 2 November 2017, www.bbc.co.uk/news/uk-41838386#:~:text=A%20phrase%20consistently%20in%20the,he%20railed%20against%20the%20media.

4 Information Commissioner's Office, 'Microtargeting', https://ico.org.uk/for-the-public/microtargeting/.

Data analytics techniques, which underpin microtargeting and serve as a vector for the dissemination of fake news, can lead to voter surveillance and interfere with the right to privacy. Elucidating the phenomenon of microtargeted online disinformation (MOD) and its effects on human rights and democracy propels my discussion, which is guided by three questions: What harms to human rights and democracy are produced by MOD? How can human rights law respond to these harms? What are the limits of human rights law?

How to respond to worries over MOD poses complex conceptual, sociological, and legal challenges. Regulatory efforts that seek to curb disinformation rub against legal protections of the right to freedom of expression, which is enshrined, for example, in Article 10 of the European Convention on Human Rights (ECHR) and in Article 11 of the Charter of Fundamental Rights of the EU.[5] There is also a real need to map and analyse the impact of microtargeted disinformation on a wider range of rights, including the right to privacy, and to unpack its broader implications for Article 10, such as its effect on the rights of minoritised voices. Paradoxically, despite the harmful effects of microtargeted disinformation on human rights, the chapter asserts that human rights law is ill-suited to address the full range of these harms. Considering the processing of personal data in the dissemination of disinformation, the chapter suggests that the protection of human rights has become displaced onto other legal regimes, such as data protection law, and is increasingly reliant on legal instruments with horizontal effect. Acknowledging the extensive regulatory activities within the EU, the chapter analyses a 'European approach'[6] to microtargeted disinformation, examining selected recent EU legislative initiatives, the General Data Protection Regulation (GDPR),[7] the Digital Services Act (DSA),[8] the Artificial Intelligence Act (AIA),[9] and the Regulation on Transparency Political Advertising,[10] and considers their capacity to regulate MOD and to mitigate potential harms to human rights and democracy. There are further reasons

5 All references to freedom of expression will refer to the ECHR. The Convention provides a benchmark for human rights protection across the member states of the Council of Europe and has special legal standing within the EU.

6 I. Nenadić, 'Unpacking the "European approach" to tackling challenges of disinformation and political manipulation' (2019) 8 *Internet Policy Review* 4, 1–22, https://policyreview.info/articles/analysis/unpacking-european-approach-tackling-challenges-disinformation-and-political.

7 Regulation (EU) 2016/679 of the European Parliament and of the Council of 27 April 2016 on the protection of natural persons with regard to the processing of personal data and on the free movement of such data, and repealing Directive 95/46/EC (GDPR).

8 Regulation (EU) 2022/2065 of the European Parliament and of the Council of 19 October 2022 on a single market for digital services and amending Directive 2000/31/EC (Digital Services Act).

9 Regulation (EU) 2024/1689 of the European Parliament and of the Council of 13 June 2024 laying down harmonised rules on AI and amending Regulations (EC) No 300/2008, (EU) No 167/2013, (EU) No 168/2013, (EU) 2018/858, (EU) 2018/1139 and (EU) 2019/2144 and Directives 2014/90/EU, (EU) 2016/797 and (EU) 2020/1828 (AIA).

10 Regulation (EU) 2024/900 of the European Parliament and of the Council of 13 March 2024 on the transparency and targeting of political advertising.

for examining the EU's regulatory initiatives. First, EU legal instruments, such as the GDPR, are said to provide a regulatory 'gold standard', which is emulated in non-EU jurisdictions. Second, the extraterritorial dimension of EU law, the much invoked 'Brussels effect',[11] sets regulatory standards beyond the jurisdictional borders of the EU. Third, while EU human rights provisions defer to the norm-setting power of the Council of Europe and the jurisprudence of the European Court of Human Rights (ECtHR), EU secondary law, specifically EU regulations, provide bespoke regulatory tools with horizontal direct effect.

The chapter is structured as follows. Section 15.2 expounds the phenomenon of online disinformation and surveys concerns about the threat of disinformation to human rights and democracy. Drawing on the ECHR, specifically Article 10, and on selected case law of the ECtHR, Section 15.3 discusses the intersection of the right to freedom of expression with online disinformation and analyses the potential consequences for the regulation of disinformation and for a wider suite of Convention rights. Section 15.4 centres on the role and impact of microtargeting in the dissemination of disinformation, while Section 15.5 examines selected regulatory initiatives in the EU, focusing on the GDPR; the DSA, the AIA, and the Regulation on Transparency Political Advertising. Section 15.6 summarises the main points covered in the chapter and identifies areas that require further work.

15.2 FROM FAKE NEWS TO (ONLINE) DISINFORMATION: CHALLENGES FOR HUMAN RIGHTS AND DEMOCRACY

The rapid spread of online communication and the attendant ease of access to online content, facilitated by the rise of social media platforms such as Facebook, X, or TikTok, and by search engines such as Google, has enhanced the capacity for disseminating and receiving information, and increased the range and scope of civic engagement. These new opportunities for communicating and connecting have been welcomed as a way of informing and empowering people, and helping them to enjoy their human rights, such as the right to assembly and association.[12] However, online content can also propel the dissemination of inaccurate and frequently misleading content to levels previously unimaginable. The term 'fake news', which was popularised during Donald Trump's first tenure as US president (2017–21) has become shorthand for this type of content. Despite its widespread use, 'fake news' lacks an agreed definition and there is no consensus on the range of expressions that it refers to. These can vary from the entertaining barb of political satire to maleficent

[11] A. Bradford, *The Brussels Effect: How the European Union Rules the World* (Oxford: Oxford University Press, 2020).

[12] UN High Commissioner for Human Rights (UNHCHR), 'Impact of new technologies on the promotion and protection of human rights in the context of assemblies, including peaceful protests', UN Doc. A/HRC/44/24, 2020), 24 June 2020, 3–4.

attempts that seek to damage public trust and confidence in the integrity of electoral processes and elected representatives,[13] and in public policy. For example, concerns over fake news accompanied the UK Brexit referendum in 2016 and the US presidential elections of 2016 and 2020.[14] Fake news stories included inaccurate reports about Turkey joining the EU, playing on fears of UK voters over immigration, and erroneous claims that the 2020 US presidential election was 'stolen'.[15] There have also been concerns about mistaken and misleading information with respect to the COVID-19 pandemic that has sought to undermine public policy efforts aimed at combating the disease.[16] Moreover, it should be stressed that faking is not limited to the dissemination of written text, such as tweets or Facebook posts. It extends to the manipulation of voices and images – so-called deepfakes – that can heighten mistrust in political leaders, institutions, and even national security.[17] Deepfakes gained notoriety when a speech delivered by Nancy Pelosi, the former leader of the Democrats in the United States House of Representatives, was altered to make it sound slurred. This alteration created the inaccurate impression that Pelosi was intoxicated. Such alteration is deceitful, and it can undermine the credibility of democratically elected politicians or of those preparing to stand for public office.[18] Furthermore, despite the contemporary interest in online disinformation, it is worth noting that fake news is not an invention of the digital age: from Octavian's fake news info war against Mark Anthony,[19] to the humorous 1835 hoax of batmen hunting bison on the moon,[20] and Joseph Goebbels' Nazi propaganda apparatus, fake news has been part of public political life for more than two millennia. However,

[13] House of Commons Digital, Culture, Media and Sports Committee, 'Disinformation and "fake news": Final Report', HC 1791 (House of Commons 2019); henceforth referred to as DCMS Report. See also House of Lords Select Committee on Communications, 'Regulating in a digital world. 2nd Report of Session 2017–19', HL Paper 299 (House of Lords 2019).

[14] C. Cadwalladr, 'The great British Brexit robbery: how our democracy was hijacked', 7 May 2017, *The Guardian*, www.theguardian.com/technology/2017/may/07/the-great-british-brexit-robbery-hijacked-democracy.

[15] C. H. Powell et al., 'Disinformation', in T. Pajuste (ed.), *Specific Threats to Human Rights Protection from the Digital Reality* (Tallinn: Tallinn University, 2022), https://graphite.page/GDHRNet-threats-to-human-rights-protection/assets/documents/GDHRNet-ThreatsReport-EditedVolume.pdf.

[16] See e.g., AVAAZ, 'How Facebook can flatten the curve of the coronavirus infodemic', 15 April 2020, https://secure.avaaz.org/campaign/en/facebook_coronavirus_misinformation/; Center for Humane Technology, 'Ledger of harms' (2021), available at https://ledger.humanetech.com.

[17] See e.g., D. K. Citron and R. Chesney, 'Deep fakes: a looming challenge for privacy, democracy, and national security' (2019) 107 *California Law Review* 6, 1753–819; B. Paris and J. Donovan, 'Deepfakes and cheap fakes: the manipulation of audio and visual evidence' (2019) *Data & Society Research Institute*, 18 September.

[18] B. Schippers, 'Artificial intelligence and democratic politics' (2020) 11 *Political Insight* 1, 32–5, at 33.

[19] BBC Bitesize, 'A brief history of fake news', www.bbc.co.uk/bitesize/articles/zwcgn9q. See also Report of the Special Rapporteur on the promotion and protection of the right to freedom of opinion and expression, Irene Khan, 'Disinformation and freedom of opinion and expression', UN Doc. A/HRC/47/25, 13 April 2021.

[20] BBC Four, 'Ian Hislop's fake news: a true history: moon hoax', 26 September 2019, www.bbc.co.uk/programmes/p07pd8dg.

developments in the field of digital technologies, propelled by advances in artificial intelligence (AI), have put the propensity to spread fake news on steroids: fake news created by a few can reach millions of users at the push of a button.

How to deal with fake news has emerged as a central issue for policymakers and scholars. One of the key challenges relates to the aptness of the expression 'fake news'. Despite its widespread use, the term has been discarded as loaded, deployed to discredit political opponents and critical media coverage of politicians and policies. For example, the UK House of Commons Digital, Culture, Media and Sports Committee report *Disinformation and 'fake news': Final Report*,[21] in one of the most thorough treatments of this topic, rejects the term and suggests instead the adoption of the words 'misinformation' and 'disinformation'. The report defines misinformation as the 'inadvertent sharing of false information', while disinformation constitutes 'the deliberate creation and sharing of false and/or manipulated information that is intended to deceive and mislead audiences, either for the purpose of causing harm, or for political, personal or financial gain'.[22] These definitions align with proposals developed by the EU's High Level Expert Group on Fake News and Online Disinformation. It conceives of disinformation as 'verifiably false or misleading information … which cumulatively … is created, presented and disseminated for economic gain or to intentionally deceive the public … and may cause public harms [as] threats to democratic political and policymaking processes as well as public goods such as the protection of EU citizens' health, the environment or security'.[23] A third category of fake news, malinformation, refers to 'genuine information shared with the intention to cause harm',[24] such as defamatory content.

Despite a broad preference for the term 'disinformation', there is no consensus regarding its impacts, whether these impacts constitute harm; who or what is being harmed, and how to address such harms. Counselling against an 'overdose of US perspectives',[25] Bodo et al. contend that worries over disinformation amount to a moral panic, which is said to originate in US political culture and in the dominance of US perspectives on disinformation, and which is not applicable beyond

[21] DCMS Report; House of Lords Select Committee on Communications, 'Regulating in a digital world'.

[22] Government response to DCMS Interim Report, quoted in DCMS Report, 10.

[23] European Commission, 'A multi-dimensional approach to disinformation: report of the independent high level group on fake news and online disinformation' (Brussels: European Union, 2018), https://digital-strategy.ec.europa.eu/en/library/final-report-high-level-expert-group-fake-news-and-online-disinformation. See also European Commission, 'The strengthened code of practice on disinformation 2022', 16 June 2022, https://digital-strategy.ec.europa.eu/en/policies/code-practice-disinformation; C. H. Powell et al., 'Disinformation'.

[24] C. Wardle and H. Derakhshan, 'Information disorder: toward an interdisciplinary framework for research and policymaking', Council of Europe report, EU Doc. DGI(2017)09, 2017), 5. See also C. H. Powell et al., 'Disinformation', p. 34.

[25] B. Bodo, N. Helberger, and C. H. de Vreese, 'Political micro-targeting: a Manchurian candidate or just a dark horse?' (2017) 6 *Internet Policy Review* 4, 1–13, at 9.

the US.[26] Meyer and Marsden also assert that 'evidence of large-scale harm is still inconclusive in Europe'.[27] In particular, there is a dearth of verifiable empirical evidence, which could demonstrate a significant effect of disinformation campaigns on electoral outcomes. However, this lack of empirical evidence does not diminish widespread concerns about the politically dangerous and potentially harmful impact of disinformation on democracy and on the integrity of electoral processes. For example, the EU regards online disinformation practices as 'public harms' and 'threats to our way of life'.[28] These harms and threats are said to undermine trust and confidence in democracy, in public discourse, and in human rights.[29] Within public political discourse, concerns about disinformation harms have conjoined with broader worries over online harms, adding force to calls for the regulation of online content. To date, the debates have centred on harms to individuals regarded as vulnerable, specifically individuals with protected characteristics such as children, women, LGBTQ+ people, or people from ethnic minority backgrounds – social demographics who are frequently subjected to misogynistic, homophobic, transphobic, or racist hate speech online, or to online sexual abuse or threats of violence.[30] An emerging consensus that 'the online and offline worlds cannot neatly be separated',[31] that what is prohibited offline should be prohibited online, underpins the deliberations about the regulation of online communications.

However, the format and precise modalities of regulation remain contested and have emerged as a key challenge. Commenting on broader attempts to come up with a suitable regulatory design, Lillian Edwards asks whether we should 'regulate by law … refuse to regulate till a clear path can be seen, or … turn to soft law, self-regulation, "co-regulation", codes of conduct, technical standards, trustmarks, ethical charters, user democracy, who knows?'.[32] While attempts to regulate the dissemination of illegal content have turned to criminal law,[33] there are no quick and easy fixes that can offer effective, meaningful, and lawful ways to deal with disinformation.

26 Ibid., p. 8.

27 T. Meyer and C. Marsden, *Regulating Disinformation with Artificial Intelligence: Effects of Disinformation on Freedom of Expression and Media Pluralism* (Brussels: European Parliamentary Research Service, 2019), pp. 3–4.

28 European Commission, 'The Strengthened Code of Practice on Disinformation 2022'.

29 J. Bayer et al., *The Fight Against Disinformation and the Right to Freedom of Expression* (Brussels: European Union, 2021), p. 13, www.europarl.europa.eu/RegData/etudes/STUD/2021/695445/IPOL_STU(2021)695445_EN.pdf.

30 D. K. Citron, *Hate Crimes in Cyberspace* (Cambridge, MA: Harvard University Press 2014).

31 Law Commission, 'Modernising communication offences', Law Com. No. 399 (2021), 3, https://assets.publishing.service.gov.uk/media/61ba022ad3bf7f05539de6f5/Modernising-Communications-Offences-2021-Law-Com-No-399.pdf.

32 L. Edwards, 'Introduction', in L. Edwards (ed.), *Law, Policy and the Internet* (Oxford: Hart Publishing, 2019), p. l.

33 Law Commission, 'Modernising communication offences'. UK Online Safety Act 2023, www.legislation.gov.uk/ukpga/2023/50. On the role of criminal law, see also R. K. Helm and H. Nasu, 'Regulatory responses to "fake news" and freedom of expression: normative and empirical evaluation' (2020) 21 *Human Rights Law Review* 2, 322–5.

Designing regulatory instruments that can address the threats and harms posed by online disinformation generate seemingly intractable problems, which converge on three aspects: first, the diffuse and opaque nature and extent of disinformation harms and their typically intangible effects on society and on societal values such as human rights and democracy complicate regulatory efforts.[34] Scholarship on the societal harms of new technologies is only beginning to emerge,[35] while, as highlighted earlier, the harms caused by disinformation, notwithstanding significant normative concerns, remain empirically unproven. Second, disinformation operates in a novel information landscape, which lacks traditional (editorial) gatekeepers, creates online filter bubbles, and facilitates the spread of online (dis-)information to previously unimaginable levels and across jurisdictional boundaries. National regulatory landscapes have been described as opaque and fragmented, with overlaps and gaps,[36] while the speed and global reach with which the disinformation 'infodemic' infects public discourse limits the effectiveness of national regulation and requires instead collaboration,[37] and the difficult work of consensus building, at international, or at the very least regional, level.[38] There is also considerable unease about the role of private companies in the regulatory architecture, for example, whether they should be tasked with the sensitive role of regulating, and possibly censoring, online content. Third, tools such as algorithmic content moderation can be used to remove or block content, but these are blunt instruments that lack contextual understanding, such as the ability to distinguish satire from harmful disinformation or illegal content.[39] Moreover, different platforms and search engines operate differently and may require bespoke regulatory tools. For example, while X (formerly Twitter) is an open platform, others, such as WhatsApp, offer end-to-end encryption, making them less transparent but no less effective in the spread of disinformation.[40]

These are important considerations for any analysis of disinformation, but this chapter's main concern, and the focus of Section 15.3, is the linkage between

34 S. Wood et al., *Review of Literature Relevant to Data Protection Harms* (London: Plum Consulting, 2022), pp. 4–5, 24–5, https://ico.org.uk/media/about-the-ico/documents/4020142/plum-review-of-literature-relevant-to-data-protection-harms-v1-202203.pdf; Information Commissioner's Office 'Overview of data protection harms and the ICO's taxonomy' (2022), https://ico.org.uk/media/about-the-ico/documents/4020144/overview-of-data-protection-harms-and-the-ico-taxonomy-v1-202204.pdf, pp. 5–7.

35 For a broader consideration of the effects of AI on democracy and the rule of law, see, e.g., N. A. Smuha, 'Beyond the individual: governing AI's societal harm' (2021) 10 *Internet Policy Review* 3, Article 1574.

36 House of Lords Select Committee Report, 'Regulating in a digital world', pp. 3, 9.

37 Helm and Nasu, 'Regulatory responses to "fake news" and freedom of expression', p. 325.

38 A. Murray '"The time has come for international regulation on artificial intelligence" – an interview with Andrew Murray', 25 November 2020, *OpinioJuris*, http://opiniojuris.org/2020/11/25/the-time-has-come-for-international-regulation-on-artificial-intelligence-an-interview-with-andrew-murray/.

39 T. Dias Oliva, 'Content moderation technologies: applying human rights standards to protect freedom of expression' (2020) 20 *Human Rights Law Review* 4, 607–40.

40 E. Magrani, *Hacking the Electorate: On the Use of Personal Data in Political Campaigning* (Berlin: Konrad Adenauer Stiftung, 2020), p. 15.

disinformation and human rights that crystallises around the right to freedom of expression. To preview my argument, the ill-considered regulation of online content, including disinformation, may lead to potentially unlawful, unnecessary, and disproportionate interferences with the right to freedom of expression.[41] Rather than addressing the threats posed by disinformation, such interferences may generate new harms: they may undermine the functioning and values of the democratic processes that critics of unregulated speech worry about. Therefore, online disinformation is not amenable to broad-brush regulation, a factor that adds substantially to the difficulty of responding effectively to its harmful impact.

15.3 FREEDOM OF EXPRESSION, DEMOCRACY, AND ONLINE DISINFORMATION

The challenges posed by the spread of online disinformation are significant, but they should not deter efforts to develop regulatory instruments. As one commentator quipped, 'the time for simply admiring the problem is over'.[42] However, as already stated, regulating online content, including disinformation, faces major hurdles. One such hurdle stems from states' obligations with respect to the right to freedom of expression: these obligations generate a complex terrain for regulatory interventions into disinformation and pose significant barriers to actions that could be construed as interfering in human rights. Drawing on the framework of the ECHR, this section plots how the right to freedom of expression intersects with the spread of online disinformation. The discussion begins with an exposition of the right to freedom of expression in Europe's regional human rights regime before problematising the legal and conceptual limitations of such a focus. The discussion demonstrates, first, that the right to freedom of expression limits states' scope to regulate disinformation. Second, it will be argued that reading disinformation harms exclusively through the lens of freedom of expression does not suffice. The section proposes instead a nuanced human rights analysis, which attends to the impact of disinformation on diverse groups and which considers how disinformation impacts a range of other human rights beyond freedom of expression. Third, despite disinformation's threat to human rights, I suggest that human rights law does not provide sufficient protection from the human rights harms caused by online disinformation.

The right to freedom of expression is enshrined in the system of international human rights law, which emerged in the aftermath of the Second World War. This right imposes negative and positive obligations on states to respect, protect

[41] Helm and Nasu, 'Regulatory responses to "fake news" and freedom of expression'.

[42] B. Epstein, 'Why it is so difficult to regulate disinformation online', in W. L. Bennett and S. Livingston (eds.), *The Disinformation Age: Politics, Technology, and Disruptive Communication in the United States* (Cambridge: Cambridge University Press, 2020), pp. 190–210, at 203.

and promote human rights.[43] Complementing international legal obligations, European human rights provisions for freedom of expression derive from Article 10 of the ECHR and from the jurisprudence of the ECtHR (or Strasbourg Court). Article 10 stipulates that:

1. Everyone has the right to freedom of expression. This right shall include freedom to hold opinions and to receive and impart information and ideas without interference by public authority and regardless of frontiers. This Article shall not prevent States from requiring the licensing of broadcasting, television or cinema enterprises.
2. The exercise of these freedoms, since it carries with it duties and responsibilities, may be subject to such formalities, conditions, restrictions or penalties as are prescribed by law and are necessary in a democratic society, in the interests of national security, territorial integrity or public safety, for the prevention of disorder or crime, for the protection of health or morals, for the protection of the reputation or rights of others, for preventing the disclosure of information received in confidence, or for maintaining the authority and impartiality of the judiciary.[44]

The protections provided by Article 10 are not limited to speech and cover instead a wide range of expressions. These include artistic and commercial expressions, the publication of photographs, forms of conduct, rules governing clothing, and the use of the 'Like' button or similar expressions on social media networks. Article 10 also protects media freedom and grants a limited margin of appreciation with respect to interferences with journalistic expressions.[45] Moreover, freedom of expression extends to different modes of receiving and imparting information and disseminating one's right to expression.[46] However, not all forms of expression are granted equal protection. Two related aspects are noteworthy in this context: first, the ECtHR presumes a hierarchy of expressions, which accords political speech the highest form of protection, followed by artistic and commercial speech.[47] Second, freedom of expression has special significance within the context of a democratic society. This principle is enshrined in the ECHR Preamble, which confirms a 'profound belief in those fundamental freedoms which are … best maintained on the one hand by

43 For a general overview see, e.g., I. Bantekas and L. Oette, *International Human Rights Law and Practice* (Cambridge: Cambridge University Press, 2024); O. de Schutter, *International Human Rights Law: Cases, Materials, Commentary* (Cambridge: Cambridge University Press, 2019).

44 Convention for the Protection of Human Rights and Fundamental Freedoms, 4 November 1950, Council of Europe Treaty Series 005, Article 10.

45 On interference with journalistic expressions, see, e.g., *Lingens v. Austria*, Application no. 9815/82, Judgment of 8 July 1986.

46 European Court of Human Rights, *Guide on Article 10 of the European Convention on Human Rights: Freedom of Expression* (Strasbourg: Council of Europe/European Court of Human Rights, 2022), pp. 12–13.

47 Bayer et al., *The Fight Against Disinformation and the Right to Freedom of Expression*, p. 26.

an effective political democracy and on the other by a common understanding and observance of the human rights upon which they depend'.

The importance of the right to freedom of expression within the system of ECHR rights is reflected in the case law of the ECtHR.[48] The leading case of *Handyside v. the UK* (1976) established that freedom of expression is '[i]ndissociable from democracy',[49] and 'one of the essential foundations of … a [democratic] society, one of the basic conditions for its progress and for the development of every man'. This assertion is stressed in an often-cited section in *Handyside*, which asserts that freedom of expression

> is applicable not only to 'information' or 'ideas' that are favourably received or regarded as inoffensive or as a matter of indifference, but also to those that **offend, shock or disturb the State or any sector of the population**. Such are the demands of that pluralism, tolerance and broadmindedness without which there is no 'democratic society'. … every 'formality', 'condition', 'restriction' or 'penalty' imposed in this sphere must be proportionate to the legitimate aim pursued.[50]

Subsequent judgments have reinforced the view that 'freedom of political debate is at the very core of the concept of a democratic society which prevails throughout the Convention'.[51] For example, in *Lingens v. Austria* (1986), the Strasbourg Court proclaims that:

> freedom of expression … constitutes one of the essential foundations of a democratic society and one of the basic conditions for its progress and for each individual's self-fulfilment. … it is applicable not only to 'information' or 'ideas' that are favourably received or regarded as inoffensive or as a matter of indifference, but also to those that offend, shock or disturb.[52]

That Article 10 'enjoys a very wide scope, whether with regard to the substance of the ideas and information expressed, or to the form in which they are conveyed',[53] is further emphasised in *Mathieu-Mohin and Clerfayt v. Belgium* (1987), which reiterates the ECHR Preamble's link between fundamental human rights and freedoms as 'best maintained by "an effective political democracy"',[54] and which enshrines in particular the 'prime importance' of free expression in free elections.[55] *Bowman v. the United Kingdom* (1998), which draws on *Lingens v. Austria* (1986), further

[48] See ibid. for a survey of relevant ECtHR case law. See also European Court of Human Rights, *Guide on Article 10 of the European Convention on Human Rights*.

[49] Ibid., p. 11.

[50] *Handyside v. UK*, Application no 5493/72, Judgment of 7 December 1976, para. 49 (emphasis added).

[51] *Lingens v. Austria*, Application no. 9815/82, Judgment of 8 July 1986, para. 42.

[52] Ibid., paras. 41–2.

[53] European Court of Human Rights, *Guide on Article 10 of the European Convention on Human Rights*, p. 12.

[54] Ibid.

[55] *Mathieu-Mohin and Clerfayt v. Belgium*, Application no. 9267/81, Judgment of 2 March 1987, para. 47.

emphasises the protection of freedom of expression and of protection of political speech, described as 'the bedrock of any democratic system':

> Free elections and freedom of expression, particularly freedom of political debate ... are inter-related and operate to reinforce each other ... freedom of expression is one of the 'conditions' necessary to 'ensure the free expression of the opinion of the people in the choice of the legislature' ... For this reason, it is particularly important in the period preceding an election that opinions and information of all kinds are permitted to circulate freely.[56]

The protection of the right to freedom of expression, its special role in democratic societies, and the extension of this right to different modes of imparting and receiving information has also been confirmed in a series of cases relating to digital communication, specifically the digital dissemination of political speech.[57] Flipping the claim that what is prohibited offline should be prohibited online, one may read the ECtHR jurisprudence as an assertion of the claim that what should be protected offline should be protected online. In its 'Guide to Article 10', the Court confirms the 'innovative character of the Internet' and states that 'user-generated expressive activity on the Internet provides an unprecedented platform for the exercise of freedom of expression'.[58] The wide scope of Article 10, together with the principles articulated in the ECHR Preamble and in subsequent ECtHR jurisprudence, suggest that online disinformation may not be inherently unlawful and may, in fact, be protected in accordance with Article 10. Therefore, attempts to regulate online disinformation may constitute an interference with the right to freedom of expression. As is well known, interferences into Article 10, for example in the interest of national security, public safety, or other matters, as specified in Article 10(2), must be assessed against the ECtHR's tripartite test of legality, proportionality, and necessity; they must also consider the additional import bestowed on political speech. These protections impose limits on interferences with the right to freedom of expression, and it is reasonable to surmise that these limits extend to attempts at interference with online disinformation.

Human rights law, specifically Article 10, creates a knotty problem for tackling online disinformation: as argued earlier, there are compelling normative concerns about the harmful impact of disinformation on human rights, yet we may plausibly conclude that disinformation can avail itself of the protections offered by Article 10. Addressing this problem requires a shift in perspective. Two aspects merit particular attention. First, although the regulation of disinformation risks disproportionate and unlawful interference in the right to freedom of expression, unfettered

56 *Bowman v. the United Kingdom*, Case no. 141/1996/762/959, Judgment of 19 February 1998, para. 42.

57 See, e.g., *Delfi AS v. Estonia* [GC], Application no. 64569/09, Judgment of 16 June 2015; *Cengiz and Others v. Turkey*, Application nos. 48226/10 and 14027/11, Judgment of 1 December 2015; *Ahmet Yıldırım v. Turkey*, Application no. 3111/10, Judgment of 18 December 2012.

58 European Court of Human Rights, *Guide on Article 10 of the European Convention on Human Rights*, p. 107.

speech, whether offline or online, can also harm the wider communication ecosystem by silencing minoritarian voices.[59] Judit Bayer argues that 'paradoxically from the perspective of Article 10 of ECHR, freedom of speech was to be restricted with the objective to preserve a sound informational environment; because pluralism of views, and ultimately the democratic process would otherwise have been distorted by the speech in question'.[60] Acknowledging these broader effects of disinformation calls for more granular analyses, which study how disinformation impacts the right to freedom of expression for a diverse range of individuals and groups. Online disinformation can generate structural conditions, which silence and exclude marginalised voices, and thus restrict their enjoyment of the right to freedom of expression. Second, conjoining critical analyses of disinformation exclusively with the right to freedom of expression risks losing sight of the effects of disinformation on the wider communication and information ecosystem and on a wider range of human rights, including the right to privacy (Article 8 ECHR), freedom of assembly and association (Article 11), the prohibition of discrimination (Article 14), or the prohibition of an abuse of rights (Article 17). This calls for a broader engagement with human rights law, beyond Article 10, and, as will be discussed in the remainder of the chapter, with legal regimes that offer new or additional protections for human rights.

15.4 MICROTARGETING: BENEFITS AND HARMS TO HUMAN RIGHTS AND DEMOCRACY

What compounds concerns about the impact of online disinformation on human rights and democracy and complicates regulatory efforts is the practice of microtargeting. The term 'microtargeting' describes the surgical, selective, and frequently opaque dissemination of tailored political or commercial communication to pre-identified, typically homogeneous audiences.[61] Through the use of data analytics, microtargeting can generate audience profiles based on social demographics such as gender, age, or ethnicity, but also philosophical beliefs or political opinions. These segmented audiences, for example, of consumers or voters, can be strategically targeted with bespoke messages.[62] The data typically required for microtargeting is personal data, defined in Article 4(1) of the GDPR as:

> any information relating to an identified or identifiable natural person ('data subject') … who can be identified, directly or indirectly, in particular by reference to

[59] See, e.g., Citron, *Hate Crimes in Cyberspace*. For a broader discussion see, e.g., M. Beard, 'The public voice of women' (2014) 36 *London Review of Books* 6, 11–4. See also J. Bayer, 'Double harm to voters: data-driven micro-targeting and democratic public discourse' (2020) 9 *Internet Policy Review* 1, 1–17, at 7.

[60] Bayer, 'Double harm to voters', p. 7.

[61] Information Commissioner's Office, 'Microtargeting'.

[62] C. J. Bennett and D. Lyon, 'Data-driven elections: implications and challenges for democratic societies' (2019) 8 *Internet Policy Review* 4, Article 1433, 3–4.

an identifier such as a name, an identification number, location data, an online identifier or to one or more factors specific to the physical, physiological, genetic, mental, economic, cultural or social identity of that natural person.

How such personal data is acquired can vary. It can be provided by the data subject ('provided data'), such as a person's political opinions, which he or she may share on social media platforms. It can also be processed through the use of cookies or tracking pixels ('observed data'). Or it can involve inferred data, which is based on probabilities emerging from the analysis of provided or observed data by finding 'correlations between datasets and using these to categorise or profile people, e.g., calculating credit scores or predicting future health outcomes'.[63]

Microtargeting has attracted significant public interest since the mid-2010s, when its deployment became associated with the practices of the data analytics company Cambridge Analytica.[64] Cambridge Analytica created data profiles of typically undecided voters, which aligned with their social media profiles, and which were used to target comparatively small cohorts of voters with selective and often inaccurate messages, especially on highly emotive issues such as immigration. However, it is important to stress that microtargeting is not inherently political in either content or objectives, and that it can be deployed for a range of purposes, including commercial goals.[65] This is because microtargeting techniques are equally amenable for commercial or political ends, or a combination of both.[66] Moreover, there is no inherent reason to associate microtargeting with disinformation: microtargeting is not intrinsically wedded to the spread of disinformation, while disinformation can proliferate without resorting to microtargeting practices. However, the conjoining of online disinformation with the practice of microtargeting adds to the significant concerns about harms to elections, to democratic practices and democratic political cultures, and to human rights. This also extends the remit of analysis, beyond a focus on freedom of expression, to include data protection and privacy issues.

63 Information Commissioner's Office, 'Guidance for the use of personal data in political campaigning' (2021), http://ico.org.uk/for-organisations/direct-marketing-and-privacy-and-electronic-communications/guidance-for-the-use-of-personal-data-in-political-campaigning-1/, 68. See also DCMS report, 17–8. Information Commissioner's Office, 'Big data, artificial intelligence, machine learning and data protection' (2017), https://ico.org.uk/media2/migrated/2013559/big-data-ai-ml-and-data-protection.pdf, 12–3.

64 J. Zhu and R. Isaacs, 'Campaign microtargeting and AI can jeopardize democracy', 29 May 2024, LSE British Politics and Policy, https://blogs.lse.ac.uk/politicsandpolicy/campaign-microtargeting-and-ai-can-jeopardize-democracy/. DCMS Report, 17. For a recent account by a protagonist involved in CA, see C. Wylie, *Mindf*ck: Inside Cambridge Analytica's Plot to Break the World* (London: Profile Books, 2019).

65 Demarcating political from non-political disinformation is a complex issue, which would lead beyond the scope of this chapter. Issues that present, at first blush, as non-political, e.g., debates on the use of COVID-19 vaccinations, can relate political issues and agendas. See, e.g., AVAAZ, 'How Facebook can flatten the curve of the coronavirus infodemic'.

66 I. S. Rubinstein, 'Voter privacy in the age of big data' (2014) *Wisconsin Law Review* 4, 861–936.

Despite extensive scholarly and public political interest in microtargeting and its respective benefits and harms, its effectiveness remains contested. For example, Borgesius et al. remind us that voters do not live in digital bubbles and may not be receptive to microtargeted messages.[67] This may diminish the capacity of microtargeted messages to influence the outcome of elections. We may also surmise that companies that offer microtargeting services may exaggerate their value.[68] This lack of empirical evidence on the effectiveness of microtargeting could, potentially, alleviate concerns over its harms. However, suggestions that microtargeting, whether deployed in political or commercial marketing campaigns, may offer benefits to the sender and receiver of targeted messages, indicates a continued confidence in its usefulness.[69] One of its alleged benefits is said to derive from its shift from 'broadcasting', a term that depicts the wide-ranging spread of political or commercial messages to general audiences, to 'narrowcasting', which provides receivers, such as voters or consumers, with information on issues that selected audiences regard as relevant, and that speak directly to their interests, needs, or concerns.[70] For example, in the field of commercial advertising, microtargeting can support the marketing of goods and services to consumers in search of specific products, and reduce advertisement overload for those who are not interested in these products. Microtargeting can also support the transmission of public policy messages in fields such as health or welfare.[71] For example, microtargeting has been deployed to communicate tailored skin cancer prevention messages to young women using sunbeds,[72] or to disseminate information about welfare programmes to people living in deprived areas.[73]

Targeting segmented audiences with bespoke messages is also said to offer distinct benefits in the democratic process. For example, microtargeting may engage hard-to-reach individuals and communities, typically those who are 'switched off' from the political process. (Re-)engaging sections of the electorate with political issues and electoral processes may offer non-partisan benefits that, rather than undermining democratic politics, may in fact strengthen democratic systems. However, its main advantage is said to lie in the partisan benefits to political campaigns. Although there is no consensus on whether microtargeting can mobilise

67 F. J. Zuiderveen Borgesius et al., 'Online political microtargeting: promises and threats for democracy' (2018) 14 *Utrecht Law Review* 1, 82–96, at 91–2.

68 Ibid.

69 Ibid., p. 82.

70 Rubinstein, 'Voter privacy in the age of big data', p. 882; see also Zuiderveen Borgesius et al., 'Online political microtargeting'.

71 Bayer, 'Double harm to voters', p. 9.

72 A. Gaysynsky, K. Heley, and W. Y. S. Chou, 'An overview of innovative approaches to support timely and agile health communication research and practice' (2022) 19 *International Journal of Environmental Research and Public Health* 22, Article 15073.

73 I. S. Smythe and J. E. Blumenstock, 'Geographic microtargeting of social assistance with high-resolution poverty maps', 1 August 2022, PNAS, www.pnas.org/doi/full/10.1073/pnas.2120025119.

undecided voters, there is a view that it can 'activate the base … and improve partisan turnout'.[74] This explains why microtargeting has been deployed so widely in election campaigns and referenda.

Critical perspectives on microtargeting contend that a focus on empirical evidence about its effectiveness with respect to elections is blind to the substantial threats, including its weaponisation of personal data and its effect on democratic infrastructures.[75] These analyses ground their arguments in normative claims about the harmful effects of microtargeting that are bound up with three interrelated issues: first, the capacity of microtargeting to disseminate disinformation to selected audiences; second, its effects on the information ecosystem and on the right to freedom of expression, and third, the consequences for privacy and data protection. For example, there are concerns that microtargeted disinformation may suppress voter turnout, and that the use of microtargeting to mobilise small groups of voters, typically in swing states in US elections, can focus on so-called wedge issues. These are polarised issues that can frame and dominate public political discourse and undermine the coherence of the wider polity by detracting attention from issues that concern voters across the party-political spectrum.[76] These concerns intersect with worries over the impact of microtargeting on privacy, specifically with the harvesting of personal data, and attendant concerns over data protection, data security, and voter surveillance, based on the use of predictive analytics and the processing of inferred data.[77] There are additional normative concerns that the impact of microtargeting extends beyond individual privacy. For example, Bennett and Lyon contend that it generates collective and societal effects, which are 'not just about privacy, but even more so about data collection and governance, freedom of expression, disinformation, and democracy itself'.[78] Zittrain asserts that what he calls 'digital gerrymandering' is 'not a wrong to a given individual user, but rather to everyone, even non-users'.[79]

Such worries about the collective and systemic effects of microtargeting also inform the work of Judit Bayer. Addressing the impact of microtargeting on democracy, she calls for a restriction of microtargeting, not because of its alleged manipulation of voters and interferences with the right to privacy, but because it fragments public discourse and threatens the democratic process. According to Bayer, microtargeting presents a double-harm: it comprises the harm of being targeted, but also the harm of not being targeted, which, according to her, constitutes a violation of

74 Rubinstein, 'Voter privacy in the age of big data', p 882. For a discussion of further benefits, see Zuiderveen Borgesius et al., 'Online political microtargeting'.

75 V. Bashyakarla, 'Towards a holistic perspective on personal data and the data-driven election paradigm' (2019) 8 *Internet Policy Review* 4, Article 1445.

76 See, e.g., Bennett and Lyon, 'Data-driven elections', and Bayer, 'Double harm to voters'.

77 Bennett and Lyon, 'Data-driven elections'.

78 Ibid., p. 8.

79 J. Zittrain, 'Engineering an election' (2014) 127 *Harvard Law Review Forum*, 335–42, at 335, 338.

informational rights, a potential 'mass violation of human rights' of all those who are not targeted.[80] She declares that the right to receive information and the right to freedom of expression are complementary: '[w]hen the right to receive information is violated, it is freedom of expression in its broader sense, which is violated.'[81] Conjoining the analyses offered by Bennett and Lyon, Zittrain, and Bayer, we may conclude that the profiling and microtargeting of online users, based on the 'analysis of their data profile' creates an information asymmetry,[82] which violates informational rights,[83] and shatters the 'shared world' of political deliberation.[84] A fragmented and opaque (dis-)information basis of public political discourse, which targets selected social media users with personalised (dis-)information based on data analytics techniques poses harm to the democratic polity, culminating in the 'polarisation and fragmentation of the public sphere'.[85] It leaves in its wake citizens who are informationally isolated and atomised.

Despite these normative concerns about MOD's harms to human rights and democracy, a consensus on how it should be regulated remains elusive. As highlighted in Section 15.3, human rights law creates significant barriers to interferences with freedom of expression; these barriers extend, potentially, to disinformation practices. There is as yet no ECtHR jurisprudence on the issue of disinformation,[86] and we may conclude that online content, including disinformation, and the mode of delivery – microtargeting – are protected under the broad umbrella of Article 10. Attention has turned instead to legal regimes beyond human rights law. Section 15.5 illustrates this shift in focus with respect to selected EU legal instruments.

15.5 REGULATING MOD: THE EU'S LEGISLATIVE ACTIONS

The notion of a 'marketplace of ideas' popularised by Justice Holmes's dissenting judgment in *Abrams v. United States* implies that the self-regulatory capacity of a public realm, constituted by uncoerced dialogue, is sufficiently inoculated against the effects of harmful speech.[87] More than a century later, there are well-founded concerns that Holmes's vision of self-regulation may not suffice to counter the harms generated by unfettered online content. Therefore, despite the affordances of online platforms and search engines to expand opportunities for freedom of expression and

80 Bayer, 'Double harm to voters', p. 3.
81 Ibid., p. 4.
82 DCMS Report, p. 17.
83 Bayer, 'Double harm to voters'.
84 H. Arendt, *The Origins of Totalitarianism* (Boston: Harcourt Books, 1951/1968).
85 Bayer, 'Double harm to voters', p. 9.
86 E. Shattock, 'Fake news in Strasbourg: electoral disinformation and freedom of expression in the European Court of Human Rights (ECtHR)' (2022) 13 *European Journal of Law and Technology* 1.
87 *Abrams v. United States*, 250 US 616 (1919).

other human rights, there are persistent worries that online disinformation compounds harms to individuals and communities and exerts chilling effects on democracy and human rights.[88] It is against this backdrop that interest in the regulation of online expression and of platforms and search engines has garnered attention.[89] However, as discussed earlier in the chapter, balancing the right to freedom of expression, which includes the right to 'offend, shock or disturb',[90] with protection from the individual, collective, and societal harms generated by MOD poses seemingly intractable challenges. Regulating online expressions may not provide a sufficiently granular response to the specific threats posed by MOD. In fact, one could plausibly argue that content regulation constitutes a regulatory scattergun, which risks missing the desired aim – that of MOD – because it is blind to diverse types of online communications and their attendant set of challenges.

Recent EU policy and legislative initiatives promise more granular approaches to deal with this problem. They are anchored in EU primary law, including Article 16 of the Treaty on the Functioning of the EU and the Charter of Fundamental Rights (hereinafter the Charter), the EU's premier human rights instrument. The latter includes the right to privacy (Article 7 of the Charter), the right to protection of personal data (Article 8 of the Charter), and the right to freedom of expression and information (Article 11 of the Charter). The EU's legislative programme is supported by a series of agenda-setting policy recommendations, Communications, and soft law instruments, which offer additional, albeit ultimately non-enforceable, ways to regulate the dissemination of disinformation via the practices of microtargeting. They include the European Commission's '2030 Digital Compass: the European way for the Digital Decade',[91] the European Democracy Action Plan;[92] the Strengthened Code of Practice on Disinformation,[93] and the European Declaration on Digital Rights and Principles for the Digital Decade.[94] Also noteworthy are statements and opinions issued by the Article 29 Data Protection Working Party, the European Data

[88] Citron, *Hate Crimes in Cyberspace*.

[89] These include self-regulation, co-regulation, information correction, and the use of criminal sanctions. See, e.g., Meyer and Marsden, *Regulating Disinformation with Artificial Intelligence*; Helm and Nasu, 'Regulatory responses to "fake news" and freedom of expression', pp. 315, 326.

[90] *Handyside v. UK*, Application no 5493/72, Judgment of 7 December 1976.

[91] European Commission, 'Communication from the Commission to the European Parliament, the Council, the European Economic and Social Committee and the Committee of the Regions '2030 Digital Compass: the European way for the Digital Decade', EU Doc. COM(2021) 118, 9 March 2021.

[92] European Commission, 'Communication from the Commission to the European Parliament, the Council, the European Economic and Social Committee and the Committee of the Regions on the European democracy action plan', EU Doc. COM(2020) 790, 3 December 2020.

[93] European Commission, 'The strengthened Code of Practice on Disinformation 2022', 16 June 2022, https://digital-strategy.ec.europa.eu/en/library/2022-strengthened-code-practice-disinformation.

[94] European Commission, 'European Declaration on Digital Rights and Principles for the Digital Decade', 15 December 2022, https://digital-strategy.ec.europa.eu/en/library/european-declaration-digital-rights-and-principles#:~:text=The%20Declaration%20on%20Digital%20Rights%20and%20Principles%20presents%20the%20EU's,EU%20values%20and%20fundamental%20rights.

Protection Board (EDPB) and the European Data Protection Supervisor (EDPS).[95] Of key interest is an emerging suite of EU secondary law, which centres on the main elements involved in the dissemination of MOD, such as the regulation of data processing, the regulation of online platforms and search engines, the regulation of AI systems, and the regulation of political advertising. Despite differences in material scope, these laws share three features: first, they have direct horizontal effect, which imposes rights obligations not just on states or an emanation of a state, but also on non-state actors, including private companies. Second, they share loopholes, wide-ranging exemptions, and monitoring and enforcement gaps, which are compounded by the significant regulatory roles accorded to private actors. Third, they manifest an unresolved tension between the EU's twin objectives of protecting the internal market and promoting innovation on the one hand, and its obligation to protect fundamental rights.

15.5.1 *Regulating Data Processing: The GDPR*

The use of data analytics in microtargeting underscores the imperative to protect personal data, as enshrined in Article 8 of the Charter, and highlights the importance of data protection laws in the regulation of online content. The GDPR, the EU's most established and perhaps most widely known legislative instrument, centres on the processing of personal data (Article 4 of the GDPR), while its provisions pursue two goals: first, respect for fundamental rights and freedoms, including the right to protection of personal data; and second, the creation of harmonised rules within the EU internal market (Recital 2).[96] To deliver on these objectives, the GDPR put forward a series of data protection principles, including transparency, purpose limitation, data minimisation, accuracy, and integrity and confidentiality (Article 5),[97] which are intended to guide the processing of personal data. As stated

[95] They include Article 29 Data Protection Working Party, 'Guidelines on automated individual decision-making and profiling for the purposes of Regulation 2016/679', 6 February 2018, https://ec.europa.eu/newsroom/article29/items/612053/en; Article 29 Data Protection Working Party, 'Guidelines on transparency under Regulation 2016/679', 11 April 2018, www.edpb.europa.eu/system/files/2023-09/wp260rev01_en.pdf; European Data Protection Board (EDPB), 'Statement 2/2019 on the use of personal data in the course of political campaigns', 13 March 2019, www.edpb.europa.eu/sites/default/files/files/file1/edpb-2019-03-13-statement-on-elections_en.pdf; European Data Protection Board (EDPB), 'Guidelines 8/2020 on the targeting of social media users; version 2.0', 13 April 2021, www.edpb.europa.eu/system/files/2021-04/edpb_guidelines_082020_on_the_targeting_of_social_media_users_en.pdf; European Data Protection Supervisor, 'Opinion 3/2018: EDPS opinion on online manipulation and personal data', 19 March 2018, www.edps.europa.eu/sites/default/files/publication/18-03-19_online_manipulation_en.pdf.

[96] Regulation (EU) 2016/679 of the European Parliament and of the Council of 27 April 2016 on the protection of natural persons with regard to the processing of personal data and on the free movement of such data, and repealing Directive 95/46/EC.

[97] Additional data protection principles include lawfulness and fairness, storage limitation, and accountability.

in Recital 4, the GDPR 'respects all fundamental rights and observes the freedoms and principles recognised in the Charter as enshrined in the Treaties', including the right to freedom of expression (Article 11 of the Charter). Thus, data protection principles, and the right to the protection of personal data, are not absolute but must be balanced against other Charter rights.

The GDPR is 'technologically neutral' (Recital 15); it is not designed to regulate the dissemination of disinformation in general or the use of microtargeting techniques in particular. However, its provisions for the processing of personal data provide tools that can be used to regulate the microtargeting of voters via the use of inferred data. Four aspects are particularly noteworthy. First, the GDPR's extraterritorial scope (Article 3) extends the application of the Regulation beyond the EU and may affect the dissemination of microtargeted online content that originates outside the EU. Second, it connects the right to the protection of personal data with the right to freedom of expression and information, including processing for journalistic purposes (Article 85(1)). Third, it prohibits the processing of 'special categories of data', including that of racial or ethnic origin, political opinion, philosophical beliefs, or health data (Article 9(1)). And fourth, it includes the right not to be subject to a decision based solely on automated processing, including profiling (Article 22(1)). Articles 9(1) and 22(1), separately as well as combined, appear to offer robust protection against the harmful effects of data analytics practices, including those that underpin microtargeting. However, each of the two articles is diluted with a range of exemptions. For example, Article 9(2d) provides exemptions for the processing of special category data for associations with political aims or where data subjects have made their personal data public (Article 9(2e)).

Analysing the GDPR's provisions, Blasi Casagran and Vermeulen have also identified compliance issues with respect to political microtargeting, specifically with the data protection principles as outlined in Article 5 of the GDPR, including lawful processing, purpose limitation, data minimisation, data accuracy, and data accountability.[98] Their concerns align with those of the EDPB, which highlights the risks of microtargeting not only for 'individuals' rights to privacy and data protection, but also to wider trust in the integrity of democratic processes themselves.[99] The EDPB has counselled that derogations from Article 9 'should be interpreted narrowly, as it cannot be used to legitimate inferred data'.[100] There are additional concerns over the enforcement of GDPR provisions, and tensions between the way that human

98 C. Blasi Casagran and M. Vermeulen, 'Reflections on the murky legal practices of political microtargeting from a GDPR perspective' (2021) 11 *International Data Privacy Law* 4, 348–59, at 349.

99 Ibid., p. 352. European Data Protection Supervisor, 'Opinion 3/2018: EDPS opinion on online manipulation and personal data', 19 March 2018, www.edps.europa.eu/sites/default/files/publication/18-03-19_online_manipulation_en.pdf, 5.

100 European Data Protection Board (EDPB), 'Statement 2/2019 on the use of personal data in the course of political campaigns', 13 March 2019, www.edpb.europa.eu/sites/default/files/files/file1/edpb-2019-03-13-statement-on-elections_en.pdf, 2.

rights protection is balanced against other interests, including the development of harmonised rules across the EU's internal market.

15.5.2 *Regulating Online Platforms: The DSA*

While the GDPR focuses on the processing of personal data, the DSA, which entered into force on 19 November 2022, is the EU's bespoke tool for dealing with the business models and practices of online service providers.[101] Like other EU legislative actions, the DSA speaks to the EU's twin concerns of protecting the internal market via a harmonisation of 'uniform, effective and proportionate mandatory rules' (Recital 4) while also protecting fundamental rights enshrined in the EU Charter. Its main objectives are 'to prevent illegal and harmful activities online and the spread of disinformation'.[102] Recognising the 'inherently cross-border nature of the internet' (Recital 2), the DSA establishes a graduated and tailored approach, which imposes increasingly stringent due diligence obligations on intermediary service providers, depending on their size and reach. The most stringent obligations are imposed on very large online platforms and very large online search engines, which Article 33(1) defines as having a number of average monthly active recipients of the service in the EU equal to or higher than 45 million.

The regulatory guidelines presented in the DSA are technology neutral. Its primary concern lies with a 'safe, predictable and trusted online environment' (Recital 9) through a graded, risk-based approach. Three categories of risk are identified: first, the dissemination of illegal content and conduct of illegal activities, such as child sexual abuse or terrorist content; second, the impact of digital services on the exercise of fundamental human rights; and third, the manipulation of platform services which have an impact, among other things, on civic discourse and electoral processes. The DSA requires intermediary service providers to have due regard to relevant international standards for the protection of human rights, including freedom of expression, media freedom, and pluralism (Recital 47). It acknowledges the wider impact of disinformation on fundamental rights (Recitals 9 and 86) and on democratic processes (Recital 82), and it recognises the systemic risks of disinformation and its impact on society and democracy (Recital 104), including the risk of online services to 'civic discourse and electoral processes, and public security' (Article 34(1)(c)). More specifically, the DSA acknowledges risks stemming from the use of online advertisements and associated targeting techniques. It stipulates that 'providers of online platforms should not present advertisements based on profiling as defined in Article 4, point (4), of Regulation (EU) 2016/679, using special

[101] Regulation (EU) 2022/2065 of the European Parliament and of the Council of 19 October 2022 on a single market for digital services and amending Directive 2000/31/EC (Digital Services Act).

[102] European Commission, 'The Digital Services Act: ensuring a safe and accountable environment online', https://commission.europa.eu/strategy-and-policy/priorities-2019-2024/europe-fit-digital-age/digital-services-act_en.

categories of personal data referred to in Article 9(1) of that Regulation, including by using profiling categories based on those special categories'. (Recital 69). Despite its recognition of the harm from disinformation, references to disinformation are relegated to the non-binding recitals. With its focus on illegal activities, the DSA offers few effective interventions into disinformation practices.

15.5.3 *Regulating Techniques: The AIA*

Broadly mirroring the approach of the DSA, the AIA focuses on the regulation of AI systems.[103] An AI system is defined as a 'machine-based system that is designed to operate with varying levels of autonomy and that may exhibit adaptiveness after deployment, and that, for explicit or implicit objectives, infers, from the input it receives, how to generate outputs such as predictions, content, recommendations, or decisions that can influence physical or virtual environments' (Article 3(1)). The Act's purpose, as outlined in Recital 1, is 'to improve the functioning of the internal market by laying down a uniform legal framework' that strikes a balance between fostering the development of a single market for lawful, safe, and trustworthy AI applications while ensuring the protection of fundamental rights and societal values, including democracy and the rule of law. To deliver on this goal, the AIA adopts a risk-based approach, which categorises AI systems into four risk levels, ranging from unacceptable and thus prohibited risks through high risk and limited risk to minimal or no risk. Its legally binding provisions delineate obligations and responsibilities for AI developers and users, seeking to foster an AI landscape that promotes human-centric and trustworthy AI systems and ensures a high level of protection of health, safety, and fundamental rights (Article 1(1)).

Although the Act has not been designed as a bespoke human rights instrument – the AIA refers to fundamental rights – it acknowledges concerns about AI's impact on rights at various stages of the AI lifecycle, from design and development to the placing of AI systems on the market. Its provisions for human rights protection are part of a broader mission, which seeks to harmonise the legal regulation of AI across the EU, and foster innovation aimed at establishing the EU as a 'global leader in the development of secure, trustworthy and ethical AI' (Recital 8). Concerns over AI's impact on human rights feature prominently in the (non-binding) recitals and in the articles. The Act promotes alignment with EU values of 'respect for human dignity, freedom, equality, democracy and the rule of law and fundamental rights' (Recital 28). To operationalise these concerns, the Act introduces a series of regulatory

[103] Regulation (EU) 2024/1689 of the European Parliament and of the Council of 13 June 2024 laying down harmonised rules on AI and amending Regulations (EC) No 300/2008, (EU) No 167/2013, (EU) No 168/2013, (EU) 2018/858, (EU) 2018/1139 and (EU) 2019/2144 and Directives 2014/90/EU, (EU) 2016/797 and (EU) 2020/1828 (AIA). This section draws on B. Schippers, C. Ferreira, and P. Veiga, 'The European Union Artificial Intelligence Act: challenges for fundamental rights protection' (2024), https://gdhrnet.eu/wp-content/uploads/EU-Artificial-Intelligence-Act.pdf.

governance techniques. These include an obligation to conduct fundamental rights impact assessments for high-risk AI systems,[104] which apply to AI deployers governed by public law or private entities providing public services (Article 27), transparency obligations (Article 50), and the reporting of serious incidents (Article 73). The Act also stipulates the voluntary application of codes of conduct, including adherence to EU guidelines on ethical AI (Article 95(2)(a)), facilitating inclusive and diverse AI design through inclusive and diverse development teams and stakeholder participation (Article 95(2)(d)), assessing and preventing the negative impact of AI on vulnerable groups and on gender equality (Article 95(2)(e), and establishing an advisory forum to the AI Board with civil society representation (Article 67(2)).

There is a recognition of the potentially maleficent impact of high-risk AI systems on democracy and democratic processes, primarily in the recitals. Recital 110 addresses the capabilities of general-purpose AI models, specifically their capacity to facilitate the spread of disinformation and pose threats to democratic values and human rights. Developing this theme, Recital 120 considers how AI systems deployed by very large online platforms and very large online search engines can disseminate artificially generated or manipulated content, with 'actual or foreseeable negative effects on democratic processes, civic discourse and electoral processes, including through disinformation' (see also Recital 136). The AIA makes specific reference to deepfakes, defined as 'AI-generated or manipulated image, audio or video content that resembles existing persons, objects, places, entities or events and would falsely appear to a person to be authentic or truthful' (Article 3(60)). It imposes a specific obligation on the deployers of deepfakes to disclose that the content has been artificially generated or manipulated if text is published 'with the purpose of informing the public on matters of public interest' (Article 50(4)). Overall, though, there is limited engagement with the issue of microtargeted disinformation, and it is fair to conclude that the AIA's provisions reveal a substantial gap between its normative commitments to protect human rights and the exemptions and regulatory loopholes in the legally binding provisions.

15.5.4 *Regulating Political Advertising: The Regulation on the Transparency and Targeting of Political Advertising*

Despite the huge public and scholarly interest in the DSA and the AIA, neither of these two instruments offer wide-ranging or bespoke regulatory tools to address the problem of MOD. The new Regulation on the Transparency and Targeting of

[104] For a classification of high-risk AI-systems see Article 6(1) and Annex III. Annex III (8(b)) classifies as high-risk those AI systems 'intended to be used for influencing the outcome of an election or referendum or the voting behaviour of natural persons in the exercise of their vote in elections or referenda'. Exempt from this classification are AI systems 'whose output natural persons are not directly exposed to, such as tools used to organise, optimise and structure political campaigns from an administrative and logistical point of view' (Recital 62).

Political Advertising (TTPA), which entered into force on 13 March 2024 and applies from 10 October 2025, promises to fill this gap by becoming the EU's most tailored legislative response to the challenge of the microtargeting of political advertising to date. A relatively short regulation – it consists of thirty articles – the TTPA seeks to create synergies with the GDPR and the DSA. For example, the TTPA utilises the GDPR's provisions for the processing of personal data. Building on the DSA, the TTPA foregrounds the principle of transparency and presents a risk-based approach. Its two objectives are to contribute to 'the proper functioning of the internal market for political advertising and related services' (Article 1(4a)) and 'to protect the fundamental rights and freedoms' enshrined in the Charter, 'in particular the right to privacy and the protection of personal data' (Article 1(4b)). It seeks to achieve these objectives by creating 'harmonised rules, including transparency and related due diligence obligations, for the provision of political advertising and related services' (Article 1(1a)) and 'harmonised rules on the use of targeting techniques and ad-delivery techniques that involve the processing of personal data in the context of the provision of online political advertising' (Article 1(1b)).

Underpinning the TTPA's provisions is a recognition that '[p]olitical advertising can be a vector of disinformation' (Recital 4) and that 'the misuse of personal data through targeting, including microtargeting … may present particular threats to legitimate public interests' (Recital 6), including threats to fundamental rights, such as freedom of expression, privacy, and equality. Three aspects are significant in this context: first, the TTPA establishes a direct link between microtargeting, disinformation, and political advertising, which is defined as 'the preparation, placement, promotion, publication or dissemination, by any means, of a message' (Article 3(1)). Second, the TTPA recognises that the targeting and amplification techniques, which disseminate political advertising, can negatively impact the democratic process and exploit the vulnerabilities of data subjects, with 'specific and detrimental effects on citizens' fundamental rights and freedoms with regard to the processing of their personal data and their freedom to receive objective information' (Recital 74). Targeting or amplification techniques are 'techniques that are used either to address a tailored political advertisement only to a specific person or group of persons or to increase the circulation, reach or visibility of a political advertisement' (Article 2(8)). These techniques, which are used to disseminate political advertising, should be prohibited unless explicit consent by the data subject has been given and appropriate safeguards are in place. In this respect, the TTPA seeks to close some of the derogations established in Article 9(2) of the GDPR, but it does not stipulate a prohibition of targeting techniques, provided that explicit consent from the data subject has been provided and that the targeting does not involve profiling (Article 18(1c)). Political parties, foundations, associations, or other non-profit bodies are exempt from these requirements provided that their communications are based on subscription data (Article 18(3)). Article 19 specifies additional transparency requirements, including publications of internal policies, record keeping, and internal annual risk assessments. Third, the TTPA rejects interferences with the substantive content of political messages and seeks to protect the content of political advertising from unlawful interference.

The TTPA is designed to go further than other EU instruments with respect to the practice of microtargeting. As distinct from the DSA, it is not focused on the regulation of illegal online content. Moreover, it expounds the wider impact of targeting and amplification techniques on a broader range of fundamental rights and on democracy itself. However, by exempting the editorial freedom of the media (Recital 29) and 'the sharing of information through electronic communication services, such as electronic message services ... provided that no political advertising service is involved' (Recital 48), the TTPA's scope excludes significant avenues for the dissemination of targeted disinformation; for example through platforms such as WhatsApp.[105] Moreover, its requirement for informed consent with respect to targeting and amplification is ill-suited to the practice of microtargeting, especially if it involves interferences by foreign states or bad actors. This will require further thought and new regulatory tools.

15.6 CONCLUSION

This chapter has surveyed the phenomenon of MOD and critically assessed whether human rights law is equipped to respond to this complex and complicated challenge. Through a focus on selected EU legislative instruments, and being cognisant of the broader legal-normative order of the ECHR and the jurisprudence of the ECtHR, the discussion has identified considerable hurdles with respect to the regulation of MOD. Given the wide-ranging protections for the right to freedom of expression, the chapter has contended that the scope for human rights law to address the harms generated by MOD is limited. The chapter began by expounding the concept of disinformation before discussing the right to freedom of expression and the limitations it poses on regulating disinformation – a form of communication not normally regarded as unlawful. Building on this discussion, the chapter then proceeded to examine the practice of microtargeting and attendant data analytics and their effects on the right to privacy. A survey and analysis of recent legislative initiatives in the EU illustrated how human rights protection has extended beyond human rights law; for example, by regulating the practices of very large online platforms, or by harnessing the tools of data protection law. While this 'European approach' can offer important lessons for the protection of human rights,[106] the chapter also highlighted important shortcomings related to issues such as enforcement and the wide-ranging scope for derogations and exemptions.

105 Magrani, *Hacking the Electorate*, pp. 15–17.

106 Nenadić, 'Unpacking the "European approach" to tackling challenges of disinformation and political manipulation'.

The regulation of MOD remains an evolving area. As emphasised in scholarly work and in policy debates, legal regulation is no panacea to counter the harms to human rights and democracy caused by fake news. The chapter therefore echoes the recommendation of Meyer and Marsden, who call for a holistic approach to disinformation that includes the development of digital literacy across all age groups.[107] This focus on digital literacy should be aligned with a broader political literacy strategy, which supports the capacity of citizens to access and analyse information and to participate in political discourse, both online and offline. As the recent push against the regulation of tech companies suggests,[108] there are worrying changes in the international political climate, which propel an anti-regulatory move. Whether EU law can withstand these powerful global actors remains to be seen.[109]

[107] Meyer and Marsden, *Regulating Disinformation with Artificial Intelligence*.

[108] L. McMahon, Z. Kleinman, and C. Subramanian, 'Facebook and Instagram get rid of fact checkers', 7 January 2025, *BBC Technology*, www.bbc.co.uk/news/articles/cly74mpy8klo.

[109] L. Graves, 'Will the EU fight for the truth on Facebook and Instagram?', 13 January 2024, *The Guardian*, www.theguardian.com/technology/2025/jan/13/meta-facebook-factchecking-eu.

16

Digital Boom: Current Issues from International Investment to Human Rights

Cristina Elena Popa Tache, Cătălin-Silviu Săraru, and Sergio de Souza Salles

16.1 INTRODUCTION

The study presented in this chapter is based on the hypothesis that today, more than ever, we need legal regulations adapted to the interaction between technology, human rights, and investments. In this context, international investors, as influential providers of digital services, must respect human rights by adapting their investment activities. At the same time, it has become a priority for states to find a balance between national sovereignty and the protection of investments and fundamental rights, especially in light of the dramatic decline in investment treaties.[1]

Sociability, as the ability of people to live in society, is a cornerstone of the digital era. Since the law reflects the structure of society, the law of sociability is a natural norm applicable to both individuals and states, highlighting the importance of international cooperation to meet the heightened human needs of civilisation. International investments have a profound impact on human rights, and the standards of legal treatment and the attitudes of host or origin states can influence inclusive and sustainable development. The question is: in light of these priorities, is it better to include new reference clauses in investment contracts or to enhance the dynamics of investment treaties that encompass these standards?

Either way, UN General Assembly Resolution 67/171 emphasises that human rights should be the main framework in negotiations regarding international legal instruments in the field of foreign investments. Current legal regulations need to create a fair and clear framework for all participants, balancing innovation, investment protection, and respect for human rights. In the latter case, we must consider both access to digitalisation as a human right and the individual autonomy to choose not to use the internet or technologies.[2]

[1] F. Cristani, M. Trunk-Fedorova, and C. E. Popa Tache, 'Editorial: the workshop 'pursuing fairness in times of crisis: reflections on the future of international economic law' held within the 2023 ESIL Annual Conference' (2024) 4 *International Investment Law Journal* 2, 131–6.

[2] C. E. Popa Tache, C.-S. Săraru, and K. Kouroupis, 'Different perspectives concerning the right not to use the internet and some analogies with education | Diverse prospettive sul diritto a non

The close interaction between international investment and significant advances in digital technologies points to the need for legal regulation adapted to this convergence. International law is facing a dynamic that reflects a complex and close interaction between the global business world and rapid technological developments. In general, the legal regime of foreign investment has its origins in the same law of sociability from which trade developed. Sociability, as an appropriation and capacity of people to live in society, resulting from the human character of being sociable, is a spring of the digital era, an era in which international investors as digital service providers have to comply by adapting to respect human rights in investment activities.

In the past, the law of sociability was considered a natural law not only for individuals but also for states.[3] It is a perfectly valid rule even now. The more humankind advances towards civilisation, the more our needs increase, and as these cannot always be satisfied by the products and industry of our own country, we are obliged to have recourse to neighbouring countries, so that it may be said that from the particular needs of individuals have been born relations between states.[4]

As a result, the diversity of human rights is directly proportional to the level of sociability. As things were in the past, so they are today. Why? Because we have a 'today' characterised by the digital boom as a new kind of sociability with new laws of sociability between individuals and states, and human rights can only be seen in their fundamental and vertical dimensions.

Therefore, international investment clearly has a profound impact on human rights, contextually given that the standards of their legal treatment, as well as the attitude of host states or even home states, may not always result in inclusive, sustainable and equitable development.[5]

General Assembly Resolution 67/171 states that human rights are a primary guiding framework in negotiations for international law instruments in the field of foreign investment. The resolution includes among its provisions the following:

> (30) also recognizes that good governance and the rule of law at the national level assist all States in the promotion and protection of human rights, including the right to development, and agrees on the value of the ongoing efforts being made by States to identify and strengthen good governance practices, including transparent, responsible, accountable and participatory government, that are responsive and appropriate to their needs and aspirations, including in the context of

usare internet ed alcune analogie con l'istruzione' (2024) 1 *European Journal of Privacy Law and Technologies*, 179–93.

3 See H. Bonfils and P. Fauchille, *Manuel de Droit International public (Droit Des Gens)*, 3rd edn (Paris: Arthur Rousseau, 1901), pp. 3–4, as cited in C. E. Popa Tache, *Legal Treatment Standards for International Investments. Heuristic Aspects* (Bucharest: Adjuris International Academic Publisher, 2021), p. 10.

4 See G. Meitani, *Course on Public International Law* (Bucharest, Al.T. Doicescu, 1930), p. 3, as cited in Popa Tache, *Legal Treatment Standards for International Investments*, p. 10.

5 See generally, C. E. Popa Tache, 'Ranking of treatment standards in international investments' (2021) 1 *International Investment Law Journal* 1, 79–87.

agreed partnership approaches to development, capacity-building and technical assistance.[6]

Increasing concerns for good regulation through the harmonisation of the international investment regime with regard to human rights have been driven by their overlap and interference with intellectual property, technology transfer, climate change, and energy regimes. Legal research analyses and assessments need to address the impact of the convergences, divergences, and intersections of these very different regimes on the realisation of human rights.

Digital technologies have become a key tool in this strategy of globalising business. Many international investments focus on areas of research and development, including digital technologies. Cross-border collaboration in these areas stimulates innovation and brings together expertise from different regions of the world. Legal regulations are currently focused on cross-border data transfer, global intellectual property rights protection, and cyber risk management. Legal initiatives must create a fair and clear framework for all participants. The balance depends on facilitating innovation, protecting investment and ensuring respect for human rights in the context of digital technologies. The focus remains on the protection of individual rights in the digital age, in particular privacy and data security, but also modern compliance with international standards on the human rights for inclusion and diversity.

16.2 IS A LEGAL APPROACH OF DIFFERENT THEORIES AND REGIMES USEFUL FOR REACHING A SINGLE UNIFIED THEORY?

Recent doctrine and case law have approached international investment through a human rights lens, taking into account a wide range of issues such as: (a) the impact that states' obligations (implicitly their liability) under Bilateral Investment Treaties (BITs) or Treaties with Investment Provisions (TIPs) would have on their capacity to respect human rights or to adopt new provisions in this respect – in this context, the phenomenon of digitisation is central; (b) the package of measures that states and other actors would need to adopt or pursue in order to ensure a positive impact and avoid negative impacts; and (c) how to address these new challenges through international cooperation. All this continues in an upward and multifunctional trend aiming at holistic, people-centred development.

In this context, the transdisciplinary approach to human rights would be advisable in the sense of an integrative research strategy.[7] Through transdisciplinarity as a

6 UN General Assembly, 'Resolution adopted by the General Assembly on 20 December 2012 [on the report of the Third Committee (A/67/457/Add.2 and Corr.1)] in the Sixty-seventh session, Agenda item 69 (b), regarding The right to development'.

7 C. E. Popa Tache, *Le dynamisme du droit international public contemporain et la transdisciplinarité* (Paris: L'Harmattan Paris, 2023), pp. 12–23.

shared space, we can seek to accumulate new knowledge from the dialogue between two or more disciplines. This is an approach that understands reality as a whole and analyses it from that complete perspective without addressing each of the different parts that make it up separately. Finally, transdisciplinarity is also present in technologies, where integrated knowledge allows the development of technological tools with immediate application in solving specific problems.[8]

When successfully used in the social sciences, we note that transdisciplinarity, if approached correctly, has the potential to overcome the singular vision of the specialist fields that form it, seeking to achieve a unity of knowledge. Human beings are a dynamic and ever-changing object of study, especially from the perspective of human rights and especially in the digital age. In this way, the transdisciplinary approach is necessary to obtain a complete assessment of human behaviours and the communities in which they develop, since they cannot be examined in isolation when we refer to the internet, new technologies, and so on.

The socialisation discussed in Chapter 15, together with integration and social control (notions that should be used with caution in the field of law), are the main concepts used in social psychology, sociology, and cultural anthropology, which define the processes, mechanisms, and institutions that ensure in any society the conformity of members of society to its ethical, normative, and cultural model, but also prevent deviation.[9] It is, therefore, impossible to analyse the subject of this chapter in isolation. However, the importance of a legal analysis that could bring together several reference extracts from different disciplines in order to arrive at a single legal theory focused on a particular theme of study, as we often find in human rights, is obvious. In other words, even if we pursue very concrete themes (such as digital impact), the legal concept must be the subject of a rigorous discipline with its own language and its own requirements.[10]

This mode of analysis chosen for the exposition of my theory was inspired, at the level of the structure of the analysis, by the ideas of E. O. Wilson, who affirmed the unified theory of knowledge in disciplines as an Esperanto between physics, biology, social sciences, and humanities. The level of legal research can concentrate, as we have shown, on different and comparative legal regimes, especially when it comes to defending and regulating human rights as comprehensively as possible. We have found that applying this theory can open new doors to new, broader, more effective solutions. In fact, since in the process of scientific knowledge it is always worth noting the success of several scientists' attempts to bring together certain different concepts for comparative analysis, Wilson's book, *Consilience*, is also a revelation in the

8 R. Burnett, 'Disciplines in crisis: transdisciplinary approaches in the arts, humanities and sciences, critical approaches to culture' (2005), www.eciad.ca/~rburnett/transdisciplinary.html.

9 See D. Banciu, S. M. Rădulescu, and M. Voicu, *Introduction to the Sociology of Deviance* (Bucharest: Științifică și enciclopedică, 1985), pp. 15–20.

10 R. Treves, *Introduction to the Sociology of Law* (Milan: Cisalpino-Goliardica, 1972), p. 11.

same sense.[11] This *jump together* of specialists from different fields that also involves substantially different concepts can indeed provide unified theories.

The aim is to obtain a unified human rights theory of international digital investment, which can be derived from the analysis of substantially different notions, such as the promotion of social progress and better living standards; greater freedom; use of specific international mechanisms to promote the economic and social progress of all peoples; and identification of interferences between intellectual property regimes, technology transfer, consumer protection, digital green infrastructure, and investment policies.

We find an example related to the theme of this chapter in addressing human rights, trade, economic value creation and capture, law enforcement, and national security for tailored digital regulation. However, the speed at which states respond differs, resulting in gaps caused by the speed of technological progress. As a consequence, these gaps are reflected in the rights of individuals, businesses, international trade, and policymaking. It is becoming increasingly important to address the issue of establishing legal frameworks that are as compatible as possible at national, regional, and multilateral levels. In the digital economy, the focus must be constantly on foreign digital and technology start-ups, as experts believe that they can become the major players of tomorrow.

Alongside all these aspects, we have discovered an equation in previous work that is applicable in such analyses. It is one of the newest legal customs: the triangle of equal sides formed by human rights–digitalisation–security; in other words, following the same correspondence: legality, necessity, and proportionality. We have often said that in law we are more likely to discover and not innovate. The following theory is one of our discoveries that we have written about and promoted in the last year at international conferences. The definitions and explanations of each component of the New International Triangle (human rights, digitisation, and security) and how they interact with each other are based on the observation that the triangle is, in fact, a modern paradigm of international relations that focuses on the interconnectedness of its three equal sides. In other words, following the same correspondence, we can observe legality, necessity, and proportionality. Since Cristina Popa Tache personally discovered this geometry, we named it 'DoDS triangle' or, in English, 'HrDS triangle'.

Using this equation has the potential to clarify regulatory lines in the area of international investment. We can see how, as digitisation intensifies, many states are having to develop new legislation to protect sensitive data belonging to individuals or institutions. Protection takes place to prevent their use for malicious or even illegal or commercial purposes, or against their use in the unauthorised surveillance of individuals (or the masses) by the state or other natural or legal persons who might have this interest. In this way, privacy and data protection will become a standard in

[11] E. O. Wilson, *Consilience: The Unity of Knowledge* (New York: Random House, 1998).

cross-border trade and investment, as many commercial transactions require cross-border data flows that meet minimum legal requirements (UNCTAD, 2019).[12] From this point of view, this standard is not only preferred by the population but is also pursued by international investors who expect to find the best possible standards for their investments in host countries. Experts believe that investors and consumers are likely to start prioritising privacy and data protection as a fundamental human right and to censure companies operating in countries that do not provide adequate privacy and data protection.[13]

The relationship to human rights highlights the connection between international investment and digitisation, going beyond data protection, and references the groundbreaking Digital Economy Partnership Agreement (DEPA), the first of its kind, signed in 2020. In its content, the following are brought into the spotlight: 'the importance of corporate advocacy, social responsibility, cultural identity and diversity, environmental protection and preservation, gender equality, indigenous rights, labour rights, inclusive trade, sustainable development and traditional knowledge'.[14] In the same vein, problems arise when human rights and freedoms conflict with the acceptance and use of digitisation. One example may be the religion or faith of certain groups of individuals that prohibits them from using modern digital means (in the same way that they refuse to take medication, for example). It has also been highlighted that there have been and continue to be cultural or traditional differences that should be given more consideration by digital service providers. The history of the investment system has seen opposition to certain types of investment, which leads us to think now about strategies for reconciling the discrepancies that can arise from relating the freedom of human belief to certain ideologies and a certain qualification of foreign investment. At one time, Canada and France, for example, invoked cultural criteria to prevent the American entertainment industry from entering these countries and dominating their national entertainment industries. The danger of a certain kind of dominance appears on the horizon for national digital industries, to be treated with particular attention because there may exist or may arise national security problems that may overlap, knowing that the limits of national security and safety are regulated at the level of domestic law and, as a consequence, are usually related to certain human rights.[15] Alternatively, precisely these

[12] UNCTAD, *Digital Economy Report* (2019), https://unctad.org/en/pages/PublicationWebflyer.aspx?publicationid=2466.

[13] See P. N. Satyanand, 'Foreign direct investment and the digital economy', ARTNeT on FDI Working Paper Series, No. 2 (2021), https://artnet.unescap.org/fd. See also C. E. Popa Tache, 'About the human rights and consumer protection in the digital age of Digital Services Act 2022 or what aspects interested investors should pay attention to' (2023) 3 *International Investment Law Journal* 2, 121–32.

[14] For a literature review, see C. E. Popa Tache and C-S. Săraru, 'Evaluating today's multi-dependencies in digital transformation, corporate governance and public international law triad' (2024) 10 *Cogent Social Sciences* 1, Article 2370945.

[15] In 2024 in Romania, proposals for new national security laws generated a wave of criticism from civil society. They were seen as incompatible with democracy and reminiscent of the dark days of

premises can lead to various contemporary problems (some marked by the unpredictability) of digital manifestation because is it not the case that 'everyone has the right to freedom of thought, conscience and religion; this right includes freedom to change his religion or belief, and freedom to manifest his religion or belief [...]'.[16]

The Universal Declaration of Human Rights itself reinforces respect for these values, which are considered to be among the highest aspirations of humanity.[17] It is equally true that all these rights and freedoms will have to be adapted at the government level so that, through the development of digitisation, social progress and improved living conditions can be fostered within the framework of greater freedom, as provided for in the Declaration.

In order to avoid discrepancies and conflicts between different jurisdictions, international regulations and especially common standards are essential. Collaboration between countries can help create a predictable and coherent environment. The convergence of international investment and the digital boom brings to the fore new paradigms, such as state–private sector relations in digital innovations. This process is not without some limits that can generate significant effects if not dealt with seriously, promptly and competently. For example, the rapid pace of innovation can lead to rapid advances in digital technologies that can outpace the ability of legislation to keep up with new developments. Regulations may become outdated before they are updated, leaving gaps in relevant legal matters. These are compounded by significant differences between jurisdictions in terms of legal regulations and practices. Obstacles to adopting global standards or maintaining a coherent framework in the context of international digital investment may be created. It is not easy to come up with regulations that take into account all the variables and ensure a fair balance between divergent interests. If we discuss individual rights and cybersecurity, the balance between data access and data privacy can become a point of contention in the regulation of international technology investments.

communism. This draft law stirred up much controversy. The Romanian Intelligence Service would become a national authority including in the field of the interception of communications. The draft also states that 'within the Service, activities may be set up financed entirely from its own revenues' and the service is authorised 'to request data, regardless of the form in which it is stored, information and, where appropriate, objects from natural and legal persons, under the conditions of this law'. The draft extended the list of threats to national security: it would include organised crime and actions or inactions targeting the administration, health, education, cultural heritage, critical communications and information technology infrastructures, as well as Romania's 'financial, economic, national energy, scientific and research interests'. For more details, see V. Burlă, 'Noile legi ale securității naționale și pericolul militarizării statului. Expert: "Este o încercare de întoarcere în timp"', 1 June 2022, https://romania.europalibera.org/a/31878826.html.

16 United Nations, Universal Declaration of Human Rights, GA Res. 217A (III), UN Doc. A/810, at 71 (1948).

17 The Universal Declaration of Human Rights itself states in its Preamble 'that the disregard and contempt of human rights have resulted in barbarous acts which outrage the conscience of mankind, and that the creation of a world in which human beings shall enjoy freedom of speech and belief and freedom from fear and want has been proclaimed as the highest aspiration of the common people'. Article 3 of the Declaration also states that 'Everyone has the right to life, liberty and security of person'.

Other limits may be given by implementation costs or resistance to change by some sectors or entities that enjoy existing regulations. Let us not forget that in this way, the process of adaptation and adoption of innovative legal practices needed in the digital environment can be slowed down. This phenomenon is amplified by the fact that regulations can be difficult to monitor and implement in practice; especially given the cross-border nature of many international investments and digital operations. The effects can be disastrous when combined with the limitation of appropriate civil society and industry consultations, as it can lead to the absence of important insights and increase the risk of the inappropriateness of norms.

Any initiative must consider the delicate balance between promoting investment and protecting human rights. The analysis of the rights and obligations of international investment actors in the information and communications technology (ICT) sector underlines the complexity of the legal issues involved in this rapidly developing area.

16.3 TYPES OF INTERNATIONAL INVESTMENT – DIGITISATION – HUMAN RIGHTS

International investment branches out into all areas: in the vertical sense, we have investments in maritime, land, air and space, while horizontally, there is an unlimited horizon of areas and fields we can find foreign investment. The recognised fact that investment activities can no longer function outside digitisation is one of the main reasons they are seen as shaping the global economy. The use of artificial intelligence is just one step further towards more advanced automation and robotics. The analytical perspectives include the legal, social, economic, and political spheres.

In contemporary society, there is an endless variety of types of international investment, including projects such as building and launching satellites, building renewable power plants, building and operating blood plasma fractionation facilities, and many and various media services. In this landscape, ICT is co-ordinated by the big investors providing social media platforms without much transparency in respect to human rights. Special treaties to regulate this area in a clear way do not exist at the multilateral level, and no clauses have been identified in investment treaties to cover this issue. Therefore, the existence of these situations of non-regulation affects the protection of human rights, which is so sensitive to legal interpretation. In the process of globalisation, the national system of regulation, adjudication, management, or dissemination of information has a significant impact.[18] In the face of these developments, states generally play an active role,

[18] J. Pauwelyn, R. A. Wessel, and J. Wouters (eds.), *Informal International Lawmaking* (Oxford: Oxford University Press, 2012); K. E. Davis et al. (eds.), *Governance by Indicators: Global Power through Quantification and Rankings* (Oxford: Oxford University Press, 2012); J. E. Alvarez, *International Organizations as Law-Makers* (Oxford: Oxford University Press, 2005).

preferring the status of policymaker rather than policy-taker in the international community.[19]

All of this requires the close cooperation of experts in these fields, and continuous research, debate, and critical analysis in order to respond to various issues that arise in relation to the effective legal regulation of the foreign investment–digitisation–human rights relationship. Like all other issues in law, the issue of human rights in this context can only achieve its social and economic objectives to the extent that all aspects are made known and are subject to critical analysis.[20] In this process, information becomes the focus of attention and acquires the characteristics of an effective tool for promoting and ensuring human rights. The rapid development of digitalisation has a serious impact on society and on culture, and experts must identify each element of this impact in relation to human rights. According to Resolution A/HRC/RES/20/8: 'Information is a source that activates the economy, making it possible for people to participate in government activities through public forums and contribute to the decision-making process.'[21] In this context, international investors interested in the correct application of legal regulations are increasingly engaging in major investments in start-ups operating in this field. These investments are often made in collaboration with human rights groups or in partnership with various social organisations, focusing on adopting appropriate digital technologies and testing their compliance with human rights standards. Information technologies will continue to deliver progress, but the way in which their use will be achieved requires both a detailed knowledge of every element of the technology, as well as human rights protection to cover each element. They inherently come with new and hard-to-anticipate risks related to non-discrimination, privacy, children's rights, freedom of expression, access to public services, and the right to work. We are therefore at the intersection of human rights and technological development.[22]

In this context, access to digitisation itself becomes a human right that needs to be expressed in specific regulations, a fact confirmed by recent developments according to which customary international law is ready to accept rules that identify internet access as a human right.[23] If we analyse the theoretical framework corresponding to this hypothesis, we will notice that there are very few recent works, even fewer in

[19] T. Pajuste (ed.), *Specific Threats to Human Rights Protection from the Digital Reality. International Responses and Recommendations to Core Threats from the Digitalized World* (Tallinn: Tallinn University, 2022), pp. 13–7.

[20] As stated in the inaugural Editorial of the *International Investment Law Journal* – C. E. Popa Tache, 'Editorial' (2021) 1 *International Investment Law Journal* 1, 9–10.

[21] United Nations, Human Rights Council Resolution 20/8, Promotion and protection of all human rights, civil, political, economic, social and cultural rights, including the right to development, A/HRC/RES/20/8, 16 July 2012.

[22] G. Sharma, 'Implementation of information and communication technology for human rights awareness and promotion' (2020) 1 *HighTech and Innovation Journal* 1, 33–8.

[23] Ibid., 35.

the field of digitisation, that address human rights in general or in investment law in particular. Discussions should also focus on the extent of the regulatory right available to states.[24] Attention must be fairly directed to the contradictory issues that can be generated between the right to regulate and the protection offered to foreign investors under international investment law.

At a theoretical level, it is also important to explore whether the host states of certain investments in technology have the right to regulate, and also how they exercise that right. For example, there are a small number of articles in which theorists have raised the issue of the possibility of adopting new and adapted regulations to improve social standards and living conditions for populations. If these regulations do not exist, then states could face a wide range of investment disputes.[25]

A case in point is financial technology, where the latest international law instruments with more tailored clauses are emerging. The model put forward by these instruments could be followed in all other investment sectors where there is the imprint of digitisation, as the global use of financial technologies is just one example with a great impact on current human rights regulations. Perhaps the ultimate goal ideally pursued by the fundamental and vertical analysis of human rights in the digital age is even the development of international law instruments, such as digital bridges, whereby states protect their populations in this respect. Of course, these new instruments come with accountability built in for those who violate human rights in the digital sphere, but accountability is the subject of a wider debate, which follows hierarchically from the normative establishment of these new rights.

Inspired by the international FinTech Bridge agreements (bilateral agreements between two national governments and their respective relevant regulatory bodies), we believe it is possible for all types of international investments to be subject to new or amended regulations. To that end, the following pillars of rights and obligations should be considered as relevant in the investment–digitalisation–human rights relationship:

(a) *Government-to-government pillar*. A framework in which implementing authorities – according to the administrative system in each country – agree to hold regular working discussions, which could, for example, be organised quarterly to help realise existing options. There are several contributors to this type of regulation that help elaborating specific norms – among them, political officials, legal experts, and regulatory authorities. From here, parties can launch discussions of the development of policies to suit the type

[24] See, for an exhaustive analysis, C. Titi, *The Right to Regulate in International Investment Law* (Oxford: Hart Publishing, 2014).

[25] C. Onyejekwe, 'International investment law and the right to regulate: a human rights perspective' (2019) 53 *The Law Teacher* 1, 125–6.

of investment-digitalisation-human rights in each jurisdiction.[26] The aim is to explore innovative ways to mitigate the impact of digitisation on human rights, to explore the challenges faced by international investors, and to gather relevant evidence, in particular on the protection and promotion of this sector. These aspects are particularly important and have been qualified in theory as part of the Great Digital Game.[27] There has even been talk of these concerns forming a Digital Silk Road (inspired by China's modus operandi for various activities – commercial and diplomatic – of interest to governments in the cyber domain).[28] In this sense, we consider the circumstances of the acceleration of the formation of a new development model that presents domestic circulation as the main body consolidated by the dual circulation of the domestic and international economy. This relationship is reciprocal, and China is one example of a large economy that has addressed it.[29] Here, a note can be added that relates to modern international law: possible bridging agreements could be established through specific clauses that dialogue between governments, regulators, and what we call industry, to identify emerging digital trends and specific issues. In FinTech, for example, blockchain, security and data exchange, RegTech,[30] SupTech,[31] and WealthTech,[32] have already been the subject of international cooperation. With these, the desirability

[26] Researchers have observed some limited participation of many social groups in digital life. The reasons were: the price of certain assets, underlying risks and household characteristics such as age, education, financial literacy, and marital status. In this sense, see: C. Christiansen, J. S. Joensen, and J. Rangvid, 'Understanding the effects of marriage and divorce on financial investments: the role of background risk sharing' (2015) 53 *Economic Inquiry* 1, 431–47; M. van Rooij, A. Lusardi, and R. Alessie, 'Financial literacy and stock market participation' (2011) 101 *Journal of Financial Economics* 2, 449–72; See also C. Xu and B. Jin, 'Digital currency in China: pilot implementations, legal challenges and prospects' (2022) 12 *Juridical Tribune/Tribuna Juridica* 2, 177–94.

[27] A. Klimburg, *The Darkening Web* (London: Penguin, 2017), p. 324.

[28] M. Willett, 'China's investment in digital technologies and the Digital Great Game' (2020) 60 *Adelphi Series* 487–9, 23–36; See also G. Austin, *Cyber Policy in China* (Cambridge: Polity, 2014), p. 1.

[29] C. Guo, X. Wang, and G. Yuan, 'Digital finance and the efficiency of household investment portfolios' (2022) 58 *Emerging Markets Finance and Trade* 10, 2895–909.

[30] According to established definitions, RegTech, or regulatory technology, is a technology system that assists a bank, credit union, or other financial institution in managing regulatory compliance. RegTech helps streamline the compliance process. Financial regulators enable institutions to develop risk and compliance management strategies that are appropriate for their size and complexity, and to better understand regulatory challenges, allowing them to direct resources to the most important areas rather than using a scattered strategy.

[31] Supervisory technology, often known as SupTech for regulators, refers to technology solutions that assist financial supervisors in managing regulatory compliance. SupTech provides regulators with technology tools to improve efficiency through automation. Technically, the definition is according to the official Sanction Scanner page: Team Sanction Scanner, 'What is the difference between RegTech, FinTech, and SupTech?', 27 September 2024, www.sanctionscanner.com/blog/whats-the-difference-between-regtech-fintech-and-suptech-519.

[32] As is well known, the words 'wealth' and 'technology' have come together to give birth to a new generation of financial technology companies creating digital solutions to transform the investment and asset management industry.

of establishing legitimate and effective international institutions is logically raised. Institutions mean public law regulations and international institutions as international public authorities will be covered by a part of public international law that should be more appropriately understood as part of (international) public law, given their hybrid typology.[33] This is also the aim of this chapter: namely, to highlight by reference to a concrete example (i.e., international investment), the emergence of a new era of legal regulation that can be used as a model for all other subsequent emergences. As developed in another publication, this coexistence of radically different visions of international institutions has proven useful in specialist theory.[34] From this perspective, public international law has the potential to transform and adapt its own ecosystem. Regulatory demands in the legal relationship between foreign investment, digitalisation, and human rights call for identifying, reforming, and advancing the aspects of public international law that govern the exercise of international public authority.[35]

(b) *Regulator-to-regulator pillar*. This is the second type of regulation, built on a cooperation agreement between implementing authorities and between regulators. Again, public international law reacts to challenges and manifests its regulatory role through these types of public authorities. The rights of the consumer of digital services are an area that must be constantly updated with the latest protections.[36] The industrial transformation of the digital ecosystem, especially but not least digital communication, has reflected the adaptations and reinterpretations of the user within the interface where there is a

33 See A. von Bogdandy, M. Goldmann, and I. Venzke, 'From public international to international public law: translating world public opinion into international public authority' (2017) 28 *European Journal of International Law* 1, 115–45.

34 C. E. Popa Tache, 'Public international law and FinTech challenge' (2022) 11 *Perspectives of Law and Public Administration* 2, 11–15. I also add here E. Benvenisti, *The Law of Global Governance* (Leiden: Brill, 2014); J. Brunnée and S. Toope, *Legitimacy and Legality in International Law: An Interactional Account* (Cambridge: Cambridge University Press, 2010); S. Cassese, 'Administrative law without the state? The challenge of global regulation' (2005) 37 *New York University Journal of International Law and Policy* 4, 663–94; B. S. Chimni, 'International institutions today: an imperial global state in the making' (2004) 15 *European Journal of International Law* 1, 1–37; B. Kingsbury, N. Krisch, and R. B. Stewart, 'The Emergence of Global Administrative Law' (2005) 68 *Law and Contemporary Problems* 3/4, 15–61; J. Klabbers, A. Peters, and G. Ulfstein (eds.), *The Constitutionalization of International Law* (Oxford: Oxford University Press, 2009) as cited in von Bogdandy, Goldmann, and Venzke, 'From public international to international public law', p. 116. A specific view in O. Șaramet and G.-B. Spîrchez, 'Limits of the discretionary power established through enforcing the European principle of proportionality' (2018) 7 *Perspectives of Law and Public Administration* 2, 260–9.

35 According to von Bogdandy, Goldmann, and Venzke, the terminology is used by S. Kadelbach, 'From public international law to international public law', in A. von Bogdandy et al. (eds.), *The Exercise of Public Authority by International Institutions* (Berlin: Springer, 2010), pp. 33–49, at 33, cited in Popa Tache, *Legal Treatment Standards for International Investments*, p. 14.

36 D. B. Ibáñez, M. R. da Cunha, and J. H. Toledo, 'Comunicación digital, redes sociales y procesos en línea: estudios en una perspectiva comparada entre América Latina y la península ibérica' (2020) 26 *Journal of Iberian and Latin American Research* 3, 275–83.

permanent dialogue with the strategies proposed by industry. The web has become the symbolic space where human-to-human interactions take place and not with the machine as it was believed.[37]

Here, we can mention the characteristic attributions of regulatory authorities: improvement of licensing procedures for innovative companies already licensed or authorised in another jurisdiction, and developing research and testing solutions (and publishing the results for the benefit of industry, regulators, and consumers). What is relevant here are the factors that prioritise or influence the elaboration of rules in international law. This argument is based precisely on the emphasis on common international interests, not on the interest of a single state.[38] The digital domain is increasingly under the purview of various international authorities. That is why the emphasis must be placed on the legal relationship of public international law (private law already presents its limits). Private international law has been criticised for its lack of meaningful contribution to global governance issues, such as the equal distribution of wealth, the fight against transnational human rights violations, and the protection of collective planetary goods such as the environment. All this, as well as many other issues, such as those pertaining to digitalisation, somehow remained within the scope of public international law.[39]

For example, through an instrument of international law, preferably through a treaty as a *hard law* instrument, states can agree to work to enhance the various digital bridges between them and the benefits of this cooperation for digital investment activities. How? By establishing cooperation at expert level, tailor-made strategic advice, assisting and supporting the process of identifying opportunities, establishing contacts between the relevant staff at trade and investment implementing authorities, developing innovation programmes, and, of course, setting up joint working groups.

37 Ibid., p. 275. For the same opinion, see A. L. Rivoir and M. J. Morales, *Tecnologías Digitales. Miradas Críticas de la Apropiación en América Latina* (Buenos Aires: CLACSO & RIAT, 2019); J. A. H. Toledo, *Medios y Mediación en la Cultura Digital. Cambios Estructurales y Construcciones Teóricas para la Comprensión de la Cultura Digital* (Valencia: Tirant lo Blanch, 2018); C. Scolari, *Las Leyes de la Interfaz: Diseño, Ecología, Evolución, Tecnología* (Barcelona: Gedisa, 2018); and L. Manovich, *Software Takes Command: Extending the Language of New Media* (New York: Bloomsbury Publishing, 2013).

38 N. Krisch, 'The decay of consent: international law in an age of global public goods' (2014) 108 *American Journal of International Law* 1, 1–40.

39 M. Lehmann, 'Regulation, global governance and private international law: squaring the triangle' (2020) 16 *Journal of Private International Law* 1, 1–30: 'The lack of a specific legal provision could be compensated by a reference to minimum standards under public international law and transnational rules built from comparative law'; H. M. Watt, 'Private international law: beyond the schism' (2011) 2 *Transnational Legal Theory* 3, 347–427, at 354; and L. Carballo Piñeiro and X. Kramer, 'The role of private international law in contemporary society: global governance as a challenge' (2014) 7 *Erasmus Law Review* 3, 109–12, at 110.

(c) *Business-to-Business pillar*. A subsequent pillar built on the ability of governments to support active engagement between digital industry bodies and human rights bodies. How? Through regular high-level business-to-business discussions involving joint human rights and industry representative groups co-chaired by signatory states.

Also under this pillar, governments would approve the initiatives of digital industry bodies. One of the topics of these discussions may be the exploration of collaboration around certain areas, such as (the list is only illustrative) supply chain finance, digital assets, and the use of blockchain in government applications, such as social care, estates or pensions, or data sharing.

In the face of these activities, there has been widespread criticism and mobilisation against trade agreements and investment treaties, which is perpetuated because solutions are not always adopted. One of the issues that has been the subject of this criticism has focused on the tendency of governments to focus more on trade interests without taking into account their obligations to address human rights, the environment, and development. In other words, the way states are preoccupied with ensuring a business-friendly environment has led to the undermining of the protection and realisation of human rights. Along with the tech giants, as the big digital investors are known in theory, states really have to bend to regulatory updates.[40] The era of *datafication* has come with issues such as surveillance capitalism, digital welfare, and the government use of data about its citizens that reconfigures rights and power and minimises the role of individuals and citizens in decisions about their own future.[41] In a United Nations (UN) report, the UN Special Rapporteur on extreme poverty, Philip Alston, states that 'social protection and assistance systems are increasingly driven by data and digital technologies that are used to automate, predict, identify, monitor, detect, target and punish'.[42]

A number of papers have gone through specific analyses of international investors' decisions and actions that extend to respect for human rights in their operations, products, and services.

In this context, it is worth recalling the UN Guiding Principles on Business and Human Rights (UNGP),[43] which establishes that investors should take into account in their investment activities the responsibility to ensure that their

[40] R. F. Jørgensen, 'Data and rights in the digital welfare state: the case of Denmark' (2021) 26 *Information, Communication & Society* 1, 123–38; D. Bigo, E. F. Isin, and E. Ruppert, 'Data politics', in D. Bigo, E. F. Isin, and E. Ruppert (eds.), *Data Politics: Worlds, Subjects, Rights* (Abingdon: Routledge, 2018), pp. 1–18.

[41] In general, S. Zuboff, *The Age of Surveillance Capitalism: The Fight for a Human Future at the New Frontier of Power* (London: Profile Books, 2019).

[42] Report of the Special Rapporteur on extreme poverty and human rights, Philip Alston, submitted in accordance with Human Rights Council resolution 35/19, UN Doc A/74/48037, 11 October 2019.

[43] United Nations, *Guiding Principles on Business and Human Rights: Implementing the United Nations 'Protect, Respect and Remedy' Framework* (New York: United Nations, 2011).

investments in the technology sector avoid negative impacts. These guiding principles are built on three pillars: the duty of the state to protect human rights, the responsibility of business to respect human rights in its own operations and along the value chain, and the right of access to redress for victims of human rights abuses. Of particular importance is the delineation of investors' responsibilities and the identification of current trends in practice, together with useful recommendations for investors.[44]

An official enumeration of the main internationally recognised human rights is found in the International Bill of Human Rights (the Universal Declaration of Human Rights and the main instruments by which it was codified: the International Covenant on Civil and Political Rights and the International Covenant on Human Rights, the Covenant on Economic, Social and Cultural Rights, together with the fundamental rights principles of the eight fundamental International Labour Organization Conventions as set out in the Declaration on Fundamental Principles and Rights at Work). They play a guiding role for other social actors who evaluate the impact of investments and business in general on human rights.

The responsibility of the international investor in general, and of commercial enterprises in particular, is to respect human rights. But along these lines, responsibilities may differ from matters of legal liability and enforcement, which remain largely defined by the provisions of national law in the relevant jurisdictions. Uniformity is a difficult goal to achieve.

Depending on the circumstances, international investors may need to follow additional standards. For example, businesses should respect the human rights of people belonging to specific groups or populations that require special attention when the businesses may have a negative impact on human rights. For this, the UN instruments further developed the rights of indigenous peoples, women, national, ethnic, religious and linguistic minorities, children, persons with disabilities, and migrant workers and their families. Special attention is also given to the elderly. The international community has felt its own low level of digital literacy against the backdrop of digitisation. At the level of older generations, its impact has been huge (social exclusion and restricted access to certain natural human rights). Theorists have analysed the power that universal human rights instruments can have to impose on states a certain concern for what is called 'the inclusion of older generations in the information society'. The same concerns are transferred horizontally to investors in digital services. A world convention is being worked on at the UN that protects the rights of elderly people and through which rights such as

[44] United Nations, B-Tech Project, *Rights-Respecting Investment in Technology Companies: A-B Tech Investors Briefing, OHCHR and Business and Human Rights* (2021), www.ohchr.org/sites/default/files/Documents/Issues/Business/B-Tech/B-Tech-Briefing-Investment.pdf.

education, information, transparency, and other aspects related to the degree of the standard of living have been brought into the spotlight.[45] Additionally, in the event of an armed conflict, investors should comply with the standards of international humanitarian law.

Establishing a system of accountability is essential because the important risks to people and the material risks to technology investments are converging rapidly, as current studies show. These continue to be highlighted in venture capital investments, as well as by the recognition of digital rights as material rights by investors and by those empowered to regulate new standards, which would lead to uniformity of data points and different methodologies today.

The UN Human Rights B-Tech Project notes that while sustainable investment practices have been around for decades, investments in Environmental, Social, and Governance funds reached approximately $40.5 trillion in global assets under management in 2020.[46] It also points out that human rights are often narrowly understood as individual aspects of human rights, such as forced labour or discrimination (correlated with certain narrow parts of business, particularly in dealing with customers and end-users), rather than encompassing the full range of human rights.[47]

The role of technologically responsible investment is becoming the benchmark for civil society seeking protection through the accountability of investors for their practices but also appropriate mechanisms to enforce these rights. Responsible investors promote public policies that encourage responsible investment in technology in a particular area of interest.[48]

16.4 WHAT IS NEW IN THE WORLD OF DIGITISATION? NEW STANDARDS FOR THE LEGAL TREATMENT OF FOREIGN INVESTMENT IN DIGITAL MATTERS

In this context, the DEPA is a first step, whereby Singapore, New Zealand, and Chile signed this as the world's first digital trade treaty in June 2020. DEPA is pioneering because it creates international rules and practices for cross-border business in the digital economy, anchored by strongly stated sustainable development goals.

45 B. Mikołajczyk, 'Universal human rights instruments and digital literacy of older persons' (2022) 27 *The International Journal of Human Rights* 3, 403–24.

46 B-Tech Project, *Rights-Respecting Investment in Technology Companies*.

47 See C. Rees, 'Transforming the way business influences people: unlocking the collective power of five distinct narratives' (November 2020), Corporate Responsibility Initiative, Harvard Kennedy School, Working Paper no. 75, www.hks.harvard.edu/sites/default/files/centers/mrcbg/files/Final_AWP_CRI_75.pdf.

48 See the recent work of the Investor Alliance for Human Rights – a collective action platform for responsible investment based on respect for fundamental human rights, Investor Alliance for Human Rights, 'About the Investor Alliance for Human Rights', https://investorsforhumanrights.org/about.

The Agreement highlights 'the importance of the digital economy in promoting inclusive economic growth … in particular Goal 8 and Goal 9'.

Meanwhile, we have seen China, South Korea, and Canada's intentions to join DEPA along with joining the Comprehensive Regional Economic Partnership, driven by the growing importance of digital trade and its evolution, leading to cooperative efforts in scientific research and international education. This development aligns with the widely accepted principle that digital trade represents the future of global trade and investment, playing a dynamic and transformative role in shaping the global economy. It is focused on blockchain, artificial intelligence, and internet technologies to guide the expansion of e-commerce and cross-border payments, issues that highlight the priority of mapping new trade technologies, including cloud services, Distributed Ledger Technology, and 3D printing.

As we have outlined the solutions in the pillars in Section 16.3, through DEPA, the parties will convene a 'Digital SME (small and medium-sized enterprises) Dialogue' to promote the benefits of the Agreement for the parties' SMEs through consultations with experts from the private sector, non-governmental organisations, academia, and other stakeholder groups.

Importantly, this international law instrument is intended to inspire international law actors in negotiations, and 'will generate new ideas and approaches in the international digital economy or digital trade'.

On the other hand, international organisations concerned with these issues have produced specific reports following global crises affecting high and volatile food prices, climate change, and financial turmoil. Public international law has felt obliged to react to the international economic order. We have seen how civil society has pushed states to turn (in parallel with the attention paid to business) to the social implications for human rights vis-à-vis the new set of international investment law policies and instruments.

In these efforts, human rights impact assessments consider the right to development and its implementation, the importance of policy coherence, taking into account human rights obligations, standards and principles, the need for human rights audits and impact assessments, flexibilities and exemptions, such as in the WTO Agreement on Trade-Related Aspects of Intellectual Property Rights, and remedies.[49]

In view of these moves, it is not out of the question that investment treaties will be amended by introducing new standards of treatment specific to digital activities.

[49] For a comprehensive analysis, see papers on globalisation and trade and investment. They can be listed here: UN OHCHR, 'Key messages on trade and human rights' (2021), www.ohchr.org/sites/default/files/2022-01/Key-Messages-on-Trade-and-Human-Rights.pdf; UN OHCHR, 'OHCHR and the right to development', www.ohchr.org/en/development; UN General Assembly, Globalization and its Impact on the Full Enjoyment of All Human Rights: Report of the Secretary-General, UN Doc. A/73/172, Seventy-third session, Item 74 (b) of the preliminary list, Promotion and Protection of Human Rights: Human Rights Issues, Including Alternative Approaches for Improving the Effective Enjoyment of Human Rights and Fundamental Freedoms, 17 July 2018.

When discussing all of this, we note the major role of treaties in the governance of digital investments, with an emphasis on strategic and significant international implications. Adapting legal regimes to the digital age is an essential process. The results of the analysis converge towards the need for domestic laws and existing treaties to be revised in order to bring them up to date and adapt them to the new digital realities. The approaches are based on identifying gaps or ambiguities in existing regulations and adjusting them, and formulating them in a flexible and adaptive way.

International collaboration to establish common standards is based on harmonisation, which has the purpose of facilitating cross-border interactions and helping to avoid discrepancies between jurisprudence. Adapting legal frameworks to the digital age also requires significant efforts in promoting digital literacy. Citizens need to be informed about their rights and responsibilities in the digital environment, and continuing education can contribute to a deeper understanding of digital challenges and opportunities.

The specific analysis of the ramifications at the national level requires a (re-)examination of the specific regulations at the domestic level, with an emphasis on issues such as intellectual property, national security and economic progress. National regulations can include policies and facilities to stimulate investment in digital technologies. The privacy and safety of consumers are at the centre of the debates, especially against the background of the absence of internationally uniform definitions for what it means to be a consumer, user, or recipient of technological products or services. By specifically analysing these issues at the national level, regulations can be adjusted to create a legal environment conducive to the sustainable development of digital technologies, while protecting national interests and the fundamental rights of citizens. At the international level, some concrete examples of the implications for public policy and human rights, as well as how international actors can gain control over technologies, are well known. China is a notorious example of the government using digital technologies to exert tight control over information available on the internet. Through digital censorship and monitoring systems, Chinese authorities have imposed significant restrictions on freedom of expression online, directly affecting human rights to freedom of information.

Situations where international actors, such as the big players in the technology industry, enter into technology transfer agreements can have major implications. For example, when a company from a developed country invests in a developing country, it can gain control over the local digital infrastructure, raising questions about data protection and access to cutting-edge technologies.

In the US, the use of facial recognition technologies in government and the private sector has raised concerns about privacy and individual freedom. In this context, questions have been raised about the protection of human rights, especially regarding mass surveillance and the potential abuse of the technology.

In addition to these examples, we can remember that international investments in the digital infrastructure of African countries can turn into a certain form of control over digital resources. An example can be given by the case of Chinese investments in communication networks and technologies in Africa, where there are concerns about the impact on the digital autonomy of these countries and the potential risks to human rights in the context of these partnerships.

16.5 CONCLUSIONS

This chapter has addressed a particularly dynamic and important theme in the international law landscape, namely the legal relationships in the triad of foreign investment, digitisation, and human rights. This is demonstrated by the frequent emergence of new international instruments, a dynamic unprecedented for any other field.

The digital intersection between trade and human rights, including the right to development, has revealed new elements that can inspire negotiating parties. The implications for inclusion and human rights extend, without limitation, to data protection, social responsibility, cultural identity and diversity, environmental protection and conservation, gender equality, indigenous rights, labour rights, inclusive trade, sustainable development, and traditional knowledge. All of these regulations aim to protect and promote fundamental human rights and freedoms, improve cultural links between people, including indigenous peoples, and improve digital access for women, rural populations, and low socio-economic groups.

All recommendations on measures to meet governments' human rights commitments are taken into account, developing national, regional, and continental approaches and frameworks to support digital trade worldwide.

It is advisable to continue analyses that build on the positive aspects of including the human rights and environmental rights dimensions of sustainability explicitly in mega-infrastructure plans and projects, globalisation and its impact on the full enjoyment of all human rights and policymaking, the concerns of all members of society in the negotiation, drafting, and implementation of specific international law instruments, including the search for complementary and adjustment measures, the infusion of ethical and normative objectives and processes into contracts between states and investors, and the ways in which human rights, in particular, can be incorporated.

The digital domain and its interaction with human rights, especially in the context of digital investments, is a domain totally subject to the argumentative practice of law as an interaction of formal and instrumental reasoning techniques.[50] The differences lie in those specific to the novelty of the field since we cannot discuss the

[50] A. van Mulligen, 'Framing deformalisation in public international law' (2015) 6 *Transnational Legal Theory* 3–4, 635–60.

formation of a precedent as paradigmatic modes of formalist reasoning. Attention is directed to instrumentalism: purposive reasoning, balancing, policy analysis, and casuistry.[51] Interactions will always exist between compliance with existing norms and the moral power to 'change the law into a more optimal rule'.[52]

Bringing together groups of specialists for these analyses has the potential optimistically to lead to positive results and the identification of the best solutions.

[51] D. Kennedy, 'The hermeneutic of suspicion in contemporary American legal thought' (2014) 25 *Law and Critique* 2, 91–139, at 92–8; C. R. Sunstein, *Legal Reasoning and Political Conflict* (Oxford: Oxford University Press, 1996), pp. 101–47.

[52] B. Bix, 'Law as an autonomous discipline', in P. Cane and M. Tushnet (eds.), *The Oxford Handbook of Legal Studies* (Oxford: Oxford University Press, 2003), pp. 975, 978, cited in A. van Mulligen, 'Framing deformalisation in public international law' (2015) 6 *Transnational Legal Theory* 3–4, 635–60.

PART IV

Challenges Faced by Vulnerable Groups

Introduction to Part IV

What Additional Challenges Do Vulnerable Groups Face in the Digital Realm?

Tiina Pajuste

The fourth and final part of this book looks at vulnerable groups in the digital context. The digital revolution has reshaped societies, economies, and human interactions. However, its benefits have not been equitably distributed. Vulnerable groups – those marginalised owing to socio-economic status, age, gender, ethnicity, language, geographic location, or other circumstances – often find themselves on the periphery of these advancements.[1] In many cases, the rapid adoption of digital technologies has exacerbated pre-existing inequalities and created new barriers to the enjoyment of fundamental rights. The United Nations Secretary-General has drawn attention to the fact that 'technologies can be, and increasingly are, used to violate and erode human rights, deepen inequalities and exacerbate existing discrimination, especially of people who are already vulnerable or left behind'.[2] This part explores some of these human rights challenges for vulnerable groups, aiming to provide different perspectives in relation to the question: *What additional challenges do vulnerable groups face in the digital realm?* The focus areas – the digital divide, children's rights, linguistic inclusivity in education, and the realities of vulnerable workers in the context of digital transformation – were selected because they address very different but interconnected dimensions of vulnerability in the digital environment, and to illustrate the broad range of issues that can arise in relation vulnerable groups. Together, the chapters examine how digitalisation interacts with broader social, cultural, and economic systems, often reinforcing existing disparities, but at the same time, they also draw attention to the transformative potential of inclusive and rights-based digital policies and practices.

1 For more detail on how to define 'vulnerable groups', see, e.g., A. Limantė and A. Tereškinas, 'Definition of vulnerable groups', in A. Limantė and D. Pūraitė-Andrikienė (eds.), *Legal Protection of Vulnerable Groups in Lithuania, Latvia, Estonia and Poland* (New York: Springer, 2022), 3–27, and F. Macioce, 'The vulnerable groups and their legal value', in F. Macioce, *The Politics of Vulnerable Groups. Implications for Philosophy, Law, and Political Theory* (London: Palgrave Macmillan, 2022), 31–60.

2 UN Secretary-General, *Roadmap for Digital Cooperation* (New York: United Nations, 2020), para. 42.

CHAPTER 17. THE DIGITAL DIVIDE: REINFORCING VULNERABILITIES

Chapter 17 explores the systemic inequalities exacerbated by unequal access to digital technologies, known as the digital divide. This divide disproportionately affects vulnerable populations such as women, older people, disabled people, rural communities, and low-income individuals, limiting their access to services, education, and other opportunities. The chapter looks at the root causes of the digital divide, including socio-economic disparities, geographic isolation, cultural and language barriers, technological gaps, and insufficient policy interventions. It emphasises the human rights implications of this divide, such as restricted access to education, healthcare, and democratic participation, and examines international and regional policy responses, noting their shortcomings in addressing the issue comprehensively.

In response to the core question of this part – *What additional challenges do vulnerable groups face in the digital realm?* – the chapter identifies several unique challenges faced by vulnerable groups in the digital realm: (a) greater difficulty in gaining access to digital devices, services and the internet; (b) limited digital skills preventing effective use of digital technologies (fewer educational and training opportunities tailored to these groups' needs); (c) amplification of the digital divide by existing inequalities, such as gender discrimination, generational isolation, and poverty, perpetuating cycles of disadvantage (e.g., women face online harassment and cultural restrictions, while older adults may be excluded from digital healthcare and public services); and (d) frequent overlooking of the needs of vulnerable groups by market-driven digital initiatives or inadequate regulatory frameworks.

CHAPTER 18. HOW THE EU SAFEGUARDS CHILDREN'S RIGHTS IN THE DIGITAL ENVIRONMENT: AN EXPLORATORY ANALYSIS OF THE EU DIGITAL SERVICES ACT AND THE ARTIFICIAL INTELLIGENCE ACT

Following the broad examination of the digital divide, Chapter 18 narrows the focus to a specific vulnerable group – children – and assesses whether and how legislative efforts seek to protect them in digital environments. Eva Lievens and Valerie Verdoodt scrutinise the EU's Digital Services Act (DSA) and Artificial Intelligence Act (AIA) from the perspective of children's rights in the digital environment. They explore the potential of these legislative frameworks to safeguard children from harm while enabling their safe engagement with digital platforms and artificial intelligence (AI) systems. The authors emphasise the unique vulnerabilities of children in the digital realm and assess how effectively the acts consider these vulnerabilities. They answer this part's core question by noting the following additional challenges faced by children in the digital realm: (a) exploitation of their vulnerability (AI and platform design utilise manipulative practices such as addictive design, autoplay features, and the promotion of harmful content); (b) difficulty in navigating platforms and AI systems safely (as usually there are no child-specific interfaces or adequate transparency about their operation); and (c) being less likely to benefit meaningfully from digital engagement (as there is an over-emphasis on risk and a neglect of the positive potential).

CHAPTER 19. RIGHT TO EDUCATION IN REGIONAL OR MINORITY LANGUAGES: INVASIONS, COVID-19 PANDEMIC, AND OTHER DEVELOPMENTS

Chapter 19 explores the intersection of linguistic rights, digital access, and education during the COVID-19 pandemic. It focuses on how the rapid digitalisation of education disproportionately affected students from regional or minority language communities. Vesna Crnić-Grotić demonstrates how national and regional policies frequently failed to account for linguistic diversity when implementing emergency online education measures. This lack of linguistic inclusivity in digital education threatened the right to education for these communities as their academic progress was hindered. In relation to this part's overarching question, the chapter notes the following additional challenges that students from minority language communities face in the digital realm: (a) less access to the internet and the digital tools necessary for participating in online education; (b) linguistic marginalisation (the dominance of major languages in digital content and platforms excluding regional and minority language speakers, denying them equitable access to education and information online); and (c) systemic neglect of linguistic diversity (and thus the unique needs of minority language groups) in educational policy and planning.

CHAPTER 20. TECHNOLOGICAL ACCELERATION AND THE PRECARISATION OF WORK: REFLECTIONS ON SOCIAL JUSTICE, THE RIGHT TO LIFE, AND ENVIRONMENTAL EDUCATION

Chapter 20 examines how digital transformations have reshaped labour dynamics in Brazil, exacerbating inequalities for vulnerable workers. Raizza da Costa Lopes, Samuel Lopes Pinheiro, and Florent Pasquier show how the 'gig economy' and the 'uberisation' of work are driving a shift towards precarious working conditions, including financial instability, lack of legal protections, and opaque algorithmic control. Additionally, the chapter connects labour issues with environmental education, emphasising its role in addressing socio-economic and ecological inequalities. It advocates for integrating human rights principles, particularly the right to life and social justice, into labour and environmental policies. The chapter answers the core question of this part of the volume by drawing attention to the following additional challenges for vulnerable workers in the digital realm: (a) opaque algorithmic management, which controls their tasks and incomes while offering little transparency or recourse (leading to insecurity and potential exploitation); (b) unpredictable earnings owing to the gig economy model (often resulting in problems covering basic living expenses); (c) lack of labour protection (platform work may not have health insurance, pensions, or even adequate safety standards); and (d) stress owing to the demand for constant availability and productivity (which undermines their well-being and work–life balance).

SHARED THEMES AND INTERCONNECTIONS

The four chapters collectively highlight the complex challenges vulnerable groups face in the digital realm, with each chapter addressing a specific issue regarding inequality and vulnerability. Despite the different focus areas, there are commonalities in the problems faced by vulnerable groups in those specific contexts. The main parallels follow, framed around the overarching themes that connect the chapters.

A. STRUCTURAL INEQUALITIES IN DIGITAL ACCESS

Each chapter emphasises how structural inequalities in access and design deepen exclusion, reinforcing systemic barriers for vulnerable populations in different contexts.

- Chapter 17 on the digital divide explores how foundational barriers, such as a lack of internet connectivity, devices, and digital literacy, disproportionately exclude vulnerable groups.
- Chapter 18 on children's rights shows how children are uniquely affected by systemic inequalities, such as inadequate privacy safeguards, harmful content, and a lack of user-friendly design on digital platforms.
- Chapter 19 on minority language education demonstrates how digital education platforms (mostly designed for dominant languages) marginalise minority language speakers, especially during crises such as the COVID-19 pandemic.
- Chapter 20 on the precarisation of work shows how gig workers, particularly in the Global South, are excluded from equitable digital participation owing to platform-centric labour models that prioritise profits over worker well-being.

B. INSUFFICIENT POLICY AND GOVERNANCE FRAMEWORKS

The absence or inadequacy of regulatory frameworks is noted across all chapters. Gaps in regulation and policymaking can have the effect of perpetuating inequalities or leaving vulnerable groups at the mercy of exploitative systems (which is why the authors advocate for improved lawmaking and policymaking in the area).

- Chapter 17 critiques the lack of comprehensive policies regarding digital inclusion, leaving the needs of vulnerable populations insufficiently addressed.
- Chapter 18 notes how regulatory frameworks, such as the DSA and AIA, while promising, are often limited in scope and lack robust enforcement mechanisms for safeguarding children's rights.

- Chapter 19 draws attention to how policy has failed to ensure linguistic inclusivity during the COVID-19 pandemic, pointing out the lack of foresight and planning for marginalised communities.
- Chapter 20 discusses resistance from digital platforms to regulatory efforts, illustrating how weak governance leaves gig workers without basic labour protections.

C. AMPLIFICATION OF VULNERABILITIES DURING CRISES

Most chapters in this part also look at the impact of the COVID-19 pandemic on vulnerable groups. The authors show how crises can act as accelerants, amplifying pre-existing vulnerabilities and exposing gaps in infrastructure, policy, and protection mechanisms across sectors.

- Chapter 17 notes how the pandemic deepened existing digital disparities, bringing the example of telemedicine during COVID-19 that excluded older people who lack digital skills.
- Chapter 19 focuses on the pandemic's impact on educational access, with minority language speakers disproportionately left behind owing to digital unpreparedness.
- Chapter 20 shows how global crises, such as COVID-19, exacerbate the precarisation of platform workers, particularly in the Global South.

And as the fourth common theme, the authors emphasise the transformative potential of inclusive rights-based interventions to counter digital exclusion and exploitation.

By progressing from structural issues to specific case studies and concluding with a global perspective, this part of the book seeks to respond to the question *What additional challenges do vulnerable groups face in the digital realm?* and to provide a nuanced understanding of how the digital domain interacts with the rights of vulnerable groups. Digitalisation, while offering opportunities, can disproportionately harm vulnerable groups by deepening systemic inequalities (or even exposing them to exploitation – see Chapter 21) and failing to adequately safeguard their rights. The authors draw attention to different aspects and contexts of this problem and emphasise the need for inclusive policies and practices that prioritise equity and human dignity in the digital age.

17

The Digital Divide: Reinforcing Vulnerabilities

Tiina Pajuste

17.1 INTRODUCTION

Digital technologies have permeated almost every aspect of modern life. The potential for such technologies to enhance the enjoyment of human rights is coupled with risks of exclusion, surveillance, and growing inequality, particularly for vulnerable populations. We need to ensure that everyone benefits from digitalisation, even those who currently lack the skills or the means necessary for it. As the European Parliament has highlighted, digital technologies 'can either help create a more inclusive society and reduce inequities, or they can amplify existing inequalities and create new forms of discrimination'.[1] It is often the most vulnerable sectors of society that are not benefiting from digitalisation (as they tend to have fewer resources and more obstacles to access). Accordingly, their needs and human rights require special attention in this process.

The gap between demographics and regions that have access to digital technology and those that do not is called the 'digital divide'. There is nothing new about the digital divide; it started receiving attention from the mid-1990s.[2] Despite long-standing awareness of the problem, it persists. As the United Nations (UN) General Assembly noted in 2016: 'Despite the previous decade's achievements in information and communications technology connectivity, [...] many forms of digital divides remain, both between and within countries and between women and men. [...] [D]ivides are often closely linked to education levels and existing inequalities, and we recognize that further divides can emerge in the future, slowing sustainable development'.[3]

1 European Parliament resolution of 13 December 2022 on the digital divide: the social differences created by digitalisation (2022/2810(RSP)), para. D. Also see UN Secretary-General, *Roadmap for Digital Cooperation* (New York: United Nations, 2020), p. 2.

2 Overview of early discussions is provided in P. K. Yu, 'Bridging the digital divide: equality in the information age' (2002) 20 *Cardozo Arts and Entertainment Law Journal* 1, 1–52, at 2.

3 UN General Assembly Resolution 70/125, Outcome document of the high-level meeting of the General Assembly on the overall review of the implementation of the outcomes of the World Summit on the Information Society, 1 February 2016, para. 21.

Such divides are problematic as they demonstrate how a significant number of individuals are lacking access to the plethora of benefits that digitalisation has brought (such as faster bureaucracy, access to information at all hours, new ways to express oneself). The European Parliament has recognised that digital divides 'may accentuate social differences by reducing some workers' opportunities to obtain quality employment', and acknowledged the especially problematic position of vulnerable groups in relation to the digital divide by noting the potential 'negative impact of the digitalisation of public and private services on workers and people such as older people and persons with disabilities, low-income, socially disadvantaged or unemployed citizens, migrants and refugees or people in rural and remote areas'.[4] As M. N. Cooper has highlighted, those on the right side of the digital divide 'find themselves better trained, better informed, and better able to participate in democracy', whereas the 'disconnected become disadvantaged and disenfranchised', with exclusion manifesting in all aspects of society.[5]

Vulnerable groups are disproportionately impacted by the digital divide, making it both a symptom and a driver of systemic inequities.[6] In the words of the UN Secretary-General, '[d]igital divides reflect and amplify existing social, cultural and economic inequalities'.[7] The digital divide can perpetuate a cycle of disadvantage for vulnerable groups. Bridging the digital divide and ensuring equal access to digital technology is crucial for promoting equity and social inclusion in our increasingly digital world. This divide not only restricts access to critical services such as education, healthcare, and employment, but also undermines fundamental human rights, including the right to equality, dignity, and participation in societal decision-making. Some of the human rights implications of the digital divide are studied in this chapter to illustrate that the digital divide is not just a practical problem but also a legal one.

This chapter focuses on the digital divide in relation to women and older people as sample groups because they are uniquely positioned at the intersection of systemic exclusion and under-representation, making them illustrative of how the digital divide magnifies inequalities and contributes to human rights violations. By examining these groups, the chapter seeks to illustrate the barriers that vulnerable groups are up against, draw attention to the human rights issues that they face and demonstrate the need for tailored solutions within broader efforts to address digital inequities. The chapter also examines international action regarding the digital

4 European Parliament resolution of 13 December 2022 on the digital divide: the social differences created by digitalisation (2022/2810(RSP)), para. H.

5 M. N. Cooper, 'Inequality in the digital society: why the digital divide deserves all the attention it gets' (2002) 20 *Cardozo Arts and Entertainment Law Journal* 1, 73–134, at 73–4.

6 The relationship of the digital divide and social inequality is aptly demonstrated in a recent paper: K. Baraka, 'Digital divide and social inequality' (2024) 3 *International Journal of Humanity and Social Sciences* 3, 30–45.

7 UN Secretary-General, *Roadmap for Digital Cooperation*, 10.

divide and whether additional steps need to be taken to adequately respond to the multitude of challenges that the digital divide presents.

17.2 THE DIGITAL DIVIDE AND ITS CONTRIBUTING FACTORS

There is a plethora of different definitions of the digital divide. The European Union (EU) has referenced the Organisation for Economic Co-operation and Development (OECD) definition of the digital divide,[8] which refers to 'the gap between individuals, households, businesses and geographic areas at different socio-economic levels with regard both to their opportunities to access information and communication technologies (ICTs) and to their use of the internet for a wide variety of activities'.[9] When the term 'digital divide' first emerged in the late twentieth century, it was used to describe the gap between people who had access to mobile phones and those who did not. Over time, its meaning has broadened to encompass the technical and financial ability to use technology and access the internet. As technology evolves, the concept of the digital divide continues to change.[10]

The digital divide is influenced by a range of interconnected factors that determine access to and use of technology for individuals and communities. Such factors include socio-economic disparities, geographic isolation, cultural and language differences, technological barriers, and gaps in law and policy. Each of these elements plays a role in determining who can benefit from the opportunities provided by digital technologies and who remains excluded. Understanding these underlying causes helps design effective strategies to bridge the divide and promote equitable digital inclusion.

First, socio-economic inequalities, such as education, employment status and income levels directly influence access to digital technologies and the internet. Low-income households often cannot afford devices or reliable internet connections. And individuals with a limited educational background may lack the skills to effectively use digital tools.[11] This disparity is evident across various demographics and regions. For instance, in India, the digital divide is heavily influenced by income and educational attainment, particularly among disadvantaged caste groups.[12] Second, remote or rural regions often suffer from a lack of investment in broadband and mobile networks (owing to higher costs and logistical challenges).

[8] European Parliament resolution of 13 December 2022 on the digital divide: the social differences created by digitalisation (2022/2810(RSP)).

[9] OECD, *Understanding the Digital Divide* (Paris: OECD Publications, 2001), p. 5.

[10] This is also highlighted in K. Taylor (reviewed by E. Rasure), 'The digital divide: what it is and what's being done to close it', 28 April 2024, Investopedia, www.investopedia.com/the-digital-divide-5116352.

[11] See further, e.g., K. Bagchi, 'Factors contributing to global digital divide: some empirical results' (2005) 8 *Journal of Global Information Technology Management*, 3, 47–65, and Yu, 'Bridging the digital divide', 16.

[12] V. Rajam, A. Bheemeshaw Reddy, and S. Banerjee, 'Explaining caste-based digital divide in India' (2021) 65 *Telematics and Informatics*, 101719.

Geographic isolation hinders digital accessibility, creating a stark gap compared with urbanised areas that have robust technological infrastructure. A similar tendency persists at the international level, with developing countries lagging behind developed nations in technology uptake. Third, cultural norms and language differences often limit the inclusivity of online spaces. Many websites and digital tools are predominantly available in a small number of global languages, creating obstacles for non-native speakers or those of linguistic minorities.[13] Cultural attitudes towards technology, such as mistrust or unfamiliarity, can further deepen this impact. Fourth, technological and infrastructure barriers are among the more obvious causes of the digital divide. The lack of broadband networks and high device costs clearly restrict access to digital technologies. The quality and speed of available internet also vary, affecting user ability to engage fully with digital services. And fifth, regulatory frameworks and government policies can play a critical role in determining the availability and affordability of digital infrastructure. Moreover, inadequate support for public digital initiatives or over-reliance on market-driven models can exclude marginalised populations. It has also been argued that sometimes groups or entities can use 'political institutions to enact policies that block the spread of the Internet'.[14]

Summing up, these challenges perpetuate unequal access to technology and its benefits. Recognising the interconnected nature of these factors is essential for fostering digital equity and ensuring that the benefits of technology are accessible to all.

17.3 GENDER GAP

The digital divide manifests differently across various groups, highlighting distinct patterns of exclusion. Among these, the gender gap and the age gap are particularly significant, as they reflect systemic barriers rooted in social, cultural, and economic inequalities. These gaps not only reveal the unique challenges faced by specific populations but also illustrate the broader structural issues that perpetuate digital inequities worldwide.

One of the most widely recognised digital divides is the gender digital divide (gender gap). According to the International Telecommunications Union (ITU), 70 per cent of men are using the internet worldwide, compared with 65 per cent of women, meaning that globally there were 244 million more men than women using the internet in 2023.[15] In low-income countries only 20 per cent of women have

[13] For a more detailed consideration of geographical and linguistic aspects, see, e.g., R. Cullen, 'Addressing the digital divide' (2001) 25 *Online Information Review* 5, 311–20.

[14] H. Milner, 'The digital divide' (2006) 39 *Comparative Political Studies* 2, 176–99.

[15] ITU, 'Facts and Figures 2023. The gender digital divide. Digital gender parity is still a distant prospect in regions with low Internet use', www.itu.int/itu-d/reports/statistics/2023/10/10/ff23-the-gender-digital-divide/.

access to the internet (compared with 35 per cent of men).[16] Yet, as UN Women has emphasised, 'digital inclusion and literacy are critical to the well-being and success of women and girls in society, including their ability to take an informed part in electoral processes and exercise their right to vote and to stand for election'.[17]

17.3.1 *Specific Issues Faced by Women and Their Human Rights Implications*

The gender digital divide highlights the problems women and girls can encounter in accessing and using digital technologies, particularly in developing countries.[18] While digital tools offer opportunities for education, economic empowerment, and social engagement, systemic barriers rooted in cultural norms, economic inequalities, and safety concerns disproportionately hinder the digital inclusion of women. This section explores the distinct obstacles women face in their digital journey and looks at the impact of the gender gap on women in relation to various aspects of their lives, including employment opportunities, education, and social inclusion. The effects are placed in the context of human rights to pinpoint the potential human rights infringements arising from the gender gap.

Women in many regions face significant barriers to accessing digital technologies owing to affordability issues and limited infrastructure, particularly in low-income and rural areas. The lack of affordable devices and reliable internet disproportionately affects women, as they are more likely to have lower incomes and fewer economic opportunities.[19]

A particularly difficult aspect to grapple with is the existence of entrenched gender norms and societal expectations, which may discourage women from using digital technologies or pursuing education in digital skills. Cultural biases can restrict women's access to public spaces such as internet cafés or limit their ownership of devices.[20] For example, in Jordan, societal attitudes even result in university educated men being uneasy about allowing women equal access to the internet and computers, reinforced by cultural mores and educational institutions.[21]

16 Ibid.

17 UN Women, 'Statement: from clicks to progress – equality in digital access advances rights for young women and girls', 9 August 2024, www.unwomen.org/en/news-stories/statement/2024/08/statement-from-clicks-to-progress-equality-in-digital-access-advances-rights-for-young-women-and-girls.

18 See further, e.g., A. Antonio and D. Tuffley, 'The gender digital divide in developing countries' (2014) 6 *Future Internet* 4, 673–87; M. Hilbert, 'Digital gender divide or technologically empowered women in developing countries? A typical case of lies, damned lies and statistics' (2011) 34 *Women's Studies International Forum* 34, 479–89; C. Kularski and S. Moller, 'The digital divide as a continuation of traditional systems of inequality' (2012) 5151 *Sociology*, 1–23.

19 For more detail on this, see Antonio and Tuffley, 'The gender digital divide in developing countries'.

20 See, e.g., P. Banerjee, 'Gender digital divide – examining the reality' (2019) 8 *International Journal of Innovative Technology and Exploring Engineering* 11S, 214–19.

21 E. Abu-Shanab and N. Al-Jamal, 'Exploring the gender digital divide in Jordan' (2015) 19 *Gender, Technology and Development* 1, 91–113.

Moreover, in many (especially developing) countries, women tend to have fewer opportunities for formal education and training, which results in them lacking digital literacy and skills. This limits their ability to use technology effectively and benefit from its advantages. For example, in India, women's digital competencies are significantly lower than men's, influenced by household dynamics, caste, and limited digital exposure.[22] And if women do access the internet, they often end up having a more negative experience than men, owing to online harassment and abuse, which disproportionately affects women, deterring them from engaging with digital platforms. Online abuse infringes upon their right to privacy and security, as laid down in human rights instruments such as the Universal Declaration of Human Rights (UDHR): '[n]o one shall be subjected to arbitrary interference with his privacy, family, home or correspondence, nor to attacks upon his honour and reputation'.[23] Women are often targeted with gender-based violence online, such as cyberstalking, threats, and harassment, which creates a hostile environment that limits their digital participation. Many studies have concluded that women are significantly more likely to experience cyberstalking and gender-based abuse than men.[24]

The gender gap brings with it many detrimental effects on the everyday lives and opportunities of women and girls. The digital divide negatively affects women's educational prospects, impacting women and girls' right to education and exacerbating existing gender disparities in learning opportunities. Digital tools provide critical access to educational resources, online courses, and skills building programmes, yet many girls, particularly in low-income and rural areas, are excluded owing to economic, infrastructural, and cultural barriers.[25] This exclusion restricts their ability to gain necessary competencies for academic and professional success. This educational gap further aggravates the employment divide, as women are less

[22] M. Vimalkumar, J. B. Singh, and S. K. Gouda, 'Contextualising the relationship between gender and computer self-efficacy: an empirical study from India' (2021) 58 *Information and Management* 4, Article 103464.

[23] UDHR, GA Res. 217A (III), UN Doc. A/810, at 71 (1948) Art. 12. Also, European Convention on Human Rights, Rome, 4 November 1950, Council of Europe, ETS No. 5, Art. 8; International Covenant on Civil and Political Rights (ICCPR), New York, 16 December 1966, 999 UNTS 171, Art. 17; American Convention on Human Rights, San Jose, 22 November 1969, 1144 UNTS 123, Art. 11; Convention on the Rights of the Child, New York, 20 November 1989, 1577 UNTS 3, Art. 16.

[24] See, e.g., S. Mas'udah et al., 'Gender-based cyber violence: forms, impacts, and strategies to protect women victims' (2024) 26 *Journal of International Women's Studies* 4, Article 5; E. L. Backe, P. Lilleston, and J. McCleary-Sills, 'Networked individuals, gendered violence: a literature review' (2018) 5 *Violence and Gender* 3, 135–46; N. Henry and A. Powell, 'Technology-facilitated sexual violence: a literature review of empirical research' (2016) 19 *Trauma, Violence and Abuse* 2, 195–208.

[25] For more on this issue in the Latin American context, see L. Camacho Gutiérrez, 'Addressing the Digital Divide among students at risk of school dropout in Latin America' (2024), Global Campus Policy Briefs 2024, https://repository.gchumanrights.org/server/api/core/bitstreams/fc5e90b1-f8c6-428f-8d84-81acf7258080/content.

prepared for the digital economy.[26] Women are less likely to work in technology-related fields,[27] and are often excluded from higher-paying jobs that require technological proficiency, perpetuating economic disparities between genders and impacting the human right to work. As proclaimed in the UDHR, '[e]veryone has the right to work, to free choice of employment, to just and favourable conditions of work and to protection against unemployment'.[28] This free choice of employment is restricted if women are not given the opportunity to develop the skills necessary to have a choice to work in ICT or in higher-paying jobs that require technological proficiency. Moreover, the lack of digital literacy can hinder women's ability to participate in lifelong learning opportunities, which are crucial for adapting to the rapidly changing job market.

The gender digital divide extends beyond individual impacts to affect women's roles in their communities. Women with limited access to ICTs are less able to engage in social, community, and civic activities that are increasingly mediated through digital platforms. This exclusion can lead to a diminished voice in community decision-making processes and reduced social capital. This, in turn, impacts their human right to participate in public affairs.[29] In contrast, women who do have access to ICTs can leverage these tools for community building and advocacy, underscoring the stark contrast in opportunities based on digital access. Women with limited or no digital access often also lack confidence in their ability to learn ICT skills and have a perception that technology is not meant for them, which further limits their ability to engage with digital tools, thereby reinforcing the gender gap.[30]

Consequently, the gender gap also significantly restricts women's freedom of expression, limiting their ability to participate in public discourse, advocate for their rights, and engage with conversations on different levels (local, regional, global). Digital platforms offer spaces for women to voice opinions, share experiences, and connect with wider communities. When women cannot access such platforms, their marginalisation is perpetuated and traditional power dynamics reinforced. Restricted access to technology leads to their perspectives remaining under-represented in both local and global dialogues. And, of course, overall, the gender digital divide significantly undermines the right to non-discrimination and

26 For more on the gender digital divide in education, see, e.g., I. C. Peláez-Sánchez, C. E. G. Reyes, and L. D. Glasserman-Morales, 'Gender digital divide in education 4.0: a systematic literature review of factors and strategies for inclusion' (2023) 1 *Future in Educational Research* 2, 129–46.

27 E.g., women occupy only 22 per cent of all tech roles across European companies: S. Blumberg et al., 'Women in tech: the best bet to solve Europe's talent shortage', 24 January 2023, McKinsey Digital, www.mckinsey.com/capabilities/mckinsey-digital/our-insights/women-in-tech-the-best-bet-to-solve-europes-talent-shortage.

28 UDHR, Art 23, para. 1.

29 As recognised, e.g., in ICCPR, Art. 25, and UDHR, Art. 21.

30 S. Singh, 'Bridging the gender digital divide in developing countries' (2017) 11 *Journal of Children and Media* 2, 245–7.

equality,[31] as it perpetuates and exacerbates systemic gender disparities in access to opportunities and resources.[32]

To avoid such overarching negative impacts on women and ensure the protection of their core human rights, it is essential to find ways to bridge the gender digital divide, in order to foster equality, empower women, and ensure their full participation in the digital society and economy.

17.3.2 *International Action in Relation to the Gender Gap*

As the gender digital divide remains a critical barrier to achieving gender equality in the digital age, several international organisations have adopted declarations, policies, or programmes to address this issue. These organisations have aimed to bridge gaps in digital access, skills, and representation, but the approach has been haphazard and inconsistent. There has not been systematic engagement with the gender gap in high-level policy documents. This section outlines the most significant efforts in some of the international organisations that have addressed the problem at least to a certain extent.

The UN has been one of the organisations drawing attention to the gender digital divide. Already in 1995, the Fourth World Conference on Women in Beijing recognised the transformative potential of ICTs for women's empowerment. The declaration identified 'Women and the Media' as a critical area, calling for equitable access 'to expression and decision-making in and through the media and new technologies of communication' and the promotion of 'balanced and non-stereotyped portrayal of women in media'.[33] A prominent step, twenty years later, was to include target 5b of '[e]nhanc[ing] the use of enabling technology, in particular information and communications technology, to promote the empowerment of women' in the Sustainable Development Goals.[34] Unfortunately, the only indicator that was chosen for assessing the achievement of this target was the '[p]roportion of individuals who own a mobile telephone, by sex', which has limited the follow-up activity and analysis to aspects connected to this narrow indicator.

A year later, the General Assembly called for 'immediate measures to achieve gender equality in Internet users by 2020, especially by significantly enhancing women's and girls' education and participation in information and communications

[31] The prohibition of non-discrimination is contained in both general international human rights instruments and specialised treaties such as the Convention on the Elimination of All Forms of Discrimination Against Women (CEDAW), New York, 18 December 1979, 1249 UNTS 13, which mandates state parties to eliminate gender-based disparities in all areas of life.

[32] See further, e.g., M. P. Treuthart, 'Connectivity: the global gender digital divide and its implications for women's human rights and equality' (2019) 23 *Gonzaga Journal of International Law* 1, 1–53.

[33] UN Fourth World Conference on Women, Beijing Declaration and Platform for Action, September 1995, www.un.org/womenwatch/daw/beijing/pdf/BDPfA%20E.pdf, strategic objective J.1. and J.2.

[34] UN General Assembly, Sustainable Development Goals and targets, 25 September 2015, GA Res. A/RES/70/1.

technologies, as users, content creators, employees, entrepreneurs, innovators and leaders', and reaffirmed its 'commitment to ensure women's full participation in decision-making processes related to information and communications technologies'.[35] Clearly, the goal was not reached as no concrete large-scale action followed that document.

An important development in the digital sphere was the 2020 UN Secretary-General Roadmap for Digital Cooperation.[36] Its thematic areas include digital human rights, achieving universal connectivity and digital inclusion. The implementation of the roadmap is managed and coordinated by the Office of the Secretary-General's Envoy on Technology, established at the beginning of 2021. For women's rights, the most important aspects of the roadmap are digital inclusion (as it emphasises the need to address the gender digital divide) and cyber-violence.

The Commission on the Status of Women (CSW; a functional commission of the UN Economic and Social Council) is the main global inter-governmental body exclusively dedicated to the 'promotion of gender equality, the rights and the empowerment of women'.[37] The CSW's annual sessions regularly include discussions on ICTs and digital equity. The 2023 priority theme was 'innovation and technological change, and education in the digital age for achieving gender equality and the empowerment of all women and girls'. The agreed conclusions of that session urge governments at all levels to '[p]rioritiz[e] digital equity to close the gender digital divide' and to '[l]everag[e] financing for inclusive digital transformation and innovation towards achieving gender equality and the empowerment of all women and girls'.[38] The document includes a plethora of well-founded recommendations and declarations of the importance of the issues, but fails to include specific measurable targets that would help ensure implementation. As there are no binding commitments coming from this document, it is unlikely that it will lead to tangible action in the short term, but it could serve as guidance to the states genuinely invested in tackling this issue.

The UN also supports gender equality in ICT through its specialised agency, the International Telecommunication Union (ITU). Since 1998, the ITU has adopted several resolutions to promote gender equality and its mainstreaming. The first resolution was on gender and telecommunications policy in developing countries.[39] In

35 UN General Assembly, Outcome document of the high-level meeting of the General Assembly on the overall review of the implementation of the outcomes of the World Summit on the Information Society, 1 February 2016, GA Res. A/RES/70/125, para. 27.

36 UN Secretary-General, *Roadmap for Digital Cooperation*.

37 UN Women, 'Commission on the Status of Women', www.unwomen.org/en/how-we-work/commission-on-the-status-of-women.

38 CSW, 'Innovation and technological change, and education in the digital age for achieving gender equality and the empowerment of all women and girls. Agreed conclusions', 20 March 2023, ECOSOC Resolution E/CN.6/2023/L.3.

39 ITU, 'Gender and telecommunication policy in developing countries', 1998, www.itu.int/en/ITU-D/Digital-Inclusion/Women-and-Girls/Documents/Resolutions/WTDC%20Valetta%20Res-7.pdf.

2018, the ITU adopted a resolution on gender mainstreaming in the ITU and the promotion of gender equality and the empowerment of women through telecommunications/ICT.[40] A year earlier, in 2017, the ITU Working Group on the Digital Gender Divide adopted 'Recommendations for action: bridging the gender gap in Internet and broadband access and use', but follow-up activities have been very limited (just two progress reports – from 2017 and 2018).[41]

The EU's efforts in relation to the gender gap are mostly limited to the last ten years. The main relevant strategy is the EU's Women in Digital policy, which has the aim of ensuring that 'everyone, regardless of gender, gets a fair chance to benefit from and contribute to the digital age'.[42] In 2019, twenty-six EU countries, along with Norway and the UK, signed the Women in Digital Declaration to achieve equality in tech.[43] The signatories of the declaration agreed to take action to create a national strategy to encourage women's participation in digitalisation, stimulate companies to combat gender discrimination at work, and advance a gender-balanced composition of boards, committees, and bodies dealing with digital matters.[44]

The 2022 European Declaration on Digital Rights and Principles addresses the gender digital divide by emphasising inclusivity and gender balance as necessary elements of the digital transformation. The Declaration has the ambitious aim of 'promot[ing] a European way for the digital transformation, putting people at the centre, built on European values and EU fundamental rights, reaffirming universal human rights, and benefiting all individuals, businesses, and society as a whole'.[45] Chapter 2 on Solidarity and inclusion proclaims that 'technology should be used to unite, and not divide, people' and that the 'digital transformation should contribute to a fair and inclusive society and economy in the EU'. The EU committed to 'a digital transformation that leaves nobody behind' and 'should benefit everyone, achieve gender balance […]'. And with Chapter 4, the EU committed to 'promoting high-quality digital education and training, including with a view to bridging

40 E.g., ITU, 'Mainstreaming a gender perspective in ITU and promotion of gender equality and the empowerment of women through telecommunications/information and communication technologies', 2018, www.itu.int/en/ITU-D/Digital-Inclusion/Documents/Resolutions/RESOLUTION%20 70%20(REV.%20DUBAI,%202018).pdf.

41 Broadband Commission for Sustainable Development, 'Working Group on the gender digital divide. How can we bridge the gender digital divide?', https://broadband.itu.int/working-groups/digital-gender-divide-2017/.

42 European Commission, 'Shaping Europe's digital future. Women in digital', https://digital-strategy.ec.europa.eu/en/policies/women-digital.

43 European Commission, 'Shaping Europe's digital future. EU countries commit to boost participation of women in digital', 9 April 2019, https://digital-strategy.ec.europa.eu/en/news/eu-countries-commit-boost-participation-women-digital.

44 Ibid.

45 European Parliament, the Council and the Commission, European Declaration on Digital Rights and Principles for the Digital Decade (2022), https://ec.europa.eu/newsroom/dae/redirection/document/94370, preamble.

the digital gender divide'. The broad language (e.g., 'achieve gender balance' and 'promoting [...] digital education') lacks measurable targets and enforcement mechanisms to ensure accountability.

The EU 2022 Digital Compass & Digital Decade Policy Programme 2030 (DDPP) is unique as it sets concrete targets for 2030 in areas such as digital skills, digital infrastructure, and making public services more digital.[46] It also emphasises the importance of women having equal opportunities in the ICT work sector and sets an ambitious target to increase the number of female ICT professionals, which involves increasing the number of girls and women studying ICT, both at school and at university. Importantly, EU Member States have to submit national strategic roadmaps about their actions to achieve all DDPP targets, which are published online, and report to the Commission about progress, which should add pressure on states to take action to meet the targets. This type of approach should also be adopted in relation to other aspects of the gender gap.

Other regional organisations are also addressing some facets of the gender gap in their policy. The Digital Transformation Strategy for Africa (2020–30) recommends promoting 'gender-inclusive education frameworks and policies and boosting relevant education opportunities and digital skills development for women and girls in STEAM-subjects to narrow the gender digital divide'.[47] And at the fifteenth session of the Regional Conference on Women in Latin America and the Caribbean, the member states of the Economic Commission for Latin America and the Caribbean (ECLAC) signed the Buenos Aires Commitment, underscoring the need to support women's participation in Science, Technology, Engineering, and Mathematics, and eliminating occupational segregation.[48] While these regional initiatives recognise the importance of addressing the gender digital divide through education and occupational inclusion, they fall short of creating systemic change. The policies lack implementation plans, mechanisms, and funds, and do not tackle deeply rooted socio-economic and cultural barriers.

In addition to policy documents, there have been several global initiatives targeted at closing the gender digital divide, including, among others, International Girls in ICT Day (ITU), the Global Partnership for Gender Equality in the Digital Age (the EQUALS initiative), the EQUALS in Tech Awards (ITU, UN Entity for Gender Equality and the Conference on Trade and Development), Gender-Sensitive Indicators for Media (UNESCO), Women on the Homepage (UNESCO), the Global Survey on Gender and Media (UNESCO), the Broadband

[46] European Commission, '2030 Digital Compass: the European way for the Digital Decade', 9 March 2021, COM(2021)118 final.

[47] African Union, 'The digital transformation strategy for Africa (2020–2030)' https://au.int/sites/default/files/documents/38507-doc-dts-english.pdf, p. 16. The acronym STEAM stands for Science, Technology, Engineering, Art, and Mathematics.

[48] ECLAC, Buenos Aires Commitment, LC/CRM.15/6/Rev.1, (Santiago: United Nations, 2023).

Commission Working Group on Broadband and Gender, and the Best Practice Forum on Gender and Access of the Internet Governance Forum.[49]

Despite various regional and international policy commitments and global initiatives, the gender digital divide persists (albeit slowly decreasing). While efforts by organisations such as the UN highlight the importance of integrating gender equality into the digital agenda, the lack of binding commitments and systematic implementation frameworks limits progress. There is a need for cohesive, measurable, and actionable strategies to ensure that the digital transformation benefits everyone, regardless of gender, and that the human rights of women and girls are not negatively impacted. The gender gap undermines their ability to fully exercise their rights to education, work, freedom of expression, and access to information. This not only limits individual potential but also hampers progress towards gender equality more broadly. The gender digital divide exacerbates existing vulnerabilities by reinforcing systemic inequalities that disproportionately affect women, particularly those in marginalised communities. Limited access to digital tools and skills excludes women from opportunities in education, employment, and civic participation, deepening poverty and social exclusion. The lack of representation and participation in the digital economy and technology design also preserves biases, further entrenching gender inequality. To avoid perpetuating such issues, promises on paper need to be translated into concrete action.

17.4 AGE GAP

The digital divide disproportionately affects older populations. According to the ITU, younger generations are significantly more likely to use the internet than older populations. Globally, internet usage rates are highest among individuals aged fifteen to twenty-four, reaching over 75 per cent, while fewer than 55 per cent of people aged sixty-five and older are online.[50] And only around one-third of those aged fifty-five to seventy-four, the retired and the inactive, have at least basic digital skills.[51] This age-based digital divide (grey digital divide, age gap) limits older adults' access to vital services, social connections, and opportunities for lifelong learning. As societies digitise, the inability to engage with technology not only marginalises older individuals but also raises human rights concerns. As the EU Agency for Fundamental Rights has noted, '[o]lder persons, a heterogeneous group with diverse socio-economic backgrounds, are among those whose enjoyment of fundamental

49 UN Economic and Social Council, Resolution 2021/28. Assessment of the progress made in the implementation of and follow-up to the outcomes of the World Summit on the Information Society, 22 July 2021, UN Doc. E/RES/2021/28.

50 ITU, 'Measuring digital development: facts and figures 2024', www.itu.int/itu-d/reports/statistics/facts-figures-2024/.

51 Digital Economy and Society Index (DESI) 2022, 'Human capital', https://ec.europa.eu/newsroom/dae/redirection/document/88765

rights might be at risk from digitalisation'.[52] Their right to participate in civic and public life, the right to work, to health, and to education, can all be impacted by digital exclusion. The age gap exacerbates existing inequalities, as those excluded from digital connectivity face challenges in accessing services, healthcare, and opportunities for social inclusion.

17.4.1 *Specific Issues Faced by Older People and Their Human Rights Implications*

The age-based digital divide highlights the significant barriers older generations face in accessing and effectively using digital technologies.[53] The rapid digitalisation of services and social interaction is leaving many older people behind, owing to obstacles such as lack of digital literacy, limited access to devices or internet connectivity, and design biases in technology that cater predominantly to younger users.[54] Moreover, technophobia and cyberphobia can pose significant self-imposed barriers to engaging with ICT.[55] This section examines the specific issues stemming from the age gap in digital inclusion and looks at their human rights implications.

FRA emphasises that only one in four people aged sixty-five to seventy-four in the EU 27 have at least basic digital skills, which, along with up-to-date technological tools, are essential to participate in public life.[56] The right to access to public services is part of the right to good administration protected, for example, under Article 41 of the EU Charter of Fundamental rights.[57] This includes equal access to public services that are in the process of being digitalised.[58] As governments and businesses shift services online, older individuals without digital access often struggle to apply for benefits, schedule government appointments, or use banking services. This creates a dependency on others or exclusion from essential services.

[52] FRA, *Fundamental Rights of Older Persons: Ensuring Access to Public Services in Digital Societies* (Luxembourg: Publications Office of the European Union, 2023), p. 7.

[53] For more on the age-based digital divide, see, e.g., B. Mikołajczyk, 'Universal human rights instruments and digital literacy of older persons' (2022) 27 *The International Journal of Human Rights* 3, 403–24; T. N. Friemel, 'The digital divide has grown old: determinants of a digital divide among seniors' (2016) 18 *New Media and Society* 2, 313–31; M. Sourbati, '"It could be useful, but not for me at the moment": older people, internet access and e-public service provision' (2009) 11 *New Media and Society* 7, 1083–100; B. Jæger, 'Trapped in the digital divide? Old people in the information society' (2004) 17 *Science Studies* 2, 5–22.

[54] See, e.g., I. Mannheim et al., 'Ageism in the discourse and practice of designing digital technology for older persons: a scoping review' (2023) 63 *The Gerontologist* 7, 1188–1200.

[55] P. K. Yu, 'Bridging the Digital Divide: Equality in the Information Age' (2002) 20 *Cardozo Arts and Entertainment Law Journal* 1, 1–52, at 15.

[56] FRA, *Fundamental Rights of Older Persons*, p. 6.

[57] Charter of Fundamental Rights of the European Union, 26 October 2012, OJ C 326.

[58] FRA, *Fundamental Rights of Older Persons*, p. 8.

The lack of digital skills can also prevent older individuals from accessing the information necessary for informed decision-making. Many voting resources and election updates are primarily available online. Older adults without digital skills or internet access struggle to find essential information about candidates, polling locations, or registration deadlines. This limits their ability to make informed decisions or participate fully in democratic processes. Voter registration, government consultations, and even voting are increasingly moving online, which reduces the ability of older people (without digital skills or access) to participate in such processes, and may end up infringing their right to participate in civic and public life. As much of today's political mobilisation and discussion occurs in digital spaces, but older individuals with limited digital access are often excluded from these forums, the perspectives of older people end up under-represented.[59] This exclusion not only diminishes their influence but also perpetuates generational divides in political representation and policymaking.

Older persons may also struggle with accessing digital healthcare services and information. People without internet access miss out on crucial health information, such as vaccination updates and preventive care guidance, exacerbating health inequities, especially in underserved areas.[60] Telemedicine, vital for remote care and during emergencies such as the COVID-19 pandemic, often excludes older individuals lacking digital skills, leading to delayed diagnoses and untreated conditions. Being unable to use digital healthcare systems, including electronic health records and online appointment platforms, creates further barriers and impacts the ability to manage one's healthcare effectively. Such problems may end up impacting older persons' right to health.

The age gap can fuel social isolation by limiting the ability of older adults to connect in an increasingly digital world. Without internet access or digital skills, many miss out on video calls, social media, and online communities that sustain relationships and combat loneliness. Human rights instruments, such as the EU Charter of Fundamental Rights, recognise the 'rights of the elderly to lead a life of dignity and independence and to participate in social and cultural life'.[61] But if older people lack digital literacy or access to social media and messaging platforms, they are at a higher risk of social exclusion and loneliness, as family and friends increasingly rely on digital communication to stay connected. This disconnect is especially impactful for those with mobility challenges or in rural areas, where

59 See further, e.g., M. Sànchez-Valle, 'The perception of older adults regarding socio-political issues disseminated on social networks' (2023) 11 *Communication for Seniors' Inclusion in Today's Society* 3, 112–23.

60 R. M. Tappen et al., 'Digital health information disparities in older adults: a mixed methods study' (2021) 9 *Journal of Racial and Ethnic Health Disparities* 1, 82–92.

61 Article 25 of the EU Charter of Fundamental Rights states that EU 'recognises and respects the rights of the elderly to lead a life of dignity and independence and to participate in social and cultural life – Charter of Fundamental Rights of the European Union, 26 October 2012, OJ C 326.

digital tools often replace in-person interactions.[62] This exclusion from (digital) social life negatively affects mental health, increasing the risk of depression and cognitive decline.[63]

The age-related digital divide can also impact older adults' rights to education and work. As (adult) education shifts online, those without sufficient digital skills face barriers to lifelong learning and skill development, limiting their ability to adapt in a changing job market. Many older individuals looking to stay in or re-enter the workforce struggle with the technological skills required in many jobs, widening economic inequality and reducing their employability. Similarly, as job applications and interviews are increasingly digital, older adults struggle to access employment opportunities.[64] Being excluded from online platforms for networking, remote work, and training can deepen economic and social inequalities.

Summing up, the age gap exacerbates age-based discrimination, undermining older people's human right to participate in civic and social life, the rights to education and work, the right to vote, and the right to health, among others. Without intervention, this digital exclusion deepens systemic inequalities, further marginalising older individuals.

17.4.2 *International Action in Relation to the Age Gap*

In order to achieve the equitable inclusion of older adults in the digital realm, some international organisations have introduced policies to address this disparity. Yet efforts remain limited and fragmented. High-level policy documents have yet to systematically engage with the unique challenges faced by older individuals because of the digital divide. This section highlights some (sporadic) policy initiatives by international organisations to tackle the age gap specifically; it does not look at broader instruments that address the (human) rights of older persons not limited to the context of digitalisation.

One of the main UN instruments in this area is the Madrid International Plan of Action on Ageing.[65] The plan emphasises the need to enhance the quality of life of older persons by ensuring their full participation in society, which includes access to ICTs. It encourages the development of programmes to reduce the digital divide and promote digital literacy among older persons.[66] In 2010, the UN's Open-Ended

62 For more on this, see, e.g., A. Seifert, S. R. Cotton, and B. Xie, 'A double burden of exclusion? Digital and social exclusion of older adults in times of COVID-19' (2021) 76 *The Journals of Gerontology: Series B* 3, e99–e103.

63 Y. Wang et al., 'Digital exclusion and cognitive impairment in older people: findings from five longitudinal studies' (2024) 24 *BMC Geriatrics* 406.

64 G. Karaoglu, E. Hargittai, and M. H. Nguyen, 'Inequality in online job searching in the age of social media' (2021) 25 *Information, Communication and Society* 12.

65 UN, Second World Assembly on Ageing, Madrid 8–12 April 2002, *Political Declaration and Madrid International Plan of Action on Aging* (New York: UN, 2002).

66 E.g., ibid., para. 40(b).

Working Group on Ageing was established.[67] It has advanced the promotion of a rights-based approach towards ageing, but has not paid much attention to addressing the age gap.

In 2022, ministers from the member states of the UN Economic Commission for Europe committed to 'promoting user-friendly digitalisation, enhancing digital skills and literacy to enable older persons to participate in an increasingly digital world, while also ensuring the right to access to information, participation, and services through access to digital devices and the Internet, and to suitable offline or other secure alternatives in user-friendly and accessible formats'.[68] However, this is a regional commission, which includes fifty-six member states, so the declaration does not reflect a global consensus. In 2013, the UN Human Rights Council established the mandate of the independent expert on the enjoyment of all human rights by older persons.[69] One of its annual thematic reports addressed the impact of automation on the human rights of older persons,[70] but the independent expert has not engaged with the age gap in detail.

The 2020 UN Roadmap for Digital Cooperation addresses the age-related digital divide through its broader focus on inclusivity and equitable digital access.[71] The roadmap highlights the importance of leaving no one behind, emphasising the need to close gaps in digital access and skills for vulnerable groups (including older people). The roadmap calls for partnerships across governments, private sectors, and civil society to address barriers, such as those faced by older populations in adopting digital technologies. The ITU as a UN specialised agency also has relevant policy goals. Its Connect 2030 Agenda has the ambitious target to bridge all digital gaps, including the age gap.[72] Other relevant targets include broadband services being affordable to all, broadband access to every household, universal access to the internet by all individuals, the majority of individuals having digital skills, and the majority of individuals accessing government services online. If successful, this would be a significant step towards eliminating the age gap. Yet the targets are very broad and do not have any specific actions or binding commitments attached to them.

The EU's approach is focused on inclusion in general and does not have many instruments specifically targeting older people (e.g., Europe's Digital Decade

[67] UNDESA, 'Open-ended Working Group on Ageing for the purpose of strengthening the protection of the human rights of older persons', https://social.un.org/ageing-working-group/.

[68] 2022 Rome Ministerial Declaration, 'A sustainable world for all ages: joining forces for solidarity and equal opportunities throughout life', https://unece.org/sites/default/files/2022-06/Rome__Ministerial_Declaration.pdf, para. 25.

[69] HRC, Resolution 24/20. 'The human rights of older persons'

[70] HRC, 'Report of the Independent Expert on the enjoyment of human rights by older persons. Robots and rights: the impact of automation on the human rights of older persons', UN Doc. A/HRC/36/48, 21 July 2021.

[71] UN Secretary-General, *Roadmap for Digital Cooperation*.

[72] ITU, 'Connect 2030 – An agenda to connect all to a better world', www.itu.int/en/mediacentre/backgrounders/Pages/connect-2030-agenda.aspx, target 2.1.

policy programme sets targets such as achieving basic digital skills for 80 per cent of adults by 2030, but does not specify how high this percentage should be among older people).[73] The main document with a distinct focus on older people and the digital divide is the 2020 Council of the EU conclusions on the human rights, participation, and well-being of older persons in the era of digitalisation.[74] The conclusions advocate for tailored strategies to enhance digital literacy among older people, improve their access to digital infrastructure, and foster their active engagement in the digital society. But the document is phrased in a very soft manner, with the Council inviting member states and the European Commission to consider, promote, and enable different steps that would improve the situation of older persons.

There are no EU directives or regulations dedicated specifically to protecting the fundamental rights of older persons or addressing the age gap. Two directives that do have a somewhat positive impact on accessibility are the Web Accessibility Directive and the European Accessibility Act.[75] The former directive obliges states to ensure that public sector websites and mobile apps have specific technical accessibility standards, which are accessible to everybody, including persons with disabilities. And the latter has the aim of improving cross-border trade in accessible products and services between EU Member States. The EU Agency for Fundamental Rights (FRA) has drawn attention to the fundamental rights implications of digital exclusion among older adults, in the particular context of access to public services. Its 2023 report underscores the risk of marginalisation in accessing essential services, including healthcare and social benefits, and advocates for inclusive digital policy frameworks.[76] Despite the acknowledgement of the issue in the EU, action is lagging.

In general, regional and specialised organisations have not been focusing on the age-related digital divide. Although many organisations have general policies in relation to the digital divide, the specific issues that older people face have not received much attention. Yet the age-related digital divide continues exacerbating existing vulnerabilities among older adults by amplifying their risk of exclusion across multiple domains. It can further marginalise those already disadvantaged by factors such as low income, poor health, or geographic isolation, particularly in

[73] European Commission, 'Europe's Digital Decade: digital targets for 2030', https://commission.europa.eu/strategy-and-policy/priorities-2019-2024/europe-fit-digital-age/europes-digital-decade-digital-targets-2030_en.

[74] Council of the EU, 'Human rights, participation and well-being of older persons in the era of digitalisation. Council Conclusions', EU doc. 11717/2/20 REV 2, 9 October 2020.

[75] Web Accessibility Directive: Directive (EU) 2016/2102/EC of the European Parliament and of the Council of 26 October 2016 on the accessibility of the websites and mobile applications of public sector bodies, OJ 2016 L 327. European Accessibility Act: Directive (EU) 2019/882/EC of the European Parliament and of the Council of 17 April 2019 on the accessibility requirements for products and services, OJ 2019 L 151.

[76] FRA, *Fundamental Rights of Older Persons.*

rural areas where digital infrastructure is often less developed. Older individuals who lack digital skills or access to technology may struggle to book medical appointments, access telehealth services, or manage financial transactions, leaving them more vulnerable to unmet needs and financial instability. Social vulnerabilities are also intensified as digital technologies have become central to communication and community engagement. Older people without digital literacy are at greater risk of loneliness and social isolation, as family, friends, and community networks have become reliant on digital platforms for connection. This isolation can contribute to mental health issues, such as depression and anxiety, which are already prevalent among older populations.

An aspect to bear in mind when addressing the age gap (and the digital divide in general), is intersectionality. Intersectionality highlights how overlapping vulnerabilities, such as age, gender, socio-economic status, and geographic isolation, compound the impacts of the digital divide.[77] Older women in rural areas exemplify this, facing barriers from age-based exclusion, entrenched gender norms, and limited infrastructure. These intersecting disadvantages amplify the risk of marginalisation. Addressing the age-related digital divide thus requires policies that account for the complex, intersecting needs of marginalised groups to ensure that digital inclusion efforts are equitable and effective.

In sum, the age-related digital divide magnifies the disparities older adults face, reinforcing cycles of exclusion that intersect with economic, social, and health vulnerabilities. Bridging this divide is not merely a matter of technological advancement but a fundamental requirement for ensuring dignity, autonomy, and inclusion for older individuals in contemporary society. Addressing this issue holistically is essential to mitigating its broader societal impacts and safeguarding the human rights of an ageing population.

17.5 CONCLUSIONS

The digital divide represents a critical fault line in the global move toward digitalisation. Despite decades of attention, the problem persists owing to the interplay of systemic factors, including socio-economic disparities, geographic isolation, cultural norms, insufficient policy interventions, and inadequate resources. This chapter has examined the gender and age dimensions of the digital divide, illustrating how these gaps perpetuate and exacerbate exclusion and vulnerability among women and older populations. Bridging this divide requires a more cohesive, enforceable, and inclusive approach that prioritises the voices and needs of marginalised groups. This has been acknowledged by the UN Secretary-General, who has noted that '[r]isk factors that affect the ability of vulnerable and marginalized groups to

77 See further, e.g., P. Tsatsou, 'Vulnerable people's digital inclusion: intersectionality patterns and associated lessons' (2021) 25 *Information, Communication & Society* 10, 1475–94.

have access to connectivity should be specifically identified and addressed'.[78] The same has been recognised by the European Parliament, which 'call[ed] for careful examination of people's needs when it comes to digital developments and innovation, especially the needs of vulnerable groups, in order to assess how they can benefit from these new technologies' as 'the digital transition must take place in a way that benefits everyone'.[79]

Both covered dimensions of the digital divide reflect broader systemic failures to address structural inequalities. While international and regional bodies have adopted policies to address these gaps, their efforts are often inconsistent, fragmented, and lack enforceable commitments. For instance, international instruments such as the UN's Sustainable Development Goals include digital inclusion targets, but fail to address the problem in a comprehensive manner. Similarly, the EU's Digital Decade policy programme and other regional initiatives advocate for inclusivity but provide limited mechanisms to enforce digital equity for women and older individuals. The organisations themselves are also calling for more action. Some of the concrete aspects that have been noted as key to bridging the digital divide are 'better metrics, data collection, and coordination of initiatives' (UN Secretary-General),[80] and 'strengthened enabling policy environments and international cooperation to improve affordability, access, education, capacity-building, multilingualism, cultural preservation, investment and appropriate financing' (UN Economic and Social Council).[81] The European Parliament has emphasised the need to design 'online services in a comprehensible way so that they can be accessed and used by people of all ages and levels of educational attainment',[82] and the importance of promoting 'basic and specialised skills with a specific focus on the most vulnerable groups of people, and the development of education and training systems including lifelong learning, re-skilling and up-skilling'.[83] Such calls for action have yet to lead to significant results.

Addressing the digital divide is not merely a matter of technological advancement but a profound human rights imperative. Civil society groups such as AGE Platform Europe have emphasised that human rights need to be used as a compass for digitalisation more broadly.[84] International and regional frameworks must

78 UN Secretary-General, *Roadmap for Digital Cooperation* (2020), at p. 7.

79 European Parliament resolution of 13 December 2022 on the digital divide: the social differences created by digitalisation (2022/2810(RSP)), para 1.

80 UN Secretary-General, *Roadmap for Digital Cooperation* (2020), at p. 10.

81 UN Economic and Social Council, Resolution 2021/28. Assessment of the progress made in the implementation of and follow-up to the outcomes of the World Summit on the Information Society, 22 July 2021, UN Doc. E/RES/2021/28.

82 European Parliament resolution of 13 December 2022 on the digital divide: the social differences created by digitalisation (2022/2810(RSP)), para 7.

83 Ibid., para 15.

84 AGE Platform Europe, 'Digitalisation and older people: our call to EU policy makers', 28 June 2024, www.age-platform.eu/content/uploads/2024/07/AGE_Paper-on-Digitalisation-and-Older-People_June-2024_FINAL-1.pdf.

go beyond aspirational targets and implement binding commitments and concrete initiatives that address the specific barriers faced by vulnerable groups. Achieving digital equity is essential not only for fostering individual empowerment but also for advancing broader societal goals of inclusivity, fairness, and human rights in an increasingly digital world.

18

How the EU Safeguards Children's Rights in the Digital Environment

An Exploratory Analysis of the EU Digital Services Act and the Artificial Intelligence Act

Eva Lievens and Valerie Verdoodt

18.1 INTRODUCTION: CHILDREN'S RIGHTS IN THE DIGITAL ENVIRONMENT

Digital technologies have a significant impact on the lives of children and the rights that are specifically attributed to them by the United Nations Convention on the Rights of the Child (UNCRC), Article 24 of the European Union (EU) Charter of Fundamental Rights (CFEU) and many national constitutions. The Council of Europe Committee of Ministers' 2018 Recommendation on Guidelines to respect, protect, and fulfil the rights of the child in the digital environment recognises that the digital environment is 'reshaping children's lives in many ways, resulting in opportunities for and risks to their well-being and enjoyment of human rights'.[1] This has also been acknowledged by the United Nations Committee on the Rights of the Child (CRC Committee), which adopted a General Comment on the rights of the child in relation to the digital environment in 2021. In General Comment no. 25, the Committee affirms that '[i]nnovations in digital technologies affect children's lives and their rights in ways that are wide-ranging and interdependent [...]'.[2] Over

[1] The digital environment is understood as 'encompassing information and communication technologies (ICTs), including the internet, mobile and associated technologies and devices, as well as digital networks, databases, content and services', Council of Europe, 'Recommendation CM/Rec(2018)7 of the Committee of Ministers to Member States on guidelines to respect, protect, and fulfil the rights of the child in the digital environment (2018)', https://search.coe.int/cm/Pages/result_details.aspx?ObjectId= 09000016808b79f7, 12. At the level of the Council of Europe, children enjoy all human rights attributed to individuals under the European Convention on Human Rights. The Steering Committee on the Rights of the Child guides the Council of Europe's work by advising the Committee of Ministers on appropriate action and proposals concerning the overall priorities regarding children's rights.

[2] UN Committee on the Rights of the Child, 'General Comment no. 25 on the rights of the child in the digital environment', CRC/C/GC/25 (2021), https://tbinternet.ohchr.org/_layouts/15/treatybodyexternal/Download.aspx?symbolno=CRC/C/GC/25&Lang=e.

the years, the EU has been relying on the guidance of the UNCRC when adopting and interpreting fundamental human rights instruments.[3] This is demonstrated for instance in Article 24 of the CFEU,[4] which contains language that is very similar to that of the UNCRC. The EU's commitment to the UNCRC was again confirmed in the 2021 EU Strategy on the Rights of the Child, built on six key pillars of which 'the digital and information society' is one.[5] In a recent case, the Court of Justice of the EU has confirmed that CFEU Article 24 represents the integration into EU law of the principal rights of the child referred to in the UNCRC.[6] Hence, the UNCRC functions as a comprehensive framework that must duly be taken into account when legislative proposals that directly or indirectly affect children are proposed and adopted.

In the past decade, regulatory action by the European Community (EC) has increasingly been targeted at the digital environment, leading to the adoption of influential legislative instruments such as the General Data Protection Regulation (GDPR),[7] and the Network and Information Security Directive. Other instruments, such as the Audiovisual Media Services Directive (AVMSD), were amended to extend their scope to also cover video-sharing platforms. Two recent legislative initiatives at the level of the EU, the Digital Services Act (DSA) and the Artificial Intelligence Act (AIA), touch upon platforms and technologies that have a significant impact on children and their rights.[8] Digital services, often provided through platforms, provide children with immense opportunities to communicate, learn,

3 European Union Agency for Fundamental Rights, 'Handbook on European law relating to the rights of the child' (2015), http://fra.europa.eu/en/publication/2015/handbook-european-law-child-rights, 30.

4 See: that '1. Children shall have the right to such protection and care as is necessary for their well-being. They may express their views freely. Such views shall be taken into consideration on matters which concern them in accordance with their age and maturity. 2. In all actions relating to children, whether taken by public authorities or private institutions, the child's best interests must be a primary consideration. [...]'.

5 European Commission, 'Communication to the European Parliament, the Council, the European Economic and Social Committee and the Committee of the Regions EU strategy on the rights of the child', COM/2021/142 final, (2021), https://eur-lex.europa.eu/legal-content/en/TXT/?uri=CELEX%3A52021DC0142.

6 See also CJEU Case C-490/20, *V.M.A. v. Stolichna obshtina, rayon "Pancharevo"* [2021], para. 59: 'Since Article 24 of the Charter, as the Explanations relating to the Charter of Fundamental Rights note, represents the integration into EU law of the principal rights of the child referred to in the Convention on the rights of the child, which has been ratified by all the Member States, it is necessary, when interpreting that article, to take due account of the provisions of that convention.'

7 Regulation (EU) 2016/679 of the European Parliament and of the Council of 27 April 2016 on the protection of natural persons with regard to the processing of personal data and on the free movement of such data, and repealing Directive 95/46/EC (General Data Protection Regulation).

8 Regulation (EU) 2022/2065 of the European Parliament and of the Council of 19 October 2022 on a Single Market for Digital Services and amending Directive 2000/31/EC (Digital Services Act); Regulation (EU) 2024/1689 of the European Parliament and of the Council of 13 June 2024 laying down harmonised rules on artificial intelligence and amending Regulations (EC) No 300/2008, (EU) No 167/2013, (EU) No 168/2013, (EU) 2018/858, (EU) 2018/1139 and (EU) 2019/2144 and Directives 2014/90/EU, (EU) 2016/797 and (EU) 2020/1828 (Artificial Intelligence Act).

and play, and artificial intelligence (AI)-based applications may offer children personalised learning or medical treatments.[9] At the same time, the use of tech platforms and AI may also pose risks to children's rights. Rights that might be negatively affected are, for example, the right to privacy and data protection, freedom of thought, the right to freedom of expression, and the right to protection from violence and exploitation. The AIA acknowledges, for instance, that this technology 'can also be misused and provide novel and powerful tools for manipulative, exploitative and social control practices'.[10] The question arises to what extent the protection and fulfilment of children's rights is addressed in these most recent legislative acts, the DSA and the AIA. In order to answer this question, the proposals are analysed, the legislative process is scrutinised, and an assessment is made of how each contributes to the effective realisation of children's rights in the digital realm. The chapter also suggests some strategies for moving forward, drawing on recent recommendations from the UN children's rights framework. We propose that EU policymakers adopt a children's rights approach in their attempts to regulate platform services and AI, so that children's rights and interests can be a strong regulatory focus rather than a regulatory afterthought.

18.2 OPPORTUNITIES FOR AND RISKS TO CHILDREN'S RIGHTS FROM PLATFORM SERVICES AND AI SYSTEMS

Before analysing the legislative acts, this section zooms in on existing evidence about children's experiences with platform services and AI systems. The aim is to provide a better understanding of both the potential opportunities for and risks to children's rights offered by these services and applications. Platform services and other AI-based applications have become an integral part of children's lives. While AI-enabled toys and voice assistants have infiltrated children's homes and schools, AI-powered tutors, learning assistants, and personalised educational programmes are becoming more commonplace.[11] Children are also avid users of (commercial) AI-enabled platform services, such as social media, video-sharing, and interactive gaming platforms. For instance, platforms such as Instagram, Snapchat, and TikTok use advanced machine learning to deliver content and personalise, to use their own word 'improve',[12] the user experience, provide filters that rely on augmented reality technology, and employ natural language processing tools to monitor and remove hate speech and other harmful content. The specific features of these platforms and

[9] UNICEF, 'Policy guidance on AI for children' (2020), www.unicef.org/globalinsight/media/1171/file/UNICEF-Global-Insight-policy-guidance-AI-children-draft-1.0-2020.pdf.

[10] AIA, Recital 28.

[11] UNICEF, 'The state of the world's children 2017: children in a digital world' (2017) www.unicef.org/reports/state-worlds-children-2017, 58.

[12] For instance, TikTok's For You feed, see https://newsroom.tiktok.com/en-us/how-tiktok-recommends-videos-for-you.

systems make them particularly appealing to children, but also carry risks.[13] The lack of transparency and insight into how exactly AI systems generate certain output makes it very difficult for end users to anticipate the potential risks, harms, or violations of their rights.[14]

Research capturing the opinions of children and youth themselves about the opportunities and risks of platform services and AI shows that they have a balanced perspective.[15] On the one hand, they realise that these services offer many opportunities for entertainment, socialising, and learning, but are never completely safe. On the other hand, children express a great deal of concern, and cite as the main risks being confronted with harmful and illegal content, cyberbullying and hate speech, and violations of their privacy and data protection rights.[16] In relation to this, questions arise about the long-term impact of platform services and AI on children's well-being and development. For instance, it has been reported that researchers within Instagram, owned by Meta, who studied user experiences, found that 'thirty-two percent of teen girls said that when they felt bad about their bodies, Instagram made them feel worse'.[17] The introduction of AI-based applications into children's lives could also have side effects at the societal level.[18] More specifically, it could lead to the normalisation of surveillance, datafication, and commercialisation. Many of these applications are driven by commercial interests and deliberately designed and used to ensure maximum engagement of children, and even to establish behavioural patterns and habits for the future.[19] Furthermore, lower quality AI-based technologies with a greater focus on entertainment and pacification rather than education and learning might be available for children from disadvantaged backgrounds compared with those from privileged backgrounds.[20]

[13] OECD, 'Children in the digital environment – revised typology of risks' (2021), www.oecd-ilibrary.org/docserver/9b8f222e-en.pdf?expires=1637159913&id=id&accname=guest&checksum=5C9D56C713550043EBF2F5EAACD4990D,5.

[14] M. Schaake, 'The European Commission's Artificial Intelligence Act' (2021) https://hai.stanford.edu/sites/default/files/2021-06/HAI_Issue-Brief_The-European-Commissions-Artificial-Intelligence-Act.pdf, 2.

[15] UNICEF, 'Adolescents perspectives on artificial intelligence' (2021), www.unicef.org/globalinsight/sites/unicef.org.globalinsight/files/2021-02/UNICEF_AI_AdolescentPerspectives_20210222.pdf; European Schoolnet, 'How to make Europe's digital decade fit for children and young people?' (2021), www.betterinternetforkids.eu/documents/167024/6847388/How+to+make+Europe%E2%80%99s+Digital+Decade+fit+for+children+and+young+people+-+A+report+from+the+consultation+with+children+and+young+people+-+October+2021.pdf/ae344db2-5b56-0f67-625e-a66244aa023c?t=1633359093370.

[16] Ibid.

[17] G. Wells, J. Horwitz, and D. Seetharaman, 'Facebook knows Instagram is toxic for teen girls, company documents show', *The Wall Street Journal*, 14 September 2021.

[18] For instance, in the context of smart toys, see E. Fosch-Villaronga et al., 'Toy story or children story? Putting children and their rights at the forefront of the artificial intelligence revolution' (2021) 38 *AI and Society* 1, 133–52.

[19] B. Kidron, A. Evans, and J. Afia, 'Disrupted childhood – the cost of persuasive design' (2018) 5Rights Foundation, https://5rightsfoundation.com/static/5Rights-Disrupted-Childhood.pdf.

[20] Fosch-Villaronga et al., 'Toy story or children story?', p. 139.

Because of the impact of platform services and AI on society at large, policymakers and legislators around the world are debating and developing instruments to counteract these risks. However, scholars have identified a disconnect and lack of adequate redress between the potential negative impact of AI on children and the regulatory means to address them.[21] UNICEF also underlines that most of the recent initiatives targeting AI only refer superficially to children and their rights and interests.[22] Considering the EU's commitment to safeguarding children's rights in the digital environment,[23] the following section will analyse two of these recent initiatives through the lens of children's rights and principles. It is important to note that both the DSA and the AIA are likely to have a standard-setting impact around the world, given what scholars and policymakers call the Brussels Effect.[24] In this sense, these initiatives also present an important opportunity to shape global norms and standards for the design and deployment of digital technologies that are used by and impact children.

18.3 CHILDREN'S RIGHTS IN THE DSA

18.3.1 *The Commission Proposal for a DSA*

The proposal for the DSA aimed to regulate intermediary services and to 'set out uniform rules for a safe, predictable and trusted online environment, where fundamental rights enshrined in the Charter are effectively protected'.[25] This proposal reflects a shift at the EU level from relying on self- or co-regulatory efforts from tech companies to imposing strong legislative obligations on those companies that offer services used by a vast number of EU citizens and affect individuals and society at the same time.[26]

[21] Ibid.

[22] In this regard, UNICEF has also warned that an overfocus on the opportunities of AI-systems for children (e.g., for educational purposes) could lead to an underestimation of the risks and challenges such systems may hold for this group. M. Penagos, S. Kassir, S. Vosloo, 'National AI strategies and children, Reviewing the landscape and identifying windows of opportunity' (UNICEF, 2020), www.unicef.org/innocenti/documents/national-ai-strategies-and-children.

[23] European Commission, 'Communication to the European Parliament, the Council, the European Economic and Social Committee and the Committee of the Regions EU strategy on the rights of the child' (2021) COM/2021/142 final, https://eur-lex.europa.eu/legal-content/en/TXT/?uri=CELEX%3A52021DC0142.

[24] Schaake, 'The European Commission's AIA', p. 2. This effect entails that companies end up complying with EU regulations even in other countries because it is more practical to have one global approach. Hence, this de facto extends EU laws internationally.

[25] European Commission, 'Proposal for a Regulation of the European Parliament and of the Council on a single market for digital services (Digital Services Act) and amending Directive 2000/31/EC' (2020) COM/2020/825 final, https://eur-lex.europa.eu/legal-content/en/TXT/?uri=COM%3A2020%3A825%3AFIN, hereafter: Proposal for a DSA.

[26] E. Lievens, 'Is self-regulation failing children and young people? Assessing the use of alternative regulatory instruments in the area of social networks', in S. Simpson, M. Puppis, and H. van den Bulck (eds.), *European Media Policy for the Twenty-First Century: Assessing the Past, Setting Agendas for the Future* (New York, Abingdon: Routledge, 2016), pp. 77–94; Recital 75 Digital Services Act.

Throughout the proposal by the European Commission, children or minors and their rights are referred to a few times. The preamble to the proposal, for instance, states that it will 'contribute to the protection of the rights of the *child* and the right to human dignity online'. Recital 34 clarifies that the proposal intends to impose a clear and balanced set of harmonised due diligence obligations on providers of intermediary services, aiming in particular 'to guarantee different public policy objectives such as the safety and trust of the recipients of the service, including *minors* and vulnerable users'.[27]

The most important provision for children (Article 26, Recital 57) in the proposal relates to the supervised risk assessment approach towards 'very large online platforms' (VLOPs). VLOPs are platforms 'where the most serious risks often occur' and which 'have the capacity to absorb the additional burden'. A platform is considered a VLOP when the 'number of recipients exceeds an operational threshold set at 45 million; that is, a number equivalent to 10% of the [EU] Union'.[28] This includes many large platforms that are popular with children, such as YouTube, TikTok, or Instagram. According to the proposal, VLOPs should identify, analyse, and assess any significant systemic risks stemming from the functioning and use made of their services in the Union. All three categories of systemic risks that are listed are especially relevant to children. The first category refers to 'the dissemination of illegal content through their services', with a mention in Recital 57 of child sexual abuse material as a type of illegal content. The second category relates to 'any negative effects for the exercise of the fundamental rights to respect for private and family life, freedom of expression and information, the prohibition of discrimination and the rights of the *child*'.[29] The third category refers to the 'intentional manipulation of their service, including by means of inauthentic use or automated exploitation of the service, with an actual or foreseeable negative effect on the protection of public health, *minors*, civic discourse, or actual or foreseeable effects related to electoral processes and public security'.[30] In order to mitigate the risks, the VLOPs must put in place reasonable, proportionate, and effective measures, tailored to the specific systemic risks (Article 27). Another mechanism that can be used to tackle different types of illegal content and systemic risks are codes of conduct (Article 35). According to the proposal, the creation of an EU-wide code of conduct will be encouraged by the Commission and the new Board for Digital Services to contribute to the proper application of the DSA. Recital 68 refers to the appropriateness of drafting codes of conduct regarding disinformation or other manipulative and abusive activities that might be particularly harmful for vulnerable recipients of the service, such as *children*.

The explicit references to children in the proposal for the DSA were welcomed by children's rights organisations but by some considered to be too weak.[31]

27 Emphasis added by the authors.

28 Proposal for a DSA, Recital 54.

29 Emphasis added by the authors.

30 Emphasis added by the authors.

31 5Rights Foundation, 'The Digital Services Act must deliver for children' (2021), https://5rightsfoundation.com/in-action/the-digital-services-act-must-deliver-for-children.html.

18.3.2 *Amendments Proposed by the LIBE Committee*

During the legislative process, and specifically in the context of the activities of the Committee on Civil Liberties, Justice and Home Affairs (LIBE), a number of child-centric amendments were proposed by a number of LIBE committee members.[32] Amendment no. 129 introduced a specific reference to Article 24 of the Charter, the UNCRC, and General Comment no. 25 to Recital 3. Amendment no. 412 suggested adding a new Article 12a, requiring the carrying out of a detailed child impact assessment. Amendment no. 414 put forward a specific article on the mitigation of risks to children that aims to address many of the existing concerns regarding children's rights in the context of VLOPs. The amendment includes, for instance, a reference to taking into account children's best interests when implementing mitigation measures in general and adapting content moderation or recommender systems in particular; adapting or removing 'system design features that expose children to content, contact, conduct, and contract risks, as identified in the process of conducting child impact assessments'; 'proportionate and privacy preserving age assurance'; ensuring 'the highest levels of privacy, safety, and security by design and default for users under the age of 18'; the prevention of profiling, including for commercial purposes such as targeted advertising; age appropriate terms that uphold children's rights; and 'child-friendly mechanisms for remedy and redress, including easy access to expert advice and support'. Amendment no. 427 concerned the publication of child impact assessments and reports about the mitigation measures taken. Finally, amendment no. 772 included a requirement for the Commission to 'support and promote the development and implementation of industry standards set by relevant European and international standardisation bodies for the protection and promotion of the rights of the child'.

In its Opinion, the LIBE committee only included the amendments regarding Recital 3,[33] leaving the more substantial amendments out.

18.3.3 *Amendments by the Council and European Parliament*

Both in the general approach of the Council of November 2021,[34] and the amendments adopted by the European Parliament (EP) on 20 January 2022, there are

[32] European Parliament Committee on Civil Liberties, Justice and Home Affairs, 'Amendments no. 126–910 Draft Opinion' (2021) PE692.898v01-00, www.europarl.europa.eu/doceo/document/LIBE-AM-693830_EN.pdf.

[33] European Parliament Committee on Civil Liberties, Justice and Home Affairs, 'Opinion' (2020) 2020/0361(COD), www.europarl.europa.eu/doceo/document/LIBE-AD-692898_EN.pdf.

[34] Council of the European Union, 'Proposal for a Regulation of the European Parliament and of the Council on a single market for digital services (Digital Services Act) and amending Directive 2000/31/EC' – general approach' (2021), 13203/21, https://data.consilium.europa.eu/doc/document/ST-13203-2021-INIT/en/pdf.

remarkably more references to children and minors compared to the Commission proposal.[35]

The general approach by the Council adds that when assessing risks to the rights of the child, 'providers should consider how easily understandable to minors the design and functioning of the service is, as well as how minors can be exposed through their service to content that may impair minors' health, physical, mental and moral development'. Risks may arise, for example, 'in relation to the design of online interfaces which intentionally or unintentionally exploit the weaknesses and inexperience of minors or which may cause addictive behaviour' (Recital 57). Recital 58 builds on this by requiring that the design and online interface of services primarily aimed at minors or predominantly used by them should consider their best interests and ensure that their services are organised in a way that minors are easily able to access mechanisms within the DSA, including notice and action and complaint mechanisms. Moreover, VLOPs that provide access to content that may impair the physical, mental, or moral development of minors should take appropriate measures and provide tools that enable conditional access to the content. Article 12 refers to explaining the conditions and restrictions for the use of the service in a way that minors can understand, where an intermediary service is primarily aimed at minors or is predominantly used by them. Finally, in Article 27, a reference was added to taking targeted measures to protect the rights of the child, including age verification and parental control tools, or tools aimed at helping minors signal abuse or obtain support.

The EP suggested adding an explicit reference to the UNCRC and General Comment no. 25 in Recital 3. Unlike in the Commission proposal, but reminiscent of guidelines from the Article 29 Working Party,[36] the EP put forward a prohibition of '[t]argeting or amplification techniques that process, reveal or infer personal data of minors or sensitive categories of personal data for the purpose of displaying advertisements'.[37] A second amendment relates to ensuring that conditions for and restrictions on the use of a service are explained in a way that minors can

[35] European Parliament, 'Amendments adopted by the European Parliament on 20 January 2022 on the proposal for a regulation of the European Parliament and of the Council on a Single Market for Digital Services (Digital Services Act) and amending Directive 2000/31/EC' (2022) COM(2020)0825 – C9-04 18/2020 – 2020/0361(COD), www.europarl.europa.eu/doceo/document/TA-9-2022-0014_EN.html.

[36] Article 29 Working Party, 'Guidelines on automated individual decision-making and profiling for the purposes of Regulation 2016/679' (2018), https://ec.europa.eu/newsroom/article29/items/612053, 29.

[37] European Parliament, 'Amendments adopted by the European Parliament on 20 January 2022 on the proposal for a regulation of the European Parliament and of the Council on a Single Market for Digital Services (Digital Services Act) and amending Directive 2000/31/EC' (2022) COM(2020)0825 – C9-0418/2020 – 2020/0361(COD), www.europarl.europa.eu/doceo/document/TA-9-2022-0014_EN.html, proposed Recital 52 ('Online platforms should also not use personal data for commercial purposes related to direct marketing, profiling and behaviourally targeted advertising of minors[; t]he online platform should not be obliged to maintain, acquire or process additional information in order to assess the age of the recipient of the service') and proposed Article 24.1.b.

understand.[38] This, however, would only be required for intermediary services that are 'primarily directed at minors or predominantly used by them'. Along the same lines, other amendments aim to ensure the internal complaint-handling systems are easy to access and user-friendly, including for minors, and that online interfaces and features are adapted to protect minors as a measure to mitigate risks.[39] A more general obligation is proposed to adapt design features to ensure a high level of privacy, safety, and security by design for minors.[40] Also potentially important for children's rights was the suggestion to change the wording of 'any negative effects' in Article 26 to 'any actual and foreseeable negative effects' on the rights of the child. Arguably, this could trigger the application of the precautionary principle.[41] Regarding the mitigation measures, the EP also proposed to add 'targeted measures aimed at adapting online interfaces and features to protect minors' to Article 27. Finally, the suggested Recital 69 encourages the development of codes of conduct to facilitate compliance with obligations regarding the protection of minors, and the proposed Article 34 1a refers to the support and promotion by the Commission of the development and implementation of voluntary standards set by the relevant European and international standardisation bodies aimed at the protection of minors.

18.3.4 *The Final Text of the DSA*

The DSA, or, as its formal title is expressed, 'the Regulation (EU) 2022/2065 of the European Parliament and of the Council on a Single Market for Digital Services and amending Directive 2000/31/EC', was adopted on 19 October 2022 and published in the Official Journal on 27 October 2022.[42] Not only are the references to *child, children*, and *minors* in the adopted text vastly more numerous than in the Commission proposal, but the substance of what is proposed is also much more extensive and arguably promising, depending on actual implementation and enforcement.

These recitals and articles that refer to children and minors can be classified in five broad categories: (a) provisions that are related to child sexual abuse material and the measures in place to tackle this type of material,[43] (b) transparency obligations regarding terms and conditions, (c) obligations for all online platforms to protect minors,[44] (d) risk assessment and mitigation obligations towards children

38 Ibid., proposed Article 12.1.c.

39 Ibid., proposed Article 17.2. and Article 27.1.

40 Ibid., proposed Article 13.3.

41 E. Lievens (2021) 'Growing up with digital technologies: how the precautionary principle might contribute to addressing potential serious harm to children's rights', 39 *Nordic Journal of Human Rights* 2, 128–45.

42 Regulation (EU) 2022/2065 of the European Parliament and of the Council of 19 October 2022 on a single market for digital services and amending Directive 2000/31/EC (Digital Services Act).

43 Ibid., Recitals 12, 61, 64, 80, 119 and Article 34.

44 Ibid., Recital 46 and Article 14.3.

for VLOPs and very large online search engines (VLOSEs),[45] and (e) references to implementation tools such as standards and codes of conduct.

In what follows, the final three categories are examined in depth.

18.3.4.1 Obligations for All Online Platforms to Protect Minors

Article 28 (an article not included in the Commission proposal) formulates extensive obligations for online platforms 'accessible to minors'. First, such platforms must put in place 'appropriate and proportionate measures to ensure a high level of privacy, safety, and security of minors, on their service'. This is an obligation that has the potential to safeguard a number of children's rights (i.e., the right to privacy and the right to protection). One point of contention is the interpretation of which platforms are considered 'accessible to minors'. This is in part clarified in Recital 71, which states that this includes (a) platforms whose terms and conditions permit minors to use the service, (b) platforms offering services that are directed at or predominantly used by minors, or (c) platforms that are aware that some of the recipients of their service are minors, 'for example, because it already processes personal data of the recipients of its service revealing their age for other purposes'. In reality, research shows that many children (including very young children) use platforms that are not directed at them and that explicitly state in their terms and conditions that their service is not to be used by children under a certain age (most often set at thirteen years).[46] It may be expected that certain platforms will try to argue that their platforms should not be considered to be 'accessible to minors'. Independent research into children's online experiences and use of platforms might be helpful in this regard, both for the platforms and for oversight bodies. Aside from this issue in relation to which platforms fall within the scope of Article 28, it might also be a challenge for platforms to decide what are 'appropriate and proportionate measures to ensure a high level of privacy, safety, and security of minors', particularly when considering that different age groups of children have different privacy and safety needs. In this regard, Recital 71 refers to standards, codes of conduct, and best practices, and Article 28.4 indicates that the Commission (after consulting the European Board for Digital Services, which is established by the DSA in Article 61) may formulate guidelines to support providers of online platforms. Work on such guidelines started in 2024.[47]

Second, Article 28.2 prohibits targeting advertisements based on profiling 'when they are aware with reasonable certainty that the recipient of the service is a minor'.

45 In the final text of the DSA, the obligations for VLOPs were also extended to very large online search engines, see ibid., Recital 41, Article 33.

46 H. Vanwynsberghe et al., 'Onderzoeksrapport Apestaartjaren: de digitale leefwereld van kinderen en jongeren' (2022), https://assets.mediawijs.be/2022-05/apestaartjaren_2022_210x210_issuu.pdf.

47 European Commission, Third meeting of the European Board for Digital Services, 29 April 2024, https://digital-strategy.ec.europa.eu/en/news/third-meeting-european-board-digital-services. A public consultation and workshops took place in May- June 2025, with the final version expected soon after. For more information, see https://digital-strategy.ec.europa.eu/en/library/commission-seeks-feedback-guidelines-protection-minors-online-under-digital-services-act.

Such types of advertisements have long been a concern for scholars,[48] and organisations such as the Article 29 Working Party, which in one of its Guidelines had stated before that 'organisations should, in general, refrain from profiling [children] for marketing purposes',[49] even though this was not explicitly prohibited by the GDPR. In this light, it can only be commended that this is now also explicitly prohibited in the DSA. Yet the question could be raised whether it would not have made sense to include a broader prohibition of profiling children for commercial purposes rather than just targeted advertising. This would have been more in line with the CRC Committee's call to 'prohibit by law the profiling or targeting of children of any age for commercial purposes' in its General Comment no. 25.[50] Moreover, profiling may also be used to target harmful types of content (e.g., relating to self-harm or eating disorders). Arguably, this could be covered under the risk assessment provisions, but their scope is limited to VLOPs and VLOSEs (see Section 3.5.2). Another doubt that may be raised is how the notion 'reasonable certainty' will be interpreted and whether this would require age verification. It would seem from the text of the DSA that this is not necessarily the case, as Article 28.3 states that compliance with the obligations of Article 28 'shall not oblige providers of online platforms to process additional personal data in order to assess whether the recipient of the service is a minor', and Recital 71 adds that this obligation 'should not incentivise providers of online platforms to collect the age of the recipient of the service prior to their use'. While this may be in line with the principle of data minimisation laid down in the GDPR,[51] it is uncertain whether the protective aim of the prohibition as well as taking measures to ensure a high level of privacy, safety, and security of minors will be effectively realised if platforms are not incentivised to know which users are actually minors. In any case, the desirability and effectiveness of age verification or age assurance has been the subject of heated debates since the emergence of the internet, and until now, this debate has not been settled.

18.3.4.2 Risk Assessment and Mitigation Obligations towards Children for the VLOPs and VLOSEs

A third category of obligations is aimed at VLOPs and VLOSEs. The first VLOPs and VLOSEs were designated by the EC on 25 April 2023. They include platforms and search engines that are hugely popular with children such as TikTok, Snapchat,

[48] S. van der Hof et al., 'The child's right to protection against economic exploitation in the digital world' (2020) 28 *The International Journal of Children's Rights* 4, 833–59.

[49] Article 29 Working Party, 'Guidelines on automated individual decision-making and profiling for the purposes of Regulation 2016/679' (2018), https://ec.europa.eu/newsroom/article29/items/612053.

[50] UN Committee on the Rights of the Child, 'General Comment no. 25 on the rights of the child in the digital environment' (2021) CRC/C/GC/25, https://tbinternet.ohchr.org/_layouts/15/treatybodyexternal/Download.aspx?symbolno=CRC/C/GC/25&Lang=, para. 42.

[51] GDPR, Article 5(1)c.

Instagram, Wikipedia, Google Play, and Google Search.[52] Article 34 requires VLOPs and VLOSEs to undertake an assessment of the systemic risks in the EU 'stemming from the design or functioning of their service and its related systems, including algorithmic systems, or from the use made of their services'. There are four categories of risks that are listed, and as mentioned earlier, at least three of these types of risks are directly relevant for children: '(a) the dissemination of illegal content through their services'; '(b) any actual or foreseeable negative effects for the exercise of fundamental rights, including rights of the *child*', and '(d) any actual or foreseeable negative effects in relation to gender-based violence, the protection of public health and *minors* and serious negative consequences to the person's physical and mental well-being'. From a children's rights perspective, it is particularly interesting to observe that in the course of the legislative process, the word *foreseeable* was added, as this could potentially trigger the precautionary principle. There is still much uncertainty about the occurrence and extent of actual harm when it comes to digital technologies.[53] There are certain indications that certain platform services might have an impact on the mental health of children in the short and long term,[54] and that certain features lead to an impact on day-to-day life and, for instance, sleep. Yet there is still little hard evidence about certain impacts on children and their rights in the long run. There is simply not enough research, there are ethical questions that surround research with children, and certain technologies have not existed long enough to draw conclusive results. We have argued before that with respect to delicate issues such as the well-being of children, the *precautionary principle* might thus come into play.[55] Simply put, this concept embraces a *better safe than sorry* approach and compels society to act cautiously if there are certain – not necessarily absolute – scientific indications of a potential danger and not acting upon these indications could inflict harm.[56] It could of course be up for discussion whether the threshold for triggering the precautionary principle and the threshold for an effect to be *foreseeable* in the sense of Article 34 are in alignment. From a linguistic point of view, *foreseeable* does not equate with *potential*. A foreseeable event is, according to the Cambridge Dictionary, 'one that can be known about or guessed before it happens'. Whether an effect can be known about will to a large extent depend on research and expert advice from a variety of disciplines. From a children's rights perspective, however, this notion would need to be interpreted broadly in the best interests of the child, in line with UNCRC Article 3 and CFEU Article 24.

52 European Commission, 'DSA: very large online platforms and search engines' (2023), https://digital-strategy.ec.europa.eu/en/policies/dsa-vlops.

53 Lievens, 'Growing up with digital technologies'.

54 Wells et al., 'Facebook knows Instagram is toxic'; S. Livingstone et al., 'Young people experiencing internet-related mental health difficulties: the benefits and risks of digital skills' (2022), https://doi.org/10.5281/zenodo.7372552.

55 Lievens, 'Growing up with digital technologies'.

56 E. Lievens, *Protecting Children in the Digital Era: The Use of Alternative Regulatory Instruments. International Studies in Human Rights* (Leiden, Boston: Brill/Nijhoff, 2010).

As to the methodology for the assessment of risks and their effect on the rights of the child, inspiration could be drawn from existing methodologies for Children's Rights Impact Assessments (CRIAs).[57] With regard to CRIAs, best practices are available that could be useful. From a children's rights perspective, in any case, it is crucial that the impact on the full range of children's rights is assessed, and rights are not looked at in isolation but as interacting with each other.

Following the assessment of the risks, Article 35 requires VLOPs and VLOSEs to take 'reasonable, proportionate and effective mitigation measures, tailored to the specific systemic risks'. One type of such mitigation measure that is proposed is 'targeted measures to protect the rights of the child, including age verification and parental control tools, tools aimed at helping minors signal abuse or obtain support'. The explicit reference to targeted measures is helpful. Recital 89 seems to indicate that such targeted measures might for instance be needed to protect minors from content that may impair their physical, mental, or moral development. The examples that are given could be helpful as well, although both age verification and parental control tools are not without their difficulties. Regarding age verification, the lack of consensus on desirability and effectiveness has already been pointed to; regarding parental control tools, it has been argued before that these types of *empowerment* tools should not be used to solely shift the burden for safeguarding the interests and rights of children from platforms to parents.[58] In addition, other non-child specific risk mitigation measures that are proposed, such as adapting the design, features, or functioning of services, including online interfaces, may also have a positive impact on children's rights. Recital 89 explains in that regard that VLOPs and VLOSEs must take the best interests of the child into account when taking such measures, particularly when their services are aimed at minors or predominantly used by them.

18.3.4.3 Standards and Codes of Conduct

Finally, as the formulation of the obligations that are imposed on VLOPs and VLOSEs still remains rather abstract, the actual implementation of them will be of the utmost importance. The tools that can support platforms in that regard are standards and codes of conduct.

[57] S. Mukherjee, K. Pothong, and S. Livingstone, 'Child rights impact assessment: a tool to realise child rights in the digital environment' (2021), https://digitalfuturescommission.org.uk/wp-content/uploads/2021/03/CRIA-Report.pdf. Additionally, inspiration could also be drawn from methodologies for Data Protection Impact Assessments: see Article 35 GDPR, Article 29 Working Party, 'Guidelines on Data Protection Impact Assessment (DPIA) and determining whether processing is "likely to result in a high risk" for the purposes of Regulation 2016/679' (2017), https://ec.europa.eu/newsroom/article29/items/611236. However, such impact assessments should take into account the impact on the full range of children's rights and not be restricted to the impact on the right to privacy or the right to data protection.

[58] E. Lievens, 'The rights of the child in the digital environment: from empowerment to de-responsibilisation', in 5Rights Foundation, *Freedom, Security and Privacy: The Future of Childhood in the Digital World* (2020), pp. 152–7.

Article 44 states that the Commission, after consultation with the Board, shall support and promote the development and implementation of voluntary standards set by relevant European and international standardisation bodies, including in respect of 'targeted measures to protect minors online'. In this regard, it is relevant to observe the efforts that are currently being undertaken by the Institute of Electrical and Electronics Engineers (IEEE) regarding the drafting of a standard for Age Appropriate Design for Children's Digital Services.[59]

Recital 104 explains that an area for consideration for which codes of conduct could be drafted (Article 45) is 'the possible negative impacts of systemic risks on society and democracy, such as disinformation or manipulative and abusive activities or any adverse effects on *minors*'. In the Commission's 2022 BIK+ Strategy, it was announced that the Commission will 'facilitate a comprehensive EU code of conduct on age-appropriate design, building on the new rules in the DSA and in line with the AVMSD and GDPR. The code aims to ensure the privacy, safety and security of children when using digital products and services. This process will involve industry, policymakers, civil society and children.'[60] It continues:

> [u]nder the DSA, the Commission may invite providers of very large online platforms to participate in codes of conduct and ask them to commit themselves to take specific risk mitigation measures, to address specific risks or harms identified, via adherence to a particular code of conduct. Although participation in such codes of conduct remains voluntary, any commitments undertaken by the providers of very large online platform shall be subject to independent audits.

At the end of 2022, a call was published by the Commission for members for a Special Group on the EU Code of Conduct on Age-Appropriate Design.[61] However, work on the Code of Conduct seems to have halted in favour of the drafting of guidelines by the European Commission (supra).

18.4 CHILDREN'S RIGHTS IN THE PROPOSAL FOR THE AIA

18.4.1 *The EU Policy Agenda on AI (and Children's) Fundamental Rights*

A second legislative initiative at the EU level that has the potential to significantly impact children's rights in the digital environment is the AIA. Developing a regulatory framework for AI has been high on the EU policy agenda for some

59 IEEE, 'IEEE publishes new standard to address age appropriate design for children's digital services' (2021), https://standards.ieee.org/news/ieee-2089/.

60 European Commission, 'Communication to the European Parliament, the Council, the European Economic and Social Committee and the Committee of the Regions – a digital decade for children and youth: the new European strategy for a better internet for kids (BIK+)' (2022) COM/2022/212 final, https://eur-lex.europa.eu/legal-content/EN/TXT/?uri=COM:2022:212:FIN.

61 See European Commission, 'Special group on the EU Code of conduct on age-appropriate design' (2023), https://digital-strategy.ec.europa.eu/en/policies/group-age-appropriate-design.

time. Initially, the EC adopted a soft-law approach consisting of non-binding recommendations and ethical guidelines. In June 2018, an independent High-Level Expert Group on Artificial Intelligence (AI HLEG) was established, which was tasked with drafting ethics guidelines for AI practitioners, as well as offering advice concerning the adoption of policy measures.[62] However, this approach changed in 2021, when the EC explicitly recognised that certain characteristics of AI, such as the opacity of algorithms and the difficulties in establishing causality in algorithmic decision-making, pose specific and potentially high risks to fundamental rights.[63] As existing legislation failed to address these risks, both the EP and the Council called for legislative action in this area.[64] Echoing these calls, the AI HLEG also stated the need to explore binding regulation to tackle some of the critical issues raised by AI. In particular, the expert group stressed the need for mandatory traceability, auditability, and *ex ante* oversight obligations for AI systems that have the potential to significantly impact human lives. According to the AI HLEG coordinator, AI is nothing more than an application, system, or tool developed by humans that can be used in different ways: (a) ways that cause harm, (b) ways that cause unintended harm, (c) ways that counteract harm, and (d) ways that cause good.[65] Therefore, 'if we are intelligent enough to create AI systems, we must be intelligent enough to ensure appropriate governance frameworks that harness the good use of those systems, and avoid those that lead to (un)intentional harm'.[66] In its framework for achieving Trustworthy AI, the AI HLEG also pays (limited) attention to children's rights. More specifically, as part of the key ethics guidelines, the AI HLEG advises to pay particular attention to situations involving more vulnerable groups,[67] such as children, and refers specifically to CFEU Article 24.[68]

[62] N. A. Smuha, 'The EU approach to ethics guidelines for trustworthy artificial intelligence' (2019) SSRN Scholarly Paper ID 3443537, https://papers.ssrn.com/abstract=3443537.

[63] European Commission, 'Communication to the European Parliament, the Council, the European Economic and Social Committee and the Committee of the Regions on fostering a European approach to artificial intelligence' (2021), https://digital-strategy.ec.europa.eu/en/library/communication-fostering-european-approach-artificial-intelligence.

[64] See, for instance, European Parliament, 'Resolution of 20 October 2020 with recommendations to the Commission on a framework of ethical aspects of artificial intelligence, robotics and related technologies (2020/2012(INL))', (2020), www.europarl.europa.eu/doceo/document/TA-9-2020-0275_EN.html; Council of the European Union, 'Council conclusions on shaping Europe's digital future' (2020) https://data.consilium.europa.eu/doc/document/ST-8711-2020-INIT/en/pdf.

[65] Smuha, 'The EU approach', p. 19.

[66] Ibid.

[67] AI HLEG, 'Ethics guidelines for trustworthy AI' (2019) https://ec.europa.eu/futurium/en/ai-alliance-consultation, 38. Regarding vulnerable persons and groups, HLEG mentions that 'there is no commonly accepted or widely agreed legal definition of vulnerable persons, due to their heterogeneity. Vulnerability is considered context-specific, and dependent on temporary life events, economic factors, identity. A vulnerable group is a group of persons who share one or several characteristics of vulnerability.'

[68] Ibid., 2.

The fact that the regulation of AI is a hot topic is evidenced by the responses to the EC's open consultation on AI in February 2020, which attracted far more feedback submissions than any other technology Act.[69] In these submissions, concerns about AI and children were raised by a range of stakeholders, including companies, academic institutions, and non-governmental organisations (NGOs), mostly in relation to education. For instance, the submissions mentioned that the use of AI in education may have serious consequences on the child's life course and should therefore be considered as high risk, as it may lead to discrimination, have a serious negative impact on their learning, and their consent might not be properly secured.[70] More generally, children's digital rights and AI,[71] and the use of AI in connection with the evaluation, monitoring, and tracking of children were also mentioned as areas of concern.[72]

18.4.2 *The Commission Proposal for an AI Act*

In response to these calls for legislative action, in April 2021 the EC unveiled its proposal for the AIA, the first Act of its kind in the world.[73] It aimed to lay down harmonised rules on the development, deployment, and use of AI systems in the EU,[74] based on the values and fundamental rights of the EU.[75] Through a risk-based approach and by imposing proportionate obligations on all participants in the value chain, the proposal aimed to ensure a high level of protection of fundamental rights in general and a positive impact on the rights of special

[69] L. Clarke, 'Here are the most contentious issues in the AI Act debate', *Tech Monitor*, 24 September 2021, https://techmonitor.ai/policy/meps-are-preparing-to-debate-europes-ai-act-these-are-the-most-contentious-issues. The submissions mentioned in the footnotes below are available at https://ec.europa.eu/info/law/better-regulation/have-your-say/initiatives/12527-Artificial-intelligence-ethical-and-legal-requirements/public-consultation_nl.

[70] W. Holmes, Submission by Nesta (academic/research institution), reference F530284, 14 June 2020.

[71] V. Hilmann, Submission by the informal working group, affiliates and alumni of Berkman Klein Centre for Internet & Society at Harvard University (academic/research institution), reference F514778, 27 April 2020.

[72] G. Hasselback, Submission by DataEthics.eu (NGO), reference F530283, 14 June 2020.

[73] European Commission, 'Proposal for a Regulation of the European Parliament and of the Council laying down harmonised rules on artificial intelligence (Artificial Intelligence Act) and amending certain union legislative acts (2021) COM(2021)', https://eur-lex.europa.eu/legal-content/EN/TXT/?uri=celex%3A52021PC0206, 206 (hereafter 'proposal for an AIA'); Schaake, 'The European Commission's AIA'. The proposal for an AIA is part of a number of proposals that shape the digitalisation in the EU – including the DSA analysed earlier – which should be viewed together. In addition, there are also the Digital Markets Act, the draft Machinery Regulation, and the Data Governance Act.

[74] It is based on article 114 TFEU, which allows the EU to regulate those elements of private law which create obstacles to trade in the internal market; R. Manko, European Parliament, and European Parliamentary Research Service, *EU Competence in Private Law: The Treaty Framework for a European Private Law and Challenges for Coherence: In-Depth Analysis* (European Parliament, 2015), p. 5.

[75] Proposal for an AIA, 1.

groups, including children.[76] More specifically, a risk-based categorisation of AI systems was introduced, where different levels of risk correspond to a different set of requirements. The intensity of risks determines the applicability of the requirements, and as such, a lighter regime applies to AI systems with minimal risks, while unacceptable risks are prohibited. The idea is that (groups of) individuals at risk and vulnerable to health, safety, and rights infringement by new AI developments need a higher level of protection.[77]

One category of prohibited practices as proposed by the Commission that is relevant for children are 'practices that exploit vulnerabilities of specific vulnerable groups such as children or persons with disabilities in order to materially distort their behaviour in a manner that is likely to cause them or another person *psychological or physical harm*', because such systems contradict Union values, for instance, by violating fundamental rights (emphasis added).[78] This is confirmed in Recital 16 and Article 5.1 (b) of the proposal, although the latter does not explicitly refer to children but to 'a specific group of persons due to their age'. As an example of such an exploitative AI system, the EC referred to a doll with an integrated voice assistant, which, under the guise of a fun or cool game, encourages a minor to engage in progressively dangerous behaviour or challenges.[79] While this is an extreme example, children's rights advocates argued that a number of persuasive design features often found in AI systems used by children could fall under this prohibition.[80] They cited, for example, the autoplay features of social media companies that aim to increase user engagement, and which could be said to affect children's sleep and education, and ultimately their health and well-being.[81] Moreover, when such recommender systems promote harmful content, they might even lead to sexual exploitation and abuse.[82] Nevertheless, the prohibition was criticised by various stakeholders for its limitations, in particular the limitation to

76 Proposal for an AIA, Preamble, 11.

77 B. Townsend, 'Decoding the proposed European Union Artificial Intelligence Act' (2021) 25 *American Society of International Law Insights* 20, 7.

78 Proposal for an AIA, Explanatory Memorandum, section 5.2.2, 12–13.

79 As cited by M. Veale and F. Zũiderveen Borgesius, 'Demystifying the draft EU Artificial Intelligence Act' (2021) 22 *Computer Law Review International* 4, 97–112.

80 5Rights Foundation, 'AI systems that put children at risk to be banned under EU's AI Act' (2021), https://5rightsfoundation.com/in-action/ai-systems-that-put-children-at-risk-to-be-banned-under-eus-ai-act.html.

81 Such features are particularly appealing to children, as research shows that they reduce children's autonomy and the likelihood of them self-regulating their media consumption, leading to longer video-viewing times; A. Hiniker et al., 'Coco's videos: an empirical investigation of video-player design features and children's media use', *Proceedings of the 2018 CHI Conference on Human Factors in Computing Systems* (Association for Computing Machinery, 2018), https://doi.org/10.1145/3173574.3173828.

82 E. Gómez, V. Charisi, and S. Chaudron, 'Evaluating recommender systems with and for children: towards a multi-perspective framework' (2021), Fifteenth ACM Conference on Recommender Systems, https://ceur-ws.org/Vol-2955/paper2.pdf, 6.

physical and psychological harm,[83] the requirement of malicious intent,[84] and the lack of references to fundamental rights.[85]

The Commission proposal also mentions children and their rights in the context of the classification of AI systems as high risk and the related requirements for the provision or use of such systems. According to Recital 28 of the proposal, the extent of the adverse impact on fundamental rights caused by AI systems is of particular relevance when classifying them as high risk.[86] In this regard, Recital 28 contains an explicit reference to CFEU Article 24, which grants children the right to such protection and care as is necessary for their well-being. Moreover, it mentions the UNCRC and the recently adopted General Comment no. 25 on children's rights in the digital environment,[87] which sets out why and how State parties should act to realise children's rights in a digital world. On reflection, however, this does not mean that the proposal considers AI systems that are likely to be accessed by children or impact upon them to be considered high risk by default. The Commission proposal also does not impose any real obligation on providers or users of high-risk AI systems to carry out and publish an assessment of the potential impact on children's rights. Instead, providers of high-risk AI systems will have to conduct a conformity assessment,[88] to demonstrate compliance with a list

83 Scholars argued that such harms may be difficult to prove or may accumulate without a single event exceeding a threshold for severity of harm; Veale and Zuiderveen Borgesius, 'Demystifying the draft EU AIA', 5; D. Keats Citron and D. J Solove, 'Privacy harms' (2021) SSRN Scholarly Paper ID 3782222, https://papers.ssrn.com/abstract=3782222. Furthermore, consumer protection organisations have emphasised that the prohibition left out important consumer harms that AI systems can facilitate, such as monetary loss or economic discrimination; BEUC (2021) 'Regulating AI to protect the consumer: position paper on the AI Act', www.beuc.eu/publications/beuc-x-2021-088_regulating_ai_to_protect_the_consumer.pdf, 11. This is also problematic in light of children's right to protection from economic exploitation under Article 32 UNCRC and related rights; S. van der Hof et al., 'The child's right to protection', 833.

84 BEUC, 'Regulating AI to protect the consumer: Position Paper on the AI Act' (2021), www.beuc.eu/publications/beuc-x-2021-088_regulating_ai_to_protect_the_consumer.pdf., 11; Veale and Zuiderveen Borgesius, 'Demystifying the draft EU AIA'.

85 European Economic and Social Committee, 'Working document section for the single market, production and consumption proposal for a Regulation of the European Parliament and of the Council laying down harmonised rules on artificial intelligence (Artificial Intelligence Act) and amending certain Union legislative Acts [COM(2021) 206 Final – 2021/106 (COD)]' (2021) https://allai.nl/wp-content/uploads/2021/09/INT940-%E2%80%93-EESC-2021-02484-00-00-DT-TRA-EN-Draft-Opinion-final.pdf. 'The EESC is a consultative body that gives representatives of Europe's socio-occupational interest groups and others a formal platform to express their points of view on EU issues'; for more information see www.eesc.europa.eu/en/about.

86 Proposal for an AIA, Recital 28.

87 UN Committee on the Rights of the Child, General Comment no. 25.

88 With regard to these conformity assessments, it is important to note the role of standardisation organisations in the process. There are currently three European standardisation organisations that can mandate the development of harmonised standards for such assessments, which providers of AI systems can follow rather than having to interpret the essential requirements themselves. By following the standard, providers can then enjoy a presumption of conformity. For a critical analysis of this mechanism, see Veale and Zuiderveen Borgesius, 'Demystifying the draft EU AIA', pp. 14–17.

of essential requirements, before placing the system on the market or putting it into service.[89] These requirements include setting up a risk management system;[90] ensuring that the data sets used comply with data quality criteria; obliging providers to guarantee accuracy, robustness, and data security; preparing technical documentation; logging; and building in human oversight to minimise risks to health, safety, and fundamental rights.[91] Regarding the latter, human–machine interface tools and measures should be integrated into the design of the AI system.[92] Users of high-risk AI systems must use the systems in accordance with the provider's instructions for use. While this seems like a solid set of requirements, how the full implementation of the risk management as described in Article 9 of the AIA proposal can be ensured without a real obligation to first identify and evaluate risks to children could still be questioned. In addition, the Commission proposal lacks individual rights and remedies against infringements by the provider or user, in contrast to, for instance, data subject rights under the GDPR.[93]

Finally, the Commission proposal also contains transparency requirements that apply to some specific limited-risk AI systems. This category essentially covers systems that can mislead people into thinking they are dealing with a human (e.g., automated chatbots such as the 'My AI' tool used by Snapchat).[94] The proposal requires AI providers to design their systems in such a manner that individuals interacting with these systems are informed that they are interacting with a bot (i.e., 'bot disclosure') unless it is contextually obvious. Second, the proposal requires users of emotion recognition systems to inform exposed persons of this and users of AI systems that generate deep fakes to disclose the AI nature of the resulting content. These transparency requirements raised a number of questions (e.g., does this mean that there is a right to an explanation?),[95] including about the standard of transparency when children are involved. More specifically, do providers have an obligation

89 Proposal for an AIA, Article 3(2).

90 Article 9 proposal for an AIA specifies that 'the risk management system shall consist of a continuous iterative process run throughout the entire lifecycle of a high-risk AI system, requiring regular systematic updating'. It shall comprise the identification and analysis of known and foreseeable risks, evaluation of potentially arising risks and adopting suitable risk management measures.

91 Proposal for an AIA, Article 14(2).

92 In contrast, for *users* of high-risk AI systems, there are no direct obligations in the proposal for an AIA regarding human oversight. Users have discretion to organise their own resources and activities for the purpose of implementing the human oversight measures indicated by the manufacturer (Article 29 (2), Proposal for an AIA).

93 This has been criticised by the EDPB and EDPS. EDPB and EDPS, 'Joint Opinion 5/2021 on the proposal for a Regulation of the European Parliament and of the Council laying down harmonised rules on artificial intelligence (Artificial Intelligence Act)' (2021) https://edps.europa.eu/system/files/2021-06/2021-06-18-edpb-edps_joint_opinion_ai_regulation_en.pdf., 9.

94 For a discussion of the potential impact of such an AI chatbot on children and young people, see Childnet, 'Snapchat's new AI chatbot and its impact on young people' (2023), www.childnet.com/blog/snapchats-new-ai-chatbot-and-its-impact-on-young-people/#:~:text=What%20is%20"My%20AI"%20and,information%2C%20and%20formulates%20a%20response.

95 For an overview, see Veale and Zuiderveen Borgesius, 'Demystifying the draft EU AIA', pp. 17–20.

to offer information in a child-friendly manner – similar to the GDPR transparency obligations – when their AI systems are likely to be accessed by a child? This remained unclear in the Commission proposal.

18.4.3 *Amendments Proposed by the IMCO and LIBE Committees*

The discussions in the EP were led by the Committee on Internal Market and Consumer Protection (IMCO) and the LIBE under a joint committee procedure.[96] Additional references to children were added in the IMCO-LIBE draft report.[97] The first was amendment 208, which proposed a requirement for the future EU advisory body on AI, the so-called AI Board, to provide guidance on children's rights, in order to 'meet the objectives of this Regulation that pertain to children'. Second, and perhaps more interesting, was amendment 289, which added to the list of high-risk AI systems 'AI systems intended to be used by children in ways that have a significant impact on their personal development, including through personalised education or their cognitive or emotional development'. Amendment 23 specified in this context that children constitute 'an especially vulnerable group of people that require additional safeguards'. Depending on how broadly this category is interpreted (e.g., does it go beyond an educational context?), this could lead to stronger protection. The draft report also did not contain a general obligation for specific protection for children in the context of AI.

Furthermore, in a public event following the publication of the Commission proposal, one of the shadow rapporteurs of the IMCO Committee on the proposal for an AIA openly criticised the fact that the Commission proposal contained no obligation to carry out fundamental rights impact assessments.[98] In this regard, amendment 90 of the draft report specified that the obligation of risk identification and analysis for providers of high-risk AI systems should also include the known and reasonably foreseeable risks to the fundamental rights of natural persons.[99] In addition, the shadow rapporteur argued that the Commission proposal overlooked the fact that AI systems that are transparent and meet the conformity requirements – and can thus move freely on the market – could still be used in violation of fundamental rights. This criticism was reflected in the draft report, which underlined that 'users

96 At the time of writing, the IMCO-LIBE Committees had published their draft report, and a vote is scheduled for the first quarter of 2023.

97 Committee on the Internal Market and Consumer Protection Committee on Civil Liberties, Justice and Home Affairs, 'Draft report on the proposal for a regulation of the European Parliament and of the Council on harmonised rules on artificial intelligence (Artificial Intelligence Act) and amending certain Union legislative Acts' (2022) COM2021/0206 – C9-0146/2021 – 2021/0106(COD) (hereafter 'IMCO-LIBE Draft Report').

98 K. van Sparrentak, IMCO shadow rapporteur, during the BEUC seminar 'The AI Act: machine rule or consumer rules?'; for more information, see www.beuc.eu/ai-act-machine-rule-or-consumer-rules.

99 As part of the risk management system of Article 9, proposal for an AIA.

of high-risk AI systems also play a role in protecting the health, safety and fundamental rights of EU citizens and EU values',[100] and placed more responsibilities on the shoulders of said users.[101]

18.4.4 *Amendments by the Council and the EP*

Both the general approach of the Council and the amendments adopted by the EP introduced a number of noteworthy changes.

The Council adopted its common position (General Approach) on 6 December 2022, which includes several noteworthy elements concerning children and their rights.[102] First, as Malgierie and Tiani argue, it adopted a wider and more commercially relevant definition of vulnerability.[103] More specifically, the Council proposed to prohibit not only the exploitation of age, but also of vulnerabilities based on disability, and the social or economic situation of the individual. This was an improvement in light of children's rights concerning accessibility and protection from economic exploitation. The Council also deleted the malicious intent requirement, and included the possibility that harms may be accumulated over time (Recital 16), thereby resolving some of the criticisms mentioned earlier. In addition, more attention was given to fundamental rights more generally in the context of the requirements for providers of high-risk AI systems. Regarding classification, the Council proposed that AI systems that are unlikely to cause serious fundamental rights violations or other significant risks should not be classified as high risk. Regarding the requirements for providers of high-risk systems, the Council text included a requirement for the 'identification and analysis of the known and foreseeable risks most likely to occur to health, safety, and fundamental rights in view of the intended purpose of the high-risk AI system'.[104]

Following lengthy discussions on the more than 3,000 amendments tabled in response to the draft report by the IMCO-LIBE committees, the EP plenary session adopted its negotiating position (Compromise Text) on 14 June 2023.[105] However,

[100] IMCO-LIBE Draft Report, 160.

[101] For instance, amendments: 136 on human oversight requirements; 220 containing a requirement for users to enter data in the EU database; 227 on reporting duties for serious incidents or malfunctioning of high-risk AI systems. IMCO-LIBE Draft Report, Ibid.

[102] Council of the European Union, 'Proposal for a Regulation of the European Parliament and of the Council laying down harmonised rules on artificial intelligence (Artificial Intelligence Act) and amending certain Union legislative acts – general approach'(2022), https://data.consilium.europa.eu/doc/document/ST-14954-2022-INIT/en/pdf, 5 (hereafter 'Council general approach').

[103] G. Malgieri and V. Tiani, 'How the EU Council is rewriting the AI Act' (2021), https://brusselsprivacyhub.eu/publications/how-the-eu-council-is-rewriting-the-ai-act.

[104] Article 9 2. a) Council general approach.

[105] European Parliament, Amendments on the proposal for a regulation of the European Parliament and of the Council on laying down harmonised rules on artificial intelligence (Artificial Intelligence Act) and amending certain Union legislative acts (2023), www.europarl.europa.eu/doceo/document/TA-9-2023-0236_EN.pdf (hereafter 'EP compromise text').

despite numerous amendments being tabled with the potential to directly impact children and their rights, none of these child-specific amendments were included in the Compromise Text of the EP. Consequently, these amendments were not part of the trilogue negotiations.[106] In relation to this, children's rights organisations raised concerns about the level of consideration given to children's rights during the legislative process.[107] Nevertheless, the Compromise Text does include several notable amendments that could impact children and their rights. First, it included a ban on AI systems inferring the emotions of a natural person in education institutions, which has implications for school children.[108] Second, the EP proposed to include as part of the risk management system for providers of high-risk AI systems a requirement to identify, estimate, and evaluate known and reasonably foreseeable risks to fundamental rights (including children's rights). Third, the introduction of general principles applicable to all AI systems under the proposed Article 4a is noteworthy. This article requires operators of AI systems to make their best efforts to develop and use these systems in accordance with these principles. The principles encompassed various aspects, including the preservation of human agency and oversight, technical robustness and safety, privacy and data governance, transparency, diversity, non-discrimination and fairness, as well as social and environmental well-being. To foster the voluntary application of these principles to AI systems other than high-risk AI systems, the EP proposed the establishment of codes of conduct. These codes should particularly 'assess to what extent their AI systems may affect vulnerable persons or groups of persons, including *children*, the elderly, migrants and persons with disabilities or whether measures could be put in place in order to increase accessibility, or otherwise support such persons or groups of persons'.[109] Finally, a new Article 4d outlined requirements for the EU, its Member States, as well as providers and deployers of AI systems to promote measures fostering AI literacy, which could be beneficial for children. This included teaching basic notions and skills regarding AI systems and their functioning.

106 L. Bertuzzi, 'AI regulation filled with thousands of amendments in the European Parliament', 2 June 2022, www.euractiv.com/section/digital/news/ai-regulation-filled-with-thousands-of-amendments-in-the-european-parliament/. E.g., amendments 862 and 1454, which categorised AI systems that are likely to interact with children as high-risk, and linked to these, amendments 2710 and 2711, which proposed applying the precautionary principle in this context. There were also amendments that clarified that a 'child' means any person below the age of eighteen years (amendments 1114 and 1119).

107 Children's rights organisations have called for the inclusion of children as a specific group that needs protection under the ban on AI systems exploiting vulnerabilities, as per the EC proposal. 5Rights Foundation, 'AI Act trilogues: the EU's last chance to protect children' (2023), https://5rightsfoundation.com/uploads/Coalition-statement_Childrens-rights-in-AI-Act-Trilogues.pdf?_cchid=f599ca7d73d2d3bf41d7204ecc95dabd.

108 EP compromise text, Article 5, para. 1, point d c.

109 Ibid., Article 69, para. 2; emphasis added.

18.4.5 *The Final Text of the AIA*

The final text of the AIA was adopted by the EP on 13 March 2024 and endorsed by the Council on 21 May 2024.[110] The specific references to children and their rights have remained, with noteworthy changes.

First, with regard to the prohibited practices, Article 5b now states:

> the placing on the market, the putting into service or the use of an AI system that exploits any of the vulnerabilities of a natural person or a specific group of persons due to their age, disability or a specific social or economic situation, *with the objective, or the effect*, of materially distorting the behaviour of that person or a person belonging to that group in a manner that causes or is reasonably likely to cause that person or another person *significant harm* [emphasis added].

Thus, the final text does not contain a malicious intent requirement (i.e., 'with the objective, or the effect'), and adopts the broader concept of vulnerability ('disability, 'social or economic situation'). Furthermore, Article 5 now covers 'significant harm' to 'that person or another person', extending beyond physical or psychological harm (infra).[111] However, a lack of clarity regarding the actual scope of the prohibition remains. A crucial point that needs clarification concerns the threshold for significant harm. For instance, would a violation of children's rights meet this threshold? According to Recital 29, this may include harms accumulated over time. In addition, this provision is rather broad regarding who suffers harm and seems to cover third-party effects as well.[112]

Second, the references to children's rights in the context of the classification (AIA Recital 48) and requirements for (AIA Article 9.9) high-risk AI systems have also remained, with some subtle changes. At first glance, these references give the impression that the EU considers that children's rights and their best interests play an important role in the regulation of high-risk AI systems. Article 9.9 of the AIA, for example, states that 'when implementing the risk management system as provided for in paragraphs 1 to 7, providers shall *give consideration* to whether in view of its intended purpose the high-risk AI system is likely to have an adverse *impact on persons*

[110] Regulation (EU) 2024/1689 of the European Parliament and of the Council of 13 June 2024 laying down harmonised rules on artificial intelligence and amending Regulations (EC) No 300/2008, (EU) No 167/2013, (EU) No 168/2013, (EU) 2018/858, (EU) 2018/1139 and (EU) 2019/2144 and Directives 2014/90/EU, (EU) 2016/797 and (EU) 2020/1828 (Artificial Intelligence Act).

[111] In relation to this, Recital 29 of the AIA specifies that Article 5 is complementary to the provisions contained in the Unfair Commercial Practices Directive (Directive 2005/29/EC, hereafter UCPD), 'in particular unfair commercial practices leading to economic or financial harms to consumers are prohibited under all circumstances, irrespective of whether they are put in place through AI systems or otherwise'. The AIA and UCPD will apply alongside each other, and thus the AIA will only have an independent function for practices that are not already covered by the UCPD; C. Bush and A. Fletcher, 'Harmful online choice architecture' (2024), Centre on Regulation in Europe, https://cerre.eu/wp-content/uploads/2024/05/CERRE-Final-Report_Harmful-Online-Choice-Architecture.pdf.

[112] By analogy, see Bush and Fletcher, 'Harmful online choice architecture'.

under the age of 18' (emphasis added). However, as mentioned, this does not mean that AI systems that are likely to be accessed by children or impact them are considered high risk by default. Notably, the word *specific* was omitted from the final text, arguably reducing the emphasis compared with the EC proposal. The AIA classifies all systems used within a list of predetermined domains as high risk.[113] A distinction is made between two sub-categories of AI systems: (a) AI systems that are products or safety components of products that are already covered by EU health and safety legislation, and (b) standalone AI systems used in specific (fixed) areas.[114] Regarding the latter, one of the areas included that is particularly relevant for children is educational and vocational training – both in terms of determining access to such training and evaluating individuals.[115] This could include, for example, AI-enabled online tracking, monitoring, and filtering software on educational devices, which could have a chilling effect on children's right to freedom of expression or violate their right to privacy. This is reminiscent of the Ofqual algorithm debacle in the United Kingdom, where an automated decision-making system was employed to calculate exam grades, leading to discriminatory outcomes for children from lower socio-economic backgrounds.[116] Such systems can clearly violate children's right to education, as well as their right not to be discriminated against and perpetuate historical patterns.[117] Another area where AI systems are likely to present high risks to children (as well as adults) is in the allocation of public assistance benefits and services.[118] Recital 37 specifies that, owing to the vulnerable position of persons depending on such benefits and services, AI systems used in this context may have a significant impact on the livelihoods and rights of the persons concerned – including their right to non-discrimination and human dignity. A concrete example is the so-called benefits scandal in the Netherlands, where an AI-enabled decision-making system withdrew and reclaimed child benefits from thousands of families, disproportionally affecting children from ethnic minority groups.[119] Aside from these two areas, Annex III lists biometric identification, categorisation, and emotion recognition; management and operation of critical infrastructure; employment; law enforcement; migration; and administration of justice and democratic processes as high-risk areas. The EC can also add sub-areas within these areas (subject to a veto from the EP or Council).[120] However, other domains where AI systems and automated decision-making are employed would not be considered high risk, even if they are likely to

[113] Townsend, 'Decoding the proposed European Union Artificial Intelligence Act'.

[114] Fixed in AIA, Annex III.

[115] AIA, Recital 56.

[116] A. Kelly, 'A tale of two algorithms: the appeal and repeal of calculated grades systems in England and Ireland in 2020' (2021) 47 *British Educational Research Journal* 3, 725–41.

[117] AIA, Recital 56.

[118] AIA, Recital 58.

[119] Amnesty International, 'Xenophobic machines – discrimination through unregulated use of algorithms in the Dutch childcare benefits scandal' (2021), www.amnesty.nl/content/uploads/2021/10/20211014_FINAL_Xenophobic-Machines.pdf?x42580.

[120] AIA, Articles 7 and 97.

be accessed by children or impact them or their fundamental rights. This leaves out a whole range of AI systems that could affect the daily lives of children, such as online profiling and personalisation algorithms, connected toys, and content recommender systems on social media.[121]

The final text includes only voluntary commitments for low-risk AI systems. Given the rapid development of AI technologies and how difficult it is at this stage to imagine the future impact on children and their rights, this feels like a very light regulatory regime. A more cautious approach – based on the precautionary principle – could have been to include a binding set of general principles (supra), including the best interests of the child (similar to recital 89 of the DSA), fairness, and non-discrimination for all AI systems in the AIA.[122]

With regard to the transparency requirements for certain AI systems, the final text includes a specific reference to children – or at least to 'vulnerable groups due to their age'. Article 50 of AIA states that AI systems should be designed so that individuals are informed that they are interacting with an AI system, unless it is contextually obvious. In relation to this, Recital 132 of AIA specifies that when implementing this obligation, the characteristics of vulnerable groups owing to their age or disability should be taken into account, if these systems are intended to interact with those groups as well.[123]

Finally, the final text also grants rights to individuals (including children) affected by the output of AI systems, including the right to lodge a complaint before a supervisory authority,[124] and the right to an explanation in certain instances.[125] However, children are not specifically mentioned in these provisions.

18.5 DISCUSSION: A CHILDREN'S RIGHTS PERSPECTIVE ON THE DSA AND THE AIA

It can only be welcomed that both instruments refer to children and their rights. The question is, however, whether the proposals have the potential to ensure that children's rights will be effectively implemented. For the DSA, the answer is quite clear: it holds great promise for advancing children's rights, depending on the actual implementation and enforcement. Where references to children in the proposal were few and far between in the Commission proposal, the final text appears to take

[121] BEUC, 'Regulating AI to protect the consumer: position paper on the AI Act' (2021), www.beuc.eu/publications/beuc-x-2021-088_regulating_ai_to_protect_the_consumer.pdf, 17.

[122] Such an approach is also advocated by BEUC, not in a child-specific manner but more generally in the context of consumer protection: ibid.

[123] Article 50 of AIA also mentions codes of practices to facilitate the effective implementation of these transparency requirements.

[124] Article 85 of AIA grants a right to lodge a complaint with a market surveillance authority to 'any natural or legal person having grounds to consider that the AI Act has been infringed'.

[125] AIA, Article 86.

children and their interests (finally) seriously by imposing obligations on VLOPs that could make a difference. Moreover, in addition to the provisions that directly refer to children that have been discussed earlier, there are of course other provisions that will indirectly have an impact on children as a subgroup of individuals in general. Examples are the provisions regarding recommender systems (Articles 27 and 38) and the design of online interfaces (Article 25). While the text of the law provides indeed many opportunities, the actual realisation of children's rights will depend on the implementation and enforcement. The DSA does create enforcement mechanisms and oversight bodies that are responsible for ensuring this.[126] In 2024, the Commission already launched formal proceedings against, among others, TikTok and Meta (Facebook and Instagram) related to the protection of minors.[127] The Commission expresses concerns about, for example, age verification, default privacy settings, and behavioural addictions that may have an impact on the rights of the child. It thus seems that the enforcement of the DSA will move forward faster than, for instance, the enforcement of the GDPR.

For the AIA, it remains to be seen whether it will succeed in guaranteeing children's rights. Children's rights are mentioned in the Preamble and provisions of the Act – which is laudable – and it clearly acknowledges the potential negative impact of AI systems on their rights. However, whether these acknowledgements are sufficient for protecting and promoting children's rights in an increasingly AI-driven world is questionable. First, the prohibition of AI systems that exploit vulnerable groups leaves questions about the threshold for significant harm and its interplay with other instruments. Second, while the final text mentions that the impact of AI systems on children's rights is considered 'of particular relevance' when classifying them as high risk,[128] and in the implementation of the risk management system. As a final consideration, the AIA does not explicitly introduce a general obligation for 'specific protection' for children when AI systems and automated decision-making infiltrate their lives – in contrast to, for instance, the GDPR when it comes to the processing of their personal data (recital 38) or – arguably – the DSA requirement to ensure a high level of privacy, safety, and security for minors. By introducing an obligation to ensure the best interests of children for all AI systems that are likely to impact children, this could have led to more effective rights implementation in practice.

[126] See AIA, chapter 4 on implementation, cooperation, penalties, and enforcement.

[127] European Commission, 'Commission opens formal proceedings against TikTok under the Digital Services Act', 19 February 2024, https://digital-strategy.ec.europa.eu/en/news/commission-opens-formal-proceedings-against-tiktok-under-digital-services-act; European Commission, 'Commission opens formal proceedings against Facebook and Instagram under the Digital Services Act', 30 April 2024, https://ec.europa.eu/commission/presscorner/detail/en/ip_24_2373; European Commission, 'Commission opens formal proceedings against Meta under the Digital Services Act related to the protection of minors on Facebook and Instagram', 16 May 2024, https://ec.europa.eu/commission/presscorner/detail/en/ip_24_2664.

[128] AIA, Recital 48.

From a children's rights perspective, a few questions remain. First, the adoption of any legislative initiative that affects children should be accompanied by a thorough Children's Rights Impact Assessment (CRIA).[129] Although both proposals have been preceded by an impact assessment, it can hardly be said that they would qualify as CRIAs. A true CRIA would assess the impact of the proposed measures on the full range of children's rights and would balance conflicting rights (both where children's rights would conflict with each other and where children's rights would conflict with the rights of adults, businesses, or other actors). A CRIA is also the way to evaluate whether a proposed measure takes the best interests of the child as a primary consideration. The best interests of the child is a key children's rights principle, which is laid down in Article 3 of UNCRC and Article 24 of CFEU. This principle should guide all actions and decisions that concern children. This is also very closely linked to another children's rights principle, laid down in Article 12 of UNCRC, which is the right to be heard. Children's views must be taken on board and must be given due weight. Although in the preparatory steps leading towards the adoption of the proposals, children's rights organisations have had opportunities to share their views and suggestions, this does not replace the actual engagement of children in that process. This is – again – a lesson to be learnt. Moreover, CRIAs might also be helpful for the addressees of the legislative acts, when assessing risks that their services or systems pose for children and their rights.

Second, experiences with other legislative instruments, such as the GDPR, have shown that the vague wording in the legislative instruments leaves addressees often at a loss for how to implement obligations (notwithstanding their often-well-meant intentions). Hence, fast and concrete guidance,[130] for instance, by means of Commission Guidelines (Article 28.4 DSA), codes of conduct or guidelines by the newly established European Board for Digital Services or the European Artificial Intelligence Board will be essential. In addition, whereas enforcement by Data Protection Authorities of the GDPR has been argued to be slow, lacking, or not prioritising children, it will be up to Member States to ensure that the DSA and AIA oversight bodies are well resourced, and it will be up to the Commission to take up its supervisory role when it comes to the VLOPs and VLOSEs.

Finally, both instruments adopt an approach that predominantly focuses on safety and risks. There are few to no obligations for platforms to take measures to support

[129] UN Committee on the Rights of the Child, General Comment no. 14 on the right of the child to have his or her best interests taken as a primary consideration (Art. 3, para. 1), CRC/C/GC/14 (2013) www2.ohchr.org/english/bodies/crc/docs/gc/crc_c_gc_14_eng.pdf; UN Committee on the Rights of the Child, General Comment no. 25, para. 24; Mukherjee, Pothong and Livingstone, 'Child rights impact assessment'.

[130] The European Data Protection Board announced that it was going to adopt guidelines on children's data in its 2019/2020 Work Programme. Yet up until June 2025 these guidelines have not been published.

children, to enable them to use the services to fully benefit them, and explore the opportunities that such services offer. Although this is for instance something that the BIK+ Strategy has more attention for, it is perhaps a missed opportunity to put into practice some of the more positive measures the General Comment no. 25 requires States to take.

18.6 CONCLUSION

The EU legislator is determined to minimise risks that are posed by platforms and AI-based systems by imposing various obligations on a range of actors. While many of those obligations are not child-specific, some of them are. Children who grow up today in a world where platforms and AI-based systems are pervasive might be particularly vulnerable to certain risks. The EU legislator is aware of this and pays increasing attention to the risks to children and their rights, although this is not necessarily the case to the same extent across different legislative initiatives. While the DSA emphasises the protection of minors quite heavily, the AIA is less outspoken. Both during the legislative process, and in the stages of implementation and enforcement, the rights and principles contained in the UNCRC should be duly taken into account in order to effectively realise children's rights in the digital environment.

19

Right to Education in Regional or Minority Languages

Invasions, COVID-19 Pandemic, and Other Developments

Vesna Crnić-Grotić

19.1 INTRODUCTION

How can we define linguistic rights and their role in human rights protection? According to the United Nations (UN) Special Rapporteur on minority issues: 'Linguistic rights can be described as a series of obligations on state authorities to either use certain languages in a number of contexts, or not interfere with the linguistic choices and expressions of private parties.'[1] Linguistic rights include the right to use one's language in private and public and not to be discriminated against for it. In respect to education, it is usually the competence of the state to organise this and set up rules for public but also for private schools. The school curricula prescribe the basic values and goals pursued by education and also the language of instruction. Could it be claimed that states have a duty to provide education in the minority languages used by portions of its population?[2]

The protection of the linguistic rights of minorities, including in education varies. We shall compare this protection at the level of the UN and the Council of Europe and look into some more recent developments in international law including during the COVID-19 pandemic.

19.2 UN: A HOUSE MUCH DIVIDED

Linguistic rights are endorsed in a number of international human rights treaties and standards, especially regarding the prohibition of discrimination, the right to freedom of expression, the right to a private life, the right to education, and the right of linguistic minorities to use their own language with others in their group. These

[1] UN Special Rapporteur on minority issues, *Language Rights of Linguistic Minorities – A Practical Guide for Implementation* (Geneva: OHCHR, 2017), p. 5.

[2] De Varennes claims that at least with respect to private schools 'there is widespread recognition of this right in legal and political documents, despite some differences in the way it is formulated'. F. de Varennes, *The Right to Education and Minority Language* (2004), www.researchgate.net/publication/242595391_The_right_to_education_and_minority_language.

treaties and standards are both universal and regional. The most significant contributor at the universal level is, of course, the UN with its many declarations and opinions. In that respect, the most important is the Declaration on the Rights of Persons Belonging to National or Ethnic, Religious or Linguistic Minorities, adopted in 1993.[3] Even though the General Assembly's declarations are not legally binding, they still have a certain legal authority. According to Article 1 of the Declaration, 'States shall protect the existence and the national or ethnic, cultural, religious and linguistic identity of minorities within their respective territories.' Consequently, linguistic identity is recognised to be an integral part of the identity of minorities and must be protected. Nevertheless, in Article 4 that speaks about education, provisions for learning and instruction in the mother tongue (para. 3) 'are qualified and ambiguous' when it comes to the teaching of or in the minority language.[4]

However, perhaps not so surprisingly, today there is still no binding treaty at the UN level on the rights of minorities nor is there a universally accepted definition of minorities other than the famous Article 27 of the 1966 International Covenant on Civil and Political Rights (ICCPR).[5] Article 27 refers to the duty of state parties 'not to deny' minorities some fundamental (collective and individual) human rights. The monitoring body under this treaty – the Human Rights Committee – provided an interpretation of this article as requiring also positive measures 'to ensure that the existence and the exercise of this right are protected against their denial or violation. Positive measures of protection are, therefore, required....'[6] Positive measures by state parties may also be necessary to protect the identity of a minority and the rights of its members to enjoy and develop their culture and language.[7] The ICCPR does not deal with the right to education but it left this to the complementary International Covenant on Economic, Social and Cultural Rights, also adopted by the UN General Assembly in 1966.[8] This treaty recognises the right of everyone to education. Its Article 13 paragraph 4 reserves 'the liberty of individuals and bodies to

3 Declaration on the Rights of Persons Belonging to National or Ethnic, Religious or Linguistic Minorities, GA res. 47/135, annex, 47 U.N. GAOR Supp. (No. 49), 210.

4 P. Thornberry and M.A.M. Estébanez, *Minority Rights in Europe* (Strasbourg: Council of Europe, 2004), p. 15. The relevant provision reads: 'States should take appropriate measures so that, wherever possible, persons belonging to minorities may have adequate opportunities to learn their mother tongue or to have instruction in their mother tongue.'

5 International Covenant on Civil and Political Rights, 16 December 1966, 999 UNTS 171. De Varennes and Kuzborska observe: 'Oddly, UN documents, with the exception of the recent 2017 UN Special Rapporteur on Minority Issues' Language Rights of Linguistic Minorities: A Practical Guide for Implementation, had never fully explored or explicated this rather fundamental dimension of language rights.' F. de Varennes and E. Kuzborska, 'Minority language rights and standards: definitions and applications at the supranational level', in G. Hogan-Brun and B. O'Rourke (eds.), *The Palgrave Handbook of Minority Languages and Communities* (London: Palgrave Macmillan, 2019), pp. 21–72, at 40.

6 Human Rights Committee, General comment No. 23(50) (art. 27), CCPR/C/21/Rev.1/Add.5.

7 Ibid.

8 International Covenant on Economic, Social and Cultural Rights, 16 December 1966, 993 UNTS 3.

establish and direct educational institutions', which may be construed (!) as including the right of minorities to run their own schools and teach (in) their own language, especially when read in conjunction with Article 2.2 (non-discrimination clause).[9] State parties are obliged to establish 'minimum educational standards' to which all educational institutions established in accordance with Article 13 (3) and (4) are required to conform. UNESCO – a specialised UN agency for education, science and culture – is more specific about the right to have education in one's own language. The Convention against Discrimination in Education provides for the 'rights of members of national minorities' in Article 5.1.c., including the use or the teaching of their own language.[10] This right, nevertheless, depends on some requirements:

> (i) That this right is not exercised in a manner which prevents the members of these minorities from understanding the culture and language of the community as a whole and from participating in its activities, or which prejudices national sovereignty; (ii) That the standard of education is not lower than the general standard laid down or approved by the competent authorities; and (iii) That attendance at such schools is optional.[11]

In this context, it is also necessary to look into the UN Convention on the Rights of the Child (CRC), adopted in 1998 and in force in an extraordinary number of 196 states.[12] Article 30 of the CRC, following Articles 28 and 29 on education, follows the formulation of Article 27 of the ICCPR so children belonging to a minority 'shall not be denied the right, in community with other members of his or her group, to enjoy his or her own culture, to profess and practise his or her own religion, or to use his or her own language'.

Finally, among other relevant UN instruments, we have to mention the International Convention on the Elimination of All Forms of Racial Discrimination, 1966 (CERD).[13] This refers to 'the right to education and training' as among the rights to be protected against discrimination (Art. 5 (e)v).[14]

9 However, there is no specific mentioning of the word 'language' even in the commentary made by the Committee for ESCR. Committee on Economic, Social and Cultural Rights, General comment No. 13: The right to education (Art. 13). (Report No. E/C.12/1999/10). The opposite claim is made in: Z. Bayat, R, Kircher, and H. Van de Velde, 'Minority language rights to education in international, regional, and domestic regulations and practices: the case of Frisian in the Netherlands' (2023) 24 *Current Issues in Language Planning* 1, 81–101.

10 UNESCO Convention against Discrimination in Education, 14 December 1960, 429 UNTS 93.

11 See also comparison in UNESCO, *UNESCO Convention against Discrimination in Education (1960) and Articles 13 and 14 (Right to Education) of the International Covenant on Economic, Social and Cultural Rights: A Comparative Analysis* (Paris: UNESCO, 2006).

12 UN Convention on the Rights of the Child, 20 November 1989, G.A. res. 44/25, annex, 44 U.N. GAOR Supp. (No. 49). Only the US has not ratified this convention. https://indicators.ohchr.org/.

13 International Convention on the Elimination of All Forms of Racial Discrimination, 7 March 1996, 660 UNTS 195.

14 P. Thornberry, 'Article 12. Education', in M. Weller (ed.), *The Rights of Minorities in Europe: A Commentary on the European Framework Convention for the Protection of National Minorities* (Oxford: Oxford University Press, 2005), pp. 397–412.

CERD provides for the jurisdiction of the International Court of Justice (ICJ), and it was used by Ukraine to bring a case against the Russian Federation concerning, among other issues, education in Ukrainian and Crimean Tatar languages on the occupied territory of Crimea.[15] Ukraine alleged that the measures taken by the Russian Federation in education since the invasion in 2014 led to a dramatic decline in accessibility and quality of education in these two languages. The Court started from the premise that:

> even if Article 5 (e) (v) of CERD does not include a general right to school education in a minority language, the prohibition of racial discrimination under Article 2, paragraph 1 (a), of CERD and the right to education under Article 5 (e) (v), may, under certain circumstances, set limits to changes in the provision of school education in the language of a national or ethnic minority. (para. 354)

The Court then considered that:

> Language is often an essential social bond among the members of an ethnic group. Restrictive measures taken by a State party with respect to the use of language may therefore in certain situations manifest a 'distinction, exclusion, restriction or preference based on … descent, or national or ethnic origin' within the meaning of Article 1, paragraph 1, of CERD. (para. 355)

Recognising the right of every state to decide on the primary language of instruction in its public schools, the Court warns against a discriminatory adverse effect of such decisions so 'as to make it unreasonably difficult for members of a national or ethnic group to ensure that their children, as part of their general right to education, do not suffer from unduly burdensome discontinuities in their primary language of instruction' (para. 357). Finally, the Court established that there was an 80 per cent decline in the accessibility of education in Ukrainian during the first year after 2014 and a further decline of 50 per cent by the following year.[16] The Russian Federation was not able to provide convincing reasons for such a decline, so the Court concluded that it violated the relevant articles of CERD.[17]

In conclusion, it seems that there has been certain progress at the level of the UN in recognising education for members of linguistic minorities. However, the majority of the analysed instruments either limits its scope to the non-discrimination obligation or imposes certain limitations and requirements on such education.[18]

[15] Application of the International Convention for the Suppression of the Financing of Terrorism and of the International Convention on the Elimination of All Forms of Racial Discrimination (Ukraine v. Russian Federation), ICJ Judgment of 31 January 2024, available at: www.icj-cij.org/sites/default/files/case-related/166/166-20240131-jud-01-00-en.pdf.

[16] The claim regarding education in the Crimean Tatar language concerned the quality of such education. The Court concluded that such a claim is not covered by CERD.

[17] The provision of Ukrainian language education was still available, so the ICJ rejected the claims that the Russian Federation violated the Court's Order of 19 April 2017 requiring the Russian Federation to ensure that education in the Ukrainian language remains 'available'.

[18] De Varennes and Kuzborska observe: 'The prevailing consensus would seem to indicate that while currently human rights do not require the funding of private minority schools unless there is a

19.3 COUNCIL OF EUROPE: GENERAL HUMAN RIGHTS VERSUS SPECIAL TREATIES

The protection of national minorities and their languages is among the core activities of the Council of Europe as part of the protection and promotion of human rights. Today, the Council of Europe has forty-six Member States after expelling the Russian Federation in March 2022 owing to its aggression against and invasion of Ukraine.[19] All forty-six Member States are bound by the European Convention for the Protection of Human Rights and Fundamental Freedoms, the Council's flagship treaty, and the jurisdiction of the European Court of Human Rights (ECtHR).[20] However, the Convention has a somewhat limited scope with regard to minorities' rights and freedoms.[21]

Post-Second World War Europe has been a champion in many aspects of the protection and promotion of human rights. Case in point, the European Convention for the Protection of Human Rights and Fundamental Freedoms (ECHR) was already adopted in 1950, only two years after the adoption of the Universal Declaration on Human Rights by the General Assembly of the UN.[22] Nevertheless, the ECHR and consequently the case law of the ECtHR has limited application in the field of the protection of minority rights and education in minority languages.

The right to education is protected by Article 2 of Protocol No. 1 to the Convention. In 1968, the ECtHR ruled in the *Belgian Linguistic* case that states have no obligation to ensure education in one's own language.[23] The right to education implied the right to be educated in the national language (in public schools).

This firm position was seemingly challenged in the interstate case between Cyprus and Turkey before the Grand Chamber in 2001.[24] The case concerned Greek-language

situation which might be discriminatory, authorities must not prevent the establishment of such schools' (De Varennes and Kuzborska, 'Minority language rights and standards', p. 44). Similarly, M. Paz, 'The failed promise of language rights: a critique of the international language rights regime' (2013) 54 *Harvard International Law Journal* 1, 157–218.

19 Committee of Ministers Resolution CM/Res(2022)2 on the cessation of the membership of the Russian Federation to the Council of Europe (Adopted by the Committee of Ministers on 16 March 2022 at the 1,428th meeting of the Ministers' Deputies), available at: https://search.coe.int/cm/Pages/result_details.aspx?ObjectID=0900001680a5da51.

20 Complete information available at the Court's web page, www.echr.coe.int/.

21 Judgments of the European Court of Human Rights, Selection of judgments of the European Court of Human Rights relevant for the protection of national minorities, www.coe.int/en/web/minorities/judgments-of-the-european-court-of-human-rights.

22 Universal Declaration of Human Rights, 10 December 1948, GA res. 217 A.

23 Case *'Relating to certain aspects of the laws on the use of languages in education in Belgium' v. Belgium*, Application no 1474/62 et al., Judgment of 23 July 1968. The case concerned a specific linguistic situation in Belgium where three languages enjoy official status. According to the national legislation, the language of education shall be Dutch in the Dutch-speaking region, French in the French-speaking region, and German in the German-speaking region. However, in some Dutch-speaking districts there were schools open to French speaking children, depending solely on their residence. The Court concluded, with a very small margin of eight to seven judges, that such practice was discriminatory.

24 *Cyprus v. Turkey* [GC], Application no. 25781/94, Judgment of 10 May 2001.

education in the occupied part of Cyprus where the Turkish Republic of Northern Cyprus (TRNC) was in power. Primary education was available but if children wanted 'to pursue a secondary education through the medium of the Greek language' they were obliged to transfer to schools in the south or to continue education at a Turkish or English-language school in the north. The Court admits that:

> In the strict sense, accordingly, there is no denial of the right to education, which is the primary obligation devolving on a Contracting Party under the first sentence of Article 2 of Protocol No. 1. Moreover, this provision does not specify the language in which education must be conducted in order that the right to education be respected (see the above-mentioned Belgian linguistic judgment, pp. 30–31, § 3).[25]

However, and here comes the twist:

> the option available to Greek-Cypriot parents to continue their children's education in the north is unrealistic in view of the fact that the children in question have already received their primary education in a Greek-Cypriot school there. The authorities must no doubt be aware that it is the wish of Greek-Cypriot parents that the schooling of their children be completed through the medium of the Greek language… [T]he failure of the "TRNC" authorities to make continuing provision for it at the secondary-school level must be considered in effect to be a denial of the substance of the right at issue. (para. 278)

Finally, the Court concluded 'that there has been a violation of Article 2 of Protocol No. 1 in respect of Greek Cypriots living in Northern Cyprus in so far as no appropriate secondary-school facilities were available to them' (para. 280).

More recently, the ECtHR adopted two judgments concerning schools in a minority language (Russian) in Latvia. Both cases concerned legislative amendments from 2018 increasing the proportion of subjects to be taught in the state language (Latvian) in public and private schools, so the use of Russian as the language of instruction was consequently being reduced.

The first case, *Valiullina and Others v. Latvia*,[26] concerned the use of Latvian in public schools. The Court returned to its conclusions reached in the *Belgian Linguistic* case that Article 2 of Protocol No. 1 does not include the linguistic preferences of the parents and explained that this judgment, as well as the one in the *Cyprus v. Turkey* case, and some others, dealt with education in (one of) the national language(s).[27] Accordingly, 'the right enshrined by Article 2 of Protocol No. 1 does not include the right to access education in a particular language; it guarantees the

[25] Ibid., para. 277. Cyprus has two national languages in the government-controlled area – Greek and Turkish.

[26] *Valiullina and Others v. Latvia*, Applications nos. 56928/19, 7306/20 and 11937/20, Judgment of 14 September 2023.

[27] E.g., in *Catan and Others v. the Republic of Moldova and Russia* [GC], Application no. 43370/04, 8252/05 and 18454/06, Judgment of 19 October 2012.

right to education in one of the national languages or, in other words, official languages of the country concerned' (para. 135).

In *Džibuti and Others v. Latvia*,[28] the Court examined the complaints by Russian speakers concerning the effect of the same 2018 legislation reform with respect to private schools. Prior to the reform, education in the state language had been mandatory only in public schools, but the authorities claimed that private schools form part of the state education system and should therefore respect the need to have a certain proportion of classes in the national language.[29] The Court would not accept that Article 2 of Protocol No. 1 covers education in minority languages and concluded that the claim must be rejected as incompatible *ratione materiae* with the provisions of the Convention.

In both Latvian cases, the Court also dismissed allegations of discrimination and concluded that there was no violation of Article 14 taken together with Article 2 of Protocol No. 1.[30] Furthermore, the applicants tried to rely on the Framework Convention for the Protection of National Minorities (FCNM).[31] This convention refers to education in several articles, but the Court 'emphasized that the principle of instruction in one's mother tongue, which the applicants referred to, is far from being the rule among the Member States of the Council of Europe'.[32] Ironically, this conclusion was extended with praise for Latvia for ensuring the protection of minority rights in their Constitution.[33]

[28] *Džibuti and Others v. Latvia*, Application no. 225/20 and 2 others, Judgment of 16 November 2023. At the time, the number of private schools in Latvia was insignificant and they mainly operated in Latvian (out of fifty-eight private schools active in 2018/2019, only eleven were teaching in Russian and eighteen were teaching only in Latvian). S. Ganty and D. V. Kochenov, 'Hijacking human rights to enable punishment by association: Valiullina, Džibuti and outlawing minority schooling in Latvia', 23 November 2023, Strasbourg Observers, https://strasbourgobservers.com/2023/11/23/hijacking-human-rights-to-enable-punishment-by-association-valiullina-dzibuti-and-outlawing-minority-schooling-in-latvia/.

[29] The authorities did not dispute the right to start and run a private school, but submitted that such an educational establishment had to comply with the requirements set by domestic law, which, in the present case, also included requirements as to how much the state language should be used in education (paragraph 86). According to the reform, Latvian should be used for 50 per cent in lower grades up to 100 per cent in final grades, with the exception of subjects related to the minority language, culture and identity, and, obviously, foreign languages.

[30] Article 14 of the Convention connects allegations of discrimination with other articles of the Convention and relevant protocols. It requires that all of the rights and freedoms set out in the Convention must be protected and applied without discrimination. Discrimination occurs when a person is treated less favourably than another person in a similar situation and this treatment cannot be objectively and reasonably justified.

[31] Latvia is a state party since 2005.

[32] The applicants further relied on Article 13 of the FCNM that speaks of the right 'to set up and to manage their own private educational and training establishments'. However, the Court emphasised that 'the Framework Convention does not provide for an obligation to finance private schools (see Article 13 § 2 of the Framework Convention)' and concluded 'that no positive obligation for the States to subsidise private schools arises from the Convention or its Protocols' (*Džibuti v. Latvia*, para. 145).

[33] The concept of 'constitutional identity' was already accepted in the Grand Chamber judgment in the case of *Savickis and Others v. Latvia* [GC], Application no. 49270/11, Judgment of 9 June 2022.

Almost simultaneously, in October 2023, the Advisory Committee (AC) of the FCNM adopted their fourth monitoring report on Latvia. The AC adopted a very stark warning about the second education reform legislation following the one from 2018 adopted in 2022 that:

> will result in the phasing out of teaching in minority languages in most public and private preschools, schools and universities by 2025. [T]he termination of teaching in Belarusian and Russian will affect about 20% of all children of schooling age. With plans also underway to discontinue the teaching of Russian as a foreign language, the offer will be reduced to extracurricular courses of language and culture. Should all these measures be implemented as planned, Latvia's system of minority education will no longer comply with the Framework Convention's provisions regarding equal access to education, the right to set up private minority educational establishments, and the right to being taught the minority language or for receiving instruction in this language.[34]

With these two judgments, the Court further confirmed that the ECHR has very limited application concerning minority rights and that their protection is better ensured through the treaties especially dedicated to the protection of minorities, namely, the FCNM and the European Charter for Regional or Minority Languages (ECRML).[35] However, these treaties apply only to state parties. So far, the Court has refused to apply some of their principles as customary law or general principles of international law extending their application beyond state parties.[36]

The ECRML has not been invoked in these two cases, since Latvia is not a state party to it. In general, the ECRML is hardly ever discussed by the Court. In one of the more recent cases, the Court simply established that the ECRML expressly recognises that the protection and encouragement of minority languages should not be to the detriment of official languages and the need to learn them.[37]

34 Advisory Committee on the FCNM, 'Fourth opinion on Latvia', 9 October 2023, ACFC/OP/IV(2023)1, https://rm.coe.int/4th-op-latvia-en/1680ae98f6.

35 Council of Europe, National Minorities, 'The Framework Convention for the Protection of National Minorities', www.coe.int/en/web/minorities/home.; Council of Europe, 'European Charter for Regional or Minority Languages', www.coe.int/en/web/european-charter-regional-or-minority-languages/home.

36 In the *Chapman* case, the Court observed

> that there may be said to be an emerging international consensus amongst the Contracting States of the Council of Europe recognising the special needs of minorities and an obligation to protect their security, identity and lifestyle [...] However, the Court is not persuaded that the consensus is sufficiently concrete for it to derive any guidance as to the conduct or standards which Contracting States consider desirable in any particular situation. The Framework Convention, for example, sets out general principles and goals but the signatory States were unable to agree on means of implementation. This reinforces the Court's view that the complexity and sensitivity of the issues involved in policies balancing the interests of the general population, in particular with regard to environmental protection, and the interests of a minority with possibly conflicting requirements renders the Court's role a strictly supervisory one.

Chapman v. UK [GC], Application no. 27238/95, Judgment of 18 January 2001, para. 94.

37 *Ádám and others v. Romania*, Applications nos. 81114/17 and 5 others, Judgment of 13 October 2020.

Nevertheless, the two treaties of the Council of Europe dealing specifically with national minorities (FCNM and ECRML), in force since 1998, have their own peculiarities. The former has thirty-eight state parties,[38] and the latter only twenty-five. They both have specific monitoring mechanisms that include the Committee of Ministers of the Council of Europe. The Framework Convention monitoring body is the AC and the Charter has the Committee of Experts.[39] The system is based on recommendations by all three bodies. Both special instruments of the Council of Europe dedicated to the protection of national minorities provide for the need and indeed the obligation to offer education in minority languages. The state parties of the Framework Convention 'undertake to promote equal opportunities for access to education at all levels for persons belonging to national minorities' (Art. 12.3). The Charter is even more precise as one of its objectives includes 'the provision of appropriate forms and means for the teaching and study of regional or minority languages at all appropriate levels' (Art. 7.1.f). In addition, state parties may choose to provide education at all levels or a substantial part in the selected languages. Finally, the last option is to provide for the teaching of the relevant regional or minority languages (Art. 8).[40]

19.4 COVID-19 PANDEMIC AND EDUCATION

During the COVID-19 pandemic, both monitoring mechanisms issued statements and recommendations to state parties that were also valid for a wider circle of states. The statements identified and focused on specific problems that minorities faced during the COVID-19 pandemic and that the majority population was not. Furthermore, as part of their monitoring processes, both bodies now routinely ask questions about the measures taken during the pandemic that affected the national minorities and the use of their languages.

In addition, a newly established intergovernmental body within the Council of Europe called the Committee on Anti-discrimination, Diversity and Inclusion (CDADI) specifically carried out an investigation to shed light on this worrying problem.[41] It seems that education in minority languages has been most affected.

From the start of the pandemic, the Committee of Experts as the monitoring body included the question of the measures taken during COVID-19. The pandemic had

[38] The Russian Federation remained a state party after being expelled from the Council of Europe, but denounced it in 2024. The withdrawal took effect on 1 August 2024.

[39] For complete information about their results, visit the web pages noted in footnote 35.

[40] Description of the ECRML can be found in V. Crnić-Grotić and A Oszmiańska-Pagett, 'The European Charter for Regional or Minority Languages: its origins, structure, and process' (2022), Linguistic Minorities in Europe Online, www.degruyter.com/database/LME/entry/lme.16303552/html.

[41] Council of Europe, Steering Committee on Anti-discrimination, Diversity and Inclusion (CDADI), 'National minorities', www.coe.int/en/web/committee-antidiscrimination-diversity-inclusion/national-minorities.

a terrible impact on all aspects of our lives – social, mental, financial, political, educational, and, of course, it affected our health. It was often heard that the virus does not discriminate; that we are all in it together. Nevertheless, research shows that this is not necessarily true and that there are some social groups that were more affected than others.

These social groups may be called *vulnerable*, and they represent different kinds of minority populations – mostly ethnic, racial, national, or sexual minorities. Evidence shows that these groups suffered the consequences of the pandemic disproportionally to their share in the population. The consequences ranged from a lack of access to sanitary information and vaccines to exposure to hate speech and physical violence. The latter especially affected LGBTQI people but also Asian-looking people at the beginning of the pandemic, as they were perceived as responsible for the virus. Roma and travellers also suffered from hate speech, and a trend known as anti-gypsism was exacerbated during this period.

These trends were confirmed, for example, by the European Network of Equality Bodies (EQUINET) and ombudsmen across Europe. They noted increases in xenophobia and racism against pretty much every minority group. The people responsible for leadership – politicians at different levels – were marked as those who often incited hate speech and discrimination.[42]

The usual targets, at least in Europe, where such trends are concerned are the Roma, a community that were already marginalised and discriminated against even before the start of the pandemic. According to a study by the Council of Europe for the CDADI,[43] in addition to general measures that affected the general population, Roma were targeted by some measures directly discriminating against them. For example, in Bulgaria and Slovakia there were militarised quarantines imposed on Roma settlements as, allegedly, they were the people who would not respect the sanitary restrictions. In Bulgaria, they were even using drones with thermal sensors to take the temperature of the residents of these settlements and to monitor their movements.

Restrictions on free movement during the pandemic affected the Roma also in a more indirect form. Their way of life and making a living often includes travelling and collecting materials for sale. That was obviously not possible during the lockdowns, but they were not entitled to financial assistance for losing their jobs because, technically, they did not lose their jobs as they did not have jobs to lose. A real Catch-22.

Finally, there is data in many states that minorities, including the Roma, suffered more infections and COVID-19 related illnesses. Namely, belonging to a minority

42 EQUINET, 'Recommendation for a fair and equal Europe: rebuilding our societies after Covid-19' (2020), https://equineteurope.org/wp-content/uploads/2020/06/equinet_rebuilding-recommendation_A4_03-web.pdf.

43 S. C. Marsal, C. Ahlund, and R. Wilson for CDADI, *COVID-19: An Analysis of the Anti-Discrimination, Diversity and Inclusion Dimensions in Council of Europe Member States* (Strasbourg: Council of Europe, 2020).

ethnic group was an additional health risk factor. As far as the Roma were concerned, most of them did not have any health insurance and were not entitled to free health services, so many stayed away from hospitals for as long as they could.

Let us think back to those first few weeks of the pandemic. We were receiving hourly and daily information and instructions on how to behave and what measures we had to take to stay safe. How much of it was given in minority languages, in real time? According to research carried out by the Committee of Experts for regional or minority languages, which I am a member of, many states failed to provide early information in regional or minority languages. Put that in the context of the non-available sanitary facilities in Roma settlements, for example, then add the lack of sanitary material such as disinfectants or facial masks together with big families living together in small houses, and the result was quite devastating for these communities. In the early days of the pandemic, in March 2020, the Committee of Experts warned about the need to use regional or minority languages in providing information to the population about the sanitary measures required to prevent the spread of the disease.[44] In the early days of the COVID-19 pandemic, people were confused and scared and the lack of proper information made it even worse. The Committee of Experts invited states to take language-related issues into account when developing further policies and instructions to address this exceptional medical crisis. In its view, the authorities should not forget that national minorities are an integral part of their societies, and in order for the measures adopted to have full effect, they should be made available and easily accessible to the whole population.

It is very common to say – well, they all speak the official language. However, this is not always true. There are parts of societies in some countries where a minority language is so dominant that many people do not master the official language of the state. This is especially the case with the Roma, whose social isolation also results in poor language skills in the official language.

A positive example in this context comes from Croatia, where the Institute for Public Health published sanitary instructions in Romani on their webpage in April 2020 along with other minority languages.[45] There are, however, at least two problems with this commendable example: (a) How many Roma had access to the internet? (b) Romani is not the only language spoken by Roma in Croatia, as the majority speaks Boyash Romanian, a completely different language. However, the Red Cross organisation in one of the counties where the Roma community in Croatia lives distributed sanitary packages with instructions in Croatian and Boyash.[46]

44 Committee of Experts of the European Charter for Regional or Minority Languages, 'Communication in RMLs of utmost importance in global medical crises' (2020), https://go.coe.int/siybY.

45 Institute for Public Health, 'Preporuke za pripadnike romske nacionalne manjine [COVID-19]' (2020), https://stampar.hr/hr/novosti/preporuke-za-pripadnike-romske-nacionalne-manjine-covid-19.

46 Ibid. The Boyash Romanian language is spoken by 80 per cent of Roma in Croatia according to some data. F. Radonić Mayr, 'Bajaški i/ili ćhib, pitanje je sad…' (2021), https://h-alter.org/kultura/tko-je-romski-jezik/.

As far as education is concerned, at the start of the pandemic the first measure across the world was the lockdown affecting all aspects of public life, including schools at all levels of education. According to UNESCO data, 1.6 billion learners were affected by school closures in more than 190 countries.[47] Therefore, realising the importance of education, one of the first measures undertaken by public authorities to counter the lockdown and the closing of schools was the shift to online education and/or TV classes.[48] This was a quick fix for an unprecedented situation.[49] However, the Committee of Experts realised the downsides of online education that quickly became a dominant model of education with respect to regional or minority languages. Many states took care of the education in the majority official language only, neglecting sometimes the needs of the speakers of regional or minority languages to also access quality education. The Committee of Experts made a public statement in July 2020 highlighting this potentially discriminatory treatment.[50] In addition, and bearing in mind the insufficient availability of teaching materials in regional or minority languages noticed during several monitoring cycles in many states, the Committee of Experts encouraged public financing of the development of quality open access textbooks in all languages protected under the Charter. Such textbooks, registered under open licences, should be made accessible online for the use of pupils, students, teachers, and the larger public. This was done for the majority languages, so the same standard was necessary also for regional or minority languages.

In view of the AC under the Framework Convention, the suspension of classes in schools and pre-school education during the COVID-19 pandemic has regrettably often resulted in unequal access to education and discrimination of children belonging to national minorities, particularly those who were not proficient enough in the official languages to be provided with appropriate

47 The closures also had long-term effects. Some gains already made towards the goals of the 2030 Education Agenda were lost: UNESCO, 'UNESCO's education response to COVID-19' (2023), www.unesco.org/en/covid-19/education-response/initiatives. In particular, girls were affected even more by the consequences: UNESCO, 'When schools shut: gendered impacts of COVID-19 school closures' (2021), https://unesdoc.unesco.org/ark:/48223/pf0000379270.

48 Online teaching is a well-known concept, but in this case it was 'emergency online teaching'. Therefore, there was no time or capacity to fully prepare the technical and human resources for such a sudden switch. UNESCO, 'Distance learning strategies in response to COVID-19 school closures' (2020), https://unesdoc.unesco.org/ark:/48223/pf0000373305.

49 Soon, however, concerns were raised about the shortcomings of this approach and the negative effects on the mental health of the children in addition to economic inequalities. Z. Blaskó and S. Schnepf, 'Educational inequalities in Europe and physical school closures during Covid-19' (2020), European Commission Joint Research Centre, https://knowledge4policy.ec.europa.eu/publication/educational-inequalities-europe-physical-school-closures-during-covid-19_en.

50 Council of Europe, European Charter for Regional or Minority Languages, 'COMEX statement on RMLs in online education in the context of the COVID-19 pandemic', 3 July 2020, https://go.coe.int/z7aut.

educational content. As a result, children of national minorities were at risk of learning delays and dropping out.[51]

Although some of these inequalities were justified by the sudden onset of the pandemic and the need to deal with such an unforeseen public health situation, it is still not acceptable to treat members of ethnic or national and linguistic minorities as second-class citizens. Furthermore, it is also clear that some aspects of COVID-19-style education will remain, and it is therefore important to be aware of the needs of the members of national and linguistic minorities.

Let us pause here for another *best practice* example from Croatia. The Ministry of Education realised the problem of Roma children's inability to follow classes online or on television. The classes were in Croatian since Croatia did not provide for education in Romani or Boyash. In fact, the school authorities are obliged to give Roma children enhanced teaching of Croatian to improve their language skills so that they can follow classes in Croatian.[52] Living in settlements meant that the vast majority of children had no access to the internet; television sets, if available, were not at the disposal of the children or, even more often, had to be shared by many children in the household. The Ministry of Science and Education provided tablets and vouchers for the internet for all children who could not afford it otherwise in order to be able to follow the online classes. Most of them were Roma. However, some comments suggested that there was no real control or assistance for these families so the vouchers were often misused. Almost 60 per cent of Roma pupils barely participated in online education. Among the reasons given, lack of support by the family and inadequate conditions at home were predominant, but lack of tablets or no access to the internet were high on the list.[53] It is clear that the consequences will be difficult to remedy since Roma children have a very high drop-out rate from school even at the best of times.[54]

In Slovakia, on 28 April 2020, the Ministry of Education issued the first guidelines on the content and organisation of education for primary school pupils during that time and released material by the State Pedagogical Institute entitled 'Content of education at primary schools during the extraordinary interruption of teaching at schools' including minority languages: German, Hungarian, Romani, Russian, Ruthenian, and Ukrainian. However, the Committee of Experts noted that, as in

[51] Advisory Committee on the Framework Convention for the Protection of National Minorities, 'Statement on the COVID-19 pandemic and national minorities', 28 May 2020, https://rm.coe.int/acfc-statement-covid-19-and-national-minorities-28-05-2020-final-en/16809e8570.

[52] Compare the case of *Oršuš and Others v. Croatia* [GC], Application no. 15766/03, Judgment of 16 March 2010.

[53] Reyn Hrvatska, 'Djeca Romi koja su nastavom na daljinu ostala na obrazovnoj distanci', 23 April 2020, www.reyn-hrvatska.net/index.php/2020/04/23/djeca-romi-koja-su-nastavom-na-daljinu-ostala-na-obrazovnoj-distanci/.

[54] UNICEF Moldova, 'Roma children – inclusion and reintegration of Roma children into the education system', www.unicef.org/moldova/en/what-we-do/roma-children.

other state parties, there were significantly more alternative audiovisual education materials available in the official language from official and unofficial sources.[55]

In the UK, the authorities undertook a number of measures considering the needs of regional or minority languages, in particular when it was the remit of regional authorities.[56] The Welsh Government has taken measures in education by ensuring that children and parents/carers received support during school closures and their reopening. The Scottish Government, through Bòrd na Gàidhlig, also provided funding for resources to help students with distance learning in Scottish Gaelic during the closure of schools. Many resources have been produced to help with distance learning. Additionally, the BBC published resources for 'lockdown learning' in Irish, Scottish Gaelic, and Welsh.

In Austria, a study was carried out on the perception of a possible decrease in knowledge of the languages of instruction (Slovene and German) in three minority secondary schools in Carinthia. After the overnight shift to online teaching, one favourable fact was that the majority of pupils were from economically solid backgrounds and were able to follow online lessons. Nevertheless, there seems to be a decline in knowledge of both languages in monolingual speakers owing to a lack of contact with the languages at school.[57]

19.5 CONCLUSIONS

The right to education in minority languages has been challenged recently in the proceedings of several international courts with not so satisfying results for minority language speakers. The arguments accepted by the courts were limited to non-discrimination. However, wider arguments should have been propagated in favour of the protection and promotion of minority languages in education. While not every language can be catered for in the school system, states should be persuaded that they have more positive obligations to preserve and promote languages spoken by parts of their population.

The COVID-19 pandemic has shown just how easy it is to fall into discriminatory patterns in the treatment of minorities and how easy it is to find excuses for this. Instead, the authorities should always keep in mind their responsibility to manage social trends and correct those with negative potential.

Council of Europe treaties specifically dedicated to the protection of minorities and their languages, in particular the ECRML, seem to be better suited to

55 Evaluation on the recommendations for immediate action from the fifth evaluation report on the Slovak Republic, 22 March 2021, https://hudoc.ecrml.coe.int/?i=SK-5th-ERIA-CM-2021-61E-0.

56 Evaluation on the recommendations for immediate action from the fifth evaluation report on the United Kingdom, 22 March 2021, https://hudoc.ecrml.coe.int/?i=UK-5th-ERIA-CM-2021-60E-0.

57 S. Zorčič, 'Dimensions of remote learning during the Covid-19 pandemic in minority language schools (the case of Austrian Carinthia)' (2020) 85 *Treatises and Documents, Journal of Ethnic Studies* 85, 223–52.

promoting a different approach to education at least for their state parties. It makes sense, therefore, to promote their ratification even more.

In the words of the former UN Special Rapporteur Mr de Varennes:

> Minority language education is more of an asset than it is a liability when understood and applied properly. It is not a right which is applicable in every situation where one individual simply demands it. It is rather a result which is consistent with the values of respect for diversity, tolerance and accommodation – rather than rejection – of differences which have become cornerstones of most democratic societies.[58]

[58] De Varennes, *The Right to Education and Minority Language*.

20

Technological Acceleration and the Precarisation of Work

Reflections on Social Justice, the Right to Life, and Environmental Education

Raizza da Costa Lopes, Samuel Lopes Pinheiro, and Florent Pasquier

20.1 INTRODUCTION

This chapter aims to provide the reader with a comprehensive overview of contemporary discussions surrounding labour and human rights in the context of technological acceleration using the context of Brazil. In times of profound digital transformation, labour relations have been shaped by growing platformisation, precarisation, and inequality, demanding a critical analysis of the new forms of exploitation and the social and political responses to these challenges.

The chapter is structured around a bibliographical review of authors who address the intersection of labour, technology, and human rights, including Rafael Grohmann, Ricardo Antunes, Ludmila Costhek Abílio, Trebor Scholz, Paul Singer, and Renato Dagnino. These scholars provide a solid foundation for understanding how platformisation processes and algorithmic management have redefined labour dynamics, exacerbating social and economic inequalities. In particular, it discusses how the gig economy and the 'uberisation' of work have transformed labour relations, increasing worker vulnerability while reducing their protections and rights.

Throughout the chapter, we investigate how the regulation of digital work and the recognition of labour rights, especially on digital platforms, have become topics of debate in Brazil, particularly in a scenario of increasing automation and social exclusion. We analyse initiatives such as Fairwork, which has emerged from the fight to promote decent working conditions in the context of digital platforms. Additionally, we highlight the difficulties faced by workers involved in this digital economy, such as the lack of security, income instability, and the opaque control exercised by companies through algorithmic management.

Finally, we bring environmental education to these discussions, showing how it can significantly contribute to addressing the socio-economic and environmental inequalities associated with platform capitalism. Environmental education, especially from the perspective of environmental justice, offers a critical lens that not only addresses ecological issues but also reflects on the social and political conditions that affect the most vulnerable workers. The connection between education, human rights, and technology thus becomes an important avenue for building more just socio-environmental relations.

20.2 CONTEXTUALISING THE DISCUSSION: DIGITAL TRANSFORMATIONS AND LABOUR INEQUALITIES IN BRAZIL

In recent years, the rapid advancement of digital technologies has profoundly transformed labour markets worldwide. As Brazil navigates this wave of digitalisation, a critical issue arises: that of the inequalities faced by vulnerable workers in this evolving landscape. Although digitalisation offers remarkable opportunities for efficiency and innovation, it also introduces new forms of disparity and exclusion. Vulnerable workers – often those in low-paying jobs, informal sectors, or with limited access to technology – are particularly susceptible to the adverse effects of this transformation, which directly impacts their well-being and economic stability.

Globally, and especially in Brazil, the intensification of labour exploitation has been used as a measure to revitalise and stabilise capitalist accumulation.[1] According to Neves, processes of precarisation, outsourcing, and informal labour are essential for the expansion of capitalism. The shift in the labour organisation model, which makes it increasingly flexible, is strongly marked by the platformisation of work.[2] The accelerated advancement of digital technologies and the growing automation of production processes have generated profound transformations in the world of work, while simultaneously accentuating socio-economic inequalities.

In this context, workers face the risk of alienation and exclusion as technological development advances at an ever-increasing pace without adequate social protection mechanisms and adaptation to the new labour realities. According to the Economic Commission for Latin America and the Caribbean, technological progress has been accompanied by a series of socially negative outcomes, such as the exclusion of a significant portion of the population from the benefits of digitalisation, mainly owing to insufficient incomes that limit access to quality connectivity, suitable devices, and reliable domestic connections. Additional problems include the proliferation of fake news, the increase in cyberattacks, growing privacy risks, and the issue of electronic waste.[3]

The COVID-19 pandemic exacerbated these issues, bringing negative impacts on jobs, wages, and efforts to combat poverty and inequality, especially in countries such as Brazil, where structural constraints, such as connectivity problems and

1 D. Neves, 'A exploração do trabalho no Brasil contemporâneo' (2022) 25 *Revista Katálysis* 1, 11–21.

2 R. Grohmann, 'Plataformização do trabalho: entre dataficação, financeirização e racionalidade neoliberal' (2020) 22 *Revista EPTIC* 1, 106–22.

3 Comisión Económica para América Latina y el Caribe (CEPAL), *Tecnologías Digitales para un Nuevo Futuro* (LC/TS.2021/43) (Santiago: CEPAL, 2021).

social inequalities, further limit the benefits of digital technologies.[4] While common elements can be identified in the digitalisation process across different countries, it is crucial to recognise the particularities of each location and region. The social dynamics and inequalities that characterise each context are accentuated by digitalisation, which often does not allow collective struggles to take shape or rights to be strengthened.

Rafael Grohmann, in his book *Os Laboratório do Trabalho Digital* (*The Digital Labor Laboratories*), argues that contextualising the geopolitics of platform labour also means understanding the different meanings of work in the economies of each country, distinguishing experiences between the global North and South.[5] Grohmann and Abílio et al. highlight that while the term 'gig economy' emerged in the global North to describe the platform work landscape, in Brazil, this nomenclature does not apply in the same way, as the Brazilian economy has always been characterised by a management of survival for the working class, now intensified by the transition to the digital under a liberal rationality.[6] Thus, platform-mediated subordinate labour is embedded in contemporary dilemmas related to mapping and recognising worker exploitation and its centrality in current forms of capitalist accumulation.[7]

Ricardo Antunes, one of Brazil's most prominent labour sociologists, notes that before 2020, more than 40 per cent of the Brazilian working class was in informal situations, a situation that worsened further with the COVID-19 pandemic.[8] According to him, 'we are living in a new level of real subordination of labour to capital under algorithmic governance, with the working class living between the disastrous and the unpredictable'.[9] In our view, this scenario reinforces Grohmann's analysis of the gig economy where workers, placed in precarious and unstable conditions, struggle to secure only the bare minimum for their survival.[10] These workers, constantly pressured by low wages and volatile conditions, cannot surpass the subsistence barrier, leaving them with only the effort to cover basic expenses, without the possibility of reaching an income that provides any kind of stability or economic progress.

Despite the over-exploitation of labour being a constant in Brazil and Latin America, it is evident that technological advances are transforming the ways in which the working class faces precarisation and exploitation.[11] In this context,

4 Ibid.

5 R. Grohmann (ed.), *Os Laboratórios do Trabalho Digital: Entrevistas* (São Paulo: Boitempo Editorial, 2021).

6 Ibid.; L. C. Abílio, H. Amorim, and R. Grohmann, 'Uberização e plataformização do trabalho no Brasil: conceitos, processos e formas' (2021) 23 *Sociologias* 57, 26–56.

7 Abílio et al., 'Uberização e plataformização do trabalho no Brasil'.

8 R. Antunes, 'Capitalismo de plataforma e desantropomorfização do trabalho', in R. Grohmann (ed.), *Os Laboratórios do Trabalho Digital: Entrevistas* (São Paulo: Boitempo Editorial, 2021), pp. 33–8.

9 Ibid., p. 33.

10 Grohmann, *Os Laboratórios do Trabalho Digital*.

11 Antunes, 'Capitalismo de plataforma e desantropomorfização do trabalho'.

Fairwork emerges as a relevant initiative both in Brazil and globally.[12] This project, based at the Oxford Internet Institute and the WZB Berlin Social Science Centre, works closely with workers, platforms, lawyers, and legislators in various parts of the world to think about and develop a fairer future for work. The Brazilian team is co-ordinated by professors Rafael Grohmann, Julice Salvagni, Roseli Figaro, and Rodrigo Carelli. Additionally, we highlight the efforts of researchers, such as Ludmila Costhek Abílio, Abílio et al., Grohmann, Rebechi et al., and many others who are fighting for the recognition and defence of the labour rights of workers within the context of digital platforms.[13]

In 2023, the second Fairwork Brazil report was published, continuing to examine how the major digital labour platforms in the country align with Fairwork's decent work principles amid intense disputes and debates about platform labour regulation.[14] The document highlights that after the election of Luiz Inácio Lula da Silva for his third term as president of Brazil, a working group was established to discuss the regulation of platform labour in the country, involving the participation of companies, workers, and government representatives. Another important fact concerns how digital platforms use lobbying practices to influence legislation and public policies, often using subtle tactics and data manipulation to distort and contest notions of decent work.

In this regard, the phenomenon of uberisation exemplifies the adverse conditions faced by digital platform workers in Brazil, as described by Abílio and Santiago in the 'Dossiê das violações dos Direitos Humanos no Trabalho Uberizado' ('Dossier on Human Rights Violations in Uberised Work').[15] Uberisation, as the dossier defines it, refers to the growing precarisation of labour relations promoted by digital platforms such as Uber and iFood. In Brazil, workers face structural problems, including the lack of basic labour rights, unsafe working conditions, and the absence of the formal recognition of their activities as regular employment. Platform-mediated work has given rise to various terms worldwide and in Brazil that attempt to describe the specific forms of precarisation associated with this reality.

[12] See Centro de Pesquisa em Comunicação e Trabalho (CPCT), 'Relatório Fairwork Brasil 2023' (2023), https://comunicacaoetrabalho.eca.usp.br/publicacoes_cpct/relatorio-fairwork-brasil-2023/.

[13] L. C. Abílio, 'Uberização e juventude periférica. Desigualdades, autogerenciamento e novas formas de controle do trabalho' (2020) 39 *Novos Estudos. CEBRAP* 3, 579–97; L. C. Abílio, 'Uberização: a era do trabalhador just-in-time?' (2020) 34 *Revista Estudos Avançados – IEA – USP* 98, 111–26; L. C. Abílio, 'Uberização: manicures, motoboys e a gestão da sobrevivência', in L. Marques (ed.), *Trajetórias da Informalidade no Brasil Contemporâneo* (São Paulo: Fundação Perseu Abramo, 2021), pp. 173–91; Abílio et al., 'Uberização e plataformização do trabalho no Brasil'; Grohmann, 'Plataformização do trabalho', Grohmann, Os Laboratórios do Trabalho Digital; and C. N. Rebechi et al., 'Trabalho decente no contexto das plataformas digitais: uma pesquisa-ação do Projeto Fairwork no Brasil' (2023) 74 *Revista do Serviço Público* 2, 370–89.

[14] CPCT, 'Relatório Fairwork Brasil 2023'.

[15] L. C. Abilio and S. M. Santiago, *Dossiê das violações dos direitos humanos no trabalho uberizado: o caso dos motofretistas na cidade de Campinas* (Campinas, SP: UNICAMP/Diretoria Executiva de Direitos Humanos, 2024).

Besides the terms 'gig economy' previously mentioned, and 'uberisation', we highlight new vocabularies that have been incorporated into research on the world of work. Among them is the concept of the 'just-in-time worker',[16] 'crowdwork', and 'work on demand'.[17] These terms reflect the different dimensions of the gig economy, which encompasses both crowdwork (work performed through online platforms) and on-demand work managed by apps ('work on demand via apps').

Based on De Stefano's contributions, we understand that crowdwork involves the performance of tasks through online platforms that connect clients and workers globally, ranging from simple microtasks to more complex jobs.[18] On-demand work via apps includes traditional activities such as transportation and cleaning, managed by apps that set quality standards. While crowdwork has global characteristics and on-demand work responds to local aspects, both share characteristics such as payment and management methods. We know these terms are more complex than presented here, but the goal is not to exhaust the concepts, but rather to highlight the reflections of these practices in the world of work. Additionally, differences between platforms can impact legal issues, such as the validity of contracts and applicable legislation.

Therefore, the problems faced by platform workers include income instability, where earnings vary significantly and often do not cover living costs. Additionally, these workers do not have access to benefits such as health insurance, pensions, or protection against work-related accidents, and they bear the full cost of work tools, such as vehicles and smartphones, exacerbating their financial vulnerability.[19] Another critical aspect is algorithmic management, which subjects workers to opaque control, meaning there is no transparency in this relationship.[20] Abílio et al. add that algorithmic management is based on automated instructions that process large volumes of data, influencing both the workers' daily actions and consumer dynamics.[21] This work organisation model generates instability and a lack of clarity in the rules.

20.3 FORMS OF RESISTING THE DEEPENING OF PLATFORM CAPITALISM INEQUALITIES

The book *Platform Cooperativism: Challenging the Corporate Sharing Economy* by Trebor Scholz, translated and commented on in Portuguese by Rafael Zanatta, emphasises that platform capitalism deepens labour precarisation, offering unstable

[16] Abílio, 'Uberização'.

[17] V. De Stefano, 'The rise of the "just-in-time workforce": on-demand work, crowdwork and labour protection in the "gig-economy"' (2016) 37 *Comparative Labor Law Journal* 3, 471–504.

[18] De Stefano, 'The rise of the "just-in-time workforce"'.

[19] Abílio and Santiago, Dossiê das Violações dos Direitos Humanos No Trabalho Uberizado.

[20] T. A. C. Moreira, 'Gestão algorítmica', in A. S. P. Oliveira and P. Jerónimo (eds.), *Liber Amicorum Benedita Mac Crorie. Volume II* (Braga: UMinho Editora, 2022), pp. 551–68.

[21] Abílio et al., 'Uberização e plataformização do trabalho no Brasil'.

and rights-deprived conditions while concentrating wealth and power in the hands of a few, thereby intensifying economic inequality.[22] The lack of regulation allows these companies to operate without social responsibility, exploiting workers under the false promise of autonomy and flexibility. Furthermore, this model contributes to the erosion of traditional labour rights, such as paid vacation and health insurance, aggravating de-regulation and worker vulnerability – a point already addressed by other authors throughout this publication. However, Scholz's main contribution, in our view, lies in his proposal for platform cooperativism, which offers a fairer and more democratic alternative to this exploitation.[23]

Scholz's proposal opposes the logic of the sharing economy, advocating for the creation of worker-controlled labour platforms, offering a more equitable and democratic alternative to the exploitation inherent in current corporate models.[24] In this same book, Rafael Zanatta discusses the origins of cooperativism in Brazil, which is linked to the early days of the Republic and the immigration process aimed at replacing slave labour and adapting to urbanisation and changes in productive structures. However, the dimension of cooperativism in Brazil followed a business logic, only giving way to more solidarity-based proposals during the Lula administration (2002–10) with the creation of the National Secretariat for Solidarity Economy within the Ministry of Labour and Employment.

In this context, it is essential to highlight the importance of the solidarity economy and social technologies, which have been gaining strength in Brazil since the 1980s and 1990s. These initiatives, whose names are associated with Paul Singer and Renato Dagnino, aim to promote solidarity-based and democratic forms of labour organisation, serving as resistance to capitalist exploitation methods. As previously mentioned, Brazil faces a legacy of social inequality and the exploitation of the working class since its origins. Therefore, we believe that platform cooperativism shares the same goals as social technology and the solidarity economy.

Social technology emerges as a tool that promotes collaboration, inclusion, and social transformation, designed to meet the specific needs of communities. By characterising technology as 'social', we recognise that it is not neutral and that its applications can have varying impacts.[25] This understanding challenges the traditional view of technology, which often prioritises profit over social and environmental well-being. It is within this context that the movement for social technology arises, which, according to Dagnino, constitutes a rejection of conventional technology, seeking alternatives that prioritise the collective and sustainability.[26]

[22] T. Scholz, *Cooperativismo de Plataforma* (São Paulo: Elefante, 2016).

[23] Ibid.

[24] Ibid.

[25] R. Dagnino, *Tecnologia Social: Contribuições Conceituais e Metodológicas* (Campina Grande, PB: EDUEPB, 2014).

[26] R. Dagnino, *Tecnociência Solidária: Um Manual Estratégico* (Marília, SP: Lutas Anticapital, 2019).

Paul Singer, in turn, argues that the solidarity economy presents itself as an alternative to the neoliberal model, seeking fairer forms of production and trade.[27] Singer discusses the solidarity economy as a response to the context of inequality, highlighting its capacity to generate income and empower communities.[28] Singer argues that 'there is no way to ignore that the solidarity economy is an integral part of the capitalist social formation, in which capital concentration incorporates technical progress and thus determines the conditions of competitiveness in each market'.[29]

Singer adds that the formation of cooperatives or cooperative complexes reveals an organisational strategy aimed at strengthening cooperativism in the face of capitalist dynamics.[30] In a scenario where capital is concentrated in the hands of a few, technological advances tend to favour this concentration, resulting in growing inequalities. Therefore, while the solidarity economy tries to mitigate the negative effects of capital concentration, it is also influenced by these conditions, revealing the interdependence between the two systems.

In this context, platform cooperativism emerges as an alternative that enhances this logic of collaboration and coordination among cooperatives. Social technology aligns with this perspective of platform cooperativism by proposing technological alternatives to facilitate collaboration between cooperatives and their members, promoting an organisational model that values community participation and autonomy. These platforms not only offer tools for management and commercialisation but also foster the exchange of knowledge and experiences, essential for strengthening cooperativism and the solidarity economy. Alvear et al. argue that:

> Among the numerous difficulties faced by cooperatives and solidarity economy enterprises, one of them is access to technology, particularly technologies that are suited to their organizational structures and values. Authors such as Dagnino (2004; 2019) and Varanda and Bocayuva (2009) emphasize how conventional technologies reinforce capitalist values and organizational forms, and thus, Social Technology would be the appropriate technology for solidarity enterprises.[31]

Social technology and the solidarity economy, when integrated into platform cooperativism, can help build more robust networks where cooperatives from different sectors can come together and develop solutions adapted to their local realities. This is especially relevant in contexts of vulnerability, where communities need support to overcome economic and social challenges. All these theoretical and methodological efforts share a common denominator – building foundations to achieve decent work.

[27] P. Singer, 'Economia solidária: geração de renda e alternativa ao liberalismo' (1997) 26 *Proposta* 72, 7–13.

[28] Ibid.

[29] P. Singer, 'Economia solidária versus economia capitalista' (2001) 16 *Sociedade e estado* 1-2, 100–12, at 109.

[30] Ibid.

[31] C. A. Alvear, R. Neder, and D. Santini, 'Economia solidário 2.0: por um cooperativismo de plataforma solidário' (2023) 9 *P2P e Inovação* 2, 42–61, at 50.

20.4 HUMAN RIGHTS AND WORKER PROTECTION IN THE ERA OF TECHNOLOGICAL ACCELERATION

The concept of fair and decent work has its roots in the labour struggles of the twentieth century, formally defined in 1999 by the International Labour Organization (ILO). Even in the twenty-first century, this remains a central demand within the United Nations (UN) 2030 Agenda, as part of the Sustainable Development Goals (SDGs).[32] The UN recognises that decent work is essential for eradicating poverty and promoting prosperity. This concept encompasses working conditions that ensure fundamental rights, social protection, and equal opportunities. SDG 8 emphasises the importance of decent work and sustainable economic growth, acknowledging that promoting proper working conditions is essential not only for eradicating poverty but also for fostering prosperity and social well-being.

Achieving this goal involves ensuring labour rights, combating unemployment, promoting job security, and encouraging social dialogue. In an increasingly globalised and constantly changing world, the challenge of ensuring fair and dignified working conditions becomes even more relevant, requiring collective efforts from governments, businesses, and civil society. Amid these changes, human rights emerge as a crucial anchor for safeguarding the dignity and working conditions of millions of people around the world.

The right to work, enshrined in Article 23 of the Universal Declaration of Human Rights (UDHR), constitutes a central principle to ensure that, even in times of intense technological transformation, everyone can have access to dignified employment opportunities. The growing automation of jobs – especially in industries and service sectors – puts millions of jobs at risk. This results in a paradox between technological progress and increasing precarisation of work.

Hartmut Rosa, in *Alienation and Acceleration: Towards a Critical Theory of Late-Modern Temporality*, describes 'time compression' and 'technical expansion' as central features of a world driven by the imperatives of growth and speed. As the economy accelerates, technology not only transforms production dynamics but also redefines social relations and the experience of time and space.[33] Rosa argues that we are living in a 'late modernity,' marked by a process of social acceleration in three dimensions: 'technological acceleration, acceleration of social changes, and acceleration of the pace of life'.[34]

According to Rosa, technological acceleration 'constantly displaces the spaces of security' that were once guaranteed by stable jobs and continuous careers, creating new forms of insecurity and alienation.[35] This acceleration intensifies the pressures on

[32] Rebechi et al., 'Trabalho decente no contexto das plataformas digitais'.

[33] H. Rosa, *Alienação e Aceleração: Por Uma Teoria Crítica da Temporalidade Tardo-Moderna* (São Paulo: Editora Vozes, 2022).

[34] Ibid., p. 20.

[35] Ibid.

workers, who face both the insecurity of losing their jobs to machines and algorithms and the difficulty of adapting their skills to new contexts.[36] In this sense, it is crucial to ensure that workers have not only access to jobs but also fair and equitable working conditions, along with opportunities for reskilling and professional development.

The ILO advocates that the protection of fundamental labour rights must include job security and access to decent working conditions. Technological acceleration, while bringing innovation, also exacerbates social inequalities. As Rosa points out, the dynamics of acceleration tend to benefit those already in privileged positions, widening the gap between the rich and the poor.

This issue is reflected in the Fairwork Report in 'Life Stories', where we see workers such as João.[37] João's story clearly illustrates that, in scenarios of labour precarisation, such as those he faces, the principles of Article 23 of the UDHR, which establishes the right to decent work, are violated. This, in turn, impedes the fulfilment of what is guaranteed by Article 25, which ensures an adequate standard of living. In light of this scenario, human rights, such as the right to a safe working environment, fair wages, and protection against unemployment, must be reaffirmed in the contexts of digitalised labour. The regulation of platforms and the inclusion of informal workers in social security networks are necessary measures to combat exploitation and ensure that technology is used to promote social well-being, rather than deepening inequalities.

20.5 ENVIRONMENTAL EDUCATION AS A RESPONSE TO INEQUALITIES AND THE DEFENCE OF HUMAN RIGHTS

Environmental education, according to Reigota, emerges as a response to the need to address the environmental problems generated by the capitalist economic model, which is predatory and unsustainable.[38] The starting point for the environmental discussion occurred at the First World Conference on the Human Environment, held in Stockholm, Sweden, in 1972. This meeting resulted in agreements between the UN signatory countries, emphasising the importance of educating people to solve environmental issues. From this conference onwards, global environmental concern gained prominence, followed by other significant events, such as the Belgrade Conference (1975), Tbilisi (1977), Moscow (1987), Rio (1992), and Rio+10 (2002) in Johannesburg, all of which contributed to the implementation of public policies on environmental education at the international level.

The concerns that gave rise to environmental education were primarily conservationist in nature and often resembled a 'manual of etiquette',[39] with proposals

36 Ibid.

37 CPCT, 'Relatório Fairwork Brasil 2023', p. 26.

38 M. Reigota, *O Que é Educação Ambiental* (São Paulo: Brasiliense, 2004).

39 J. S. Leite Lopes, *A Ambientalização Dos Conflitos Sociais: Participação e Controle Público da Poluição Industrial* (Rio de Janeiro: Relume Dumará, 2004).

that were more behavioural than critical of the capitalist system. Initially, environmental education was a concern of ecological movements; however, as the debate deepened, works by authors such as Layrargues and Carvalho became essential in expanding the field's discourse.[40]

In this regard, it is worth noting that environmental education is a constantly evolving field, shaped by socio-environmental issues: 'Refounding the historical, anthropological, philosophical, sociological, ethical, and epistemological foundations of Environmental Education means providing new representations to the signs that these sciences come to symbolise within the horizon of a plurality of knowledge within a unity of meanings.'[41] Considering that we live in a time when crises seem to overlap at a frenetic pace – something we can call polycrises, as reported by Pinheiro and Pasquier – we understand that the necessary debate in the field of environmental education is one that seeks to comprehend the conditions surrounding the emergence of epidemics and pandemics, particularly COVID-19, climate catastrophes, and wars spreading across different parts of the planet.[42] In all cases, there is always a segment of society disproportionately affected by the damages and negative consequences of these processes.

From this perspective, Isabelle Stengers, in her book *In Catastrophic Times*, discusses the relationship between the economic crisis in the US and the devastation caused by Hurricane Katrina.[43] The author asserts that economic and climate crises share a common denominator. Similarly, Henri Acselrad argues that the COVID-19 pandemic, which emerged in 2020, cannot be understood in isolation, but rather as an intrinsic product of neoliberal capitalism.[44] The health crisis emerged in a context already marked by impending financial crisis, resulting in a general collapse of economic activities. For Acselrad, the notions of environmental crisis and disaster must be analysed in light of the processes of capitalist reproduction and crisis.

Carvalho and Ortega support Stengers and Acselrad by pointing to the intertwining of the pandemic, environmental issues, and the climate crisis.[45] In the same

40 P. P. Layrargues, 'Para onde vai a educação ambiental? O cenário político ideológico da educação ambiental brasileira e os desafios de uma agenda política crítica contra-hegemônica' (2012) 7 *Revista contemporânea de educação* 14, 388–411; I. C. M. Carvalho, 'A perspectiva das pedras: considerações sobre os novos materialismos e as epistemologias ecológicas' (2014) 9 *Pesquisa em Educação Ambiental* 1, 69–79.

41 C. R. S. Machado, H. Calloni, and G. K. Adomilli, 'Pensares e fazeres sobre e na Educação Ambiental: reflexões sobre/desde os fundamentos ao campo atual Brasileiro' (2016) 21 *Ambiente e Educação* 1, 3–25, at 11.

42 S. L. Pinheiro and F. Pasquier, 'Consciousness and environmental education: transdisciplinary urgencies from the post-pandemic context' (2023) 14 *Transdisciplinary Journal of Engineering & Science*.

43 I. Stengers, *No Tempo Das Catástrofes: Resistir à Barbárie que Se Aproxima* (São Paulo: Cosac Naify, 2015).

44 H. Acselrad, 'Os desastres e a ambientalidade crítica do capitalismo' (2021) 45 *Ciência & Trópico* 2, 89–103.

45 I. C. M. Carvalho and M. A. A. Ortega, 'Aprendizagens em tempos de fim de um mundo e de abertura de múltiplos mundos. Reflexões desde a educação ambiental' (2024) 23 *Revista Cocar*; Stengers, *No Tempo Das Catástrofes*; Acselrad, 'Os desastres e a ambientalidade crítica do capitalismo'.

paragraph, the authors reflect on the war between Russia and Ukraine. Therefore, the pandemic, environmental issues, and geopolitical tensions are deeply intertwined, revealing an interconnected global system in which crises not only accumulate but mutually intensify.

Based on Abílio et al., Grohmann, and the Fairwork Report, we add that platform capitalism is an emergent factor within these crises, interconnected within a complex global system in which each crisis amplifies the others.[46] This reality, described as a polycrisis, demands a relational approach, which has already been addressed and to which we aim to contribute through the field of environmental education. From the perspective already emphasised, environmental education must not only address environmental degradation but also the social and political conditions that contribute to these emergencies. Therefore, environmental education must include a critical analysis – based on critical thinking – of epidemics, climate disasters, and conflicts, recognising that their consequences disproportionately affect vulnerable groups.[47] This is an environmental education for environmental justice.[48]

Environmental education provides a conducive space for strengthening the fight against the socio-economic and environmental inequalities faced by workers, especially in the context of environmental crises and technological acceleration. By expanding its boundaries beyond environmental preservation, environmental education becomes a field of study aimed at promoting educational projects in which individuals are engaged in the fight for life in its entirety.

In this sense, Carlos Frederico Loureiro, in his book *Environmental Education: Questions of Life*, places life at the centre of the debate, highlighting the urgency of a utopia that allows the overcoming of the limiting situations imposed by an exclusionary, oppressive system that destroys nature, including humans.[49] Loureiro's view of environmental education is anchored in a broad understanding of the struggle for life. For him, this struggle is not limited to the environmental field but involves transforming the social structures that perpetuate inequalities and the exploitation of workers. He emphasises the need for hope and the imagination of other possible worlds, resisting the logic of a system that generates human misery and environmental destruction.[50]

This conception resonates with discussions on the centrality of life as a fundamental right within the framework of human rights. Rossane Bigliardi and Ricardo Cruz,

46 Abílio et al., 'Uberização e plataformização do trabalho no Brasil'; Grohmann, 'Plataformização do trabalho'; CPCT, 'Relatório Fairwork Brasil 2023'.

47 M. Sawada and F. Pasquier, 'Discourses of Japanese history textbooks: from Doxa to critical thinking', in M. Sawada and F. Andres, *Impacts of Museums on Global Communication* (Hershey, PA: IGI Global, 2024), pp. 45–86.

48 C. F. Santos, L. D. Gonçalves, and C. R. Da Silva Machado, 'Educação ambiental para justiça ambiental: dando mais uns passos' (2015) 32 *REMEA-Revista Eletrônica do Mestrado em Educação Ambiental* 1, 189–208.

49 C. F. Loureiro, *Educação Ambiental: Questões de Vida* (São Paulo: Cortez, 2019).

50 Ibid.

in their article, reinforce this view by stating that the right to life, beyond mere biological existence, includes access to the minimum conditions necessary for the constitution of a healthy and dignified subjectivity, allowing human beings to fully and equitably develop their potential.[51] In this sense, environmental education aligns with human rights education, promoting a praxis oriented towards justice, equality, solidarity, and freedom.

Amorim et al. provide another key reading for environmental education by discussing the need for environmental educators to reflect on the temporal dynamics of contemporary society.[52] In their article 'A resonance of time: the contemporary challenges of environmental education', the authors point out that contemporary time is marked by an acceleration imposed by neoliberal dynamics, which creates challenges for the full development of humanity. According to the authors, environmental education should engage in a resonance of time, rescuing the importance of educational practices that consider the multiple and complex temporalities of human existence and life on the planet, challenging the utilitarian view of time promoted by a society focused on consumption and productivity.

Moreover, they suggest that environmental education needs to reformulate its foundations, taking into account temporal dynamics and how they affect human and environmental relationships. They propose a critical analysis of social temporalities, articulating individual and collective time, and point to the need for new 'synchronisers' that enable formative practices more suited to the complexity of life. This critical reflection on time is also directly connected to the inequalities faced by Brazilian workers in a context of technological hyper-acceleration.[53]

New technologies, by accelerating production rhythms, impose increasing demands on workers, deepen labour precarisation, and exacerbate social inequalities. To address this challenge, environmental education must adopt a perspective that problematises the impact of temporal dynamics on labour relations and society as a whole, promoting a critique of neoliberal models that alienate individuals and fragment their temporal experiences.

Articulating environmental education with human rights is not only possible but also necessary given that both fields share fundamental principles such as human dignity, social justice, and the right to life. Bigliardi and Cruz argue that environmental education, when oriented towards human rights, fosters a civic education that promotes solidarity and cooperation, essential elements for building a more just and sustainable society.[54] Moreover, this education provides workers

51 R. V. Bigliardi and R. G. Cruz, 'As (im)possibilidades de uma sociedade sustentável e o inextricável embricamento entre educação ambiental e direitos humanos' (2013) 23 *Revista Eletrônica do Mestrado em Educação Ambiental* 1, 22–35.

52 F. V. Amorim, S. L. Pinheiro, and H. Calloni, 'Uma ressonância do tempo: os desafios contemporâneos da educação ambiental' (2019) 14 *Revista Pesquisa em Educação Ambiental* 1, 48–57.

53 Ibid.

54 Bigliardi and Cruz, 'As (im)possibilidades de uma sociedade sustentável'.

with a critical understanding of structural inequalities and prepares them to face the challenges imposed by a system that commodifies life and destroys nature.

By incorporating human rights principles and placing life at the centre of the debate, environmental education becomes a field of reflection capable of building, together with workers, the necessary tools to confront socio-environmental inequalities and participate in constructing a more just society. As Loureiro, Bigliardi, and Cruz, and Amorim et al. argue, this education goes beyond environmental preservation and involves transforming social structures that perpetuate exploitation and the destruction of life in all its forms.[55] Therefore, environmental education is an education for life and human rights, preparing us for the struggle for a more just and equitable world.

20.6 CONCLUSION

This chapter has sought to provide a critical analysis of technological transformations and their implications for labour, as in Brazil, particularly for the most vulnerable workers. Throughout the chapter, we have discussed how platformisation, precarisation, and algorithmic management – topics emphasised by authors such as Rafael Grohmann, Ricardo Antunes, and Ludmila Costhek Abílio – are reconfiguring labour dynamics, exacerbating inequalities, and excluding millions of people from basic conditions of dignity at work. The phenomena of the gig economy and the uberisation of work have emerged as symbols of this new landscape, in which workers face financial instability, lack of legal protections, and the invisible control of digital platforms.

The chapter has also highlighted the importance of initiatives such as Fairwork, which aim to regulate platform labour and promote fairer working conditions. Regulation and the recognition of digital workers' rights are essential in a context where technological acceleration has deepened exploitation, necessitating new forms of protection and worker participation in decisions that affect their lives.

However, the discussion is not limited to formal labour rights. By connecting labour issues with environmental education, this text broadens the reflection to encompass the right to life in its entirety, integrating social, economic, and ecological dimensions. The struggle for environmental and social justice is intimately connected to the fight for decent working conditions, as both involve the right to a full and sustainable life. Environmental education, when grounded in principles such as justice and solidarity, proposes a critical perspective that goes beyond environmental preservation, addressing the roots of the inequalities that perpetuate the exploitation of workers and the destruction of the environment.

55 Loureiro, *Educação Ambiental*; Bigliardi and Cruz, 'As (im)possibilidades de uma sociedade sustentável'; Amorim et al., 'Uma ressonância do tempo'.

In addition, one of the central issues discussed throughout the chapter has been the acceleration of time, a theme explored by Hartmut Rosa. Late modernity is characterised by acceleration in technological, social, and life dimensions, transforming not only labour relations but also workers' experience of time. This acceleration, driven by the neoliberal logic of productivity, fragments temporal experiences and intensifies pressures on individuals, calling for a response that embraces more human and balanced rhythms. In this sense, environmental education can also be seen as a proposal to reclaim a different rhythm of life, one that considers the complexity of natural, social, and individual temporalities, in contrast to the alienation promoted by technological acceleration.[56]

Consequently, this chapter aims to contribute to discussions about technological transformations in the workplace by proposing an integrated approach that links the right to decent work with the right to life and environmental justice. By recognising that the accelerated pace of contemporary life affects not only work but also human and ecological relations, this chapter suggests that any response to the challenges of digitalisation must include a critical analysis of the foundations of environmental education. Only through a broad perspective that comprehends life in its fullness will it be possible to build alternatives that promote a more just, equitable, and sustainable future.

[56] F. Pasquier, D. Galeffi, and J. Collado-Runao, 'Educação transdisciplinar para um mundo complexo', in B. Letellier et al., *IIIe Congrès Mondial de la Transdisciplinarité – Adopter un Langage Transdisciplinaire Commun Face à la Complexité du Monde* (Paris: Rencontres Transdisciplinaires-PlasticitéS, 2024), Vol. IV, pp. 53–98.

Bibliography

BOOKS

Alexander, L., and Sherwin, E., *Demystifying Legal Reasoning* (Cambridge: Cambridge University Press, 2008)

Alvarez, J. E., *International Organizations as Law-Makers* (Oxford: Oxford University Press, 2005)

Aristotle, *The Nicomachean Ethics* (London: Penguin Books, 2004)

Von Arnauld, A., von der Decken, K., and Susi, M., (eds.), *The Cambridge Handbook on New Human Rights: Recognition, Novelty, Rhetoric* (Cambridge: Cambridge University Press, 2020)

Austin, G., *Cyber Policy in China* (Cambridge: Polity, 2014)

Banciu, D., Rădulescu, S. M., and Voicu, M., *Introduction to the Sociology of Deviance* (Bucharest: Științifică și enciclopedică, 1985)

Bantekas, I., and Oette, L., *International Human Rights Law and Practice*, 3rd ed. (Cambridge: Cambridge University Press, 2024)

Baudenbacher, C., and Planzer, S. (eds.), *International Dispute Resolution. The Role of Precedent* (Stuttgart: German Law Publishers, 2010)

Belmessous, S., (ed.), *Native Claims: Indigenous Law against Empire, 1500–1920* (Oxford: Oxford University Press, 2012)

Belov, M., *Rule of Law at the Beginning of the Twenty-first Century* (The Hague: Eleven International Publishing, 2018)

Benedek, W., and Kettemann, M. C., *Freedom of Expression and the Internet*, 2nd ed. (Strasbourg: Council of Europe Publishing, 2020)

Benkler, Y., Faris, R., and Roberts, H., *Network Propaganda: Manipulation, Disinformation, and Radicalization in American Politics* (Oxford: Oxford University Press, 2018)

Bennett, T. W., Munro, A., and Jacobs, P. J., *Ubuntu: An African Jurisprudence* (Cape Town: Juta, 2018)

Bently, L., Sherman, B., Gangjee, D., and Johnson, P., *Intellectual Property Law*, 6th ed. (Oxford: Oxford University Press, 2022)

Benvenisti, E., *The Law of Global Governance* (Leiden: Brill, 2014)

Berman, H. J., *Law and Revolution, II: The Impact of the Protestant Reformations on the Western Legal Tradition* (Cambridge, MA & London: Harvard University Press, 2003)

Bonfils, H., and Fauchille, P., *Manuel de Droit International public (Droit Des Gens)*, 3rd ed. (Paris: Arthur Rousseau, 1901)

Borges, G., and Sorge, C. (eds.), *Law and Technology in a Global Digital Society: Autonomous Systems, Big Data, IT Security and Legal Tech* (Cham: Springer Nature, 2022)

Bradford, A., *The Brussels Effect: How the European Union Rules the World* (Oxford: Oxford University Press, 2020)

Brenner, S., and Spaeth, H. J., *Stare Indecisis: The Alteration of Precedent on the Supreme Court, 1946–1992* (Cambridge: Cambridge University Press, 1995)

Brodie, R., *Virus of the Mind: The New Science of the Meme* (Carlsbad: Hay House, Inc, 2009)

Brunnée, J., and Toope, S., *Legitimacy and Legality in International Law: An Interactional Account* (Cambridge: Cambridge University Press, 2010)

Bustamante, T., and Pulido, C. B., *On the Philosophy of Precedent: Proceedings of the 24th World Congress of the International Association for Philosophy of Law and Social Philosophy, Beijing, 2009* (Stuttgart: Franz Steiner Verlag, 2012)

Bychawska-Siniarska, D., *Protection the Right to Freedom of Expression under the Convention on Human Rights: A Handbook for Legal Practitioners'* (Strasbourg: Council of Europe, 2017)

Chamberlain, P., *Drones and Journalism – How the Media is Making Use of Unmanned Aerial Vehicles* (London: Routledge, 2016)

Citron, D. K., *Hate Crimes in Cyberspace* (Cambridge, MA: Harvard University Press 2014)

Citron, D. K., *The Fight for Privacy: Protecting Dignity, Identity, and Love in the Digital Age* (New York: W.W. Norton & Company, 2022)

Cortez, E. K. (ed.), *Data Protection Around the World: Privacy Laws in Action* (The Hague: T.M.C. Asser Press, 2021)

Cross, R., and Harris, J. W., *Precedent in English Law* (Oxford: Clarendon Press, 2004)

Dagnino, R., *Tecnologia Social: Contribuições Conceituais e Metodológicas* (Campina Grande, PB: EDUEPB, 2014)

Dagnino, R., *Tecnociência Solidária: Um Manual Estratégico* (Marília, SP: Lutas Anticapital, 2019).

Davis, K. E., et al. (eds.), *Governance by Indicators: Global Power through Quantification and Rankings* (Oxford: Oxford University Press, 2012)

Deva, S., and Bilchitz, D. (eds.), *Human Rights Obligations of Business: Beyond the Corporate Responsibility to Respect* (Cambridge: Cambridge University Press, 2013)

Feinberg, J., *Harm to Others* (New York: Oxford University Press, 1984)

Finnis, J., *Natural Law and Natural Rights* (Oxford: Oxford University Press, 1980)

Fuchs, R. G., *Contested Paternity: Constructing Families in Modern France* (Baltimore: Johns Hopkins University Press, 2008)

Fuller, L. L., *The Morality of Law: Revised Edition* (New Haven: Yale University Press, 1969)

Goldstein, P., and Hugenholtz, B., *International Copyright: Principles, Law, and Practice* (Oxford: Oxford University Press, 2019)

De Gregorio, G., *Digital Constitutionalism in Europe* (Cambridge: Cambridge University Press, 2022)

Grohmann, R. (ed.), *Os Laboratórios do Trabalho Digital: Entrevistas* (São Paulo: Boitempo Editorial, 2021)

Habermas, J., *The Structural Transformation of the Public Sphere: An Inquiry into a Category of Bourgeois Society* (Cambridge, MA: The MIT Press, 1991)

Harari, Y. N., *21 Lessons for the 21st Century* (New York: Vintage Publishing, 2019)

Harlow, C., and Rawlings, R., *Law and Administration*, 2nd ed. (London: Butterworths, 1997)

Harvey, D., *Collisions in the Digital Paradigm: Law and Rule-making in the Internet Age* (Oxford: Hart Publishing, 2017)

Holmes, S., *Passions and Constraint: On the Theory of Liberal Democracy* (Chicago and London: The University of Chicago Press, 1995)

Horty, J. F., *Rules and Reasons in the Theory of Precedent* (Cambridge: Cambridge University Press, 2011)

Jackson, V., and Tushnet, M. (eds.), *Proportionality: New Frontiers, New Challenges* (Cambridge: Cambridge University Press, 2017)
Jacob, M., *Precedents and Case-Based Reasoning in the European Court of Justice* (Cambridge: Cambridge University Press, 2014)
Kelsen, H., *General Theory of Law and State*, translated by Andreas Wedberg. (Cambridge, MA: Harvard University Press, 1945)
Klabbers, J., Peters, A., and Ulfstein, G. (eds.), *The Constitutionalization of International Law* (Oxford: Oxford University Press, 2009)
Klimburg, A., *The Darkening Web* (London: Penguin Books, 2017)
Kohlberg, L., *The Philosophy of Moral Development* (New York: Harper & Row, 1981)
Krishnamurthi, R., Nayyar, A., and Hassanien, A. E. (eds.), *Development and Future of Internet of Drones (IoD): Insights, Trends and Road Ahead* (Cham: Springer International Publishing, 2021)
Leite Lopes, J. S., *A Ambientalização Dos Conflitos Sociais: Participação e Controle Público da Poluição Industrial* (Rio de Janeiro: Relume Dumará, 2004)
Llewellyn, K. N., *Jurisprudence: Realism in Theory and Practice* (New Brunswick: Transaction Publishers, 2008)
Llewellyn, K. N., *The Bramble Bush: On Our Law and Its Study* (New York: Oceana Publications, 1991)
Locke, J., *Two Treatises of Government* (Cambridge: Cambridge University Press, 1967)
Locke, J., *Two Treatises of Government* (Vermont: Everyman, 1997)
Loureiro, C. F., *Educação Ambiental: Questões de Vida* (São Paulo: Cortez, 2019)
Lyon, D., *Surveillance Society: Monitoring Everyday Life* (Buckingham: Open University Press, 2001)
Magrani, E., *Hacking the Electorate: On the Use of Personal Data in Political Campaigning* (Berlin: Konrad Adenauer Stiftung, 2020)
Manovich, L., *Software Takes Command: Extending the Language of New Media* (New York: Bloomsbury Publishing, 2013)
Mantelero, A., *Beyond Data: Human Rights, Ethical and Social Impact Assessment in AI* (New York: Springer, 2022)
McLeod, I., *Legal Method* (London: Palgrave Macmillan, 2007)
Megele, C., and Longfield, A., *Safeguarding Children and Young People Online: A Guide for Practitioners* (Bristol: Bristol University Press, 2017)
Meitani, G., *Course on Public International Law* (Bucharest: Al.T. Doicescu, 1930)
Melo, V. E., *Fake News* (Buenos Aires: La Ley, 2022)
Merleau-Ponty, M., *The Visible and the Invisible*, edited by C. Lefort, translated by A. Lingis, Northwestern University Studies in Phenomenology and Existential Philosophy (Evanston: Northwestern University Press, 1968)
Pajuste, T. (ed.), *Specific Threats to Human Rights Protection from the Digital Reality: International Responses and Recommendations to Core Threats from the Digitalized World* (Tallinn: Tallinn University, 2022)
Pauwelyn, J., Wessel, R. A., and Wouters, J. (eds.), *Informal International Lawmaking* (Oxford: Oxford University Press, 2012)
Pollicino, O., *Judicial Protection of Fundamental Rights on the Internet: A Road Towards Digital Constitutionalism?* (Oxford: Hart Publishing, 2021)
Popa Tache, C. E., *Le dynamisme du droit international public contemporain et la transdisciplinarité* (Paris: L'Harmattan Paris, 2023)
Popa Tache, C. E., *Legal Treatment Standards for International Investments: Heuristic Aspects* (Bucharest: Adjuris International Academic Publisher, 2021)

Raz, J., *The Authority of Law: Essays on Law and Morality* (Oxford: Clarendon Press, 1979)
Raz, J., *The Morality of Freedom* (Chicago: Clarendon Press, 1986)
Reigota, M., *O Que é Educação Ambiental* (São Paulo: Brasiliense, 2004)
Riordan, J., *The Liability of Internet Intermediaries* (Oxford: Oxford University Press, 2016)
Rivoir, A. L., and Morales, M. J., *Tecnologías Digitales: Miradas Críticas de la Apropiación en América Latina* (Buenos Aires: CLACSO & RIAT, 2019)
Rosa, H., *Alienação e Aceleração: Por Uma Teoria Crítica da Temporalidade Tardo-Moderna* (São Paulo: Editora Vozes, 2022)
Ross, A., *On Law and Justice* (Clark, NJ: The Lawbook Exchange Ltd., 2004)
Sajó, A., and Uitz, R., *The Constitution of Freedom: An Introduction to Legal Constitutionalism* (Oxford: Oxford University Press, 2017)
Santos-D'Amorim, K., and Fernandes de Oliveira Miranda, M. K., 'Misinformation, disinformation, and malinformation: Clarifying the definitions and examples in disinfodemic times' (2021) 26 *Revista eletrônica de biblioteconomia e ciência da informação*, e76900, 7
Sartre, J.-P., *Existentialism and Human Emotions* (New York: Philosophical Library Book, 1957)
Scholz, T., *Cooperativismo de Plataforma* (São Paulo: Elefante, 2016)
De Schutter, O., *International Human Rights Law: Cases, Materials, Commentary* (Cambridge: Cambridge University Press, 2019)
Schwab, K., *The Fourth Industrial Revolution* (Geneva: World Economic Forum, 2016)
Scolari, C., *Las Leyes de la Interfaz: Diseño, Ecología, Evolución, Tecnología* (Barcelona: Gedisa, 2018)
Singh, R., *Profiling Humans from their Voice* (Singapore: Springer, 2019)
Solove, D. J., *Understanding Privacy* (Cambridge: Harvard University Press, 2008)
Stahl, B. C., *Artificial Intelligence for a Better Future: An Ecosystem Perspective on the Ethics of AI and Emerging Digital Technologies* (Cham: Springer, 2021)
Stengers, I., *No Tempo Das Catástrofes: Resistir à Barbárie que Se Aproxima* (São Paulo: Cosac Naify, 2015)
Stone, J., *Precedent and Law: Dynamics of Common Law Growth* (Sydney: Butterworths, 1985)
Sullivan, C., *Digital Identity: An Emergent Legal Concept. The Role and Legal Nature of Digital Identity in Commercial Transactions* (Adelaide: University of Adelaide Press, 2011)
Sunstein, C. R., *Legal Reasoning and Political Conflict* (Oxford: Oxford University Press, 1996)
Sunstein, C., *Designing Democracy: What Constitutions Do* (Oxford: Oxford University Press, 2001)
Sunstein, C., *Liars: Falsehoods and Free Speech in an Age of Deception* (Oxford: Oxford University Press, 2021)
Sunstein, C., *One Case at a Time: Judicial Minimalism on the Supreme Court* (Cambridge, MA: Harvard University Press, 1999)
Susi, M., et al., *Governing Information Flows during War: A Comparative Study of Content Governance and Media Policy Responses after Russia's Attack on Ukraine* (Hamburg: Verlag Hans-Bredow-Institut, 2022)
Susi, M., *The Non-Coherence Theory of Digital Human Rights* (Cambridge: Cambridge University Press, 2024)
Thomas, J., *Public Rights, Private Relations* (Oxford: Oxford University Press, 2015)
Titi, C., *The Right to Regulate in International Investment Law* (Oxford: Hart Publishing, 2014)
Toledo, J. A. H., *Medios y Mediación en la Cultura Digital: Cambios Estructurales y Construcciones Teóricas para la Comprensión de la Cultura Digital* (Valencia: Tirant lo Blanch, 2018)
Treves, R., *Introduction to the Sociology of Law* (Milan: Cisalpino-Goliardica, 1972)

Veiga, P., *Direito Constitucional e Direito Internacional no Contexto do Constitucionalismo Global: Um Roteiro Pedagógico* (Lisbon: Petrony, 2020)

Vermeule, A., *Common Good Constitutionalism: Recovering the Classical Legal Tradition* (Cambridge: Polity Press, 2022)

Wardle, C., and Derakhshan, H., *Information Disorder: Toward an Interdisciplinary Framework for Research and Policymaking* (Strasbourg: Council of Europe Publishing, 2017)

Wilson, E. O., *Consilience: The Unity of Knowledge* (New York: Random House, 1998)

Wylie, C., *Mindf*ck: Inside Cambridge Analytica's Plot to Break the World* (London: Profile Books, 2019)

Žaltauskaitė-Žalimienė, S., et al., *Europos Sąjungos Pagrindinių teisių chartijos taikymas supra- ir nacionaliniu lygmenimis* (Vilnius: Vilnius University Press, 2019)

Zuboff, S., *In the Age of the Smart Machine: The Future of Work and Power* (New York: Basic Books, 1988)

Zuboff, S., *The Age of Surveillance Capitalism: The Fight for a Human Future at the New Frontier of Power* (New York: Public Affairs, 2019)

CHAPTERS IN EDITED VOLUMES

Abílio, L. C., 'Uberização: manicures, motoboys e a gestão da sobrevivência', in Marques, L. (ed.), *Trajetórias da Informalidade no Brasil Contemporâneo* (São Paulo: Fundação Perseu Abramo, 2021) 173–91

Antunes, R., 'Capitalismo de plataforma e desantropomorfização do trabalho', in Grohmann, R. (ed.), *Os Laboratórios do Trabalho Digital: Entrevistas* (São Paulo: Boitempo Editorial, 2021) 33–8

Arneson, R. J., 'Liberal neutrality on the good: An autopsy', in Wall, S., and Klosko, G. (eds.), *Perfectionism and Neutrality: Essays in Liberal Theory* (Lanham, MD: Rowman & Littlefield Publishers, 2003) 191–208

Benedek, W., 'International organizations and digital human rights', in Wagner, B., Kettemann, M. C., and Veith, K. (eds.), *Research Handbook on Human Rights and Digital Technology: Global Politics, Law and International Relations*, 2nd ed. (Cheltenham: Edward Elgar 2024) 311–26

Benedek, W. 'Internet Governance and Human Rights', in Benedek, W., Bauer, V., and Kettemann, M. C. (eds.), *Internet Governance and the Information Society* (The Hague: Eleven, 2008) 31–50

Benedek, W., 'Multi-stakeholderism in the development of international law', in Fastenrath, U., Geiger, R., and Khan, D.-E., et al. (eds.), *From Bilateralism to Community Interest: Essays in Honour of Judge Bruno Simma* (Oxford: Oxford University Press, 2011) 201–10

Benedek, W., and Kettemann, M. C., 'The Council of Europe and the Information Society', in Kicker, R. (ed.), *The Council of Europe, Pioneer and Guarantor for Human Rights and Democracy* (Strasbourg: Council of Europe Publishing, 2010) 88–93

Beširević, V., 'The constitution in the European Union: The state of affairs', in Dupeyrix, A., and Raulet, G. (eds.), *European Constitutionalism: Historical and Contemporary Perspectives* (Brussels: Peter Lang, 2014) 15–35

Beširević, V., 'Introduction', in Beširević, V. (ed.), *Public Law in Serbia: Twenty Years After* (London: European Public Law Organization & Esperia Publications Ltd, 2012) 15–19

Beširević, V., 'A short guide to militant democracy: Some remarks on the Strasbourg jurisprudence', in Benedek, W., Benoît-Rohmer, F., Karl, W., and Nowak, M. (eds.), *European Yearbook of Human Rights 2012* (Antwerp: Intersentia, Vienna: NW Verlag, 2012) 243–58

Bigo, D., Isin, E. F., and Ruppert, E., 'Data politics', in Bigo, D., Isin, E. F., and Ruppert, E. (eds.), *Data Politics: Worlds, Subjects, Rights* (Abingdon: Routledge, 2018) 1–17

Bix, B., 'Law as an autonomous discipline', in Cane, P., and Tushnet, M. (eds.), *The Oxford Handbook of Legal Studies* (Oxford: Oxford University Press, 2003) 975–87

Cali, B., 'The right to meaningful access to the internet', in von Arnauld, A., von der Decken, K., and Susi, M. (eds.), *The Cambridge Handbook on New Human Rights: Recognition, Novelty, Rhetoric* (Cambridge: Cambridge University Press, 2020) 276–84

Cane, P., 'Theory and values in public law', in Craig, P., and Rawlings, R. (eds.), *Law and Administration in Europe: Essays in Honour of Carol Harlow* (Oxford: Oxford University Press, 2003) 3–21

Dworkin, R., 'Liberalism', in Hampshire, S. (ed.), *Public and Private Morality* (Cambridge: Cambridge University Press, 1978) 113–43

Edwards, L., 'Introduction', in Edwards, L. (ed.), *Law, Policy and the Internet* (Oxford: Hart Publishing, 2019) 49–50

Epstein, B., 'Why it is so difficult to regulate disinformation online', in Bennett, W. L., and Livingston, S. (eds.), *The Disinformation Age: Politics, Technology, and Disruptive Communication in the United States* (Cambridge: Cambridge University Press, 2020) 190–210

Finn, R. L., Wright, D., and Friedewald, M., 'Seven types of privacy', in Gutwirth, D., Leenes, R., de Hert, P., et al. (eds.), *European Data Protection: Coming of Age* (Dordrecht: Springer, 2013) 3–32

Gardbaum, S., 'The structure and scope of constitutional rights', in Dixon, R., and Ginsburg, T. (eds.), *Research Handbook in Comparative Constitutional Law* (Cheltenham: Edward Elgar Publishing, 2011) 387–403

Gillespie, J., and Nicholson, P., 'Taking the interpretation of legal transfers seriously: The challenge for law and development', in Gillespie, J., and Nicholson, P. (eds.), *Law and Development and the Global Discourses of Legal Transfers* (Cambridge: Cambridge University Press, 2012) 1–26

Gomez, F., and Artigot i Golobardes, M., 'Intrinsic and extrinsic motivations to comply with legal rules: Comment on B. Deffains and D. Demougin, "Class Actions, Compliance, and Moral Cost"', in Grundmann, S., Möslein, F., and Riesenhuber, K. (eds.), *Contract Governance: Dimensions in Law and Interdisciplinary Research* (Oxford: Oxford Academic, online ed., 2015) 241–8

Hargittai, E., and Hsieh, Y. P., 'Digital inequality', in Dutton, W. H. (ed.), *The Oxford Handbook of Internet Studies* (Oxford: Oxford University Press, 2013) 129–50

Hunter-Henin, M., 'Horizontal application of human rights in France: The triumph of the European Convention on Human Rights', in Dawn, O., and Fedtke, J. (eds.), *Human Rights and the Private Sphere – a Comparative Study* (Cavendish, London and New York: Routledge, 2007) 98–124

Kadelbach, S., 'From public international law to international public law', in von Bogdandy, A., et al. (eds.), *The Exercise of Public Authority by International Institutions* (Berlin: Springer, 2010) 33–49

Katselli, E., 'The rule of law and the role of human rights in contemporary international law', in Dickinson, R., Katselli, E., Murray, C., and Pedersen, O. W. (eds.), *The Rule of Law and the Role of Human Rights in Contemporary International Law* (Cambridge: Cambridge University Press, 2012) 131–52

Kettemann, M., and Peukert, A., 'Conclusion', in Kettemann, M., Peukert, A., and Spiecker gen. Döhmann, I. (eds.), *The Law of Global Digitality* (London: Routledge, 2022) 250–5

Khan, E., Sperotto, A., van der Ham, J., and van Rijswijk-Deij, R., 'Stranger VPNs: Investigating the geo-unblocking capabilities of commercial VPN providers', in Brunstrom, A., Flores,

M., and Fiore, M. (eds.), *Passive and Active Measurement: PAM 2023* (Cham: Springer, 2023) 46–68

King, D. L., and Delfabbro, P. H., 'The natural history of problematic Internet use and gaming: Recent findings, challenges, and future directions', in Potenza, M. N., Faust, K. A., and Faust, D. (eds.), *The Oxford Handbook of Digital Technologies and Mental Health* (Oxford: Oxford University Press, 2020) 65–74

Kulesza, J., 'Multistakeholderism – meaning and implications', in Susi, M. (ed.), *Human Rights, Digital Society and the Law: A Research Companion* (London: Routledge, 2019) 117–31

Kumm, M., and Ferreres Comella, V., 'What is so special about constitutional rights in private litigation? A comparative analysis of the function of state action requirements and indirect horizontal effect', in Sajó, A., and Uitz, R., *The Constitution of Freedom: An Introduction to Legal Constitutionalism* (Oxford: Oxford University Press, 2017) 241–86

Lauk, E., Uskali, T., Kuutti, H., and Hirvinen, H., 'Drone journalism: The newest global test of press freedom', in Carlsson, U. (ed.), *Freedom of Expression and Media in Transition: Studies and Reflections in the Digital Age* (Gothenburg: Nordicom, 2016) 117–25

Lee, H. K., and Chung, S., 'Conceptualization of Internet addiction based on the public health perspective', in Potenza, M. N., Faust, K. A., and Faust, D. (eds.), *The Oxford Handbook of Digital Technologies and Mental Health* (Oxford: Oxford University Press, 2020) 87–96

Lievens, E., 'The rights of the child in the digital environment: from empowerment to de-responsibilisation', in 5 Rights Foundation, *Freedom, Security and Privacy: The Future of Childhood in the Digital World* (2020) 152–7

Lievens, E., 'Is self-regulation failing children and young people? Assessing the use of alternative regulatory instruments in the area of social networks', in Simpson, S., Puppis, M., and van den Bulck, H. (eds.), *European Media Policy for the Twenty-First Century: Assessing the Past, Setting Agendas for the Future* (New York, Abingdon: Routledge, 2016) 77–94

Limantė, A., and Tereškinas, A., 'Definition of vulnerable groups', in Limantė, A., and Pūraitė-Andrikienė, D. (eds.), *Legal Protection of Vulnerable Groups in Lithuania, Latvia, Estonia and Poland* (New York: Springer, 2022) 3–27

Looschelders, D., and Makowsky, M., 'The impact of human rights and basic rights in German private law', in Trstenjak, V., and Weingerl, P. (eds.), *The Influence of Human Rights and Basic Rights in Private Law* (Cham, Heidelberg, New York: Springer, 2016) 295–317

Macioce, F., 'The vulnerable groups and their legal value', in Macioce, F., *The Politics of Vulnerable Groups: Implications for Philosophy, Law, and Political Theory* (London: Palgrave Macmillan, 2022) 31–60

Magarin, G. P., 'The Internet and social media', in Stone, A., and Schauer, F. (eds.), *The Oxford Handbook of Freedom of Speech* (Oxford: Oxford University Press, 2021) 350–70

Maroni, M., 'The liability of Internet intermediaries and the European Court of Human Rights', in Petkova, B., and Ojanen, T. (eds.), *Fundamental Rights Protection Online: The Future Regulation of Intermediaries* (Cheltenham: Edward Elgar Publishing, 2020) 255–78

Mawby, R. I., 'Comparing police systems across the world', in Bruinsma, G., and Weisburd, D. (eds.), *Encyclopedia of Criminology and Criminal Justice* (New York: Springer, 2014) 478–88

Miller, J., 'The influence of human rights and basic rights in private law in the United States', in Trstenjak, V., and Weingerl, P. (eds.), *The Influence of Human Rights and Basic Rights in Private Law* (Cham, Heidelberg, New York: Springer, 2016) 473–86

Moreira, T. A. C., 'Gestão algorítmica', in Oliveira, A. S. P., and Jerónimo, P. (eds.), *Liber Amicorum Benedita Mac Crorie. Volume II* (Braga: UMinho Editora, 2022) 551–68

Nayyar, A., Nguyen, B.-L., and Nguyen, N. G., 'The Internet of drone things (IoDT): Future envision of smart drones', in Luhach, A., Kosa, J., Poonia, R., et al. (eds.), *First International Conference on Sustainable Technologies for Computational Intelligence: Advances in Intelligent Systems and Computing* (Singapore: Springer, 2020) 563–80

Pajuste, T., 'The protection of personal data in the digital society: The role of the GDPR', in Susi, M. (ed.), *Human Rights, Digital Society and the Law: A Research Companion* (London: Routledge, 2019) 303–15

Pasquier, F., Galeffi, D., and Collado-Runao, J., 'Educação transdisciplinar para um mundo complexo', in Letellier, B., et al., *IIIe Congrès Mondial de la Transdisciplinarité – Adopter un Langage Transdisciplinaire Commun Face à la Complexité du Monde* (Paris: Rencontres Transdisciplinaires-PlasticitéS, 2024), Vol. IV, 53–97

Postema, G., 'Implicit law', in Witteveen, W. J., and van der Burg, W. (eds.), *Rediscovering Fuller: Essays on Implicit Law and Institutional Design* (Amsterdam: Amsterdam University Press, 1999) 253–75

Powell, C. H., and Schonwetter, T., 'Africa, the Internet and human rights', in Susi, M. (ed.), *Human Rights, the Digital Society and Law: A Research Companion* (New York: Routledge Publishing, 2019) 316–34

Preuß, U., 'The German Drittwirkung doctrine and its socio-political background', in Sajó, A., and Uitz, R. (eds.), *The Constitution in Private Relations: Expanding Constitutionalism* (Utrecht: Eleven International Publishing, 2005) 23–32

Puccinelli, O., 'The right to be forgotten 2.0', in von Arnauld, von der Decken, K., and Susi, M. (eds.), *The Cambridge Handbook on New Human Rights: Recognition, Novelty, Rhetoric* (Cambridge: Cambridge University Press, 2020) 300–10

Rumpf, H.-J., 'General population-based studies of problematic Internet use: Data from Europe', in Potenza, M. N., Faust, K. A., and Faust, D. (eds.), *The Oxford Handbook of Digital Technologies and Mental Health* (Oxford: Oxford University Press, 2020) 57–64

Saunders, C., 'Constitutional rights and the common law', in Sajó, A., and Uitz, R. (eds.), *The Constitution in Private Relations: Expanding Constitutionalism* (Utrecht: Eleven International Publishing, 2005) 183–216

Sawada, M., and Pasquier, F., 'Discourses of Japanese history textbooks: From Doxa to critical thinking', in Sawada, M., and Andres, F. (eds.), *Impacts of Museums on Global Communication* (Hershey, PA: IGI Global, 2024) 45–86

Siddappaji, B., and Akhilesh, K. B., 'Role of cyber security in drone technology', in Akhilesh, K. B., and Möller, D. P. F. (eds.), *Smart Technologies* (Singapore: Springer, 2020) 169–78

Stalla-Bourdillon, S., and Thorburn, R., 'The scandal of intermediary: Acknowledging the both/and dispensation for regulating hybrid actors', in Petkova, B., and Ojanen, T. (eds.), *Fundamental Rights Protection Online: The Future Regulation of Intermediaries* (Cheltenham: Edward Elgar Publishing, 2020) 141–74

Susi, M., 'Novelty in new human rights: The decrease in universality and abstractness thesis', in von Arnauld, A., von der Decken, K., and Susi, M. (eds.), *The Cambridge Handbook on New Human Rights: Recognition, Novelty, Rhetoric* (Cambridge: Cambridge University Press, 2020) 21–33

Susi, M., 'The right to be forgotten', in von Arnauld, A., von der Decken, K., and Susi, M. (eds.), *The Cambridge Handbook on New Human Rights: Recognition, Novelty, Rhetoric* (Cambridge: Cambridge University Press, 2020) 287–99

Sweeney, J. A., 'Freedom of religion and democratic transition', in Buyse, A., and Hamilton, M. (eds.), *Transitional Jurisprudence and the ECHR, Justice, Politics and Rights* (Cambridge: Cambridge University Press, 2011) 103–30

Teubner, G., 'Societal constitutionalism: Alternatives to state-centred constitutional theory?', in Joerges, C., Sand, I.-J., and Teubner, G. (eds.), *Transnational Governance and Constitutionalism* (Oxford: Hart Publishing, 2004) 3–28

Thornberry, P., 'Article 12. Education', in Weller, M. (ed.), *The Rights of Minorities in Europe: A Commentary on the European Framework Convention for the Protection of National Minorities* (Oxford: Oxford University Press, 2005) 397–412

Troper, M., 'Who needs a third party effect doctrine? – The case of France', in Sajó, A., and Uitz, R. (eds.), *The Constitution in Private Relations: Expanding Constitutionalism* (Utrecht: Eleven International Publishing, 2005) 115–28

De Varennes, F., and Kuzborska, E., 'Minority language rights and standards: Definitions and applications at the supranational level', in Hogan-Brun, G., and O'Rourke, B. (eds.), *The Palgrave Handbook of Minority Languages and Communities* (London: Palgrave Macmillan, 2019) 21–72

Veiga, P., 'Uma lição da pandemia: Renúncia à globalização ou limites a essa renúncia? Ressignificação do Estado', in Pinto Oliveira, A. S., and Jerónimo, P. (eds.), *Liber Amicorum Benedita Mac Crorie*, II vol (Braga: UMinho Editora, 2022) 381–90

Verma, V., Rohilla, M., Sharma, A., and Gupta, M., 'Fake news detection on Twitter', in Tiwari, S., et al. (eds.), *Advances in Data and Information Sciences: Proceedings of ICDIS 2022* (New York: Springer, 2022) 141–9

Wagner, B., 'Ethics as an escape from regulation. From "ethics-washing" to ethics-shopping?', in Bayamlioğlu, E., Baraliuc, I., and Janssens, L. (eds.), *Being Profiled: Cogitas Ergo Sum. 10 Years of Profiling the European Citizen* (Amsterdam: Amsterdam University Press, 2018) 84–8

Weingerl, P., 'The influence of fundamental rights in Slovene private law', in Trstenjak, V., and Weingerl, P. (eds.), *The Influence of Human Rights and Basic Rights in Private Law* (Cham, Heidelberg, New York: Springer, 2016) 535–58

Wischmeyer, T., 'What is illegal offline is also illegal online: the German Network Enforcement Act 2017', in Petkova, B., and Ojanen, T. (eds.), *Fundamental Rights Protection Online: The Future Regulation of Intermediaries* (Cheltenham: Edward Elgar Publishing, 2020) 28–56

JOURNAL ARTICLES

Abílio, L. C., Amorim, H., and Grohmann, R., 'Uberização e plataformização do trabalho no Brasil: conceitos, processos e formas' (2021) 23 *Sociologias* 57, 26–56

Abílio, L. C., 'Uberização: a era do trabalhador just-in-time?' (2020) 34 *Revista Estudos Avançados – IEA – USP* 98, 111–26

Abílio, L. C., 'Uberização e juventude periférica. Desigualdades, autogerenciamento e novas formas de controle do trabalho' (2020) 39 *Novos Estudos. CEBRAP* 3, 579–97

Abiri, G., and Buchheim, J., 'Beyond true and false: Fake news and the digital epistemic divide' (2022) 29 *Michigan Technology Law Review* 59–109

Abu-Shanab, E., and Al-Jamal, N., 'Exploring the gender digital divide in Jordan' (2015) 19 *Gender, Technology and Development* 1, 91–113

Acselrad, H., 'Os desastres e a ambientalidade crítica do capitalismo' (2021) 45 *Ciência & Trópico* 2, 89–103

Alexander, L., and Sherwin, E., 'Judges as rulemakers' (2004) 15 *University of San Diego Public Law and Legal Theory Research Paper Series*, 1–36

Allam, H., et al., 'Prevalence of problematic social media use among residents and teaching assistants in Ain Shams University Hospitals and faculty of medicine and its relationship to emotional distress' (2021) 114 (Supplement 1) *QJM: An International Journal of Medicine* i216

Alston, P., 'Conjuring up new human rights: A proposal for quality control' (1984) 78 *American Journal of International Law* 3, 607–21

Altawy, R., and Youssef, A. M., 'Security, privacy, and safety aspects of civilian drones: A survey' (2016) 1 *ACM Transactions on Cyber-Physical Systems* 2, 1–25

Alvear, C. A., Neder, R., and Santini, D., 'Economia solidário 2.0: por um cooperativismo de plataforma solidário' (2023) 9 *P2P e Inovação* 2, 42–61

Amorim, F. V., Pinheiro, S. L., and Calloni, H., 'Uma ressonância do tempo: os desafios contemporâneos da educação ambiental' (2019) 14 *Revista Pesquisa em Educação Ambiental* 1, 48–57

Antonio, A., and Tuffley, D., 'The gender digital divide in developing countries' (2014) 6 *Future Internet* 4, 673–87

Antonova, S., 'Internet and the emerging global community of rights: The human-rights debate at the internet governance forum' (2013) 4 *Journal of International Law* 1, 84–98

Augner, C., et al., 'The association between problematic smartphone use and symptoms of anxiety and depression – a meta-analysis' (2023) 45 *Journal of Public Health* 1, 193–201

Backe, E. L., Lilleston, P., and McCleary-Sills, J., 'Networked individuals, gendered violence: A literature review' (2018) 5 *Violence and Gender* 3, 135–46

Bagchi, K., 'Factors contributing to global digital divide: some empirical results' (2005) 8 *Journal of Global Information Technology Management* 3, 47–65

Baker, C. E., 'Scope of the First Amendment freedom of speech' (1977) 25 *UCLA Law Review* 5, 964–1040

Banerjee, P., 'Gender digital divide – examining the reality' (2019) 8 *International Journal of Innovative Technology and Exploring Engineering* 11S, 214–19.

Baraka, K., 'Digital divide and social inequality' (2024) 3 *International Journal of Humanity and Social Sciences* 3, 30–45

Barker, J. C., 'The politics of international law-making: Constructing security in response to global terrorism' (2007) 3 *Journal of International Law and International Relations* 1, 5–24

Barnett, S. R., 'The right to one's own image: Publicity and privacy rights in the United States and Spain' (1999) 47 *The American Journal of Comparative Law* 4, 555–81

Bashyakarla, V., 'Towards a holistic perspective on personal data and the data-driven election paradigm' (2019) 8 *Internet Policy Review* 4, Article 1445

Bayat, Z., Kircher, R., and Van de Velde, H., 'Minority language rights to education in international, regional, and domestic regulations and practices: The case of Frisian in the Netherlands' (2023) 24 *Current Issues in Language Planning* 1, 81–101

Bayer, J., 'Double harm to voters: Data-driven micro-targeting and democratic public discourse' (2020) 9 *Internet Policy Review* 1, 1–17

Beard, M., 'The public voice of women' (2014) 36 *London Review of Books* 6, 11–14

Beckers, A., and Teubner, G., 'Human–algorithm hybrids as (quasi-)organizations? On the accountability of digital collective actors' (2023) 50 *Journal of Law and Society* 1, 100–19

Bénabou, R., and Tirole, J., 'Intrinsic and extrinsic motivation' (2003) 70 *Review of Economic Studies* 3, 489–520

Benedek, W., 'Digital human rights and artificial intelligence' (2023) 14 *Pravni Zapisi* 2, 227–37

Benka, J., Orosova, O., and Hricova, L., 'Risk and protective factors of problematic internet use in the context of prevention: Jozef Benka' (2016) 26 (Supplement 1) *European Journal of Public Health* 367–8

Benka, J., et al., 'Internalization of rules and risk-behavior among early adolescents and relevance for public health' (2019) 29 *European Journal of Public Health* Issue Supplement 4, 485–6

Bennett, C. J., and Lyon, D., 'Data-driven elections: Implications and challenges for democratic societies' (2019) 8 *Internet Policy Review* 4, Article No. 1433

Beširević', V., '"Uhvati me ako možeš": o (ne)odgovornosti transnacionalnih korporacija zbog kršenja ljudskih prava' ["Catch me if you can": reflections on legal (un)accountability of transnational corporations for human rights violations] (2018) 9 *Pravni zapisi* 1, 22–45

Bigliardi, R. V., and Cruz, R. G., 'As (im)possibilidades de uma sociedade sustentável e o inextricável embricamento entre educação ambiental e direitos humanos' (2013) 23 *Revista Eletrônica do Mestrado em Educação Ambiental* 1, 22–35

Bjola, C., 'Legitimating the use of force in international politics: A communicative action perspective' (2005) 11 *European Journal of International Relations* 2, 266–303

Blank, P., Kirrane, S., and Spiekermann, S., 'Privacy-aware restricted areas for unmanned aerial systems' (2018) 16 *IEEE Security and Privacy* 2, 70–9

Blasi Casagran, C., and Vermeulen, M., 'Reflections on the murky legal practices of political micro-targeting from a GDPR perspective' (2021) 11 *International Data Privacy Law* 4, 348–59

Blum, A. W., and Grant, J. E., 'Legal aspects of problematic Internet usage' (2022) 45 *Current Opinion in Behavioral Sciences* 101142

Bodo, B., Helberger, N., and de Vreese, C. H., 'Political micro-targeting: A Manchurian candidate or just a dark horse?' (2017) 6 *Internet Policy Review* 4, 1–13

Von Bogdandy, A. 'Globalization and Europe: How to square democracy, globalization and international law' (2004) 15 *European Journal of International Law* 5, 885–906

Von Bogdandy, A., Goldmann, M., and Venzke, I., 'From public international to international public law: Translating world public opinion into international public authority' (2017) 28 *European Journal of International Law* 1, 115–45

Borges, G., 'Liability for AI systems under current and future law: An overview of the key changes envisioned by the Proposal of an EU Directive on Liability for AI' (2023) 24 *Computer Law Review International* 1, 1–8

Boxler, H., 'Quest for the grail? Searching for critical thinking in adult education' (2002) *43rd Annual Adult Education Research Conference*, Conference Proceedings, North Carolina University, Raleigh, NC

Bradford, L., Aboy, M., and Liddell, K., 'COVID-19 contact tracing apps: A stress test for privacy, the GDPR, and data protection regimes' (2020) 7 *Journal of Law and the Biosciences* 1, 1–34

Van den Broeck, A., et al., 'Beyond intrinsic and extrinsic motivation: A meta-analysis on self-determination theory's multidimensional conceptualization of work motivation' (2021) 11 *Organizational Psychology Review* 3, 240–73

Brunée, J., and Toope, S., 'International law and constructivism: Elements of an interactional theory of international law' (2000) 39 *Columbia Journal of Transnational Law* 1, 19–74

Campo, L., et al., 'Methodologies for fostering critical thinking skills from university students' points of view' (2023) 13 *Education Sciences* 2, Article 132

Cannie, H., and Voorhof, D., 'The abuse clause and the freedom of expression in the European Convention on Human Rights – an added value for democracy and human rights protection' (2011) 29 *Netherlands Quarterly of Human Rights* 1, 54–83

Carballo Piñeiro, L., and Kramer, X., 'The role of private international law in contemporary society: Global governance as a challenge' (2014) 7 *Erasmus Law Review* 3, 109–12

Carvalho, I. C. M., 'A perspectiva das pedras: considerações sobre os novos materialismos e as epistemologias ecológicas' (2014) 9 *Pesquisa em Educação Ambiental* 1, 69–79

Carvalho, I. C. M., and Ortega, M. A. A., 'Aprendizagens em tempos de fim de um mundo e de abertura de múltiplos mundos. Reflexões desde a educação ambiental' (2024) 23 *Revista Cocar* 1–23

Casey, C., and Vermeule, A., 'Myths of common good constitutionalism' (2022) 45 *Harvard Journal of Law and Public Policy* 1, 103–46

Cassese, S., 'Administrative law without the state? The challenge of global regulation' (2005) 37 *New York University Journal of International Law and Policy* 4, 663–94

Ceccato, V., 'Special issue: Crime and control in the digital era' (2019) 20 *Criminal Justice Review* 10, 1–6

Celeste, E., 'Digital constitutionalism: A new systematic theorization' (2019) 33 *International Review of Law, Computers & Technology* 1, 76–99

Celso, J., 'Droning on about the Fourth Amendment: Adopting a reasonable Fourth Amendment jurisprudence to prevent unreasonable searches by unmanned aircraft systems' (2014) 43 *University of Baltimore Law Review* 3, 461–94

Chemerinsky, E., 'Rethinking state action doctrine' (1985) 80 *Northwestern University Law Review* 503–57

Cheng, H. H. L., 'Beyond forms, functions and limits: The interactionism of Lon L. Fuller and its implications for alternative dispute resolution' (2013) 26 *The Canadian Journal of Law and Jurisprudence*, 2, 257–92

Chiarella, M. L., 'Digital Markets Act (DMA) and Digital Services Act (DSA): New rules for the EU digital environment' (2023) 9 *Athens Journal of Law* 1, 33–58

Chimni, B. S., 'International institutions today: An imperial global state in the making' (2004) 15 *European Journal of International Law* 1, 1–37

Choi, D. W., et al., 'The association between parental depression and adolescent's Internet addiction in South Korea' (2018) 17 *Annals of General Psychiatry*, Article 15

Christiansen, C., Joensen, J. S., and Rangvid, J., 'Understanding the effects of marriage and divorce on financial investments: The role of background risk sharing' (2015) 53 *Economic Inquiry* 1, 431–47

Ciacchi, A. C., 'The direct horizontal effect of EU fundamental rights: ECJ 17 April 2018, Case C-414/16, Vera Egenberger v Evangelisches Werk für Diakonie und Entwicklung e.V. and ECJ 11 September 2018, Case C-68/17, IR v JQ' (2019) 15 *European Constitutional Law Review* 2, 294–305

Citron, D. K., and Chesney, R., 'Deep fakes: A looming challenge for privacy, democracy, and national security' (2019) 107 *California Law Review* 6, 1753–819

Clarke, R., 'The regulation of civilian drones' impacts on behavioural privacy' (2014) 30 *Computer Law and Security Review* 3, 286–305

Clayton, G., 'Safeguarding the world's new currency' (2002) 36 *Information Management Journal* 3, 18–24

Columb, D., Griffiths, M. D., and O'Gara, C., 'Fantasy football (soccer) playing and Internet addiction among online fantasy football participants: A descriptive survey study' (2022) 20 *International Journal of Mental Health and Addiction* 2, 1200–11

Congiu, L., and Moscati, I., 'A review of nudges: Definitions, justifications, effectiveness' (2022) 36 *Journal of Economic Surveys* 1, 188–213

Cooper, M. N., 'Inequality in the digital society: Why the digital divide deserves all the attention it gets' (2002) 20 *Cardozo Arts and Entertainment Law Journal* 1, 73–134

Craig, P., 'Theory, "pure theory" and values in public law' (2005) *Public Law* 440–7

Cremer, F., et al., 'Cyber risk and cybersecurity: A systematic review of data availability' (2022) 47 *The Geneva Papers on Risk and Insurance – Issues and Practice* 3, 698–736

Cristani, F., Trunk-Fedorova, M., and Popa Tache, C. E., 'Editorial: The workshop 'pursuing fairness in times of crisis: reflections on the future of international economic law' held within the 2023 ESIL Annual Conference' (2024) 4 *International Investment Law Journal* 2, 131–6

Cullen, R., 'Addressing the digital divide' (2001) 25 *Online Information Review* 5, 311–20

Dallmayr, F., 'The discourse of modernity: Hegel and Habermas' (1987) 84 *The Journal of Philosophy* 11, 682–92
Decker, E., 'Full count? Crime rate swings, cybercrime misses and why we don't really know the score' (2020) 10 *Journal of National Security, Law and Policy* 583–604
Dias Oliva, T., 'Content moderation technologies: Applying human rights standards to protect freedom of expression' (2020) 20 *Human Rights Law Review* 4, 607–40
Donaldson, P., 'Covid-19 vaccines. A global common good' (2020) 1 *The Lancet Healthy Longevity* 1, e6–e8
Dror-Shpoliansky, D., and Shany, Y., 'It's the end of the (offline) world as we know it: From human rights to digital human rights – a proposed typology' (2021) 32 *The European Journal of International Law* 4, 1249–82
Duff, R. A., and Marshall, S. E., '"Abstract endangerment", two harm principles, and two routes to criminalisation' (2015) 3 *Bergen Journal of Criminal Law and Criminal Justice*, 2, 131–61
Enciso, O. L. U., et al., 'Critical thinking and its importance in education: Some reflections' (2017) 19 *Rastros Rostros* 34, 78–88
Fabbrini, F., and Celeste, E., 'The right to be forgotten in the digital age: The challenges of data protection beyond borders' (2020) 21 *German Law Journal* S1, 55–65
Fineberg, N. A., et al., 'Manifesto for a European research network into problematic usage of the Internet' (2018) 28 *European Neuropsychopharmacology* 11, 1232–46
Floridi, L., 'The fight for digital sovereignty: What it is, and why it matters, especially for the EU' (2020) 33 *Philosophy & Technology* 3, 369–78
Foran, M., 'Rights, common good, and the separation of powers' (2023) 86 *The Modern Law Review* 3, 599–628
Fosch-Villaronga, E., van der Hof, S., Lutz, C., and Tamò-Larrieux, A., 'Toy story or children story? Putting children and their rights at the forefront of the artificial intelligence revolution' (2021) 38 *AI and Society* 1, 133–52
Frantziou, E., 'The horizontal effect of the Charter: Towards an understanding of horizontality as a structural constitutional principle?' (2020) 22 *Cambridge Yearbook of European Legal Studies* 208–32
Frantziou, E., 'The horizontal effect of the Charter of Fundamental Rights of the EU: Rediscovering the reasons for horizontality' (2015) 21 *European Law Journal* 5, 657–79
Friemel, T. N., 'The digital divide has grown old: Determinants of a digital divide among seniors' (2016) 18 *New Media and Society* 2, 313–31
Frosio, G., 'Why keep a dog and bark yourself? From intermediary liability to responsibility' (2018) 26 *Oxford International Journal of Law and Information Technology* 1, 1–33
Gardbaum, S., 'The "horizontal effect" of constitutional rights' (2003) 102 *Michigan Law Review* 2, 387–459
Garrison, D. R., 'Critical thinking and adult education: A conceptual model for developing critical thinking in adult learners' (1991) 10 *International Journal of Lifelong Education* 4, 287–303
Gates, C., and Matthews, P., 'Data Is the New Currency' (2014) *Proceedings of the 2014 New Security Paradigms Workshop* 105–16
Gaysynsky, A., Heley, K., and Chou, W. Y. S., 'An overview of innovative approaches to support timely and agile health communication research and practice' (2022) 19 *International Journal of Environmental Research and Public Health* 22, Article 15073
Glowacka, M., 'A little less autonomy? The future of working time flexibility and its limits' (2021) 12 *European Labour Law Journal* 2, 113–33
Golda, T., et al., 'Perception of risks and usefulness of smart video surveillance systems' (2022) 12 *Applied Sciences* 20, Article 10435

Goodhart, A. L., 'Determining the ratio decidendi of a case' (1930) 40 *Yale Law Review* 2, 161–83
Goodhart, A. L., 'The ratio decidendi of a case' (1959) 22 *Modern Law Review* 2, 117–30
Gordon, J., 'John Stuart Mill and the "marketplace of ideas"' (1997) 23 *Social Theory and Practice* 2, 235–49
Gray, D. C., and Citron, K. D., 'A shattered looking glass: The pitfalls and potential of the mosaic theory of Fourth Amendment privacy' (2013) 14 *North Carolina Journal of Law and Technology* 2, 381–429
Greenstein, S., 'Preserving the rule of law in the era of artificial intelligence' (2022) 30 *Artificial Intelligence and Law* 3, 291–323
De Gregorio, G., 'Digital constitutionalism across the Atlantic' (2022) 11 *Global Constitutionalism* 2, 297–324
De Gregorio, G., and Radu, R., 'Digital constitutionalism in the new era of internet governance' (2022) 30 *International Journal of Law and Technology* 1, 68–87
Grohmann, R., 'Plataformização do trabalho: entre datificação, financeirização e racionalidade neoliberal' (2020) 22 *Revista EPTIC* 1, 106–22
Guo, C., Wang, X., and Yuan, G., 'Digital finance and the efficiency of household investment portfolios' (2022) 58 *Emerging Markets Finance and Trade* 10, 2895–909
Habermas, J., 'The crisis of the European Union in the light of a constitutionalization of international law', (2012) 23 *European Journal of International Law* 2, 335–48
Haggart, B., and Keller, C. I., 'Democratic legitimacy in global platform governance' (2021) 45 *Telecommunications Policy* 6, Article 102152
Harlow, C., 'Public law and popular justice' (2002) 65 *Modern Law Review* 1, 1–18
Helm, R. K., and Nasu, H., 'Regulatory responses to "fake news" and freedom of expression: Normative and empirical evaluation' (2020) 21 *Human Rights Law Review* 2, 322–5
Henry, N., and Powell, A., 'Technology-facilitated sexual violence: A literature review of empirical research' (2016) 19 *Trauma, Violence and Abuse* 2, 195–208
Hesselberth, P., 'Discourses on disconnectivity and the right to disconnect' (2018) 20 *New Media & Society* 5, 1994–2010
Hilbert, M., 'Digital gender divide or technologically empowered women in developing countries? A typical case of lies, damned lies and statistics' (2011) 34 *Women's Studies International Forum* 34, 479–89
Hiniker, A., Heung, S., Hong, S., and Kientz, J., 'Coco's videos: An empirical investigation of video-player design features and children's media use' (2018) *Proceedings of the 2018 CHI Conference on Human Factors in Computing Systems*, Paper No. 254, pp. 1–13
Van der Hof, S., et al., 'The child's right to protection against economic exploitation in the digital world' (2020) 28 *The International Journal of Children's Rights* 4, 833–59
Hoffmann, S., Lazanski, D., and Taylor, E., 'Standardising the splinternet: How China's technical standards could fragment the internet' (2020) 5 *Journal of Cyber Policy* 2, 239–64
Huang, J., and Sang, G., 'Conceptualising critical thinking and its research in teacher education: A systematic review' (2022) 29 *Teachers and Teaching: Theory and Practice* 6, 638–60
Huhn, W. R., 'The state action doctrine and the principle of democratic choice' (2005) 34 *Hofstra Law Review* 4, 1379–460
Ibáñez, D. B., da Cunha, M. R., and Toledo, J. H., 'Comunicación digital, redes sociales y procesos en línea: estudios en una perspectiva comparada entre América Latina y la península ibérica' (2020) 26 *Journal of Iberian and Latin American Research* 3, 275–83
Ingber, S., 'The marketplace of ideas: A legitimizing myth' (1984) 33 *Duke Law Journal* 1, 1–91
Ishihara, K., Yamada, H., and Otani, T., et al., 'Introducing Face Express, A new boarding procedure using face recognition (One ID at Narita Airport)' (2021) 16 *NEC Technical Journal* 1, 49–53

Ivanov, A., Gorelik, D., and Prokofiev, K., 'Law enforcement in the context of digitalization: problems and prospects for improving efficiency' (2020) 171 *Advances in Economics, Business and Management Research, volume*, Proceedings of the 1st International Scientific Conference "Legal Regulation of the Digital Economy and Digital Relations: Problems and Prospects of Development" (LARDER 2020)

Jæger, B., 'Trapped in the digital divide? old people in the information society' (2004) 17 *Science Studies* 2, 5–22

Jansen, A. M., et al., 'The influence of the presentation of camera surveillance on cheating and pro-social behavior' (2018) 9 *Frontiers in Psychology*, Article 1937

Jiang, B., Yang, J., and Song, H., 'Protecting privacy from aerial photography: state of the art, opportunities, and challenges' (2020) *IEEE Conference on Computer Communications Workshops* 799–804

Johnson, D. R., and Post, D., 'Law and borders: the rise of law in cyberspace' (1996) 48 *Stanford Law Review* 5, 1367–402

Johnstone, I., 'Legislation and adjudication in the Security Council: Bringing down the deliberative deficit' (2008) 102 *American Journal of International Law* 2, 275–308

Jørgensen, R. F., 'Data and rights in the digital welfare state: The case of Denmark' (2021) 26 *Information, Communication & Society* 1, 123–38

Karaoglu, G., Hargittai, E., and Nguyen, M. H., 'Inequality in online job searching in the age of social media' (2021) 25 *Information, Communication and Society* 12, 1679–97

Kaufmann, C., 'Responsible business in a digital world – what's international law got to do with it?' (2021) 81 *Heidelberg Journal of International Law* 3, 781–815

Keats Citron, D. and Solove, D. J, 'Privacy harms' (2021) SSRN Scholarly Paper ID 3782222, https://papers.ssrn.com/abstract=3782222.

Kelly, M. D., 'Challenging common good constitutionalism' (2024) 15 *Jurisprudence* 1, 418–40

Kelly, A., 'A tale of two algorithms: The appeal and repeal of calculated grades systems in England and Ireland in 2020' (2021) 47 *British Educational Research Journal* 3, 725–41

Kennedy, D., 'The hermeneutic of suspicion in contemporary American legal thought' (2014) 25 *Law and Critique* 2, 91–139

Kerr, O. S., 'The mosaic theory of the Fourth Amendment' (2012) 111 *Michigan Law Review* 3, 311–54

Kim, M., 'Legalization and norm internalization: An empirical study of international human rights commitments eliciting public support for compliance' (2019) 7 *Journal of Law and International Affairs* 2, 337–81

Kingsbury, B., Krisch, N., and Stewart, R. B., 'The Emergence of Global Administrative Law' (2005) 68 *Law and Contemporary Problems* 3/4, 15–61

Klabbers, J., 'Constitutionalism and the making of international law: Fuller's procedural natural law' (2008) 5 *No Foundations: An Interdisciplinary Journal of Law and Justice* 84–112

Klar, M., 'Binding effects of the European General Data Protection Regulation (GDPR) on US companies' (2020) 11 *Hastings Science & Technology Law Journal* 2, 101–54

Kleijssen, J., and Perri, P., 'Cybercrime, evidence and territoriality: issues and options' (2017) 47 *Netherlands Yearbook of International Law* 147–73

Koloß, S., 'Facebook and the rule of law' (2020) 80 *Heidelberg Journal of International Law* 2, 509–31

Königs, P., 'Government surveillance, privacy, and legitimacy' (2022) 35 *Philosophy & Technology* 1, Article 8

Krisch, N., 'The decay of consent: International law in an age of global public goods' (2014) 108 *American Journal of International Law* 1, 1–40

Kuczerawy, A., 'The power of positive thinking: Intermediary liability and the effective enjoyment of the right to freedom of expression' (2017) 8 *Journal of Intellectual Property, Information Technology and Electronic Commerce Law* 3, 226–37

Kuczerawy, A., 'Intermediary liability & freedom of expression: Recent developments in the EU notice & action initiative' (2015) 31 *Computer Law and Security Review* 1, 46–56

Kularski, C., and Moller, S., 'The digital divide as a continuation of traditional systems of inequality' (2012) 5151 *Sociology* 1–23

Kumm, M., 'Who is afraid of the total constitution? Constitutional rights as principles and the constitutionalization of private law' (2006) 7 *German Law Journal* 4, 341–69

Lambach, D., 'The territorialization of cyberspace' (2020) 22 *International Studies Review* 3, 482–506

Lamond, G., 'Do precedents create rules?' (2005) 11 *Legal Theory* 1, 1–26

Landes, W. M., and Posner, R. A., 'Legal precedent: A theoretical and empirical analysis' (1976) 19 *Journal of Law and Economics* 2, 249–307

Larcom, S., et al., 'Follow the leader? Testing for the internalization of law' (2019) 48 *The Journal of Legal Studies* 1, 217–44

Larsson, K., 'Understanding and teaching critical thinking – a new approach' (2017) 84 *International Journal of Educational Research* 32–42

Lareki, A., et al., 'Fake digital identity and cyberbullying' (2022) 45 *Media, Culture & Society* 2, 338–53

Layrargues, P. P., 'Para onde vai a educação ambiental? O cenário político ideológico da educação ambiental brasileira e os desafios de uma agenda política crítica contra-hegemônica' (2012) 7 *Revista contemporânea de educação* 14, 388–411

Leerssen, P., 'An end to shadow banning? Transparency rights in the Digital Services Act between content moderation and curation' (2023) 48 *Computer Law & Security Review* 105790

Lehmann, M., 'Regulation, global governance and private international law: Squaring the triangle' (2020) 16 *Journal of Private International Law* 1, 1–30

Lievens, E., 'Growing up with digital technologies: How the precautionary principle might contribute to addressing potential serious harm to children's rights' (2021) 39 *Nordic Journal of Human Rights* 2, 128–45

Lomborg, S., and Ytre-Arne, B., 'Advancing digital disconnection research: Introduction to the special issue' (2021) 27 *Convergence* 6, 1529–35

Loughlin, M., 'Theory and values in public law: An interpretation' (2005) *Public Law* 48–66

Lv, Z., 'The security of Internet of drones' (2019) 148 *Computer Communications* 208–14

Machado, C. R. S., Calloni, H., and Adomilli, G. K., 'Pensares e fazeres sobre e na Educação Ambiental: reflexões sobre/desde os fundamentos ao campo atual Brasileiro' (2016) 21 *Ambiente e Educação* 1, 3–25

MacLennan, J. F., 'Facing the digital future: Public service broadcasters and state aid law in the European Union' (2017) 2 *Cambridge Yearbook of European Legal Studies* 159–202

Mannheim, I., et al., 'Ageism in the discourse and practice of designing digital technology for older persons: A scoping review' (2023) 63 *The Gerontologist* 7, 1188–200

Mannion, C., 'Data imperialism: The GDPR's disastrous impact on Africa's e-commerce markets' (2020) 53 *Vanderbilt Journal of Transnational Law* 2, 685–711

Maras, M. H., and Alexandrou, A., 'Determining authenticity of video evidence in the age of artificial intelligence and in the wake of Deepfake videos' (2019) 23 *The International Journal of Evidence and Proof* 3, 255–62

Marengo, N., et al., 'Cyberbullying and electronic media communication problematic use in Piedmont. Data from HBSC study' (2020) 30 (Supplement 5) *European Journal of Public Health* v869

Marique, E., and Marique, Y., 'Sanctions on digital platforms: Beyond the public-private divide' (2019) 8 *Cambridge University Law Journal* 2, 258–81

Mas'udah, S., et al., 'Gender-based cyber violence: forms, impacts, and strategies to protect women victims' (2024) 26 *Journal of International Women's Studies* 4, Article 5

May, P. J., 'Regulation and compliance motivations: Examining different approaches' (2005) 65 *Public Administration Review* 1, 31–44

May, P. J., 'Compliance motivations: Affirmative and negative bases' (2004) 38 *Law and Society Review* 1, 41–68

Mboya, I. B., et al., 'Internet addiction and associated factors among medical and allied health sciences students in northern Tanzania: A cross-sectional study' (2020) 73 *BMC Psychology* 8, Article 73

McBride, P., 'Beyond Orwell: The application of unmanned aircraft systems in domestic surveillance operations' (2009) 74 *Journal of Air Law and Commerce* 3, 627–62

McClain, L. C., and Fleming, J. E., 'Toward a liberal common good constitutionalism for polarized times' (2023) 46 *Harvard Journal of Law and Public Policy* 1123–48

McRae, J. N., Nielsen, B. M., Gay, C. J., et al., 'Utilizing drones to restore and maintain radio communication during search and rescue operations' (2021) 32 *Wilderness and Environmental Medicine* 1, 41–6

Michalkiewcz-Kadziela, E., and Milczarek, E., 'Legal boundaries of digital identity creation' (2022) 11 *Internet Policy Review* 1, 1–13

Mikołajczyk, B., 'Universal human rights instruments and digital literacy of older persons' (2022) 27 *The International Journal of Human Rights* 3, 403–24

Miller, M. L., and Vaccari, C., 'Digital threats to democracy: Comparative lessons and possible remedies' (2020) 25 *The International Journal of Press/Politics* 3, 333–56

Milner, H., 'The digital divide' (2006) 39 *Comparative Political Studies* 2, 176–99

Mikołajczyk, B., 'Universal human rights instruments and digital literacy of older persons' (2022) 27 *The International Journal of Human Rights* 3, 403–24

Mitrus, L., 'Potential implications of the Matzak judgment (quality of rest time, right to disconnect)' (2019) 10 *European Labour Law Journal* 4, 386–97

Molina, M. D., Sundar, S. S., Le, T., and Lee, D., '"Fake news" is not simply false information: A concept explication and taxonomy of online content' (2021) 65 *American Behavioral Scientist* 2, 180–212

Montrose, J. L., 'Ratio decidendi and the House of Lords' (1957) 20 *Modern Law Review* 2, 124—30

Moore, K., 'The three-part harmony of adult learning, critical thinking, and decision-making' (2010) 39 *Journal of Adult Education* 1, 1–10

Morris, L. S., et al., 'On what motivates us: A detailed review of intrinsic v. extrinsic motivation' (2022) 52 *Psychological Medicine* 10, 1801–16

Moses, L. B., 'Adapting the law to technological change: a comparison of common law and legislation' (2003) 26 *UNSW Law Journal* 2, 394–417

Moyn, S., 'On human rights and majority politics' (2019) 52 *Vanderbilt Law Review* 5, 1135–66

Van Mulligen, A., 'Framing deformalisation in public international law' (2015) 6 *Transnational Legal Theory* 3–4, 635–60

Murawski, L. M., 'Critical thinking in the classroom…and beyond' (2014) 10 *Journal of Learning in Higher Education* 1, 25–30

Murphy, C., 'Lon Fuller and the moral value of the rule of law' (2005) 24 *Law and Philosophy* 3, 239–62

Neal, P., 'Liberalism & neutrality' (1985) 17 *Polity* 4, 664–84

Nenadić, I., 'Unpacking the "European approach" to tackling challenges of disinformation and political manipulation' (2019) 8 *Internet Policy Review* 4, 1–22

Neves, D., 'A exploração do trabalho no Brasil contemporâneo' (2022) 25 *Revista Katálysis* 1, 11–21

Nolan, A., 'Holding non-state actors to account for constitutional economic and social rights violations: Experiences and lessons from South Africa and Ireland' (2014) 12 *International Journal of Constitutional Law* 1, 66–93

Nussbaum, M. C., 'Animal rights: The need for a theoretical basis' (2001) 114 *Harvard Law Review* 5, 1506–52

O'Brien, B., 'Digital ethics in higher education' (2020) 55 *Educause Review* 2, 11–43

Olcott, D. Jr, et al., 'Ethics and education in the digital age: Global perspectives and strategies for local transformation in Catalonia' (2015) 12 *RUSC* 2 Special Issue, 59–72

O'Leary, S., 'Balancing rights in a digital age' (2018) 59 *Irish Jurist* 59–92

Onyejekwe, C., 'International investment law and the right to regulate: A human rights perspective' (2019) 53 *The Law Teacher* 1, 125–6

Ott, T., and Tiozza, M., 'Digital media ethics: Benefits and challenges in school education' (2022) 14 *International Journal of Mobile and Blended Learning* 2, 1–8

Padovan, P. H., Martins, C. M., and Reed, C., 'Black is the new orange: How to determine AI liability' (2023) 31 *Artificial Intelligence and Law* 1, 136–67

Palladino, N., 'The role of epistemic communities in the "constitutionalization" of Internet governance: The example of the European Commission High-Level Expert Group on Artificial Intelligence' (2021) 45 *Telecommunications Policy* 6, Article 102149

Pansu, L., 'Evaluation of "right to disconnect" legislation and its impact on employee's productivity' (2018) 5 *International Journal of Management and Applied Research* 3, 99–119

Paris, B., and Donovan, J., 'Deepfakes and cheap fakes: The manipulation of audio and visual evidence' (2019) *Data & Society Research Institute*, 18 September 2019

Park, A., and Youm, K. H., 'Fake news from a legal perspective: The United States and South Korea compared' (2019) 25 *Southwestern Journal of International Law* 1, 100–19

Paz, M., 'The failed promise of language rights: A critique of the international language rights regime' (2013) 54 *Harvard International Law Journal* 1, 157–218

Peláez-Sánchez, I. C., Reyes, C. E. G., and Glasserman-Morales, L. D., 'Gender digital divide in education 4.0: A systematic literature review of factors and strategies for inclusion' (2023) 1 *Future in Educational Research* 2, 129–46

Pettrachin, A., 'Towards a universal declaration on Internet rights and freedoms?' (2018) 80 *International Communication Gazette* 4, 337–53

Pezoa-Jares, R., and Espinoza-Luna, I., '629 – neurobiological findings associated with Internet addiction: A literature review' (2013) 28 (Supplement 1) *European Psychiatry* 1

Phillipson, G., 'The Human Rights Act, "horizontal effect" and the common law: A bang or a whimper?' (1999) 62 *The Modern Law Review* 6, 824–49

Pigatto, J. T., Datysgeld, M. W., and Silva, L. G. P. D., 'Internet governance is what global stakeholders make of it: a tripolar approach' (2021) 64 *Revista Brasileira de Política Internacional* 2, e011

Pinheiro, S. L., and Pasquier, F., 'Consciousness and environmental education: transdisciplinary urgencies from the post-pandemic context' (2023) 14 *Transdisciplinary Journal of Engineering & Science* 1–15

Pohle, J., and Thiel, T., 'Digital sovereignty' (2020) 9 *Internet Policy Review* 4, 1–19

Pollman, E., 'A corporate right to privacy' (2014) 99 *Minnesota Law Review* 1, 27–88

Popa Tache, C. E., Săraru, C.-S., and Kouroupis, K., 'Different perspectives concerning the right not to use the internet and some analogies with education | Diverse prospettive sul diritto a non usare internet ed alcune analogie con l'istruzione' (2024) 1 *European Journal of Privacy Law and Technologies* 179–93

Popa Tache, C. E., and Săraru, C-S., 'Evaluating today's multi-dependencies in digital transformation, corporate governance and public international law triad' (2024) 10 *Cogent Social Sciences*, 1, Article 2370945

Popa Tache, C. E., 'About the human rights and consumer protection in the digital age of Digital Services Act 2022 or what aspects interested investors should pay attention to' (2023) 3 *International Investment Law Journal* 2, 121–32

Popa Tache, C. E., 'Public international law and FinTech challenge' (2022) 11 *Perspectives of Law and Public Administration* 2, 11–15

Popa Tache, C. E., 'Ranking of treatment standards in international investments' (2021) 1 *International Investment Law Journal* 1, 79–87

Popa Tache, C. E., 'Editorial' (2021) 1 *International Investment Law Journal* 1, 9–10

Quach, S., et al., 'Digital technologies: Tensions in privacy and data' (2022) 50 *Journal of the Academy of Marketing Science* 6, 1299–323

Rahman, K. T., and Arif, Z. U., 'Impact of binge-watching on Netflix during the Covid-19 pandemic' (2017) 2 *South Asian Journal of Marketing* 1, 97–112

Rajam, V., Bheemeshaw Reddy, A., and Banerjee, S., 'Explaining caste-based digital divide in India' (2021) 65 *Telematics and Informatics* 101719

Randall, M. H., 'Human rights within a multilayered constitution: The example of freedom of expression and the WTO' (2012) 16 *Max Planck Yearbook of United Nations Law* 1, 183–280

Raposo, V. L., 'The doctor just poked you: Os novos desafios da e-health' (2014) 57 *Boletim das Ciências Económicas* 3, 2903–33

Ratner, S. R., 'Corporations and human rights: A theory of legal responsibility (2001) 111 *The Yale Law Journal* 3, 468–9

Ratner, C., 'When "sweetie" is not so sweet: Artificial intelligence and its implications for child pornography' (2021) 59 *Family Court Review* 2, 386–401

Rebechi, C. N., et al., 'Trabalho decente no contexto das plataformas digitais: uma pesquisa-ação do Projeto Fairwork no Brasil' (2023) 74 *Revista do Serviço Público* 2, 370–89

Redeker, D., Gill, L., and Gasser, U., 'Towards digital constitutionalism? Mapping attempts to craft an Internet Bill of Rights (2018) 80 *International Communication Gazette* 4, 302–19

Reed, C., 'Online and offline equivalence: Aspiration and achievement' (2010) 18 *International Journal of Law and Information Technology* 3, 248–73

Reich, P. L., 'Regime Change and Legal Change – The Legacy of Mexico's Second Empire' (2015) *Oxford University Comparative Law Forum* 1

Reiter, E. H., 'Personality and patrimony: Comparative perspectives on the right to one's image' (2002) 76 *Tulane Law Review* 3, 673–726

Rivera-Perez, W., 'What the constitution got to do with it: Expanding the scope of constitutional rights into the private sphere' (2012) 3 *Creighton International and Comparative Law Journal* 1, 189–214

Robinson, K., 'Corporate rights and individual interests: The corporate right to privacy as a bulwark against warrantless government surveillance' (2015) 36 *Cardozo Law Review* 6, 2283–320

Van Rooij, M., Lusardi, A., and Alessie, R., 'Financial literacy and stock market participation' (2011) 101 *Journal of Financial Economics* 2, 449–72

Rosenberg, A. S., 'Motivational law' (2008) 56 *Cleveland State Law Review* 1, 111–36

Rosenfeld, M., 'Rethinking the boundaries between public law and private law for the twenty-first century: An introduction' (2013) 11 *International Journal of Constitutional Law* 1, 125–8

Rubinstein, I. S., 'Voter privacy in the age of big data' (2014) *Wisconsin Law Review* 4, 861–936

Rule, T. A., 'Airspace in an Age of Drones' (2015) 95 *Boston University Law Review* 1, 155–208

Rumpf, H.-J., Effertz, T., and Montag, C., 'The cost burden of problematic internet usage' (2022) 44 *Current Opinion in Behavioral Sciences* 101107

Rundle, K., 'The impossibility of an exterminatory legality: Law and the Holocaust' (2009) 59 *University of Toronto Law Journal* 1, 65–125

Ryan, R., and Deci, E. L., 'Intrinsic and extrinsic motivations: Classic definitions and new directions' (2000) 25 *Contemporary Educational Psychology* 1, 54–67

Sànchez-Valle, M., 'The perception of older adults regarding socio-political issues disseminated on social networks' (2023) 11 *Communication for Seniors' Inclusion in Today's Society* 3, 112–23

Santos, C. F., Gonçalves, L. D., and Da Silva Machado, C. R., 'Educação ambiental para justiça ambiental: dando mais uns passos' (2015) 32 *REMEA-Revista Eletrônica do Mestrado em Educação Ambiental* 1, 189–208

Şaramet, O., and Spîrchez, G.-B., 'Limits of the discretionary power established through enforcing the European principle of proportionality' (2018) 7 *Perspectives of Law and Public Administration* 2, 260–9

Sartor, G., 'The right to be forgotten: Balancing interests in the flux of time' (2016) 24 *International Journal of Law and Information Technology* 1, 72–98

Savin, A., 'Digital sovereignty and its impact on EU policymaking', (2022) CBS LAW Research Paper, 22-02, Copenhagen Business School

Savin, A., 'The EU Digital Service Act: Toward a more responsible Internet' (2021) 24 *Journal of Internet Law* 7, 15–25

Savolainen, L., 'The shadow banning controversy: Perceived governance and algorithmic folklore' (2022) 44 *Media, Culture & Society* 6, 1091–109

Schaap, D., and Scheeper, P., 'Comparing citizens' trust in the police across European countries: An assessment of cross-country measurement equivalence' (2014) 24 *International Criminal Justice Review* 1, 82–98

Schippers, B., 'Artificial Intelligence and democratic politics' (2020) 11 *Political Insight* 1, 32–5

Seifert, A., Cotton, S. R., and Xie, B., 'A double burden of exclusion? Digital and social exclusion of older adults in times of COVID-19' (2021) 76 *The Journals of Gerontology: Series B* 3, e99–e103

Seo, M., Kim, J.-H., and David, P., 'Always connected or always distracted? ADHD symptoms and social assurance explain problematic use of mobile phone and multicommunicating' (2015) 20 *Journal of Computer-Mediated Communication* 6, 667–81

Sevignani, S., 'Digital transformations and the ideological formation of the public sphere: Hegemonic, populist, or popular communication?' (2022) 39 *Theory, Culture and Society* 4, 91–109

Shany, Y., 'Digital rights and the outer limits of international human rights law' (2023) 24 *German Law Journal* 3, 461–72

Sharma, G., 'Implementation of information and communication technology for human rights awareness and promotion' (2020) 1 *HighTech and Innovation Journal* 1, 1–6

Shattock, E., 'Fake news in Strasbourg: Electoral disinformation and freedom of expression in the European Court of Human Rights (ECtHR)' (2022) 13 *European Journal of Law and Technology* 1

Sheehy, B., et al., 'Shifting from soft to hard law: Motivating compliance when enacting mandatory corporate social responsibility' (2023) 24 *European Business Organization Law Review* 4, 693–719

Simmonds, N. E., 'Constitutional rights, civility and artifice' (2019) 78 *The Cambridge Law Journal* 1, 175–99

Singer, P., 'Economia solidária versus economia capitalista' (2001) 16 *Sociedade e estado* 1-2, 100–12

Singer, P., 'Economia solidária: geração de renda e alternativa ao liberalismo' (1997) 26 *Proposta* 72, 7–13

Singh, S., 'Bridging the gender digital divide in developing countries' (2017) 11 *Journal of Children and Media* 2, 245–7

Smuha, N. A., 'Beyond the individual: governing AI's societal harm' (2021) 10 *Internet Policy Review*, 3, Article No. 1574

Smuha, N. A., 'The EU Approach to ethics guidelines for trustworthy artificial intelligence' (2019) SSRN Scholarly Paper ID 3443537, https://papers.ssrn.com/abstract=3443537

Smyrnaios, N., and Baisnée, O., 'Critically understanding the platformization of the public sphere' (2023) 38 *European Journal of Communication* 5, 435–45

Sourbati, M., '"It could be useful, but not for me at the moment": Older people, internet access and e-public service provision' (2009) 11 *New Media and Society* 7, 1083–100

Spohr, D., 'Fake news and ideological polarization: Filter bubbles and selective exposure on social media' (2017) 34 *Business Information Review* 3, 150–60

De Stefano, V., 'The rise of the 1"just-in-time workforce": On-demand work, crowdwork and labour protection in the "gig-economy"' (2016) 37 *Comparative Labor Law Journal* 3, 471–504

Stein, D. J., and Hartford, A., 'Health-policy approaches for problematic Internet use: Lessons from substance use disorders' (2022) 46 *Current Opinion in Behavioral Sciences* 101151

Sturm, D., 'Lon Fuller's multidimensional natural law theory' (1965-1966) 18 *Stanford Law Review* 3, 612–39

Susi, M., 'The internet balancing formula' (2019) 25 *European Law Journal* 2, 198–212

Tappen, R. M., et al., 'Digital health information disparities in older adults: Amixed methods study' (2021) 9 *Journal of Racial and Ethnic Health Disparities* 1, 82–92

Tasioulas, J., 'Saving human rights from human rights law' (2021) 52 *Vanderbilt Law Review* 5, 1167–207

Teubner, G., 'Horizontal effects of constitutional rights in the Internet: A legal case on the digital constitution' (2017) 3 *The Italian Law Journal* 1, 193–205

Thurman, N., Sly, J., Wilczek, B., and Fletcher, R., 'Forbidden fruit or soured grapes? Long-term effects of the temporary unavailability and rationing of US news websites on their consumption from the European Union' (2022) 84 *International Communication Gazette* 7–8, 698–720

Ting, M., 'The role of the WTO in limiting China's censorship policies' (2011) 41 *Hong Kong Law Journal* 285–310

Tinmaz, H., et al., 'A systematic review on digital literacy' (2022) 9 *Smart Learning Environments*, Article 21

Tourkochoriti, I., 'The Digital Services Act and the EU as the global regulator of the Internet' (2023) 24 *Chicago Journal of International Law* 1, 129–47

Townsend, B., 'Decoding the Proposed European Union Artificial Intelligence Act' (2021) 25 *American Society of International Law Insights* 20

Treuthart, M. P., 'Connectivity: The global gender digital divide and its implications for women's human rights and equality' (2019) 23 *Gonzaga Journal of International Law* 1, 1–53

Trouille, H., 'Private life and public image: Privacy legislation in France' (2000) 49 *International and Comparative Law Quarterly* 1, 199–208

Tsatsou, P., 'Vulnerable people's digital inclusion: Intersectionality patterns and associated lessons' (2021) 25 *Information, Communication & Society* 10, 1475–94

Tsitsika, A. K., et al., 'Association between problematic internet use, socio-demographic variables and obesity among European adolescents' (2016) 26 *European Journal of Public Health* 4, 617–22

Turner, A., 'How does intrinsic and extrinsic motivation drive performance culture in organizations?' (2017) 4 *Cogent Education* 1, Article 1337543

Vanden Abeele, M. M., and Mohr, V., 'Media addictions as Apparatgeist: What discourse on TV and smartphone addiction reveals about society' (2021) 27 *Convergence* 6, 1536–57

de Varennes, F., 'The right to education and minority language' (2004), www.researchgate.net/publication/242595391_The_right_to_education_and_minority_language

Varul, P., and Pisuke, H., 'Louisiana's Contribution to the Estonian Civil Code' (1999) 73 *Tulane Law Review* 4, 1027–34

Veale, M., and Zuiderveen Borgesius, F., 'Demystifying the draft EU Artificial Intelligence Act' (2021) 22 *Computer Law Review International* 4, 97–112

Vimalkumar, M., Singh, J. B., Gouda, S. K., 'Contextualising the relationship between gender and computer self-efficacy: An empirical study from India' (2021) 58 *Information and Management* 4, Article 103464

De Vries, D. A., 'Balancing fundamental rights with economic freedoms according to the European Court of Justice' (2013) 9 *Utrecht Law Review* 1, 169–92

Waldron, J., 'Is the rule of law an essentially contested concept (in Florida)?' (2002) 21 *Law and Philosophy*, 2, 137–64

Wang, Y., et al., 'Digital exclusion and cognitive impairment in older people: findings from five longitudinal studies' (2024) 24 *BMC Geriatrics*, Article 406

Warren, S. D., and Brandeis, L. D., 'The right to privacy' (1890) 4 *Harvard Law Review* 5, 193–220

Watt, H. M., 'Private international law: Beyond the schism' (2011) 2 *Transnational Legal Theory* 3, 347–427

Willett, M., 'China's investment in digital technologies and the Digital Great Game' (2020) 60 *Adelphi Series* 487–489, 23–36

Wong, D., and Floridi, L., 'Meta's Oversight Board: A review and critical assessment' (2023) 33 *Minds and Machines* 2, 261–84

Wueste, D. E., 'Fuller's Processual philosophy of law' (1986) 71 *Cornell Law Review* 6, 1205–30

Wulandari, E., and Triyanto, W., 'Digital citizenship education: Shaping digital ethics in society 5.0' (2021) 9 *Universal Journal of Educational Research* 5, 948–56

Wulff, C. M., 'The right to be forgotten in post-Google Spain case law: an example of legal interpretivism in action?' (2020) 26 *Comparative Law Review* 1, 255–79

Xu, C., and Jin, B., 'Digital currency in China: Pilot implementations, legal challenges and prospects' (2022) 12 *Juridical Tribune/ Tribuna Juridica* 2, 177–94

Yu, P. K., 'Bridging the digital divide: Equality in the information age' (2002) 20 *Cardozo Arts and Entertainment Law Journal* 1, 1–52

Ziller, C., and Helbling, M., 'Public support for state surveillance' (2021) 60 *European Journal of Political Research* 4, 994–1006

Zittrain, J., 'Engineering an election' (2014) 127 *Harvard Law Review Forum* 335–42

Zorčič, S., 'Dimensions of remote learning during the Covid-19 pandemic in minority language schools' (2020) 85 *Treatises and Documents Journal of Ethnic Studies* 85, 223–52

Zufall, F., Kimura, R., and Peng, L., 'A simple mathematical model for the legal concept of balancing of interests' ICAIL '21: Proceedings of the Eighteenth International Conference on Artificial Intelligence and Law, June 2021, 270–1

Zuiderveen Borgesius, F. J., Möller, J., Kruikemeier, S., et al, 'Online political microtargeting: Promises and threats for democracy' (2018) 14 *Utrecht Law Review* 1, 82–96

Zuluaga, Y. E. L., et al., 'A study of critical thinking in higher education students' (2020) 16 *Revista Latinoamericana de Estudios Educativos* (Colombia), 2, 256–79

Zvereva, E., 'Digital ethics in higher education: Modernizing moral values for effective communication in cyberspace' (2023) 13 *Online Journal of Communication and Media Technologies* 2, e202319

Index

Printed by Integrated Books International,
United States of America